TIME AND ENVIRONMENTAL LAW

Disciplined by industrial clock time, modern life distances people from nature's biorhythms such as its ecological, evolutionary, and climatic processes. The law is complicit in numerous ways. It compresses time through 'fast-track' legislation and accelerated resource exploitation. It suffers from temporal inertia, such as 'grandfathering' existing activities that limits the law's responsiveness to changing circumstances. Insouciance about past ecological damage, and neglect of its restoration, are equally serious temporal flaws: we cannot live sustainably while Earth remains degraded and unrepaired. Applying international and interdisciplinary perspectives of these issues, *Time and Environmental Law* explores how to align law with the ecological 'timescape' and enable humankind to 'tell nature's time'. Lending insight into environmental behaviour and impacts, this book pioneers a new understanding of environmental law for all societies, and makes recommendations for its reform. Minding nature, not the clock, requires regenerating Earth, adapting to its changes, and living more slowly.

BENJAMIN J. RICHARDSON is Professor of Environmental Law at the University of Tasmania, and the 2017 Global Law Visiting Chair at Tilburg University. Earlier, he held the Canada Research Chair in Environmental Law and Sustainability at the University of British Columbia. His global recognition includes winning the Research Excellence Prize of the UN Principles for Responsible Investment Academic Network and the Senior Scholar Prize of the IUCN Academy of Environmental Law. Professor Richardson is a member of the Australian Panel of Experts on Environmental Law and practises environmental stewardship on his Tasmanian eco-sanctuary, Blue Mountain View.

TIME AND ENVIRONMENTAL LAW

Telling Nature's Time

BENJAMIN J. RICHARDSON
University of Tasmania

CAMBRIDGE
UNIVERSITY PRESS

CAMBRIDGE
UNIVERSITY PRESS

University Printing House, Cambridge CB2 8BS, United Kingdom

One Liberty Plaza, 20th Floor, New York, NY 10006, USA

477 Williamstown Road, Port Melbourne, VIC 3207, Australia

314-321, 3rd Floor, Plot 3, Splendor Forum, Jasola District Centre, New Delhi - 110025, India

79 Anson Road, #06-04/06, Singapore 079906

Cambridge University Press is part of the University of Cambridge.

It furthers the University's mission by disseminating knowledge in the pursuit of education, learning and research at the highest international levels of excellence.

www.cambridge.org
Information on this title: www.cambridge.org/9781316641736
DOI : 10.1017/9781108120678

© Benjamin J. Richardson 2017

This publication is in copyright. Subject to statutory exception and to the provisions of relevant collective licensing agreements, no reproduction of any part may take place without the written permission of Cambridge University Press.

First published 2017
First paperback edition 2018

A catalogue record for this publication is available from the British Library

ISBN 978-1-107-19124-2 Hardback
ISBN 978-1-316-64173-6 Paperback

Cambridge University Press has no responsibility for the persistence or accuracy of URLs for external or third-party internet websites referred to in this publication, and does not guarantee that any content on such websites is, or will remain, accurate or appropriate.

For Kiri

'Only time (whatever that may be) will tell'.
—Stephen Hawking

'Well, here we are, Mr Pilgrim, trapped in the amber of this moment. There is no why'.
—Kurt Vonnegut

'An hour, once it lodges in the queer element of the human spirit, may be stretched to fifty or a hundred times its clock length'.
—Virginia Woolf

'The longer you can look back, the farther you can look forward'.
—Winston Churchill

'One moment of patience may ward off great disaster'.
'One moment of impatience may ruin a whole life'.
—Chinese proverb

'Time destroys the speculation of men, but it confirms the judgement of nature'.
—Marcus Tullius Cicero

CONTENTS

Acknowledgements   xi
List of Abbreviations   xiii

1 It's Time   1
   Minding Nature, Not the Clock   1
   Time and Space in Environmental Law   9
   The Nature of Time   19
   Time in Nature   30
   Telling the Story   41

2 Temporalities of Change   46
   Time-Lapsed Environmental Change   46
   Eden Besieged   52
   Evolutionary Time Lags   59
   Time and Law   80
   Timelines of Modern Environmental Law   98

3 The Ever-Present Now   121
   Pull of the Future; Drag of the Present   121
   Governing the Future   125
   Governing Change   146
   Ungrandfathering the System   180

4 Rear Vision   187
   Nature's Ghosts   187
   Nature's Enclaves   192
   Restoring the Environment   197
   Environmental Restoration Law   206
   Ecological Restoration Law   226
   Restoring Culture with Nature   250
   Reflections   261

5 *Rallentare*   264
    Life in the Fast Lane   264
    Keeping Up with the Jones   271
    Compressing Time in Law   287
    Slowness   306
    Slow Food   311
    Slow Money   330
    Patience and Timing   347

6 Telling the Time   350
    On Borrowed Time   350
    Listening to Nature   360
    Adjudicating for Nature   368
    Living with Nature   382
    Arcadia   399

Index   405

ACKNOWLEDGEMENTS

All big books take time. I began contemplating nature's time while visiting some of the most beautiful and inspiring wild places, both in my homeland – Tasmania – and in other places, including some in Canada where I resided for many years. That experience of time struck me as dramatically unlike the contrived, social time of our daily lives, a difference I came to see as increasingly relevant to understanding our environmental behaviour. This book thus owes a lot to nature itself.

It also owes a lot to my former student assistants Nicole Bakker, Olivia French, Angela Lee, and Meghan Trepanier. All helped me research the literature. Also, I am deeply indebted to anthropologist Mary Jackes for our many conversations about time in human culture and evolution. Among my academic colleagues in the field of law with whom I discussed some of my ideas, I thank Natasha Affolder, Tom Baxter, Lauren Butterly, Scott Findlay, Doug Harris, Louis Kotze, Peter Lawrence, Helen Locher, Ted Lefroy, Di Nichol, Jeff McGee, Jan McDonald, Beate Sjafjell, Heather Forrest, and Afshin Akhtar-Khavari.

ABBREVIATIONS

ANZ	Australian and New Zealand Bank
ASIC	Australian Securities and Investments Commission
CBA	Cost-benefit analysis
CDP	Carbon Disclosure Project
CERCLA	Comprehensive Environmental Response, Compensation and Liability Act (US)
CERES	Coalition for Environmentally Responsible Economies
CJEU	Court of Justice of the European Union
CLCP	Comprehensive Land Claims Process
CLRP	Collaborative Landscape Restoration Program
CO_2	Carbon dioxide
CSR	Corporate social responsibility
DoC	Department of Conservation (New Zealand)
EC	European Commission
EEZ	Exclusive economic zone
EIA	Environmental impact assessment
EIS	Environmental impact study
EPBCA	Environment Protection and Biodiversity Conservation Act (Australia)
ETS	Emissions trading system
EU	European Union
FAO	UN Food and Agricultural Organization
FERC	Federal Energy Regulatory Commission (US)

FoF	Friends of Flora
FSC	Forest Stewardship Council
GDP	Gross domestic product
GFC	Global Financial Crisis
GHG	Greenhouse gases
GMO	Genetically modified organism
IASB	International Accounting Standards Board
ICANN	Internet Corporation for Assigned Names and Numbers
ICJ	International Court of Justice
ILO	International Labour Organization
ISDS	Investor-state dispute settlement
ITQ	Individual transferable quota
IUCN	International Union for Conservation of Nature
MSC	Marine Stewardship Council
NASA	National Aeronautics and Space Administration
NEPA	National Environmental Policy Act (US)
NGO	Nongovernmental organisation
NGPFG	Norwegian Government Pension Fund Global
OECD	Organisation for Economic Cooperation and Development
PMAA	Pulp Mill Assessment Act (Tasmania)
RAC	Resource Assessment Commission (Australia)
REDD	Reduced Emissions from Deforestation and Degradation
RMA	Resource Management Act (New Zealand)
RPDC	Resource Planning and Development Commission (Tasmania)
SARA	Species at Risk Act (Canada)
SER	Society for Ecological Restoration
SEZ	Special economic zone
SRI	Socially responsible investment/investing

SWF	Sovereign wealth fund
TAC	Total allowable catch
TfL	Trees for Life
UK	United Kingdom
UN	United Nations
UNEP	United Nations Environment Programme
UNEP-FI	United Nations Environment Programme – Finance Initiative
UNESCO	UN Educational, Scientific and Cultural Organization
UNPRI	UN Principles for Responsible Investment
UPOV	International Union for the Protection of New Varieties of Plants
US	United States of America
VDR	Vintage differentiated regulation
WBCSD	World Business Council for Sustainable Development
WWF	Worldwide Fund for Nature
Y2Y	Yellowstone to Yukon

1

It's Time

Minding Nature, Not the Clock

We once habitually watched nature to tell the time. It was perhaps first contemplated while gazing at the heavens, tracking celestial objects to gauge the timing of notable occasions. The oldest known image of a star constellation, Orion, was found on a tablet carved from mammoth tusk about 35,000 years ago.[1] Archaeologists speculate that the tablet's many notches were a pregnancy calendar, in which human fertility cycles were linked to the stars' presence. People were also deeply attuned to Earth's temporalities for their own survival: the fruiting and flowering of vegetation and the mating and migration of animals were among natural cycles that people scrutinised for cues in organising their lives. Ancient communities were also mindful of time's greater expanses – from the primordial past to the eternal future. In Australian Aboriginal spirituality, the Dreamtime stories connect the living to their ancestor spirits and the landscapes they fashioned, passing treasured knowledge and belief systems to later generations.[2] Palaeolithic cave paintings with evocative renderings of animals, such as those adorning the Lascaux Caves in France, gave successive human generations insights into the appearances and habits of wildlife that their forebears saw. People also acknowledged the need to support, not sacrifice, posterity; the ancient 'seventh generation' principle of the Native American Iroquois behoved individuals to consider how their actions might affect their descendants seven generations to come. And the prospect of an immortal future shows in archaic *Homo sapiens*' burial sites preserving artefacts such as tools and weapons for the presumed afterlife.[3]

---

[1] D. Whitehouse, '"Oldest star chart" found', *BBC News* 21 January 2003, at www.bbc.com/news.
[2] C. Hammond and M. Fox, *Creation, Spirituality and the Dreamtime* (Millennium Books, 1991).
[3] J. Riel-Salvatore and G.A. Clark, 'Grave markers: Middle and early upper Paleolithic burials and the use of chronotypology in contemporary Paleolithic research' (2001) 42(4) *Current Anthropology* 449.

Time continues to prove indispensable to our modern lives, but in a jarringly different guise. As American historian Lewis Mumford observed in his 1934 classic *Technics and Civilization*, 'the first characteristic of modern machine civilization is its temporal regularity . . . From the moment of waking, the rhythm of day is punctuated by the clock'.[4] Time has assimilated the plasticity of space, as something to be filled up, diced up, and even compressed through time-saving devices. As a valuable good, time also cannot sit idle, with popular adages reminding us that 'the early bird catches the worm' or 'never put off to tomorrow what you can do today'. Timetables, diaries, clocks, calendars, and other time-keeping wares not only discipline our personal lives through scheduling, deadlines, and so on, they pervasively regiment social institutions from the market to the law through an intensely commodified time.[5] For all its success in boosting economic productivity and efficiency through 'time savings', this mechanical, industrial time lessens our sensitivity to Earth's timescales. Modern economic systems and their governance are moored to the present and immediate, at odds with nature's stretching across expansive time frames from the distant past to the long-term future. While ancient *Homo sapiens* were complicit in some major ecological disturbances, our recent 'mastery' of time has disconnected people from the rhythms of nature to the point where far greater upheaval beckons, as evident in species extinctions, climatic shifts, and other turmoil of the Anthropocene.

By detaching time from its organic cycles and sequences, nature shows increasing signs of time-distorted decay and damage. Forests and fisheries have dissipated for short-term economic gains that prevent nature's capital from fully regenerating. Some species have gone extinct, shearing from the tree of life some of its branches of evolutionary potential. Agriculture has become dependent on massive artificial inputs, such as petrochemicals, to enable production to 'defy' nature's potentialities. Non-biodegradable plastics designed for durability litter the oceans in ever-greater gyres, resistant to natural decay. And greenhouse gas emissions have accumulated to the point at which Earth's climate threatens to shift abruptly, beyond natural permutations. These and other temporalities of change in nature we have unleashed of course threaten ourselves as well.

---

[4] L. Mumford, *Technics and Civilization* (Routledge and Kegan Paul, 1934), 269.
[5] On the development of time-keeping technologies and their social context and consequences, see D.S. Landes, *Revolution in Time: Clocks and the Making of the Modern World* (Harvard University Press, 2000).

It's time for change: humanity must mind nature, not the clock. Although hunter–gatherer livelihoods encompassed 99 per cent of human history, returning to them is no longer possible for most of us, and instead we must find other lifestyles that bond us with our natural environment. That human beings have socialised nature for millennia cannot lead to the conclusion that we can exist independently of Earth's life-sustaining systems. Our social temporalities must be aligned with the timescales of the rest of nature, respecting the processes of ecological succession and biological evolution, as well as the timescales by which nature can safely absorb anthropogenic disturbances – whether from harvesting fisheries or emitting greenhouse gases, for example. Telling nature's time will result in moderating our behaviour in order that environmental change occurs within manageable natural permutations. The law, as a means of articulating cultural values and influencing behaviour, has a seminal role in meeting this challenge. As legal governance has been deeply complicit in our time-distorted environmental practices, especially in markets and industrial development, from which ecological stresses emerge, telling nature's time will require law reform in addition to other social and institutional changes.

A book about this subject might, however, strike a scholar of environmental law, as much as anyone with an interest in environmental policy and practice, as superfluous. For surely we have been accustomed to appreciate time as central to environmental decision-making at least since the ascendancy of the philosophy of sustainable development. It behoves us to act for the enduring well-being of future generations and the health of the planet that we all depend on. Yet, although the mantra of sustainability has sensitised environmental decisions to time, it's an ersatz understanding of nature's time, rather incomplete and inadequate. Many important dimensions of time are missing or marginalised from environmental governance. The world has suffered vast ecological losses, yet the need for restoration, which requires orienting ourselves towards the past, is poorly acknowledged in legislation. Likewise, the frenzied pace of economic development and its collateral environmental damage defies control, and indeed the law is complicit in this acceleration of time, through contrivances such as 'fast-track' regulation. Even the capacity to govern future threats, the main legacy of sustainability, is in fact mired in temporal inertia, as numerous existing developments are grandfathered from change. Society needs to slow down and have the capacity to change and adapt to new circumstances in order to live with its natural surroundings. This book is devoted to rescuing these temporalities so that we can, through the law, align ourselves with the timescales and motions of the natural world. Telling nature's time will contribute to better timed decisions, enabling society to choose the ecologically appropriate time for action.

A useful way to decipher these challenges and solutions comes from the visual arts, which can enliven our imagination about nature's time. Some artists humble us through their works, which evoke feelings of timelessness and slowness. Andy Goldsworthy, one of the world's foremost ecological artists, explores tempo in many of his works, as documented in his film *Rivers and Tides: Andy Goldsworthy Working with Time*. We may drift into meditative bliss watching his igloo made from beach driftwood; as the tide creeps in, the wooden assemblage begins to float and then slide out to sea in a delicate swirl. Similar contemplation comes with Polish artist Marzena Wasikowska's serene paintings, such as *Waterfall*, embodying calm, beauty, and hope, and some of her works adorn hospitals to facilitate patients' healing. In the metropolis, the seeming antithesis of tranquil slowness, perhaps the most extreme depiction of deceleration is Andy Warhol's *Empire*, featuring some eight hours of continuous slow motion footage of New York's iconic Empire State Building.

These portrayals of slowness will resonate with those who have eloped to the wilderness. Our sense of time in nature is sometimes dramatically unlike the hurried tempo of modern living. For visitors to Antarctica, the remotest and wildest nature left, timelessness is commonly felt where 'time melts into yesterday, today and tomorrow'.[6] When time appears 'frozen' while immersed in these ancient places of breathtaking beauty, we seemingly focus and appreciate the moment. Slowness, as this book will argue, is a vital temporality that our environmental laws must cultivate to reduce the intensity of pressures on Earth while fostering more careful and sensitive decision-making. Slowness must also be linked to knowing *when* to act, to ensure that the timing of environmental decisions is correctly attuned to nature's temporalities such as when to harvest natural resources or mitigate degrading impacts.

Another way that artists can help reimagine Earth's timescales is to connect us to the past. Saving nature requires not just ceasing damage but healing past losses, an imperative evoked in the intriguing work of New York artist Alan Sonfist, who erected numerous natural monuments in cities around the globe to commemorate and 'heal' their lost ecology.[7]

---

[6] R. Kohn, 'The great unseen continent', *ABC Radio National* (The Spirit of Things) 14 February 2014, at www.abc.net.au/radionational/programs/spiritofthings.

[7] A. Sonfist (ed.), *Art in the Land: A Critical Anthology of Environmental Art* (Dutton, 1983).

His archetypal work, *Time Landscape*, was began in 1965 in Manhattan in cooperation with the Metropolitan Museum of Art and municipal planners. His landscape recreated the original indigenous vegetation of New York with plants (such as oak and red cedar) selected after consulting with botanists. The project represents the processes of nature reclaiming itself and evoking the memory of the revegetated site. Sonfist repeated similar projects in many cities, creating narrative landscapes to show how the reclaimed sites looked in different epochs, and thereby engaging with his audiences about how humankind's survival depends on better understandings of the interrelationships between culture and nature. Hungarian artist Agnes Denes evokes similar restorative impulses. In the 1990s she engineered an ambitious project in Ylojarvi, Finland, called *Tree Mountain – A Living Time Capsule*, involving the planting of 10,000 pines on an artificial mountain sculpted from refuse material left in a gravel pit. The trees were placed in an intricate mathematical pattern derived from a combination of the patterns in a sunflower and pineapple. The restoration project, intended to last for at least 400 years, was presented as a communication from the late twentieth century generation to posterity to express society's reawakened reverence for nature.[8] In 1996, the President of Finland dedicated the site as a national monument.

These artists' work accentuates the need for humankind to accept its responsibility to help restore nature. This of course may not always be necessary. Robert Smithson, one of the leading practitioners of the Land Art movement of the 1960s and 1970s, drew attention to nature reclaiming itself in his iconic piece *Partially Buried Woodshed*, a work done on the grounds of Kent State University in 1970. To Smithson, it symbolises nature's forces of entropy as the mounds of earth gradually envelop and bury the derelict and decaying structure. Sometimes art itself evidences the past natures we wish to restore. Anglo-Australian painter John Glover's many vivid depictions of the landscape of the state of Tasmania during his sojourn there in the 1830s and 1840s have since been studied by local environmentalists trying to decipher the former conditions they seek to restore. Similarly, climate scientists have scrutinised European winter landscape paintings from the medieval and more recent periods to obtain clues about the magnitude and impact of shifting climatic conditions over time.[9]

Our capacity to respond deftly and lightly to an evolving future, without irreparably burdening nature, is another temporality that some artists

---

[8] J. Clark, 'Fields of thought: the art of Agnes Denes' (1997) 16 *Public Art Review* 9.
[9] P.J. Robinson, 'Ice and snow in paintings of Little Ice Age winters' (2005) 60(2) *Weather* 37.

embrace, as does this book. 'Walking artists', such as Richard Long and Hamish Fulton, whose *A Line in the Himalayas* and *The Pilgrim's Way*, respectively, move through nature on long, solitary walks, leaving no trace other than their photographic record. Other artists fashion temporary structures in nature, without any lasting impact, such as sculptor John Davis, whose *Tree Piece* was made in 1973 by enclosing the trunks of several trees on the edge of the Murray River, Australia, with materials such as mud, latex, and twigs bound, which were then allowed to weather and rot away. Or consider landscape photographer Jem Southam, renowned for his patient surveillance of subtle changes in sites in southwest England over months or even several years, such as his *The Pond at Upton Pyne* series that tracks the transformation of a neglected village pond.

This book isn't about environmental art, but how the social practice of time deviates from nature's timescales and how to reform environmental law to help society realign itself with nature's temporalities. These artistic gestures vividly arouse some of the temporalities of our strained relationship with nature that need repair. Time matters greatly to our personal lives and social systems, yet despite being forever in our minds and almost constantly in view, as seen on clocks, computers, calendars, and other timekeepers, it remains abstruse and subject to diverse understandings. Most fundamentally, time serves to mark changes in our surroundings, including the environment and the changes wrought by humankind. In this guise, time is best understood as an intellectual framework by which we can measure change, sequence, and compare events and choose timeframes for action such as when to phase out greenhouse gas emissions expeditiously. As a way to identify change and draw connections between the past, present, and future, time enables us to see associations between present environmental conditions with their former state and how they might alter in the future. Time is also about great expanses of change – evolutionary, geological, and other dimensions of change of Earth – that we must grasp in order to see our species within an exponentially larger temporal field.

Unfortunately, such temporal expanses, continuities, and shifts are fragmented in the human conceptualisation of time. Time is rendered discontinuous, so that past environmental changes are often not seen as relevant to the present, while the near-sighted behaviour of today's generation causes the future to be discounted into irrelevance. Such discontinuities lead humankind's timescales to diverge from Earth's, and this lack of synchronisation may widen as cultural evolution dramatically accelerates our trajectory away from Earth's temporal rhythms. Natural resources are depleted more quickly than they can regenerate, past ecological damage remains unrepaired, and future environmental changes are not adequately guarded against, the result of which is that natural systems lose their capacity to change and evolve according to their own biorhythms. The Anthropocene has become the potent epochal signifier of human-induced environmental change.

Although time, including nature's tempo, is anthropomorphically framed, in that we comprehend it through our individual cognition and collective culture, we are not locked into any single or invariable view of time that condemns humankind to perpetuate its misguided ways. To deprive nature of its own reality, to subsume it within culture, as an artefact of cultural practice, would merely trap society in a destructive determinism that eviscerates its capacity to critique the Anthropocene. Just as artists can help reconceptualise how we see changes in nature, and promote dialogue about past, present, and future environments, the legal system also has a formative role. Environmental law codifies human understandings of environmental change and provides directions on how to manage it. The law can direct us to remedy the consequences of past mistakes or avoid actions that would engender new ones. The law's operation itself also embodies a temporality, such as by requiring environmental decisions to occur within designated time frames or the law only taking notice of events or impacts that occur within a stipulated period. Despairingly, environmental law often fails to acknowledge changes in the natural world and is complicit in the Anthropocene. The law is too temporally one-dimensional, and indeed quite static, often lacking the adaptive flexibility to adjust to new circumstances and unwilling to acknowledge past losses. Mired in an overly contemporaneous time frame, preoccupied with the present, environmental law has failed to help human culture become attuned to Earth's timescales. Emerging environmental threats such as climate change are downplayed because addressing them would be too costly for today's generation and interfere with more immediate considerations. Past environmental losses, of which many continue to reverberate, receive little attention, let alone lead to any legal accountability. The temporally stilted approach resonates in regulatory controls, such as environmental assessment and licensing, that resist adjustment to accommodate shifting circumstances. It is rare for governance to be recalibrated, such as through relicensing, and indeed environmental regulation often 'grandfathers' existing developments, shielding them from necessary change over time.

This book seeks to inculcate an *ecological timescape* in the law that synchronises human and ecological timescales.[10] The term 'timescape' describes the totality of the time-context of the natural world in which human beings live. As Barbara Adam explains, where 'landscapes, cityscapes and seascapes mark the spatial features of past and present activities of organisms and matter, timescapes emphasise their rhythmicities, their timings and tempos, their changes and contingencies'.[11] To align social time with nature's timescape requires environmental governance to foster a slower, more flexible, and holistic understanding of time. The assumption, for instance, that new developments can be fast-tracked for one-off approval should be replaced by regulation offering greater due diligence and foresight before making commitments, and a willingness to periodically adjust standards because of changing circumstances. Concomitantly, the commitment to sustainability – perpetuating current environmental conditions – needs a parallel devotion to addressing past damage and engaging in ecological restoration. Further, the pace of environmentally burdensome development must dramatically slow, in line with a wider deceleration of social and economic life as championed by social movements for Slow Food and Slow Money.

A demanding agenda, no doubt, as any appeal to nature's timescales as existing 'outside' human contrivance creates a methodological conundrum of how to understand the natural world even though it includes humankind.[12] This challenge transcends this book's subject matter, as environmental law worldwide confronts similar difficulties of 'knowing' the plants, animals, and landscapes that it seeks to protect. The law, as a product of human culture, is thus shaped by the limits of its thinking. Scientific knowledge provides an invaluable resource to unveil natural timescales and other ecological phenomena, insights that the law must strengthen. But because scientific expertise is neither values-free nor able to solve every environmental challenge,[13] it must be supplemented by other insights into nature's tempo, such as the ecological wisdom of indigenous peoples or community know-how pioneering restoration

---

[10] The expression 'timescape' was apparently coined by science fiction writer Gregory Benford in 1980 for his novel of that name, a novel which also spoke about ecological disaster. Barbara Adam used the term effectively to underpin her critique of the temporalities of human environmental behaviour: *Timescapes of Modernity: The Environment and Invisible Hazards* (Routledge, 1998).

[11] Adam, *Timescapes of Modernity*, 11.

[12] On the constructions of time, and space, see D. Massey, *Space, Place and Gender* (University of Minnesota Press, 1994).

[13] S. Jasanoff, *The Fifth Branch: Science Advisers as Policymakers* (Harvard University Press, 1990).

and slowness. In overcoming the nature-culture dichotomy, Kate Soper emphasises that 'it is an error to suppose that defending the possibility of an objective knowledge of natural processes one is committed to an uncritical acceptance of the "authority" of science'.[14]

A further reason to supplement scientific accounts of the natural world is that alone they will unlikely engender adequate behavioural changes; we also need strategies to engage communities, to expand their imagination and altruism for the forests, animals, and rivers they share. As Aldo Leopold observed, 'we can only be ethical in relation to something we can see, feel, understand, love, or otherwise have faith in'.[15] A hermeneutical approach to nature, as some describe this challenge, reflects on and mediates between various interpretations or narratives about environmental issues, thereby complementing (but not rejecting) the positivist, scientific accounts of nature in seeking to nurture greater environmental affinity and respect.[16] Such narratives of the natural world permeate the stories and arts of aboriginal peoples,[17] and so too for Western cultures many landscapes are layered with myths and memories.[18]

This agenda, clearly, involves much more than just legislative reform; the challenges fester deeply in social, political, and economic systems. Human beings' perceptions of time and change are grounded in complex institutional and cultural settings that the law must respond to and shape.[19]

Time and Space in Environmental Law

This book aims to deepen knowledge of the role of time in environmental law, in order to better comprehend why environmental law is not particularly effective and thereby stimulate debate about its reform. It's an ambitious agenda, departing from the spatial vista that dominates the practice and analysis of environmental law. While some scholars might disagree that such a spatial bias exists, and would cite the profusion of interest in time in environmental law coming with the philosophy of sustainable

---

[14] K. Soper, 'Nature/"Nature"' in G. Robertson, et al. (eds), *Future Natural: Nature, Science, Culture* (Routledge, 1996), 21, 30.
[15] A. Leopold, *A Sand County Almanac* (Oxford University Press, 1949) xxvi.
[16] See generally F. Clingerman, et al. (eds), *Interpreting Nature: The Emerging Field of Environmental Hermeneutics* (Fordham University Press, 2015).
[17] F. Besson, C. Omhovère and H. Ventura, *The Memory of Nature in Aboriginal, Canadian and American Contexts* (Cambridge Scholars Publishing, 2014).
[18] S. Schama, *Landscape and Memory* (Alfred A. Knopf, 1994).
[19] B.J. Richardson, 'A damp squib: environmental law from a human evolutionary perspective' (2011) 7(3) *Law and Prosociality eJournal* 2.

development, as well as the interest in environmental history, this embrace of time is very much unfinished business. The linear, prospective temporality of sustainability falls to capture the multi-stranded temporalities of nature that governance must grapple with. The discipline of environmental history has greatly enlightened us about changes in the natural world, from the biological to geological, as well as knowledge of human interaction with our environment over time.[20] Environmental law itself is increasingly studied in its historical context.[21] But academic curiosity about the past has had insufficient impact on the practice of contemporary environmental law.

The spatial bias not only informs environmental decision-making, it also pervades society. As French philosopher Henri Lefebvre observed, 'let everyone look at the space around them. What do they see? Do they see time? They live time after all; they are in time. Yet all anyone sees is movement. In nature, time is apprehended within space'.[22] The environmental law literature often dwells on property rights, jurisdictional authority, the spatial connections between ecological impacts and sources of harm, and the sheer physicality of ecological problems.[23] The celebrated motto of the modern environmental movement – 'Think Globally, Act Locally' – is the ultimate expression of the spatial vista in environmental policy and practice. The focus on space in the doctrinal and theoretical development of environmental law dovetails with the wider fascination with space in much legal scholarship. 'Space', from physical places to socially and politically constructed spaces, has been elevated by socio-legal scholarship and law and geography literature as a privileged framework for enquiry about the exercise of legal power and structuring of legal relationships. Edward Soja's work on 'spatial justice' focuses on unjust geographies in urban America.[24] While Soja believes the spatial turn is necessary to counteract

---

[20] For recent synopses of the scholarly field, see A.C. Isenberg (ed), *The Oxford Handbook of Environmental History* (Oxford University Press, 2014); E. Vaz, C.J. de Melo, and L.M. Costa Pinto (eds), *Environmental History in the Making: Volume I: Explaining* (Springer, 2016).

[21] See the Environment, Law and History Blog, at https://environmentlawhistory.blogspot.com.au.

[22] H. Lefebvre, *The Production of Space* (Basil Blackwell, 1991), 95.

[23] E.g. J. Holder and C. Harrison (eds), *Law and Geography: Current Legal Issues*, Volume 5 (Oxford University Press, 2003); R. Verchick, 'Critical space theory: keeping local geography in American and European environmental law' (1998) 73(3) *Tulane Law Review* 739; D. Grinlinton and P. Taylor, *Property Rights and Sustainability* (Brill, 2011); C. Rootes (ed), *Acting Locally: Local Environmental Mobilizations and Campaigns* (Routledge, 2008); A. Philippopoulos-Mihalopoulos, *Spatial Justice: Body, Lawscape, Atmosphere* (Routledge, 2015).

[24] E. Soja, *Seeking Spatial Justice* (University of Minnesota Press, 2010).

the tradition of privileging time in justice studies, David Delaney, one of the pioneers of the law and geography genre, has been accused of 'reifying the spatial and privileging, a priori, spatial over temporal analyses'.[25] Legal scholars in this tradition tend to borrow heavily from literature in politics, sociology, and other disciplines that accentuates the significance of space over time. Frederick Jameson and David Harvey, among such examples, both use space as a key lens for understanding social and economic phenomenon of the late-capitalist, postmodern world.[26]

Scholars of law have engaged with time in various contexts, such as legal anthropology, legal history, and critical legal studies. Carol Greenhouse, notably, critiques the dominance of 'linear time' in Western legal traditions, and from case studies spanning ancient China to recent American politics shows that 'time arises ... from the temporal assumptions embedded in specific state practices – bureaucratic administration, taxation and the regulation of economic life, and through a variety of executive, legislative and judicial powers'.[27] Scholars of indigenous law such as John Borrows sometimes draw heavily on the temporalities of injustice and redemption.[28] A rich body of legal history, both doctrinal and socio-legal in character,[29] uses the past to debunk legal norms portrayed as 'timeless' or 'natural'.[30] Legal historians have illuminated how the law renders history into legal procedure, and uses it to delineate the official record of the past, and then to vindicate the present and control the future.[31] David Bederman, for instance, probes the instrumentality behind the

[25] M. Valverde, '"Time thickens, takes on flesh". Spatiotemporal dynamics in law' in I. Braverman, et al. (eds), *The Expanding Spaces of Law* (Stanford University Press, 2015), 53, 57 (discussing D. Delaney, *The Spatial, the Legal and the Pragmatics of World-Making: Nomospheric Investigations* (Routledge, 2010)).
[26] F. Jameson, 'The end of temporality' (2003) 29(4) *Critical Inquiry* 695; D. Harvey, *Cosmopolitanism and the Geographies of Freedom* (Columbia University Press, 2009).
[27] C. Greenhouse, *A Moment's Notice: Time Politics Across Cultures* (Cornell University Press, 1996), 7.
[28] J. Borrows, *Recovering Canada: The Resurgence of Indigenous Law* (University of Toronto Press, 2002).
[29] E.g. R. Lesaffer, *European Legal History: A Cultural and Political Perspective*, trans. J. Arriens (Cambridge University Press, 2099); J. Seutter, *The Origins and Effects of Early Developments in English Common Law, 1066-1400* (Anchor Academic Publishing, 2015); J. Getzler, *A History of Water Rights at Common Law* (Oxford University Press, 2004).
[30] R.W. Gordon, 'Critical legal histories' (1984) 36(1–2) *Stanford Law Review* 57.
[31] For many examples, see e.g. D.W. Hamilton and A.L. Brophy (eds), *Transformations in American Legal History: Law, Ideology, and Methods: Essays in Honor of Morton J. Horwitz* (Harvard University Press, 2010); H. Foster, B.L. Berger, and A.R. Buck (eds), *The Grand Experiment: Law and Legal Culture in British Settler Societies* (University of British Columbia Press, 2008).

manipulation of the past and historical sources used in international legal practice.[32] The doctrine of precedent, limitation limits, eligibility periods, risk management, and many other temporal devices structure the operation and lived experience of law. In critiquing how the state builds narratives to anchor its legitimacy, historians also unveil how the past is forever wedged in the partialities of memory, selection of facts, and their ideological framing.[33] Likewise, across the social sciences, such as cultural studies, anthropology, and sociology, interest is growing in the social construction of time, including through the law, with analyses spanning critiques of temporality in postcolonial studies[34] to chronotopes.[35] The foregoing scholarship may aid understandings of how law mediates the experience of time in human environmental behaviour, although this research does not directly deal with the natural world.

The scholarly discipline of environmental history deals most directly with the human interactions with nature over time. It fascinates many people, as exemplified by the plethora of bestsellers by John McNeil, Tim Flannery, Jared Diamond, and others, plus endless television documentaries and abundant scientific research.[36] Environmental history draws from many disciplines including geography, geology, and palaeontology, to name a few. It illuminates changes in nature over time, including anthropogenic impacts and nature's influence on us.[37] Some of this knowledge has implications for contemporary environmental law. Climatologists, for instance, extract ancient ice-core samples in Antarctica, from as far back as 800,000 years, in order to measure and compare temporal fluctuations in atmospheric concentrations of carbon dioxide.[38] Conservation biologists decipher past wildlife populations and their habitats in order to

---

[32] D.J. Bederman, 'Foreign Office international legal history', in M. Craven, M. Fitzmaurice, and M. Vogiatzi (eds), *Time, History and International Law* (Martinus Nijhoff, 2007) 43.
[33] G. Schopflin and G. Hosking (eds), *Myths and Nationhood* (Routledge, 1997).
[34] D. Scott, *Omens of Adversity: Tragedy, Time, Memory, Justice* (Duke University Press, 2014).
[35] G.C. Spivak, 'Time and timing: law and history', in J.B. Bender and D.E. Wellbery (eds), *Chronotypes: The Construction of Time* (Stanford University Press, 1991), 99.
[36] T. Flannery, *The Eternal Frontier: An Ecological History of North America and Its Peoples* (Grove Press, 2002); J. McNeill, *Something New Under the Sun* (WW Norton, 2001); J. Diamond, *Collapse: How Societies Choose to Fail or Succeed* (Viking, 2005).
[37] The literature is vast; see e.g. M. Williams, *Deforesting the Earth: From Prehistory to Global Crisis. An Abridgement* (University of Chicago Press, 2006); J.D. Hughes, *An Environmental History of the World: Humankind's Changing Role in the Community of Life* (Routledge, 2001); R.H. Huggett, *The Natural History of Earth: Debating Long-Term Change in the Geosphere and Biosphere* (Routledge, 2014).
[38] D. Lüthi, et al., 'High-resolution carbon dioxide concentration record 650,000–800,000 years before present' (2008) 453 *Nature* 379.

guide new management decisions. Understanding environmental history helps to evaluate the causes and nature of ecological damage. An ambitious example that puts human endeavour into the context of the Earth's evolving ecology and geology is David Christian's *Maps of Time*.[39] From the origins of our planet, Christian steps through many varied economic, social, and ecological dimensions of human history with a call for humankind to learn the lesson of history so as to save the global environment. Its history, however, should be more than a repository of interesting 'lessons' about our predecessors' mistakes; environmental history should deepen our understanding of nature's evolution and its former, unimpaired conditions that we should sometimes strive to restore.

The history of environmental law itself has also become quite a scholarly niche, investigating the evolution of conservation law and resource management, their political and economic contexts, and the philosophical foundations of legal responses.[40] Much of this genre covers recent history, tracing the emergence of modern environmental law since the 1960s, such as Richard Lazarus' *The Making of Environmental Law*.[41] But some tackle much earlier periods, such as Kieko Matteson's *Forests in Revolutionary France: Conservation, Community, and Conflict, 1669–1848*,[42] Mark Kanazawa's *Golden Rules: The Origins of California Water Law in the Gold Rush*,[43] and Douglas Harris' *Landing Native Fisheries: Indian Reserves and Fishing Rights in British Columbia, 1849–1925*.[44] This enthralling scholarship reveals the diverse ways in which the law has shaped environmental behaviour through time, and provides an intricate record of past mistakes and successes to eschew or emulate.

---

[39] D. Christian, *Maps of Time: An Introduction to Big History* (University of California Press, 2004).

[40] R.J. Lazarus, *The Making of Environmental Law* (University of Chicago Press, 2004); and also P.H. Sand, *The History and Origin of International Environmental Law* (Edward Elgar Publishing, 2015); S. Coyle and K. Morrow, *The Philosophical Foundations of Environmental Law: Property, Rights and Nature* (Hart Publishing, 2004); K.B. Brooks, *Before Earth Day: The Origins of American Environmental Law, 1945-1970* (University of Kansas Press, 2009); W.H. Rodgers, Jr., 'The most creative moments in the history of environmental law: "the whats"' (2000) *University of Illinois Law Review* 1.

[41] Z.J.B. Plater, 'From the beginning, a fundamental shift of paradigms: a theory and short history of environmental law' (1993–4) 27 *Loyola of Los Angeles Law Review* 981.

[42] K. Matteson, *Forests in Revolutionary France: Conservation, Community, and Conflict, 1669–1848* (Cambridge University Press, 2015).

[43] M. Kanazawa, *Golden Rules: The Origins of California Water Law in the Gold Rush* (University of Chicago Press, 2015).

[44] D. Harris, *Landing Native Fisheries: Indian Reserves and Fishing Rights in British Columbia, 1849–1925* (University of British Columbia Press, 2008).

Time is a constitutive element of several other clusters of environmental law research. Some use it to help explain the workings of specific legal doctrines, such as environmental liability.[45] Others investigate the future impulse of environmental regulation; here, the ethos of sustainable development and associated concepts, including intergenerational equity and the precautionary principle, have generated many writings that both critique existing practices and chart new directions to avoid apocalyptic scenarios.[46] Some explore the notion of adaptive governance, highlighting the benefits of regulation that allow societies and ecosystems to respond resiliently to environmental change and uncertainty.[47] While these scholarly endeavours are important, especially the adaptive governance literature, none provides an adequate picture of the temporalities of the natural world, and human impacts and their regulation. Most crucially, time as a social construct mediated by environmental law is under-theorised.

The architecture of environmental law itself resonates a lop-sided temporality, narrowly framed around a 'present-future' outlook: specifically, governing present human behaviours that may have future environmental effects.[48] Sustainable development, environmental governance's pre-eminent norm and temporal ballast, reinforces this bias through its attention to avoiding risks, mitigating impending damage, and other prospective actions.[49] Environmental law also embodies respect for history, such as

---

[45] E. Stavang, 'Tolerance limits and temporal priority in environmental civil liability' (1997) 17 *International Review of Law and Economics* 553; C. Boyd, 'Temporal severance and the exclusion of time in determining the economic value of regulated property' (2001–2) 36 *University of San Francisco Law Review* 793.

[46] K. Bosselmann, *The Principle of Sustainability: Transforming Law and Governance* (Ashgate, 2008); B.J. Richardson and S. Wood (eds), *Environmental Law for Sustainability* (Hart Publishing, 2006); E. Brown Weiss, *In Fairness to Future Generations: International Law, Common Patrimony, and Intergenerational Equity* (Transnational Publishers, 1989); J. Cameron and J. Abouchar, 'The precautionary principle: a fundamental principle of law and policy for the protection of the global environment' (1990) 14 *Boston College International and Comparative Law Review* 1; J. Owley and K.H. Hirokawa (eds), *Rethinking Sustainability to Meet the Climate Change Challenge* (Environmental Law Institute, 2015); D.A. Farber, 'From here to eternity: environmental law and future generations' (2003) 2 *University of Illinois Law Review* 289.

[47] D. Armitage and R. Plummer (eds), *Adaptive Capacity and Environmental Governance* (Springer, 2010); A.S. Garmestani and C.R. Allen (eds), *Social-Ecological Resilience and Law* (Columbia University Press, 2014).

[48] L. Heinzerling, 'Environmental law and the present future' (1999) 87 *Georgetown Law Journal* 2025.

[49] M. De Iuliis and P. Brandon, 'The time horizon in the evaluation of sustainable development' (2012) 6(3) *Journal of Civil Engineering and Architecture* 344.

its deference to common law property rights, a legacy that continues to constrain the law's evolution, such as limiting the scope to coerce conservation of biodiversity on private tenure or allocating natural resources equitably.[50] Neither the present-future perspective, which speaks to our collective destiny, nor our legal heritage, which undervalues respect for the natural environment, adequately aligns human behaviour with the ecological timescape. Specifically, the future orientation of environmental law can be a mirage, with little flexibility for adjustment in the light of new circumstances; the law also ignores nature's history and the massive injuries we have inflicted on it; and the law is complicit in the acceleration of time that intensifies environmental pressures.

The sparse commitment to ecological restoration is governed by myriad factors including the economic costs and biases in human psychology against valuing timescales beyond the present. When damage accretes gradually, the present generation may also not appreciate the extent of past losses and thus the consequences of further degradation. Declines in fisheries, for instance, may seem worrying from the vantage of recent decades, but disastrous from a longer time frame of over a century.[51] And in trying to explain the aetiology of environmental decline, we tend to look at temporally proximate causes, when the real cause may be much older. Loss of biodiversity might be attributed to the presence of a new invasive species, when in fact historic climatic shifts, which enable such intruders to thrive, may also inform the explanation. A further struggle for environmental law is to acknowledge the frequently slow and temporally dispersed impacts on nature.[52] Insidious ones, such as the growing amount of plastic debris littering the oceans, take their time to inflict mayhem rather than erupt spectacularly to jolt our complacency, which may help explain why such impacts rarely incur legal sanctions. Even many victims of the worst environmental catastrophes of the late twentieth century – at Bhopal in 1984 and Chernobyl in 1986 – have not obtained environmental justice, both because of the tardiness of authorities and because the poisonous fallout from these toxic monstrosities has leached beyond the horizons of

---

[50] P. Martin and M. Verbeek, *Cartography for Environmental Law. Finding New Paths to Effective Resource Use Regulation* (Profit Foundation, 2000).
[51] J. Hsu, 'Overfishing goes back centuries, log books reveal', 25 May 2009, at www.livescience.com/5445-overfishing-centuries-log-books-reveal.html.
[52] B.H. Thompson Jr, 'The trouble with time: influencing the conservation choices of future generations' (2004) 44 *Natural Resources Journal* 601.

conceivable time and allowed the responsible parties to defuse and evade responsibility.[53]

Knowledge of the past can improve contemporary environmental management, helping to curb the scourge of 'shifting' environmental baselines that determine what to sustain. One cannot assume that sustainability will accrue by basing legal protections and standards on current environmental conditions; rather, some restoration to recapture more complex and robust prior ecological conditions may be necessary. Lands may need to be replanted with trees, fish stocks replenished to their former riches, and landscapes cleansed of contaminants. The 're-wilding' movement speaks most directly to this task,[54] although its implications for legal governance have not yet been comprehensively investigated.[55] Essentially, environmental law must recover from the slough of temporal amnesia that has marginalised the past as an inspiration for future action.

A second pathway to the ecological timescape is adaptive governance that can flexibly adjust environmental decisions to changing circumstances. Adaptive governance, a term promoted by Thomas Dietz and others,[56] appeals to academics and practitioners for coordinating and adjusting resource management in the face of the complexity and uncertainty accompanying rapid ecological change. Adaptive governance is associated with broader theoretical enquiries into improving the resilience of human and natural systems to cope with adversity.[57] Governing for these purposes requires expanding the role of law and other governance institutions beyond limiting adverse change in the belief that the status quo can be maintained indefinitely, to nurturing the ability of human and natural systems to adapt to further change.[58] The capacity to adapt may also include restoration of past ecological losses, such as reforestation, to improve responses to further changes, such as climatic

---

[53] R.E. Hernan, *The Borrowed Earth: Lessons from the Fifteen Worst Environmental Disasters Around the World* (Palgrave Macmillan, 2010); R. Nixon, *Slow Violence and the Environmentalism of the Poor* (Harvard University Press, 2011).

[54] G. Monbiot, *Feral: Rewilding the Land, the Sea, and Human Life* (Allen Lane, 2013).

[55] P. Burdon, *Exploring Wild Law: The Philosophy of Earth Jurisprudence* (Wakefield Press, 2011).

[56] T. Dietz, E. Ostrom, and P.C. Stern, 'The struggle to govern the commons' (2003) 302 *Science* 1907.

[57] E.g. C. Folke, 'Resilience: the emergence of a perspective for social ecological systems analyses' (2006) 16 *Global Environmental Change* 253; C.S. Holling, 'Understanding the complexity of economic, ecological, and social systems' (2001) 4 *Ecosystems* 390.

[58] L.H. Gunderson and S.S. Light, 'Adaptive management and adaptive governance in the everglades ecosystem' (2006) 39 *Policy Sciences* 323.

shifts. Environmental law has yet to embody this agenda adequately; legislation commonly 'grandfathers' existing resource uses and polluters from transitions to tougher standards; new developments are frequently governed by licensing regimes with limited scope for adjustment to accommodate changing circumstances; and strategic planning frameworks downplay experimentation and learning processes that could generate feedback to improve governance.

Another temporality, the 'pace' of time, occupies much of this book. The tendency of technological innovations and economic globalisation to 'compress' time and accelerate the frenzied pace of modern life intensifies environmental stress.[59] The global financial agora presents one of the most pernicious sources of this impetus. The obscene rapidity of industrialisation in China and other emerging economies, much of it fuelled by cheap credit from liberalised financial markets, is now the world's major incubator of environmental pressure. Of specific economic sectors, the food business is organised on an industrial scale through gigantic factory farms that aim to get produce from the paddock to the plate by the quickest and most economical route. Major infrastructure projects also often enjoy privileged treatment by regulators to ensure their timely approval. Through 'fast-track' approval of prestige projects, restrictions on the period to evaluate environmental impacts, and arbitrary brief periods for public challenges to development decisions, the law compresses time. Legal systems are thus complicit in economic activity that accelerates changes in ecological systems that may not adapt.

This book advocates patience (going beyond the related, but much better known, 'precautionary' approach), in which we slow the speed of economic activity and its environmental sequelae and thereby get the timing right in environmental decisions. Case studies on the 'slow' movement – Slow Food and Slow Money (aka socially responsible investing) – provide potential role models for all of us.[60] The theory of adaptive management may also help govern environmental activities in a more tentative and slower manner.[61] While adaptive management theory has been utilised

---

[59] T. Eriksen, *Tyranny of the Moment: Fast and Slow Time in the Information Age* (Pluto Press, 2001); D. Harvey, *Spaces of Global Capitalism* (Verso, 2006); L. Karsten, *Globalization and Time* (Routledge, 2013).

[60] C. Honoré, *In Praise of Slow: How a Worldwide Movement Is Challenging to Cult of Speed* (AA Knoff Canada, 2004); H. Mayer and P. Knox, 'Slow cities: sustainable places in a fast world' (2006) 28 *Journal of Urban Affairs* 321; B.J. Richardson, *Socially Responsible Investment Law: Regulating the Unseen Polluters* (Oxford University Press, 2008).

[61] C.S. Holling, *Adaptive Environmental Assessment and Management* (Blackburn Press, 2005).

primarily to improve responsiveness to unpredictable and uncertain futures, Shannon Hagerman and others' work on resilience theory focuses on the past record of governance as a guide for improving adaptive management capacities.[62] A pollution-licensing regime, for instance, may need overhauling in the light of new information about ecological conditions. Slowness may ensue from a wide variety of other law reforms, from animal welfare (to end fast factory farms) to changes to corporate law (to stimulate long-term business practices).

Taking this multi-stranded approach to time should not mean abandoning space in our understanding of environmental law: space and time inform one another in many contexts of governance.[63] Because of the dynamic qualities of ecosystems, physical spaces may literally move, with consequences for legal rights and relationships. Take climate change, for instance: as sea levels rise in response to global warming, some coastal lands will be inundated and displace people and wildlife. Property rights may be lost and land use planning authorities will encounter new legal responsibilities to manage changes along vulnerable seashores. Conversely, the so-called 'tide of history' can eviscerate legal claims to spaces, as has occurred for some indigenous peoples in Canada and Australia seeking restoration of their traditional homelands – with significant repercussions for environmental management in such contested places. In the *Yorta Yorta* case, Justice Olney of the Federal Court of Australia foreshadowed the obstacle that many Aboriginal communities encounter:

> the tide of history has indeed washed away any real acknowledgment of their traditional laws and any real observance of their traditional customs. The foundation of the claim to native title in relation to the land previously occupied by those ancestors having disappeared, the native-title rights and interests previously enjoyed are not capable of revival.[64]

As the preceding remarks suggest, legal spaces or relationships that were formally abolished or 'washed away' may nonetheless persist as informal practices or memories. These 'lingering spaces', as some legal geographers explain, may continue because some people do not accept the legitimacy

---

[62] S. Hagerman, H. Dowlatabadi, and T. Satterfield, 'Observations on drivers and dynamics of environmental policy change: insights from 150 years of forest Management in British Columbia' (2010) 15(1) *Ecology and Society* 2.

[63] Valverde, '"Time thickens, takes on flesh"'.

[64] *Members of the Yorta Yorta Aboriginal Community v. Victoria and Ors*, [1998] FCA 1606, para. 129.

of the changed legal order.[65] Not only may Aboriginal people defy governments that ignore their traditional land rights, others in our socially heterogeneous societies may cling to old laws. Farmers can oppose new land use controls that limit their traditional prerogatives to manage their properties as they see fit: laws protecting remnant native vegetation and wetlands have been sources of great controversy in some jurisdictions.[66] These examples illustrate an important spatio-temporal dynamic of environmental law, in which time influences the status of legal spaces, even allowing them to persist as memories after the law is formally revoked or changed.

Most of this book, however, focuses on time rather than attempting a full-blown synthesis of time and space. While the following chapters occasionally acknowledge the spatio-temporal dynamics of environmental law, the priority is to explain the under-appreciated temporalities of environmental law and to advance a better timescape for governance. With that knowledge we can in future research engage in the spatial and temporal interactions in environmental law.

So what exactly is 'time', and how does time manifest in nature?

The Nature of Time

At Cambridge University hangs an unusual public artwork called the Corpus Clock or the Chronophage (meaning 'time eater', in Greek). Spanning nearly five feet, the clock's face is a bristling gold-plated steel disc. Without hands or numbers, the seconds, minutes, and hours are projected by a clock face backlit with blue LED lights exposed by opening slits in three concentric rings. The pendulum moves not always consistently, and sometimes tends to lag and then hurry up, a feature that may remind us that time and life itself do not always flow at a steady pace. The clock is dominated by a disquieting metallic sculpture of a locust or lizard-like creature that motions its mouth hypnotically to suggest the eating up of time as the moments pass. Conceived by John Taylor, a member of Corpus Christi College, and unveiled in 2008, the Chronophage provokes observers in a rather vivid and disturbing way to see the ravaging march of time whose seconds we can seemingly never recover.

---

[65] F. von Benda-Beckmann and K. von Benda-Beckmann, 'Places that come and go', in I. Braverman, et al. (eds), *The Expanding Spaces of Law* (Stanford University Press, 2015), 30, 41.
[66] E.g. in Australia, the Native Vegetation Act 2003 (NSW); Vegetation Management Act 1999 (Qld).

The Chronophage offers one of the most startling examples of how we may conceive time, a most inscrutable phenomenon. We constantly check it with clocks and watches, keep diaries, calendars, and other tools for scheduling, and often hurry to complete tasks 'on time'. Although we live in the present, it 'is the knife edge on which the past and future balance'.[67] People also often dwell on past experiences, sometimes with nostalgia or regret: being a passenger on a train with a rear-facing seat may resemble how we experience life, relentlessly unfolding into our past. We also anticipate the future with anxiety, excitement, or other conflicting emotions. The prospect of our own mortality and the question of whether life endures after death is the most powerful and inevitable perspective we have of our own futures. But despite all this familiarity and preoccupation with time's passage, it remains 'strangely elusive'.[68] Time in the abstract has proved to be an extraordinarily abstruse concept for physicists, philosophers, psychologists, and others exploring its multiple dimensions.[69] Jacques Derrida declared there is 'no non-metaphysical concept of time',[70] while Immanuel Kant argued that time cannot be directly known as it defies observation by the human mind, instead functioning as a precondition for other dimensions of our lives.[71] Whereas space is directly comprehensible, such as through surrounding objects that can be seen and touched, we lack a sensory organ connected with time.

Of the various denominations of time, firstly and obviously for most people, time denotes the continuum of past, present, and future, or the idea of history and destiny. Secondly, time has a rhythmic quality, being associated with sequences and cycles, such as seasonal weather changes to the daily day/night alternation. Another dimension is 'tempo', which frames time around the speed of activities and changes. Time is also evaluated in terms of 'temporality', denoting the time embedded in events and things, such as the ageing process, species evolution, or more cyclical processes such as the shedding and budding of leaves. 'Timing' is an

---

[67] Quoted in P.J. Nahin, *Time Machines: Time Travel in Physics, Metaphysics, and Science Fiction* (Springer-Verlag, 1993), 416.
[68] J.T. Fraser, 'Time felt, time understood' (2003) 3 *KronoScope* 15.
[69] P.J. Corfield, *Time and the Shape of History* (Yale University Press, 2007); L.N. Oaklander and Q. Smith (eds), *The New Theory of Time* (Yale University Press, 1994); J. Brough and L. Embree (eds), *The Many Faces of Time* (Kluwer Academic, 2000); P.K. McInerney, *Time and Experience* (Temple University Press, 1991); J.T. Fraser, *Of Time, Passion, and Knowledge: Reflections on the Strategy of Existence* (Princeton University Press, 1990).
[70] G. Bannington, *Interrupting Derrida* (Routledge, 2000), 173.
[71] I. Kant, *Critique of Pure Reason*, trans. N.K. Smith (St Martin's Press, 1965, original 1781), 70–1.

important touchstone of understanding time, denoting the particular point or period of time when natural and cultural things occur. Finally, some writers, including myself, use the language of 'timescape' to evoke the collective elements of time. Barbara Adam describes timescape as a temporal equivalent of landscape, linking together the diverse and complex dimensions of time in socio-environmental contexts in order not to understand 'what time is but what we do with it and how time enters our system of values'.[72]

Scholarly enquiries into time have clustered into three main fields – the philosophy of time, the sociology of time, and the psychology of time perception, and within each a variety of theoretical views jostle for supremacy. While some of these explorations seemingly lack practical relevance to contemporary environmental regulation, they highlight that the conceptualisation of time is a social practice. The basic questions over which protagonists debate the meaning of time include: is time only what we sense or does it exist throughout the universe; how can time be measured; and does time flow in the direction through which we perceive? Philosophical theories of time focus on fundamental issues such as the origins of time, whether it is real, and how time interacts with space and other fundamental dimensions of the universe. The sociological perspectives range from explicit enunciations of the social construction of time, such as cross-cultural differences in the experience and scheduling of time, to corollary theories that use time explicitly or implicitly as elements of theories of other social phenomena. Time perception has become a specialised field of study in psychology and neuroscience that investigates its subjectivity and how perceived time may differ from measured time because of emotion, personality, and other individual qualities.

Several cleavages stand out in conceptualisations of time.[73] First, we have substantivist and relational approaches to time, or namely between the assumption that time exists independently of the processes or events that fill it, and time defined by its relationship with events in a continuing process. A second cleavage in understandings of time is between time as 'tensed', in the sense of having linear order along a past to future continuum, and 'tenseless' time without direction or any privileged vantage. Finally, wrangling occurs over an objective definition of time as

---

[72] B. Adam, 'The temporal gaze: the challenge for social theory in the context of GM food' (2000) 51 *British Journal of Sociology* 125, 137.

[73] See P. Ricoeur, *Time and Narrative*, Volume 3 (University of Chicago Press, 1998); K.M. Jaszczolt, *Representing Time: An Essay on Temporality as Modality* (Oxford University Press, 2009).

opposed to one culturally or mentally mediated. These debates are worth describing in a little more detail.

Of the first split, the substantival concept of time departs from notions of time in ancient philosophy, such as Aristotle's view that time serves to ascertain changes and relationships between objects or events, although temporality itself neither causes nor resists change,[74] or the subjectivity and relativity of time in Confucianism and Taoism that reject any absolute or fixed time.[75] Until Einstein's reinterpretation of the relationship between time and space, time was portrayed in the Newtonian framework as the same throughout the universe, and existing independently of any observer. Einstein's theory of general relativity, however, asserted that time is affected by its surroundings. Speed and gravity affect time's flow, with high speed and high gravity slowing time: for instance, a planet's colossal mass warps time, slowing it more for a person standing on Earth than a more distant orbiting satellite. Relatedly, Einstein suggested that time passes differently for observers if their motion differs, and if one accelerates fast enough the passage of time can slow to a mere trickle. A person's position and movement in space will thus influence time, according to this view. Recently, quantum physicists exploring the temporal frontier beyond the 'Planck time' – the smallest known unit of discernible time – have speculated that time may actually disappear entirely at the most basic level of physical reality, and that therefore the universe could be fundamentally timeless.[76] In this world of illusionary time, time may simply mean, as ancient philosophers surmised, how we perceive and delineate changes in our physical world.

The debate over 'tensed' and 'tenseless' time in our cosmology is sometimes described as dynamic versus static time.[77] Tenseless time depicts it as 'an undifferentiated continuum'[78] without any objective flow or direction. Instead of a remorseless passage from the past to the future, the fundamental temporal properties of the tenseless world are the famous 'B-relations' described by philosopher John McTaggart. Without a temporal ordering of events, the past, present, and future are considered as equally real,

---

[74] U. Coope, *Time for Aristotle: Physics IV.11-14* (Oxford University Press 2005).
[75] C.C. Hunag and J.B. Henderson (eds), *Notions of Time in Chinese Historical Thinking* (Chinese University Press, 2006).
[76] T. Folger, 'Newsflash: time may not exist', *Discover: Science for the Curious* 12 June 2007, at http://discovermagazine.com/2007/jun/in-no-time.
[77] R. Le Poidevin and M. MacBeath (eds), *The Philosophy of Time* (Oxford University Press, 1993).
[78] K.B. Denbigh, *Three Concepts of Time* (Springer-Verlag, 1981), 4.

and the 'present' for some activity is simply those activities simultaneous with it.[79] Einstein himself, by prioritising the observation point, implies that its frame of reference fixes how the order or succession of events will appear to unfold. Thus any change in our surroundings does not reflect a real change in the event's intrinsic properties but only in the observer's relationship to the event. In *Slaughterhouse Five*, Kurt Vonnegut described this tenseless time allusively:

> Billy Pilgrim says that the Universe does not look like a lot of bright little dots to the creatures from Tralfamadore. The creatures can see where each star has been and where it is going, so that the heavens are filled with rarefied, luminous spaghetti. And Tralfamadorians don't see human beings as two-legged creatures, either. They see them as great millipedes – 'with babies' legs at one end and old people's legs at the other', says Billy Pilgrim.[80]

In the tenseless cosmos, the more important issue thus becomes how events are spatially connected rather than their temporal connections.[81] The human lived sense of time also may be construed as having a tenseless quality in that apprehension of the past, present, and future comes from the vantage of the present, or as philosopher Peter Osborne puts it, the present embraces 'the totality of the temporal spectrum within itself'.[82] But time in human affairs, especially in its modern guise, has a strong linear direction.

To reduce time to a tenseless unreality would appear to fail to account for its significance in human-scale phenomena, reducing the passage of time and our changing world to just labels that connote events in the universe that has only one 'now'. Arguing from the laws of nature, American philosopher Tim Mauldin argues that 'the passage of time is an intrinsic asymmetry in the temporal structure of the world . . . there are facts about what happened in the past that are independent of the present state of the world and independent of all knowledge or beliefs about the past'.[83] This tensed concept of time, pioneered by Arthur Prior, thus posits time as embodying a dynamic but linear quality in which the present continually flows, turning the unreal future into the real past.[84] The astronomer-philosopher

---

[79] J.E. McTaggart. 'The unreality of time' (1908) 17 *Mind: A Quarterly Review of Psychology and Philosophy* 456.
[80] K. Vonnegut, *Slaughterhouse-Five, Or the Children's Crusade* (Delacorte, 1969), 87.
[81] R. Read, 'Against "time slices"' (2003) 26(1) *Philosophical Investigations* 24.
[82] P. Osborne, *The Politics of Time: Modernity and Avant-Garde* (Verso, 1995), 49.
[83] T. Maudlin, *The Metaphysics within Physics* (Oxford University Press, 2010). 107–8.
[84] C. Broad, 'Time and change' (1928) supp. 8 *Proceedings of the Aristotelian Society* 175; A. Prior, *Past, Present and Future* (Clarendon Press, 1967).

Arthur Eddington in the 1920s identified the gradual dispersal of energy (from Lord Kelvin's second law of thermodynamics) as evidence of an irreversible 'arrow of time'.[85] This movement of time across a past–future continuum dovetails more closely with the intuitive and everyday perception of time people have. Typically, we think of time as past, present, and future sequences and, concomitantly, we imagine that our behaviour today can affect the flow of events tomorrow. This idea of a one-way motion of time has been influential for many human affairs, including the legal system in identifying relationships between persons and events, such as liability,[86] and the social sciences' reliance on linear sequencing in tracking causal flows.[87]

An idea of time derived from our lived experience rather than presented as an objective given also infuses much philosophical debate. Although technology allows calculation of time ever more precisely and minutely, time also has a strong subjective experience. Claudia Hammond's bestseller *Time Warped* explores this subjectivity, pondering whether 'this stretching and shrinking of time is simply an illusion or whether the mind processes time differently at different moments of our lives'.[88] Memories are our portal to the experience of time, enabling the hoarding of information, reconstructing the past, and anticipating the future.[89] Age, emotional state, body temperature, and stress are among variables that seemingly influence perception of time, including the formation of memories and the sense of tempo. For instance, individuals' time perception changes as they age: time is experienced slowly for children and faster for the elderly, and while the elderly often recall experiences from their youth as though they were yesterday they may struggle to remember events a mere week ago. Personality traits also seem relevant, suggests Stanford University professor Philip Zimbardo. His 'Time Perspective Inventory' divides personalities into six temporal types: past-negative, past-positive, present-hedonistic, present-fatalistic, future, and transcendental future.[90] Those with the present-hedonistic outlook live for the moment and indulge

---

[85] A. Eddington, *The Nature of the Physical World* (Macmillan, 1928).
[86] B.G. Peabody, 'Reversing time's arrow: law's reordering of chronology, causality, and history' (2007) 40 *Akron Law Review* 587, 589–90.
[87] For a critique, see A. Abbott, *Time Matters: On Theory and Method* (University of Chicago Press, 2001).
[88] C. Hammond, *Time Warped: Unlocking the Mysteries of Time Perception* (House of Anansi Press, 2012), 5.
[89] S. Klein, *Time: A User's Guide* (Penguin Books, 2006), 102–3.
[90] P. Zimbardo and J. Boyd, *The Time Paradox: The New Psychology of Time That Will Change Your Life* (Free Press, 2009).

in short-sighted pleasures, while future-oriented individuals lead busy, successful careers but risk fatigue and social isolation because they may neglect immediate circumstances. Neuroscience has also revealed how time perception is influenced by individuals' neurotransmitter systems,[91] and neurological and psychiatric conditions, such as attention deficit hyperactivity disorder.[92] The temporalities of everyday human behaviour have been mapped by Michael Flaherty in his *The Textures of Time*, identifying five seminal temporal dimension behaviours – duration (how long things appear to take), frequency (how often things happen), sequence (the ordering of things that happen), timing (determining when to do things), and allocation (budgeting time for various tasks) – that are implicated in a wide range of personal activities from work hours to leisure time.[93] This relativity of individual experience with time thus raises challenges about how nature's timescales can ever be authentically known by governance decision-makers.

While time perception has an intensively subjective dimension, it's felt within the penumbra of social context, which adds to the complexity of telling nature's time.[94] According to Edward Hall, time is part of culture's 'silent language' that influences daily routines, such as behavioural norms about punctuality, scheduling, multi-tasking, and distinctions between work and leisure time.[95] The sociology of time has explored cross-cultural and historical differences in the understanding of time, especially how temporality responds to economic and technological factors. In the early twentieth century, Emile Durkheim pioneered the recognition of time as a sociological phenomenon.[96] While he acknowledged the force of the subjective sense of time, Durkheim argued that events and activities are temporally located within a social setting. In the early 1930s, George Mead's theorisation of time challenged the linear model by suggesting that the past, present, and future have, socially, a more interdependent nexus.[97] Mead saw the present as the paramount temporality or the 'locus of

---

[91] W.H. Meck, 'Neuropharmocology of timing and time perception' (1996) 3(3–4) *Cognitive Brain Research* 227.
[92] M. Allman and W. Meck, 'Pathophysiological distortions in time perception and timed performance' (2012) 135(3) *Brain: A Journal of Neurology* 656.
[93] M. Flaherty, *The Textures of Time: Agency and Temporal Experience* (Temple University Press, 2011).
[94] C.D. Laughlin and C.J. Throop, 'Continuity, causation and cyclicity: a cultural neurophenomenology of time-consciousness' (2008) 1(2) *Time and Mind* 159.
[95] E. Hall, *The Silent Language* (Doubleday, 1959).
[96] E. Durkheim, *The Elementary Forms of Religious Life* (Free Press, 1965, original 1915), 23.
[97] G.H. Mead, *The Philosophy of the Present* (Open Court Publishing, 1932).

reality'; from this stance, the past conveys to the present assorted facts whose effects are mediated by personal and social interpretation that render their impact uncertain rather than the billiard-ball causality implied by linear temporal relationships. Later, sociologists such as Georges Gurvitch identified not one but a multiplicity of social times associated with different social groups and settings,[98] while Wilbert Moore and Julius Roth discussed the variety of ways that time is organised and scheduled such as in the family and workforce.[99] In the 1970s, Eviatar Zerubavel attempted to push these enquiries into a distinct field of research into an overarching social theory of time.[100]

As societies have become more time-obsessive and time-scheduled, the nature of time has similarly been harnessed as a corollary of scholarly enquiry.[101] Many scholars explore time not as an end in itself, but as a lens to investigate other phenomena, such as religion, economic behaviour, the legal system, and technological innovations. Some use time for understanding the impact of information technologies on communities,[102] urban social patterns,[103] postmodern economies,[104] labour practices and retirement living,[105] and environmental impacts.[106] Time also features in Anthony Giddens' theory of structuration (the creation and reproduction of social systems) and Niklas Luhmann's related work on systems theory.[107] Some sociologists also explore cultural changes in attitudes to or experiences of time. Norbert Elias, in this regard, argued that with the evolution of more complex societies, and the need for people's behaviour and work

---

[98] G. Gurvitch, *The Spectrum of Social Time* (D. Reidel Publishing Company, 1964).
[99] W.E. Moore, *Man, Time, and Society* (Wiley, 1963); J.A. Roth. *Timetables: Structuring the Passage of Time in Hospital Treatment and Other Careers* (Bobbs-Merrill Company, 1963).
[100] E. Zerubavel, 'Timetables and scheduling: on the social organization of time' (1976) 46 *Sociological Inquiry* 87; E. Zerubavel, 'The standardization of time: a sociohistorical perspective' (1982) 88 *American Journal of Sociology* 1.
[101] W.H. Sewell Jr, *Logics of History: Social Theory and Social Transformation* (University of Chicago Press, 2005).
[102] M. Castells, *The Rise of the Network Society*, Volume 1 (Blackwell, 1996).
[103] M.F. Goodchild and D.G. Janelle, 'The city around the clock: space-time patterns of urban ecological structure' (1984) 16 *Environment and Planning A* 807.
[104] D. Harvey, *The Condition of Postmodernity: An Enquiry into the Origins of Cultural Change* (Blackwell, 1989).
[105] M. Young and T. Schuller, *Life After Work: The Arrival of the Ageless Society* (Harper Collins, 1991).
[106] Adam, *Timescapes of Modernity*.
[107] A. Giddens, *The Constitution of Society: Introduction of the Theory of Structuration* (University of California Press, 1984); N. Luhmann, *Social Systems* (Stanford University Press, 1995).

to be temporally aligned, social time has become more prescriptive.[108] Michel Foucault, echoing concerns about the disciplined time management of Taylorism, observed the micro-division of time as a manifestation of organisation and control.[109] Stephen Kern identifies technological change during the late Industrial Revolution, such as cinema and the telephone, as a formative influence on new enunciations and experiences of time in literature, music, architecture, and other cultural productions: film and photography for instance allow unprecedented 'preservation' of the past.[110]

Time also permeates the study of past societies, as by archaeologists, anthropologists, and historians. Their capacious vistas of time harvest a wide variety of historical data as well as relying on diverse temporal concepts related to understanding origins, antecedents, turning points, and consequences.[111] Their work sometimes reveals cultural timescapes dramatically unlike that found in modern industrial capitalism. Some anthropologists find hunter–gatherer groups lacking a well-developed sense of time.[112] The Amondawa tribe in the Amazon, whose first contact with the outside world was apparently only in 1986, have no words for time or for temporal demarcations such as month or year, even though they can talk about the sequence of events. Researchers hypothesise that this omission is due to their lack of 'time technology' – a calendar system or clocks.[113] Also unlike Western chronological time is the 'Dreamtime' of Aboriginal Australians; the Dreamtime cosmology has an eternal quality in which the world is continually re-created through the present, linking ancestors and descendants.[114]

Historians and anthropologists also appreciate that because their enquiries flow through the portal of the present, the past is continually reinterpreted by each generation and that their enquiries into temporality

---

[108] N. Elias, *Time: An Essay* (Blackwell, 1992).
[109] M. Foucault, *Discipline and Punish: The Birth of the Prison* (Pantheon Books, 1977).
[110] S. Kern, *The Culture of Time and Space 1880-1918* (Harvard University Press, 1983).
[111] See, in particular, articles in the specialist periodical *Time and Mind: The Journal of Archaeology, Consciousness and Culture*.
[112] See J. Fabian, *Time and the Other: How Anthropology Makes Its Object* (Columbia University Press, 2002); T.R. Kidder, 'Transforming hunter-gatherer history at poverty point' in K.E. Sassaman and D.H. Holly (Jr.) (eds), *Hunter-gatherer Archaeology as Historical Process* (University of Arizona Press, 2011), 95.
[113] C. Sinha, et al., 'When time is not space: the social and linguistic construction of time intervals and temporal event relations in an Amazonian culture' (2011) 3(1) *Language and Cognition* 137.
[114] D. Bell, *Daughters of the Dreaming* (Spinifex Press, 2002), 46–7.

are strongly biased to the present and immediate.[115] Many debates in the study of history are infused with ideological, religious, imperialist, nationalist, and other biases, and societies can 're-create' their past through new narratives and myths about their history and origins.[116] Jeremy Black's boldly entitled *Curse of History* dissects these ideological rifts and the historical revisionism. [117] As Walter Murphy has put it, we regularly 'acknowledge that the present and the future may change views we hold about the past, [although] we nonetheless would reject the notion that the [present or] future can affect the past'.[118] Sometimes these 're-creations' of the past are beneficial in overcoming past injustices. Australia and Canada have started to acknowledge their Aboriginal history more critically,[119] previously bleached from the national psyche and legally expunged by the doctrine of 'terra nullius'.[120] The burgeoning field of environmental history is another example; what was once glorified as heroic mastery of nature through the spear or spade is reinterpreted as barbaric greed or struthiousness.[121] But consensus about these matters remains elusive. Historian Penelope Corfield tries pragmatically to chart a middle ground between rejecting belief in one true historical message on which all can agree and despairing that the past is so mangled, unfathomable, and controversial as to defy all systematic enquiries.[122]

Time's direction and tempo are seminal themes that inform many social constructions of time. The former resonates in the rival temporal metaphors of time's arrow and time's cycle.[123] Time's arrow evokes the distinctive character of unfolding, sequential events and progress, whereas time's cycle renders change more predictable and routine. Time's circles are often

---

[115] R. Fox, 'Time out of mind: anthropological reflections on temporality' (2001) 1(1–2) *KronoScope: Journal for the Study of Time* 129.

[116] J. Willette, 'Postmodernism and the past', Art history Unstuffed 31 August 2012, at www.arthistoryunstuffed.com/postmodernism-and-the-past.

[117] J. Black, *Curse of History* (Social Affairs Unit, 2008).

[118] W.F. Murphy, 'Merlin's memory: the past and future imperfect of the once and future polity' in S. Levinson (ed), *Responding to Imperfection: The Theory and Practice of Constitutional Amendment* (Princeton University Press, 1995), 164, 171–2.

[119] See B.J. Richardson, K. McNeil, and S. Imai (eds), *Indigenous Peoples and the Law: Comparative and Critical Perspectives* (Hart Publishing, 2009).

[120] R.J. Miller, J. Ruru, L. Behrendt, and T. Lindberg, *Discovering Indigenous Lands: The Doctrine of Discovery in the English Colonies* (Oxford University Press, 2010).

[121] E.g. J.R. McNeill and E.S. Mauldin (eds), *A Companion to Global Environmental History* (Wiley Blackwell, 2015).

[122] Corfield, *Time and the Shape of History*.

[123] S.J. Gould, *Time's Arrow, Time's Cycle: Myth and Metaphor in the Discovery of Geological Time* (Harvard University Press, 1987).

associated with the 'ceaselessly recurrent cycles or nature's constancies' – the diurnal, lunar, and seasonal rhythms, along with the predictable quotidian habits of eating and sleeping, and life and death of individual creatures.[124] This view of time thus dilutes belief in the irreversibility of change implied by linear time. Cyclical time is sometimes associated with agriculturalists tied to nature's seasonal rhythms, while urban denizens may experience time as lineal. A cyclical model is also associated with some ancient cultures such as the Incan and Mayan, and some indigenous peoples.[125] Other intercultural differences in time concern how some indigenous peoples, such as Maori, perceive the past, present, and future as more interconnected, such as the past being 'not necessarily the precursor to the present, but an inextricable part of it'.[126]

With the Enlightenment, Western societies experienced a pronounced shift in understanding of time as preordained life cycles to a directional arrow. The linear progression of time, frequently coupled with the Modernist idea of the onward march of progress, was furthered with scientific advances and new theories such as evolutionary biology, coupled with economic and technological advancement. Modernity 'relocated' the relationship between the past and future, bringing the future closer through an accelerating social tempo powered by the prospect of attaining utopian fulfilment.[127] This oeuvre has taken some knocks in recent years as doubts fester about enlightened progress.[128] Climate change, the Global Financial Crisis (GFC), the war on terrorism and other recent breakdowns in the narrative of 'enlightened' advance challenge the comfort of linear continuity and progression. Francis Fukuyama's preposterous 'end of history' declaration was certainly premature.[129] And the Marxist alternative of the historical dialectic of economic change (feudalism to capitalism and finally communist utopia) imploded with the demise of the Soviet bloc.[130]

---

[124] D. Lowenthal, 'Reflections on humpty-dumpty ecology' in M. Hall (ed), *Restoration and History: The Search for a Usable Environmental Past* (Routledge, 2010), 13, 15.

[125] K. Baffoe, 'Cultural eclipse: the effect on the Aboriginal peoples in Manitoba' (2004–5) 5 *Tribal Law Journal* 2.

[126] K.D. Lo and C. Houkamau, 'Exploring the cultural origins of differences in time orientation between European New Zealanders and Māori' (2012) 12(3) *New Zealand Journal of Human Resources Management*, 105, 117.

[127] R. Koselleck and K. Tribe, *Futures Past: On the Semantics of Historical Time* (Columbia University Press, 1985).

[128] P. Coveney and R. Highfield, *The Arrow of Time: A Voyage through Science to Solve Time's Greatest Mystery* (Ballantine Books, 1992).

[129] F. Fukuyama, *The End of History and the Last Man* (Free Press, 1992).

[130] P.J. Corfield, 'Teaching history's big pictures: including continuity as well as change' (September 2009) *Teaching History: Journal of the Historical Association* 136.

On tempo, sociologists and historians have also had much to say. Technological advances have radically transformed the way in which the *hoi polloi* experience time. The invention of motorised transportation such as automobiles and airplanes, and the concomitant spread of modern telecommunications and the Internet, has seemingly compressed and accelerated time. In industrial production, the philosophies of Fordism and Taylorism reshaped business management and labour relations to spur mass production systems that further commoditised time into a fungible unit to measure economic efficiency and productivity. This industrial time is environmentally problematic, contends Barbara Adam, and as we will explore later, because its invariant deterministic structure and emphasis on linear causal links violates the temporalities of environmental change that are more contextual, multidimensional, and nonlinear.[131] There also appear to be measurable differences in societies' tempos that correlate with economic livelihoods. Social psychologists Robert Levine and Ara Norenzyan compared the tempo of life in 31 diverse countries using three indicators: how quickly people walk, the value they place on time-keeping, and their time-efficiency in completing tasks.[132] They discovered that the hastiest countries were also associated with the most robust economies, which raises a question of caution – namely, do people in active economies act quicker because time holds more value, or does a hurried approach to life foster economic prosperity? Other studies verify salient international differences in how national cultures experience some aspects of temporality,[133] although global media and communication technologies have fostered some convergence in time perception.[134]

Time in Nature

Earth's Timescales

Our understanding of 'time', generally qualified as 'social time', simply evokes one of the possible ways of interpreting physical time. As we shift from theoretical notions of time to a functional understanding, the choice

---

[131] Adam, *Timescapes of Modernity*.
[132] R.V. Levine and A. Norenzyan, 'The pace of life in 31 countries' (1998) 30(2) *Journal of Cross-Cultural Psychology* 178.
[133] E.g. S. Armagan, et al, 'Temporality in negotiations: a cultural perspective' in Y.R. Chen (ed), *National Culture and Groups (Research on Managing Groups and Teams*, Volume 9 (Emerald Group Publishing, 2006), 115.
[134] P. Tsatsou, 'Reconceptualising time and space in the era of electronic media and communications' (2009) 1 *PLATFORM: Journal of Media and Communication* 11.

of time frame for decision-making on environmental issues becomes crucial. The preferred viewpoints about time will influence what becomes privileged or downplayed. Modern physics tends to express an invariant quality of natural phenomena, a paradigm of an everlasting world lacking a true past and future. A homogeneous, tenseless time may be plausible, but such a changeless void lacks relevance for a planet marked by evolution, and cycles and movements of growth, succession, and decline. One notable exception to physics' directionless time, of relevance to understanding Earth's systems, is the second principle of thermodynamics (entropy increases towards the future), but to be meaningful time needs to elicit a more comprehensive notion of change.

In the phenomenal natural world, time acquires infinite complexity. Evolutionary, biological, geological, seasonal, and human timescales are among the diverse constituents of time in nature. The intertwined actions of creatures' short lifespans and the more protracted processes of ecological and climatic cycles, in addition to anthropogenic influences, perpetually shape Earth. The academic disciplines of geology, physical geography, and environmental science are schooled to look at Earth systems from an epochal perspective, over millennia, vastly beyond the time frames of individual human beings or their societies. This disjuncture between social and natural time influences poor environmental governance.[135] The obdurate philosophical tradition of human/nature dualism conceives humankind as different and superior in kind to the non-human world, which not only legitimates its exploitation but also fosters a perilous illusion that denies human inclusion within and dependency on nature's temporalities. An ecological timescape requires acknowledging our lives as ecologically embodied rather than outside of Earth's ecological systems, and that social time must be synthesised and integrated with those systems. Instead of the mechanical, commodified clock time of Modernity, we need to respect the variable timescales, tempos, and timings of ecological processes such as seasons, evolution, succession, regeneration, and decay.

Our understanding of the workings of time in nature has changed through scientific scrutiny. From the mid-nineteenth century, evolutionary biology displaced classical natural history and concentrated on the functional interactions between organisms and their surroundings. In place of the classical assumption of a timeless continuity in nature there emerged a view of changing ecosystems in which species were seen

---

[135] Adam, *Timescapes of Modernity*; M. Bastian, 'Fatally confused: telling the time in the midst of ecological crises' (2012) 9(1) *Environmental Philosophy* 23.

as discontinuous entities evolving under the influence of their fluctuating environment.[136] Dynamic processes may span daily, seasonal, yearly, and longer cycles in the growth and lives of individual creatures, from the monthly menstrual cycles of females to the nightly sleeping cycles of all. These temporalities of individual life are themselves ensconced in longer-term dynamic processes. Over successive generations, the gene frequencies in the population of each species fluctuate, giving rise to evolutionary changes. Further elongating the time frame, these life processes are nested within planetary and cosmological changes: entire continents drift, break apart or merge, and the Earth oscillates through recurrent climatic shifts, from greenhouse to icehouse. And in the wider cosmos, entire planets and stars form, grow and die, some of which likely nurture life during their existence.

Earth's timescales can be mapped at various levels, several of which are directly important for environmental governance.[137] In nature, time's cycle reflects the movement of the Earth and the Moon, producing changes ranging from the daily ebb and flow of tides to longer-term seasonal weather cycles. Time's arrow in nature, by contrast, is a function of the growth of individual living creatures and their collective adaptation to selective pressures from the dynamic geosphere and dynamic atmosphere. Evolution through natural selection may imply teleological progress, but that simply reflects a response to changes from above and below the biosphere and can be, at any time, regressive. The uncertain and contingent character of many natural phenomena and processes, however, also cautions against assuming any inevitable processes of change in the natural world. One primary natural timescale is the seasonal climate, which has relevance in several dimensions, such as the timing of spring thaws, timing of rainfall events (e.g. monsoons), relationships to fertility and reproduction of plants and animals, and consequences for agriculture (e.g. the time to plant fields or leave fallow to rejuvenate). Another timescale is climate oscillations, of which of the most globally significant is ENSO (El Nino/La Nina Southern Oscillation); it occurs in the tropical Pacific approximately every five years, causing extreme weather, such as droughts or flooding, in different regions.[138]

---

[136] G. Gerstner, 'Temporal integrations and rhythms: that's what language and animal behavior are made of' (1995) 6 *Journal of Contemporary Legal Issues* 329, 354–6.

[137] This discussion draws partly on G. Chapman and T. Driver (eds), *Time-Scales and Environmental Change* (Routledge, 1997).

[138] El Nino is associated with warm ocean temperature and high air surface pressure. La Nino is associated with cold ocean temperature and low air surface pressure.

A further temporality is ecological succession, a process that denotes the regeneration of a disturbed ecosystem into a mature community that has 'climaxed'.[139] The process of maturation though varies considerably for individual plants and animals, as well as for other ecosystem components such as the formation of soil or the replenishment of groundwater. Scientists also identify alternative stable states in ecosystems rather than an inevitable trajectory to a climax community; thus, multiple states are possible following some disturbance and a return to a prior trajectory may not be possible.[140] Knowledge of successional processes and their time frames is relevant for resource harvesting, especially for forestry management in deciding when to log and replant. Attaining and perpetuating successional recovery, however, should not be viewed as necessarily ecologically desirable, as occasional violent disturbances, such as major fires or storms, unleash crucial processes for renewal of biodiversity and ecosystem integrity. That fire can be a powerful ecosystem engineer was recognised by indigenous peoples in Australia and North America for thousands of years, and is today similarly advocated by scientists as an indispensable rhythm of ecological time to be released rather than suppressed.[141]

Time is also relevant for measuring rates of environmental responses to pollution. Rates of decomposition are a variable environmental timescale, and significant for pollution regulation in many contexts, such as heavy metal contamination. The rates at which garbage, plastics, or nuclear materials decompose vary enormously, and some take several million years to disappear according to Weisman's analysis of how long nature would take to recover in a 'world without us'.[142] The time for carbon emissions to have effects discernible by humans is debatable, depending on whether dangerous concentration thresholds are breached.[143] But their potential for harm is much faster than the time it takes for greenhouse

---

[139] P. Osborne, *Tropical Ecosystems and Ecological Concepts* (Cambridge University Press, 2012), 253–4.
[140] B.E. Beisner, D.T. Haydon, and K. Cuddington, 'Alternative stable states in ecology' (2003) 1(7) *Frontiers in Ecology and the Environment* 376.
[141] D. Bowman, et al., 'Fire in the earth system' (2009) 324 *Science* 481; D. Bowman, 'The impact of aboriginal landscape burning on the Australian biota' (1998) 140 *New Phytologist* 385.
[142] A. Weisman, *The World Without Us* (Harper, 2008).
[143] E. Biber, 'Climate change and backlash' (2009) 17 *New York University Environmental Law Journal* 1295, referencing G.A. Meehl, et al., 'Global climate projections' in S. Solomon, et al. (eds), *Climate Change 2007: The Physical Science Basis: Contribution of Working Group I to the Fourth Assessment Report of the Intergovernmental Panel on Climate Change* (IPCC, 2007), 747, 822–31.

gases to leave the atmosphere or otherwise to be rendered harmless. At least two-thirds of carbon dioxide released into the atmosphere dissolves into the ocean over 20–200 years (where it can still cause adverse changes), and the remainder is removed by more glacial processes that may take thousands of years, including chemical weathering and rock formation.[144] Chlorofluorocarbons, which are also a greenhouse gas, are ozone-depleting substances with lifespans in the stratosphere from 25 to 400 years. The Antarctic ozone hole is already recovering, a process that may take until 2030 or even longer to complete.[145] By contrast, metal-bearing air pollutants tend to last from three to seven days in the atmosphere, and over three days they can travel up to 1,300 km.[146]

Another, often hauntingly beautiful, portal into environmental change is the places abandoned by human beings that nature reclaims. Surprisingly, within a few decades many such places show signs of ecological recovery. The Chernobyl environs offer one of the best vantages of Mother Nature prevailing over civilisation. In a no-go zone rarely visited by people since the 1986 disaster, wildlife such as elk and wolves have rebounded along with the forests that now envelope the crumbling ruins around the nuclear facility. The abandoned fishing village on Gouqi Island, China, is another ghost settlement slowly being consumed by nature; the coastal village was deserted when fishermen moved to the mainland where their catch could more easily be transported and sold. Micronesia's Truk Lagoon, once a formidable wartime Japanese stronghold in the Pacific, is now an aquatic military graveyard providing habitat for abundant marine life. Nature can even prevail in the midst of crowded cities; the New World Shopping Mall in Bangkok, which closed in 1999, became flooded with monsoon rains and is now one of the world's largest urban fish ponds. Polish photographer Anna Mika, whose work brings hope of nature's capacity to recover even without human intervention, captures many more examples of the beauty of decay and renewal.[147]

The evolution and demise of species is one of Earth's seminal time-scales.[148] Life began about 3.8 billion years ago, giving rise to the first main

---

[144] Carbon Brief, 'How long do greenhouse gases stay in the air?', *The Guardian* 16 January 2012, at www.theguardian.com.
[145] Environment Canada, 'Depletion of the ozone layer', at www.ec.gc.ca/ozone/default.asp?lang=En&n=2ED3F6DA-1.
[146] World Health Organization, *Health Risks of Heavy Metals from Long-range Transboundary Air Pollution* (WHO Regional Office for Europe, 2007).
[147] See www.annamika.pl.
[148] S.J. Gould, *The Book of Life* (WW Norton, 2002).

groups of life: bacteria and archaea. It took another 2.9 billion years for the first multicellular life to develop, some 900 million years ago. By about 530 million years ago, the first vertebrates appear, and by 465 million years ago plants begin to inhabit the land. Insects appear in the fossil record around 400 million years ago, and about 245 million years ago the dinosaurs emerge, to eventually dominate Earth for about 180 million years. Mammals emerged before the dinosaurs, around 358 million years ago, but would dominate after their demise. The earliest primates, our closest branch of the tree of life, appeared between 55 and 65 million years ago, depending on definitions,[149] and modern *Homo sapiens* evolved only about 200,000 years ago in Africa. Scientists estimate that the planet is presently home to about 8.7 million species.[150]

While the theory of natural selection – by which variability in reproductive success allows certain populations to survive environmental changes more successfully than others – is the most influential account of these evolutionary stages, the development of life has such a multifactorial nature, involving countless contingent and random elements, that it would be wrong to assume that life evolves under any predetermined pathway. Evolutionary change has also been shaped, in particular, by periodic disturbances that have resulted in mass extinctions, although it could be said that natural selection is also relevant here in explaining which species became extinct and which populations had sufficient variability to adapt and soldier on. Scientists continue to discover new dimensions of evolutionary adaptations to a changing world, such as how animals' behaviour can be affected by events, such as an unpleasant smell, that previous generations that have passed on to their offspring through a type of genetic memory.[151] The contemporary wave of extinctions foreshadows the planet's sixth mass extinction, the most recent prior such episode being some 70 million years ago, when the dinosaurs were wiped out. The worst mass extinction occurred between the Permian and Triassic geological periods some 252 million years ago, obliterating 90 per cent of marine species and 70 per cent of land species.[152] Although extinction is assumed to have permanency, some scientists hope to recover some lost species through

---

[149] W.C. Hartwig (ed), *The Primate Fossil Record* (Cambridge University Press, 2013).
[150] L. Sweetlove, 'Number of species on Earth tagged at 8.7 million', *Nature News* 24 August 2011, at www.nature.com/news/2011/110823/full/news.2011.498.html.
[151] B.G. Dias and K.J. Ressler, 'Parental olfactory experience influences behavior and neural structure in subsequent generations' (2014) 17(1) *Nature Neuroscience* 89.
[152] C. Shultz, 'How a single act of evolution nearly wiped out all life on Earth', *Smithsonian.com* 1 April 2014, at www.smithsonianmag.com.

biotechnology advances, with the Tasmanian thylacine and mammoth among the candidates. Even so, in the tree of life species alive today carry genetic traces of others gone, as birds do for dinosaurs.

At a larger timescale are planetary orbital cycles and their effect on global temperatures and glacial cycles. Milutin Milankovitch identified these astronomical cycles and how they influence the amount of solar radiation Earth receives, which in turn influences global temperatures.[153] These orbital cycles correspond with the glacial–interglacial periods, which have cycled approximately every 100,000 years. Some scientists (primarily climate sceptics) rely on Milankovitch cycles to explain recent climate change, but most believe that this could not have been the only driver and that other mechanisms such as atmospheric concentration of greenhouse gas emissions must be involved.[154] Shorter orbital cycles (axial: 41,000 years, and precession: 22,000 years) that correspond to climate change have been directly correlated to variations in atmospheric concentrations of methane (from ice core samples).[155] Further elongating the temporal scale is geologic time: the Earth's history is divided into eons, which are further divided into eras, periods, epochs, and ages. Eons reflect major variations in the geology of the planet and the rocks that formed during these periods. The Phanerozoic is the current geologic eon, and covers 541 million years to the present. Environmental science generally does not concern itself with eras prior to the Cenozoic (starting 66 million years ago) and generally focuses on the recent epochs of the Quaternary period, the Pleistocene (2.588 million years ago to 11,700 years), and the Holocene (11,700 years ago to present). The Anthropocene is gaining recognition as a third epoch.

Respecting the Ecological Timescape

While other species evidently have awareness of the passage of time, human beings may be unique in our capacity to cogitate beyond the immediate to the very distant past or remote future. This uncanny ability to perceive time in such manifold dimensions, including how the past shapes the present and in turn moulds the future, has no doubt contributed to our evolutionary success. Our ancestors told the time via natural cycles, such as diurnal light/dark rhythms and climatic sequences. Hunter–gatherer and farming

---

[153] G. Roe, 'In defense of Milankovitch' (2006) 33(24) *Geophysical Research Letters* L24703.
[154] See 'Milankovitch cycles', at www.skepticalscience.com/Milankovitch.html.
[155] N. Roberts, 'Long-term environmental stability and instability in the tropics and subtropics' in Chapman and Driver, *Time-Scales and Environmental Change*, 25, 28.

communities have always been intensely tied to seasonal cycles, whether of animal migration patterns or when trees bear nuts or fruits. These were indispensable temporal markers that determined social behaviour, including when and where to live, feed, and breed. Some societies also began to calculate time by tracking the Moon and the Sun, as appears from ancient monuments such as Stonehenge (its alignments may have allowed its users to track lunar eclipses and solstices).

Several innovations have influenced and shifted our relationship to nature's time. The discovery of fire was revolutionary because it loosened our dependency on day/night cycles.[156] With agriculture, the cyclical understanding of time continued, as knowing the optimal times for sowing and harvesting was essential for survival, but farming also started to distance people from other biorhythms outside of farming. The dramatic shift in time perception that really unhinged society from Earth's timescales came with the economic and technological changes of the last few centuries. Increasing social complexity has disciplined the organisation of time – its scheduling and management – as mirrored in the continuous refinement of time measurement devices. The dependence on natural cycles for regular economic and cultural activities has for most people been supplanted by industrial clock time. The current system of time-keeping originated in the Sumerian civilisation of the third millennium BCE; they developed the sexagesimal system of counting (a system using the number sixty as its base). The quantification and measurement of time intensified after 1700 when the first pendulum was created, enabling clocks to become more precise. Time is now universally organised and ordered by a spectrum of units, from small durations of time (second, minute, hour, day, week) to larger timescales (month, year, century), which receive near unanimous acceptance with some minor variations, notably in the calendar (e.g. between the Julian and Gregorian calendars and the Chinese new years).[157] Other important structures of social time are its linearity (past, present, and future) and zonal division (namely, international time zones).

The increasing precision in measuring time has enabled its commodification and unification into a global standard. The spread of this machine time enabled new associations and activities to develop, such as in the organisation of workforces. Technological breakthroughs in communication and transportation, combined with the greater need for exactness in timing standards, facilitated an international, universalised framework

---

[156] See R. Wrangham, *Catching Fire: How Cooking Made Us Human* (Basic Books, 2009).
[157] D. Flechon and F. Cologni, *The Mastery of Time* (Flammarion, 2012).

in how societies measure time. Aeroplanes and trucks have replaced the sailboat and oxcart, enabling goods to be traded and people to travel at speeds that save time and hence save money. Most importantly, explains Barbara Adam in her critique, industrial clock time has become 'disassociated from planetary rhythms and seasons, from change and ageing, from experience and memory. It became independent from time and space, self-sufficient, empty of meaning and thus apparently neutral'.[158]

The 'mastery' of time by modern society has thus been a crucial factor in the economic and technological developments of recent centuries that drive anthropogenic environmental change. While human beings have been disturbing ecological equilibria for at least 50,000 years,[159] the great surge in human activity since the Industrial Revolution has enlarged our environmental impacts from local to global scales. And as the scale has expanded, the pace of time has intensified, and with it collateral environmental damage. When time is money, as capitalism decrees, speed becomes a competitive advantage, as the faster an activity can be produced, traded, and consumed, the shorter the period in which an economic resource is tied up. The built-in obsolescence of many products is another legacy of the cult of speed, as the more quickly a product reaches its use-by-date the quicker a consumer will likely return to buy another. The ecological footprint of this frenzied pace is canvassed in detail in the next two chapters. Our capacity to restore degraded environments will be severely compromised if the worst climate change scenarios materialise, while our ability to sustain and protect the existing intact ecosystems will similarly diminish as temperatures increase, sea levels rise, and rainfall changes.

But another possibility exists. While we cannot escape how individual psychology and culture mediates our experience of time, human ingenuity, through institutions such as the law, science and community participation, can reshape our perception and use of time, and help society to tell nature's time. A concrete, physical time in nature exists, as manifested through changing cycles and processes from individual species to entire ecosystems and planetary motions. A social construction of time also exists, in which time is abstracted as an object of thought but nonetheless has tangible implications, such as timetables and deadlines. The dualist distinction between society and nature stands behind this bifurcated understanding of time. Understanding nature's timescape to overcome

---

[158] B. Adam, *Time* (Polity, 2004), 113–14.
[159] T. Flannery, *The Future Eaters* (Reed Books, 1995).

this dualism begins with grasping the relationship between time and change, and the importance of deep time.

Conceptualising time around change is essential for successful environmental governance because nature does not stand still.[160] As Graham Chapman and Thackwray Driver explain, 'there are conservationists who see the protection of a particular plant communities on stable sand-dunes as a priority, as though there is or ought to be a natural permanence to what is at other scales transient and ephemeral'.[161] In other words, we should not assume any pre-disturbance or natural state of the environment as an inviolable benchmark for modern environmental management. Understanding time as about change makes it easier to appreciate that environmental law should limit rates of change so that ecosystems and social systems can adapt successfully; in particular, climate change must not go unchecked such that natural systems cannot cope. Nonetheless, simply equating time with change leaves many questions to resolve when it comes to extrapolating what change means for natural and social systems, such as the direction, pace, or duration of change. The Anthropocene implies linear change, yet ecological restoration (a vital management practice) envisions reversing change and undoing past damage. It can be equally difficult to agree on an acceptable rate of environmental change to accommodate when setting standards such as for water quality or biodiversity management. To identify tolerable rates of change requires consideration of longer timescales that enable comparison of current rates of environmental change to past permutations and – where major anthropogenic environmental disturbance has occurred – to understand what the unaffected condition of the environment was.

Aligning ourselves with Earth's timescales also requires appreciation of deep time. It will extend the human story into a non-human realm, into the immensities of time from the distant past to the eternal future. Deep time is radically unlike the conventional, experience of social time that people know, a time measured, at its furthest margins, in merely a few human generations either side of the present. Novelist John McPhee evidently coined the phrase 'deep time' in his 1981 book on geological thought entitled *Basin and Range*.[162] It reminds us of the parallel of 'deep space' that we became familiar with in the era of space travel, conjuring up the enormous

---

[160] Adam, *Time*, 26-7.
[161] G.P. Chapman and T.S. Driver, 'Time, mankind and the Earth' in Chapman and Driver, *Time-Scales and Environmental Change*, 1.
[162] J. McPhee, *Basin and Range* (Farrar, Straus, and Giroux, 1981).

expanses of the universe within which Earth is a mere pin prick. Deep time evokes the vast timescales within which we now have to contemplate life on Earth beyond on our species' history. While humankind can theoretically measure long timescales, it is altogether another challenge to assimilate that insight into our behaviour. Biologist Stephen Jay Gould reflects on the same challenge: 'an abstract, intellectual understanding of deep time comes easily enough ... Getting it into the gut is quite another matter'.[163] The growing popularity of deep environmental histories, such as in the writings of Tim Flannery[164] and Jared Diamond,[165] help familiarise many with the great depths of time and may provide a springboard for complementary changes in environmental laws and policies.

Our awareness of deep time surely ranks alongside the Copernican and Darwinian revolutions as one of the most momentous and humbling insights for humanity. Gould described it as 'geology's most frightening fact', relegating human beings to a tiny moment in cosmological history.[166] The deep time of Earth over numerous epochs and eons reduces a human lifetime to a fleeting instant that is hard to comprehend. As Mark Twain said about humankind's existence: 'If the Eiffel Tower were now representing the world's age, the skin of paint on the pinnacle-knob at its summit would represent man's share of that age'.[167] An awareness of deep time not only helps sharpen perspective of the cataclysmic impact of *Homo sapiens*, especially the recent environmental destructiveness of industrialisation, it also gives us hope. The deep historical perspective that Tim Flannery took in his tour de force *The Future Eaters* not only unveiled the depth of environmental impact the first wave of Aborigines had on Australia, but also how they learned from their mistakes to live sustainably within the ecological constraints of the continent for many thousands of years until the European invasion. With time (but acting quickly), we might learn to emulate their success.

We must overcome the separation of social time from natural time. As human beings are embedded in and inseparable from nature, our notion of time cannot remain indefinitely divorced from the behaviour of natural systems. The physical processes of nature impose limits on the human

---

[163] Gould, *Time's Arrow*, 3.
[164] Flannery, *The Future Eaters*.
[165] Diamond, *Collapse*.
[166] S.J. Gould, *Wonderful Life: The Burgess Shale and the Nature of History* (Penguin Books, 1989), 44.
[167] M. Twain, 'Was the world made for man?' (unpublished, 1903); reprinted in B. DeVoto, *Letters from the Earth* (Fawcett Publications, 1962), 211.

constructions of time. The psychological and social constructions of time are also a natural fact, rooted in a time-limited body and nature-dependent society. Like all animals, *Homo sapiens* have built-in, natural temporalities: we are guided by our circadian rhythms, which are synchronised by the brain's pineal gland – with light and dark cycles governed by the Earth's rotation.[168] Our millions of years of evolution even more concretely subsume *Homo sapiens* within Earth's time. Our recent attempt to disregard our embeddedness in nature's time is not sustainable.

Telling the Story

As the 'problem' with time concerns its social practice, this book takes a socio-legal approach that includes the timescales and temporal orientations that inform social and economic life, while putting aside other fascinating but less relevant enquiries about time (e.g. cosmological and ontological). Our social institutions, including the law, filter our awareness of and interpretation of time.[169] Human beings have constantly remade their understandings of the temporal structure of their surroundings in order to forecast and control their destiny. In recent decades environmental law has helped inculcate a longer-term outlook in decision-making about natural resources, biodiversity conservation, and climate change, a temporal shift associated with the philosophy of sustainable development. Although gaps and deficiencies in both the law's conceptualisation and implementation of sustainability continue, even larger unresolved challenges in regard to past time and the pace of time persist, as well as deficiencies in realising the ambitions of adaptive governance to cope with change. This book addresses these challenges.

The interdisciplinary, multijurisdictional, and conceptual approaches of this research deprive it somewhat of the benefit of the well-crafted positivist methodologies of the natural sciences based on hypothesis testing and empirical evaluation. While this volume draws heavily on other research grounded in such methodologies, such as conservation biology and restoration ecology, the governance dimensions of the subject lack a widely accepted, comprehensive research methodology. Few scholars of environmental law have evaluated it through the lens of time.

---

[168] M. Amir, 'Bio-temporality and social regulation: the emergence of the biological clock' (2002) 18 *Polygraph: An International Journal of Culture and Politics* 47.
[169] A. Giddens, *A Contemporary Critique of Historical Materialism*, Volume 1 (University of California Press, 1981), 36.

Legal scholarship commonly rests on arguments about doctrinal and philosophical issues rather than addressing empirical questions about the impact or efficacy of governance.[170] Empirical evaluation of environmental law and policy faces a variety of practical barriers, including the difficulty of measuring parameters that we cannot easily quantify, and the associated challenge of correlating cause and effect in complex phenomena whose relationships we may not decipher except over a very long period. Environmental law innovations require considerable time to be devised and implemented, and their actual effects may be indecipherable in the near term. Environmental law research has a strong axiological quality, meaning that it dwells primarily on ethics and norms. This book, similarly, is value-oriented, in that it is predicated on the assumption of the importance of the natural environment to human well-being and the importance of social and institutional changes to align environmental practices with Earth's timescales. Core concepts that underpin this book relating to community participation, shared governance, restoration, slow living, and environmental stewardship reflect value-laden and contested choices.

The policy research framework developed by Ann Majchrzak and Lynne Markus should help the investigations promoted by this book, as some other scholars of environmental law recommend.[171] Majchrzak and Markus use an empirical-inductive approach, emphasising discourse and reasoning, in contrast to the scientific hypothesis-testing approach. One must begin by learning about the dimensions of the social problem, such as environmental degradation, and identifying relevant concepts and causal explanations.[172] In our context, this will include the social construction of time, scientific knowledge about natural systems, and economic drivers of environmental behaviour. The second dimension of their approach evaluates options, namely to assess the merits of future courses of action that may resolve these social problems. These actions might comprise different legislative schemes, participation by non-state actors in governance, and hybrid approaches, as all acknowledged in this book. Thirdly, the methodology has a normative approach, by

---

[170] C. McGrath, *Does Environmental Law Work? How to Evaluate the Effectiveness of Environmental Legal Systems* (Lambert Academic Publishing, 2010).

[171] P. Martin and D. Craig, 'Accelerating the evolution of environmental law through continuous learning from applied experience' in P. Martin and A. Kennedy (eds), *Implementing Environmental Law* (Edward Elgar Publishing, 2015), 27, 42–43.

[172] A. Majchrzak and L. Markus, *Methods for Policy Research: Taking Socially Responsible Action* (SAGE, 2014).

recommending future action that may resolve these public problems. Overall, the policy analysis approach is partly descriptive by harnessing scholarly disciplines that seek to understand the causes and consequences of public policies and regulations, and also normative (and thus value-dependent) by recommending better laws and other types of decisions. Advantageously, it helps to explain not only what happens, but also why it happens and how we might do better. The prospective and pragmatic orientation of this applied research approach dovetails with my book's focus on investigating a multi-faceted contemporary problem, and incorporating norms and values to improve solutions. We need to consider both why environmental law is misaligned with nature's temporalities and how that dissonance can be overcome.

In this light, the book adopts a comparative and multi-jurisdictional approach to evaluate trends from representative and significant examples in order to understand environmental law and its societal context. Much of the discussion refers to Anglophile jurisdictions, notably Australia, Britain, Canada, New Zealand, and the United States, both because of their major role in pioneering environmental law as well as my personal familiarity with these countries over my academic career. Environmental law in the European Union (EU) and the international system is also important and often considered. While not ignored, environmental law in other countries or regions gets less attention. Thus, readers should appreciate that on a case-by-case basis the book's analysis and conclusions might differ somewhat according to the country concerned. Most of the research came from existing primary and secondary literature, and is occasionally supplemented by interviews with stakeholders such as regulators and environmental managers to glean further insights into practices and behaviours undocumented in the literature.

The ensuing discussion flows over five further chapters. Chapter 2 investigates the temporalities of change in three interrelated settings. First, it maps environmental change, such as the harm and disturbance caused by people, so as to understand how the legal system can respond better to adverse changes. Second, humankind's own history of change and evolutionary context, both biological and cultural, is considered so as to decipher whether and how human beings can change to become more environmentally literate and compassionate. Thirdly, the chapter considers the law for its temporal qualities, including its contradictory impulses to solidify tradition and unleash change. The timelines of environmental law that the chapter identifies can thus be evaluated against the ecological, cultural, and evolutionary context of humankind.

Chapters 3 to 5 examine specific temporal weaknesses of environmental law. Chapter 3 critiques its dominant 'present-future' outlook, as evident in the philosophy of sustainable development, and associated concepts and methodologies such as cost-benefit analysis. Humankind's seeming obsession with the future is a mirage, however, as social practice, including environmental governance, remains subject to expedient considerations that ground us firmly in the present. This limits the scope for responsive governance to address changing circumstances and thus reduces the resilience of socio-ecological systems to cope with adversity. Environmental licensing, including grandfather clauses and relicensing provisions, illustrates the constraints to adaptive governance in responding to an uncertain and variable future. Of great importance, Chapter 4 considers how environmental law addresses past losses, and demonstrates the limited success in containing cumulative environmental losses and initiating ecological restoration. It looks at the 'rewilding' movement and other approaches to restoration, and their influence on law reform. While many jurisdictions have laws that mandate environmental restoration, such as remediation of former mines or recovery of endangered species, few have *ecological* restoration as their focus that would regenerate entire landscapes and ecosystems. Restoration also has an important cultural dimension. The restoration of indigenous land and sea rights serves both to enrich and sustain their cultures as well as sometimes improve the quality of environmental stewardship. The chapter devotes some space to indigenous rights and their implications for environmental governance. The pace of time features in Chapter 5. It begins by examining the intertwined paths between the acceleration of time and environmental degradation. Among the issues, the insatiable 'fast consumerism' of modern life depletes and pollutes natural resources. The chapter considers 'fast-track' legislation as the most overt manifestation of this path in the legal domain, and analysis of Tasmania's pulp mill assessment legislation illustrates its pernicious effects. The chapter also shows how some people seek to live more slowly in order to align themselves with nature's rhythms. The movements for Slow Food and Slow Money provide directions towards the ecological timescape, although their legal framework remains undeveloped.

The closing chapter, *Telling the Time*, expounds the implications of the preceding discussions for governance reform within countries and internationally. The law must encourage ecological restoration, respond better to future environmental changes, and slow the pace of life. Many institutional reforms are conceivable, including stewardship trusts to care for natural places indefinitely, and new duties on companies and other economic actors to pursue more patient, long-term development. But the kernel of reform should be ecological restoration, as it will not only help us recover nature's past, but also provide a range of collateral benefits to address other dimensions of the ecological timescape. In all cases, legislators should collaborate with the progressive social movements that are pursuing this agenda. The primary purpose of my book, however, is not to prescribe a specific blueprint for law reform, but to initiate a serious conversation about the major frailty of environmental law worldwide and options for better governance. I hope to unveil the temporal shortcomings of environmental law practice in its broader institutional, policy, and socio-economic setting, and thereby help decision-makers tell nature's time. Telling it will take us beyond the limited purview of the future tense of the sustainability model. In addition, I hope this book stimulates a wider appreciation of 'time' as a powerful framework for evaluating the efficacy and impact of environmental governance to complement and enrich the scholarly focus on 'space'.

2

Temporalities of Change

Time-Lapsed Environmental Change

Although seemingly at the pinnacle of its evolutionary success, humankind has deeply unsustainable tendencies that environmental law has barely mitigated. Perched on the precipice of a collapse in planetary ecological systems, we struggle to genuinely acknowledge how quickly nature is unravelling, despite abundant scientific evidence.[1] A spectacular, and quite disturbing way to visualise these trends is Google Earth's time-lapse bird's-eye panoramas. In a partnership with the US Geological Survey and NASA, Google displays vivid satellite pictures of Earth over approximately three decades.[2] Users of the 'Earth Engine' can zoom into any spot on the planet to watch time-lapse sequences of images between 1984 and 2012. Taken from Landsat satellites, they evoke a dramatic retrospective of changes in the Earth's landscape over a mere few decades – a fleeting moment for many of its timescales. One time-lapse series reveals Dubai surging into a mega-metropolis, with artificial islands; another tracks the booming sprawl ringing Las Vegas; while a further shows the ravenous deforestation of the Amazon jungle.

The spectacle of planetary decline through these panoramas unveils a shocking story that we cannot glean so easily from the vantage of the present or a single image of the past. Rather, it's the compilation of numerous images, over time, and on a large spatial scale, that reveals the death by a thousand cuts: the encroachment of cities into bucolic spaces, the retreat and disappearance of glaciers, and the paving of ever more terrain with concrete. We struggle to understand the enormity of our environmental impacts without a sense of changes over time. And particularly alarming about the time-lapse sequences is the rapidity of change in many corners

---

[1] C. Fowler and L. Hobbs, 'Is humanity sustainable?' (2003) 270 *Proceedings of the Royal Society of London, Series B: Biological Sciences* 2579.
[2] See http://earthengine.google.org/#intro. Users can also view the images on *Time Magazine*, at http://world.time.com/timelapse.

of the planet, just within our own lives. If we could stretch these timescales over longer periods to capture other environmental menaces, we would be even more alarmed. The depletion of marine fisheries, for instance, troubles many from the perspective of recent decades, but becomes frightening when tracked over the last century.[3] The time-lapse imagery helps to visualise how the growing *hoi polloi* and its insatiable demand for environmental resources is literally altering the very face of the planet. Throughout human history, the scale, intensity, and frequency of anthropogenic permeations on the biosphere have grown exponentially, spurred by technological advances, rising material consumption, and the sheer number of people. One must dread how these trends will likely intensify in the coming decades as economic behemoths such as China and India ramp up their frenzied development.

This chapter concerns the temporalities of environmental change, including that of humankind itself. It puts anthropogenic environmental changes in their historical context, highlighting how ecological impacts pose major temporal challenges for decision-makers. Humankind, as part of nature, also lives within forces of change, and we assess how *Homo sapiens*' evolutionary legacy, including human perception of time, influences our environmental behaviour. The acceleration of cultural change, ahead of biological change, is the source of environmental infamy, but also the potential cure. The chapter examines the structural forces or inertia and movement within the legal system itself, a system that articulates society's response to a changing world. These insights inform the history of environmental law, and how space and time have shaped its evolution, on which the chapter concludes.

The window of time, as seen via time-lapse footage, presents a mixed blessing. It helps people to recognise and understand the gravity of environmental change by putting impacts in temporal perspective from the distant past to the long-term future. The passage of time enables comparisons of the 'before' and 'after' in the environment from which we might identify human agency. But time also complicates managing those impacts: we may be unprepared to incur costs now to reduce environmental impacts for the benefit of posterity, or be reluctant to remedy harms perpetrated by our ancestors long ago, harms for which we feel no moral or legal responsibility. A mismatch can thus arise between awareness and action, and between who incurs the costs and who receives the benefits of action.

---

[3] J.B. Jackson, et al., 'Historical overfishing and the recent collapse of coastal ecosystems' (2001) 293 *Science* 629.

In raising awareness, the 'turning point' is a well-established temporal metaphor for defining time frames, chronologies, and shifts. Turning points provide a structure and interpretative framework to narratives about changes in environmental history, such as the onset of environmental decline, the birth of a new environmental idea, or the onset of a regulatory trend.[4] As a tool of historians, turning points can be criticised if they invoke simplistic periodisation or mono-causal explanations when more nuanced and complex accounts should prevail. As a tool for environmental activists and policy-makers desiring to highlight a problem and motivate action, the 'turning point' has been quite effective. Sometimes transformations in environmental law occur quite suddenly, being triggered by community outrage over major catastrophes such as the 1967 *Torrey Canyon* oil tanker spill.[5] But some catastrophes arise not from a single event but from the aggregation of many over years, as epitomised by the Anthropocene epoch – for which the epochal shift is only judged as a 'turning point' by viewing environmental changes across longer expanses of time.

Another identified turning point is the emergence of the global environmental movement in the 1970s and the concomitant flurry of laws to protect or moderate exploitation of the natural environment.[6] The Club of Rome report of 1972 was one of the formative markers of shifting awareness, conveying the message that, given a planet of finite resources, humankind risked bumping into its physical limits in the early twenty-first century unless we drastically curbed our eco-footprint.[7] The growing public debate in the 1970s about environmental impacts, especially in Western societies, reflected several political and social factors, including scientific knowledge and public education, rather than any specific, tangible decline in Earth's health at this time. The warnings of the Club of Rome and others during this decade helped pave the way for the notions

---

[4] F. Uekoetter (ed), *Turning Points of Environmental History* (University of Pittsburgh Press, 2010).

[5] Shocked by the *Torrey Canyon* disaster, the International Maritime Organization convened an extraordinary session of its council and sponsored a conference to draft an international agreement establishing new legal standards to minimise contamination of the oceans from ships: International Convention for the Prevention of Pollution from Ships, 2 November 1973, as modified by the Protocol of 1978 Protocol relating to the International Convention for the prevention of pollution from ships, in force 2 October 1983, (1973) 12 ILM 131; (1978) 17 ILM 546.

[6] J.I. Engels, 'Modern environmentalism' in F. Uekoetter, *Turning Points of Environmental History* (University of Pittsburgh Press, 2010), 119.

[7] D. Meadows, et al., *The Limits to Growth* (Universe Books, 1972).

of 'sustainable development' and 'sustainability' in environmental law – a conceptual innovation of huge importance given that, as ecological systems function over indefinite time horizons, their long-term future must be valued.

Yet the temporal trajectories of many environmental changes have differed from those projected by the Club of Rome. It focused on those with a degree of tangibility and immediacy, such as depletion of forests, pollution of water, and energy consumption. Numerous environmental problems have uncertain, latent, or non-linear trajectories, perhaps only becoming a manifest scourge after crossing irreparable tipping points. Such 'hidden' features can dampen the perception of an emerging problem and reduce policy-makers' motivation to intervene. The latency of many environmental impacts that accrete slowly over many years creates uncertainty and difficulties for lawmakers to determine whether and when regulatory interventions are worthwhile.[8] We may not know whether the modification of a particular landscape will precipitate the demise of an endangered species or whether the release of a new chemical is hazardous until it is too late to act. Concomitantly, banning the chemical or preserving the species' habitat may not be straightforward when the costs and benefits of such actions today are calibrated over time to take into account unclear future costs and benefits spanning several generations. The trade-offs and the choice of metric to reconcile them infuriate some and resonate in long-standing ethical debates about intergenerational equity.[9] The introduction in many countries of the precautionary principle to guide environmental governance acknowledges the heightened risks and uncertainties associated with these anthropogenic changes.

The gradual pace of ecological change in particular challenges governance premised on much shorter time frames for action. The protocols for determining the conservation status of species illustrate this difficulty. The International Union for Conservation of Nature's (IUCN) Red List of Threatened Species is the most authoritative global mechanism of its kind, and used by many governments.[10] The Red List classifies species into nine groups, such as 'endangered' or 'vulnerable', according to criteria such as population size, rate of decline, and distribution. The time frames for

---

[8] B. Adam, *Timescapes of Modernity: The Environment and Invisible Hazards* (Routledge, 1998), 10.
[9] J. O'Neil, R.K. Turner, and I. Bateman, *Environmental Ethics and Philosophy* (Edward Elgar Publishing, 2001).
[10] See www.iucnredlist.org.

determining a negative shift in species' status may overlook long-term changes. The Red List criteria for a species listed as vulnerable include a 'population size reduction of ≥ 30 per cent over the last 10 years or three generations, whichever is longer', while the criteria for endangered species listing include a 'population size reduction of ≥ 70 per cent over the last 10 years or three generations, whichever is the longer'.[11] Unfortunately, these criteria don't capture the gradual decline in abundance of many species, as evident from environmental history. The Late Pleistocene megafauna extinctions at the hands of the Clovis transpired over only about 250 years.[12] New Zealand's nine species of moa, the large flightless birds, disappeared within a roughly similar time frame after the first humans arrived – both intervals not 'brief' enough to show a negative trajectory under Red List criteria.[13] More recent and relevant is that Australia's koala population has plunged, from in the millions in the nineteenth century (about 1 million were slaughtered in 1919–20 alone in a Queensland open season) to a few hundred thousand lately;[14] but its 'vulnerable' status on the Red List and legislation in Queensland and New South Wales is criticised by the Australia Koala Foundation as complacent given the demographic trends.[15] Moreover, determining conservation status on recent population shifts ignores the question of how valuable a species is to ecosystem health and may result in resources being wasted in emergency responses to bring a species back from the brink when those resources could have been better spent on protective measures at the outset.

The 'slow violence' of much environmental trauma, as Robert Nixon describes it,[16] also obfuscates determining a correlation between their causes and impacts. We tend to view environmental changes within a short time frame, privileging circumstances of temporal immediacy or proximity, such as clearance of a forest that suddenly diminishes wildlife habitat. Some environmental impacts have particular longevity. Depletion

---

[11] IUCN, 'The criteria for critically endangered, endangered and vulnerable' (2001 Categories and Criteria; version 3.1), at www.iucnredlist.org/static/categories_criteria_3_1.

[12] D. Peacock, *In the Shadow of the Sabertooth* (AK Press, 2013), passim.

[13] V. Morell, 'Why did New Zealand's Moas go extinct?', *Science* 14 March 2014, at www.sciencemag.org/news/2014/03/why-did-new-zealands-moas-go-extinct.

[14] C. McAlpine, et al., *Conserving Koalas in the 21st Century: Synthesising the Dynamics of Australia's Koala Populations* (Australian Centre for Ecological Analysis and Synthesis, 2012).

[15] Australia Koala Foundation, 'The koala – endangered or not?', at www.savethekoala.com/about-koalas/koala-endangered-or-not.

[16] R. Nixon, *Slow Violence and the Environmentalism of the Poor* (Harvard University Press, 2011).

of the stratospheric ozone layer by chlorofluorocarbons and other compounds will remain a long-term problem because some of these chemicals linger in residence for many decades, eating away our UV radiation shield.[17] But some air pollution, such as city smog, persists briefly and thus is a lesser temporal challenge for environmental law. Unlike atmospheric or water pollution, where some pollutants can rapidly disperse, deposition of solid and liquid wastes often remains a relatively concentrated, festering problem: it tends not to degrade, except over very long periods.[18] Consider nuclear waste, which is difficult to isolate safely over millennia while it slowly decays. Other elements, such as mercury, remain toxic forever for all practical purposes because they cannot be destroyed. Such hazards must remain in safe, stable locations in perpetuity.

The extended time horizons of nature make it difficult to accommodate a dynamic system when environmental regulations and policies often assume an unchanging nature. An area designated as a national park may become a less suitable habitat for a particular species whose distributions will shift in response to climatic influences. Likewise, water quality standards set for a river to ensure its suitability for fish may become obsolete due to wider changes in its catchment not targeted by the standard. Human infrastructure and development can be stranded by nature's dynamism: the rising seawaters of a warming planet risk submerging low-lying, coastal real estate.

Time also complicates efforts to restore injured environments. When ecological damage accretes gradually, originating ages ago, we may not appreciate the extent of past injuries or their real causes. The demise of a rare mammal might be attributed to the presence of a new invasive predator, when in fact historic climatic shifts, which enable such intruders to thrive, may offer a more valid explanation. As Barton Thompson explains in his illustration, 'faced by declining populations of stellar sea lions, for example, environmentalists have focused on current fishing and human predation, while the best explanation may be destructive whaling practices in the early- and mid-twentieth century'.[19] This temporal distortion is also relevant to deciding how to restore damaged environments;

---

[17] U.L. McFarling, 'Hole in ozone may stay longer than expected', *Los Angeles Times* 7 December 2005, at www.latimes.com.
[18] J.S. Applegate, 'The temporal dimension of land pollution: another perspective on applying the breaking the logjam principles to waste management' (2008–09) 17 *New York University Environmental Law Journal* 757.
[19] B.H. Thompson Jr, 'The trouble with time: influencing the conservation choices of future generations' (2004) 44 *Natural Resources Journal* 601, 603.

we should not assume that sustainable development may ensue from prevailing ecological conditions used as baselines for legal protections. Attaining sustainability may require some backtracking to regenerate damaged ecologies through restoration projects, but as Chapter 4 discusses, scientific disagreements rage as to the most appropriate historic baseline for restoration.

Baselines are twisting further, with the pace of environmental change accelerating – global warming, invasive species, oceans awash with plastic debris, and so on. The upheaval shockingly displayed by time-lapse satellite imagery helps to verify the epochal dimensions of these changes, in which biological evolution is seemingly becoming an artefact of human cultural evolution. This distortion of nature's temporal rhythms needs further reflection before looking at changes in human culture, including legal responses to this environmental devastation.

Eden Besieged

References to time are sometimes evoked to convey the gravity of environmental permeations sweeping the Earth. An oft-used allegory is to depict the entire 4.5 billion years of the planet's history condensed into 24 hours, of which the existence of humankind, and especially our industrialised era, is mere seconds (if that) of that day.[20] Alternatively, if the planet's history were crunched into the more manageable timescale of 1 year, modern human civilisation only appeared at about 5 minutes before the year ends. When the intense planetary impacts of humankind are calibrated into such a relatively short interval, it may help jolt our sense of complacency.

A potent and scientifically verified temporality that evokes similar concerns is the 'Anthropocene'. Coined by Paul Crutzen and Eugene Stoermer,[21] the Anthropocene signifies the unprecedented epochal effects of human-induced damage that have moved the Earth from its natural geological phase, the interglacial period called the Holocene.[22] Since the early twentieth century the range and magnitude of our ecological

---

[20] Taking the last 10,000 years of human history, marked by the rise of agriculture and other changes of environmental significance, this amounts to only 0.2 seconds on the clock. The time since the Industrial Revolution is only 0.004 seconds: P. Danesi and H. Cherif, 'Environmental changes in perspective: the global response to challenges' (1996) 2 *IAEA Bulletin* 2.
[21] P.J. Crutzen and E.F. Stoermer, 'The "Anthropocene"' (2000) 41 *Global Change Newsletter* 17.
[22] J. Zalasiewicz, et al., 'The new world of the Anthropocene' (2010) 44 *Environmental Science and Technology* 2228–31.

footprint has surged exponentially, with scientists warning that Earth's ecosystems are teetering on a 'state shift', with severe repercussions for ecological integrity.[23] Clarence Glacken in the 1960s spoke of similar emerging epochal shifts, although without this label.[24] Etymologically, Anthropocene stems from the ancient Greek *anthro* and *cene*, which mean 'human' and 'new' respectively.[25] In the geo-ecological context, it denotes a new period since the onset of the Industrial Revolution when human beings became a major influence in modifying the environment, rivalling the great forces of nature. Industrialisation powered by cheap fossil fuels engendered a cornucopia of material riches, but a gravely poorer Earth.[26]

While it has yet to receive official designation as a new epoch,[27] the Anthropocene is increasingly acknowledged by scientists as a new planetary phase exhibiting changes 'well outside the range of the natural variability exhibited over the last half million years at least'.[28] The onslaught is not recent, as humankind has been an 'ecological serial killer' for thousands of years, first as hunter–gatherers decimating megafauna and then as agriculturalists simplifying entire ecosystems, well before the greater carnage of the Industrial Revolution.[29] As environmental violence surpasses tipping points of resilience and as landscapes shift into 'novel ecosystems',[30] human beings themselves will suffer repercussions as drastic as having to flee for sheer survival. This grim prognosis awaits the inhabitants of some islands whose ancestral homes will be inundated by rising seas, thereby possibly facing the cultural impoverishment of migration to wealthier countries most responsible for climate change.[31]

---

[23] About 43 per cent of the world's land area has been converted to agricultural or urban use to support the human population. This number may exceed 50 per cent by 2025: A. Barnosky, et al., 'Approaching a state shift in earth's biosphere' (2012) 486 *Nature* 52.

[24] C.J. Glacken, *Traces on the Rhodian Shore: Nature and Culture in Western Thought from Ancient Times to the End of the Eighteenth Century* (University of California Press, 1967).

[25] R.A. Slaughter, 'Welcome to the Anthropocene' (2012) 44 *Futures* 119–26.

[26] See, more generally, M. Raupach, and J. Canadell, 'Carbon and the Anthropocene' (2010) 2 *Current Opinion in Environmental Sustainability* 210.

[27] D. Carrington, 'The Anthropocene epoch: scientists declare dawn of human-influenced age', *The Guardian* 29 August 2016, at www.theguardian.com.

[28] International Geosphere-Biosphere Programme, '2001 Amsterdam Declaration on Earth Science'.

[29] Y.N. Harari, *Sapiens: A Brief History of Mankind* (Harper, 2015); T. Flannery, *The Future Eaters: An Ecological History of the Australasian Lands and People* (Reed 1995).

[30] R.J. Hobbs, E.S. Higgs, and C. Hall (eds), *Novel Ecosystems: Intervening in the New Ecological World Order* (Wiley-Blackwell, 2013).

[31] M. Gerrard, *Threatened Island Nations; Legal Implications of Rising Seas and a Changing Climate* (Cambridge University Press, 2013).

The hypothesis of the Anthropocene has been nuanced through another temporal metaphor, the 'Great Acceleration', denoting a supplementary epoch of intensified environmental pressure and dislocation. Paul Crutzen and others identify it as beginning in the mid-twentieth century.[32] Writing in 2007, they observe how 'nearly three-quarters of the anthropogenically driven use of CO_2 concentration has occurred since 1950 (from about 310 to 380 ppm), and about half of the total rise (48 ppm) has occurred in just the last 30 years'.[33] A similar accelerating tempo applies to the demise of much biodiversity, with the IUCN warning that 'humans [are] driving extinction faster than species can evolve', with extinction rates presently '100–1000 times that suggested by the fossil records before humans'.[34] Christian Pfister has identified a similar 'acceleration' of environmental impacts, which he calls the '1950s Syndrome': an economic 'boom lasting from 1950 until 1973 [that] was the longest and the most pronounced in human history, with average growth rates in world per capita GDP of 2.91 per cent'.[35]

A crowded planet intensifies the environmental onslaught; in the twentieth century the world's human population grew by a factor of four, from some 1.5 billion to 6 billion, and the global economy enlarged by a factor of 13.[36] Humanity devours the equivalent of 2.7 global hectares per person for resource extraction and waste assimilation each year, translating to 1.5 Earths, or a 50 per cent overshoot of the planet's carrying-capacity.[37] Eliminating this overshoot seems unlikely as the global human population, at 7.4 billion in late 2016, soars: it intensifies demand for space, food,

---

[32] W. Steffen, et al., 'The Anthropocene: conceptual and historical perspectives' (2011) 369 *Philosophical Transactions of the Royal Society* 842, 847–9.

[33] W. Steffen, P.J. Crutzen, and J.R. McNeill, 'The Anthropocene: are humans now overwhelming the great forces of nature?' (2007) 36(8) *Ambio* 614, 614.

[34] J. Jowit, 'Humans driving extinction faster than species can evolve, say experts', *The Guardian* 7 March 2010, at www.theguardian.com/. See also R. Wagler, 'The Anthropocene mass extinction: an emerging curriculum theme for science educators' (2011) 73(2) *The American Biology Teacher* 78.

[35] C. Pfister, 'The "1950s syndrome" and the transition from a slow-going to a rapid loss of global sustainability' in F. Uekoetter (ed), *Turning Points of Environmental History* (University of Pittsburgh Press, 2010), 90, 96.

[36] J. McNeill, *Something New Under the Sun: An Environmental History of the Twentieth-Century World* (W.W. Norton, 2001), 360.

[37] The ecological footprint statistics in this chapter come from the calculations by the Global Footprint Network: B. Ewing, et al., *The Ecological Footprint Atlas 2010* (Global Footprint Network, 2010). Also, see Worldwatch Institute, *State of the World 2012: Moving toward Sustainable Prosperity* (Worldwatch Institute, 2012), xxii.

energy, and other resources. With emerging economies adding to the burden, grave ecological tipping points may be irreparably passed soon.

The *Deepwater Horizon* oil spill in the Gulf of Mexico in 2010 was the worst environmental catastrophe of recent years, highlighting the frailty of US regulation in controlling severe pollution risks,[38] but the truly insidious ecological problems of the planet are far more pervasive and cumulative rather than episodic. Between one-third and one-half of the planet's land surface has already been altered or degraded by human activity,[39] thus reducing biological diversity and abundance. Species are disappearing much faster than in pre-human times,[40] with scientists warning of the sixth mass extinction.[41] Some 40 per cent of the planet's forests of 8000 years ago have gone,[42] and global deforestation clears terrain about the size of Costa Rica (or 5.2 million hectares) annually.[43] The shocking Indonesia forest fires, which incinerate some 20,000 km² annually for agricultural plantations and settlement, obliterate millions of creatures and fuel global warming.[44] Atmospheric CO_2 recorded in 2008 was at its highest level in at least 650,000 years,[45] and reportedly passed the ominous milestone of 400 ppm in May 2013.[46] Global temperatures have already climbed by 0.8 °C since the late nineteenth century and with a pending increase of about 0.4 °C this century due to past fossil fuel emissions. The disparate corollaries of these perturbations could include food shortages, poisoned food, more pathogens, damaged infrastructure, resource conflicts, poverty, and other socio-economic trauma.[47] Climate change, according to the

---

[38] B. Bush, 'Addressing the regulatory collapse behind the Deepwater Horizon oil spill' (2011) 26 *Journal of Environmental Law and Litigation* 535.

[39] P.M. Vitousek, et al., 'Human domination of earth's ecosystems' (1997) 277 *Science* 494.

[40] J.H. Lawton and R.M. May (eds), *Extinction Rates* (Oxford University Press, 1995), 10–22; see also Lowlett, 'Humans driving extinction faster than species can evolve, say experts'.

[41] A. Barnosky, et al., 'Has the Earth's sixth mass extinction already arrived?' (2011) 471 *Nature* 51.

[42] A. Shvidenko, C. Barber, and R. Persson, 'Forests', in R. Hassan, R. Scholes, and N. Ash (eds), *Ecosystems and Human Well-Being: Current State and Trends* (Millennium Ecosystem Assessment, 2005), 585, 588.

[43] UN Food and Agriculture Organization (FAO), *Global Forest Resources Assessment 2010: Key Findings* (FAO, 2010).

[44] 'The catastrophe of Indonesian forest fires', ABC Radio National (Science Show) 14 November 2015, at www.abc.net.au/radionational/programs/scienceshow.

[45] D. Adam, 'World carbon dioxide levels highest for 650,000 years, says US report', *The Guardian* 13 May 2008, at www.theguardian.com.

[46] R. Keeling, 'Record 400 ppm CO_2 milestone "feels like we're moving into a another era"', *The Guardian* 15 May 2013, at www.theguardian.com.

[47] See the various impacts and predictions discussed in D. Montgomery, *Dirt: The Erosion of Civilizations* (University of California Press, 2007); G. Monbiot, *Bring on the Apocalypse:*

2014 Fifth Assessment Report of the Intergovernmental Panel on Climate Change (IPCC), already hurts us and poses much graver harm this century.[48] The likelihood of these scenarios should not surprise us; archaeological records unveil how many civilisations that ignored environmental constraints ultimately suffered ruin.[49]

While the prognosis for many species and ecological systems is bleak, if we enlarge the timescale sufficiently much of the carnage will largely dissipate, albeit not in a time frame that brings solace for current human generations and other species. In his bestseller *The World Without Us*, Alan Weisman predicts that, liberated from humankind's poisonous burden, the planet will recover from most damage within a few thousand years, and within a few million only the most indestructible plastics and radioactive debris would linger, quite possibly buried out of harm's way.[50] The ability of nature to recover from some assaults has been show already, such as at Chernobyl, where animal life has blossomed after the 1986 deadly radiation leak in an area where few people still dare to visit. In other words, just as the depiction of humankind's presence on Earth can be compressed into 1 day or year in order to jolt public consciousness about the speed and scale of anthropogenic environmental changes, by the same calibrated infinitesimal moments, we might sense how 'quickly' nature can bounce back. Of course, this is no ethical excuse for avoiding urgent action to stop further ecological damage and repair past losses.

Nor should environmental law's occasional triumphs, such as eliminating ozone-depleting chemicals[51] or rescuing iconic species from extinction,[52] lull us into complacency. Ostensibly, some jurisdictions, particularly in

---

  Essays in Self-Destruction (Anchor Canada, 2008); V. Shiva, *Water Wars, Privatization, Pollution, and Profit* (South End Press, 2002).

[48] Intergovernmental Panel on Climate Change (IPCC), *Climate Change 2014. Impacts, Adaptation and Vulnerability: Summary for Policymakers* (Working Group II, IPCC, 2014).

[49] see C. Redman, *Human Impact on Ancient Environments* (University of Arizona Press, 1999); J. Diamond, *Collapse: How Societies Choose to Fail or Succeed* (Viking, 2005); But cf. P.A. McAnany and N. Yoffee (eds), *Questioning Collapse: Human Resilience, Ecological Vulnerability and the Aftermath of Empire* (Cambridge University Press, 2010).

[50] A. Weisman, *The World Without Us* (Picador, 2008).

[51] Montreal Protocol on Substances that Deplete the Ozone Layer, 16 September 1987, in force 1 January 1989, (1987) 6 ILM 1550; for an analysis on why this instrument succeeded, see S. Barrett, *Environment and Statecraft: The Strategy of Environmental Treaty-Making* (Oxford University Press, 2003), 221–52.

[52] A national symbol of the United States, the American Bald Eagle (*Haliaeetus leucocephalus*) was virtually extinct when the Endangered Species Preservation Act, 80 Stat. 926) was passed in late 1966. Today, in 2010, all populations except those in the far southwestern United States were transferred from the endangered to the threatened species list.

Western Europe and North America, have amassed extensive and ambitious environmental regulations. On some indicators they appear to work. Cleaner air was one of their first achievements, with American and European cities today vastly more breathable than a century ago, when smog was regarded as a necessary corollary of the industrial boom.[53] Forested areas in these regions have also been maintained or increased between 1990 and 2010.[54] Europe's climate change policy and emissions trading scheme lowered greenhouse gas emissions by 17.4 per cent below 1990 levels as of 2009,[55] and the United States nearly doubled its renewable energy generation from 2008 to 2011.[56] A reported 6 per cent increase in biodiversity in the Eurasian biogeographic realm since 1970[57] provides additional evidence that, sometimes, human intervention including legal controls can halt adversity.

Such successes, unfortunately, do not reflect the broader track towards unsustainability.[58] The ostensible successes in the West are due partly to their 'exporting' some damaging activities to countries, such as China, with less stringent regulations: China's largest export market is the United States, followed closely by the main European economies.[59] As labour standards and environmental practices in China and other emerging economies improve, manufacturers may simply move their factories – and the eco-footprint – to more impoverished countries eager for the economic opportunities.[60] On a per capita basis, the footprint of developed countries with the 'best' environmental laws are brought into

---

[53] R. Percival, *Against All Odds: How America's Century-Old Quest for Clean Air May Spur a New Era of Global Environmental Cooperation* (University of Utah Press, 2016).

[54] FAO, *Global Forest Resources Assessment 2010*, 18.

[55] V. Bolla, et al. (eds), *Sustainable Development in the European Union: 2011 Monitoring Report of the EU Sustainable Development Strategy* (Eurostat, 2011).

[56] From 72.6 terawatt hours in 2008 to 140.8 in 2011: US Energy Information Administration (EIA), *Annual Energy Outlook 2012: Early Release* (EIA, 2012).

[57] As based on populations of 535 indicator species in the Palearctic biogeographic region: M. Grooten, et al. (eds), *Living Planet Report 2012: Biodiversity, Biocapacity and Better Choices* (WWF, 2012), 35.

[58] See e.g. D. Boyd, *Unnatural Law: Rethinking Canadian Environmental Law and Policy* (UBC Press, 2003); B. Ackerman and R.B. Stewart, 'Reforming environmental law: the democratic case for market incentives' (1985) 37 *Stanford Law Review* 1333; A. Gillespie, *The Illusion of Progress; Unsustainable Development in International Law* (Earthscan, 2001).

[59] US-China Business Council, *US-China Trade Statistics and China's World Trade Statistics* (2011), at www.uschina.org/statistics/tradetable.html.

[60] D. Roberts, 'Why factories are leaving China', *Bloomberg Businessweek* at www.businessweek.com/magazine/content/10_21.

sharper relief: the 5 per cent of the world's population in the United States accounts for about 25 per cent of annual global fossil fuel consumption.[61]

Although the foregoing epochal shift is primarily associated with industrialisation over the past two centuries, it has much older antecedents and we should not assume that human beings once lived in any blissful harmony with nature.[62] The environmental practices of our ancestors have attracted some interesting research. The vivid depictions of animals in the 15,000-years-old Lascaux Caves in France plausibly reveal their awe and appreciation of nature. Incongruously, however, others were killing off megafauna, as well as feuding among themselves over scarce resources.[63] Large, ungainly creatures unaccustomed to the presence of human beings were easily dispatched, as occurred with the arrival of Aborigines in Australia some 50,000 years ago and the Clovis people in North America 12,000 years ago.[64] The spread of agriculture unleashed further environmental pressures, beginning with the deforestation of vast areas of Western Europe and Southeast Asia.[65] William Ruddiman attributes the increase in atmospheric carbon and methane at 8000 and 5000 years ago, respectively, as verified in ice-core samples, to these landscape changes.[66] Farming also generated the resources to usher in the first great urban civilisations in the Levant and Mesopotamia, which in later millennia would exert a crushing ecological burden around the world.[67]

---

[61] Worldwatch Institute, *State of the World 2011: Innovations That Nourish the Planet* (Worldwatch Institute, 2011).

[62] L. Shields, 'Are conservation goals and aboriginal rights incompatible?' (2000) 10 *Journal of Environmental Law and Practice* 187; A. Stearman, 'Revisiting the myth of the ecologically noble savage in Amazonia: implications for indigenous land rights' (1994) 49 *Culture and Agriculture* 2.

[63] T. Goldsmith and W. Zimmerman, *Biology, Evolution and Human Nature* (John Wiley, 2001), 340.

[64] L. Dayton, 'Mass extinctions pinned on ice age hunters' (2001) 292 *Science* 1819; Flannery, *The Future Eaters*, 195. The evidence of such impacts is disputed by some: e.g. D. Grayson and D. Meltzer, 'Clovis hunting and large mammal extinction: a critical review of the evidence' (2002) 16 *World Prehistory* 313.

[65] F. Oldfield, 'The role of people in the Holocene' in R.W. Battarbee and H.A. Binney (eds), *Natural Climate Variability and Global Warming: A Holocene Perspective* (Wiley-Blackwell, 2008), 58, 64; B. Maloney, 'Pollen analytical evidence for early forest clearance in North Sumatra' (1980) 324 *Nature* 287.

[66] W.F. Ruddiman, 'The anthropogenic greenhouse era began thousands of years ago' (2003) 61(3) *Climatic Change* 261.

[67] G. Barker, *The Agricultural Revolution in Prehistory: Why Did Foragers Become Farmers?* (Oxford University Press, 2006), 1–2.

The Anthropocene thus feeds off a much older and deeper unsustainable impulse of humankind. This ancient legacy has important implications for environmental law, as the obstacles to its success are perhaps not simply deficits in scientific knowledge, regulatory design, or public education; instead, more fundamental obstacles rooted in the evolutionary makeup of humankind may need to be reckoned. People have evolved diverse cognitive and behavioural predilections that shape understandings of the past and future, evaluation of risks and uncertainty, and motivations to cooperate or conflict. Human beings have the capacity to identify and respond positively to environmental shifts, even over quite expansive time frames, but also are mired by countervailing tendencies that can skew behaviour towards more immediate and expedient considerations. The understanding of time itself, as a social construct, must thus be placed in this evolutionary context.

Evolutionary Time Lags

The Primitive Mind and Modern Civilisation

Homo sapiens' misaligned cultural and biological evolution helps to explain our environmental wantonness. This two-speed evolutionary motion, with cultural change galloping ahead of our biological shuffle, has left human beings retaining traits maladaptive for their modern context. Eons ago, in a world inhabited by few people with archaic technologies, humankind didn't threaten the Earth's environmental stability even though localised impacts were sometimes severe. But subsistence behaviours that succeeded under ancestral conditions become dysfunctional when the perpetrators number billions and wield destructive technologies. A desire to catch any available prey or hoard all resources to survive a bad season might have been advantageous for a vulnerable hunter–gatherer clan, but becomes counter-productive when done by modern societies. As evolution happens slowly, over countless generations, contemporary generations remain imprinted with cognitive and biological traits formed long ago, despite dramatic cultural shifts that necessitate different environmental behaviours. The mismatch between the primitive mind and modern 'civilisation' results in *Homo sapiens* being an evolutionary time lag:[68] we

---

[68] The phrase 'primitive mind and modern civilization' was the title of a pioneering book on human psychology: C.R. Aldrich, *The Primitive Mind and Modern Civilization* (Routledge, Trench, Trubner and Co, 1931).

may seem to be at the apogee of evolutionary success, but the pinnacle climbed has become the precipice from which an earth-shattering collapse looms.

The human evolutionary endowment must be deciphered to identify behaviours deeply ingrained and resistant to change, through law or other mechanisms, and behaviours amenable to redemption. Environmental regulation already makes assumptions about human traits, though regulators may be unaware of their implicit reliance on behavioural models or complacent about their accuracy. In the modern history of environmental law one influential exposition of human nature is Garrett Hardin's parable of the 'tragedy of the commons'.[69] His tale of the 'inevitable' degradation of a communal grazing pasture reflects a particular view of human nature as selfish, materialistic, and uncooperative. This scenario has fascinated many, especially game theorists interested in the 'prisoner's dilemma',[70] and it has informed neoclassical economic assumptions about behavioural drivers.[71] Hardin highlighted the challenges to cooperative resource use, although his one-sided assumptions about human nature, in addition to his confusion between a lawless, open-access resource and one managed communally, detracts somewhat from his intellectual legacy.[72] Environmental law has evolved to harness other behavioural and cognitive models, including risk perception (in controlling environmental hazards)[73] and 'nudge' theory (about non-coercive ways to change daily routines and conveniences).[74] The design of environmental legislation thus draws, implicitly or explicitly, on understandings about human desires, fears, preferences, and biases, but given significant disagreement about human psychology it remains open how to craft the most behaviourally effective laws.

Philosophers have long debated human nature, often scrutinising our most primitive and seemingly unadulterated form for answers. Some mythologise a golden age from which we have been corrupted by civilisation. Moral sentimentalists such as Francis Hutcheson and David Hume

---

[69] G. Hardin, 'The tragedy of the commons' (1968) 162 *Science* 1243.
[70] E.g. R.A. McCain, *Game Theory and Public Policy* (Edward Elgar Publishing, 2009).
[71] C. Doucouliagos, 'Note on the evolution of homo economicus' (1994) 28 *Journal of Economic Issues* 469.
[72] M. Ridley, *The Origins of Virtue* (Penguin Books, 1997), 232.
[73] A. Bostrom, 'Risk perceptions: "experts" vs. "lay people"' (1997) 8 *Duke Environmental Law and Policy Forum* 101.
[74] R. Thaler and C. Sunstein. *Nudge* (Penguin Books, 2008).

believed that people have natural inclinations to be altruistic.[75] Perhaps more than any other Enlightenment thinker, Jean-Jacques Rousseau saw humankind's original state of nature as utopian, born without original sin and blessed with benevolence.[76] For Rousseau, it was the trappings of 'civilisation', such as property ownership, monarchies, and religion, which depraved people. Alternatively, some welcome it for improving the human character from its supposedly barbaric, primitive beginnings. In this view, any 'human morality is presented as just a thin crust under which boil antisocial, amoral, and egoistic passions'.[77] Thomas Hobbes famously depicted humankind as naturally selfish, brutal, and nasty, for which his solution was enlightened despotism by strong government.[78] Hobbes' sombre view of humankind has influenced many environmental thinkers, from Thomas Robert Malthus[79] to William Ophuls,[80] who foreshadowed authoritarianism to rescue a depleting planet from the ravenous masses. They believed that the fecklessness of modern democracy would be unable to make the hard choices necessary in a diminishing environment. From a similar sentiment, Australian Tim Flannery, in his wake-up call the *Weather Makers*, speculates about a hypothetical 'carbon dictatorship' where an 'Earth Commission for Thermostatic Control' runs the economy to safeguard against a looming climate crisis.[81] Refuting behavioural innatism, another perspective interprets human nature as largely socially conditioned. Over three centuries ago, John Locke postulated that individuals are born as a *blank slate* (except perhaps for a penchant to acquire property), out of which life experience and culture moulds each person's character.[82] Many social psychologists (e.g. John Watson),[83] sociologists

---

[75] see L. Schneider, *The Scottish Moralists on Human Nature and Society* (University of Chicago Press, 1967), 7–9.
[76] J.J. Rousseau, *Discourse on Inequality* (Aziloth Books, 2013, original in 1754).
[77] S. Neiman, *Moral Clarity: A Guide for Grown-Up Idealists* (Vintage, 2011), 267 (quoting F. de Waal). This idea, often known as 'veneer theory', originated with T.H. Huxley, *Evolution and Ethics* (Macmillan, 1894).
[78] T. Hobbes, *Leviathan* (Penguin Books, 1982, original in 1651).
[79] T.R. Malthus, *An Essay on the Principle of Population* (J. Johnson, 1798).
[80] W. Ophuls, 'Leviathan or oblivion' in H.E. Daly (ed), *Toward a Steady State Economy* (W.H. Freeman, 1973), 215.
[81] T. Flannery, *The Weather Makers* (HarperCollins, 2005), 290–5.
[82] J. Locke, *An Essay Concerning Humane Understanding* (Oxford University Press, 1979, original in 1690).
[83] J.B. Watson, *Behavior: An Introduction to Comparative Psychology* (Henry Holt, 1914).

(e.g. Emile Durkheim),[84] and anthropologists (e.g. Margaret Mead)[85] similarly view human behaviour as imprinted mainly by its social environment rather than biological predisposition.

Contemporary behaviourists appreciate that human nature, as verified by empirical research, is more complex than some of these stark perspectives. The intertwined forces of nature and nurture engender a range of traits, depending on the context: aggression, selfishness, empathy, cooperation, and altruism. But the precise triggers of individuals' ensemble of lighter and darker instincts, how they are modified culturally, remain highly debatable. Behavioural scientists have spilt much ink debating the relative significance of our selfish and altruistic impulses – traits that shape our capacity to deal with environmental problems. The debate infuses the titles of polemics such as *Biological Constraints on the Human Spirit*,[86] *The Moral Animal*,[87] *How Morality Evolved*,[88] and *The Modern Denial of Human Nature*.[89] Our enquiry here is not to dwell on these quarrels but rather to focus on how people perceive time and its implications for our environmental behaviour. The abilities to reflect on the past and plan for the future are critically important for how societies deal with environmental change.

Foresight

Human nature in its most unadulterated, archaic form can reveal a lot. Evolutionary psychology, with other cognitive disciplines, can illuminate whether environmental behaviour is ingrained or amenable to education, law, or other influences. The savannahs of Africa were the canvas on which much human evolution was etched.[90] People survived in small, highly interdependent hunter–gatherer groups, dominated by kin and

---

[84] E. Durkheim, *Rules of Sociological Method* (Free Press, 1966), 106 (contending that 'individual natures are merely the indeterminate material which the social factor determines and transforms').

[85] M. Mead, *Coming of Age in Samoa: A Psychological Study of Primitive Youth for Western Civilization* (William Morrow, 1928).

[86] M. Konner, *The Tangled Wing: Biological Constraints on the Human Spirit* (Henry Holt, 2002).

[87] R. Wright, *The Moral Animal. Why We Are the Way We Are: The New Science of Evolutionary Psychology* (Da Capo Press, 1994).

[88] F. De Waal, *Primates and Philosophers: How Morality Evolved* (Princeton University Press, 2006).

[89] S. Pinker, *How the Mind Works* (WW Norton, 1999).

[90] F. Marlowe, 'Hunter gatherers and human evolution' (2005) 14 *Evolutionary Anthropology* 54.

allies, but probably in competition with unrelated groups over territory and resources. Evolutionary psychology examines the human mind for psychological adaptations that evolved from such ancestral environments.[91] It challenges understandings of sex, family, and friendship, as well as environmental conduct, by showing that much is bred in the bone, with culture a secondary influence.[92]

Like other species, *Homo sapiens* heeds natural selective pressures regarding its preferences, emotions, and cognition that serve to enhance opportunities for individuals' survival and reproduction.[93] From the theory of 'socio-biology' pioneered in the 1970s,[94] evolutionary psychologists such as David Buss and Steven Pinker interpret much human behaviour as highly specialised psychological adaptations that evolved to solve challenges in our ancestral environments.[95] Behaviours present worldwide, transcending specific cultures, such as fear of spiders and snakes, may reflect evolved adaptations. Evolutionary psychology, however, doesn't imply rigid biological determinism; rather, evolutionary models recognise that human behaviour reflects the *mutual* interaction between biological variation and environmental selection, or, as often described, between nature and nurture. Local cultural and ecological conditions can generate variations within the broad parameters set biologically. Evolutionary psychology also builds on a variety of related disciplines, such as paleoneurology and bioarchaeology, in seeking to identify and describe the neural characteristics that selection pressures during human evolutionary history have forged to define the human mind.

They give insights into how our ancestors perceived time that can shed light on current environmental conduct.[96] Some of the earliest human

---

[91] D.M. Buss, *Evolutionary Psychology: The New Science of the Mind* (Allyn and Bacon, 2004), 49–50.

[92] Many scholars see cultural memes as more significant, however. see R. Brodie, *Virus of the Mind: The New Science of the Meme* (Hay House, 2011), A. Lynch, *Thought Contagion: How Belief Spreads Through Society* (Basic Books, 1998); R. Aunger, *Darwinizing Culture: The Status of Memetics* (Oxford University Press, 2001); S. Blackmore, *The Meme Machine* (Oxford University Press, 2000).

[93] C. Darwin, *On the Origins of Species by Means of Natural Selection, or the Preservation of Favoured Races in the Struggle for Life* (J. Murray, 1859).

[94] E.O. Wilson, *Sociobiology: The New Synthesis* (Harvard University Press. 1975).

[95] D.M. Buss, 'Evolutionary personality psychology' (1991) 42 *Annual Review of Psychology* 439; Pinker, *How the Mind Works*.

[96] See generally C.D. Laughlin, and C.J. Throop, 'Continuity, causation and cyclicity: a cultural neurophenomenology of time-consciousness' (2008) 1(2) *Time and Mind: The Journal of Archaeology, Consciousness and Culture* 159; E. Bruner (ed), *Human Paleoneurology* (Springer, 2015).

remains reveal a sophisticated awareness of time because the evidence implies strong consciousness of the future and past. One clue is burial of the dead, and in particular inclusion of artefacts in burials, presumably from the belief that the deceased was entering the afterlife and would need tools and weapons. Burials would presumably also have allowed for veneration of one's ancestors, suggesting a consciousness of the past. Evidence of funerary practices in *Homo sapiens* and *Homo neanderthalensis* is traced to the Middle Palaeolithic about 100,000 years ago.[97] Early examples of burials with ornaments include a 74,000-year-old perforated *Conus* shell excavated in an infant's grave from the Border Cave in southern Africa.[98] The practice may be much older, because the interments may well have been accompanied by organic material that rotted away. While the authenticity of this and other evidence is disputable because of bioturbation, clearly *Homo sapiens* have buried their dead, and sometimes with ornaments, for a very long time.

The construction of tools, which seemingly began much earlier than burials, being traced back to early hominids 3.3 million years ago in Kenya,[99] also suggests an inchoate future consciousness. The effort to make a tool such as a hunting weapon occurred with anticipation of its future use.[100] The development of language is another powerful sign of temporal perception in humans. Early cave art, such as paintings of animals or hunting scenes, demonstrates a capacity for imagination, by representing objects and events not perceptually present but having once been observed.[101] The use of ochre at the Qafzeh cave in Israel has been dated to 92,000 years ago.[102] Similarly, verbal storytelling no doubt emerged at some point in this prehistoric era. Language thus provided the means to express our capacity to contemplate another reality beyond the present.

---

[97] J. Zilhão, 'Lower and middle Palaeolithic mortuary behaviours and the origins of ritual burial' in C. Renfrew, M. Boyd, and I. Morley (eds), *Death Rituals and Social Order in the Ancient World: Death Shall Have No Dominion* (Cambridge University Press, 2016), 27.

[98] F. d'Errico and L. Blackwell, 'Earliest evidence of personal ornaments associated with burial: the Conus shells from Border Cave' (2016) 93 *Journal of Human Evolution* 91. See also R. Leaky, *Origins Reconsidered: In Search of What Makes Us Human* (Anchor, 1993).

[99] S. Harmand, et al., '3.3-million-year-old stone tools from Lomekwi 3, West Turkana, Kenya' (2015) 521 *Nature* 310.

[100] P.V. Tobias, 'The brain of Homo habilis: a new level of organization in cerebral evolution' (1987) 16(7–8) *Journal of Human Evolution* 741.

[101] R. White, *Prehistoric Art: The Symbolic Journey of Humankind* (Harry N. Abrams, 2003).

[102] E. Hovers, et al., 'An early case of color symbolism: ochre use by modern humans in Oafzeh Cave' (2003) 44(4) *Current Anthropology* 491.

Through this perceptual awareness of time, people became aware of duration, continuity, and change; of patterns, rhythms, and forms of change; and thereby to connect a sequence of events in their lives or surroundings. Increasing future consciousness enabled people to forecast or fantasise about tomorrow, to have hopes and fears about what lies ahead, and to have goals, make choices, and implement plans for another day.[103] Likewise, time perception enabled us to contemplate the past, such as the birth or loss of loved ones, or knowledge of previous hardships and successes, with the potential to learn from such memories.

While consciousness of timescales beyond the present may be hailed as one of *Homo sapiens'* unique attributes, other animals also display it. Some apes and other species, such as crows, fashion materials such as sticks and rocks into tools and display evidence of episodic memory (i.e. mental time travel).[104] Elephants and horses apparently mourn their dead kin.[105] An idea of time and knowledge of the future in fact is likely to occur widely in the animal world. Carnivores that follow migratory species will understand the importance of being in a certain location at a given time of year to catch prey. Even insects that eat fruits and nuts will know that they need to find specific types of trees in certain areas at a given season. Some of these behaviours may be instinctive rather than contemplated, but this is unlikely in all cases.[106]

Human beings' more sophisticated consciousness of time, which yields the capacity to imagine future prospects and ponder past deeds, has profound implications for environmental behaviour. It aids survival by enabling people to understand how seasonal cycles and other temporalities alter the availability of food and other essentials. William Burroughs identifies environmental sensitivity among early hunter–gatherers based on their intricate knowledge of the resources they depended on, such as 'watching movements of migratory birds, which are very sensitive to climatic shifts' and 'observing the timing of the different stages of vegetation'.[107] Our own impacts on nature can also be bought into sharper

---

[103] A. Reading, *Hope and Despair: How Perceptions of the Future Shape Human Behavior* (John Hopkins University Press, 2004).

[104] J. Bräuer and J. Call, 'Apes produce tools for future use' (2015) 77(3) *American Journal of Primatology* 254; G.R. Hunt, 'Manufacture and use of hook-tools by New Caledonian crows' (1996) 379 *Nature* 249.

[105] B.J. King, *How Animals Grieve* (University of Chicago Press, 2013).

[106] P. Skorupski and L. Chittka, 'Animal cognition: an insect's sense of time?' (2006) 16(19) *Current Biology* R851.

[107] W. Burroughs, *Climate Change in Prehistory: The End of the Reign of Chaos* (Cambridge University Press, 2005), 163–4.

relief through time awareness – having foresight gives individuals the capacity of 'recognizing the threat posed by their own natural propensities'.[108] Veneration of animal totems and sacred sites by indigenous peoples today may have an ancient lineage in cautious practices designed to avoid over-harvesting treasured species or damaging their breeding grounds.

Awareness of the great expanses of time beyond the present also surely fostered social cooperation and altruism – both crucial traits for environmental stewardship. Evolutionary psychologists have suggested several drivers of mutual aid beyond familial consanguinity. In 1971, Robert Trivers suggested that caring for others is favoured among nonrelatives through reciprocal interactions. Cooperative big game hunting and sharing the spoils of the kill was likely one seminal incubator of such interactions.[109] Later, Richard Alexander coined the phrase 'indirect reciprocity' to explain the development of moral systems in societies, in which social reputation drives individuals to be good Samaritans.[110] Kristen Hawkes argued that the more valuable rewards of reciprocal altruism are often intangible, involving social recognition for one's sharing and public-spiritedness.[111] In a further extension of the altruistic circle, Robert Frank identified emotions such as love and trust as predisposing people to act against their self-interest.[112] Sarah Hrdy's *Mothers and Others* pinpoints the human practice of alloparenting as our most unique attribute (among primates) to foster selective pressures that favour individuals who empathise and cooperate.[113] Unlike wild salmon, humans do not spawn and then perish, but spend many years nurturing their progeny, and the resulting generational overlaps would themselves have also lengthened human empathy. Marc Hauser in *Moral Minds* goes further and argues that our capacity for morality is innate, like the capacity for language itself, honed by thousands of years of evolution rather than being a recent cultural advance.[114] Penny Spikins makes similar claims in her analysis of the roots of empathy and

---

[108] J. Karr, 'Attaining a sustainable society' in L. Westra, K. Bosselmann, and R. Westra (eds), *Reconciling Human Existence with Ecological Integrity* (Earthscan, 2008), 1, 24.
[109] R. Trivers, 'The evolution of reciprocal altruism' (1971) 46 *Quarterly Review of Biology* 35.
[110] K. Hawkes, 'Sharing and collective action' in E. Smith and B. Winterhalder (eds), *Evolutionary Ecology and Human Behavior* (Aldine de Gruyter, 1992), 269.
[111] R. Alexander, *Darwinism and Human Affairs* (University of Washington Press, 1979).
[112] R.H. Frank, *Passions within Reason: The Strategic Role of the Emotions* (Norton, 1988).
[113] S.B. Hrdy, *Mothers and Others: The Evolutionary Origins of Mutual Understanding* (Belknap Press, 2009), 175–208.
[114] M.D. Hauser, *Moral Minds: How Nature Designed Our Universal Sense of Right and Wrong* (Harper Perennial, 2006).

mores.[115] Under these circumstances perhaps the ethical time frame of the present, procreating generation can be stretched both back and forward in time by many years to the point where the well-being of many others and the health of the biosphere become shared concerns.

But why, then, do many persons behave as though there is no tomorrow, oblivious to the environmental adversity foreshadowed by scientific research? Most societies have shown themselves to be not particularly farsighted in dealing with ecological threats. Their gravity is commonly denied or trivialised until they materialise to the point of demonstrably interfering with our self-interest, such as engendering diseases, droughts, and other harms to personal health or economic well-being. Despite improving scientific evidence of these environmental risks and impacts, humankind often ignores the advice. We may seem incandescent about climate change, but continue to travel in aeroplanes, eat meat, and indulge in other incongruities. So why?

Well, human propensities for kindness and cooperation compete with tendencies to be selfish and violent. The propensity for aggression has been debated for centuries, at last since Hobbes surmised that the 'natural condition of mankind' was violence. In recent decades anthropologists and bioarchaeologists have entered the fray. Theorising about primate behaviour and its applicability to *Homo sapiens* led many researchers in the 1950s and 1960s to see competition and aggression over access to food and sexual partners as a fundamental driver of the human condition.[116] While this so-called 'killer ape' thesis has since been jettisoned as a too one-dimensional portrait of human character, many agree that our predilection for lethal violence against 'out-group' members (for whom there is no consanguinity or other close association) has a deep evolutionary basis.[117] Traumatic injuries in ancient skeletons that suggest projectile wounds and blunt force trauma are grisly reminders of our bloody lineage.[118] Tribalism and parochialism continue to flourish, often organised at a higher scale in nation-states and religious sects. Competition rather than cooperation

---

[115] P. Spinkins, *How Compassion Made Us Human: The Evolutionary Origins of Tenderness, Trust and Morality* (Pan and Sword Books, 2015).

[116] see R. Dart, 'The predatory transition from ape to man' (1953) 1 *International Anthropology and Linguistic Review* 201; R. Ardrey, *African Genesis: A Personal Investigation into the Animal Origins and Nature of Man* (Athenaeum, 1961).

[117] E. Staub, *The Roots of Evil: The Origins of Genocide and Other Group Violence* (Cambridge University Press, 1989).

[118] P.L. Walker, 'A bioarchaeological perspective on the history of violence' (2001) 30 *Annual Review of Anthropology* 573.

over scarce environmental resources is thus a plausible outcome, and is already widely evident in international affairs, such as disputes over fishing on the high seas or shirking responsibility for climate change. Such conflict and competition clearly undermine planetary stewardship for the long-term benefit of all.

Another reason why foresight does not necessarily translate into actions that prioritise future well-being is their costs relative to benefits. The harm-reducing benefits of environmental protection may be so distant in time that they do not materialise until after the people taking the responsible measures have died. Actions to save biodiversity or reduce pollution may have no discernible benefits for decades. The incentive to act presciently is thus blunted by misaligned timing: the costs of environmental improvements and protections are usually quite tangible and upfront, while the promised benefits seem vague and occur over the long term, which is problematic for individuals or groups when faced with competing demands on their time and resources. We see this discrepancy in environmental law, with the most robust laws commonly enacted to address near-term threats and impacts, especially those menacing our personal health or property. For example, in the 1970s many countries eliminated lead from gasoline, paints, and other sources of contamination because of evidence that cumulative exposure to it poisons our bodies. The benefits of these anti-lead measures accrue to both current and future generations. By contrast, mitigating climate change has not received the same decisive commitment. Interestingly, American environmental law professor Lisa Heinzerling contends that some paternalistic laws that speak mainly to the distant future can provide solace to the current generation, such as by lessening fear of future harms, a benefit that she sees as improving psychological and social well-being now.[119] But still, the evidence asserts that long-term environmental changes that require costly actions now in order to reap benefits later are more difficult to address than where the costs and benefits align temporally.

Another explanation for the discrepancy between awareness and action is because of the spatial qualities of much environmental harm. Many impacts are diffused not only across wide timescales, but also wide spatial scales, with harm manifesting far from the originating pressures. Marine plastic pollution, a growing global problem, is a good example. The spatial diffusion of environmental impact makes it difficult to grasp

---

[119] L. Heinzerling, 'Environmental law and the present future' (1999) 87 *Georgetown Law Journal* 2025, 2029.

conceptually or to experience directly. As Rolf Lidskog puts it, 'these threats are becoming more remote from our perceptual apparatus and acquiring form as abstract prognoses that are beyond lay people's knowledge and experience'.[120] Unlike temporally immediate and spatially proximate pollution that we can sense and observe, such as city smog, other harms such as climate change are invisible and remote, being understood usually only vicariously through academic research.

Apart from temporally (and spatially) mismatched benefits and costs, the passage of time carries uncertainty and risk. A decision to ward off future peril reflects a prediction about the future – whether in fact the peril would arise if nothing is done and whether preventive measures would work and provide the anticipated benefits. The future, of course, is largely uncertain or unknown, and the risk of making a wrong turn tends to increase as the time horizon lengthens. Too much uncertainty can stifle even the most optimistic to invest resources now for a possible payoff many years away. Even when one's personal health is at stake, individuals can be astonishingly careless: many cancers and diseases have long latency, but inexpensive protective actions, such as wearing sunscreen to prevent melanoma, are often insouciantly ignored by those at risk.

The perception of environmental risks, and the measures people adopt to avoid them, have intrigued scholars.[121] They suggest a discrepancy between how ordinary people and experts perceive risks, with lay opinions sometimes not being rational according to statistical probabilities. The public tends to acutely fear radioactive contamination from nuclear facilities, yet underestimates what experts warn is a greater cumulative harm from lifelong exposure to X-rays.[122] Individuals are prone to 'temporal discounting', in which environmental threats that manifest slowly tend to be perceived as of lesser importance than the same threat that has more immediacy.[123] Heinzerling explains that the discrepancies between lay and expert perception of environmental risks are partly because of 'laypeople's

---

[120] R. Lidskog, 'Scientific evidence or lay people's experience: on risk and trust with regard to modern environmental threats' in M. Cohen (ed), *Risk in the Modern Age: Social Theory, Science, and Environmental Decision-Making* (Macmillan, 2000), 196, 202.

[121] G. Bohm and H.R. Pfister, 'Antinomies of environmental risk perception: cognitive structure and evaluation' in M.J. Casimir (ed), *Culture and the Changing Environment: Uncertainty, Cognition, and Risk* (Berghahn Books, 2008), 61; M. Douglas and A. Wildavsky, *Risk and Culture* (University of California Press, 1982).

[122] B.L. Cohen, *The Nuclear Energy Option* (Plenum Press, 1990), Chapter 5.

[123] R. Gifford, et al., 'Temporal pessimism and spatial optimism in environmental assessments: an 18-nation study' (2008) 29(1) *Journal of Environmental Psychology* 1, 7.

tendency to consider a wider set of factors when judging risks' such as 'controllability, familiarity, immediacy, diffuseness, voluntariness, equity, reversibility, and naturalness of the hazard'.[124] These considerations are not necessarily invalid; the longevity of some environmental threats increases the uncertainty and stress that potential victims may suffer; and the temporal lag between the pollution and illness can foster pervasive anxieties for many people over the loss of knowledge over when or if the harm may result.

Evolutionary psychology also suggests that the ancestral environments of human evolution continue to influence our apprehension of risks. People commonly loath spiders, snakes, sharks, and tigers,[125] as well as dread heights and darkness,[126] even though many of these fears are exaggerated given the unlikeliness of encountering them in our modern lives. Conversely, contemporary people tend not to have evolved the requisite fears of new environmental dangers: we seemingly lack instinctive wariness about pollution and other insidious threats posed by modern lifestyles, such as car fumes, food contaminants, and plastics. In other words, risks that were notable in our ancestral environments can continue to disproportionately worry us, despite their rarity compared to other hazards commonly encountered, such as crossing a busy street. This insouciance may also be explained, suggests evolutionary psychology, by the widely observed tendency of individuals to be overly optimistic and concomitantly to self-deceive about their prospects.[127] Optimism may benefit individuals by increasing morale, determination, or persistence, and generating a self-fulfilling prophecy in which inflated confidence actually improves success.[128] As an evolutionary advantage, Trivers suggests 'that there are intrinsic benefits to having . . . a more optimistic view of the future than the facts would seem to justify',[129] while Edward

---

[124] Heinzerling, 'Environmental law and the present future', 2030.
[125] Of the human fear of predators, see D. Quammen, *Monster of God: The Man-Eating Predator in the Jungles of History and the Mind* (W.W. Norton, 2004).
[126] J.A. Gray, *The Psychology of Fear and Stress* (Cambridge University Press, 1987), 11–12.
[127] D. Goleman, *Vital Lies, Simple Truths: The Psychology of Self-Deception* (Simon and Schuster; 1996); R.L. Trivers, 'The elements of a scientific theory of self-deception' (2000) 907 *Annals of the New York Academy of Science* 114; J. Chambers, P. Windschitl, and J. Suls, 'Egocentrism, event frequency and comparative optimism: when what happens frequently is "more likely to happen to me"' (2003) 29(11) *Journal of Personality and Social Psychology Bulletin* 1343.
[128] D. Johnson and J. Fowler, 'The evolution of overconfidence' (2011) 477 *Nature* 317.
[129] Trivers, 'The elements of a scientific theory of self-deception', 125.

O. Wilson elaborates that 'without it the mind, imprisoned by fatalism, would slow and deteriorate'.[130]

Conversely, faulty assessments and dangerous decisions may ensue from overconfidence. Erroneous optimism intersects with risk perception, such as individuals trusting that, in environmental terms, they are safer than others. One study found that residents felt less vulnerable to radon contamination than their neighbours when they had not tested their homes.[131] Overconfidence can have hazardous consequences that become amplified when the bravado is scaled-up through political and legal mechanisms to societal decisions. Marc Pratarelli and Connie Aragon surmise that perhaps only 'environmental pressures in the form of imminent catastrophic ecological and/or economic collapse on a scale not seen in recorded human history are likely to compel humans to adapt their value systems to focus on conservation practices and sustainable economic policies'.[132] Crises may unseat misplaced optimism and trigger major structural reform, as observed when the Great Depression of the 1930s motivated sweeping economic policy changes in many countries. The dilemma is that numerous environmental threats, particularly climate change, unfold too slowly in human perception to provoke similar anxiety.

Extinguishing the Past: Environmental Amnesia

Humankind's warped perception of its future prospects is matched by equally problematic memories of the past. Environmental blunders are habitually ignored or trivialised, thereby condemning society to repeat them. And nonchalance about past losses can mislead us about the relative health of the natural environment today and thereby encourage complacency when behavioural changes are needed.

People's view of nature is relative and conditioned by what they regard as normal. If one grows up in a smoggy city devoid of trees and parks, one might regard those conditions as 'normal'. A 1995 study by Peter Kahn and Batya Freidman of how children perceive their environmental surroundings found, in their case study of a black community in inner city

---

[130] E.O. Wilson, *Consilience: The Unity of Knowledge* (Vintage, 1998), 120.
[131] N. Weinstein, M. Klotz, and P. Sandman, 'Optimistic biases in public perceptions of the risk from radon' (1988) 78(7) *American Journal of Public Health* 796.
[132] M.E. Pratarelli and C.M. Aragon, 'Acknowledging the "primitive origins of human ecological dysfunction": a view toward efficacy and global ecological integrity' (2008) 8(1) *Globalisation*, at http://globalization.icaap.org.

Houston, Texas – one of the most polluted cities in the United States – that most kids did not see themselves as directly affected by the stench or contamination. As the researchers explained: 'one possible answer is that to understand the idea of pollution one needs to compare existing polluted states to those that are less polluted . . . if one's only experience is with a certain amount of pollution, then that amount becomes not pollution, but the norm against which more polluted states are measured'.[133] Kahn and Freidman described this condition as the 'environmental generational amnesia', in which people take the condition of the environment in which they grow up as the norm to measure pollution during their lives, but as the degradation increases with each generation, each successor takes that (altered) degradation as the norm. Fisheries biologist Daniel Pauly has also explored the impact of intergenerational temporal amnesia on our understanding of environmental change. He coined the phrase 'shifting baseline syndrome' to denote how current environmental policies may be based on inaccurate baselines that ignore cumulative losses.[134] Pauly critiqued how experts evaluated depleted fisheries using the state of the stock at the start of their careers as the baseline rather than the fisheries in their older, untouched state before human exploitation. The pernicious effect of shifting baselines is to accelerate stagnation of ecosystems as cumulative losses get ignored, and to make ecological restoration harder where baselines have shifted too far.

People seem to be cognitively poorly equipped to notice long-term diminution in environmental conditions. Small or gradual changes over many decades – a comparatively short period for many of nature's processes – are imperceptible to most except perhaps those who have etched a living close to the land or sea, such as farmers, fishers, or indigenous peoples. Urban denizens have little opportunity to witness shifting environmental conditions: concrete jungles of roads and buildings commonly make up their 'baselines'. Yet, there is no shortage of academic information about natural history. Climatologists study ice core samples from Antarctica to decipher variations in the global climate over many millennia. Conservation biologists educate us about the former distribution, abundance, and evolution of wildlife. Botanists can likewise reveal the history of plants and flora communities. But such knowledge may not inform

---

[133] P. Kahn Jr. and B. Friedman, 'Environmental views and values of children in an inner-city black community' (1995) 66 *Child Development* 1403, 1414.
[134] D. Pauly, 'Anecdotes and the shifting baseline syndrome of fisheries' (1995) 10 *Trends in Ecology and Evolution* 430.

how ordinary people understand their natural surroundings and nor may it influence the media, politicians, or others in positions of influence. Even major pollution disasters, such as *Deepwater Horizon*, can, within a few years, be largely forgotten except by those most directly affected or academic researchers. Since the initial public outcry and clean-up operation, with BP pledging to pay billions to settle claims, the victims have struggled to be compensated, the Gulf of Mexico holds less sea life, and the oil business continues to flirt with mishap.[135] The possibly largest environmental disaster in US history has also failed to improve the robustness of safety law: the plethora of new initiatives sponsored by the Obama administration appears to have achieved only cosmetic changes.[136] Societies, suggests this anecdote, tend to acclimatise to a new 'normal' and then forget.

A rich historical record of nature as depicted in paintings, explorers' diaries, newspapers, and other cultural resources provides a fascinating portal to its former fecundity. A walk through New Zealand's ghost forests today can be an eerie experience, unlike the astonishing dawn chorus that greeted its first European explorers in the eighteenth century. The songbirds' symphony was noted by Sir Joseph Banks, the great naturalist on board the *Endeavour* with Captain Cook, who wrote on visiting Queen Charlotte Sound in 1769:

> the ship lay at a distance of somewhat less than a quarter of a mile from the shore, and in the morning we were awakened by the singing of the birds: the number was incredible. And they seemed to strain their throats in emulation of each other. This wild melody was infinitely superior to any that we had ever heard of the same kind.[137]

Mustelids, rodents, and other bird-devouring species foolishly introduced by Europeans decimated these avian divas. One can only imagine the even richer symphony these forests resonated with for the first Polynesians, who arrived at least 500 years earlier and eventually killed off (directly or indirectly) some 38 species, including the suite of giant moa.[138] Aotearoa's biodiversity losses are among the worst, perhaps only exceeded

---

[135] B. Casselmann, 'Five years after the BP oil spill, the industry is still taking big risks', *FiveThirtyEight Economics* 20 April 2015, at http://fivethirtyeight.com; K. Reckdahl, 'Five years after the *Deepwater Horizon* oil spill, BP's most vulnerable victims are still struggling', *The Nation* 15 April 2015, at www.thenation.com.
[136] J. Weaver, 'Deepwater Horizon: four years on and offshore safety remains questionable', *The Conversation* 18 April 2015, at http://theconversation.com.
[137] Quoted in A. Kennedy, *New Zealand* (Longmans, Green, and Co, 1874), 20.
[138] M.S. McGlone, 'The Polynesian settlement of New Zealand in relation to environmental and biotic changes' (1989) 12 *New Zealand Journal of Ecology* 115.

by Australia's, losing 29 endemic mammals that 'comprise 35 per cent of the world's modern mammal extinctions'.[139] Using early explorers' writings and colonial artists' works, Bill Gammage's magnum opus *The Biggest Estate on Earth* documents that the Australian landscape encountered by the first European explorers was one socialised by Aborigines to create a 'parkland' setting with a mosaic of vegetation that enabled wildlife to flourish.[140]

Many species not yet extinct cling in remnants within vastly contracted ranges. Six Australian mammals survive only inside fenced sanctuaries or predator-free islands.[141] In Roman times, the lion roamed across North Africa and Asia Minor, as evident in its depictions in mosaics and other artistic portrayals of Roman blood sports – events that contributed to their expiration from these regions. Elephants once roamed through much of China as recently as 2000 years ago.[142] The California's state flag depicts grizzly bears, but none have apparently lived in the state since 1924. The great whales number about one-tenth of their historic population before the modern whaling era.[143] In the eighteenth century, whales could be found venturing up the Thames into London: the return of one in 2006 after two centuries' absence provoked much public curiosity.[144] J.B. MacKinnon calls this situation the '10 per cent World', a planet where 'nature as we know it today is a fraction of what it was', that fraction being about ten per cent of ecosystems and wildlife that are largely intact in their diversity and abundance as they once were, before human colonisation through agriculture, industrialisation, and settlement.[145] But many people may view this '10 per cent' as the normal state of environmental affairs, and the baseline to measure 'progress' towards sustainable development.

People are also prone to conveniently 'forget' their own ancestors' wanton practices when criticising that of others today. Westerners are often outraged by the cruel poaching of African elephants, rhinos, and other

---

[139] J. Woinarskia, et al., 'Ongoing unraveling of a continental fauna: decline and extinction of Australian mammals since European settlement' (2015) 112(15) *Proceedings of the National Academy of Sciences* 4531.
[140] B. Gammage, *The Biggest Estate on Earth: How Aborigines Made Australia* (Allen and Unwin, 2011).
[141] P. Taylor, 'Cat-proof fence spares critters the last post', *The Australian* 5–6 September 2015.
[142] M. Elvin, *The Retreat of the Elephants: An Environmental History of China* (Yale University Press, 2006).
[143] J.B. MacKinnon, *The Once and Future World* (Vintage Canada, 2014), 36.
[144] P. Hoare, 'The whale that died in the Thames in 2006 deserves its plaque', *The Guardian* 10 June 2012, at www.theguardian.com.
[145] MacKinnon, *The Once and Future World*, 38.

species for their horns or tusks, and appalled by the Asian shark finning industry; but they ignore their own bloody history. Over more than two centuries starting in the mid-1600s, the North American fur trade slaughtered hundreds of millions beaver, otter, and other creatures to supply hats and other fashion accessories in Europe. In the period 1700–70 alone, 21 million beaver and other fur hats were exported to European markets.[146] Another bloodbath occurred in England itself. Roger Lovegrove's *Silent Fields* traces Britain's unsavoury penchant for wildlife persecution, focusing on the most recent 300 years in which millions of birds and other creatures were despatched in the name of vermin control, taxidermy, and egg souveniring.[147]

Interestingly, not all losses are forgotten, and sometimes the extinction or near oblivion of a creature can enthral many, from eccentric cryptozoologists to the tabloid media. One in Tasmania, where I live, is the thylacine. The last known specimen died ignominiously in a Hobart zoo in 1936, some 59 days after the state government gave the species legal protection.[148] The demise of the so-called 'tiger' was due primarily to the callous decision of previous authorities to place a bounty on it, a creature wrongly maligned as a menace to sheep and poultry. As the years have passed since the last thylacine perished in captivity, fascination within and beyond Tasmania continues as to whether the creature survives, with numerous alleged sightings, scientific expeditions, and TV documentaries. The dodo is an even more notorious extinction, giving rise to the adage 'as dead as a dodo'. While nobody seriously imagines that it survives, with the species disappearing from Mauritius in the mid-1600s, it continues to fascinate many, an interest sparked nearly two centuries after its demise when a dodo featured in Lewis Carroll's *Alice's Adventures in Wonderland*. The American passenger pigeon, which once swarmed in flocks of millions or even billions, is another infamous extinction, with the last of its kind dying in a Cincinnati zoo in 1914. Among near extinctions, the North American bison grazed the prairies in millions before being slaughtered in the late nineteenth century, gunned down to a few hundred stragglers. But many other mass wildlife slaughters, such as the

---

[146] A. Carlos and F. Lewis, 'The economic history of the fur trade: 1670–1870' (Economic History Association), at https://eh.net/encyclopedia/the-economic-history-of-the-fur-trade-1670-to-1870.

[147] R. Lovegrove, *Silent Fields: The Long Decline of a Nation's Wildlife* (Oxford University Press, 2007).

[148] R. Paddle, *The History and Extinction of the Thylacine* (Cambridge University Press, 2000).

war against deer in the United States, or bloodlust persecution of badgers in England, have become 'vanishingly obscure'.[149] These extinctions, and other crimes against nature, should be acknowledged more openly and publicly, beyond academic writings or specialist film documentaries. For instance, civic memorials could be erected in cities to commemorate their lost wildlife, especially those deliberately persecuted. Such nature memorials would, like war memorials and other public shrines, remind everyone of past losses and enable society to reflect on and perhaps improve its values to ensure other creatures don't suffer the same fate. But that is a remote possibility, for now.

Just as denial struthiously blinds us to environmental risks and future threats, it can also banish nature's losses from our memory. Lying comes naturally, helping individuals to advance their self-interests over competitors. We also self-deceive, says Trivers, because it makes our lying more convincing to others when we believe our own fibs.[150] In other words, hiding the truth from yourself enables you to hide it more deeply from others. Self-deception can involve rationalising away the relevance or importance of opposing evidence that makes one uncomfortable, such as signs of environmental degradation that raise unsettling questions about responsibility and sustainability. Denial and self-deception are not simply operative at the level of individual psychology, but also at a group and societal level. At this higher level, denial can involve selective memories of historic events and tactical reinterpretation of the record.

These manifestations of group self-deception provide fertile ground for building environmental myths instead of environmental history. The mythology surrounding the conquest of nature by 'heroic' settlers and explorers is one of the most pernicious narratives of Western societies, such as Australia and Canada, that has served to downplay the environmental destruction and persecution of indigenous peoples inflicted by colonisers.[151] Mythologies about environmental history not only offensively attempt to conceal wrongs, they can deceptively perpetuate existing unsustainable practices that are culturally mythologised as 'normal' or 'natural' to follow, such as how some landholders believe they have a God-given right to exploit their property as they see fit. Despite the warnings of

---

[149] MacKinnon, *The Once and Future World*, 26.
[150] R. Trivers, *The Folly of Fools: The Logic of Deceit and Self-Deception* (Basic Books, 2014).
[151] E. Furniss, 'Imagining the frontier: comparative perspectives from Canada and Australia' in D. Bird Rose and R. Harding Davis (eds), *Dislocating the Frontier: Essaying the Mystique of the Outback* (ANU Press, 2005), 23.

many international scientists that human activity undermines the planet's life-supporting systems, the responses have been few and feeble. Most mainstream environmental initiatives, such as 'triple bottom line' corporate environmental policies, green entrepreneurialism, ethical consumerism, 'smart growth' models for cities, and environmental law reforms themselves, have made little difference to humanity's overall environmental burden, but have fostered the illusion of progress.[152] One of these scientists, William Rees (who co-pioneered the eco-footprint theory), bemoans, 'the world is facing a slow but ominous crisis, yet whole domains of relevant knowledge are allowed to "lie fallow" as if of no consequence to human well-being'.[153]

From Biological to Cultural Change

There is no *one* human way to which we are tied by our evolutionary history, and the varieties of human cultures worldwide point to the diversity of human practices conceivable within our evolutionary makeup. Culture refers to the knowledge and practices that we learn from others that endure long enough to generate language, technologies, arts, economic systems, political organisations, law, and many other customs and institutions. Although culture gives human beings the capacity to mitigate biological predilections and promote positive traits, cultural evolution does not spring from a blank slate. Many sociologists and anthropologists once interpreted human behaviour as socially conditioned rather than biologically driven.[154] Such socially deterministic views of human nature have since been challenged by evolutionary psychology; more plausibly, cultural change occurs within and is shaped by biological parameters. Biological change of course also occurs, but it would be far too slow to shift human environmental behaviour in time to survive the Anthropocene.[155]

---

[152] W. Rees, 'The ecological crisis and self-delusion: implications for the building sector' (2009) 37(3) *Building Research and Information* 300.
[153] Ibid, 302.
[154] Durkheim, *Rules of Sociological Method*, 106 (contending that '*Individual natures are merely* the indeterminate material which the social factor determines and transforms'); Mead, *Coming of Age in Samoa*.
[155] While behavioural adaptations sometimes occur relatively 'quickly' in other species, the time frames are far too long for our circumstances. Dogs, which diverged from wolves only over the last 15,000 years, adopted different behaviours primarily through domestication; dogs understand pointing gestures and making eye contact, whereas wolves do not: J. De Smedt, H. De Cruz, and J. Braeckman, 'Why the human brain is not an enlarged chimpanzee brain' in H. Hogh-Olesen, J. Tonnesvang, and P. Bertelsen (eds),

While culture is rooted in our biological makeup, culture supplements genetic transmission with social transmission.

Biohistorians view the emergence of culture as not only our most significant characteristic as a species, but also the factor that has made humanity the planet's dominant evolutionary force.[156] Cultural evolution has been a mixed blessing. It has spawned vast scientific knowledge about the natural world, some remarkable technological innovations, and sophisticated legal institutions that galvanise action towards sustainability. Conversely, culture has unleashed some maladaptive practices, causing much unnecessary human distress and undesirable ecological damage. These once included ancient customs such as burning witches and the foot-binding of young girls; today, we have the misguided invention of weapons of mass destruction, the rapacious burning of fossil fuels, and the eating of endangered species in the dubious belief they possess talismanic medicinal properties.

The dilemma is thus that culture can dangerously amplify our worst prejudices and biases. In the very distant past, in a world with few people and Stone Age technologies, *Homo sapiens* could act without much concern for long-term ecological constraints – the primary survival challenge was to secure food and avoid being eaten. But attitudes that were functional in ancestral environments become counter-productive under a vastly more numerous humanity wielding destructive technologies that can deplete and degrade nature in no time at all. There is an evolutionary time lag here, leading to a phenomenon called 'time-shifted rationality'.[157] It means, explains US law professor Owen Jones, a 'temporal mismatch between design features of the brain appropriate for ancestral environments, on one hand, and quite different current environments, on the other'.[158] Stephen Boyden, an Australian biohistorian, asserts likewise in

---

Human Characteristics: Evolutionary Perspectives on Human Mind and Kind (Cambridge Scholars Publishing, 2009), 168, 170. The scope for human biological evolution may even be quicker, suggest G. Cochran and H. Harpending (in *The 10,000 Year Explosion: How Civilization Accelerated Human Evolution* (Basic Books, 2007)), because of more dynamic social and physical environments, including massive population increase, urbanisation, and the dispersal and migration of people worldwide.

[156] S. Palumbi, 'Humans as the world's greatest evolutionary force' (2001) 239 *Science* 1786. Human beings, however, are not alone in the animal kingdom in having culture: see A. Whiten, *Culture Evolves* (Oxford University Press, 2012).

[157] O.D. Jones, 'Time-shifted rationality and the law of law's leverage' (2001) 95 *Northwestern University Law Review* 1141, 1173.

[158] O.D. Jones, 'Evolutionary psychology and the law' in D.M. Buss (ed), *The Handbook of Evolutionary Psychology* (Wiley, 2005), 953, 960.

this 'eco-deviation' thesis about the widening dissonance between humankind's slow biological evolution and rapid cultural advance.[159] One familiar example in another context to illustrate this clearly is our love of sweets. Historically this preference for sugary food was highly adaptive, because it was a valuable and scarce source of concentrated calories. But with cheap junk food, sugar is everywhere nowadays. Our continuing preference for it fuels numerous health problems, such as obesity and diabetes. Cultural institutions such as markets and laws can similarly amplify other cognitive tendencies of environmental significance, such as myopia and denial.[160]

Overcoming denial of past environmental losses and insouciance about future risks is a momentous, but not impossible, challenge. Our evolved biological predispositions, explains William Rees, are simply 'a *propensity* that is likely to play out in the absence of countervailing circumstances such as moral codes, cultural taboos, legal prohibitions, or other social inhibitors'.[161] For such countervailing cultural mechanisms to prevail, we must first acknowledge the underlying facts of human nature, including our expansionist tendencies, misplaced optimism, and self-deception, but also our benign capacities for altruism and cooperation. The essential social challenge is to design environmental laws, along with other societal mechanisms, that can effectively supress maladaptive traits while promoting the benign ones. In modelling the 'law of law's leverage', Jones predicts that: 'the magnitude of legal intervention necessary to reduce or to increase the incidence of any human behavior will correlate positively or negatively, respectively, with the extent to which a predisposition contributing to that behavior was adaptive for its bearers, on average, in past environments'.[162] Behaviours that can resist modification include, according to him, those relating to control of territory, resource accumulation, and kinship bias. While beliefs and traits deeply embedded in human evolutionary history are not necessarily impervious to change, they will likely resist legal influences and thus be more costly to change.

The temporalities of the law itself, as a cultural mechanism for enabling change, can now be examined to take this enquiry further.

---

[159] S. Boyden, *Western Civilization in Biological Perspective: Patterns in Biohistory* (Oxford University Press, 1987), 264–5.
[160] Douglas and Wildavsky, *Risk and Culture*.
[161] W. Rees. 'What's blocking sustainability? Human nature, cognition, and denial' (2010) 6(2) *Sustainability: Science, Practice and Policy* 13, 15.
[162] Jones, 'Evolutionary psychology and the law', 962.

Time and Law

Temporalities of the Legal System

Time is an intrinsic element of the legal system, although surprisingly few have sought to investigate this subject systematically, let alone time in environmental law.[163] Before looking at how the law mediates societal changes over time, we should review time's role as a key structural feature of the legal system, as many of these structural elements will be relevant to the following chapters that focus on specific temporal qualities of environmental law. The connections between time and law are myriad, each reflective of certain social conventions, as well as law being a mechanism to construct or shape those social conventions. Time is not something that simply exerts an influence on law, but rather law itself also structures how we perceive time, by disciplining and normalising the experience of time. Legal systems have not only worked to erode spatial barriers to economic activities, such as by facilitating global trade, they have also eroded temporal boundaries, by compressing time, speeding up economic development, and sometimes making connections between past, present, and future behaviours and impacts.

The law evokes multiple temporalities 'to encode and systematize otherwise disparate and unreferenced events and relationships'.[164] Numerous official routines are structured around time, such as the sequence of national holidays, daylight savings cycles, and permitted trading hours for business.[165] Time has even been mapped into the very surface of the Earth: Greenwich Mean Time, the international dateline, and the division of the world into multiple time zones come from international agreements.[166] Time also informs the ambit of numerous legal responsibilities, from residency durations that determine tax liabilities to overtime hours worked earning additional wages under labour law. These and other temporal

---

[163] See e.g. L.A. Khan, 'Temporality of law' (2009) 40 *McGeorge Law Review* 55: R. French, 'Time in the law' (2001) 72 *University of Colorado Law Review* 663; C.J. Greenhouse, 'Just in time: temporality and the cultural legitimation of law' (1988–9) 98 *Yale Law Journal* 1631; K. von Benda-Beckmann, 'Trust and the temporalities of law' (2014) 46 *Journal of Legal Pluralism and Unofficial Law* 1; J. Přibáň, *Legal Symbolism: On Law, Time and European Identity* (Ashgate Publishing, 2007); G.G. Posterna, 'Melody and law's mindfulness of time' (2004) 17 *Ratio Juris* 203.

[164] Greenhouse, 'Just in time', 1631.

[165] T. Edensor, 'Reconsidering national temporalities: institutional times, everyday routines, serial spaces and synchronicities' (2006) 9 *European Journal of Social Theory* 527, 530ff.

[166] V. Ogle, 'Whose time is it? The pluralization of time and the global condition, 1870s–1940s' (2013) 118(5) *American Historical Review* 1376.

orderings are means by which the legal system manipulates and disciplines the experience of time to create a social time, and as discussed later, it is a social time that can separate us from the timescales of the rest of nature.

A number of specific functional uses of time can be identified. Foremost, time is a resource for the legal system because it can help solidify tradition. Some of the most fundamental legal norms are authoritative because of their supposed 'timeless' qualities.[167] International human rights law sometimes evokes such a timeless, enduring quality.[168] In the aftermath of the Second World War, the victors sought to apply so-called natural law principles, based upon an ancient and universal morality, to legitimate their prosecution of war criminals. The Nuremburg trials were a platform to elucidate a collective moral order, standing above the laws of any nation.[169] The ensuing propagation of 'universal human rights', transcending the laws of individual countries, reflects this ideal and has emerged as a core domain of international law. The precepts of natural law have not only filled substantive legal rights and duties, they are believed to inform some of the most cherished legal procedures. For Lon Fuller, the 'inner morality' of law is these procedures, such as non-retroactivity and impartiality.[170] Whether the legal systems of the world share timeless legal principles and procedures, however, remains deeply contentious for some, as evident in raging disputes over basic political and civil rights, environmental protection, and many other issues that split countries long developing/developed lines, religious faiths, and other cleavages.[171]

Time is also used to define the law's application to persons or situations. The doctrine of precedent specifies that a judge should apply the rulings of higher courts in previous cases involving similar facts. The principle of legislative intent informs statutory interpretation; it guides judges to assess legislators' intent where a statute is unclear or does not appear to directly address an issue in dispute. Time is also intrinsic to the doctrine of desuetude, namely that laws will lapse and lose their validity because they have not been used for ages. While not all jurisdictions favour the doctrine,

---

[167] J. Finnis, *Natural Law and Natural Rights* (Oxford University Press, 1980).
[168] F. Johns, 'The temporal rivalries of human rights' (2016) 23 *Indiana Journal of Global Legal Studies* 39.
[169] R.D. Citron, 'The Nuremberg trials and American jurisprudence: the decline of legal realism, the revival of natural law, and the development of legal process theory' (2006) 2 *Michigan State Law Review* 385.
[170] L. Fuller, *Anatomy of the Law* (Greenwood Press, 1976).
[171] For a controversial perspective, see S.P. Huntington, *The Clash of Civilization and the Remaking of World Order* (Simon and Schuster, 2011).

many now address obsolescence by another temporal device – the sunset clause. Inserted into legislation, the sunset dictates that all or part of the statute ceases after a specific date, unless further legislative action extends its life.[172] A statute of limitations is a more prevalent temporal device of legal systems, serving to limit the time to litigate civil claims and criminal charges.[173] Thus, a prosecutor cannot charge someone with a crime committed more than a specified period ago, although prosecution of the most heinous crimes, such as homicide, commonly has no time limit. Limitation periods are more widely prescribed in civil law and the periods are typically between 5 and 10 years. Statutes of limitation associated with the civil law can undermine environmental justice for latent harms by limiting the time to pursue legal action.[174] They aim to ensure that a plaintiff with a valid cause of action pursues it with reasonable diligence, and that convictions or other determinations occur only upon reliable evidence that has not deteriorated with time. Also, from a policy perspective, society benefits by allowing people to get on with their lives without fear of litigation from distant events, and legal resources are supposedly better devoted to addressing more recent violations.

Time also provides triggers to activate or terminate certain procedures, rights, duties, and powers. Examples are boundless: the law sets deadlines for filing annual income tax returns; vehicle drivers must renew their licence by a specified date; and passports lose their validity if not renewed in time. Legal systems worldwide commonly distinguish civil rights according to age; a person may become eligible to vote in political elections at 18 years, or drive a car at 16 years, for example.[175] International law also relies on timing prescriptions, such as continuous cycles of treaty compliance reporting. At the other end of the demographic spectrum, social security law sets age entitlements for access to pensions and other welfare. Conversely, time can trigger the termination of legal rights or opportunities, such as setting a mandatory retirement age. Time triggers also specify when a law comes into effect, such as criminal responsibility. The prescribed age varies among nations, although the age of full criminal

---

[172] In recent years, sunset clauses have been commonly used in anti-terrorism legislation, because of the controversial nature of the legislative restrictions on civil and political rights: J. Ip, 'Sunset clauses and counterterrorism legislation' (2013) 1 *Public Law* 74.

[173] R.A. Epstein, 'The temporal dimension in tort law' (1986) 53 *University of Chicago Law Review* 1175, 1183.

[174] G. Milhollin, 'Long-term liability for environmental harm' (1979) 41(1) *University of Pittsburgh Law Review* 1.

[175] T.E. James, 'The age of majority' (1960) 4(1) *American Journal of Legal History* 22.

responsibility is commonly 18 years, while young children (e.g. under 10 years) are commonly deemed to have no criminal responsibility. In international law, too, time-related intervals are set for the entry into force of treaties. Overall, temporal triggers enable the law to allocate and terminate powers and obligations to increase convenience and efficiency in legal affairs.

Relatedly, the law also structures the timing of decisions, sometimes to the detriment of environmental management: some decisions are hastily adopted (e.g. legislation fast-tracking prestige economic developments), while others are problematically delayed (e.g. deferring regulations to cut carbon emissions). Equally perniciously, special rules sometimes shield existing practices from legal transitions (so-called 'grandfather' clauses that protect historic polluters).[176] Motivated by political expediency, such concessions may undermine the integrity and impartiality of the law. Some international treaties provide for new standards to be phased in to accommodate the disadvantaged circumstances of some developing countries: agreements on eliminating ozone-depleting chemicals and greenhouse gas emissions are examples.[177] Other ways in which the law influences the timing of environmental decision-making are triggers for the initiation of recovery plans for endangered species, requirements for undertaking an environmental impact assessment (EIA) of a proposed project, and scheduling when and for how long the public may participate in decision-making processes such as contributing a written submission to a regulator or filing a judicial appeal. The following chapters will discuss these examples in much greater detail. Other policy areas of law, including health law and employment law, display similar temporal features in shaping when decisions are made, such as obligations on when to conduct risk assessments for new drugs or mandatory notice periods for sacking workers.

Time, including triggers, is also pivotal to the ambit of any many legal rights. The ambit may be defined for prescribed periods, a practice evident in intellectual property law: patents (typically 20 years), copyright (author's lifetime plus 50–70 years), trademarks (indefinite, if continually used), and geographic indications (indefinite). These temporal demarcations assume

---

[176] H.G. Robertson, 'If your grandfather could pollute, so can you: environmental "grandfather clause" and their role in environmental inequity' (1995–96) 45 *Catholic University Law Review* 131.
[177] Montreal Protocol on Substances that Deplete the Ozone Layer; Kyoto Protocol to the United Nations Framework Convention on Climate Change, 11 December 1997, in force 16 February 2005, (1998) 37 ILM 22.

that the resulting monopoly of the benefits of an invention can incentivise the creation of knowledge and technological innovation. And the law can use temporal triggers to allocate rights to exploit natural resources, such as 'first in time' concessions to exploit water or minerals. The past can be important to substantiate one's entitlement to property, as often occurs in legal claims by indigenous peoples based on original occupation. In property law, the passage of time can allow a claim for adverse possession to mature into a superior legal right.[178] Similarly, a prescriptive easement may arise over another's land with sufficient time, typically one or two decades.

The law also relies on time to facilitate efficiency and productivity, and to stimulate cooperation. These goals are epitomised by the legal adage that 'time is of the essence' in the completion of transactions such as fulfilment of contractual responsibilities. Courts can take account of a litigant's tardiness in making an adverse costs award. The equity doctrine of laches can serve to disallow unreasonably delayed lawsuits. Strict deadlines are also routinely set by legislation for filing civil claims and lodging appeals. Escalating regulatory penalties for late payment of fines or deadlines for making submitting judicial appeals are other temporal levers for incentivising compliance.

Temporal proximity is another contrivance of the law to show correlations between events and relationships for determining legal responsibility. Thus, 'toxic tort' liability might be substantiated by exposure to a toxic substance and subsequent onset of disease within a 'reasonable' period.[179] On the other hand, a polluter who has continued harmful activities for ages may defeat a nuisance action on the basis of the changed locality and the shift in the balance of reasonableness between the parties towards the defendant.[180] Conversely, the difficulty many indigenous peoples suffer in proving ownership of their traditional territories based on historic use is associated with the lack of temporal proximity, as such claims may hinge on unverified evidence thousands of years old, or there may be discontinuity in the claimants' connections to the land because of colonial dispossession.[181]

---

[178] R.A. Epstein, 'Past and future: the temporal dimension in the law of property' (1986) 64 *Washington University Law Quarterly* 667.
[179] L. Collins and H. McLeod-Kilmurray, *The Canadian Law of Toxic Torts* (Carswell, 2014).
[180] A. Beever, *The Law of Private Nuisance* (Hart Publishing, 2013), passim.
[181] See generally B.J. Richardson, S. Imai, and K. McNeil (eds), *Indigenous Peoples and the Law: Comparative and Critical Perspectives* (Hart Publishing, 2008).

The results of law-making can also be differentiated along a continuum of temporalities.[182] One dimension concerns the *direction* of the law's outputs: the law can apply historically (typically the common law's stance) or prospectively (as with regulations). A further dimension is the *duration* of a law, spanning exceptionally enduring laws (typically a national constitution) to transient examples (e.g. administrative regulations or statutes with sunset clauses). A third parameter is the *speed* with which law is made, depending on the urgency or importance of its subject-matter, the degree of social consensus and the procedures of the law-making institution. As we will explore in Chapters 3 and 5, these temporal contrivances have important implications for environmental governance, such as the limited scope for relicensing developments (i.e. *duration*) and fast-tracking to initiate developments (i.e. *speed*).

Time not only pervades specific legal rules and outcomes, it permeates the governing organisations and the nation state itself.[183] Commemorative narratives, such as heroic revolutions or wars, are frequently mobilised by national leaders to legitimise their power and to anchor the state in an imagined past.[184] 'Accounts of the temporal constitution of national identities', explains Tim Edensor, 'continue to focus upon common traditions, myths of shared descent, and the linking of historical and future narratives'.[185] Time is further deployed by the state in its political setting to set terms for governments and presidents and the timing of elections, as well as time frames for various national agendas, such as financial budget cycles and multi-year national economic plans. Each branch of a nation's legal system also evokes a distinct temporality: the legislature is mainly prospective, the judiciary more retrospective, and the executive primarily contemporaneous. The legislature tends to be future-oriented, by enacting and amending legislation to address ongoing and future problems. The legislature rarely passes laws that have retroactive application; Plato once suggested: 'when we legislate, we make our laws with the idea that they will

---

[182] A.J. Wistrich, 'The evolving temporality of lawmaking' (2012) 44(3) *Connecticut Law Review* 737, 750.
[183] A.M. Alonso, 'The politics of space, time and substance: state formation, nationalism and ethnicity' (1994) 23 *Annual Review of Anthropology* 379.
[184] B. Havel, 'In search of a theory of public memory: the state, the individual, and Marcel Proust' (2005) 80 *Indiana Law Journal* 605, 608 (discussing how Austria used law and politics to construct, retrospectively, an 'official memory' of Nazism). And see B. Anderson, *Imagined Communities: Reflections on the Origin and Spread of Nationalism* (Verso, 2006).
[185] Edensor, 'Reconsidering national temporalities: institutional times, everyday routines, serial spaces and synchronicities' 525, 527.

be advantageous in time to come'.[186] Occasionally the law has retroactive dimensions in which it attempts to alter the past, such as granting pardons to quash the effect of a past criminal conviction or imposing liability for an activity or impact that was once lawful (e.g. an owner's liability to remediate contaminated land).[187] Another example is the UK's War Damage Act,[188] as used to retroactively exempt the Crown from any liability associated with wartime damage such as destruction of property.

The judiciary is often assumed to dwell on the past, applying tradition and precedent to adjudicate previous matters. Courts can be slow to react quickly to changing circumstances, and even occasional breakthroughs, such as the *Mabo* ruling of Australia's High Court, which precipitated wider reforms on indigenous rights,[189] or the public interest litigation in India that forged a constitutional right to a healthy environment and recognition of the public trust doctrine,[190] ensued from years of grinding litigation and periodic setbacks. The executive branch lives more immediately in the present, applying current laws and policies. Government authorities enact regulations, issue policies, and take other expedient measures to respond to current circumstances and flesh out statutes with more precise requirements to address perpetual issues. With a change of government, these regulations and policies can similarly be uprooted quite quickly. But these institutional differences in temporal focus are matters of degree rather than firm distinctions. Each branch of the state may consider any temporal perspective within its purview. Legislation is often drafted in the light of lessons learned from past experiences, the executive may be endowed with broad discretionary powers to tackle issues over any time frame, and courts may issue an injunction to ward off adversity.[191]

Legal governance at an international level also displays several temporal orientations depending on the organisation or process. Treaties tend to be highly future-oriented, setting frameworks for ongoing cooperative action among states, such as the UN Framework Convention on Climate

---

[186] Plato, 'Theaetetus', 178a, quoted in F. MacDonald Cornford, *Plato's Theory of Knowledge* (Routledge and Kegan Paul, 1935), 90.
[187] N. Duxbury, 'Ex post facto laws' (2013) 58(2) *American Journal of Jurisprudence* 135.
[188] 1965 c. 18.
[189] *Mabo v. Queensland (No. 2)*, (1992) 175 CLR 1; Native Title Act 1993 (Cth).
[190] E.g. *M.C. Mehta v. Union of India*, [1988] SC 1031; *M.C. Mehta v. Kamal Nath and Others*, (1997) 1 SCC 388.
[191] C. Mollers, *The Three Branches: A Comparative Model of Separation of Powers* (Oxford University Press, 2013).

Change.[192] Customary international law, conversely, draws on the past by solidifying practices that acquire *opinio juris* through the passage of time; the decision in the *Trail Smelter* case adjudicated between Canada and the United States was a seminal step in enunciation of an international obligation to avoid transboundary pollution.[193] Judicial forums, led by the International Court of Justice (ICJ), can have the same time horizons as domestic courts. The ICJ is occasionally trail-blazing, such as the opinion of Judge Weeramantry in the *Gabcikovo-Nagymaros* case that elaborated the legal dimensions of the doctrine of sustainable development.[194] Intergovernmental agencies, such as the United Nations Environment Programme (UNEP), tend to have a broader temporal outlook than national equivalents, as they often engage in studies into long-term global problems and facilitate international cooperation to find solutions.

The foregoing reveals a variety of temporalities in modern legal institutions and norms, without any single or coherent approach. Such multiple temporalities in law intersect in economic, social, and political life, reflective of the heterogeneous context of the law. The discontinuity of time reflected in the law, as we see later in this book, has serious implications for environmental decision-making because of the fragmentation of connections between the past, present, and future.

An important consideration with all the foregoing legal rules and institutions is that their temporal orientations and concepts are often a matter of disputed interpretation that reflects their political context and ideological wrangling. Legal processes, even in common law courts, may be much more contemporaneous when judges make *ad hoc* decisions in the light of immediate expediencies and their own personal values. The presence of discretionary powers held by judges and regulators can allow for such practices to flourish, coupled with the difficulty of codifying a clear and universal meaning to applicable legal norms. The American Legal Realists, a scholarly movement of the 1930s, revolutionised thinking about courts by showing that their precedents were artifices of tactical manipulation by judges to attain their preferred outcome beneath a veil of legitimacy.[195] Even the doyen of legal philosophy, H.L.A. Hart, recognised that legal

---

[192] (1992) 31 ILM. 849.
[193] J. Wirth, 'The trail smelter dispute: Canadians and Americans confront transboundary pollution, 1927–41' (1996) 1(2) *Environmental History* 34.
[194] *Gabcikovo-Nagymaros Project (Hungary v. Slovakia)*, (Separate Opinion of Vice President Weeramantry), [1997] ICJ Reports 7, 88.
[195] K.N. Llewellyn, 'A realistic jurisprudence: the next step' (1930) 30 *Columbia Law Review* 431; J. Frank, *Law and the Modern Mind* (Doubleday, 1963).

language is somewhat open-textured, in the sense that while words can have a clear core meaning, they also cast 'penumbras'[196] where the extension of a legal rule becomes unclear.

The cudgel against legal positivism was later wielded by critical legal studies and postmodernism. They unveiled the law's political setting and rejected the assumed objectivity or neutrality of its language. Thus, legal conventions such as *stare decisis* and original intent could be viewed as reflective of 'distinctive cultural values and social positions' of privileged decision makers in the legal system.[197] As Canadian legal philosopher Alan Hutchinson explains, 'the law is not simply there in its object-like presence, but is always waiting to be apprehended and fixed by the active crafting of its judicial interpreters and legal artisans . . . determinacy and indeterminacy are not pre-interpretive features of the law, but products of legal interpretation'.[198] If we accept, therefore, limits to the capacity of law to stand 'above the fray' to guide human behaviour and provide clear normative direction, then we should also acknowledge that the conceptualisation of time in law can be highly contingent and indeterminate. A lofty legal prescription to act in the interests of future generations may simply be viewed in the light of immediate expediencies.

A proper understanding of the relationships between time and law thus requires not only knowledge of how the legal system already functions, but how it changes. The legal system is subject to structural forces of inertia and progression, seeking stability and continuity on the one hand, but sometimes embracing or spurring change in response to shifting social values, economic downturns, or other drivers of law reform. The capacity of the law to change is pivotal to aligning it with nature's timescape.

Temporal Inertia and Motion in Law

The legal system straddles a tension between two temporalities: the veneration of tradition, predictability, and continuity versus the impetus for change and modernisation to keep the law abreast of evolving community values or to facilitate their change in order to overcome social injustices,

---

[196] B. Leiter, 'American legal realism' in W. Edmundson and M. Golding (eds), *The Blackwell Guide to Philosophy of Law and Legal Theory* (Blackwell, 2003), 50.

[197] S.M. Feldman, 'Playing with the pieces: postmodernism in the lawyer's toolbox' (1999) 85 *Virginia Law Review* 151.

[198] A. Hutchinson, 'In the park: a jurisprudential primer' (2010) 48 *Osgoode Hall Law Journal* 337, 352.

economic stagnation, or other societal challenges, including environmental damage. The adherence to precedent 'reduces the likelihood that the judiciary will indulge in radical and unexpected departures from existing law',[199] but at the risk that the law drifts out of touch with social mores or fails to address urgent societal problems in time. The bitter struggles in many societies recently over gay marriage, access to public healthcare, or tax reform – struggles fought out in courts and legislatures – are among many examples of this tension. The legal system thus sits within contradictory impulses that emphasise the past or the future whose relative influence has consequences for law to serve as an agent of change.

Because of its veneration of tradition and precedent, the law is subject to the myriad influences of the past. The stabilising effects may operate at several levels.[200] Systemic stability to the law as a whole is furthered in many levels of governance, from customary international law (i.e. state practices that persist over time) to the common law (which evolves gradually), as well as constitutional laws (being hard to repeal or amend, though subject to evolving judicial interpretations).[201] As John Finn explains, 'constitutions, much like promises, are nothing less than attempts to fashion the future – to forge the institutional patterns and cultural folkways of political and social experience'.[202] Systemic stability may also involve allegiance to a moral or political philosophy associated with the mythology of a given society or nation-state, such as that associated with their establishment through revolution or succession.[203] The appeal to tradition may also be mobilised to avoid tough decisions that would chart a new course; as Rebecca Brown explains, 'to the extent that traditions represent judgments that others in other times have made, they can provide an attractive resource to those uncomfortable with making judgments of their own'.[204] At the micro level of governance around specific issues or actors, a further temporal dimension is evident in precedential inertia, in which similar factual cases are seemingly judged alike. The doctrine is valorised for its contribution to predictability and stability in the law; as US judge Louis

---

[199] Fuller, *Anatomy of the Law*, 103.
[200] Khan, 'Temporality of law'.
[201] V.C. Jackson and J. Greene, 'Constitutional interpretation in comparative perspective: comparing judges or courts?' in T. Ginsburg and R. Dixon (eds), *Comparative Constitutional Law* (Edward Elgar Publishing, 2011), 599, 602.
[202] J.E. Finn, *Constitutions in Crisis: Political Violence and the Rule of Law* (Oxford University Press, 1991), 4.
[203] P. Fitzpatrick, *The Mythology of Modern Law* (Routledge, 1992), 111–18.
[204] R. Brown, 'Tradition and insight' (1993) 103 *Yale Law Journal* 177–9.

Brandeis noted, 'stare decisis is usually the wise policy, because in most matters it is more important that the applicable rule of law be settled than that it be settled right'.[205] Remedial inertia, a related type of temporal inertia, arises when a statute of limitations limits the time to litigate a civil claim. The price, of course, is that 'settled' legal rules can stall reform, leaving the law trailing shifted societal norms.[206] Conversely, these stabilising legal processes promote values such as consistency, equality, predictability, and efficiency.[207]

Such forces of systemic stability and tradition can result in the perpetuation of laws long after their usefulness has passed. Obsolescent laws litter the legal landscape of many countries, some of which are quite humorous. India's Treasure Trove 1878 defines treasure specifically as 'anything of any value hidden in the soil' and worth as little as 10 rupees (about 15 US cents); the finder of such treasure, according to the law, must inform the most senior local official of the 'nature and amount or approximate value of such treasure and the place where it was found'.[208] In New Orleans, Louisiana, the municipal code bans using fortune telling, astrology, or palmistry to settle lovers' quarrels.[209] A British law from 1313 apparently still on the books prohibits politicians from wearing armour in parliament.[210] Indeterminacy of statutory language and judicial discretion, as earlier noted, can mitigate the impact of precedence or cause deviations from statutory rules, though legal decision-makers rarely have open-ended discretion that allows them to make any decision they wish. More seriously, beyond these quaint illustrations, outdated or problematic assumptions and values of the past may remain embedded in legal norms and institutions as natural givens, such as assumptions that animals are mere chattels of their human masters or that 'nomadic' and 'uncivilised' indigenous peoples held no legally recognisable relationship with their ancestral lands. As a mechanism of power, the law is intertwined with discourses and strategies that can privilege or marginalise its subjects in ways that can be invisible because of the imprimatur of long-standing custom.[211]

---

[205] *Burnet v. Coronado Oil and Gas Co.*, (1932) 285 US 393, 405.
[206] N. Duxbury, *The Nature and Authority of Precedent* (Cambridge University Press, 2008).
[207] See R. Dworkin, *Taking Rights Seriously* (Harvard University Press, 1997), 111–12 (examining how judges attempt to conform their rulings with past precedent).
[208] Treasure Trove Act 1878, no. VI, s. 4(a).
[209] City of New Orleans Code of Ordinances, Ordinance No. 26972, 14 July 2016. s. 54–312.
[210] Statute Forbidding Wearing Armour, 1313, 7 Edw. 2, c. 0.
[211] M. Foucault, 'Lecture two: 14 January 1976' in C. Gordon (ed), *Power/Knowledge: Selected Interviews and Other Writings* (Pantheon Books, 1980), 78.

Many established legal rules of course are equally prospective, by aiming to regulate future conduct. The focus of criminal law, for example, is not just punishing past misdeeds but also shaping (e.g. deterring) future conduct to promote social stability and harmony. Where judges enjoy independence and discretion, they may consider long-term ramifications of legal decisions more carefully than legislatures whose members tend to be constrained by short-term electoral cycles. Judges may be prepared to safeguard the environment for posterity when legislators are reluctant. Consider the Philippines Supreme Court's decision in *Minors Oposa v. Secretary of the Department of Environment and Natural Resources*, where it recognised intergenerational environmental responsibilities to protect and wisely manage the country's forestry resources.[212] This future focus is evident in many other branches of the law, such as contract law and tort law. The latter serves to enhance social welfare by deterring accidents while the former articulates future relationships between people to ensure parties adhere to the deals they make. Some theorists would even go so far as to suggest that law's temporal arrow is only the future. As J.B. Ruhl and Harold Ruhl contend: 'all complex dynamical systems have an arrow of irreversibility; their evolutionary processes cannot be put into reverse so as to re-create the past. Law shares this property. It unfolds as part of a socio-legal system that could no more return to a prior point on its path than could the weather be reversed'.[213] However, any improbability of returning to the past is very different from the reality of how the past imprints itself on future decisions.

The theory of 'path dependency' can help illuminate how the past shapes future law. Path dependence postulates that legal changes do not proceed from a blank slate, but rather governance is constrained by the decisions made by predecessors, even though previous circumstances that justified earlier laws or policies may no longer be applicable. The theory was fashioned by economists to explain the adoption of technologies and business practices, and has since been extended to other contexts, including legal phenomena. Path dependence helps explain why certain modes of governance persist even when they are inefficient or unhelpful, and

---

[212] Reproduced at (1994) 33 ILM 173.
[213] J.B. Ruhl and H.J. Ruhl, Jr, 'The arrow of the law in modern administrative states: using complexity theory to reveal the diminishing returns and increasing risks the burgeoning of law poses to society' (1997) 30 *UC Davis Law Review* 405, 409–10.

better options are available.[214] The trajectory has two important sources. One is institution-driven, wherein certain institutional structures, such as corporate governance or government bureaucracy, remain imprinted with characteristics previously established.[215] The second source is rules-driven path dependence, which emanates from the effect that initial modalities of regulation or other governance methods have on subsequent rule preferences.[216] The common law strongly displays path dependence in its body of principles and decision rules based 'solely from usages and customs of immemorial antiquity, or from the judgments and decrees of the courts recognising, affirming, and enforcing such usages and customs'.[217] When confronted with situations that invite changes to the law, the courts may deftly refer the issue to the legislature. In the *Cambridge Water* case of 1993, in which the British House of Lords considered tortious liability for groundwater pollution, the Lords concluded that 'given that so much well-informed and carefully structured legislation is now being put in place for this [environmental protection] purpose, there is less need for the Courts to develop a common law principle to achieve the same end'.[218] The legislative realm of course may itself be mired in path-limiting options because of its political composition or constitutional law constraints on its freedom of action.

Path dependence in both institutions and rules flows not simply from a 'status quo' bias but also the political resources that can be mobilised to protect vested interests. The theory of 'regulatory capture' is relevant here, modelling how power dynamics infuse path-dependent rule-making.[219] Regulatory authorities such as pollution control agencies are susceptible to usurpation by the very industries they should govern impartially. Such capturing is particularly troublesome in environmental governance, where many industries have incentives to manipulate regulators in order to minimise compliance costs and obtain benefits such as subsidies. Thereby, the

---

[214] L. Bebchuk and M.J. Roe, 'A theory of path dependence in corporate ownership and governance' (1999) 52 *Stanford Law Review* 127, 139.
[215] P.A. David, 'Why are institutions the "carriers of history"? Path dependence and the evolution of conventions, organizations and institutions' (1994) 5(2) *Structural Change and Economic Dynamics* 205.
[216] O. Hathaway, 'Path dependence in the law: the course and pattern of legal change in a common law system' (2001) 86 *Iowa Law Review* 601.
[217] H.C. Black (ed), *Black's Law Dictionary* (Springer, 1990), 276 (defining 'common law').
[218] *Cambridge Water Company v. Eastern Counties Leather*, [1993] UKHL 12, 17.
[219] G. Stigler is an influential proponent of this theory: 'The theory of economic regulation' (1971) 2 *Bell Journal of Economics and Management Science* 3, 3 ('as a rule, regulation is acquired by the industry and is designed and operated primarily for its benefits').

public is left to incur the social and environmental externalities of such 'captures'.[220] One recent example, among many, is Canadian fossil fuel companies who lobbied their government to stymie action on climate change.[221] Another is the resistance to reforming business law to incorporate environmental performance standards. Environmental governance relies on *external* controls on economic activity rather than embedding its standards within the internal legal fabric of business organisations.[222] Environmental performance standards are rarely found in company law or securities regulation, which instead convey legal norms that can encourage businesses to prioritise their economic success even if it carries social costs.[223]

The theory of path dependence cannot satisfactory explain all dimensions of legal inertia or change because occasionally legislatures enact landmark reforms and courts pioneer breakthroughs. Big shifts sometimes happen, and legal changes can be inspired not only to correct past injustices, but also to prospectively equip society to deal with new challenges such as climate change. Such transformations may arise because of the ascendancy of new social movements, shifts in political alliances, economic pressures to the status quo, and many other factors. Empirical research suggests the growing prevalence of legal change in some jurisdictions. In the United States, commentators have observed a weakening of the authority of judicial precedent under a culture of growing judicial activism.[224] This trend is significant, explains Andrew Wistrich, as 'when a court overrules a precedent, it adopts a more future-oriented perspective. It looks to the needs of the future, rather than to the decisions of the past'.[225] In international law too, a variety of legal innovations are found; pioneering efforts include the UN Convention on the Law of the Sea[226] and

---

[220] A notorious example concerns the 2010 *Deepwater Horizon* oil spill: G. O'Driscoll, 'The gulf spill, the financial crisis, and government failure', *Wall Street Journal* 12 June 2010, at www.wsj.com.
[221] 'Oil industry successfully lobbied Ottawa to delay climate regulations', *Globe and Mail* 8 November 2013, at www.theglobeandmail.com.
[222] B. Sjafjell and B.J. Richardson (eds), *Company Law and Sustainability: Legal Barriers and Opportunities* (Cambridge University Press, 2015).
[223] Consequently, those most responsible for environmental harm face conflicting demands – the market disciplines businesses to act for their self-interest while environmental regulation expects them to accommodate a societal interest in reduce environmental impacts.
[224] See E.M. Maltz, 'Some thoughts on the death of stare decisis in constitutional Law' (1980) *Wisconsin Law Review* 467.
[225] Wistrich, 'The evolving temporality of lawmaking', 769.
[226] Adopted 10 December 1982, in force 16 November 1994, (1982) 21 ILM 1261.

the Treaty on the Non-Proliferation of Nuclear Weapons.[227] The history of domestic environmental law itself includes numerous examples of legislative innovation, as the next section of this chapter introduces.

The relationship between law reform and social change stirs fundamental questions in legal philosophy about the nature and utility of law, and the extent to which achieving social change requires working through or beyond legal institutions. The most diametrically opposed views are associated with legal positivism, on the one hand, and critical legal movements such as critical race theory, feminism, and elements of postmodernism, on the other. Legal positivism, as epitomised by the writings of John Austin and H.L.A. Hart, postulates that what the law is and what it ought to be are separate enquiries.[228] While many positivists have certainly advocated law reform, they believe that debates about law reform should be informed by political and ethical standards rather than by anything innate to the mechanics of law. The rationale for this bifurcation of law and morality is that it provides the means by which law, as a system of decision-making, can be evaluated objectively on its own terms, such as with reference to matters including the coherence of legislative drafting, the relationship between primary and secondary rules, and the canons of statutory interpretation. Thus, jurisprudence in the legal positivist academy is concerned only with an explanatory understanding of what the law is.

A number of difficulties arise from the positivist conceptual orientation. Primarily, it may be neither possible nor desirable to keep the domains of law and morality separate. The Nazi experience led to the locking of jurisprudential horns between Hart and natural law philosophers such as Lon Fuller over the implications of positivism that would accept Nazi law, no matter how barbaric, as 'law'.[229] A deeper schism erupted in the 1970s with the arrival of critical legal theorists who rejected any attempt to separate law from politics, as law was excoriated as deeply complicit in patriarchy, class, racism, and other inequities.[230] Much of this complicity, suggested the 'crits', was subtly embedded in legal language and institutions that appeared neutral and impartial. Given the nexus between law and politics,

---

[227] Adopted 1 July 1968, in force 5 March 1970, (1968) 7 ILM 8809.

[228] J. Austin, *The Province of Jurisprudence Determined and the Uses of the Study of Jurisprudence*, H.L.A. Hart (ed) (Weidenfeld and Nicolson, 1954; original in 1832); H.L.A. Hart, 'Positivism and the separation of law and morals' (1958) 71 *Harvard Law Review* 593.

[229] L. Fuller, 'Positivism and fidelity to law: a reply to professor Hart' (1958) 71 *Harvard Law Review* 630.

[230] R. Unger, *Knowledge and Politics* (The Free Press, 1975); D. Kennedy, 'Form and substance in private law adjudication' (1976) 89 *Harvard Law Review* 1685.

they doubted the capacity of law to advance social progress; and indeed to focus on law reform could perversely reinforce inequalities and injustices. Instead, they saw legal change towards social justice, environmental well-being, and other transformative goals necessitating a much broader programme beyond the traditional agenda of liberal-democratic law reform.

One alternative strategy they advocated was to abandon law reform in favour of 'trashing' or 'deconstructing' the current system to expose its contradictory and oppressive dimensions.[231] This approach, however, lacked positive direction for social change and ignored the empirical evidence of the capacity of reform of legal doctrine to sometimes yield immediate and tangible benefits, in areas such as rights for aboriginal people, gays, and women. Another strategy has been to move beyond legal doctrine to focus on altering the discourses and symbolism of the legal system so as to expose their meanings and empower those who have suffered from them. Michel Foucault's work has been particularly relevant here for investigations into how discourses and institutions, including those outside the formal legal system such as that associated with hospitals, asylums, schools, and factories, embody disciplinary power.[232] A third approach associated with some of these critical theorists has been to pragmatically accept some compromise and seek change through the legal system while vigilantly critiquing it where necessary.[233] This strategy thus remains suspicious of law for its roles in veiling and perpetuating injustice, but also acknowledges some scope to alleviate hardship opportunistically through strategic legal reforms. It recognises that in some instances legal governance has been deeply empowering; the development of the Internet and its collegial governance is one of the best examples of an open and free system of global communications that has been enormously empowering for many social movements and activists around the world.[234]

As explored later in this book, the environmental movement has embraced law reform to transform society's environmental values and practices. The agenda includes individual environmental rights, extending such rights to nature itself,[235] enhanced due diligence such as procedures

---

[231] J.M. Balkin, 'Deconstructive practice and legal theory' (1987) 96 *Yale Law Journal* 743.
[232] B. Golder and P. Fitzpatrick, *Foucault's Law* (Routledge, 2009).
[233] E.g. scholarship of feminist legal scholar, C. MacKinnon, *Feminism Unmodified: Discourses on Life and Law* (Harvard University Press, 1987).
[234] J. Mathiason, *Internet Governance: The New Frontier of Global Institutions* (Routledge, 2008).
[235] C. Stone, *Should Trees Have Standing? Law, Morality, and the Environment* (Oxford University Press, 2010).

for environmental assessment and land use planning, and legislated societal goals such as sustainable development. But after several decades of intensive legislative and judicial action, the evidence is clear that environmental conditions are still declining; at most, environmental law has mitigated what would be a direr situation. The core problem, as critical legal researchers in other fields of law would recognise, is that reform through the legal system cannot achieve enough if the broader social and economic systems that drive environmental decline remain largely unaltered. At most, evolutions in legal doctrines and procedures can alleviate some of the symptoms of unsustainability, but not achieve progression to a fundamentally different relationship between people and their environment. That does not mean that law reform is routinely irrelevant, but that it must be tied to a broader framework of social transition engaging directly with market and civil societal actors.

Among alternative modalities of cultural change that include but do not rely exclusively on state regulation are legal pluralism and new governance. Legal pluralism proceeds from the recognition that nation-state law often co-exists with other forms of social order, some of which may rival the state apparatus in shaping people's daily lives.[236] These may include informal methods of social ordering associated with the business community and civil society groups, as well as more formal legal regimes as practised by cultural and ethnic minorities such as indigenous peoples.[237] Furthermore, state law itself may accommodate a variety of different legal traditions and cultures, such as the dual civil and common law systems in Canada with distinct Anglophone and Francophone communities. Recognition of legal pluralism opens additional avenues for social change through other legal cultures and traditions, which may be more successful than working alone within the state itself or the state's dominant legal culture. Accommodation of legal pluralism may range from a state merely tolerating other legal traditions, by designating them a separate space in its legal system, to embracing plurality as a positive force to empower.[238]

Another related way to reconceptualise law and social change comes from new governance scholarship, a broad term that spans a variety of

---

[236] J. Griffiths, 'What is legal pluralism?' (1986) 24 *Journal of Legal Pluralism* 1.
[237] E.g. N. Zlotkin, 'Judicial recognition of aboriginal customary law in Canada: selected marriage and adoption cases' (1984) 4 *Canadian Native Law Reporter* 1.
[238] P. Sack, 'Legal pluralism: introductory comments' in P. Sack and E. Minchin (eds), *Legal Pluralism: Proceedings of the Canberra Law Workshop VII* (Australian National University, 1988), 1.

theories, both explanatory and normative, that address the trend away from wholly state-based regulation towards 'governance' in which the role of the state is de-centred and other institutions, such as the private sector and civil society actors, play more central roles.[239] Manifestations of this trend include industry-led codes of conduct, corporate sustainability reporting and audits, and private governance initiatives, whether in the form of industry certification schemes or transnational activist networks. These changes have been theorised under diverse banners including 'nodal governance',[240] 'networked governance',[241] 'new environmental governance'[242] and 'regulatory spaces'.[243] Some of this theorisation has been influenced by systems theory, which depicts modern society as polycentric, centrifugal, and acephalous, comprising semi-autonomous subsystems, such as the market and bureaucracy, each with its own dynamic.[244] German sociologist Niklas Luhmann, a leading exponent of this idea, describes these subsystems as 'autopoietic', implying that each has evolved its own operational codes and protocols, and therefore can respond to problems defined only in their own terms.[245] The implication is that such conditions make it difficult for a society to coalesce coherently towards shared objectives, such as environmental sustainability. This conception of social systems has led some theorists, such as Gunther Teubner and Eric Orts, to advocate legal change through 'reflexive law', in which top-down command-and-control regulation is replaced by non-coercive laws that seek to stimulate new modes of decision making with companies and other organisations that encourage internal reflection, learning, and behavioural changes.[246]

---

[239] See generally G.D. Búrca and J. Scott, *Law and New Governance in the EU and the US* (Hart Publishing, 2006).
[240] S. Burris, P. Drahos, and C. Shearing, 'Nodal governance' (2005) 30 *Australian Journal of Legal Philosophy* 30.
[241] G.A. Huppé, H. Creech, and D. Knoblauch, *The Frontiers of Networked Governance* (International Institute for Sustainable Development, 2012).
[242] C. Holley, N. Gunningham, and C. Shearing, *The New Environmental Governance* (Routledge, 2012).
[243] B. Lange, 'Regulatory spaces and interactions: an introduction' (2003) 12(4) *Social and Legal Studies* 411.
[244] See N. Luhmann, *Ecological Communication* (University of Chicago Press, 1989); N. Luhmann, *The Differentiation of Society* (Columbia University Press, 1982).
[245] N. Luhmann, *Social Systems* (Stanford University Press, 1995).
[246] G. Teubner, *Law as an Autopoietic System* (Blackwell, 1993); E.W. Orts, 'Reflexive environmental law' (1995) 89(4) *Northwestern University Law Review* 1227.

Both legal pluralism and governance scholarship help to identify additional institutions and processes beyond the nation-state that can be harnessed to promote legal and social change, going beyond both the naivety of legal positivism and the negativity of critical legal perspectives. In the following chapters of this book, we encounter a number of these governance processes beyond the state that seek to change environmental attitudes and practices. They include community-based, ecological restoration projects, the Slow Food movement, and socially responsible investing. These social and market-based movements also, as we will learn, have and will benefit from some legal undergirding. It is the combination of social and legal change that will inculcate the ecological timescape in our lives.

Timelines of Modern Environmental Law

The Evolving Environmental Acquis

Environmental laws around the world have evolved in recent decades to reflect diverse conceptual orientations from ecocentric to anthropocentric expediency, but most reflect the latter's commitment to environmental protection to the extent that it meets utilitarian criteria based on benefits to human beings. For example, the Aarhus Convention declares that 'adequate protection of the environment is essential to human well-being and the enjoyment of basic human rights, including the right to life itself' and so 'every person has the right to live in an environment adequate to his or her health and well-being'.[247] An ecocentric approach, which values ecological integrity and biological diversity, regardless of human benefits, remains uncommon despite growing support for it among academic commentators.[248] That the rise of modern environmental law has coincided with the intensification of the Anthropocene should thus come as no surprise. The law's occasional triumphs, such as banning ozone-depleting chemicals[249] or saving some iconic species from extinction,[250] gives a

---

[247] Convention on Access to Information, Public Participation in Decision-Making and Access to Justice in Environmental Matters, 25 June 1998, in force 30 October 2001, (1999) 38 ILM 517, preamble.

[248] E.g. P. Burdon (ed), *Exploring Wild Law: The Philosophy of Earth Jurisprudence* (Wakefield Press, 2011).

[249] Montreal Protocol on Substances That Deplete the Ozone Layer.

[250] A notable example is the American Bald Eagle (*Haliaeetus leucocephalus*), the national symbol of the United State, which was saved by the *Endangered Species Preservation Act*, Pub. L. 89-669, 1966.

misleading picture, as most ecological indicators show declines. By and large, environmental law is just mitigating what would be a direr situation. Several factors have converged to weaken it – both internal factors (concerning the law's guiding principles, design, and methods) and external factors (its political and economic context), which together have abetted the separation of social time from nature's temporalities. The following pages look at the history and achievements of environmental law.

Environmental law is not a recent phenomenon, although its contemporary character, which this chapter focuses on, mostly reflects reforms since the 1960s.[251] The spatiality of environmental problems, their sheer physicality and proximity to people, dominated early forms of regulation. As the first place to industrialise and experience the stench and squalor of slums and sweatshops, Victorian Britain pioneered laws to improve urban amenities. In 1863, the Alkali Act, along with tort law, restricted emissions from the burgeoning chemical industry,[252] whose visible noxious fumes were killing wildlife,[253] while the Public Health Act 1875 tackled overcrowding, disease, and odours by setting building standards, creating sewerage infrastructure, and mandating garbage collection.[254] In North America and Oceania, with their less industrialised landscapes, the conservation movement was launched to establish parks, beginning with the 1872 dedication of Yellowstone. Reliance on legislation was often necessary because the common law (e.g. tort law and property law) proved inadequate for addressing the new generation of urban and industrial challenges.[255] A third trend in this formative period was the numerous laws to facilitate the 'orderly' exploitation of natural resources – such as game hunting, mining, and forestry. The spatial carve up of nature into

---

[251] On the evolution of modern environmental law, see N. Gunningham, 'Environment law, regulation and governance: shifting architectures' (2009) 21(2) *Journal of Environmental Law* 179. For detailed accounts of specific jurisdictions, see e.g. Boyd, *Unnatural Law*; R.V. Percival, et al., *Environmental Regulation: Law, Science and Policy* (Aspen Publishers, 2009); L. Kramer, *EU Environmental Law* (Sweet and Maxwell, 2012); R.L. Revesz, P. Sands, and R.B. Stewart (eds), *Environmental Law, the Economy and Sustainable Development: The United States, the European Union and the International Community* (Cambridge University Press, 2008).

[252] B. Pontin, 'Integrated pollution control in Victorian Britain: rethinking progress within the history of environmental law' (2007) 19(2) *Journal of Environmental Law* 173.

[253] 1863, P.P. 135. See further M. Daunton, 'London's "great stink" and Victoria urban planning', *BBC History* 4 November 2004, at www.bbc.co.uk/history.

[254] 1875, c. 55.

[255] J.L. Sax, 'The public trust doctrine in natural resource law: effective judicial intervention' (1970) 68(3) *Michigan Law Review* 471.

legally defined prerogatives expressed as tenures, licences, leases, or other entitlements was not only deployed in the West, but in its colonial dominions too.[256]

The United States emerged ostensibly as an environmental leader during the second wave of law reform in the 1960s and 1970s, sparked by growing scientific knowledge of the toxic side-effects of modern economic development and technology,[257] as well as the growth of articulate social movements taking advantage of more liberal political conditions.[258] The Clean Air Act 1963[259] and National Environmental Policy Act 1969[260] were among a tranche of national regulations curbing pollution and preventing further harm that included EIA of development proposals. During the 1970s, American civil society groups also became an instrument of governance, turning to the courts to discipline government agencies or private developers. In the famous *Snail Darter* case[261] the Endangered Species Act[262] was used to thwart a water development project that threatened a rare fish species.[263] Another seminal trend of this era was the establishment of specialist administering institutions, such as the federal Environmental Protection Agency (EPA) founded in 1970. Numerous other countries followed suit, most recently with many developing countries enacting environmental laws and associated agencies, often modelled (perhaps problematically) on Western precedents.[264]

Since the 1990s, the centre of gravity in environmental law innovation seems to have shifted to the European Union (EU).[265] While American environmental legislation was rebuked during the Bush presidencies, in Europe the growing influence of green political parties and social support

---

[256] R.H. Grove, *Green Imperialism: Colonial Expansion, Tropical Island Edens and the Origins of Environmentalism, 1600–1860* (Cambridge University Press, 1996).
[257] R. Carson, *Silent Spring* (Houghton Mifflin, 1962).
[258] R. Gottlieb, *Forcing the Spring: The Transformation of the American Environmental Movement* (Island Press, 1993).
[259] Public Law No. 88–206.
[260] Public Law No. 91–190.
[261] *Tennessee Valley Authority v. Hill et al.*, 437 US 153 (1978).
[262] Public Law No. 93–205.
[263] N.M. Ganong, 'Endangered Species Act Amendments of 1978: a Congressional response to Tennessee Valley v. Hill' (1979) 5(2) *Columbia Journal of Environmental Law* 283.
[264] J. Mayda, 'Environmental legislation in developing countries: some parameters and constraints' (1985) 12(4) *Ecology Law Quarterly* 997.
[265] See S. Wood, G. Tanner, and B.J. Richardson, 'What ever happened to Canadian environmental law?' (2010) 37(4) *Ecology Law Quarterly* 981; see further R.D. Kelemen and D. Vogel, 'Trading places: the role of the United States and the European Union in international environmental politics' (2010) 43(4) *Comparative Political Studies* 427.

for government leadership in this domain enabled many reforms such as for clean energy, environmental liability, and water management.[266] For instance, the EU introduced sophisticated legislation on integrated pollution control (covering several environmental media through one licensing process),[267] strategic EIA of government plans and programs (going beyond the usual project-level focus),[268] and cradle-to-grave environmental management, such as of electrical equipment waste (thereby to extend producer responsibility for final disposal).[269] The EU has also had its fair share of failures, such as the wretched common fisheries policy, which the European Commission conceded had led to fleet over-capacity, wasteful subsidies, and depletion of fisheries stocks.[270] Any conclusions about EU success and leadership in environmental governance are thus relative to its peers.

While the transatlantic gap narrowed somewhat during the Obama administration,[271] Canadian environmental law withered under the Harper administration. In 2012 it diluted or eliminated many federal environmental laws, policies, and institutions, including abolition of the National Round Table on the Environment and the Economy.[272] The Canadian Environmental Assessment Act was repealed and replaced with an *ersatz* version that diminished the scope and stringency of project assessments.[273] The ostensible aims of the changes were to streamline and minimise regulatory clutter, and ensure more certainty and predictability for proponents of major infrastructure projects.[274] The anti-regulatory

---

[266] R. Macrory (ed), *Reflections on 30 years of EU Environmental Law – A High Level of Protection?* (Europa Law Publishing, 2005).

[267] Directive 2008/1/EC of the European Parliament and of the Council of 15 January 2008 concerning integrated pollution prevention and control. OJ L 24/ 8, 29 January 2008.

[268] Directive 2001/42/EC of the European Parliament and of the Council of 27 June 2001 on the assessment of the effects of certain plans and programmes on the environment, OJ L 197/30, 21 July 2001.

[269] Directive 2012/19/EU of the European Parliament and of the Council of 4 July 2012 on waste electrical and electronic equipment, OJ L 197/38, 24 July 2012.

[270] European Commission, *Green Paper – Reform of the Common Fisheries Policy*, COM (2009) 163 final, 3.

[271] E.g. American Recovery and Reinvestment Act 2009, Public Law 111–5, included billions in tax credits and direct spending for clean energy, green jobs and energy efficiency, enabling the United States to double its renewable energy generation within 3 years.

[272] Bill C-38, An Act to implement certain provisions of the budget tabled in Parliament on 29 March 2012 and other measures, 1st session 41st Parliament 2012.

[273] Canadian Environmental Assessment Act, 2012, SC 2012, c. 19, s. 52.

[274] D. Corcker and L. Finney, 'Federal government seeks to overhaul the environmental assessment process' (8 May 2012) *Davis LLP Environmental Law Bulletin*.

trend also precipitated Canada's shameful withdrawal from the Kyoto Protocol[275] in December 2011.[276] The subsequent Trudeau administration has initiated a major review of federal EIA law that might lead to recovery of some of this lost ground.[277] Conversely, the new Trump administration in the United States portends significant weakening of federal environmental legislation.

The evolving environmental acquis has not simply been a transatlantic duel, as innovations have come from many other jurisdictions. New Zealand is reputedly the first nation to have enshrined the concept of sustainable development (albeit expressed as 'sustainable management') in its lodestar legislation, the Resource Management Act 1991.[278] Australia pioneered new models of environmental cooperation through the Intergovernmental Agreement on the Environment 1992, negotiated between the federal and state governments,[279] and the Resource Assessment Commission, which conducted ambitious public inquiries to help settle national environmental controversies.[280] The Global South has also contributed valuable precedents, such as the recognition of the rights of nature in the national constitution of Ecuador in 2008.[281] Table 2.1 of this chapter lists these and other milestones of the acquis.

Despite international variations in addressing environmental challenges, no country has yet been particularly successful. In 2012 UNEP lamented that credible progress had only been made towards four of the 90 main global environmental goals.[282] Some countries have better records, but no jurisdiction has an effective system of environmental governance as measured by substantial ecological improvements. Even nations with ostensibly superior records owe this partly to exporting their ecological footprint to emerging economies where the majority of consumer products are manufactured or natural resources are mined, and where waste such as electronic junk is shipped. Some harm is also displaced temporally,

---

[275] Kyoto Protocol to the UN Framework Convention on Climate Change, 11 December 1997, in force 18 February 2005, (1998) 37 ILM 22.
[276] M. Winfield, 'Canada hits bottom with withdrawal from Kyoto', *Toronto Star* 15 December 2011, at www.thestar.com.
[277] J. Maclean, 'How to restore trust in Canada's environmental regulations', *Toronto Star* 23 June 2016 at www.thestar.com.
[278] Public Act 1991, No.69, s. 5.
[279] See www.environment.gov.au/about-us/esd/publications/intergovernmental-agreement.
[280] Resource Assessment Commission 1989 (Cth). The Commission was abolished in 1993.
[281] República del Ecuador Constitucion de 2008.
[282] United Nations Environment Programme (UNEP), *GEO5: Global Environmental Outlook 5* (UNEP, 2012), 5.

Table 2.1 *Timeline of modern environmental law milestones*

Date	Milestone	Jurisdiction
Circa 1450	Seven generation principle, in the Iroquois Great Law of Peace	Five Nations Indian Confederacy (later six First Nations)
1610	Aldred's case, 9 Co Rep 57b, early use of tort of nuisance to stop a neighbour's pollution	England
1822	Cruel Treatment of Cattle Act, parliamentary legislation for animal welfare	Great Britain
1863	Alkali Act, to control muriatic acid gas emissions from alkali works	Great Britain
1872	World's first national park, at Yellowstone, under the Yellowstone Act	United States
1892	Public trust doctrine invoked to protect public resources, in *Illinois Central Railroad* v. *Illinois*, 146 US 387 (1892)	Illinois, United States
1941	*Trail Smelter* arbitration decision, concerning transboundary pollution	Canada and United States
1948	International Union for Conservation of Nature established	Switzerland
1966	Endangered Species Preservation Act	United States
1967	World's first specialist Environmental Protection Agency	Sweden
1969	National Environmental Policy Act, introduces EIA of proposals	United States
1969	Swedish Environmental Protection Act is first to recognise the precautionary principle	Sweden
1971	First environmental provisions to appear in a national constitution	Switzerland
1972	OECD Council recommends its members adopt the polluter pays principle	International
1972	Stockholm Declaration on the Environment	International
1972	UNEP established	International
1979	Land and Environment Court established	New South Wales, Australia
1979	Environmental Protection Law, the first such comprehensive law in China	China

(*cont.*)

Table 2.1 (cont.)

Date	Milestone	Jurisdiction
1980	The concept of 'sustainable development' appears in international policy, in the IUCN's World Conservation Strategy	International
1982	UN Law of the Sea Convention	International
1986	Single European Act, explicitly empowers the European Community to address environmental issues	European Community
1987	World Commission on Environmental Development publishes *Our Common Future* (Brundtland Report), popularising the concept of sustainable development	International
1987	Montreal Protocol on Substances That Deplete the Ozone Layer	International
1988	*MC Mehta* v. *Union of India* (beginning of public interest, environmental litigation in India)	India
1990	World' first carbon tax	Finland
1990	European Environment Agency established as an information source	European Community
1992	UN Framework Convention of Climate Change, world's first legal agreement to mitigate greenhouse gas emissions	International
1992	Convention on Biological Diversity, the pre-eminent global treaty in this field	International
1992	Resource Management Act, world's first legislation to make sustainable management a national goal	New Zealand
1997	Kyoto Protocol adopted, for curbing greenhouse gas emissions	International
2008	First national constitution to affirm the rights of nature	Ecuador
2012	Whanganui River declared a legal person with its own guardians	New Zealand
2015	World's first climate change liability lawsuit against a government	Netherlands
2015	Paris agreement to reduce greenhouse gas emissions	International
2017	Court declares the Ganges to be a legal person	India

and efforts to control it can be compared to the motion of a lumbering ship: the ship's mass and momentum can keep it travelling for miles after the engines stop. Most ozone-depleting chemicals were banned during the 1990s, but the ozone layer is taking decades to regenerate fully.[283] Similarly, even when fossil fuel emissions finally end, the lingering effect of past releases will leave the planet warmer for decades or centuries. Conversely, some environmental degradation encountered today, notably toxic soil or contaminated food, reflects past insouciance now outlawed. This temporal mismatching between the introduction of laws and the manifestation of impacts has a critical place in the story of environmental law. The overall result, warned the Board of the Millennium Ecosystem Assessment in 2005, is that 'human activity is putting such strain on the natural functions of the Earth that the ability of the planet's ecosystems to sustain future generations can no longer be taken for granted'.[284]

The gap between the ambitions and achievements of environmental law reflects pragmatic and expedient pressures that lead the present to displace the future. Responsible for national housekeeping, the modern state resembles the *parens patriae*, tasked with creating jobs, controlling inflation, and lifting living standards. The economy does not always trump other considerations, and increasingly wealthy societies value clean air, parks, and other environmental amenities that enrich their lifestyles, as predicted by the environmental Kuznets curve.[285] But while such concerns sometimes prevail over development pressures, especially where property rights or personal health are affected, development usually wins when major jobs and investment opportunities beckon. In economic downturns, the headwinds against environmental action rage even stronger. Political and business elites may collude to unwind legislative protections scapegoated for hindering economic recovery. Canada is a quintessential example, as earlier noted: under the Harper administration a portfolio of environmental laws were trashed including the pivotal EIA legislation.[286] With similar motivations, the Australian government under Tony Abbott slashed funding for environmental programs and environmental legal

---

[283] M. Park, 'Antarctic ozone layer is gradually healing, researchers find', *CNN* 2 July 2016, at http://edition.cnn.com.

[284] Millennium Ecosystem Assessment Board (MEAB), *Living Beyond Our Means: Natural Assets and Human Well-Being* (MEAB, 2005), 5.

[285] S. Dasgupta, et al., 'Confronting the environmental Kuznets curve' (2002) 16 *Journal of Economic Perspectives* 147.

[286] 'Canada's new budget "guts" environmental provisions', *Environment News Service* 20 June 2012, at http://ens-newswire.com.

aid[287] and proposed statutory amendments to limit access to courts.[288] The Trump presidency may result in even worse outcomes. These and other examples of backsliding on environmental law inspired French scholar Michel Prieur to propose the 'non-regression' principle as a fundamental guide to environmental law reform.[289] The principle demands continuous advancement of environmental law and policy without derogation, and that any legal change should occur only if it improves environmental outcomes.

Another governance trend inspired by similar economic circumstances is to render regulation more business-friendly. The evolution of environmental law was closely associated with the norms and institutions of the welfare state, including reliance on instruments of public ownership and highly prescriptive standards.[290] In recent decades these methods of 'command and control' became increasingly unfashionable, perceived as too rigid, complex, inefficient, and adversarial, and a barrier to entrepreneurialism and business competitiveness.[291] According to some critics of the US experience, 'the present regulatory system wastes tens of billions of dollars every year, misdirects resources, stifles innovation, and spawns massive and often counterproductive litigation'.[292] The response has been more experimentation with market-based instruments, a trend that may suggest a break with the 'path dependency' trajectory of environmental law, but it can also be construed as a continuation of the tradition of minimising restrictions on economic activity. The experimentations have been labelled 'self-organisation',[293] 'responsive regulation',[294] and 'smart

---

[287] 'Funding cut to environmental defender's offices described as "barbaric"', *ABC News* 19 December 2013, at www.abc.net.au/news.

[288] Environment Protection and Biodiversity Conservation Amendment (Standing) Bill 2015 (Cth).

[289] M. Prieur, 'Non-regression in environmental law' (2012) 5(2) *SAPIENS*, at https://sapiens.revues.org/1405.

[290] C. Sunstein, 'Paradoxes of the regulatory state' (1990) 57 *University of Chicago Law Review* 407; M. Moran, 'Understanding the regulatory state' (2002) 32 *British Journal of Political Science* 391.

[291] See e.g. C. Abbott, 'Environmental command regulation' in B.J. Richardson and S. Wood (eds), *Environmental Law for Sustainability* (Hart Publishing, 2006), 6.

[292] Ackerman and Stewart, 'Reforming environmental law', 1333.

[293] G. Teubner, L. Farner, and D. Murphy (eds), *Environmental Law and Ecological Responsibility: The Concept and Practice of Ecological Self-Organisation* (John Wiley and Sons, 1994).

[294] I. Ayres and J. Braithwaite, *Responsive Regulation: Transcending the Deregulation Debate* (Oxford University Press, 1992).

regulation,[295] among various terms.[296] They share a preference for legal controls that are 'less heavy-handed, and more responsive to the demands and possibilities of their context'.[297] Informational policy instruments, economic incentives, and contractual agreements are among examples.[298] Environmental law should of course consider more cost-effective approaches that harness the private sector and other non-state actors where they yield improvements over conventional regulation; but the difficulty arises when they are applied without rigorous public oversight, which thereby enables unscrupulous behaviour to flourish. Collaborative governance that includes representation from civil society actors such as environmental NGOs and indigenous peoples can improve the integrity of these arrangements, as later chapters discuss.

At an international level, environmental treaties do not generally directly regulate the activities of private entities, and nation-states retain considerable independence not only to choose which international laws to accept but how to implement them. Global environmental rules are typically quarantined within designated environmental treaties, governing biodiversity conservation and climate change for instance, while treaties controlling investment and other economic activities have few such provisions. Trade law tends to make only limited provision for environmental standards,[299] while governance of financial capital flows is even more bereft.[300] The spread of free trade deals is controversial for some because of the perception that trade agreements give

---

[295] N. Gunningham and P. Grabosky, *Smart Regulation. Designing Environmental Policy* (Clarendon Press, 1998).

[296] D. Levi-Faur, 'Regulation and regulatory governance' in D. Levi-Faur (ed), *The Handbook on the Politics of Regulation* (Edward Elgar Publishing, 2012), 2.

[297] J. Steele and T. Jewell, 'Law in environmental decision-making' in T. Jewell and J. Steele (eds), *Law in Environmental Decision-Making. National, European and International Perspectives* (Clarendon Press, 1998), 1, 14; see further J. Black, 'Decentring regulation: understanding the role of regulation and self-regulation in a "post-regulatory world"' (2011) 54 *Current Legal Problems* 103.

[298] See D.A. Farber, 'Taking slippage seriously: noncompliance and creative compliance in environmental law' (1999) 23 *Harvard Environmental Law Review* 297; A. Iles, 'Adaptive management: making environmental law and policy more dynamic, experimentalist and learning' (1996) 13 *Environmental and Planning Law Journal* 288; E.W. Orts and K. Deketelaere (eds), *Environmental Contracts: Comparative Approaches to Regulatory Innovation in the United States and Europe* (Kluwer Law, 2000).

[299] E. Brown Weiss, J.H. Jackson, and N. Bernasconi-Osterwalder (eds), *Reconciling Environment and Trade* (Martinus Nijhoff, 2008).

[300] C. Williams, 'Corporate social responsibility in an era of economic globalization' (2002) 35 *University of California Davis Law Review* 705, 731.

foreign companies additional rights to challenge domestic environmental legislation. The most contentious are treaties that provide for investor-state dispute settlement (ISDS),[301] which allows foreign investors to use international arbitration to hear grievances against a government over regulatory measures they find economically injurious. ISDS processes may discourage governments to enact or enforce legitimate environmental regulations. Disputes using ISDS have proliferated in recent years, with many involving challenges to environmental regulations.[302] For instance, in 2016 TransCanada initiated ISDS proceedings under the North American Free Trade Agreement to challenge President Obama's rejection of its Keystone pipeline proposal.[303]

The above table captures a representative example of the major milestones in the history of environmental law, at both the domestic and international levels. It tracks innovations in new principles, methods, and institutions. The table is not exhaustive, and lawyers will certainly disagree on what qualifies as a 'milestone' and the lack of knowledge of milestones in some societies, such as among indigenous peoples or ancient civilisations such as that of the Greeks or Romans, but what ultimately matters here is appreciation of the increasing intensity of change in the architecture of environmental law in recent centuries. New institutions, techniques, and norms have enriched states' ensembles of environmental regulations and policies, with considerable growth in international cooperation (the spatial dimension) and precaution to address future risks (the temporal orientation). This contrasts with historic approaches that were much more spatially and temporally immediate, such as a legal dispute between neighbours over an unsightly development, or regulation of fishing in a local river. The depth of change should also give us hope of the potential of much more to come, which is urgently needed. To understand these needs we must begin by looking specifically at the spatial and temporal qualities of current environmental law that need attention.

Space and Time in Environmental Law

Prior to sustainable development becoming environmental law's leitmotif – as examined further in the next chapter – environmental governance was

---

[301] J.E. Kalicki and A. Joubin-Bret (eds), *Reshaping the Investor-State Dispute Settlement System* (Brill Nijhoff, 2015).
[302] E.g. *Pac Rim Cayman LLC v. Republic of El Salvador*, ICSID Case No. ARB/09/12.
[303] 'Keystone XL rejection leads TransCanada to sue Obama administration', *CBC News* 6 January 2016, at www.cbc.ca/news.

couched more strongly in spatial terms. Space remains hugely important, both underpinning the structure of legal doctrines and procedures, as well as being a key lens through which scholars study environmental law.[304] Space – the physicality of places and entities and their interrelationships – helps to define the allocation of natural resources, delineate legal associations between events and impacts, demarcate units for environmental management, and enable visualisation of nature's species and terrain and our impacts on them. Time in nature, by contrast, is intangible and imperceptible, unable to be touched or observed except on timescales that are usually beyond human experience except vicariously through time-lapse photography or scientific literature. Thus, an environmental problem that is present and visible, such as urban smog or a waste dump, is more likely to attract legal controls than invisible greenhouse gas emissions or toxins in the food chain that wreak havoc decades from now. The limiting effect of being unable to 'see' an environmental problem is also particularly acute for the oceans, which readily hide the perils of overfishing or plastic debris.[305]

The influence of space on environmental law doctrine occurs in many contexts. In property law, space delineates the ambit of entitlements to land and other resources.[306] Garret Hardin's tragedy of the commons parable, one of the most powerful concepts in the development of environmental law, reflects the converse, where legally 'empty' space invites its reckless exploitation.[307] Access to natural resources, such as minerals or forests, is commonly articulated through property or quasi-property rights, such as leases and licences. They may apply to a given terrestrial or aquatic area, or to a quantum of the resource such as volume of minerals or fish stock. Space also informs conservation law: national parks are organised

---

[304] As reflected in the field of critical legal geography, for instance. It examines how law shapes space (e.g. creating public parks) and how space affects law (e.g. one law being implemented differently in separate spatial contexts: R.T. Ford, 'Law's territory: a history of jurisdiction' (1999) 97 *Michigan Law Review* 843; D.T. Goldberg, 'Polluting the body politic: race and urban location' in N. Blomley, K.D. Delaney, and R.T. Ford (eds), *The Legal Geographies Reader* (Blackwell Publishers, 2001), 87.

[305] For example, the fecund kelp forests around the waters of southern Australia – the 'rainforests of the ocean' are dying due to infestation by sea urchins, yet the seriousness of the problem, which dates from the 1940s, received little attention until 2012 when the Australian government finally listed under its legislation the kelp forests as a threatened ecosystem. It was a case of 'out of sight out of mind' until scientists were able to press for intervention: D. Wroe, 'Decimated kelp "jungles" listed as endangered', *Sydney Morning Herald* 18 August 2012, at www.smh.com.au.

[306] N. Blomley, 'Property, law and space' (2014) 3(3) *Property Law Review* 229.

[307] Hardin, 'The tragedy of the commons'.

around specific territorial designations while in private tenures statutory covenants can delineate conservation responsibilities. Property law, of course, is not entirely a spatial phenomenon. Several types of tenure, such as the life estate and the leasehold, have an explicit time-limiting quality. Further, licenses to engage in forestry or fisheries usually endure for a specified period, with licence conditions ostensibly subject to review and possible modification over time.

Tort law also draws heavily on space, as well as time. A private nuisance action requires the plaintiff to show damage or inconvenience to her land, and that the offending impact is 'sensed' such as by sight or smell.[308] The chain of causation between the offending action and the resulting harm must also be proximate, implying some overt spatial connection such as between neighbouring properties. (Temporal proximity also matters, as a court may rule that a harm that does not manifest for many years is too 'remote' to attribute liability.[309]) The tort of trespass, while not requiring actual damage, assumes that a person physically violates another's space by walking on it or throwing objects onto it. The tort of negligence is slightly less spatial in that an injured plaintiff is more likely to be able to recover for pure economic losses that are not as overt as direct physical damage to a property.[310]

Beyond the common law, many types of environmental regulation and management rely on space to frame controls on real property. We have already touched on national parks as one example. Land use zoning, an early form of environmental regulation, has been a powerful tool to codify representations of space and to inscribe it in the physical uses of land and water. Zoning, coupled with property rights, also has the effect of fragmenting space into smaller units that can inhibit ecological connections because of potentially conflicting land use activities across different zones. International law also relies on zoning, notably the delimitation of coastal states' jurisdiction such as the exclusive economic zone (EEZ) and territorial sea. Zoning also has a temporal quality in that it can freeze land use patterns in a moment of time that limits future changes.

---

[308] S. Ball and S. Bell, *Environmental Law: The Law and Policy Relating to the Protection of the Environment* (Blackstone Press, 1991), 135.
[309] J. Murphy and C. Witting, *Street on Torts* (Oxford University Press, 2012), 178–85.
[310] As since the UK House of Lords' decision in *Hedley Byrne and Co Ltd v. Heller and Partners Ltd*, [1964] AC 465.

A relatively new spatial concept is the 'offset'.[311] This serves to compensate for the environmental effects of an activity that cannot be adequately reduced on the affected site through avoidance or alleviation. Offsets are most prevalent in climate change mitigation and biodiversity conservation. In the markets for greenhouse gas emissions, emitters may be authorised to offset their emissions by investing in carbon sequestration such as by afforestation. In the biodiversity context, an offset typically entails restoring wildlife habitat equivalent to that lost by the development, through actions such as removal of weeds and feral animals, and revegetation. The development of environmental offsets took off after the late 1980s when US President George H.W. Bush adopted a policy of 'no net loss' of wetlands, which allowed for clearance of some wetlands so long as others were created.[312] The offsets market has since expanded to many other environmental contexts, and has appealed to governments for the flexibility to make trade-offs.

Offsets are controversial for several reasons, including the potential lack of equivalence between the environments lost and gained, and the time lag between the event loss and the future gain on the restored site.[313] Clearing wildlife habitat produces immediate effects, whereas restoring a natural ecosystem may require a long maturation period with uncertain outcomes. Crude metrics such as hectares or habitat function may fail to capture these complex differences in ecological components. Likewise, carbon offsets have temporal risks: insects or fire may ravage a forest planted to sequester CO_2. Offset policies themselves have loopholes, such as the lack of legal accountability for the quality of an offset several decades from now, which governments or companies may exploit to allow environmentally dubious developments to proceed. An Australian parliamentary inquiry in 2014 found that some offsets are not 'like for like', some are not properly restored or managed, and some offset sites were in danger of incurring damage.[314]

---

[311] E.g. Department of Sustainability, Environment, Water, Population and Communities, *EPBC Act Environmental Offsets Policy* (Commonwealth of Australia, 2012).

[312] M.R. Deland, 'No net loss of wetlands: a comprehensive approach' (1992) 7(1) *Natural Resources and Environment* 3.

[313] M. Maron, et al., 'Faustian bargains? Restoration realities in the context of biodiversity offset policies' (2012) 155 *Biological Conservation* 141.

[314] Discussed in 'Background briefing: the trouble with offsets', *ABC Radio National* 16 March 2014, at www.abc.net.au/radionational.

Access to courts to enforce environmental law is also closely tied to space.[315] To have standing, the plaintiff must normally show that she is personally injured or affected by the imputed decision, such as owning property contaminated by pollution. A mere altruistic concern about nature can be insufficient. In a pioneering case on standing in environmental lawsuits, *Sierra Club* v. *Morton*,[316] the US Supreme Court held that 'a mere "interest in a problem"' does not alone confer standing. The Court conceded, however, that the Sierra Club's members could have personal standing to sue if the imputed government's decision affected their aesthetic or recreational interests as demonstrated by their having visited the affected site. A similar decision was rendered by Australia's High Court in 1980, in denying standing to the Australian Conservation Foundation to challenge a federal environmental decision because the Foundation was viewed as having no special interest in the matter beyond that of an ordinary member of the public.[317] The Court held that a 'mere intellectual or emotional concern' does not suffice to establish a special interest. Legislative reform in many jurisdictions has since broadened standing to overcome such barriers, but other obstacles to public interest litigation such as exorbitant legal fees continue to deter litigants.

A spatial bias also imbues international law. National sovereignty and its territorial connotations are fundamental to the delineation of states' rights and responsibilities over natural resources. The state enjoys, in law, dominion over its landmass, subterranean minerals, airshed, and adjacent coastal waters. Because of the economic stakes and national pride, most litigation before the ICJ has concerned disputed territorial boundaries, especially maritime waters.[318] State responsibility for transboundary pollution has similarly rested on showing a strong physical manifestation of harm, as evident in the seminal *Trail Smelter* case that led to Canada's liability for pollution that blew into the United States.[319] Despite some attempts to 'de-spatialise' international environmental law through unifying principles such as the 'common heritage of humankind', countervailing pressures remain to deploy space when demarcating legal entitlements and responsibilities. The introduction in the 1970s and 1980s of EEZs in coastal waters – the 200 nautical miles extension of state control beyond

---

[315] See further D. Farber, 'Stretching the margins: the geographic nexus in environmental law' (1996) 48(5) *Stanford Law Review* 1247.
[316] (1972) 405 US 727.
[317] *Australia Conservation Foundation* v. *Commonwealth*, (1980) 146 CLR 493.
[318] E.g. *Peru* v. *Chile*, [2014] ICJ Reports 3.
[319] J. Read, 'The trail smelter dispute' (1963) 1 *Canadian Yearbook of International Law* 213.

the traditional 12 miles of territorial sea – reflects this territorial impetus in resource management. The hope was that because of the near-exclusive nature of EEZs, states could curb the tragedy of the commons in marine waters that had been plundered unsustainably.

Space is not simply another lens, distinct from time, through which to understand environmental law; rather, space and time have interrelationships that need acknowledgement. EIA, a pillar of many environmental law systems worldwide, illustrates these. Many impacts such as climate change and loss of biodiversity, which accumulate gradually over extended time periods, become discernible only on a large scale. This is because in physical systems a positive correlation exists between characteristic timescales (the time needed to 'see' a change in the system) and spatial scales (the size of the area over which processes exert causal influence). Large scales give one the necessary depth of perspective to understand the full magnitude and significance of ecological changes. Thus, for EIA to work effectively, it must use appropriate spatial and temporal scales together. Cumulative EIA, which examines the incremental impacts of many activities together over a period of time, ostensibly attempts to address this challenge. The outcome of an EIA depends critically on the selection of these temporal and spatial parameters, as a development proposal deemed as acceptable at some scale might not be if evaluated at a broader scale.

Just as space informs the architecture of environmental law in various guises, so too has time in many ways, with three of particular importance. First, time can demonstrate legally significant relationships between persons or events, with closer temporal proximity usually carrying greater legal consequences. Conversely, latent or incremental harms unrecognised as dangerous until a long time has passed may enable responsible parties to escape liability. Temporal proximity is thus directly relevant to the next chapter's consideration of the future orientation of environmental law, as well as its consideration of past damage long ago, as taken up in Chapter 4. Second, time can differentiate the application of legal standards, such as by shielding existing environmental users from new rules (known as grandfathering) or providing for expiration dates for legislative rules (sunset provisions). This temporality is also explored in Chapter 3's analysis of how the law can govern changes over time. Third, the law influences the 'pace' of time and timing. Legal procedures to fast-track development or limit the period to exercise rights such as to lodge an appeal are ways in which the pace of time has become a deeply contested dimension of environmental governance, a theme explored in Chapter 5. Each of these three dimensions will be briefly canvassed.

Temporal proximity can demonstrate the legal existence or salience of environmental relationships. 'Proximity' as a human judgement can be very different from natural timescales of proximity. Environmental law reflects the human preoccupation with the immediate, the instantaneous, spectacular, and most visible harms wrought on nature, or those events we label 'disasters' such as the shocking Canadian wildfires of May 2016.[320] Conversely, the law struggles to recognise the slow, incremental poisoning of the environment from activities dating back decades or unfolding harms that will not manifest for many years. For example, the accumulation of excessive phosphorus in many farmed soils threatens aquatic systems with increased eutrophication, yet the full impact of phosphorus fertilisers may not become apparent, such as through erosion, for many years. To establish liability for a pollution nuisance, the plaintiff must show a relationship between cause and effect, which can be difficult for impacts that gestate slowly. Even victims of highly publicised catastrophes can fail to secure justice when effects are time-delayed. In the 1984 Bhopal gas leak, the majority of harms manifested over subsequent decades as birth defects, cancers, and lingering post-trauma. The more recent 2010 *Deepwater Horizon* catastrophe will not have public effects on this scale, but its impact on marine life in the Gulf of Mexico will linger for eons.

In isolation, at any moment in time, these accretive harms may be imperceptible or innocuous without dedicated scientific study. In the early 1960s Rachel Carson's *Silent Spring* provoked international awareness about this threat. She highlighted the protracted, insidious, and long-lasting accumulation of dichlorodiphenyltrichloroethane (DDT) and other chemicals in the environmental food chain.[321] More recently, Rob Nixon has critiqued the 'slow violence' of cumulative environmental damage, which in his words means 'a violence that occurs gradually and out of sight, a violence of delayed destruction that is dispersed across time and space, an attritional violence that is typically not viewed as violence at all'.[322] Gradual environmental decay is pervasive – the toxins wafting through the food chain, the warming climate, acidifying oceans, and numerous other insidious, percolating problems. Their slow, deathly manifestation

---

[320] A. Kassam, 'Canada wildfire: why sleeping giant awoke in Alberta and became relentless', *The Guardian* 15 May 2016, at www.theguardian.com. See further K. Erikson, *A New Species of Trouble: The Human Experience of Modern Disasters* (WW Norton, 1994), 148.
[321] Carson, *Silent Spring*.
[322] Nixon, *Slow Violence and the Environmentalism of the Poor*, 2.

has sometimes been explained through the metaphor about the unknowing frog that boils to death in a pot of water gradually heated up.

Climate change poses the greatest 'slow' threat. While a sudden environmental catastrophe can trigger an outpouring of humanitarian assistance, as after the 2004 Asian tsunami, the menace posed by slowly rising seas or declining rainfall can lull governments into complacency. The underwater cabinet meeting stunt of the Maldives government in 2009 to garner international attention to the dangers of climate change to the low-lying Indian Ocean nation was a rare moment of high media publicity.[323] The aquatic theatre, however, was not enough to precipitate a deal later that year at the Copenhagen conference to cut global carbon emissions. Time-extended phenomena such as climate change, with considerable remoteness and uncertainty as to the relationship between cause and effect, also trouble courts when asked to impose liability for the costs.[324]

Overcoming this bias to temporal immediacy or proximity has been one of the greatest challenges for environmental law, because many threats are more efficiently addressed through preventive measures even if they won't arise until the very far future. Prevention is often the only cost-effective and logical approach because damage is sometimes irreparable or more costly to repair than to prevent. This idea underpins the precautionary principle. The ICJ advised in the *Gabčikovo-Nagymaros* case that: 'in the field of environment, vigilance and prevention are necessitated by the often irreversible damage to the environment and the limitations inherent in the very mechanism of reparation of this type of damage'.[325] Environmental planning and EIA provide tools to help overcome the bias to temporal immediacy, with the 1969 National Environmental Policy Act,[326] a federal US law, the first comprehensive, national framework for EIA. Its quality, however, depends on the spatial and temporal parameters of the assessment including whether cumulative and synergistic effects are evaluated.

Temporal proximity also influences how regulations define the time frame for companies to report on their activities. The reporting tends to relate to a specific interval, such as the past year, and under securities

---

[323] 'Maldives cabinet makes a splash', *BBC News* 17 October 2009, at www.bbc.com/news.
[324] *American Electric Power Company v. Connecticut*, (2011) 564 US 131.
[325] Case Concerning the Gabcikovo-Nagymaros Project (Hungary/Slovakia) [1997] ICJ Reports 7, 78.
[326] Public Law No. 91–190.

regulation the reporting of environmental performance is usually confined to matters construed as 'financially material', a concept that also tends to be interpreted within a narrow time frame. According to the influential International Accounting Standards Board: 'information is material if its omission or misstatement could influence the *economic decisions* of users taken on the basis of the financial report'.[327] The US Securities and Exchange Commission's regulations elaborate that 'materiality' includes 'the material effects that compliance' with government environmental regulations 'may have upon the capital expenditures, earnings, and competitive position of the registrant and its subsidiaries'.[328] Because markets focus on current or near-term economic performance, financial materiality is measured in a limited temporal window. Not only are the long-term social and environmental impacts of corporations, decades from now, virtually never considered to be 'financially material', much environmental harm traceable to business will not create any legally defined liabilities or costs, and thus will also escape reporting triggers.

A second key function of time is to differentiate the application of environmental regulation, in the sense of distinguishing the time periods in which different standards or rules apply. Thus the principle of non-retroactivity shields past errors such as pollution emissions that once enjoyed the imprimatur of legality.[329] Statutes of limitations can similarly curb environmental accountability for historic harms by limiting the period in which to pursue legal action.[330] 'Grandfather' provisions in legislation, a topic the next chapter considers later in detail, exempt persons already active in the market from new, stricter regulations. Grandfathering is commonly used in pollution control, land use planning, and resource access governance, and it may involve giving beneficiaries either a grace period before the new rules apply or indefinite exemption so long as the beneficiary does not change its activity. The main rationale for time-differentiated rules is to avoid the seeming injustice of coercing a person to incur costs in adjusting to a new regulation after having made investments to conform to a prior standard. Differentiated regulation, however, can cement temporal inertia in environmental

---

[327] International Accounting Standards Board (IASB), *Framework for the Preparation and Presentation of Financial Statements* (IASB, 2004), para. 30 (my emphasis).
[328] Reg. S-K, 17 CFR, s. 229.101(c)(xii). For more detailed information, see T. Pfund, 'Corporate environmental accountability: expanding SEC disclosures to promote market-based environmentalism' (2004) 11 *Missouri Environmental Law and Policy Review* 118.
[329] C. Sampford, et al., *Retrospectivity and the Rule of Law* (Oxford University Press, 2006).
[330] Milhollin, 'Long-term liability for environmental harm'.

governance, holding back reform and the capacity to respond to change. For instance, new regulations with grandfather concessions retard investment in cleaner factories and keep inefficient, polluting plants operating longer than they otherwise would.[331]

Given the economic advantages to industry beneficiaries, it should be appreciated that grandfathering, as well as non-retroactive liability and statutes of limitations, tend to reflect corporate influence. The phenomenon of 'regulatory capture' speaks to this pernicious influence, whereby government agencies and politicians come under the sway of those whom they are supposed to regulate impartially in the public interest. The privileged access to political power that money brings may ensue from donations to political parties, intense lobbying, private meetings, and the revolving door between government bureaucrats and corporate managers. An Australian study of the corrupting influence of the mining industry in the state of Queensland found that its outcomes include 'legislative changes to remove environmental protections, federal and state government approval of projects despite serious environmental concerns, and even retrospective approval of illegal mining activities'.[332] The last chapter of this book takes up this theme again in exploring how to democratise environmental decision making.

The timing of decisions is another cog in the temporalities of environmental law. As a process for scrutinising economic activities such as to build mines or harvest forests, environmental law has a mighty influence on the timing of development. It can delay them because of the need for assessments and public consultation. The opportunities for appeal or review of executive decisions, which can cause further delay, are also subject to time frames set by law. The law may also be complicit in rushed decisions in order to minimise costly holdups for business operators. The narrative increasingly constructed by political and business elites is that environmental law creates unreasonable delays. In 2015 an Australian parliamentary committee reported in favour of amending the federal environmental legislation to limit appeal rights, with the committee citing 'the costs to proponents and consequences for economic activity when major development projects are delayed by judicial review'.[333]

---

[331] J.R. Nash and R.L. Revesz, 'Grandfathering and environmental regulation: the law and economics of new source review' (2007) 101 *Northwestern University Law Review* 1677.
[332] H. Aulby and M. Ogge, *Greasing the Wheels* (Australian Institute and Australian Conservation Foundation, 2016), 1.
[333] Senate Environment and Communications Legislation Committee, *Environment Protection and Biodiversity Conservation Amendment (Standing) Bill 2015* (Commonwealth of Australia, 2015), 27.

Similar sentiments motivated the Canadian government in 2012 to drastically alter a suite of environmental statutes in order to accelerate approval processes for coveted resource developments.[334] The legislation rewrote sections of the National Energy Board Act[335] to set a 2-year limit on the review process, and giving the federal cabinet power to allow a project that was rejected by an assessment. The government also altered the Species at Risk Act[336] to exempt the National Energy Board from having to impose conditions to protect critical habitat on approved projects. The same sentiment was reflected in the government's tactic to limit initial parliamentary debate on the amending bundle of legislation to just 7 days. We'll return to the subject of 'fast-tracking' law in Chapter 5.

The myopic and expedient character of environmental regulation, whether it be ignoring long-term future damage, grandfathering existing uses, or rushing approvals for new activities, share a preoccupation with the now, the immediate. The philosophy of sustainable development, as the following chapter examines, has had limited success in challenging the status quo.

In Closing

Nature does not stand still, and neither should environmental law. Time is about change, and for environmental law to remain relevant and effective, it must respond to nature's temporalities and especially its anthropogenic disturbances. Humankind itself has its own temporalities, from the saunter of biological evolution to the sprint of cultural change. Law is among the cultural institutions that can help align environmental behaviour with nature's timescales, but equally the law can be complicit in its wanton destruction. To avoid further degradation, humanity will need much more than cleaner technologies and thriftier use of natural resources. Already societies have at their disposal considerable knowhow that could lower our ecological footprint with only modest effort. Opinion polls over the years also show that a substantial majority profess environmental concern.[337] Yet

---

[334] J. Oliver, 'Environmental laws getting facelift to accelerate projects', *Vancouver Sun* 8 May 2012, at http://vancouversun.com.
[335] RSC 1985, c. N-7.
[336] SC 2002, c. 29.
[337] See e.g. R.E. Dunlap, 'Trends in public opinion toward environmental issues: 1965–1990' in R.E. Dunlap and A.G. Mertig (eds), *American Environmentalism: The U.S. Environmental Movement 1970–1990* (Taylor and Francis, 1992), 89: Y. Wolinsky-Nahmias and S.

a vast chasm between rhetoric and action persists.[338] While minor behavioural improvements have ensued from environmental pressures (e.g. gasoline price hikes can curb driving habits and increase demand for fuel-efficient cars), these changes have tended to be too fleeting, perfunctory, or localised to make enough difference.

Behavioural changes must arise culturally, and specifically through institutions capable of leveraging significant change. Although evolutionary scientists imply that culture is secondary to biological urges, culture itself is one of the manifestations of *Homo sapiens*' evolution. Nature circumscribes rather than determines our possibilities. We cannot condone our environmental abuses by some crude reasoning that they simply reflect the workings of nature and the laws of natural selection. Nature is not a moral authority and we shouldn't necessarily derive our values from its workings, such as 'survival of the fittest' or 'might makes right'. Concomitantly, in elevating our own moral agency and responsibility we must not lapse into fatalistic cultural relativism without any defensible truths such as about the threat of climate change or extinction of species. A rapid mutation in human cultural evolution is needed to trigger much more ambitious attitudinal and behavioural changes towards the environment. Maladaptive cultural traits, like harmful genetic mutations, could be 'selected out'. Already, history shows that some societies have occasionally shifted their moral sensibility quite dramatically, for example the abolition of slavery, the recognition of animal welfare, and the greatly improved status of women.[339] Discrimination certainly continues, even in the most enlightened societies, but it is now more often stigmatised than condoned or encouraged.

Law played a seminal role in these moral shifts, along with other social factors. The tensions between the selfish inclinations of individuals and the expectations of group living, explains Richard Alexander, fostered the

---

Young Kim, 'International public opinion on the environment: responses to inequality and globalization', ISPP 31st Annual Scientific Meeting, Paris, 9 July 2008; European Commission, *Attitudes of European Citizens Towards the Environment* (Directorate General Communication, March 2008).

[338] S. Barr, 'Are we all environmentalists now? Rhetoric and reality in environmental action' (2005) 35(2) *Geoforum* 231.

[339] S. Drescher, *Abolition: A History of Slavery and Anti-Slavery* (Cambridge University Press, 2009); K. Shevelow, *For the Love of Animals: The Rise of the Animal Protection Movement* (Macmillan, 2008); K.C. Berkeley, *The Women's Liberation Movement in America* (Greenwood Press, 1999).

development of moral systems such as law.[340] It greatly extended the sphere of cooperation for humans than would otherwise be naturally attainable for a species that lived in small clans for 99 per cent of its evolutionary history. Law disciplines people to behave in ways they otherwise would not, if left to their own devices. Law can promote cooperation both by enacting rules that direct human behaviour towards specific outcomes and by creating institutions such as corporations or states that provide decision-making regimes for coordinating and managing human activities.

Law reform, of the government variety, alone is no assurance of positive results given the obstacles, especially political intransigence, to translating the ecological timescape into workable policies and practices. Furthermore, as a language, law's capacity to convey a stable and shared meaning about time and the environment is difficult, given societal disagreements about the seriousness of environmental problems and how to solve them.[341] Postmodernism draws attention to how knowledge and 'truth' are culturally mediated. This should not imply that reality does not pre-exist language or that events and experience are not material: instead, it reminds us that language is a precondition for analysis, debate, and problem-solving.[342] As different cultural and historical contexts modulate language, reality itself can be comprehended in various ways.[343] Thus, in addition to time itself, terms like 'sustainable development' or 'environmental restoration' may be interpreted diversely according to their context. For law reform this implies a pre-eminent role for institutions that can promote scientific investigation, sharing of knowledge, public debate, and democratic processes – important constituents of building a culture that shares an understanding of the temporalities of nature and how to govern human environmental behaviour. Collaborative governance that works with progress social movements can also make a difference. The following three chapters examine the major temporal dimensions of environmental law where challenges must be overcome to align our environmental behaviour with nature's timescales.

---

[340] R. Alexander, *The Biology of Moral Systems* (Aldine Transaction, 1987).
[341] Postmodernist influences have been most evident in critical legal studies: see further A. Hunt, 'The big fear: law confronts postmodernism' (1990) 35(3) *McGill Law Journal* 508; J. Hasnas, 'Back to the future' (1995) 45 *Duke Law Journal* 84.
[342] see J. Dryzek, *The Politics of the Earth: Environmental Discourses* (Oxford University Press, 1987).
[343] See generally N. Fairclough, *Language and Power* (Longman, 1989).

3

The Ever-Present Now

Pull of the Future; Drag of the Present

The future infatuates modern society. Since the Enlightenment and the Industrial Revolution, our experience of time has shifted dramatically, away from the recurrent momentum of nature's cycles to a forward-reaching time for society advancing through its technological prowess and material prosperity. Modernity has brought greater scientific knowhow that tempts us to control our destiny as never before: we are excited about the prospect of colonising distant planets, that robots may take over tedious daily chores, and medical breakthroughs that may prolong human longevity for decades. Even some of our gravest environmental challenges might be resolvable; geo-engineering advances invite scientists to stall the Earth's warming climate, while new synthetic and genetically modified sustenance might stave off food shortages. Although the postmodernist worldview emerging since the late twentieth century has challenged the utopian, future-progressing Modernism with its concern with the under-acknowledged or marginalised aspects of history, the future impulse still dominates the centres of political and economic power, and mainstream culture.[1] As international cultural critic Hal Niedzviecki recently wrote in *Trees on Mars: Our Obsession with the Future*, we remain preoccupied with 'knowing and owning the future'.[2]

This future impulse manifests ubiquitously in the competitive world of business. Corporate jargon constantly exhorts one to be 'future-focused', 'goal-oriented', 'forward-thinking', 'mission-driven', 'growth-minded', 'proactive', and other vacuities. The market valuation of enterprises itself similarly responds to their future prospects rather than past deeds, as a company's projected earnings primarily determine its stock price. When news broke

---

[1] On the past orientation of postmodernism, see A. Dirlik, *Postmodernity's Histories: The Past as Legacy and Project* (Rowman and Littlefield, 2000).
[2] H. Niedzviecki, *Trees on Mars: Our Obsession with the Future* (Seven Stories Press, 2015), Chapter 5.

in 2015 that BP would incur the heftiest environmental fine in US history to settle legal actions against it – some US$18.7 billion, due to the *Deepwater Horizon* catastrophe – the company's share price rose on the 'good news' that it had resolved the matter.[3] Some observers also compare societies' overall business cultures by their prospectiveness, as though this yardstick singularly foreshadows success or failure. A 2007 study published in the *Harvard Business Review* ranked Singapore as the world's most 'forward-thinking' business culture, based on metrics such as investing, planning, and rewarding long-term performance.[4] Other highly ranked, future-focused cultures are supposedly Switzerland, the Netherlands, and Malaysia. Another metric is the 'Future Orientation Index', devised by British academics to identify the most forward-thinking countries, which they found in 2012 to be Germany, followed by Japan and then Switzerland, while Pakistan was identified as the most backward.[5] The Index measured how frequently the citizens of surveyed countries searched Google for 'future' or related terms.

This future impulse extends, ostensibly, to environmental governance. Through legislation and policy, many states have embraced the philosophy of sustainable development (or 'sustainability' as it's sometimes called), which behoves society to act for the long-term protection of natural capital for economic prosperity. Legislation often invokes the principles of precaution and intergenerational equity that inform sustainability, along with other future-oriented tools, including strategic environmental planning and impact assessment. The dogma that environmental protection can dovetail with economic success has been fortified through the allied concept of 'ecological modernisation', which deftly reframes the ethical and political dilemmas of industrial capitalism as surmountable technical and managerial challenges.[6] Ecological modernisation, which has garnered much interest in Japan and the European Union (EU),[7] sees

---

[3] D. Rushe, 'BP set to pay largest environmental fine in US history for Gulf oil spill', *The Guardian* 3 July 2015, 30.

[4] M. Javidan, 'Forward thinking cultures', (2007) July–August *Harvard Business Review*, at https://hbr.org/2007/07/forward-thinking-cultures.

[5] A. Sedghi, 'Which countries are the most forward thinking?', *The Guardian* 9 February 2013, at www.theguardian.com.

[6] See M. Skou Andersen and I. Massa, 'Ecological modernization – origins, dilemmas and future directions' (2000) 2 *Journal of Environmental Policy and Planning* 337; M.A. Hajer, *The Politics of Environmental Discourse: Ecological Modernisation and the Policy Process* (Oxford University Press, 1997).

[7] H. Nishimura, 'The greening of Japanese industry' in M. Rogers (ed), *Business and the Environment* (St Martin's Press, 1995), 21; P. Christensen (ed), *Governing the Environment: Politics, Policy and Organization in the Nordic Countries* (Nordic Council of Ministers, 1996).

environmental degradation as resolvable through industrial modernity, innovative technologies, business acumen, and managerial creativity.[8] By embracing it, green companies should benefit financially by gaining competitive advantages, building new markets, and improving production efficiency.[9] The rapid ascent of the creed of sustainability and ecological modernisation, however, has not greatly disturbed the status quo, and certainly hardly dented the Anthropocene. Economic well-being today remains the index of success: people's desires for holidaying abroad, commuting by cars, eating meat, renovating swanky homes, and acquiring the latest gadgets, remain largely unfettered by the law. We may act more efficiently in using natural resources and reducing waste, but with population growth and a ravenous consumer culture, the efficiency dividend gets easily overwhelmed.

The pull of the future is a mirage, however, with the present exerting far greater rein over environmental decisions and habits. The implementation of environmental laws worldwide remains deeply pragmatic and expedient, accommodating short-term pressures and conveniences such as respect for property rights and minimisation of business costs. The temporal discrepancy is reflected in the difference between the speed and determination with which governments intervene to save the economy and their prevarication on environmental protection. The Global Financial Crisis (GFC) spurred governments worldwide to restore market stability with urgency unprecedented since the Great Depression;[10] by contrast, the looming crisis of climate change has garnered only sporadic and lukewarm responses, notwithstanding the achievements in Paris in November 2015.[11] Achieving sustainability on nature's terms requires greater economic pain and social dislocation than corporate and political leaders concede. The lofty legislated rhetoric about intergenerational responsibilities and long-term prescience hardly infiltrates regulatory decisions because of the paucity of integrity mechanisms such as indicia for measuring progress and sanctions for performance failures. Proposals to price the cost of environmental

---

[8] See generally J. Huber, *New Technologies and Environmental Innovation* (Edward Elgar Publishing, 2004).
[9] E.g. World Business Council for Sustainable Development and United Nations Environment Programme, *Cleaner Production and Eco-Efficiency, Complementary Approaches to Sustainable Development* (World Business Council for Sustainable Development, 1998), 3.
[10] 'Adding up the government's total bailout tab', *New York Times* 4 February 2009, at www.nytimes.com.
[11] T. Bawden, 'COP21: Paris deal far too weak to prevent devastating climate change, academics warn', *Independent* 9 January 2016, at www.independent.co.uk.

damage, such as a carbon tax – which would greatly help prioritise the future – have been fiercely resisted by political and business elites, as evident in Australia and Canada recently.[12]

The struggle to internalise within environmental law a serious commitment to the future reflects a wider malaise in modern governments' capacity for foresight and long-term action. The fading welfare state in recent decades has been intertwined with growing scepticism about the efficacy of long-term administrative planning and the viability of its predictive capacities. Prescriptive planning about the allocation of resources and assignment of responsibilities has been challenged politically from the Right and Left on grounds ranging from economic inefficiency, imperfect knowledge, and unacceptable limits to individual choice.[13] Rising expectations on the part of competing interest groups have led to severe political overload on governments, which find themselves, under the impact of fiscal constraints, facing legitimation crises and reduced capacity to engage in long-term national development.[14] The business world as well fails to embrace the long term, with American cultural theorist Fredric Jameson remarking, 'it is scarcely fair to expect long-term projections . . . from minds trained in the well-nigh synchronic habits of zero-sum calculation and of keeping an eye on profits'.[15] Competitive market pressures drive myopic business practices to stay solvent.

The crisis in environmental law reflects not simply societies' lack of appreciation of the future or a failure to act for the long term. These are serious obstacles, for sure, but the governance problem also inheres in the lack of capacity to manage a *changing* future. Time is about change, such as changes in natural systems, shifts in social attitudes, and economic practices. Environmental change is often unpredictable in its timing, nature, magnitude, and consequences. To safeguard future natural capital along with the people who depend on it, the law must be able to respond and manage change more adroitly. This necessity clashes with the law's focus on guaranteeing the stability and predictability of relationships between

---

[12] T. Arup, 'Tony Abbott battles the future by axing carbon tax', *Sydney Morning Herald* 17 July 2014, at www.smh.com.au; L. Whittington, 'Carbon pricing just a tax grab, Stephen Harper says', *Toronto Star* 23 April 2015, at www.thestar.com.
[13] See P. McAuslan, *The Ideologies of Planning Law* (Pergamon Press, 1980): D. Yergin and J. Stanislaw, *The Commanding Heights: The Battle Between Government and the Marketplace* (Simon and Schuster, 1998).
[14] J. Habermas, *Legitimation Crisis* (Beacon Press, 1973); C. Offe, *Contradictions of the Welfare State* (MIT Press, 1987).
[15] F. Jameson, 'The end of temporality' (2003) 29 *Critical Inquiry* 695, 705ff.

legal persons. The temporally static character of much regulation, in which the law shields existing resource users and polluters through 'grandfathering', and the limited scope for relicensing facilities to accommodate new circumstances, are among the obstacles to managing change. Business moguls' incessant demands for certainty and predictability in their regulatory environment militate against legal changes except those that reduce taxes, licences, or other regulatory burdens.[16] Thus, regulators often have little appetite to adjust controls on existing developments to take account of changing social values or new environmental performance criteria.

The story of this chapter is about the ever-present now of environmental law, in which the future simmers as a mirage that the law never properly grasps. It examines the difficulties of articulating the philosophy of sustainable development and intergenerational stewardship in the law, and the challenges of improving the law's responsiveness to changing circumstances. These largely unresolved difficulties have left environmental law mired in a 'present-future' straitjacket, with the utopian embrace of the future squeezed by the pragmatic demands of the present.

Governing the Future

Sustainable Development (and Its Rivals)

As environmental issues have become mainstream concerns in many societies since the 1960s, a tension has grown between the objectives of economic development and environmental protection that is already well known to many readers of this book. The tension was brought into sharp relief by the Club of Rome's *Limits to Growth* report published in 1972,[17] which argued that the environment could not sustain continued economic expansion. Attempting to resolve this tension, the World Commission on Environment and Development (colloquially known as the 'Brundtland Commission') advanced the concept of sustainable development in its landmark report, *Our Common Future*.[18] Essentially, the concept posits that economic development must be moderated to safeguard the long-term capacity of the biosphere to sustain fundamental ecological

---

[16] E.g. W. Cole, 'Australia business leaders clamor for certainty as election closes in', *Reuters* 30 August 2013, at www.reuters.com; G. Karol, 'Small business owners want more certainty from Washington', *Fox Business* 4 April 2013, at www.foxbusiness.com.
[17] D.H. Meadows, et al., *The Limits to Growth* (Universe Books, 1972).
[18] World Commission on Environment and Development, *Our Common Future* (Oxford University Press, 1987).

services and biodiversity. Sustainable development has since enjoyed wide respect and ostensibly become the main goal for environmental law in most countries, as well as being espoused in a variety of global treaties.[19] It has also gained traction in corporate boardrooms.[20] But some academic critics and environmental groups have attempted to redefine sustainable development to emphasise its ecological considerations, as expressed through the concept of 'sustainability', with more emphasis on ethical values and remaking capitalism.[21] The language of sustainability itself has become appropriated by some political and business elites, and purged of its potentially more radical overtones that might imply prioritisation of nature conservation over its economic use.[22]

Part of sustainable development's appeal includes that its breadth and vagueness allow many to notionally embrace it while holding divergent definitions of it.[23] The 'triple bottom line'[24] approach – commonly advocated in the context of corporate social responsibility (CSR) – accentuates the economic aspect of sustainability.[25] It thereby helps justify continual economic growth and consumption on the basis that it underpins business success while corporate innovation can overcome environmental problems.[26] Ecologically focused definitions of sustainable development draw on the natural sciences, emphasising absolute (not relative) reduction of pollution and consumption to levels within the carrying capacity of ecosystems.[27] The principal recent effort to overcome the divergent

---

[19] C. Voigt, *Sustainable Development as a Principle of International Law* (Martinus Nijhoff Publishers, 2009).

[20] B. Sjåfjell and B.J. Richardson (eds), *Company Law and Sustainability: Legal Barriers and Opportunities* (Cambridge University Press, 2015).

[21] K. Bosselmann, *The Principle of Sustainability Principle: Transforming Law and Governance* (Ashgate, 2008).

[22] E.g, S.M. Livesey and K. Kearins, 'Transparent and caring corporations? A study of sustainability reports by the Body Shop and Royal Dutch/Shell' (2002) 15 *Organization and Environment* 233.

[23] A.D. Basiago, 'Methods of defining sustainability' (1995) 3 *Sustainable Development* 109; K. Pezzoli, 'Sustainable development: a transdisciplinary overview of the literature' (1997) 40(5) *Journal of Environmental Planning and Management* 549; K. Bruno and J. Karliner, *Earthsummit.Biz: The Corporate Takeover of Sustainable Development* (Food First Books, 2002), 66.

[24] J. Elkington, *Cannibals with Forks: The Triple Bottom Line of 21st Century Business* (Capstone Publishing, 1997).

[25] H.E. Daly, 'Toward some operational principles of sustainable development' (1990) 2(1) *Ecological Economics* 1.

[26] Bruno and Karliner, *Earthsummit.Biz*, 5.

[27] S. Hendry, 'Worth the paper that it's written on? An analysis of statutory duty in modern environmental law' (2005) *Journal of Planning and Environment Law* 1145.

definitions and risk of nebulousness is the United Nations Sustainable Development Goals, adopted in 2015. The resulting 17 goals with 169 targets are so encyclopaedic that that they fail to identify and differentiate the main priorities.[28] While we should commend the recognition of environmental restoration among the key 17 goals (explored further in Chapter 4),[29] the accompanying 'targets' for it are not precise and measurable. Furthermore, the use of discretionary language such as that the commitments 'will be voluntary and country-led', and they can be tailored to 'different national realities, capacities and levels of development', will surely lead to disappointing outcomes.[30]

Building on this philosophy, environmental legislation commonly espouses a variety of objects and principles that serve to allocate roles and responsibilities among decision-makers, to discipline regulators in their exercise of discretionary powers, and to specify desired outcomes. In its more robust variants, these policy principles – including inter- and intra-generational equity, the polluter pays principle[31] and the precautionary principle[32] – provide sustainable development with greater operational traction and clearer practical application. Courts, when asked to resolve uncertainty as to the meaning of statutory provisions, may consider such principles. The precautionary principle is particularly important for articulating societal responsibility to ensure future ecological health, as it fosters protective decisions that are more risk-averse despite scientific uncertainty about future impacts.

The relative weight given to ecological and economic values in such legislation varies considerably, although some general patterns are discernible. Environmental legislation essentially serves to mitigate or avoid the most serious impacts, and channel public participation into formal, institutional processes. Planning and protection legislation (e.g. environmental impact assessment (EIA), land use, pollution control laws) commonly aims to facilitate rather than restrict economic development, with restrictions limited mainly to activities that present major environmental or public health risks. Rarely would an environmental assessment of any

---

[28] United Nations, *Transforming our World: The 2030 Agenda for Sustainable Development*, Resolution A/RES/70/1 of 25 September 2015.
[29] Ibid, goal 15.
[30] Ibid.
[31] Organization for Economic Cooperation and Development (OECD), *The Polluter Pays Principle: OECD Analyses and Recommendations* (OECD 1992).
[32] N. de Sadeleer (ed), *Implementing the Precautionary Principles: Approaches from the Nordic Countries, the EU and USA* (Earthscan, 2007).

development proposal result in its rejection altogether, although some proposals never get assessed because developers abandon their plans knowing that they would probably not pass critical scrutiny. Regulators sometimes apply a cost-benefit analysis (CBA) in these contexts, including evaluation of proposed new regulations and policies, whereby a balance is sought between potential impacts and economic gains and losses (a controversial decision-making tool evaluated in some detail later in this chapter). Some laws incorporate the precautionary principle to mitigate or avoid future serious impacts, with the principle explicitly mandated in the EU Treaty,[33] and in 2005 France ambitiously incorporated the precautionary principle into its national constitution, the Charter for the Environment.[34] But surprisingly, the lodestar environmental laws of quite a few countries, such as New Zealand's Resource Management Act (RMA),[35] do not mention it, although the government interprets the legislation as implying a precautionary approach.[36]

In natural resources management, legislation tends to give economic considerations even greater preference over environmental objectives. Legislation in this sector aims primarily to facilitate access to both renewable (e.g. fisheries, forests, and water) and non-renewable (e.g. minerals, oil, and gas) resources for development purposes.[37] Alberta's Forest Act, to illustrate, has the 'purpose of establishing, growing and harvesting timber in a manner designed to provide a yield consistent with sustainable forest management principles and practices',[38] while the long title of Queensland's mining legislation declares its purpose as 'to provide for the assessment, development and utilisation of mineral resources to the maximum extent practicable consistent with sound economic and land use management'.[39] In recent decades environmental controls have improved as resource scarcities, such as with regard to water, intensify. But the ethos persists that natural resources will be harnessed for economic activity rather than left untouched.

---

[33] Article 191(2) of the Treaty on the Functioning of the European Union, OJ C 326, 26 October 2012, provides that all Community policy on the environment shall be based on the precautionary principle.
[34] D. Bourg, 'France's Charter for the Environment: of presidents, principles and environmental protection' (2007) 15(2) *Modern and Contemporary France* 117.
[35] Public Act 1991, No. 69.
[36] E.g., Department of Conservation, *New Zealand Coastal Policy Statement. Guidance Note 3: Precautionary Approach* (Department of Conservation, 2010).
[37] For examples from a representative jurisdiction, see J.R. Rasband, J. Salzman, and M. Squillace, *Natural Resources Law and Policy* (Foundation Press, 2008).
[38] Forests Act, RSA 2000, c. F-22, s. 16(1).
[39] Mineral Resources Act 1989 (Qld).

Extraordinarily, even as concerns about climate change escalate, in many jurisdictions (such as Australia and Canada) coal mining, oil extraction, and other fossil fuel industries continue to enjoy precedence over environmental protection goals.[40] The sustainability of any human activity with environmental consequences often depends on the context. The impact of the emission of greenhouse gases is not context-specific, as one tonne of carbon emitted into the atmosphere has the same impact on the climate whether it comes from China or the United States. But many environmental impacts have local ramifications depending on the time and place. A massive factory in contemporary New York that belches a cocktail of pollutants would be viewed quite differently for its environmental impacts compared to the same facility located in sparsely populated seventeenth-century Siberia.

Privileged priority to the environment is generally given in the law only for prestige areas and issues, such as iconic endangered species, scenic landscapes, and world heritage. The Canada National Parks Act, for instance, stipulates that 'maintenance or restoration of ecological integrity, through the protection of natural resources and natural processes, shall be the first priority of the Minister when considering all aspects of the management of parks'.[41] In these contexts, the law commonly limits access for economic development. However, as the perceived opportunity cost of leaving such places fallow grows, pressures for mining, tourism, and other economic activities continue, in regard to both existing and proposed conservation areas. For example, Tasmania's world heritage-listed wilderness has come under pressure for selective logging and more tourist infrastructure in order that the 'unused' expanse can yield more economic benefits.[42] Even the aforementioned Canadian legislation has been mired in controversy for allowing road developments, as discussed in Chapter 4. Again, the competition between conservation and economic imperatives permeates environmental governance.

Evidence of the increasing gravity of the Anthropocene, coupled with concerns about weakening government regulation, have spawned competing ideas and approaches. A variety of non-state actors, from enlightened business entrepreneurs to civil society activists, have tabled alternative

---

[40] K. Mech, 'Australia and Canada's climate bromance: competing for the lowest rank on climate action', OurClimate.Ca, at www.ourclimate.ca/australia_and_canada_climate_bromance.
[41] SC 2000, c. 32, s. 8(2).
[42] A. Luttrell, 'Tasmania's draft WHA plan rejected by World Heritage Committee', *Mercury* 2 July 2015, at www.themercury.com.au.

paths to environmental governance that have coalesced under banners such as fossil fuels divestment, CSR, fair trade, slow food, and other socio-ecological causes. With this agitation have come ideas to move beyond the concept of sustainable development or sustainability, and although these remain the philosophical cornerstone of modern environmental law, they occupy an increasingly contested normative space.

One dissenting approach, associated with ecocentric and deep ecology philosophy, is known as 'Earth jurisprudence' or 'wild law'. As Cormac Cullinan explains, 'wild laws . . . regulate humans in a manner that creates the freedom for all the members of the Earth Community to play a role in the continuing co-evolution of the planet',[43] in a manner that respects the 'wildness' of the biosphere. Wild law seeks to maintain or improve the integrity of ecological communities and Earth systems, with no special priority given to human well-being. The Earth Charter and the World Charter for Nature, both of which have been endorsed by many states and international organisations (though often viewed as aspirational 'soft law' instruments), exemplify efforts to codify some of these sentiments.[44] A few national constitutions and some legislation also speak to similar values, such as Bolivia's Law on the Rights of Mother Earth.[45] The ecocentric approach gives other species and ecological elements such as rivers rights to integrity and existence that limit human activity. The potential difficulty in attempting to ordain such a legal regime to guide humankind's place on Earth is that ultimately what is deemed a 'wild' or 'natural' law might just be viewed as what some human institution declares it to be so. The 'rewilding' movement, another a protégé of ecocentric philosophy, evokes similar sentiments, but with the emphasis on ecological restoration.[46] One proponent, Harvard evolutionary biologist Edward O. Wilson, wants 'half the Earth' left wild for other species.[47] Some environmental groups

---

[43] C. Cullinan, *Wild Law: Governing People for Earth* (Siber Ink, 2002), 10; and see P. Burdon (ed), *Exploring Wild Law: The Philosophy of Earth Jurisprudence* (Wakefield Press, 2011).

[44] Earth Charter Initiative, at http://earthcharter.org; World Charter for Nature, 28 October 1982, (1982) 22 ILM 455.

[45] Ley 071 del 21 diciembre 2010 (Bolivia), Asamblea Legislativa Plurinacional, Ley de Derechos de la Madre Tierra; D.R. Boyd, *The Environmental Rights Revolution: A Global Study of Constitutions, Human Rights and the Environment* (University of British Columbia Press, 2012).

[46] D. Foreman, *Rewilding North America: A Vision for Conservation in the 21st Century* (Island Press, 2004); C. Fraser. *Rewilding the World: Despatches from the Conservation Revolution* (Metropolitan Books, 2009).

[47] T. Hiss, 'Can the world really set aside half of the planet for wildlife?', *Smithsonian Magazine* September 2014, at www.smithsonianmag.com.

are voluntarily seeking to reclaim degraded landscapes, such as the massive Gondwana Link project in Western Australia,[48] and such initiatives represent an important extension of environmental governance into multi-stakeholder, community-based approaches. While the foregoing ideas have yet to displace the dominance of sustainable development in the environmental acquis, they already influence some ecological restoration practices.

Alternatively, some clamour for more social justice, a call often made under the banner of 'environmental justice'.[49] It isn't a new idea, but it has become more salient in recent years. In 1982, Murray Bookchin, the American 'eco-anarchist', linked improvements in social justice to better environmental practices, since societies wracked by violence and discrimination are unlikely to care greatly for their environment.[50] Environmental justice issues have since sprung up in numerous contexts: refugees displaced by rising rivers or shifting sands, indigenous peoples fighting for land rights, and the toxic pollution that burdens poor communities disproportionately.[51] Internationally, inequalities between developing and developed countries fester, and stymie many efforts to forge global environmental cooperation,[52] and thus poverty alleviation has become a growing dimension of global environmental law.[53] The ecocentric ethos, while certainly not indifferent to these issues, gives greater priority to nature conservation. Sustainable development also acknowledges social justice, as evident in its cognate principle of intragenerational equity and many ostensible statements of concern, such as the UN Sustainable Development Goals of 2015, but its justice agenda strikes many as timid. Instead, some believe that systemic changes to remake capitalism, such as that expressed by the 'Occupy' protest movement that erupted after the GFC,

---

[48] See www.gondwanalink.org.
[49] R. Sandler and P.C. Pezzullo (eds), *Environmental Justice and Environmentalism: The Social Justice Challenge to the Environmental Movement* (MIT Press, 2007).
[50] M. Bookchin, *The Ecology of Freedom* (Cheshire Books, 1982).
[51] R.D. Bullard, *Dumping in Dixie: Race, Class, and Environmental Quality* (Westview Press, 1990); J.R. Wennersten and D. Robbins, *Rising Tides: Climate Refugees in the Twenty-First Century* (Indiana University Press, 2017); L. Westra, *Environmental Justice and the Rights of Indigenous Peoples* (Earthscan, 2008).
[52] S. Alam, S. Atapattu, C.G. Gonzalez, and J. Razzaque, *International Environmental Law and the Global South* (Cambridge University Press, 2015).
[53] Y. Le Bouthillier, et al. (eds), *Poverty Alleviation and Environmental Law* (Edward Elgar Publishing, 2014).

offer greater hope.[54] In this agenda, structural impediments to a more benign environmental future, such as private enterprise, property rights, global trade, and measurements of societal progress based on economic growth, all face reassessment.[55]

Another important idea, blending ecological and social considerations, is 'resilience thinking'.[56] It promises better recognition of the uncertainty and non-linear changes in ecological conditions and that such thinking can 'reorient current research and policy efforts toward coping with change instead of increasingly futile efforts to maintain existing states of being'.[57] A resilient ecosystem has the capacity to withstand abrupt changes and stay within the same regime, while an environment lacking resilience may, under stress, shift to a different regime, having structural and functional qualities that are less desirable for humankind and other life forms. Resilience also applies to human cultures, which need to have the grit to cope with the Anthropocene and the fortitude to change their laws, economies, and other systems to overcome adversity. Governance for resilience is also closely affiliated with the concept of adaptive management, which focuses on the capacity to experiment, learn, and transform in response to variable ecological and social conditions. These are exceptionally important ideas relevant to the temporal setting of environmental law. As we will explore later in this chapter, they will require far greater nimbleness in the law than is currently available.[58] Grandfathering and relicensing regimes, for instance, limit the scope at present for responding to a changing future, and adaptive approaches clash with the traditions of certainty and predictability in legal governance.

Prospective Governance

Valuing the future underpins the sustainable development philosophy: to 'sustain' literally means to perpetuate a state of affairs or thing indefinitely.

---

[54] M.A. Gould-Wartofsky. *The Occupiers: The Making of the 99 Percent Movement* (Oxford University Press, 2015).

[55] K. Annelee and M. Lievens. *The Limits of the Green Economy: From Re-inventing Capitalism to Re-politicising the Present* (Routledge, 2015); N. Klein, *This Changes Everything: Capitalism vs the Climate* (Simon and Schuster, 2014).

[56] B. Walker and D. Salt, *Resilience Thinking* (Island Press, 2006).

[57] M. Benson and R. Craig, 'The end of sustainability' (2014) 27 *Society and Natural Resources* 777, 780.

[58] A. Garmestani, C.R. Allen, and M.H. Benson, 'Can law foster social-ecological resilience?' (2013) 18(2) *Ecology and Society* 37.

As the aim is to avoid adverse legacies for posterity, sustainable development implies that societal decisions will reflect time frames that dovetail with nature's temporal scales, such as those applicable to ecological succession, the capacity of species to adapt to their surroundings, and the elasticity of the environment to safely assimilate pollutants or other disturbances. Because these time frames often extend beyond the lifetimes of any individual, or involve environmental changes imperceptible to individuals during their lives, the law has a special role to inculcate awareness of the future in economic, social, and political institutions.

Of all the cognate sustainability principles, the notion of intergenerational equity evokes most tangibly the value of the future. Unlike other contexts for the application of equity, intergenerational justice focuses on distributional issues that are temporal rather than based on class, geography, or other spatial contexts. Several international instruments recognise the principle, such as the 1992 Rio Declaration on Environment and Development[59] and the 1992 UN Framework Convention on Climate Change.[60] In the 1997 International Court of Justice (ICJ) case on the Gabcikovo-Nagymaros dam project, Justice Weeramantry in his separate opinion commented that the principle is part of the 'traditional wisdom' of many 'ancient legal systems'.[61] But intergenerational equity has gained only modest recognition in domestic law. Australian legislation acknowledges it in some foundational federal and state laws, although with limited guidance on how it to implement it.[62] Some decisions of the New South Wales Land and Environment Court interpret the principle as requiring 'the assessment of cumulative impacts of proposed activities on the environment',[63] and sustainable resource utilisation and increasing replacement of polluting energy sources with cleaner ones.[64] One famous court judgement purporting to apply intergenerational equity is *Minors Oposa v. Factoran*,[65] a Philippines case that largely turned on constitutional

---

[59] Adopted 14 June 1992, principle 3.
[60] Adopted 4 June 1992, in force 21 March 1994, (1992) 31 ILM 849, article 3(1).
[61] *Gabcikovo-Nagymaros Project* (*Hungary/Slovakia*), Separate Opinion of Vice-President Weeramantry, [1997] ICJ Reports, 88, 103.
[62] E.g. Protection of the Environment Administration Act 1991 (NSW) s. 6(2)(b); National Environment Protection Council Act 1995 (SA) Schedule 1, s 3.5.2; Environment Protection Act 1970 (Vic.), s 1D.
[63] *Gray v. Minister for Planning and Ors*, [2006] NSWLEC 720, para. 122.
[64] *Taralga Landscape Guardians Inc v. Minister for Planning*, [2007] NSWLEC 59.
[65] *Minors Oposa v. Secretary of the Department of Environmental and Natural Resources*, (1993) in (1994) 33 ILM 173.

rights: the court gave the parents standing to represent their children, who were deemed the closest to speak for posterity.

Special challenges arise with stretching governance to the timescales of intergenerational relationships. These include how far into the future should decision-makers look, what value should be assigned to future interests, and how to reconcile competition between present and future interests. In addition, how can we design legal institutions that can effectively articulate solutions to these ethical and policy questions? The legal system has experience with notions of justice and fairness between contemporaries, but lacks proven tools to adjudicate equity between different generations separated by many years.[66] The following comments reflect on the legal precedents and methods rather than the philosophical debates, which have already been covered in great detail in the literature.[67]

A primary legal issue is to delineate the parameters of the 'future' or 'future generations' as objects of prospective governance. These subjects may span into eternity or be limited pragmatically to the most immediate successor generations, such as our children and grandchildren as implied in the Philippines case. How we answer this question may have knock-on effects for managing specific environmental issues. A short time frame could cause risks and threats to the environment to be underestimated because they might not be discernible or have impacts except over longer periods outside the legislated time interval. Conversely, a long time frame may lead to unreliable predictions and wasted resources in trying to protect the environment. Further, open-ended commitments without any quantified time interval, such as an obligation to manage nature for the 'long term' or 'foreseeable future', may give decision-makers too much latitude. Such latitude gives flexibility to adapt to new circumstances, but with the downside that the lack of clarity may impede public confidence and enable unscrupulous decisions.

A variety of approaches to the foregoing choices are evident in environmental legislation and policy. They often contain open-ended exhortation about the importance of long-term considerations or the needs of future generations. The objects of Australia's Environment Protection and Biodiversity Conservation Act 1999 (Cth) are: 'to promote ecologically

---

[66] J. Thompson, *Intergenerational Justice* (Routledge, 2009), 3.
[67] E.g. A. De-Shalit, *Why Posterity Matters: Environmental Policies and Future Generations* (Routledge, 1995); W. Beckerman and J. Pasek, *Justice, Posterity and the Environment* (Oxford University Press, 2003); J. Rawls, *A Theory of Justice* (Harvard University Press, 1971).

sustainable development'[68] and its accompanying list of principles include that: '(a) decision-making processes should effectively integrate both long-term and short-term . . . considerations'.[69] New Zealand's RMA expresses a duty to sustain resources in order 'to meet the reasonably foreseeable needs of future generations',[70] a phrase borrowed from the Brundtland report.[71] The Comprehensive Environmental Response and Compensation Liability Act 1980 (CERCLA), one of the most important US environmental laws, relies on the same open-ended time frames but includes some more specific guidance:

In assessing alternative remedial actions, the President shall, at a minimum, take into account:

(a) the long-term uncertainties associated with land disposal;
. . .
(d) short- and long-term potential for adverse health effects from human exposure;
(e) long-term maintenance costs;
(f) the potential for future remedial action costs if the alternative remedial action in question were to fail.[72]

In contrast, some policies and laws quantify specific time intervals. When writing this book, the most recent environmental policies express an outlook to about 2050, but occasionally longer. This mid-century time frame appears in the European Commission's roadmap to a low-carbon economy;[73] the OECD environmental outlook to 2050,[74] and the World Energy Council's energy policy scenario for the same time frame.[75] Many climate change researchers make predictions and impacts according to longer time frames, often up to 2100, and the IPCC has used models and projections as far as the year 3000 (but most of its projections are much

---

[68] Section 3(1)(b).
[69] Section 3A.
[70] Public Act 1991, No. 69, s. 5(2)(b).
[71] World Commission on Environment and Development (WCED), *Our Common Future* (WCED, 1983), Chapter 2, para. 1.
[72] Public Law No. 96–510, s. 121.
[73] European Commission, 'A roadmap for moving to a competitive low carbon economy in 2050', COM (2011) 0112 final.
[74] Organisation for Economic Cooperation and Development (OECD), *Environmental Outlook to 2050: The Consequences of Inaction* (OECD, 2012).
[75] World Energy Council (WEC), *Composing Energy Futures to 2050* (WEC, 2013).

nearer term).[76] In July 2016 the New Zealand Prime Minister John Key announced a national plan to eradicate by 2050 introduced predatory pests such as rats, possums, and stoats that have decimated the country's dwindling avifauna, with interim milestones set for 2020 and 2025.[77]

The time frames adopted in legislation rarely extend beyond the middle of this century. National park legislation commonly sets periods for the duration of management plans, such as 15 years in the Australian state of Victoria's National Parks Act 1975 (Vic.). The US Endangered Species Act 1973 requires the government to assess extinction risks of species as part of the listing process and to review the status of listed species every 5 years.[78] The time frames used in these decisions may be insufficient to capture extinction risks, as over a short time horizon threats to biodiversity may be underestimated.[79]

England's Climate Change Act 2008 commits to 'contributing to sustainable development' and specifies 2050 as the deadline for the government to ensure that the country's carbon emissions have fallen at least 80 per cent below its 1990 levels.[80] The Australian state of Tasmania also chose 2050 as the time frame in its Climate Change (State Action) Act 2008 (Tas.) for achieving its goal to reduce Tasmania's greenhouse gas emissions by 60 per cent below 1990 levels.[81] In international law, the 1997 Kyoto Protocol[82] and the UN Framework Convention on Climate Change of 1992[83] set nearer-term goals with emission targets for developed nations to be achieved by 2012 and, under the new tranche of commitments under Doha amendments to the Protocol, by 2020. The 2015 Paris Agreement, covering the period beyond 2020, envisions a bottom-up approach as each nation determines its own climate mitigation measures, for updating on a 5-yearly cycle and subject to internationally administered accounting and

---

[76] IPCC Fourth Assessment Report, *Climate Change 2007, Working Group 1: The Physical Science Basis*, 10.7.2, 'Climate change commitment to year 3000 and beyond to equilibrium'.
[77] Department of Conservation, 'Predator free by 2050', at www.doc.govt.nz/our-work/predator-free-new-zealand-2050.
[78] Public Law No. 93–205, s. 4.
[79] J. D'Elia and S. McCarthy, 'Time horizons and extinction risk in endangered species categorization systems' (2010) 60(9) *Bioscience* 751.
[80] 2008 c. 27, ss 1 and 13.
[81] Section 5.
[82] Kyoto Protocol to the United Nations Framework Convention on Climate Change, 11 December 1997, in force 16 February 2005, (1998) 37 ILM 22.
[83] Adopted 4 June 1992, in force 21 March 1994, (1992) 31 ILM 849.

reporting requirements.[84] Through this approach, the Paris Agreement aims to limit global warming to 1.5°C above pre-industrial levels. The 1987 Montreal Protocol on Substances that Deplete the Ozone Layer[85] set phase-out periods for hydrochlorofluorocarbons from 2004 to 2030 (and earlier dates for other chemicals). With such actions, the ozone hole should recover by 2060 from pre-1990 depletion. The feasibility of such time frames is contentious, as the choice of time interval depends on diverse considerations, including scientific knowledge about the nature of the impacted environment, the political feasibility of the timing of preventive action, and the availability of behaviourally effective legal instruments to influence the activities of individuals, corporations, and other entities.

Legislating time frames for action can elevate social awareness about the need to tackle environmental problems, although without necessarily improving legal accountability. For relatively distant targets, such as 2050, it would be difficult to hold any present decision-maker legally responsible because the achievement of a target depends on the effect of the aggregation of numerous actions over many years. Accountability is even more elusive with open-ended commitments to act for the long term or to safeguard the interests of posterity. In these contexts, collateral measures could be introduced as proxies for measuring progress to distant goals, such as completion of interim performance milestones and implementation of specific environmental actions on which to hinge accountability.

An alternative approach rests on fiduciary and trusts law precedents that do not rely on delineating future time frames. Edith Brown Weiss, a leading advocate here, explains that the goal should be 'every generation needs to pass the Earth and our natural and cultural resources on in at least as good condition as we received them'.[86] She proposes a 'planetary trust' to institutionalise this fiduciary responsibility, with specific obligations to: conserve the diversity of the natural resource base; ensure environmental quality is maintained; and provide equitable access across generations to Earth's resources and life-sustaining properties. Her approach thus eschews the debate about determining what future generations would

---

[84] Conference of the Parties, United Nations Framework Convention on Climate Change, *Adoption of the Paris Agreement*, 21st sess, UN Doc. FCCC/CP/2015/L.9 (12 December 2015), Annex.
[85] Adopted 16 September 1987, in force 1 January 1989, (1987) 26 ILM 1550.
[86] E. Brown Weiss, *In Fairness to Future Generations* (Transnational Publishers, 1989).

want or need, as the ethical responsibility instead becomes to ensure that options are conserved for future generations to determine for themselves how to fulfil their needs. Brown Weiss' ideas have influenced the 2016 climate change lawsuit initiated by 'Our Children's Trust' against the US federal government. The lawsuit, brought in the name of 21 young Americans, aged 8–19 years at the time, 'asserts that, in causing climate change, the federal government has violated the youngest generation's constitutional rights to life, liberty and property, as we as failed to protect essential public trust resources'.[87]

But because many environments are already degraded, Brown Weiss' prospective approach may overlook the importance of intergenerational responsibilities to restore former losses. Another reason to acknowledge ecological restoration better is that, with population growth, one generation cannot leave the same per capita amount of resources for the next, larger generation (world population increased from about 1 billion in 1820 to 7 billion on 2011, adding about 800 million per decade since the late twentieth century).[88] To increase natural capital requires restoring soil fertility, improving water quality, expanding wildlife habitat, and so on – issues that we will consider in the next chapter. Some existing formulations of the public trust are capable of including restoration as a dimension of a trustee's responsibilities. For example, the Louisiana Supreme Court upheld on this basis a state reclamation project, opposed by oyster farmers, that flooded their oyster beds; the project aimed to recover the coastline and enhance local fisheries.[89] University of Oregon scholar Mary Wood, a leading authority on this subject, has argued that trust law includes an active duty of 'vigilance' to prevent 'permissive waste' or 'decay' to the asset.[90]

Another technique widely used in prospective environmental law is economic analysis, which unlike the foregoing proposals and precedents, uses a monetary framework to compare gains and losses and resolve any trade-offs between the present and the future. But this methodology has many detractors, as the following section explains.

---

[87] 'Federal climate change lawsuit', Our Children's Trust, at http://ourchildrenstrust.org/us/federal-lawsuit.
[88] J. Peron, 'The mirage of sustainability' (2002) 1(34) *Laissez Faire Electronic Times* 7.
[89] *Avenal v. State*, 886 So. 2d 1085 (La. 2004).
[90] M.C. Wood, *Nature's Trust: Environmental Law for a New Ecological Age* (Cambridge University Press, 2014), 168.

Cost-Benefit Analysis and Intergenerational Trade-Offs

Decision-makers, from government regulators to corporate managers, rely heavily on economic calculations to evaluate choices with intergenerational dimensions. Human ingenuity has invented a way to put a monetary value on the future stream of estimated costs and benefits of an action or decision, a method known as CBA. It aims to systematically calculate and compare the benefits and costs of a project, decision, or other action in terms of economic outcomes such as income and jobs, social effects, environmental impacts such as pollution, and other variables. The benefits of economic growth and its environmental costs are, in theory, rendered comparable so that new developments, regulations, and other actions occur only where the benefits exceed the costs. The ultimate validation of CBA, say its proponents, is the promotion of economic efficiency and maximisation of societal welfare.[91]

Many jurisdictions mandate CBA, not only in environmental regulation, but also a variety of other policy contexts such as public health and education. In the 1920s the US Army Corps began evaluating decisions in terms of their benefits and costs.[92] The CBA method became more formulaic from the late 1930s, when economists Nicholas Kaldor and John Hicks argued that a 'public policy was justified if it produced social gains in excess of social losses so that it was possible for winners from the policy to compensate losers – even if such compensation did not actually occur'.[93] Today, governments often prescribe when and how to apply CBA. Whenever the US EPA proposes a major regulation, it must conduct a CBA for review by the Office of Management and Budget. A Presidential Executive Order issued by Bill Clinton in 1993 commands all federal agencies that propose or adopt regulations, including environmental regulations, to demonstrate that the benefits justify the costs.[94] The Australian government also uses CBA in a variety of contexts, including for major new regulatory proposals.[95] Likewise, the New Zealand

---

[91] D. Fuguitt and S.J. Wilcox, *Cost-benefit Analysis for Public Sector Decision Makers* (Quorom Books, 1999); M.D. Adler and E.A. Posner, *New Foundations of Cost-Benefit Analysis* (Harvard University Press, 2006).
[92] J. Persky, 'Retrospectives: cost-benefit analysis and the classical creed' (2001) 15(4) *Journal of Economic Perspectives* 199.
[93] Ibid, 202.
[94] Executive Order 12.866 – Regulatory Planning and Review, 4 October 1993, 58 Federal Register 51,735. The order applies unless a particular statute requires otherwise.
[95] Office of Best Practice Regulation, *Cost Benefit Analysis* (Department of Prime Minister and Cabinet, 2016).

government's Regulatory Impact Analysis Handbook directs CBA for such purposes because of the benefits of 'enhancing the evidence-base to inform decisions' and the additional 'transparency'.[96] The European Commission has issued guidelines that recommend CBA for proposed EU policies and legislation, with the aim to improve transparency, effectiveness, and coordination of decision-making.[97] Japan uses CBA in preparing new environmental regulations and for assessing major infrastructure projects initiated by government.[98]

The execution of CBA requires putting all costs and benefits into a common metric to enable objective comparisons. When all goods and services are traded in a market, the price system will automatically enable the comparison of costs and benefits. But where the market suffers from gaps or weaknesses the price system will not convey all the relevant information. Such market failures often arise with environmental goods and services, such as the value of biodiversity or clean air, which are not traded in the market like motor vehicles or houses. In this situation, a CBA analyst must find equivalent monetary values that reflect what individuals would potentially pay to avoid a cost or obtain a benefit. These methods include travel cost, choice modelling, and contingent valuation, which aim to determine the price that surveyed individuals would willingly pay for a given environmental outcome.[99] While the methods thereby purport to enable comparison of like for like, they have methodological challenges such as which individuals are surveyed, how the questions are framed, and whether public opinion can truly reflect what individuals would actually pay in the market. Value judgements in making such comparisons are clearly ever-present, and the distribution of benefits and costs can affect different groups or individuals unevenly.[100] For example, President George W. Bush's 'Clear Skies' legislative package, designed to avoid tougher restrictions on electricity power generators, was supported by a CBA commissioned by his administration that was manipulated to prefer the Bush proposal

---

[96] Treasury, *Regulatory Impact Analysis Handbook* (New Zealand Government, 2013), 4.
[97] European Commission, *Impact Assessment Guidelines* (SEC, 2009).
[98] T.H. Arimura and K. Iwata, *An Evaluation of Japanese Environmental Regulations* (Springer, 2015), 12.
[99] For these and other methods, see J. Bennett (ed), *The International Handbook on Non-Market Environmental Valuation* (Edward Elgar Publishing, 2011).
[100] D.A. Farber and P.A. Hemmersbaugh, 'The shadow of the future: discount rates, later generations, and the environment' (1993) 46 *Vanderbilt Law Review* 267, 280–1; D. Driesen, 'Is cost-benefit analysis neutral?' (2006) 77 *University of Colorado Law Review* 335.

over rival options that would have led to less pollution.[101] In other words, the conduct of CBA is not necessarily a neutral mechanism for environmental decisions.

Because time affects the value of money, these methodological challenges intensify when the costs and benefits are not contemporaneous. This difficulty arises with intergenerational environmental costs and benefits, which may span vast stretches of time. In these circumstances a 'discount rate' is introduced to the CBA to remove temporal distortions. The discount rate essentially measures the value of the forgone benefits had the expenditure costs been allocated elsewhere (i.e. the opportunity cost) at an interest rate that compounds over time. To describe its function more simply, in comparing the size of two objects placed at different distances from the viewer, discount rates serve to standardise the 'distance' (in time) so that they can be objectively compared.

The selection of the discount rate is highly contentious, as it can dramatically skew the relative costs and benefits.[102] Within a single generation, many economists would discount the value of additional welfare benefits at the prevailing market rate of return on financial instruments. For multigenerational effects, most CBA practitioners favour a positive discount rate to all costs and benefits.[103] A survey of over 2160 economists in 2001 found that 4 per cent was the average discount rate they would choose for valuing the current costs of long-term environmental problems.[104] Since the costs of environmental protection measures tend to accrue initially, such as loss of economically beneficial new development, compared to the delayed benefits of maintenance or enhancement of ecological services, high discount rates tend to be applied in CBA. Often, governments try to standardise the discount rate for CBAs; for instance, the state of New South Wales in Australia prescribes a rate of 7 per cent,[105] while the Canadian government has recommended 8 per cent.[106]

---

[101] D.H. Cole, '"Best practice" standards for regulatory benefit–cost analysis' (2007) 23 *Research in Law and Economics* 1, 16–18.
[102] G. Heal, 'Discounting: a review of the basic economics' (2007) 74 *University of Chicago Law Review* 59, 68–9.
[103] P. Portney and J. Weyant, 'Introduction' in P. Portney and J. Weyant (eds), *Discounting and Intergenerational Equity* (Resources for the Future 1999), 6–7.
[104] Reported in M.L. Weitzman, 'Gamma discounting' (2001) 91 *American Economic Review* 260, 268.
[105] New South Wales (NSW) Treasury, *NSW Government Guidelines for Economic Appraisal* (NSW Government, 2007), 18.
[106] Treasury Board of Canada Secretariat, *Canadian Cost-Benefit Analysis Guide: Regulatory Proposals* (Government of Canada, 2007), 37.

Defenders of discount rates, as in these examples, give a variety of reasons.[107] The principal one is the opportunity cost. If money to obtain particular benefits is spent today, we will have forgone the opportunity to invest that money and have it accrue in value, and then have greater wealth in the future with which to buy benefits. To determine the opportunity cost requires comparing the available rate of return on alternative investments. Subsidiary rationales for positive discount rates include that future generations cannot exist without the survival of the present, so its immediate sustenance is crucial to continuation of our species. Furthermore, the current generation bequeaths its knowhow and wealth to the succeeding generation at some cost to itself. A further factor is based on the empirical evidence of individuals' 'positive time preference', meaning that we prefer to receive benefits now rather than enjoy the same benefits in the future (primarily because of the risk that such benefits could disappear later).

The impact of discounting the future amplifies the further one moves into the future. Because the effect of the discount rate compounds over time exponentially, even large initial valuations of the benefits of environmental protection can be rendered trivial when dispersed over many years. For instance, at a 5 per cent discount rate per year, the value of any future cost or benefit is reduced by a factor of 131 in 100 years and by about 39 billion in 500 years.[108] Or in an example from Derek Parfit and Tyler Cowen, a discount rate of 10 per cent would calculate one life today as equivalent to 1 million lives in 145 years.[109] By the same discounting procedure, the apparent significance of policy effects on future generations is dramatically diminished in the context of ecological problems such as global warming, deforestation, and fisheries depletion.

Thus many critics disagree with such steep discounting, for ethical and economic reasons. Ethically, it violates the interests of future generations, whose welfare is acknowledged in the principle of intergenerational equity.[110] Discounting over such time frames is also ethically problematic for non-human life, whose value is reduced within metrics that serve

---

[107] See W.K. Viscusi, 'Rational discounting for regulatory analysis' (2007) 74 *University of Chicago Law Review* 209; S.L. Hsu and J. Loomis, 'A defense of cost-benefit analysis for natural resource policy' (2002) 32 *Environmental Law Reporter* 10239.

[108] T. Cowan, 'Caring about the distant future: why it matters and what it means' (2007) 74 *University of Chicago Law Review* 5, 8.

[109] D. Parfit and T. Cowen, 'Against the social discount rate' in P. Laslett and J.S. Fishkin (eds), *Justice Between Age Groups and Generations* (Yale University Press, 1992), 144–5.

[110] Portney and Weyant, 'Introduction'.

human ends.[111] Furthermore, the CBA methodology presumes by its very nature that the timing and magnitude of physical and economic effects of various environmental scenarios is predictable. Yet uncertainty pervades (we might even say defines) environmental problems. Such uncertainty explains why governments commonly recommend that CBA calculations apply to a defined time period; the New South Wales Government's CBA guidelines explain that because of 'the difficulty of forecasting costs and benefits over such long periods, caution should be exercised in adopting a project period, longer than 20 years. Certainly the project period should not exceed 30 years'.[112] Obviously, such truncated time intervals can impair valuation of long-term environmental benefits.

Specific economic arguments have also been marshalled against steep discounting – arguments that relate to valuation of the essential functions and services of natural capital. For example, application of high positive rates in CBA might discourage pollution abatement despite the substantial long-term advantages of acting now, or encourage more intensive exploitation of natural resources.[113] These concerns factored into the methodologies of the highly publicised *Stern Review on the Economics of Climate Change*.[114] In calculating the possible economic damages of future climate change, the Stern Review avoided a single discount rate in favour of a stochastic approach whereby the discount rate varied with the expected climate change and economic growth scenarios. The Stern Review applied an average discount rate of about 1.4 per cent, a number below that used in most economic studies on global warming damage. Unsurprisingly, the discounting methodology and the various assumptions made by Stern incurred much criticism from economists.[115] The heart of the controversy is that *if* we can agree to reduce carbon emissions now, future generations will reap the benefit while those alive today will bear the cost. By using a low discount rate, Stern essentially urged the present generation to make

---

[111] D.A. Kysar, 'Discounting... on stilts' (2007) 74 *University of Chicago Law Review* 118.
[112] NSW Treasury, *NSW Government Guidelines for Economic Appraisal*, 39.
[113] See A.W. Ando, 'Waiting to be protected under the Endangered Species Act: the political economy of regulatory delay' (1999) 42(1) *Journal of Law and Economics* 29; J.P. Dwyer, R.R.W. Brooks, and A.C. Marco, *The Political and Legal Causes of Regulatory Delay in the United States: Four Case Studies of Air Pollution Permitting in the U.S. and Germany* (University of California at Berkeley Public Law and Legal Theory Working Paper No. 99-2, 1999).
[114] N. Stern, *Stern Review on the Economics of Climate Change* (HM Treasury, 2006).
[115] E.g. W.D. Nordhaus, 'A review of the Stern review on the economics of climate' (2007) 45(3) *Journal of Economic Literature* 686.

sacrifices for the sake of posterity, like the Iroquois' seventh-generation principle identified on the opening of this book.

As humankind's cumulative ecological burden overwhelms the planet, CBA becomes unworkable for evaluating environmental impacts on a case-by-case basis such as that associated with proposed infrastructure or a new regulation.[116] In a sparsely populated or relatively undeveloped world, each incremental impact might have caused tolerable disturbance, as in the case of small increments of carbon emissions. But in the Anthropocene, such additions cumulatively lead to irreparable devastation that is immeasurable in total and incalculable on the basis of each incremental harm-causing project or activity. As Joseph Guth explains, 'an increment of environmental damage that seems affordable in an empty world cannot be projected at that value (or at a discounted lesser value) into a distant future where the total cost of the cumulative increments of damage will have become infinite'.[117] Furthermore, for long-term environmental effects that span multiple generations, it may be impossible to quantify time-dispersed costs and benefits and provide for their redistribution because of uncertainty about the magnitude of future injury and the difficulty of accumulating wealth over long periods to compensate for it. Consequently, no rate of discounting will likely be able to properly measure the basket of costs and benefits of individual actions when the entire system teeters towards collapse.

Such considerations draw attention to how CBA sits with the precautionary principle, one of modern environmental law's supposed foundational norms. Reliance on CBA does not sit easily with the principle because it generally calls for tougher defensive measures against risky activities, despite uncertainty, and it shifts the burden of proof so that instead of government needing to justify new regulation the proponents of risky products or activities must defend their safety. But some seasoned scholars, such as US law professor David Driesen, believe we can reconcile CBA and precaution as it 'all depends on how analysts and policymakers approach the myriad assumptions needed to carry out a CBA'.[118] Driesen goes on to recommend methodological and institutional changes to resolve the tension between precaution and CBA, essentially by incorporating

---

[116] S.A. Shapiro and C.H. Schroeder, 'Beyond cost-benefit analysis: a pragmatic reorientation' (2008) 32 *Harvard Environmental Law Review* 433.

[117] J. Guth, 'Resolving the paradoxes of discounting in environmental decisions' (2009) 18 *Transnational Law and Contemporary Problems* 95, 112.

[118] D.M. Driesen. 'Cost-benefit analysis and the precautionary principle: can they be reconciled?' (2013) 3 *Michigan State Law Review*, 771–3.

more stringent levels of risk aversion in CBA studies. Alternatively, some propose identifying the most essential components of ecological integrity (e.g. a stable climate and protection of biodiversity) whose lost would be 'catastrophic' or 'irreversible', and then investing in their protection via a precautionary approach without discount rates.[119]

Still, acceptance of the ethical and economic arguments to value the future more highly does not provide any specific guidance on how to compare the costs and benefits of particular projects or policies that can contribute to future well-being. As Weisbach and Sunstein explain, 'if we are going to increase the amount we leave for the future, it is incumbent on us not to do so in a way that wastes resources. Therefore, even if the ethicists' argument is entirely correct, we still must carefully consider the opportunity costs of projects and pick those with the highest return'.[120] Hence, once society reaches an ethical determination on how much to leave future generations, it must still ascertain how to most efficiently invest that allocation to ensure that it will yield the greatest benefit. Such investments in the future could include ecological restoration programs that rebuild natural capital and socially responsible investment (SRI) to stimulate environmentally innovative development. Other defences of CBA include that it can reduce political favouritism and regulatory capture by obliging regulators to document costs and benefits and articulate a reasoned choice,[121] and it can demonstrate the social importance of nature conservation in a monetary value that lay people will likely understand.[122] Both counter arguments, however, only bring comfort if the underlying CBA analysis is rigorous: if the numbers are skewed to economic gains over environmental losses, environmentally unacceptable outcomes may ensue.

In sum, while we may sanguinely agree that environmental regulation should protect natural capital over the long term, considerable wrangling over rival ethical and economic criteria dogs any commitments, and decision-making in practice can suffer from short-term expediency.

---

[119] See further D. Kysar, *Regulating from Nowhere: Environmental Law and the Search for Objectivity* (Yale University Press, 2011), passim; F. Ackerman and L. Heinzerling, *Priceless – On Knowing the Price of Everything and the Value of Nothing* (The New Press, 2004), 185–6.

[120] D. Weisbach and C. Sunstein, *Climate Change and Discounting the Future: A Guide for the Perplexed* (University of Harvard Public Law Working Paper No. 08-20, 2008).

[121] R.L. Revesz and M.A. Livermore. *Retaking Rationality: How Cost-benefit Analysis Can Better Protect the Environment and Our Health* (Oxford University Press, 2008), passim.

[122] I. Brauer, 'Money as an indicator: to make use of economic evaluation for biodiversity conservation' (2003) 98 *Agriculture, Ecosystems and Environment* 483–4.

Unsurprisingly, the aspirations of sustainability dogma remain unfulfilled and on most ecological trajectories the prognosis is worsening, not improving. The barrier to prospective governance, however, is not simply disagreement over the valuation of posterity's interests; a further dilemma is temporal inertia in decision-making systems that lack responsiveness to future *change*.

Governing Change

Managing Change

Because acting for the long term confronts great uncertainty and risks in a future that can only be predicted rather than known, environmental governance must have the flexibility to adapt. It may need to adapt to correct for wrong predictions, or to respond to exigencies or changing circumstances, such as new scientific knowledge, shifting economic fortunes, or different community expectations, among many reasons. The temporal challenge, in other words, is not just to value the future but also to respond and manage a *changing* future. Society can manage change through policies, regulations, and other tools that can be modernised, customised, or repealed as appropriate, while ensuring that environmental decision-making does not become arbitrary and unaccountable. Development licences, for instance, might be modified through relicensing procedures; and partnerships with the corporate sector might be updated through re-negotiated agreements. Crucially, governance must be able to *anticipate* new threats and emerging issues, such as climate change or risks to biodiversity, by introducing measures to curb threatening processes. The capacity to anticipate, of course, depends on robust scientific monitoring of environmental conditions to track trends and shifts, and feedback mechanisms that enable new knowledge to inform regulations. Anticipation also requires democratic decision-making, in which societal concerns can be articulated and taken into account in a timely manner. Besides parliamentary elections, these democratic elements include access to justice to challenge decisions in courts, and rights to participate in executive decision-making such as EIAs and pollution licensing. Without these processes, governance will lack means of knowing about changing ecological and social circumstances.

The title of this section is 'managing change' rather than 'responding to change' because the latter might misleadingly imply that governance must simply 'respond' to changes that are seemingly inexorable and unalterable. 'Managing change' means not only the capacity to adapt to new circumstances, but also the capacity to influence change itself. Societies wish to shape their destiny: to try to influence the future rather than just react to it. Ecological restoration, as examined in Chapter 4, is one way in which society can manage change by repairing past damage to strengthen ecological and social resilience. Slowing down, as through eco-friendly farming (Slow Food) and community investing (Slow Money) are other ways, as explored in Chapter 5, in which societies can manage change. Governing a changing future thus means actively shaping our future, rather than waiting for circumstances to shape ourselves. This toing and froing brings to the fore the relationship between law and society, as discussed in the previous chapter. A longstanding debate among legal philosophers and historians is whether the legal system only reacts to changes in social values or whether the law can and should engineer social change.[123] In fact, the law does both. Women's rights, gay marriage, and animal liberation are among seminal shifts in many countries in the modern era in which the law has been pushed or pulled by social agitation. The law can facilitate new social practices, but concurrently it can sometimes overreach itself and suffer loss of respect and efficacy.

Making environmental law lithe and responsive is a daunting challenge because of the economic and social costs of 'redoing' regulatory decisions, as well as the risks to legality itself if regulatory changes occur without due process. While adaptive management has been applauded for enhancing flexibility to manage uncertain and shifting ecological conditions,[124] it risks vesting power in scientific managers whose judgements may be beyond effective legal scrutiny and control.[125] Not only is scientific expertise value-laden, environmental management decisions can involve social and economic trade-offs that require community scrutiny. Thus, the virtue of greater flexibility may carry the vice of greater arbitrariness. But this tension can lessen if the rules for changing the rules (i.e. the law governing adaptation) can be set in advance. In practice, regulation has tended to insulate companies from change by 'grandfathering' their existing

---

[123] E.g. S.L. Roach Anleu, *Law and Social Change* (SAGE, 2010); G.N. Rosenberg, *The Hollow Hope: Can Courts Bring About Social Change?* (University of Chicago Press, 2008); G. de Burca, C. Kilpatrick, and J. Scott (eds), *Critical Legal Perspectives on Global Governance* (Hart Publishing, 2014).

[124] B.J. Ruhl, 'The Pardy–Ruhl dialogue on ecosystem management, Part IV: narrowing and sharpening the questions' (2007) 24 *Pace Environmental Law Review* 25.

[125] B. Pardy, 'The Pardy–Ruhl dialogue on ecosystem management, Part V: discretion, complex-adaptive problem solving and the rule of law' (2008) 25 *Pace Environmental Law Review* 341.

practices or by restricting the ambit of any relicensing to narrow technical and operational details. Thus, many reforms to environmental law in recent decades have left existing resource users relatively unscathed, or have even benefited them through deregulation programs.[126]

Managing change faces different challenges in international environmental law. Negotiating new treaties is fraught with political hurdles, but working within existing treaties is often easier because they tend to be formulated with loose and discretionary language that gives state parties considerable room to manoeuvre. Phrases such as 'as far as practicable and as appropriate' or 'subject to its national legislation', as used in the Convention on Biological Diversity for instance, give governments leeway to customise international obligations to their national circumstances.[127] Some treaties also explicitly give states the discretion to determine their own environmental goals, as the Paris Agreement does with its 'nationally determined contributions' for reducing carbon emissions.[128] States may also have the right to make reservations or withdraw from a treaty altogether, and some may even choose to violate treaties with near impunity given their weak enforcement machinery.

Beyond the state, governance may also change through private sector initiatives. The movements for corporate and investor social responsibility, as epitomised by the fossil fuels divestment and fair trade movements, seek better environmental performance through governance processes that harness the resources and discipline of the market and civil society. Reliance on non-state actors has risks and limitations, however, including accountability deficits and conflicts of interest. Later in this chapter we examine the scope for change through the private sector, and subsequent chapters also consider specific case studies of private sector initiative.

Much literature has already explored how to render governance more flexible and responsive. One cluster of ideas relates to multi-scalar, polycentric regulation in which environmental action occurs at different levels and in diverse fora. This approach has been advocated for dealing with climate change, in which local governments and cities, coupled with the private sector, take more initiative in mitigating greenhouse gases,

---

[126] U. Collier (ed), *Deregulation in the European Union: Environmental Perspectives* (Routledge, 1998); N. Heynen, et al. (eds), *Neoliberal Environments: False Promises and Unnatural Consequences* (Routledge, 2007).

[127] Adopted 5 June 1992, in force 29 December 1993, (1992) 31 ILM 818, article 8.

[128] Conference of the Parties, United Nations Framework Convention on Climate Change, *Adoption of the Paris Agreement*, 21st sess, UN Doc. FCCC/CP/2015/L.9 (12 December 2015), Annex.

developing clean energy solutions, and strengthening local adaptation to climate change.[129] 'Polycentric' governance was championed by Nobel Laureate Elinor Ostrom because of her belief that governments are not always more effective than users in managing natural resources.[130] In arguing against 'one size fits all' environmental policies, Ostrom showed that non-state actors could be a valuable resource through their expertise, entrepreneurism, and capacity to discipline compliance. Though her focus was often community resource managers, other actors, such as the business sector, may also drive innovation and experimentation. Ostrom's polycentric model has much in common with legal pluralism scholarship that examines the multiple legal communities that sometimes operate in shared spaces.[131] Other related research on multi-scalar or multi-level governance has explored the value of tiered levels of government and NGO participation in decision-making and the appropriate scale for managing environmental challenges (which vary according to the issue or threat).[132] Such inclusive and participatory approaches to environmental governance also have potential drawbacks relating to their piecemeal character, the potential lack of coordination, and risk of conflicting actions. Researchers see these risks with climate change governance if left to disparate, bottom-up initiatives.[133]

Another relevant stream of research deals with 'adaptive management'. The phrase was coined in the 1970s by Canadian ecologist Crawford Holling,[134] although the concept's antecedents have been traced several decades earlier to the ruminations of Aldo Leopold.[135] Adaptive management is an iterative, learning process of decision-making that responds

---

[129] B.J. Richardson (ed), *Local Climate Change Law: Environmental Regulation in Cities and Other Localities* (Edward Elgar Publishing, 2012); J. Peel, L. Godden, and R.J. Keenan, 'Climate change law in an era of multi-level governance' (2012) 1(2) *Transnational Environmental Law* 245.

[130] E. Ostrom, 'Beyond markets and states: polycentric governance of complex economic systems' (2010) 100 *American Economic Review* 1.

[131] See P.S. Berman, 'Global legal pluralism' (2007) 80 *Southern California Law Review* 1155; R. Michaels, 'The re-statement of non-state law: the state, choice of law, and the challenge from global legal pluralism' (2005) 51 *Wayne Law Review* 1209.

[132] I. Weibust and J. Meadowcroft, *Multilevel Environmental Governance: Managing Water and Climate Change in Europe and North America* (Edward Elgar Publishing, 2014); G. Winter (ed), *Multilevel Governance of Global Environmental Change: Perspectives from Science, Sociology and Law* (Cambridge University Press, 2006).

[133] Peel, Godden, and Keenan, 'Climate change law in an era of multi-level governance'.

[134] C.S. Holling, *Adaptive Environmental Assessment and Management* (John Wiley and Sons, 1978).

[135] B.G. Norton, 'The rebirth of environmentalism as pragmatic, adaptive management' (2005–6) 24 *Virginia Environmental Law Journal* 353, 356.

to environmental uncertainty through reversible management actions that are periodically adjusted as new knowledge emerges about ecological systems.[136] Focusing on specific localities or contexts, such as a river system or fisheries, an initial project design and management plan is continually monitored to test hypotheses in order to learn and make adjustments. The result should be that uncertainty about the behaviour of the environmental system reduces more quickly than would otherwise occur. For instance, a fisheries manager might deliberately set harvest levels above or below the best estimates of the available stock in order to understand more quickly the optimal yield curve for the fishery. This pragmatic commitment to experimentation rather than fidelity to rigid dogma is the hallmark of the adaptive approach.[137] It has been advocated by scholars of environmental law in response to static, homogenised resource management models that led to disastrous results, such as the collapse of the Newfoundland cod fishery in the early 1990s and ill-conceived attempts to farm the Everglades.[138] The adaptive approach is not always appropriate for some ecological issues and changes. Waiting for several decades to learn whether a strategy is effective might be too long. Mitigating climate change, which must happen urgently, would not be appropriate for adaptive strategies in which managers experiment with different emission control strategies and wait several decades to ascertain which works best.

Instead, we need a precautionary approach to prevent serious and irreparable harms, such as from global warming. Similarly, the 1984 discovery of the hole in the ozone layer necessitated a speedy response to phase out the offending chemicals, which was tackled robustly with the 1987 Montreal Protocol.[139] It might be said that in both such examples there was sufficient certainty about the nature of the threat to justify a pre-emptive strike. Like adaptive management, the precautionary principle addresses decision-making in uncertain and risky conditions.

---

[136] The literature is vast; see e.g. B.G. Norton, *Sustainability: A Philosophy of Adaptive Ecosystem Management* (University of Chicago Press, 2005); M. Conroy and J. Paterson, *Decision Making in Natural Resource Management: A Structured, Adaptive Approach* (Wiley-Blackwell, 2013); C. Allen and A. Garmestani (eds), *Adaptive Management of Social-Ecological Systems* (Springer, 2015).

[137] A. Light and E. Katz, 'Introduction: environmental pragmatism and environmental ethics as contested terrain' in A. Light and E. Katz (eds) *Environmental Pragmatism* (Routledge, 1996), 1.

[138] W.T. Coleman, 'Legal barriers to the restoration of aquatic systems and the utilization of adaptive management' (1998) 23(1) *Vermont Law Review* 177.

[139] Montreal Protocol on Substances that Deplete the Ozone Layer, 16 September 1987, in force 1 January 1989, (1987) 26 ILM 1550.

But unlike adaptive responses, the precautionary stance seeks not further experimentation but quick defensive responses because of the risk of dangerous, irreparable consequences. As noted earlier in this chapter, the precautionary principle is ostensibly well entrenched in some areas of international and domestic environmental law, although its implementation remains patchy and governments often prefer to use CBA for guiding decisions with intergenerational trade-offs.[140] The precautionary principle is already the subject of a vast literature that does not need further analysis here.

While the precautionary principle can clash with adaptive management where the latter assumes unforeseen problems can be adequately addressed *ex-post facto* through experimentation, both approaches can coincide where they contribute to a related goal of improving the resilience of social and ecological systems to cope with adverse change, such as climate change. Holling himself advocated more 'resilience', which he described as the ability of an ecological system to absorb disturbances, such as fire, storms or anthropogenic impacts while retaining its basic structure and functioning.[141] Disturbance is not *per se* a bad thing, as many species, such as some plants, depend on periodic disturbances like fire to flourish.[142] The resistance of ecosystems to disturbance and their speed of recovery from disruption are the kernel of resilience. Resilience can be applied to other systems, such as social and economic systems, and ecological change has ramifications for the resilience of such systems. Whereas adaptive management can improve resilience by experimenting and learning from different interventions, such as in regard to managing the effects of droughts or climbing sea levels, the precautionary principle addresses resilience via investment in defensive measures without waiting for possible harm to materialise.

The failure to respond appropriately to future change can cause societal decay or even collapse. Archaeologists have long encountered evidence of human civilisations engulfed by natural disaster. Many disasters are so-called acts of god, such as hurricanes and earthquakes, but the behaviour of societies through their economic systems and methods of governance may equally affect their capacity to cope and recover from

---

[140] J. Peel, *The Precautionary Principle in Practice: Environmental Decision-making and Scientific Uncertainty* (Federation Press, 2005).

[141] C.S. Holling, 'Resilience and stability of ecological systems' (1973) 4 *Annual Review of Ecology and Systematics* 1.

[142] L. Pringle, *Natural Fire: Its Ecology in Forests* (William Morrow and Company, 1979), 22–4.

environmental adversity. Jago Cooper and Payson Sheets, in *Surviving Sudden Environmental Change*, document case studies of human communities in different ecological contexts that survived natural adversity.[143] Jared Diamond's *Collapse* tells the story of those who were less successful.[144] Contemporary societies face more ominous adversity. According to the Millennium Ecosystem Assessment reporting in 2005, 'over the past 50 years, humans have changed these ecosystems more rapidly and extensively than in any comparable period of time in human history', and going forward 'changes being made in ecosystems are increasing the likelihood of nonlinear changes in ecosystems (including accelerating, abrupt, and potentially irreversible changes)'.[145]

While modern societies might seem much better placed than their predecessors to manage adversity, because of their scientific knowhow and resources, their solutions may be institutionally unsustainable. This is due to the costs that accompany ever-increasing social complexity. Historian Joseph Tainter's seminal theory of societal collapse, based on historic examples such as the Roman Empire, essentially posits that human societies become more socially complex as they solve the economic, ecological, and other problems they confront, and though this complexity initially yields a net benefit to society, eventually the benefits obtained from increasing complexity diminish while their relative costs enlarge.[146] Societies respond first with measures that are the simplest and yield the biggest return, resorting only later to more complex and expensive solutions. Thus, confronted with mounting environmental stresses, regulators tend to prescribe more detailed rules, seek new technologies, and commit greater financial resources. Initially, such investments can yield a good payoff; for example, in its early years during the 1950s and 1970s, environmental law delivered some tangible benefits, such as ridding cities of smog. Yet, argues Tainter, at the point when a society must conscript all its resources and knowhow just to keep on top of its problems, the society will no longer advance further and will instead begin to decline and may eventually collapse. With environmental problems, Tainter saw this dynamic evident in the investment in more complex ways

---

[143] J. Cooper and P. Sheets (eds), *Surviving Sudden Environmental Change: Answers from Archaeology* (University Press of Colorado, 2012).
[144] J. Diamond, *Collapse: How Societies Choose to Fail or Succeed* (Viking Press, 2005).
[145] Millennium Ecosystem Assessment, *Ecosystems and Human Well-being: Synthesis* (Island Press, 2005), 1 and 11.
[146] J. Tainter, *The Collapse of Complex Societies* (Cambridge University Press, 1988).

of achieving sustainability that demand ever-higher governance resources that eventually exceed the capacity of human society to provide.[147] Climate change, marine plastic pollution, and habitat degradation are among these overbearing governance problems. Societal collapse is not inevitable, but it is a risk if environmental governance cannot keep ahead of the problems it faces.

The dominant response of most societies to these environmental problems has not been to commit ever-greater resources to their resolution but to avoid serious action. Several reasons explain this reticence. One problem is the temporal mismatching between when the costs and benefits of action occur. Addressing many anthropogenic environmental impacts involves costs that the present generation prefers to defer for posterity to resolve. Conversely, exploitation of environmental riches may yield only short-term benefits before the resource is exhausted. Depletion of groundwater reservoirs or use of superphosphates, for instance, provides short-term benefits to farmers, but at long-term cost to agricultural lands. Another barrier to responsive governance is uncertainty about the ecological changes it must respond to. While ecological changes often occur gradually, sometimes they can erupt abruptly without foresight. Non-linear changes have this character, in which an ecosystem may change incrementally until a growing pressure on it crosses a critical threshold, whereupon changes ensue rapidly as the system shifts to a novel state. Examples abound, such as the eruption of algal blooms from high fertiliser runoff that result in devastation of aquatic life, or the sudden collapse of fisheries, as occurred with Canada's mismanaged Atlantic cod fishery in 1992. Recovery to the original state of an ecosystem that has undergone such spectacular shifts may take decades or longer, or may never occur.

Societies are not without knowledge about the virtues of adaptive management or resilience enhancements to respond to the foregoing challenges, but lack adequate legal institutions to give effect to such imperatives. The law displays considerable temporal inertia, as the Millennium Ecosystem Assessment Panel recognised in calling for 'substantial changes in institutions and governance'.[148] A fundamental problem of environmental law is its bias to protect existing land uses and operators; the phenomenon of 'grandfathering' is the most overt form of this temporal drag. But nor is the solution simply to empower environmental regulators to impose

---

[147] J. Tainter, 'Social complexity and sustainability' (2006) 3 *Ecological Complexity* 91.
[148] Millennium Ecosystem Assessment, *Ecosystems and Human Well-being*, 2.

changes at a whim without regard for the economic impacts on resource users. Open-ended, discretionary governance might become a curse as great as the problem it would purport to resolve. Let us now look more closely at this temporal inertia in environmental law.

Grandfathering: Frozen in Time

Sometimes when legislation changes the changes apply only selectively, with some activities or actors exempt from the new rules. 'Grandfathered'[149] refers to this situation, whereby existing pursuits such as fishing, forestry, or the by-products of activities such as pollution, remain legally sheltered. Grandfather provisions thereby constrain the law's capacity to respond to a changing future, dragging the law back to the past. The ostensible rationale is to reduce the burden on actors of having to adjust to altered environmental regulations contrary to pre-existing expectations and arrangements. Grandfather clauses appear in a variety of economic sectors, and vary in purpose, scope, and duration, depending on the context.[150] While the following discussion focuses on their pernicious effects on environmental governance, we should acknowledge that temporal inertia is sometimes evident in staunchly pro-environmental measures; US federal national parks and other priority conservation reserves can only be removed by both houses of Congress, and there have surprisingly been 'virtually no examples of national parks or wildlife refuges that have been voted off the map'.[151]

One common form of grandfathering allows existing development facilities to pollute at higher levels than newer facilities.[152] This type blunts the impact of more rigorous environmental standards by permitting exemptions based solely on factors like the age of the facility.[153] A company might have invested heavily in the then latest pollution control technology to

---

[149] The governance literature refers to the concept of grandfathering through a variety of terms: e.g. grandfather clauses, grandfather rights, grandfather provisions, and grandfather schemes.

[150] For example, grandfather clauses appear in regulations in banking, taxation, occupational health and safety, automotive safety, consumer product safety, and building codes: E. Rotenberg, 'Ending both forms of grandfathering in environmental law' (2007) 37 *Environmental Law Reporter* 10, 717.

[151] B.H. Thompson Jr, 'The trouble with time: influencing the conservation choices of future generations' (2004) 44 *Natural Resources Journal* 601, 608.

[152] H.G. Robertson, 'If your grandfather could pollute, so can you: environmental "grandfather clauses" and their role in environmental inequity' (1995–6) 45 *Catholic University Law Review* 131, 134–5.

[153] Rotenberg, 'Ending both forms of grandfathering in environmental law', 10720.

conform to a standard that applied when it began operations, and the costs of upgrading to match new control standards might be prohibitive. Robert Stavins describes this type of grandfathering as 'vintage differentiated regulation' (VDR).[154] Bruce Huber describes it as 'temporal relief', which postpones the requirements of new regulation for a period of time that is limited, unspecified, triggered by a terminating event, or indefinite.[155] However labelled, such grandfathering creates different classes of assets governed by different pollution control rules on the basis of two different time periods. Another type of grandfathering 'allocat[es] tradable pollution permits at a zero price, or a price substantially below market value, according to some historic criteria'.[156] Some carbon trading systems have distributed emissions permits on this basis. Unlike VDR systems, these grandfathered emissions permits function as direct monetary relief to actors that face a loss because of legislative changes. Joseph Huber explains that 'quite apart from dealing with the schedule of compliance, [it] provides financial assistance to existing parties in order to facilitate their compliance', which may take the form of grants, subsidies, or indirect financial mechanisms.[157]

Grandfathering in either of the foregoing forms is pervasive around the world. In the United States, the majority of environmental regulations contain grandfather provisions.[158] The contentious Clean Air Act 1963[159] and the associated pollution-control requirements under the New Source Review programme highlight the complex problems created by grandfathering.[160] Congress largely exempted facilities built before 1970 from new, more stringent environmental requirements; the standards for sulphur dioxide, nitrogen oxides, and other pollutants thus differed substantially based on whether power plants were new or existing. As Bruce Biewald and others discuss, there were several specific reasons behind Congress' choice to grandfather existing facilities under the Clean Air Act. The first was that

---

[154] Ibid.
[155] B. Huber, 'Transition policy in environmental law' (2011) 35 *Harvard Environmental Law Review* 91, 95–6.
[156] Rotenberg, 'Ending both forms of grandfathering in environmental law', 10720.
[157] Huber, 'Transition policy in environmental law', 95.
[158] G. Heutel, 'Plant vintages, grandfathering, and environmental policy' (2011) 61(1) *Journal of Environmental Economics and Management* 36, 43.
[159] Public Law No. 86-206.
[160] For a more comprehensive overview, see B. Biewald, et al., 'Grandfathering and environmental comparability: an economic analysis of air emission regulations and electricity market distortions' (National Association of Regulatory Utility Commissioners 1998), especially 19–21.

'the cost of installing pollution control technologies was assumed to be significantly higher after a power plant has been constructed'.[161] Secondly, 'a dramatic and sudden regulatory change frustrated the expectations of owners of existing facilities and would discourage investment'.[162] Thirdly, there was 'an expectation that the existing power plants would retire in the not-too-distant future, and that the different standards between the two types of plants would not persist very long'.[163] Finally, there was political expediency, as 'offering concessions to those who stood to lose from new environmental standards allowed the formation of a consensus around policy action to reduce emissions'.[164] However, although grandfathering was politically helpful – and perhaps necessary – in winning passage of the Clean Air Act, critics argue that the facilities grandfathered are no longer young, and older facilities should not continue to enjoy 'an unending windfall, at the expense of both their newer competitors and the quality of our air'.[165]

Another example is Europe's emissions trading system (ETS), launched in 2005 as the first large-scale greenhouse gas emissions market initiative in the world.[166] The ETS cap-and-trade system places an upper limit on the permissible level of emissions generated by high-emitting industry sectors, with the cap lowered by 1.74 per cent each year until 2020 so that the total emissions reduce accordingly. The ETS is mandatory for all EU member states, and the programme has been articulated through several phases. During Phase I, also known as the 'learning by doing' phase, most emissions allowances in all participating countries were distributed for free. To cover any additional emission allowances needed, companies needed to buy additional allowances.[167] This grandfathering arrangement has been interpreted as a reflection of the relative power of the various interest groups involved.[168] As with the American Clean Air Act, the

---

[161] Biewald, et al., 'Grandfathering and environmental comparability', 42.
[162] S.L. Hsu, 'What's old is new: the problem with new source review' (2006) 29(1) *Regulation* 36–7.
[163] Biewald, et al., 'Grandfathering and environmental comparability', 42.
[164] Ibid.
[165] F. Ackerman, et al., 'Grandfathering and coal plant emissions: the cost of cleaning up the Clean Air Act' (1999) 27 *Energy Policy* 929, 937.
[166] European Commission, 'The EU Emissions trading system', at http://ec.europa.eu/clima/policies/ets/index_en.htm.
[167] Ibid.
[168] M. Faure, 'Effectiveness of environmental law: what does the evidence tell us?' (2012) 36(2) *William and Mary Environmental Law and Policy Review* 293, 335.

European ETS[169] was criticised for allowing windfall profits, being less efficient than competitive auctioning, and providing insufficient incentive for market innovation to provide clean, renewable energy.[170] The European Commission later reformed the ETS in 2009 to allow for auctioning of a greater share of emission permits; by 2013, more than 40 per cent of allowances were auctioned, with this share rising progressively every year, and legislation sets the goal of phasing out free allocation completely by 2027.[171] The allocation process differs according to sector: power generators will experience the fully auctioned system first, with other sectors, such as manufacturing and aviation, transitioning gradually later.

Emissions trading systems designed in some other countries have been informed by the experience of the EU following the free allocation of permits, identifying that grandfathering is inferior to auctioning.[172] The New Zealand Emissions Trading Scheme began in 2008, covering various sectors, including forestry, energy, industry, and waste. The Climate Change Response (Moderated Emissions Trading) Amendment Act 2009 made several important changes to the country's ETS, including delaying the participation of the agriculture sector in the scheme until 2015, and to give additional emission allowances to farmers on an emissions intensity basis.[173] New Zealand also took a tradeable allowance approach to management of its inshore fisheries. Individual transferable quotas (ITQs) were introduced in 1986 by the Fisheries Amendment Act for 'preserving commercial fish stock, giving security to fishing companies and providing a basis for companies to manage their investment in plant and equipment'.[174] The quota management system has expanded from its initial 27 marine species,[175] and currently covers about 100 species

---

[169] Directive 2003/87/EC of the European Parliament and of the Council of 13 October 2003 establishing a scheme for greenhouse gas emission allowance trading within the Community and amending Council Directive 96/61/EC, OJ L 275/32, 25 October 2003.
[170] Carbon Trade Watch, 'EU emissions trading system: failing at the third attempt' (April 2011), at http://corporateeurope.org.
[171] European Commission, 'The EU emissions trading system'.
[172] R. Garnaut, *Garnaut Climate Change Review: Final Report* (Commonwealth of Australia and Cambridge University Press, 2008), 331.
[173] Public Act 2009, No. 57.
[174] Public Act 1986, No. 34; C.R. de Freitas and M. Perry, *New Environmentalism: Managing New Zealand's Environmental Diversity* (Springer, 2012), 200.
[175] J. Sanchirico and R. Newell, 'Catching market efficiencies: quota-based fisheries management' (Spring 2003) *Resources* 8, 9.

managed in several hundred management units.[176] The New Zealand Ministry of Fisheries sets an annual total allowable catch (TAC) for each fish stock, determined by taking into account the maximum sustainable yield. From the TAC, an allowance provides for recreational fishing, customary uses, and all other fishing-related mortality of any stock. The remainder is available to the ITQ holders in the commercial sector as a yearly allocation.

Initially, New Zealand authorities allocated ITQs based on absolute tonnages of fish,[177] with fishing rights allocated freely (grandfathered) according to the historic participation in the fishery. Quota shares were allocated in perpetuity once a stock entered the quota management system. In 1990 the ITQ right was denominated as a percentage of the TAC rather than a specific tonnage.[178] With quotas thus defined, the Minister was now able to alter the TAC for a given fish stock without selling or purchasing quotas from the commercial sector. This innovative change not only removed the government's financial liability, but also shifted the burden of risk associated with the uncertainty surrounding future catch limits from the government to the fishing industry. A further change, introduced in 2004, mandated that ITQs for new species introduced to the management system would be subject to a tendering process, rather than a quota allocated by catch history, a change reflecting the government's desire to discourage over-investment in the industry. The New Zealand approach with ITQs illustrates one way in which some flexibility to governance can accommodate future exigencies while also respecting the interests of historic resource users.

Grandfathering is also ubiquitous in land use planning. Existing land uses, such as farming, residential housing, and commercial development, are habitually grandfathered against changes in land use and associated development control legislation. Thus, homeowners ordinarily do not need to upgrade their properties to reflect the frequent changes to planning and building codes unless their house poses a serious health or safety risk. Farmers also typically enjoy the right to continue to engage in agriculture, although sometimes legislation may change to restrict additional

---

[176] New Zealand Ministry for Primary Industries, 'Quota management system' (2014), at http://fs.fish.govt.nz/Page.aspx?pk=81.
[177] I.N. Clark and P.J. Major, 'Development and implementation of New Zealand's ITQ management system' (1988) 5 *Marine Resource Economics* 325, 347.
[178] R. Connor, *Case Studies on the Allocation of Transferable Quota Rights in Fisheries* (Fisheries Technical Paper No 411, FAO, 2001).

land clearance or water extraction without permits. Even the later law changes can offend landowners because of the widespread assumption that property ownership should be unfettered or at least not diminished without financial compensation.[179] Efforts to regulate rampant clearance of native vegetation in some Australian states have been politically controversial, and in one recent instance led a farmer to kill an unwelcome environmental inspector.[180]

Even where historic resource users are not legally grandfathered, they may still exert political influence to equivalent effect. Consider the governance of Australia's Murray–Darling Basin, the country's largest river system (about the size of France) and historically subject to chronic environmental mismanagement. The Murray–Darling Basin Authority has trustee-like functions under the Water Act 2007 (Cth) to promote sustainable use of the Basin's water resources while protecting and restoring its ecological values, and in so doing fulfil Australia's international environmental obligations.[181] The Authority's initial plans for the Basin published in 2010 envisioned slashing existing water allocations for economic uses and a corresponding boost to ecological flows to allow the degraded Basin to recover.[182] Although an independent statutory agency, the Murray–Darling Basin Authority was not able to withstand political pressure from its unpopular proposals that would hurt rural communities.[183] The final Basin Plan adopted in November 2012 by the federal government succumbed to this pressure, much to the chagrin of scientists.[184] Their concerns have been alleviated somewhat as the Australian government started to buy back historic water allocations to bring usage within sustainable limits.[185]

---

[179] For a critique of such views, see N. Graham, 'Owning the earth', in P. Burdon (ed), *Exploring Wild Law: The Philosophy of Earth Jurisprudence* (Wakefield Press, 2011), 259.

[180] C. Hough and C. McKillop, 'Labor reignites debate on tree clearing laws in Queensland ahead of state election', *ABC Rural* 22 January 2015, at www.abc.net.au/news; N. Graham, 'Land clearing laws bring out worrying libertarian streak', *The Conversation* 4 August 2014, at http://theconversation.com.

[181] Sections 3, 20–1.

[182] Murray–Darling Basin Authority (MDBA), *Guide to the Proposed Murray-Darling Basin Plan* (MDBA, 2010).

[183] G. Williams, 'When water pours into legal minefields', *Sydney Morning Herald* 26 October 2010, at www.smh.com.au.

[184] 'Scientists want "manipulated" Basin plan scrapped', *ABC News* 19 January 2012, www.abc.net.au/news.

[185] A. Felton-Taylor and J. Gunders, 'Australian first: Darling Downs irrigators welcome successful water buyback tender', *ABC Rural* 18 March 2016, at www.abc.net.au/news.

International law also grandfathers activities. New agreements sometimes provide transitional relief for countries, usually emerging economies claiming to be disproportionately burdened by new environmental standards. A recent example is the 2016 agreement to phase out hydrofluorocarbons (HFCs), a potent greenhouse gas widely used in fridges, aerosol sprays, and air conditioning. The agreement provides that the richest countries will discontinue their HFC use by 2019 while some developing countries will not cut back until 2024, in the case of China, or 2032, in the case of India and several other developing states.[186] This agreement was an amendment to the Montreal Protocol 1987, an instrument that already contained significant transitional relief for developing countries to phase out a variety of ozone-depleting chemicals. Another international example is the climate change agreements,[187] with a similar rationale. The principle of common but differentiated responsibility, which supports such grandfathering, was introduced in 1992 to share the burdens and costs of global challenges like biodiversity conservation and climate change fairly.[188] In recent years developed nations have sought to modify the principle because of substantial economic progress in many countries such as China and Brazil, which they contend requires that these states assume a greater share of meeting global environmental goals.[189]

Proponents of grandfathering assert a variety of reasons for differential treatment. Accommodating powerful industry players is one pragmatic reason.[190] Environmental law reform is often an uphill battle, and can be difficult enough without the tricky question of how to integrate new provisions with entrenched patterns of behaviour. Through grandfather clauses, legislators can create tiered systems of regulations whereby they attempt to adopt stringent legislation while exempting some from its application based on existing conditions. Grandfathering allows legislators to delay the adverse consequences of contentious political decisions in a way that may make achievable what would otherwise be politically impossible. The costs of regulation are imposed on future, rather than present actors,

---

[186] M. McGrath, 'Climate change: 'monumental' deal to cut HFCs, fastest growing greenhouse gases', *BBC News* 15 October 2015, at www.bbc.com/news.
[187] Conference of the Parties, United Nations Framework Convention on Climate Change, *Adoption of the Paris Agreement*, 21st sess, UN Doc. FCCC/CP/2015/L.9 (12 December 2015), Annex.
[188] Rio Declaration on Environment and Development, 4 June 1992, in force 21 March 1994, (1992) 31 ILM 849, principle 7.
[189] J. Martens, 'Sharing global burdens' (2014) 12 *D+C: Development and Cooperation* 474.
[190] Robertson, 'If your grandfather could pollute, so can you', 160.

thereby sidestepping resistance from those who would be affected.[191] In this way, legislation that imposes more stringent standards, despite the blight of a grandfather clause, may be better than nothing at all.

Supposed economic fairness is another consideration. Introducing new legislation without transition relief smacks of changing the rules in the middle of the game, some believe. Steven Shavell looks at the level of past compliance with the law as an important factor in whether such actors' facilities should be grandfathered.[192] Enacting more stringent legislation without the protective effect of a grandfather clause may also compromise the expectations of recent investors; they may avoid investing in future facilities if they may face unpredictable changes in regulation and the associated expenses.[193] Furthermore, imposing more stringent standards on polluting facilities may lead to the closure of important facilities where compliance with new regulation is more onerous. As Robertson points out, 'legislators might conclude that it is more responsible to allow some existing facilities to operate under less stringent standards, rather than lose the capacity they provide, especially given the increasing difficulty in siting newer, cleaner replacement facilities'.[194]

Finally, grandfathering has a philosophical defence. Luc Bovens defends it on Lockean grounds, comparing the allocation of emission rights to the allocation procedure of land that yielded unequal property rights and arguing that none of the differences between the usage of land and the usage of atmosphere prevent the application of the Lockean argument to emission rights.[195] Carl Knight also defends grandfathering of emissions rights on several strands of political philosophy – including utilitarianism, egalitarianism, and prioritarianism. The crux of his argument is that actors with higher historical emissions are typically burdened with higher costs when transitioning to a given reduced level of emissions, and that they therefore deserve greater resources, including emission entitlements, than those in similar positions but with lower emissions.[196]

Conversely, grandfathering can offend us economically and environmentally on several grounds. One objection relates to unjust distributional

---

[191] Ibid, 169.
[192] S. Shavell, 'On optimal legal change, past behaviour, and grandfathering' (2008) 37(1) *Journal of Legal Studies* 37, 39.
[193] Robertson, 'If your grandfather could pollute, so can you', 167.
[194] Ibid, 168.
[195] L. Bovens, 'A Lockean defense of grandfathering emission rights' in D.G. Arnold (ed), *The Ethics of Global Climate Change* (Cambridge University Press, 2011), 124.
[196] C. Knight, 'Moderate emissions grandfathering' (2014) 23(5) *Environmental Values* 571.

impacts.[197] As the criticisms of Europe's ETS show, free permits serve to mitigate the impact on industry, leaving these costs to be borne elsewhere by others. By endorsing the status quo, grandfathering 'tends to favour the existing major polluters or largest resource users while creating a barrier for new entrants who must purchase permits from existing holders who receive them free of charge'.[198] The grandfathering of emissions permits also has wider implications than merely providing transition relief for industry, often creating undesirable trickle-down effects for the ultimate consumer. Shi-Ling Hsu points out, 'by creating a more favorable... regulatory environment for existing facilities than new ones, grandfathering creates an incentive to keep old, grandfathered facilities up and running. The grandfather status of a plant becomes a valuable asset'.[199] Hsu inflames his criticism of grandfathering further, labelling it 'a rotten concept. The idea that we should discriminate on the basis of timing is economically and environmentally disastrous'.[200] The perverse incentive to maintain older facilities may also have the unintended consequence of impeding new investment, and thereby reducing productivity due to the continued functioning of less efficient facilities. T.H. Tietenberg describes this effect as 'new source bias', whereby grandfathering 'imposes a bias against new sources . . . [that] could retard the introduction of new facilities and new technologies'.[201]

Although in theory an activity can be 'ungrandfathered',[202] it is much more challenging to remove privileges once exceptions are conceded. Accordingly, the 'temporary' label on many grandfather arrangements is often illusory. As Edan Rotenberg puts it, 'grandfathering is very difficult to undo because grandfathered firms see themselves as having an entitlement to their privilege'.[203] Furthermore, when grandfather clauses have

---

[197] An alternative version of the traditional economic version of this argument is put forth by Heidi Gorovitz Robertson, who argues that grandfather clause-like provisions that allow older facilities to operate under less stringent requirements have a discriminatory effect analogous to environmental racism, as 'many major sources of pollution and environmental risk are located disproportionately in low-income communities': Robertson, 'If your grandfather could pollute, so can you'.

[198] de Freitas and Perry, *New Environmentalism*, 36.

[199] Hsu, 'What's old is new', 38 (emphasis in original).

[200] Ibid, 42.

[201] T.H. Tietenberg, 'Economic instruments for environmental regulation' (1990) 6(1) *Oxford Review of Economic Policy* 17, 25.

[202] An example of ungrandfathering is discussed in Robertson, 'If your grandfather could pollute, so can you', 171–3.

[203] Rotenberg, 'Ending both forms of grandfathering in environmental law', 10722.

indefinite longevity, the initial advantage grows with the passage of time as the disparities between old and new sources of pollution increase in terms of the quality of the technology and procedures. If grandfathering remains for political expediency, at most it should be limited in time to give existing facilities a grace period in which to be upgraded, but not a permanent exception.[204] A common regulatory technique is to give existing actors some time to transition to new rules, such as to announce a forthcoming ban on a certain product or activity that will apply for everyone. For instance, the US Congress enacted in 2015 the Microbead-Free Waters Act,[205] banning the manufacture and sale of microscopic pieces of plastic contained in soaps, body washes, and toothpastes in the United States, with the law effective from 1 July 2017.

Grandfathering will not disappear in the near future, but it should be rendered a lesser bottleneck to the capacity of environmental law to innovate, respond, and manage change. We should compensate existing users who would suffer significant hardship if required to adjust to changing regulations, but not allow environmentally destructive practices to continue unabated, especially where new technologies or alternative land use practices are available. Other techniques to control the impact of new environmental legislation could also be considered; they include relicensing provisions within existing legislation and agreements negotiated between regulatees and authorities. The following section delves into these (potential) means of recalibrating environmental governance.

Relicensing and Other Recalibrations

In addition to new legislation, the relicensing provisions of existing environmental legislation offer a means to respond to a changing future. Most development activities are subject to licences, permits, or other kinds of regulatory approvals, which may be subject to periodic renewal or adjustment rather than given in perpetuity. This relicensing process provides a window, potentially, to update rules to reflect new circumstances. I say 'potentially', because the licensing process is typically front-loaded by authorities that scrutinise projects and activities when first proposed. The regulatory system invests heavily in the initial due diligence, environmental assessments, CBA studies, and public consultations that inform licensing decisions. Once approved, resource-constrained regulators often give

---

[204] Nash and Revesz, 'Grandfathering and environmental regulation'.
[205] Public Law No. 114–114.

much less attention to what ensues, such as follow-up monitoring and even ensuring compliance with licence conditions. The scope for re-opening a licence may also be quite limited under the legislation, and is usually confined to operational details rather than revisiting the appropriateness of the approved activity unless the developer has violated material terms of the licence. For the same reasons that some oppose removal of grandfather protections, relicensing is resisted to the extent that it introduces uncertainty and additional costs for business.

Licensing itself is unpopular and often perceived as an unwieldy and inefficient means of regulating environmental behaviour. Associated with the maligned 'command and control' label, licensing commonly involves regulators imposing prescriptive standards on companies supported by punitive civil and criminal sanctions.[206] A licensing regime may have up to three stages. The first is the initial approval, such as to build a dam, open a mine, or establish a manufacturing facility. The approval may be linked to local land use plans as well as the results of any environmental assessments and public consultations. Most licences come with conditions, which enable the regulator to take into account the local environment and thereby allow for bespoke standards and rules in the licence appropriate for each individual operator. The second stage of licensing covers its operational phase, which governs ongoing pollution emissions, resource harvesting, or other controlled activities. Here the regulator may adjust operational requirements, such as the allowable resource harvest or pollution load, with such adjustments implemented annually through a periodic performance review or only at predetermined license renewal dates. Occasionally a licensing regime may extend to a third, post-project phase, where the licensee must remediate an impacted site to its former condition (a subject addressed in the following chapter).

Environmental licenses may need adjustment for numerous reasons. Their standards, such as allowable harvest levels or emission loads, may in the light of subsequent scientific research be judged as inadequate. Climate change, if unmitigated, may necessitate revisiting some licence decisions; water allocations to farmers might need to be adjusted as droughts become more frequent, for instance. And a 'sudden change in economic or environmental conditions', explains researcher Carolyn Abbot, may

---

[206] On the development of environmental licensing, see D. Vogel, *National Styles of Regulation: Environmental Policy in Great Britain and the United States* (Cornell University Press, 1986).

also necessitate adjusting the terms of a licence.[207] Apart from evolving scientific knowledge or emergencies, social values may shift and with time community members might want better environmental standards. The local waste dump, a factory belching hazardous fumes, or even unsightly buildings are among potential targets for increasingly environmentally literate communities. Coal mining is becoming increasingly stigmatised as climate-conscious citizens shun fossil fuels.[208] Thus, licence conditions premised on a specific set of environmental or social variables may need revision when those criteria change, and sometimes the very continuance of a project may become questioned.

Conversely, reasons can be found to retain the status quo. The business community wants predictable and reasonably constant regulation because its investment decisions may commit long-term expenditures that cannot be easily recouped or reassigned. These sunk costs, such as those for opening a mine or building a dam, reflect business plans whose criteria include assumptions about the regulatory milieu. Prudent business planning of course allows some contingency for uncertainty (e.g. fluctuating commodity prices or changing regulations), but too much uncertainty can render any economic development too risky and unviable. Sometimes, a business operator will welcome the chance to vary its licence terms, and indeed may ask for a variation such as to allow more emissions because of expanded production or the development of a new product. But in general, the economic interests of the private sector are stacked against relicensing.

A further constraint to relicensing (as well as removal of grandfathering) comes from international law. Many trade and investment treaties include clauses to protect foreign investors, thereby reducing national regulators' discretion to relicense or make other unilateral changes to regulation. Treaties that provide for investor–state dispute settlement (ISDS) are the most contentious as they allow investors (often multinational corporations) to use international arbitration to settle claims against a government over regulatory measures that might economically damage their business.[209] Because ISDS clauses provide additional means of challenging environmental regulations, it creates differential standards

---

[207] C. Abbot, 'Environmental command regulation' in B.J. Richardson and S. Wood (eds), *Environmental Law for Sustainability* (Hart Publishing 2006), 61, 72.

[208] This occurs in Australia: M. McGowan, 'Stigma of mining may cut deepest', *Newcastle Herald* 28 September 2014, at www.theherald.com.au.

[209] K. Tienhaara, 'Regulatory chill and the threat of arbitration: a view from political science' in C. Brown and K. Miles (eds), *Evolution in Investment Treaty Law and Arbitration* (Cambridge University Press, 2011), 606.

of treatment between foreign and domestic investors. They may even lead to 'regulatory chill', namely where ISDS-related fears cause governments to avoid enacting, enforcing, or strengthening legitimate regulatory measures. For instance, some foreign investors secured an exemption from Indonesian authorities from a ban on open-pit mining in protected forests after they threatened the government with exorbitant arbitration claims.[210] But not all states are deterred. Australia's tobacco plain-packaging laws were introduced despite the industry's hostility, and the government held out and won an ISDS case brought by tobacco giant Philip Morris Asia, which argued that the legislation – the Tobacco Plain Packaging Act 2011 (Cth) – violated a 1993 agreement between the Australia and Hong Kong authorities for the promotion and protection of investments.[211]

The type of activity also influences the scope to re-regulate it. Forestry and fishing operators may adapt to changing resource availability by reducing harvests or shifting exploitation to another area. Operators with substantial sunk costs, such as a woodchip mill or large fishing fleet, will be more sensitive to any regulatory changes that reduce their resource access. Even more obdurate are large infrastructure projects such as major dams, with a life span of about a century and realistically no capacity to be relocated or redesigned, except at huge cost. An order to remove a dam would be one of the most extreme forms of re-regulation conceivable, but surprisingly it is not unheard of. The most common legal proceedings resulting in dam removal ensue from safety-related concerns, whereby periodic inspections may detect safety issues that lead authorities to direct the dam owner to either repair or remove it.[212] The owners sometimes choose the latter because it can be cheaper to remove rather than repair a large dam.

In practice, relicensing appears not to be common, despite the legislative potential for the procedure. Apart from the previously noted situation where the licensee itself requests a variation, such as to enable a change in its operations,[213] legislation may authorise authorities to review licence conditions, either on an *ad hoc* basis in the light of changing circumstances or at predetermined intervals. To illustrate the former, New Zealand's RMA allows consent authorities to review the conditions of resource consents

---

[210] K. Tienhaara, *The Expropriation of Environmental Governance: Protecting Foreign Investors at the Expense of Public Policy* (Cambridge University Press, 2009).
[211] G. Hutchens, 'Australian government wins plain packaging case against Philip Morris Asia', *Sydney Morning Herald* 18 December 2015, at www.smh.com.au.
[212] M.B. Bowman, 'Legal perspectives on dam removal' (2002) 52(8) *BioScience* 739.
[213] E.g. Protection of the Environment Operations Act 1997 (NSW), s. 58.

in several contexts, including to address new adverse environmental effects and to align consents with any new or amended regional plan or national environmental standard.[214] Whilst these provisions might seem far-reaching, the consent authority must *inter alia* have regard to 'whether the activity will continue to be viable after the change' and, in the case of a review of a discharge permit or coastal permit, to have regard to 'the financial implications for the applicant of including that [permit] condition'.[215] The case law confirms that consent conditions cannot be amended upon review to render the original activity incapable of further continuation.[216] In practice, reviews are uncommon, averaging about 1 per cent of resource consents in a 2-year survey period according to one study.[217] The reluctance of authorities to review more frequently, according to this research, is due to uncertainty about whether the costs of reviews can be recovered from consent holders, insufficient information on relevant environmental effects, and staff shortages to administer consent reviews.[218] But the New Zealand authorities have another mechanism at their disposal to address future changes, namely to limit the duration of resource consents. On average, consents are limited to about 15 years, for reasons that include giving flexibility to address changing environmental conditions and improvements in mitigation technology such as pollution control.[219]

The alternative to *ad hoc* relicensing is a predetermined licence renewal. The renewal intervals vary dramatically, depending on the jurisdiction and subject matter. Routine pollution emission licences might be subject to renewal proceedings every 5 years. Major infrastructure projects, such as dams, may operate under very lengthy license terms of half a century. In the United States, the Federal Energy Regulatory Commission (FERC) is responsible for some of this relicensing and it must be satisfied that the license renewal serves the public interest, taking equal account of both the development (i.e. dam) and non-development options of the river (e.g. fish and wildlife habitat, and recreation).[220] The FERC's policy advises that it may refuse a relicense application and thus order the removal of

---

[214] Public Act 1991, No; 69, s, 128.
[215] Ibid, s. 131.
[216] *Medical Officer of Health* v. *Canterbury Regional Council*, [1995] NZRMA 49.
[217] R. van Voorhuysen and M. Cameron, 'Resource consent durations and reviews' (2000) 2(9) *Resource Management Journal* 8, 10.
[218] Ibid.
[219] Ibid, 9–10.
[220] USC, title 16, s. 797[e}.

a dam if it determines that this serves the public interest.[221] However, the FRDC has exercised this power very rarely, such as in 1997 when it ordered removal of the Edwards Dam on the Kennebec River in Maine. Alternatively, dams have been removed in the context of the FEDC's relicensing agreements in which new conditions have proved too costly for dam operators to meet. One instance in 2011 was removal of the Condit Dam on the White Salmon River in Washington, as a result of the dam owner being unable to meet the FERC's requirement to install new fish passage devices.

Another context for relicensing relates to statutory offences.[222] Consistent with the theory of 'responsive regulation',[223] drastic sanctions such as suspension or revocation of a licence are usually only resorted to after persistent misconduct and lack of cooperation. A study of pollution licensing under English legislation seems to verify this conclusion. Between 1996 and 2001, the Environment Agency had revoked only 4 per cent of water discharge consents, despite a large number of pollution incidents during this period, including 14,400 substantiated such incidents in 1999–2000 alone.[224] The Agency during this period was 'slightly more willing to exercise its powers of suspension', with only the worst offenders targeted because of their 'high levels of non-compliance' with waste management regulations.[225] Research on enforcement of Australian environmental legislation suggests similarly that regulators rarely suspend or revoke licences, and prefer alternative compliance controls such as mandatory environmental audits, adverse publicity notices, or community service orders.[226] In regard to British Columbia, Canada, convictions for environmental law offences have dropped dramatically in recent decades. According to David Boyd's analysis of the convictions data, in the 1990s there were over 500 convictions annually, but over 2006–15 the tally drops to about 65 per year, and concomitantly the severity of penalties such

---

[221] Federal Energy Regulator Commissioner, 'Project decommissioning at relicensing: policy statement' (1995) 60(2) *Federal Register* 339.
[222] E.g. Protection of the Environment Operations Act 1997 (NSW), s. 79(4); Environment Protection Act 1993 (SA), s. 5.
[223] I. Ayres and J. Braithwaite, *Responsive Regulation: Transcending the Deregulation Debate* (Oxford University Press, 1992).
[224] Data from A. Ogus and C. Abbot, 'Pollution and penalties', in T. Swanson(ed), *Symposium on Law and Economics of Environmental Policy* (University College London, September 2001), 10.
[225] Ibid, 11.
[226] C. Abbot, 'The regulatory enforcement of pollution control laws: the Australian experience' (2005) 17(2) *Journal of Environmental Law* 161.

as fines had moderated.²²⁷ He attributes the drop to reduced enforcement capacity rather than improved environmental behaviour by residents. In this context, few companies risk suspension or change to their environmental licences, and may even not bother to apply for a licence because of the low risk of incurring sanctions. A study of the implementation of land-clearing regulations in New South Wales during 2010–13 found noticeable levels of 'unexplained' and possibly illegal vegetation clearance across the state that was not approved by authorities.²²⁸ Of 4417 properties where such clearing was found, compliance actions were taken against only 818, or about one-fifth.

To overcome the perceived inefficiencies of traditional 'command' regulation, environmental law has evolved several techniques that seek to inject more flexibility and raise standards without the necessity of a formal relicensing process. One technique is outcomes-based environmental standards, as is being advanced in Australia through the Environmental Protection and Biodiversity Conservation Act 1999 (Cth).²²⁹ Outcomes-based regulation departs from prescriptive regulation in two ways: firstly, by replacing rigid prescriptions such as on pollution control technology or allowable emission discharge loads with environmental performance outcomes that can be met by any number of means; and, secondly, using a collaborative, negotiated process between regulators and development operators to determine desired outcomes and the adaptive management process by which the developer will achieve such outcomes. The outcomes could be maintenance of a wildlife population or improvement of water quality in the project area. Outcomes-based regulation assumes outcomes that are capable of specific, measurable and objective assessment, which is not the case for some ecological impacts, and the approach requires excellent environmental baseline data and subsequent monitoring to verify progress. Because the focus is on outcomes rather than inputs, this style of regulation has the potential to offer more flexibility to manage changing conditions.

Another regulatory innovation is incentives provided to companies to go 'beyond compliance', exceeding standards prescribed by legislation.²³⁰

---

[227] D.R. Boyd, 'B.C. slow to enforce environmental laws', *Times Colonist* 28 April 2016, at www.timescolonist.com.

[228] Office of Environment and Heritage, *NSW Report on Native Vegetation 2013–14* (State of NSW, 2016).

[229] Department of Environment, *Outcomes-based Conditions Guidance: Draft* (Australian Government, 2015).

[230] N. Gunningham and D. Sinclair, *Leaders and Laggards: Next-generation Environmental Regulation* (Greenleaf Publishing, 2002).

These 'environmental leaders' programs, as they are sometimes called, empower enterprises to choose the most cost-effective methods of pollution control or other environmental goal, removing much of the decision-making from government regulators. Project XL (for eXcellence and Leadership) in the United States was introduced under the Clinton administration's 'Reinventing Environmental Regulation' initiative, with the aim to substitute government controls with standards designed by the regulatee and other stakeholders that exceeded normal performance obligations. In return for achieving outcomes that exceed the regulatory floor, participating enterprises benefitted from less costly compliance oversight from the EPA. Project XL also had an experimental, 'adaptive' nature in that the collaborations with the private sector served to road test new regulatory approaches to guide future reform.[231] In Canada, the province of Ontario in 2004 introduced its Environmental Leaders Program, in which enterprises that volunteered to commit to exceed compliance standards were offered incentives such as government technical assistance, faster turnarounds on license applications and public recognition on government websites and other communications.[232] By incentivising one to exceed minimum standards, regulation introduces a process by which shifting environmental conditions or changing social expectations can be addressed by licence holders without always changing the underlying rules.

Another governance shift to bring about more flexibility is to allow authorities and enterprises to negotiate the rules in order to tailor environmental performance expectations on a case-by-case basis.[233] Use of negotiated rule-making (in the United States)[234] and contractual or quasi-contractual agreements between regulators and business (especially in Western Europe)[235] aims to adapt regulatory controls to specific institutional and economic contexts in a more cost-effective manner than standard licensing regimes. The Netherlands and Germany have made the

---

[231] L.E. Susskind and J. Secunda, 'Improving Project XL: helping adaptive management to work within EPA' (1998–9) 17 *UCLA Journal of Environmental Law and Policy* 155.

[232] Ontario Ministry of the Environment, *A Framework for Ontario's Environmental Program* (Environmental Innovations Branch, July 2004).

[233] E.W. Orts, *Environmental Contracts: Comparative Approaches to Regulatory Innovation in the United States and Europe* (Kluwer, 2002).

[234] See P.J. Harter, 'Negotiating regulations: a cure for malaise' (1982) 71 *Georgetown Law Journal* 1; C. Coglianese, 'Assessing consensus: the promise and performance of negotiated rulemaking' (1997) 46 *Duke Law Journal* 1255.

[235] Orts, *Environmental Contracts*.

most extensive use of environmental agreements in Europe. The Dutch use them for reducing carbon emissions, via long-term agreements between the state and major industrial emitters.[236] The Federal Association of German Industry has also made agreements with authorities for similar purposes.[237] Outside of Europe, bilateral agreements figure strongly in Japanese environmental governance, often between local authorities and individual companies wishing to enter into an alternative compliance plan that entails higher and more detailed standards as evidence of their commitment to the local community.[238] The terms of these agreements may include mechanisms for review and adjustment, as with conventional relicensing.

Agreements can also be negotiated to govern land use management, including biodiversity conservation. Government authorities and private landowners may negotiate arrangements for environmental stewardship, sometimes as an alternative to regulation or purely as a voluntary commitment of an altruistic landowner. These contracts may be backed by a conservation covenant placed on the property title in perpetuity.[239] Because covenants can set in stone specific legal obligations, they can be problematic for a property that might need to be managed differently in years to come or if circumstances change. Some landowners who are wary of the permanency of a covenant prefer the flexibility of short-term contracts, of say 5 or 10 years' duration. This approach has been used in protecting biodiversity on private property in Tasmania's Midlands.[240] The trade-off, however, is that the shorter duration reduces the legal security of environmental improvements, which may be undone when the agreement expires.

The governance challenge with relicensing and these other ways of recalibrating regulation is to find an effective balance between a system that is

---

[236] P. Glasbergen, 'Partnership as a learning process; environmental covenants in the Netherlands' in P. Glasbergen (ed), *Co-operative Environmental Governance: Public-Private Agreements as a Policy Strategy* (Kluwer Academic, 1998), 133.

[237] E. Jochem and W. Eichhammer, 'Voluntary agreements as an instrument to substitute regulating and economic instruments: lessons from the German voluntary agreements on CO2 reduction' in C. Carraro and F. Leveque (eds), *Voluntary Approaches in Environmental Policy* (Kluwer Academic, 1999), 209.

[238] E. Rehbinder, 'States between economic deregulation and environmental responsibility' in K. Bosselmann and B.J. Richardson (eds), *Environmental Justice and Market Mechanisms* (Kluwer Law, 1999), 93, 104.

[239] V. Adams and K. Moon, 'Security and equity of conservation covenants: contradictions of private protected area policies in Australia' (2013) 30(1) *Land Use Policy* 114.

[240] Tasmanian Land Conservancy, 'Conservation success in Tasmanian midlands' (2008) 18 *Tasmanian Land Conservancy* 1.

lithe and responsive to change, while avoiding too much uncertainty or complexity in the system. The prospect of frequent and costly changes to the environmental rules might deter economic investment and be politically unpalatable for any government to tolerate. Another problem with modifying licenses is that each modification may trigger legal challenges, thus making responsive governance via relicensing or other adjustments a drawn out and possibly futile process. But conversely, rigid licensing unacceptably risks stifling the capacity of governance to respond and adapt to environmental adversity. One compromise might be an interim period of some duration for adjustment for specified activities associated with heightened risks and uncertainties, after which an acceptable project can continue without further relicensing checks except for performance failures. Chapter 6 discusses these ideas further in charting new directions for environmental law.

Relicensing and other recalibrations of regulation focus on *individual* entities on a case-by-case basis with thus limited scope to take account of their broader context, such as cumulative impacts from other developments, population growth, and ecological changes. In other words, relicensing of individual activities may not be enough to manage future change while the bigger picture remains unaddressed. For this reason, regulation of particular activities must be linked to other mechanisms for managing change on a wider scale, such as through land use planning and strategic environmental assessments that occur with sufficient frequency and rigour so as to inform subsidiary decisions on individual developments. Meeting this challenge will be harder in regard to existing activities than new ones, of course. For new proposals, it is easier to establish rules that incorporate periodic revisions and renewals that any developer will need to factor into their business plans. For existing uses, the political and economic challenges to changing the rules can be severe. But another option may mitigate these challenges, as the next section examines.

Responding to Change via Corporate Initiative

Although environmental regulation may often remain time-locked and resistant to shifting currents, change may still ensue through other mechanisms of governance in the market or civil society. Indeed, in recent decades an increasing share of governance has come through non-state processes. Sometimes governments have overtly encouraged it because of their fiscal and managerial constraints, with authorities increasingly delegating or sharing governance responsibilities with the corporate sector and NGOs. Of course, the business sector also seeks to control environmental governance for its own ends. Through industry codes of conduct, sustainability reports, and environmental management systems, among many initiatives, the business sector is somewhat attempting to improve its environmental performance and respond to changing circumstances. Thus, even though a company's environmental licence conditions may remain unchanged, it may in fact have updated its environmental policies and practices quite substantially. Some companies may even take the initiative to observe international environmental treaties that do not directly regulate them, especially when active in jurisdictions without effective domestic legislation, as Canadian scholar Natasha Affolder has researched.[241]

As noted in the previous chapter, this realignment of governance between the state and market has been conceptualised under a variety of labels including 'self-organization',[242] 'responsive regulation',[243] 'reflexive adaptation',[244] and 'smart regulation',[245] to name just a few. They are a reaction to the enormous extension and intensification of environmental standards and rules worldwide in the past half century.[246] Prescriptive regulations have lost ground to mechanisms that encourage reflection, learning, and behavioural change within organisations that participate in governance along with state authorities.[247] The following pages focus on this trend in the corporate sector, while Chapter 5 canvasses some examples from the non-profit sector.

In this setting for market initiative, the movement for CSR has flourished, as epitomised by the hundreds of voluntary codes developed that cater to a smorgasbord of societal concerns, from climate change

---

[241] N. Affolder, 'The private life of environmental treaties' in J.A.R. Natzinger (ed), *Cultural Heritage Law* (Edward Elgar Publishing, 2012), 257.

[242] G. Teubner, I. Farner, and D. Murphy (eds), *Environmental Law and Ecological Responsibility: The Concept and Practice of Ecological Self-Organisation* (John Wiley and Sons, 1994).

[243] Ayres and Braithwaite, *Responsive Regulation*.

[244] E.J. Kane, 'Reflexive adaptation of business to regulation and regulation to business' (1993) 15(3) *Law and Policy* 179.

[245] Gunningham and Grabosky, *Smart Regulation*.

[246] R.B. Stewart, 'A new generation of environmental regulation?' (2001) 29 *Capital University Law Review* 21, 30–1.

[247] See D.A. Farber, 'Taking slippage seriously: noncompliance and creative compliance in environmental law' (1999) 23 *Harvard Environmental Law Review* 297; A. Iles, 'Adaptive management: making environmental law and policy more dynamic, experimentalist and learning' (1996) 13 *Environmental and Planning Law Journal* 288; Orts, *Environmental Contracts*.

to blood diamonds. Disavowing the unbridled free market ethos of neoliberalism, the influential World Business Council for Sustainable Development explains: 'corporate social responsibility is the continuing commitment by business to behave ethically and contribute to economic development while improving the quality of life of the workforce and their families as well as of the local community and society at large'.[248] A parallel movement has taken root in the financial sector, known as SRI, with its own plethora of codes, standards, certifications, and other governance mechanisms that purport to improve the environmental performance of financiers and those they fund.[249]

The motivations of companies or investors to voluntarily improve their environmental performance are diverse. The dominant driver is usually financial self-interest, namely the belief that better environmental due diligence and risk management can benefit businesses through less wasteful use of resources, lower energy costs, and attracting green consumers.[250] Another influential driver is the desire to improve stakeholder relations.[251] Stakeholders, such as local communities, the media, consumers, and employees, denote those affected by or who can themselves affect a business enterprise. In the natural resources sector, such as forestry and mining, the reputation of operators may be tarnished by local environmental impacts.[252] Peer pressure may also motivate action, as where publicised corporate initiatives such as a new performance code induces other actors to join in, as evident in the bandwagon support for major codes such as the UN Principles for Responsible Investment (UNPRI) and the chemical industry's Responsible Care.[253]

An enterprise's 'social licence' to operate, which depends on the quality of its stakeholder relationships and public reputation, can motivate

---

[248] World Business Council for Sustainable Development (WBCSD), *Corporate Social Responsibility: Meeting Changing Expectations* (WBCSD, 1999), 3. Among important CSR literature, see D. Crowther and L. Rayman-Bacchus (eds), *Perspectives on Corporate Social Responsibility* (Ashgate, 2004); D. Vogel, *The Market for Virtue: The Potential and Limits of Corporate Social Responsibility* (Brookings Institution Press, 2005).

[249] See B.J. Richardson, *Socially Responsible Investment Law: Regulating the Unseen Polluters* (Oxford University Press, 2008).

[250] M.E. Porter and V. der Linde, 'Green and competitive: ending the stalemate' (1995) 73(5) *Harvard Business Review* 120.

[251] M. Clarkson, 'A stakeholder framework for analyzing and evaluating corporate social performance' (1995) 20(1) *Academy of Management Review* 92.

[252] J.R. Owen and D. Kemp, 'Social licence and mining: a critical perspective' (2003) 38(1) *Resources Policy* 29.

[253] See www.unpri.org; and www.icca-chem.org/en/Home/Responsible-care.

it to alter and improve its environmental governance over time, even though its legal licence endures. Social licence means the unwritten permission that communities may give a company to engage in an activity, such as mining or forestry, with the 'licence' reflective of the opinions and expectations of the broader community on the impacts and benefits of the industry.[254] The need for social endorsement reflects not only the growing public expectation for environmentally sustainable practices and the desire of specific stakeholders, such as a local community, for more involvement in environmental decision-making, but also tacitly acknowledges that official legal permissions such as a pollution licence may alone be insufficient to socially legitimate an environmental activity. The discrepancy between the social licence and legal licence may arise because of new environmental information, shifts in social values, or the behaviour of the company itself. When a firm loses its social licence, it risks community protests, consumer or investor boycotts, adverse media publicity, and other backlashes.

Over the past two decades the social licence has become a commonly acknowledged concept applied in corporate planning and management in a diversity of industries, including mining, oil and gas, forestry, and even eco-friendly sectors such as wind power.[255] Businesses not in the public spotlight, such as the manufacturer of obscure technical equipment for other companies, may have a lower need for a social licence. To achieve social acceptance, the industry may need to consult with affected stakeholders, disclose its environmental performance, or offer community benefits to compensate for unresolved impacts, among many options.[256] But when an entire industry sector comes under challenge, as with those currently targeted by the fossil fuels divestment movement, a social licence may be unattainable except via wholesale restructuring or closing of economic activities. The embattled coal and oil industries cannot ever

---

[254] P. Edwards, et al., 'The social licence to operate and forestry – an introduction' (2016) *Forestry*, doi:10.1093/forestry/cpw036; B.F. Yates and C.L. Horvath, 'Social license to operate: how to get it, and how to keep it', Working paper (Pacific Energy Summit, 2013).

[255] See N. Gunningham, R.A. Kagan, and D. Thornton, 'Social license and environmental protection: why businesses go beyond compliance' (2004) 29(2) *Law and Social Inquiry* 307; J.R. Owen and D. Kemp, 'Social license and mining: a critical perspective' 38 (2013) *Resources Policy* 28; N. Hall, et al., 'Social licence to operate: understanding how the concept has been translated into practice in energy industries' (2015) 86 *Journal of Cleaner Production* 301.

[256] S. Bice, 'What gives you a social licence? An exploration of the social licence to operate in the Australian mining industry' (2014) 3 *Resources* 62.

secure a social licence in the view of many divestment activists, for whom the only solution is renewable energy.[257] But different community and stakeholder groups can articulate different objectives and criteria for granting social licence, which may enable some business activities to continue with partial support. In the fossil fuels divestment campaign, some financial investors, such as university endowment funds, continue to support coal and oil companies despite opposition from student groups.[258]

Although obtaining (and maintaining) social licence remains distinct from permits issued by government authorities, they have important interconnections. Failure to hold a social licence may ensue from deficiencies in the formal licensing process, such as poor public consultation procedures or deficient EIA studies that alienated certain stakeholders, who subsequently choose to challenge the offending activity in court, or due to the lack of government enforcement against a company that contravenes its licence. On the other hand, because social licence implies an 'ongoing acceptance' of a company or industry's activities, it must be earned and actively maintained over time in contrast to an official licence that may effectively grandfather the company's development because the relicensing process is infrequent or narrowly framed. This dynamic quality of the social licence gives it the capacity to respond to a changing future and thereby play a vital role in shifting environmental governance towards the ecological timescape.

Of course, gestures such as participation in CSR codes and issuance of sustainability reports do not necessarily correlate with real changes in corporate environmental behaviour, and thus any ostensible social licence may in fact fail to reflect the quality of environmental performance. While the voluntary nature of CSR and SRI is a virtue, in that it creates room for innovative leadership by businesses and scope for being responsive to shifting stakeholder demands, voluntarism has the downside of allowing perfunctory or unscrupulous behaviour by companies interested in free-riding on the efforts of others. That downside is more likely to materialise if improvements to corporate environmental behaviour will cost more than any perceived financial reward. An abundance of literature has documented the limitations of this kind of voluntarism, colloquially

---

[257] See 350.org's 'Fossil Free' campaign, at http://gofossilfree.org.
[258] B.J. Richardson, 'Universities unloading on fossil fuels: the legality of divestment' (2016) 10(3) *Carbon and Climate Law Review* 62.

branded 'green washing', which does not need to be rehearsed here.[259] To minimise such risks, collaborative approaches to governance that involve community and government actors as well as the business sector tend to be more socially legitimate and robust. Examples include the certification programs administered by the Marine Stewardship Council and the Forest Stewardship Council.[260] The development of hybrid governance systems is also evident nationally, in which regulators incorporate voluntary CSR or SRI standards into their regulations; for instance, Denmark's Financial Statements Act provides that a financier's requirement to report annually on its sustainability performance may be fulfilled if it has submitted an equivalent progress report in connection with its accession to the UNPRI.[261]

Climate change has motivated some corporate and investor initiatives to compensate for lacklustre political leadership. Governments' prevarication on reducing greenhouse gas emissions, epitomised by recent Australian and Canadian governments' hostility to carbon taxes, as well as sluggish advances in international law, notwithstanding the 2015 Paris Agreement, has encouraged some in the business community to push for action through the market. A variety of voluntary codes have been drafted for willing businesses and financiers, including the Carbon Principles and Climate Principles.[262] The ebullient fossil fuels divestment movement, spurred by networks such as Go Fossil Free,[263] is seeking to impose financial sanctions on oil, gas, and coal-mining operators in the hope to accelerate a shift away from the carbon economy.[264] Government investors led by the Norwegian Government Pension Fund Global have also began to divest, with the Norwegians abandoning 122 coal-mining

---

[259] E.g. J. Moon, 'The firm as citizen? Social responsibility of business in Australia' (1995) 30(1) *Australian Journal of Political Science* 1; R. Gibson (ed), *Voluntary Initiatives: The New Politics of Corporate Greening* (Broadview Press, 1999); S. Wood, 'Voluntary environmental codes and sustainability' in B.J. Richardson and S. Wood (eds), *Environmental Law for Sustainability* (Hart Publishing, 2006), 229.

[260] C. Tollefson, F. Gale, and D. Haley, *Setting the Standard: Certification, Governance and the Forest Stewardship Council* (UBC Press, 2008); L.H. Gulbrandsen, *Transnational Environmental Governance: The Emergence and Effects of the Certification of Forests and Fisheries* (Edward Elgar Publishing, 2010).

[261] Act amending the Danish Financial Statements Act (Årsregnskabsloven), 2008. s. 99a(7).

[262] B.J. Richardson, 'The evolving marketscape of climate finance' (2014) 1 *Climate Law* 94.

[263] See http://gofossilfree.org.

[264] J. Ayling and N. Gunningham, 'Non-state governance and climate policy: the fossil fuel divestment movement' (2015) 17(2) *Climate Policy* 131.

companies in 2015.[265] Most mainstream financiers prefer the more collegial approach of corporate 'engagement', such as informal dialogue or exercise of shareholder rights, in order to leverage improvements in corporate behaviour. Public sector pension funds, such as the California Public Employees' Retirement System and Britain's Universities Superannuation Scheme, have become particularly active in coalitions of investors engaging with major multinational companies on climate change and other social concerns.[266] Some global banks are also scrutinising their clients' activities with regard to global warming as it has become recognised as an important facet of financial due diligence, and some lenders have rejected loans to major fossil fuel projects.[267] Megan Bowman, who has investigated this subject, asserts that 'voluntary action by the banking industry has potential to facilitate climate change mitigation and the transition to a low-carbon economy'.[268] Some financiers also serve as transactional agents to facilitate the burgeoning trade in carbon emission allowances.

Despite much goodwill and some occasional successes, such as challenging North American oil sands and fracking operations,[269] lifting corporate behaviour in the absence of credible environmental regulation faces limits. The business community continues to succumb to short-term outlooks, many doubt the link between environmental performance and business success, and competitive rivalries in the market can hinder cooperation on climate change.[270] The capacity of social investors to leverage market influence is also constrained for a variety of reasons, including the limited efficacy of divestment (when other conventional investors

---

[265] D. Carrington, 'Norway confirms $900bn sovereign wealth fund's major coal divestment', *The Guardian* 5 June 2015, at www.theguardian.com.

[266] G.L. Clark and T. Hebb, 'Pension fund corporate engagement: the fifth stage of capitalism' (2004) 59(1) *Industrial Relations* 142.

[267] M. Bowman, *Banking on Climate Change: How Finance Actors and Transnational Regulatory Regimes are Responding* (Kluwer Law, 2015).

[268] M. Bowman, 'The role of the banking industry in facilitating climate change mitigation and the transition to a low-carbon global economy' (2010) 27 *Environmental and Planning Law Journal* 448.

[269] J. Cook, 'Political action through environmental shareholder resolution filing: applicability to Canadian oil sands?' (2012) 2(1) *Journal of Sustainable Finance and Investment* 26.

[270] C. Juravle and A. Lewis, 'Identifying impediments to SRI in Europe: a review of the practitioner and academic literature' (2008) 17(3) *Business Ethics: A European Review* 285; H. Jemel-Fornetty, C. Louche, and D. Bourghelle, 'Changing the dominant convention: the role of emerging initiatives in mainstreaming ESG' in W. Sun, C. Louche, and R. Pérez (eds), *Finance and Sustainability: Towards a New Paradigm? A Post-Crisis Agenda* (Emerald Group, 2011), 85, 89–91.

can enter the market to support targeted firms) and the paucity of corporate engagement (because it is labour-intensive and time-consuming).[271] The prospects for leverage seem better in some business supply chains where large, dominant companies can dictate to suppliers that their products or services must meet environmental standards. Wal-Mart has directed its thousands of Chinese suppliers to reduce packaging and improve energy efficiency.[272] In a similar vein, Unilever declared that by 2020 it would purchase palm oil only from sustainable sources.[273]

Pricing greenhouse gas emissions, such as through a tax or cap-and-trade scheme without grandfathering, is essential to curb climate change. Of course, the politics of carbon pricing can be just as distorting as the market, as the history of carbon taxes reveals.[274] But at least in the public arena opportunities for citizen debate and media scrutiny are superior to that within clandestine corporate boardrooms. The public process can also broaden the discourse about climate change action beyond financial metrics to take into account other values such as ecological integrity, biodiversity conservation, and human rights – values that no pricing or CBA mechanism can ever meaningfully quantify.

Overall, the private sector can sometimes enable environmental governance to be more responsive to fluctuating circumstances, such as new scientific information about ecological trends or shifting social values, including heightened concern about global warming. The lithe qualities of the business sector driven by competitive market pressures can enable it to innovate quickly to address shifting circumstances, and sustainability has become one of the most potent drivers of business innovation.[275] When governments fail to act, the private sector's need for social licence can nurture improvements in corporate environmental governance, especially the capacity to respond over time to changing circumstances. Although the foregoing remarks dwell on the business community, other parts of this book showcase initiatives from other non-state, sectors such as farmers and community groups, in regard to Slow Food and ecological restoration. The contribution of NGOs to the capacity of governance to adapt may well

---

[271] B.J. Richardson, 'Are social investors influential?' (2012) 9(2) *European Company Law* 133.
[272] O. Schell, 'How Walmart is changing China', *The Atlantic* December 2011, at www.theatlantic.com/magazine.
[273] Unilever, 'Transforming the palm oil industry', at www.unilever.com/sustainable-living/what-matters-to-you/transforming-the-palm-oil-industry.html.
[274] B. Stephan and R. Lane (eds), *The Politics of Carbon Markets* (Routledge, 2015).
[275] R. Nidumolu, C.K. Prahalad, and M.R. Rangaswami 'Why sustainability is now the key driver of innovation' (2009) 87(9) *Harvard Business Review* 57.

increase in years to come given the trends towards smaller government, budget cutting, and deregulation as states struggle to survive their fiscal and legitimation crises. Proponents of the 'third way' or 'new governance' introduce another approach that envisions not a retreat of the state but its realigned relationship with markets and civil society towards more collaborative and shared governance.[276] But still, even these multi-stakeholder initiatives prove insufficient, and more systemic and radical changes may need consideration.

Ungrandfathering the System

Recalibrating the governance of existing individual activities will not on its own address the *systemic* barriers to living sustainably. The Anthropocene has materialised not because a few dirty coal mines or oil refineries have been grandfathered; the upheaval reflects pervasive institutional and cultural influences associated with capitalism, global trade, nation-states, and the mania of economic growth. At stake is thus more than disciplining outdated businesses: the agenda must tackle the broader, systemic unsustainability of economic systems and their political governance. The global 'Occupy' protest movement for greater socio-economic equality in the wake of the GFC, and the Arab Spring, the democratic uprisings that flared up around the Arab world at a similar time, are among a wave of recent global mass protests rocking the established political and economic orders.[277] Another is the fossil fuels divestment campaign, coalescing around networks such as 350.org's Fossil Free[278] and the Fossil Fuel Divestment Student Network.[279] Frustrated by government prevarication, the campaign vows to curb greenhouse gas emissions by pressuring investors to shun fossil fuel industries in the hope that they adopt more environmentally benign practices or go out of

---

[276] A. Giddens, *The Third Way: Renewal of Social Democracy* (Polity, 1998); G. de Burca and J. Scott (eds), *Law and New Governance in the EU and the US* (Hart Publishing, 2006); B.C. Karkkainen, '"New governance" in legal thought and in the world: some splitting as antidote to overzealous lumping. Reply' (2004) 89 *Minnesota Law Review* 471; O. Lobel, 'Setting the agenda for new governance research. Surreply' (2004) 89 *Minnesota Law Review* 498.

[277] P. Beaumont, 'Global protest grows as citizens lose faith in politics and the state', *The Guardian* 23 June 2013, at www.theguardian.com.

[278] See http://gofossilfree.org.

[279] See www.studentsdivest.org.

business altogether. Some climate activists also advocate a bigger agenda to remake capitalism.[280]

But protesters' anger exceeds their answers. They tell us what we need less of, such as fossil fuels or economic inequalities, but less competently articulate solutions and a strategy to attain them. Divestment, for instance, has limited market influence when other conventional investors stand by to support coal and oil companies, and even a bruised social licence may not matter greatly when most of us are so ubiquitously dependent on 'cheap' carbon.[281] Protesters give less scrutiny to the future of private enterprise, property tenure, markets, and globalisation – all needing some reassessment to enable humankind to avert ecological ruin. Yet the sheer urgency of this threat probably necessitates some pragmatic working 'within the system' for now, as it cannot realistically be 'ungrandfathered' in a short time. We therefore need greater understanding of the structural barriers and opportunities to systemic change while opportunistically pursuing deeper change promoted by social movements, some of which this book discusses later.

Understanding how to change environmental behaviour through the state takes us back to the previous chapter's reflections on the temporalities of change in the legal system. Moving change through the system has already achieved a lot, such as for women's rights, indigenous peoples, marriage equality, and healthcare, to name a few. Environmental issues, of course, involve some exceptional challenges. Although the state oversees the economy through diverse tools from monetary policy to company law, in an era of privatisation and deregulation the state has shed most of its direct control of economic production,[282] and therefore 'must either react *a posteriori* to events it cannot directly control and/or engage in ineffective *a priori* planning'.[283] The dilemma for states resides in the need to moderate the economy to minimise its environmental sequelae, such as carbon emissions or over-fishing, but concomitantly allow entrepreneurs enough free rein to generate the material wealth on which the

---

[280] See G. Dembicki, 'Fossil fuel divestment's true aim? To remake capitalism', The Tyee 20 February 2015, at http://thetyee.ca/News/2015/02/20/Fossil-Fuel-Divestment-True-Ai.
[281] B.J. Richardson, 'Universities unloading on fossil fuels: the legality of divestment'.
[282] O. Letwin, *Privatizing the World: A Study of International Privatisation in Theory and Practice* (Cassell, 1988).
[283] B. Jessop, *State Theory: Putting Capitalist State in Its Place* (Pennsylvania State University Press, 1990), 356.

state's success as an economic manager depends.[284] Governments in times of reduced investment, unemployment, or other economic negatives risk having their terms cut short, so they cannot afford to alienate the business sector.[285] It tends to perceive environmental regulation as a cost, and has been embroiled in major political disputes with environmentalists over forestry, pipelines, mining, and other issues that have rocked many countries.[286] Business tends to prevail in such disputes; in capitalist societies, those who organise the economic process enjoy great strategic influence in policy-making.

The power of business, however, isn't immutable. Companies depend on the state for many matters, including clear and effective regulations to enable markets to flourish, and to curb social unrest and mitigate the most egregious ecological damage in order to protect industry's legitimacy. The pluralist perspective of politics suggests that government policy can factor the variable influence of a smorgasbord of interests in a liberal-democratic society.[287] Sometimes local communities or networks of NGOs, operating domestically or transnationally, can assert influence and win concessions. In Australia, grassroots activism demonstrated its clout in the 1970s through the seminal 'Green Ban' movement in Sydney; trade unions and community groups collaborated to stop environmentally and socially harmful building projects, eventually winning reforms, in the form of the Environmental Planning and Assessment Act 1979 (NSW), that gave unprecedented rights of public participation in development decisions.[288] In the history of legal and political struggles over the natural environment, Tasmania stands out internationally. It saw the birth of the world's first Green Party, and was the centre of epic struggles over dams, pulp mills, and logging; the Tasmanian experience suggests that environmental

---

[284] K.J. Walker, 'The state in environmental management: the ecological dimension' (1989) 37(1) *Political Studies* 25.

[285] The evidence for this is legion: see W.P. Nordhaus, 'The political business cycle' (1975) 42 *Review of Economic Studies* 169; S. Brittan, 'The economic contradictions of democracy' (1975) 5(1) *British Journal of Political Science* 129.

[286] E.g. H. Veltmeyer and P. Bowles, 'Extractivist resistance: the case of the Enbridge oil pipeline project in Northern British Columbia' (2014) 1(1) *Extractive Industries and Society* 59; D.S. Meyer, 'Protest cycles and political process: American peace movements in the nuclear age' (1993) 46 *Political Research Quarterly* 451; A. Krien, *Into the Woods: The Battle for Tasmania's Forests* (Black Inc, 2010).

[287] D. Held and J. Krieger, 'Theories of the state: some competing claims' in S. Bornstein, D. Held, and J. Krieger (eds), *The State in Capitalist Europe* (Allen and Unwin, 1984), 1.

[288] M. Burgmann and V. Burgmann, *Green Bans, Red Union: Environmental Activism and the New South Wales Builders Labourers' Federation* (UNSW Press, 1998).

activists can sometimes get the upper hand. Their greatest success, defeating the Gunns pulp mill, however, owed a considerable amount to securing backers from the business community, including persuading key investors to boycott the project.[289] Such an alliance should remind us that the interests of particular businesses and industries are not identical. Companies in different economic sectors can have divergent interests; while the fossil fuels industry resists climate change mitigation, insurance companies increasingly want action because they are insurers of assets vulnerable to damage by global warming, as well as investors in the market.[290] Likewise, socially responsible investors, as Chapter 5 explores, discriminate between corporate laggards and leaders on environmental performance.

Also, the state itself is not homogeneous, possessing a complex and somewhat contradictory amalgam of institutions.[291] Without an 'internally coherent, organisationally pure' system,[292] the state's environmental laws and policies function within bureaucratic rivalries over control of budgets and authority. Finance ministries and environmental departments typically have different agendas and constituencies to serve, which undermines coordinated governmental regulation. Vertical linkages between national and local governments can similarly be frayed over different ambitions. If the state's separation of powers is strong, the legislature and the judiciary can also function at odds to executive power. The point of all this is that while the state is vulnerable to regulatory capture by the business sector, its influence is conditional and variable, and opportunities can come for advancing environmentally sympathetic policies and laws through the state.

Ungrandfathering industrial capitalism would thus seem a tall order for now, especially in the absence of viable alternatives to the nation-state or current economic system, but social movements with their business and political allies can sometimes leverage improvements to environmental governance. Tellingly, some of their concerns have started to percolate into mainstream policy debates. The Governor of the Bank of England has recently emphasised the need to shift from a model of pure market capitalism to one of 'social capitalism' in which individuals and financial

---

[289] Q. Beresford, *The Rise and Fall of Gunns Ltd* (NewSouth Books, 2015).
[290] E. Mills, 'A global review of insurance industry responses to climate change' (2009) 34 *The Geneva Papers* 323.
[291] See T. Skocpol, R.E. Evans, and D. Rueschemeyer, *Bringing the State Back In* (Cambridge University Press, 1985).
[292] Jessop, *State Theory*, 316.

institutions owe broader responsibilities for societal well-being.[293] Making the case for systemic reform even more bluntly, Anne Simpson, an Investment Director at the huge California Public Employees' Retirement System, explains: 'the governance systems for regulating the markets are based on nineteenth century designs. The truth is that those concerned with Responsible Investment will not make progress unless these wider issues related to the soundness of the capital markets are addressed'.[294] Others also show some unease; some conservative US Republicans have broken ranks with their peers to push for action on climate change,[295] as have some major global companies,[296] and even the Pope has declared environmental destruction a sin.[297] Clearly, something is happening.

Under the ethos of sustainability, environmental law has seemingly embraced time as one of its pillars. High expectations ensued, as sustainability promised that governance of economic development and other human activity would be liberated from the expedient preoccupation with the present. Unshackled from the ever-present, governance would become more future-oriented and thereby ensure stewardship of nature for the well-being of posterity. With this shift, environmental law would also loosen its dominant spatial orientation. But in practice, the story has unfolded rather differently. Environmental law remains tethered to the forever now, with the future often just a misty mirage. Not only is the drag of the present stronger than the pull of the future, environmental law has struggled to acquire the adaptive flexibility to respond to changing circumstances.

As nature doesn't stand still, and indeed is changing more rapidly than in any period of human history, environmental governance must become more deft and nimble. The grim prospects of ocean acidification, mass species extinction, and other apocalyptic scenarios collide with the Modernist exuberance of humankind mastering its destiny through economic growth and technological prowess. We need policies and laws

---

[293] M. Carney, 'Inclusive capitalism: creating a sense of the systemic', in Governor of Bank of England, *Conference on Inclusive Capitalism* (London, 27 May 2014).

[294] A. Simpson, 'In the wake of the financial crisis: rethinking responsible investment' (2012) 26 *Notre Dame Journal of Law, Ethics and Public Policy* 73, 76.

[295] S. Goldenberg, 'Republicans to break rank with party leaders in call for climate change action', *The Guardian* 17 September 2015, at www.theguardian.com.

[296] L. Leonard, 'Leading companies Join WWF in calling for large-scale climate action ahead of Paris talks', WWF 21 March 2015, at www.worldwildlife.org/blogs.

[297] J. McKenna, 'Pope Francis says destroying the environment is a sin', *The Guardian* 2 September 2016, at www.theguardian.com.

capable of adjustment in the light of performance failures, new environmental circumstances, changing scientific knowledge, or evolving social values. This may require that the issuance of licences and other kinds of environmental permissions aren't one-off, all-time authorisations, but rather exist contingently and open to revision. Similarly, the government's own management plans for natural resources under its dominion should be amenable to periodic adjustment. Such flexibility will also dovetail with the virtues of adaptive management, where some pragmatic experimentation can help overcome environmental uncertainty. Being more responsive to a changing future may sometimes even necessitate halting a dangerous activity, though subject to proper legal process.

Some of the tools for this task already exist. Land use planning law looks to the future, and if periodically revised, can manage change. Environmental impact assessment of proposals offers another prospective tool. Development licences also can have built-in periodic adjustments. Environmental surveying and reporting obligations can keep decision-makers informed of changing conditions. Further innovation in environmental regulation must overcome its considerable temporal inertia. Grandfathering concessions in legislation, from land use planning to fisheries management, exert a huge drag on governance that limits its capacity to respond to change except for new users. Relicensing itself is not utilised as expansively as it could be. The corporate sector, often a barrier to changing regulation, has ironically pioneered a variety of environmental initiatives that give some scope for managing change, such as through voluntary environmental reporting and codes of conduct.

Making governance more flexible requires much more, however. While the system itself cannot be entirely ungrandfathered, a variety of reforms could make it much healthier while being vigilant for opportunities to leverage more systemic change. We must set overarching environmental quality standards, with regard to biodiversity, water quality, climate, and more, coupled with clear and measurable performance markers which if not met would trigger adaptive responses. Within such parameters, the planning system should be more strategic and scaled around bioregions, and include allowances for future changes. Review mechanisms must be incorporated into natural resource allocation regimes, such as forestry and water, to enable timely adjustments to reflect changes in the quantity and health of resources. The licensing process should include a longer probationary phase, in which development approvals are phased over time with graduation to higher steps contingent on meeting performance outcomes. This stepped development approval process would, by limiting initial investment in new facilities, reduce path dependence in governance. And in the meantime, long-term structural changes must be debated in public fora to tackle the fundamental drivers of economic growth and depletion of natural capital. A commitment to a changing future also requires an equal commitment to the past, because the legacies of previous greed or ignorance must be undone where possible. The philosophy of sustainable development, with its focus on intergenerational equity, disregards the ethical importance of the past. As the present is shaped by the past and past environmental injustices continue to leave their mark, we must restore and improve the environment to ensure that our progeny will inherit a healthier planet. Not only would these recommendations help governance become more adaptive, it would have the advantage of slowing human activity – another important temporality of environmental governance that we will consider in Chapter 5.

4

Rear Vision

Nature's Ghosts

Human memory of an ecosystem and its wildlife often fades as recollection of the once intact biota becomes more remote with time. In a continually degrading environment, we may come to accept the depleted conditions we grew up amidst as 'normal', without realising what was once there. This in turn can diminish the ambitiousness of environmental laws, as people become resigned to conserving what remains rather than recovering what once flourished. But if we look hard enough, our surroundings sometimes yield clues to their former riches.

Nature's ghosts may linger in the toponyms recorded on maps – place names that memorialise animals or natural features long gone or altered. In the city of Hobart, Tasmania, where I reside, the main highway dissects a peninsula called Kangaroo Point, but alas no *Macropus giganteus* have lived there for many decades, perhaps in more than a century. In the Tasmanian official place names database, 25 entries across the island mention the emu, a large flightless bird extinct in Tasmania since about 1870. In Sydney, the sprawling Australian city crammed with over 4 million residents, one can find numerous eponymous references to vanquished nature, such as Cockatoo Island (visitors will not encounter these birds there) and Woolloomooloo (likely named after a related Aboriginal word for kangaroo, which were last present there about 200 years ago). Similarly, in many other countries one can find memories of a vestigial nature in toponyms. The United States has numerous examples, including Buffalo (New York), Eagles Nest (New Mexico), Caribou (Massachusetts), Goose Creek (South Carolina), and Hoot Owl (Texas), though in some of these places the honoured wildlife may be faring better than in the Australian examples. In Kenya, Mbusyani in the tribal language of the Kamba people means 'the place of rhinos', but the place is now a busy shopping centre.[1] In Lesotho, one can find villages with names such as Taung ('place of lions') and Litŝoeneng ('place of baboons'), creatures no longer encountered there.[2] In densely settled Britain, the Wildlife and Wetlands Trust records some 270 place names that allude to cranes that once graced the Isles in large flocks: names containing 'cran' such as Cranbourne, Cranhill, and Cranley provide clues.[3] Cranes disappeared from Britain about 400 years ago due to the usual suspects, though since 1979 a small colony has returned under the aegis of a dedicated recovery programme. Researchers have also identified some 200 places in England named after wolves, an animal even more ruthlessly exterminated, and completely gone by about 1500.[4]

Many toponyms signify landscape or vegetation features that have likewise disappeared. In Sydney, again, the suburb of Greenacre is now paved with houses and asphalt. The southeast of England is sometimes known as the 'Weald', and many settlements in the region contain 'weald' in their names, such as Sevenoaks Weald (in Kent); 'weald' is old Saxon for forest or woodland, a feature of the English countryside centuries ago but now much less common. The Canadian prairie city of Saskatoon is named after the Aboriginal Cree word for 'early berries', which once flourished in its riparian enclaves. Saskatoon is the provincial capital of Saskatchewan, another Cree word meaning 'swift flowing river', though the river, now punctuated by several dams, no longer flows so swiftly.[5] Place name etymologies may thus also signify the former presence of indigenous peoples, many of whom lived in greater harmony with nature than the colonisers who displaced or persecuted them. Sydney itself, where I grew up, has many examples. The Ku-ring-gai National Park on the city's northern edge derives its title from the Guringai people who were there until the early nineteenth century. In the United States, the Mississippi River is a name from the Ojibwe language, meaning 'big river', while the city of Seattle honours a Native American chief.[6]

---

[1] M.T.E. Mbuvi, 'Using names as a guide to past ecology and land use practices' (October 1996) 27 *PLA Notes* 83.
[2] P. Morake, *Documenting Historical Faunal Change in Lesotho and the Adjoining Eastern Free State of Southern Africa*, (Master dissertation, University of the Witwatersrand, 2010), 14.
[3] See www.thegreatcraneproject.org.uk/cranes/crane-history.
[4] C. Aybes and D. Yalden, 'Place-name evidence for the former distribution and status of wolves and beavers in Britain' (1995) 25(4) *Mammal Review* 201.
[5] W. Hamilton, *The Macmillan Book of Canadian Place Names* (Macmillan of Canada, 1978).
[6] W. Bright, *Native American Placenames of the United States* (University of Oklahoma Press, 2004).

Art, music, and literature likewise often describe wildlife or natural scenery, and have become vessels by which memories of the natural world, much of it gone, linger in our cultural topography. Contemporary environmental art in Western societies has some antecedents in the Romanticism movement, with its reverence and desire for identification with nature.[7] In the late eighteenth and nineteenth centuries, nature, as evident in landscape art in the United States and Europe, began to be welcomed as a positive presence rather than repulsed as an alien force. John Constable depicted pastoral scenery (e.g. *Dedham Vale Morning*, 1811; *Weymouth Bay*, 1816), finding in English nature a serenity that contrasted with the hustle of cities. Albert Bierstadt sought to glorify America's wildest lands (e.g. *Domes of Yosemite*, 1867; *Mount Corcoran*, 1875–7) that even more accentuated the awe of nature beyond the rapidly encroaching industrialised landscape. These and other artistic works resonate memories of nature's majesty.

This book will not dwell on art or cartography, but it is worthwhile to appreciate how contemporary environmental managers can use them to grasp earlier conditions, such as climate and vegetation. For instance, some art historians believe the roiling orange and inflamed red sky in Edvard Munch's famous *The Scream*, painted in 1893, was inspired by the brilliant sunsets that swept the planet after the colossal Mount Krakatoa eruption in Indonesia a decade earlier. Accounting for such permutations in the Earth's climate may help improve models to predict future global warming. Similarly, historic place names can help us know whether the diversity and distribution of animals and plants have shifted over time. Because accurate records of past wildlife distribution are often unavailable, place names can aid scientists restoring wildlife to identify where they may best be reintroduced. And music, paintings, and other performing arts can mobilise social action and educate the public on environmental initiatives, as done in some ecological restoration projects discussed later in this chapter.

Nature's ghosts may also be commemorated through our wider curiosity about social history, as evident from researching family ancestors to collecting heritage kitsch. Reminders of the past are pervasive, in museums, memorials, and monuments, and it is celebrated for reasons of nation building, cultural identity, and sheer melancholy and nostalgia. Numerous laws serve to protect iconic cultural heritage, such as old buildings and architectural gems, while famous historical figures are commemorated in

---

[7] E. Brady, *Aesthetics of the Natural Environment* (Edinburgh University Press, 2003), 43–5.

public statues. Some interpret the *hoi polloi's* fetish for history and heritage as enabling individuals to forge more secure personal and collective identities, and find comfort in an uncertain future.[8] This desire to collect, relive, and celebrate the past extends to the natural environment, as memorialised increasingly in natural history museums and zoos. In my neighbourhood, the Tasmanian Museum and Art Gallery's most popular exhibit is the thylacine room, featuring photos, films, skins, and other memorabilia of this (probably) extinct marsupial carnivore. Likewise, popular and academic interest in environmental history is booming, as evident in the best sellers of Tim Flannery, John McNeil, and others.[9] These writings, museums, and other interpretations of the past no doubt sometimes peddle nonsense. Even Jared Diamond's blockbuster, *Collapse*, has been challenged for its allegedly simplistic portrayal of human agency in environmental decay and societal collapse.[10] But at least the growing thirst for knowledge of our environmental past would be comforting if it signals a willingness to do something about its losses, rather than merely reminisce.

Much of our environmental history unfortunately is 'lost', in the sense that it becomes forgotten or ignored, or replaced with something very different to which we become habituated. The inhabitants of successor industrial, urban, or farmed landscapes, blistered with human detritus, may simply treat them as the 'normal' surroundings; they have evidently been that way since living memory and assumed to stay so indefinitely. A South African colleague who lives near Johannesburg gave the example of the huge abandoned mines that punctuate many townships as one such accustomed blight in his own homeland.[11] And interestingly, sometimes environmentalists will prefer the human-modified landscape to its predecessor because of the cultural or emotional affinity that a community may acquire with it. For instance, Katherine Wright found that when a large tract of an exotic pine plantation near the town of Armidale, in New South

---

[8] D. Lowenthal, *The Past is a Foreign Country* (Cambridge University Press, 1985). His book was 'revisited' in 2015 with the same title and publisher. See also R. Samuel, *Theatres of Memory: Past and Present in Contemporary Culture* (Verso, 1995).

[9] T. Flannery, *The Future Eaters: An Ecological History of the Australasian Lands and Peoples* (Reed, 1995); J. McNeill, *Something New Under the Sun* (WW Norton, 2001).

[10] Compare J. Diamond, *Collapse: How Societies Choose to Fail or Succeed* (Viking Press, 2005), to P. McAnany and N. Yoffee (eds), *Questioning Collapse: Human Resilience, Ecological Vulnerability and the Aftermath of Empire* (Cambridge University Press, 2010).

[11] From Professor Louis Kotze, North-West University; see further O. Balch, 'Radioactive city: how Johannesburg's townships are paying for its mining past', *The Guardian* 6 July 2015, at www.theguardian.com.

Wales, was cleared for logging, the local community expressed outrage at the loss of their heritage.[12] This anecdote also brings to the fore the difficulties of defending any specific historic point in time as the 'natural', pristine state on which to base environmental decisions, when such decisions may exclude cultural values and community interests.[13] This conceptual and methodological challenge for governance, especially ecological restoration, is revisited later in this book.

As anthropogenic changes spread and become normalised over time, we risk losing sight of what was once there, with environmental baselines drifting over time to become imperceptible except to the most curious natural historians. The precipitous declines in wildlife, from cetaceans to carnivores, often span several generations or longer, beyond our own life experiences. When we complacently assume that prevailing surroundings are normal or natural, we likely won't believe they need restoration. But occasionally some changes unfold rapidly within our own lifespans. A stock take of British wildlife in 2013 commissioned by 25 conservation organisations found that 60 per cent of animal and plant species studied had declined in the past 50 years, with some mighty falls in just a few decades, such as a third fewer sightings of hedgehogs since 2000 and a similar drop in harbour seals seen in Scottish waters since 1996.[14] Still, even with such knowledge, which in this story received abundant media coverage,[15] struthious denial or intransigence may ensue when we perceive the costs of taking corrective action as too onerous.

On the other hand, with overt environmental impacts that immediately and directly harm human beings, the baselines are less likely to shift and indeed may be reversed. A classic example is the success of many Western countries in improving urban air quality; London was once regularly engulfed in lethal smog until the Clean Air Act 1956 transformed its air and that of other British cities.[16] Likewise, porpoises and other marine wildlife are returning to London's River Thames, which has recovered

---

[12] K. Wright, 'Pining for the present: ecological remembrance and healing in the Armidale State Forest' (2012) 9(1) *Environmental Philosophy* 109.

[13] P.S. Alagona, J. Sandios, and Y.F. Wiersma, 'Using historical ecology and baseline data for conservation and restoration projects in North America' (2012) 9(1) *Environmental Philosophy* 49.

[14] The Wildlife Trusts, *State of Nature 2013* (RSPB, 2013), at www.rspb.org.uk/Images/stateofnaturetcm9-345839.pdf.

[15] E.g. '"Worrying declines" for UK species', *BBC News* 22 May 2013, at www.bbc.com/news.

[16] 1956, 4 and 5 Eliz. 2, c. 52.

greatly from the 1950s when it was declared biologically dead.[17] And recent news coverage of British forests' rapid regeneration to levels last recorded in 1750 is further evidence that baselines can sometimes shift for the better.[18] But such examples are exceptions to nature's general decay; on trees, for instance, globally their numbers have shrunk by about 46 per cent since human civilisation began.[19]

But one context where nature no longer presents a 'ghost' on a map, painting, book, or museum, but seems alive and well, is in national parks. We visit them in droves for the opportunity to experience 'wild' nature.

Nature's Enclaves

The proudest symbol of environmental law's embrace of the past is the national park, the legacy of some of its earliest regulations. Conservationists habitually celebrate the national park as nature in its most unadulterated glory. The parks movement took off in North America, rallying to protect the last wilderness stands before they fell to the axe or plough.[20] George Perkins Marsh's seminal book, *Man and Nature*, published in 1864, 8 years before the world's first national park was declared at Yellowstone, challenged the assumption that human use and modification of nature were generally benign and he stirred awareness about the virtue of wilderness preservation.[21] Yellowstone Park itself was directly indebted to John Muir, another influential father of the modern conservation movement. The trend soon took off elsewhere. Just 1 year after Yellowstone, Australia established its first national park just south of Sydney, now known as Royal National Park. The idea spread to Africa too under the aegis of colonial rule, albeit sometimes for different reasons. In 1898 Sabi Game Reserve (now known as Kruger National Park) was proclaimed in South Africa for protecting game for hunting, while Kenya designated its first reserve in 1906 in what is now known as Amboseli National Park. Bernard Grzimek, one of the colonial-era architects of East Africa's extensive network of protected areas, once said: 'a National Park ... must remain a primordial

---

[17] S. Hardach, 'How the River Thames was brought back from the dead', *BBC News* 12 November 2015, at www.bbc.com/news.
[18] V. Ward, 'Forest levels booming as UK woodland returns to highest level in more than 250 years', *The Telegraph* 3 October 2010, at www.telegraph.co.uk.
[19] T.W. Crowther, et al., 'Mapping tree density at a global scale' (2015) 525 *Nature* 201, 204.
[20] R.W. Sellars, *Preserving Nature in the National Parks: A History* (Yale University Press, 1997).
[21] G.P. Marsh, *Man and Nature: Or, Physical Geography as Modified by Human Action* (Charles Scribner, 1864).

wilderness to be effective. No men, not even native ones, should live inside its borders'.[22]

This philosophy of pristine nature, separated from or without much human presence, still pervades nature conservation law in some jurisdictions.[23] By harbouring these primeval refuges from the degrading pressures of urban-industrial modernity, the 'wilderness' presents itself as a spiritual and recreational antidote to our stressed lifestyles and as a biosphere sanctuary from which nature can rebound.[24] But as we have gained more awareness of environmental history, the 'wilderness' ideal has begun to be reassessed. Our ancestors have modified most of the planet for millennia, and even small hunter–gatherer tribes could and did inflict environmental changes.[25] Today, the belief that parks should continue to exclude people has also become challenged, for both economic reasons (parks offer good eco-tourism opportunities, for instance), and philosophic reasons (jettisoning the assumption of nature as separate from humankind). Yet, curiously, economic opportunities and cultural identity can also give reasons for some societies to define their identities around wilderness; notably, New Zealand's '100% Pure' advertising campaign to attract tourists, complete with gorgeous images of pristine forests and empty landscapes, seems incongruous to the long Maori history in Aotearoa, let alone the vast upheavals since the Pakeha came.[26]

The national park ideal, albeit in modified form, continues to flourish, with the area earmarked for conservation expanding remarkably. In 1962, at the first World Conference on National Parks, convened in Seattle, 9214 protected areas graced the planet, a number that by 2014 had soared to just over 209,000.[27] They now conserve 15.4 per cent of the world's land and freshwaters, as well as 3.4 per cent of the oceans.[28] Virtually all countries

---

[22] Cited in J. Adams and T. McShane, *The Myth of Wild Africa: Conservation without Illusion* (W.W. Norton, 1992), xvi.
[23] R. Poirier and D. Ostergren, 'Evicting people from nature: indigenous land rights and national parks in Australia, Russia, and the United States' (2002) 42 *Natural Resources Journal* 331.
[24] W. Cronon (ed), *Uncommon Ground: Rethinking the Human Place in Nature* (W.W. Norton, 1995), 69–90.
[25] W.M. Denevan, 'The pristine myth: the landscape of the Americas in 1492' (1992) 82 *Annals of the Association of American Geographers* 369.
[26] J. Ruru, 'Wilderness is a walled garden' in M. Abbott and R. Reeve (eds), *Wild Heart: The Possibility of Wilderness in Aotearoa New Zealand* (Otago University Press, 2010), 172.
[27] G. Worboys, 'Concept, purpose and challenges' in G.L. Worboys, et al. (eds), *Protected Area Governance and Management* (ANU Press, 2015), 9, 21.
[28] Ibid.

have enacted legislation for the designation and management of national parks and other types of conservation reserves, and international law has numerous provisions. The World Heritage Convention is the pre-eminent international gesture, and its 191 state parties must 'ensur[e] the identification, protection, conservation, presentation and transmission to future generations of [its] cultural and natural heritage'.[29] Domestic legislation evinces similar values. The National Parks and Wildlife Act 1974 (NSW) of the state of New South Wales in Australia declares its objects to include 'the conservation of ... landscapes and natural features of significance including wilderness'[30] and the stated purpose of a national park is to 'protect and conserve areas containing outstanding or representative ecosystems, natural or cultural features or landscapes or phenomena that provide opportunities for public appreciation and inspiration and sustainable visitor or tourist use and enjoyment'.[31] These are fairly representative statements of the ethos of nature conservation found in this genre of legislation.

The impressive growth in parks and their accompanying laws, however, provides a misleading picture of nature's enclaves in the early twenty-first century. Many were gazetted in areas not for their ecological representativeness but because they were redundant for human settlement or development. Further, some are merely notional: a legal designation on paper that bears no resemblance to the reality on the ground, such as encroachment by squatters, poachers, and other destructive incursions. And many protected areas explicitly authorise some level of development, from tourism to even logging and mining. While this might be unavoidable for some national parks in Western Europe, given its long history of settlement,[32] it is more problematic in some less crowded places. In my own homeland of Tasmania, a huge hydropower dam wallows in its world heritage-listed southwest 'wilderness'.[33] Tourism itself can love nature to death. Parks cater to the surging eco-tourism industry in which intrepid travellers can visit exotic lands to awe the 'timeless' scenery of the Serengeti or Yellowstone. At the same time, many have amnesia to the indigenous

---

[29] Convention Concerning the Protection of the World Cultural and Natural Heritage, 16 November 1972, in force 17 December 1975, (1972) 11 ILM 1358, Article 4.
[30] Section 2A(1)(a).
[31] Section 30E(1).
[32] See e.g. National Parks and Access to the Countryside Act 1949, 11, 12, and 14 Geo. c. 97.
[33] On the campaign for its removal, see B.J. Richardson, 'Rewilding Tasmania's Lake Pedder: past loss as nature's lex ferenda' (2014) 33(2) *University of Tasmania Law Review* 194.

peoples who once occupied these rebranded 'wildernesses', or what Robert Nixon calls 'temporal enclaves' of a bygone colonial era.[34]

Even the most seemingly stringent legislation has not been able to insulate parks from such pressures. Canada's National Park Act, which proclaims 'ecological integrity' as the 'first priority' of the government 'when considering all aspects of the management of parks', has been watered down by the courts.[35] In a dispute over a proposed road through the Wood Buffalo National Park in Alberta, the Federal Court interpreted 'ecological integrity' as not the 'determinative factor' or 'sole priority'. In taking into account other provisions in the legislation, the Court concluded that some balancing of conflicting interests is permissible, such as to allow park users and local residents to enjoy improved road access.[36] There is other bad news from Canada. A Panel on Ecological Integrity in Canada's National Parks reported in 2000 that 38 of the then 39 national parks were suffering from severe ecological stress.[37] Parks Canada's survey in report 2011 was more positive, advising that 92 per cent of the 102 ecosystems protected in its parks have been assessed are either in good or fair condition; however, 43 per cent of the ecosystems in fair condition were showing *declining* health.[38] Climate change may make these numbers even less palatable soon.

The US national parks system, comprising about 400 places (besides thousands of state-based parks and reserves), suffers even more. Joseph Sax in his insightful polemic, *Mountains Without Handrails*, observed nearly 40 years ago that tourism had become a destructive, parasitic presence in American parks.[39] Yosemite, the crown jewel, hosts about 4 million visitors annually and traffic jams of up to 2 hours are not unprecedented during peak seasons. A common interpretation of the National Parks Service Organic Act 1916[40] holds that it balances conservation with recreational needs, which has created a difficult tension with trade-offs. Many

---

[34] R. Nixon, *Slow Violence and the Environmentalism of the Poor* (Harvard University Press, 2011), 181.
[35] SC 2000, c. 32, s. 8.
[36] *Canadian Parks and Wilderness Society v. Canada (Minister of Heritage)*, (2001) 2 FC 461; affirmed [2003] 4 FC 672.
[37] Panel on the Ecological Integrity of Canada's National Parks, *Unimpaired for Future Generations?* (Department of Canadian Heritage, 2000).
[38] Parks Canada, *State of Canada's Natural and Historic Places 2011* (Government of Canada, 2012).
[39] J. Sax, *Mountains Without Handrails: Reflections on the National Parks* (University of Michigan Press, 1980).
[40] 39 Stat. F35.

other threats to American parks have been identified, with a seminal 2012 report of the National Parks Advisory Board observing:

> Environmental changes confronting the National Park System are widespread, complex, accelerating, and volatile. These include biodiversity loss, climate change, habitat fragmentation, land use change, groundwater removal, invasive species, overdevelopment, and air, noise, and light pollution. . . . Parks once isolated in a rural or wildland context are now surrounded by human development.[41]

The capacity of the US National Parks Service to meet these challenges has been undermined by budget cuts and inappropriate political appointees to its senior ranks.[42] Thus, the statutory obligation of the Service to leave the parks 'unimpaired' for posterity remains illusory.[43] A similar story pervades many other jurisdictions. In Australia, the national parks in the state of Victoria are reported as 'struggling to cope with feral animals, weeds, fire threats and degraded infrastructure after deep budget cuts' that stripped Parks Victoria's funding by 37 per cent between 2011 and 2015.[44] The story is often bleaker in developing counties. South Africa's iconic parks, such as Kruger, are withering from poachers craving rhino horns and elephant tusks.[45] The condition of Kenya's parks, with an equally bloody history of poaching and squatting, were described in 2014 as a 'national disaster'.[46]

Not only are the crown jewels of the park system tarnished, the broader goals of conserving biodiversity at large remain imperilled. The 'enclave' view of environmental protection that arose under the philosophy of conservation has proved inadequate to meet the challenges of the Anthropocene. The enclave theory posited that environmental sanctuaries could be set aside in designated spaces within which all conservation goals are met while freeing the remaining, and much larger areas, for economic development and human settlement.[47] But activities outside a park

---

[41] Science Committee, National Parks Service Advisory Board, *Revisiting Leopold: Resource Stewardship in the National Parks* (National Parks Service Advisory Board, 2012), 4–5.

[42] J. Eilperin, 'National parks face severe funding crunch', *Washington Post* 19 August 2012, at www.washingtonpost.com.

[43] National Park Service Organic Act 1916, 39 Stat. 535, s. 1.

[44] J. Gordon, 'Victoria's national parks in jeopardy after deep funding cuts', *The Age* 4 January 2016, at www.theage.com.au.

[45] A. Cruise, 'Elephant poachers take aim at South Africa's famed refuge', *National Geographic* 13 November 2015, at http://news.nationalgeographic.com.

[46] B. Mutai, 'Kenya poaching crisis "national disaster"', *Daily Nation*, 19 March 2014, www.nation.co.ke.

[47] J. Sax, 'The new age of environmental restoration' (2001) 41 *Washburn Law Journal* 1.

can dramatically affect the environment inside it, for obvious reasons that don't require explanation, especially in the case of marine protected areas. Ostensibly, the last major refuges of wilderness are the polar regions, the vast boreal forests of northern Canada and Russia, the Amazon (parts of it) and some marine environments, but even here human impacts manifest. For instance, Arctic wildlife shows traces of persistent pesticides, while plastic debris litters the remotest oceans.[48]

Consequently, we should no longer assume that nature's past will survive blissfully in special enclaves. The philosophy of sustainable development, as discussed in Chapter 3, has emerged as a response to this misplaced assumption. As a guiding norm of much environmental legislation, it addresses the need for a comprehensive approach in which environmental considerations are incorporated into all places and contexts, not just in nature reserves. For instance, to protect wildlife we often need not only to set aside sanctuaries, but also to safeguard connecting corridors between parks to allow migration of species and maintain the viability of their gene pool. The sustainability ideal, however, is an incomplete answer to these challenges, not simply for the reasons canvassed in the previous chapter but also because its prospective orientation tends to ignore past losses.

Restoring the Environment

Environmental and Ecological Restoration

Restoring environmental damage requires a societal commitment to acknowledge and value past environments as a reminder of nature's former glory and hope for future renewal. Often, unfortunately, a society has no direct experience of its former, unimpaired natural surroundings; its memories of vanquished nature are filtered through layers of history. Memories are not just within the realm of individual cognition but are also socially constructed. Fidelity to national mythology such as a state's origins in revolution or 'heroic' conquest, to give conspicuous instances, are ways that the 'past' is enlisted to help legitimise privileges enjoyed today. The British invasion of Australia, to illustrate, was legitimated by the legal doctrine of *terra nullius* that contributed to the narrative that

---

[48] M. McGrath, 'Mercury exposure linked to dramatic declines in Arctic foxes', *BBC News* 6 May 2013, at www.bbc.com/news; M. Ayre, 'Plastics "poisoning world's seas"', *BBC News* 7 December 2006, at www.bbc.com/news.

the continent was unoccupied or at least not settled by civilised beings.[49] Reclaiming an authentic understanding of nature's past in any country is not easily achieved, as the work of any historian is never a pure facsimile of the past but a culturally filtered perspective. In this sense, environmental historians, scientists, or other interested persons are no less immune than governments from biases – ideological, professional, or other sources. While an objective understanding of past nature may never be fully recoverable, environmental restoration may find a more authentic basis through multi-stakeholder (including a voice for nature) and multi-disciplinary approaches that minimise damaging biases from any single perspective while ensuring nature's recovery has broad social support.

Recovering nature must begin with overcoming ignorance about environmental history. This lack of rear vision stifles environmental law worldwide. Past environmental desecration has left a wretched legacy that limits the scope for sustaining what remains, yet mitigating new environmental impacts, rather than remedying previous ones, is the law's priority. The criteria for legal interventions tend to reflect current ecological conditions or the stock of natural resources, without taking into account past damage. Under the philosophy of sustainability, the law has (ostensibly) embraced a future tense in which the priority is averting, mitigating, or adapting to new ecological impacts. While we must of course avoid further environmental upheaval, sustaining what remains is illusory if prevailing conditions remain degraded. Encouragingly, the world's leading nature conservation organisation, the International Union for Conservation of Nature (IUCN), has begun to call for ecological restoration in protected areas.[50] The larger challenge, though, is to restore what's outside such enclaves.[51] Conserving biodiversity may be futile while invasive species run amok; sustaining agriculture may be inhibited when soils have eroded or been contaminated; and mitigating climate change may be unfeasible if few forests remain to sequester carbon. We must *improve* the environment as against merely sustain it. Ecological restoration has many potential

---

[49] B. Kercher, 'Native title in the shadows: the origins of the myth of terra nullius in early New South Wales courts' in G. Blue, M. Bunton, and R. Croizier (ed), *Colonialism and the Modern World: Selected Studies* (ME Sharpe, 2002), 100.

[50] K. Keenleyside, et al., *Ecological Restoration for Protected Areas: Principles, Guidelines and Best Practices* (IUCN, WCPA Ecological Restoration Taskforce, 2012).

[51] E.g. A. Telesetsky, 'Ecoscapes: the future of place-based ecological restoration' (2013) 14 *Vermont Journal of Environmental Law* 493; M.A. Palmer and J.B. Ruhl, 'Aligning restoration science and the future of law to sustain ecological infrastructure for the future' (2015) 3(9) *Frontiers in Ecology and the Environment* 512.

benefits including: to reduce forest loss, enhance biodiversity, improve air and water quality, and improve humanity's relationships within our natural surroundings. Ecological restoration, in other words, is the indispensable twin of sustainability.

This lacuna in environmental law might strike some observers as puzzling, because occasionally we encounter dramatic news of ghastly environmental emergencies that trigger major restoration responses. The shocking BP *Deepwater Horizon* spill in 2010 provoked a massive government and corporate cleanup operation in the Gulf of Mexico that continues. The earlier *Exxon Valdez* oil tanker spill in 1989 similarly led to billions of dollars spent on compensation and remediation of polluted Alaskan waters and shorelines. Western Europe's worst equivalent catastrophe in the modern era was perhaps the 1986 Sandoz spill on the Rhine River in Switzerland, and it too precipitated some expensive decontamination. But some other dreadful disasters, such as at Bhopal, India, in 1985 and Chernobyl, Ukraine, in 1986, did not lead to such concerted responses, perhaps because many of their environmental and human impacts were initially less visible and displaced into the future through a 'slow violence', as well as the different political context in these countries.[52]

All these interventions do not really qualify as *ecological* restoration, in the sense of improvements to whole ecosystems and landscapes; instead, they involve emergency contain-and-cleanup responses in which the primary aim is to curb further risks to human health and livelihoods. Other examples of *environmental* restoration include small-scale remediation of specific sites, such as rehabilitation of a former mine. Rehabilitation of an old quarry or a derelict brownfield can improve aesthetics and functionality, but unlike ecological restoration it doesn't re-establish the 'health, integrity and sustainability' of an entire ecosystem.[53] Overlooking this distinction can be confusing, waste resources, and engender unsatisfactory outcomes. For instance, rehabilitation of a mining pit may involve replanting an exotic tree because that species can best stabilise the soil and hold ground cover; but if we want ecological restoration, that tree species may be inappropriate because it does not provide the right habitat for native birds.[54]

---

[52] Nixon, *Slow Violence and the Environmentalism of the Poor*.
[53] Society for Ecological Restoration, International Science and Policy Working Group, *The SER International Primer on Ecological Restoration* (SER, 2004).
[54] This problem has been observed in regard to India's legislation governing post-mine restorations: R. Ravi and D.R. Priyadarsanan, 'Needs for policy on landscape restoration in India' (2015) 108(7) *Current Science* 1208.

Environmental law's limited rear vision is curious given that the legal systems of many countries respect history, both as the ballast of legal tradition and as the object of its remedies. Since the late twentieth century, the international movement for restorative justice has flourished in various guises, ranging from new modes of criminal justice that aim to reconcile victim–offender relationships, to national truth and reconciliation commissions to create accountability for historic human rights abuses.[55] Rather than simply establishing the guilt or innocence of individuals, restorative justice seeks a more comprehensive record of past wrongs as a basis for healing society. In regard to legal claims by indigenous peoples, such as for restitution of traditional land rights, the law can display an even deeper orientation to the past, stretching back many centuries. While historic injustices often go unaccounted for, such as Western powers' rebuff of calls for reparations for the slave trade,[56] even in these cases they still garner debate in legal and political circles. But the enslavement of nature mostly passes unremarked unless the damage demonstrably interferes with human interests.

Delving into this problem more closely, the insouciance about ecological damage and its restoration is attributable to diverse factors. Restoring an ecosystem may be difficult because of insufficient knowledge of its prior characteristics, as well as a lack of agreement about which past environmental baseline to return to. In some cases, any restoration can only imperfectly approximate the past because of irreversible losses such as species extinctions. Another reason is that ecosystems change; thus, there is often no definable, fixed end-point for restoration, and its results may not materialise until long after a human lifetime. This can create difficulties in defining in law the performance criteria and accountability for restoration projects. It can therefore be difficult to initiate ambitious restoration projects that require multi-generational efforts. Relatedly, climate change looms ominously, threatening ecological integrity and thereby undermining any initial restoration success. But if done properly, restoration can help mitigate climate change. Also daunting is the sheer spatial scale of restoration, across vast areas inhabited by numerous property tenures, both public and private; ecological restoration projects thus face significant challenges in coordinating societal efforts. Raising

---

[55] H. Strang and J. Braithwaite (eds), *Restorative Justice and Civil Society* (Cambridge University Press, 2001).
[56] E. Dunkley, 'David Cameron rules out slavery reparation during Jamaica visit', *BBC News* 30 September 2015, at www.bbc.com/news.

the necessary funds to undertake restoration may be just as arduous, especially when the benefits may not accrue for many years, and are collective and shared rather than accruing to any individual financial sponsor. Also, restoring ecosystems may rouse opposition from host communities, especially where residents must coexist with reintroduced species, such as dangerous carnivores or herbivores that compete for resources. In some cases, affected communities might even lose their economic livelihoods. And, finally, the laws relating to restoration can suffer from numerous flaws and lacunae in regard to elementary details such as definition of key terms, specification of restoration standards and goals, and provision of suitable implementation tools. This last issue requires further explanation.

Terminology and Goals

Ecological restoration suffers from bureaucratic wrangling over the appropriate terminology and the lack of statutory definition of key concepts and management standards. The increasingly diverse nomenclature, from the traditional language of 'remediation' and 'rehabilitation' to quirky additions like 'regardening' and 'rewilding',[57] reflects the rival values and goals of environmental managers. Their variable motivations include to steady the climate, enhance soil productivity, and slow depletion of biodiversity.[58] The scale of projects can also vary, from local initiatives to large regional interventions. Some guidance has come from the Society for Ecological Restoration (SER), the peak international body for restoration professionals. It defines 'ecological restoration' as 'an intentional activity that initiates or accelerates the recovery of an ecosystem with respect to its health, integrity and sustainability'.[59] It considers an ecosystem 'restored' when it can 'sustain itself structurally and functionally', showing sufficient 'resilience to normal ranges of environmental stress and disturbance'.[60] 'Rehabilitation', by contrast, involves the 'reparation of ecosystem processes, productivity and services', explains the SER.[61] This focus on the

---

[57] M. Hall (ed), *Restoration and History: The Search for a Usable Environmental Past* (Routledge, 2010); G. Monbiot, *Feral. Searching for Enchantment on the Frontiers of Rewilding* (Penguin, 2013); D. Foreman, 'The wildlands project and the rewilding of North America' (1998) 76 *Denver University Law Review* 535.
[58] M.P. Perring, et al., 'Advances in restoration ecology: rising to the challenges of the coming decades' (2015) 6(8) *Ecosphere article 131*, 4.
[59] Society for Ecological Restoration, *The SER International Primer on Ecological Restoration*.
[60] Ibid, Section 10.
[61] Ibid.

functional productivity of an ecosystem, such as its water, soils, or forests, distinguishes rehabilitation (and related terms) from the broader vision of restoration that re-establishes plants and animals and their ecological system as valuable in their own right. The related terms of 'reclamation' and 'remediation' also appear in some environmental laws and policies, commonly referring to the treatment of former mines or industrial areas in order to stabilise the terrain, remove pollutants, and improve appearances.

A recent entry to the lexicon is 'rewilding', an emotive ideal used to rouse popular interest in healing nature. Rewilding has garnered fame lately as high-prolife environmentalists such as George Monbiot have lauded its virtues.[62] The rewilding philosophy goes beyond the SER's understanding of ecological restoration, through its ambition to rebuild ecosystems according to their deep historical condition, perhaps before any human disturbance or presence, as well as its emphasis on our ethical and cultural relationships with nature and the need to realign that relationship to give nature priority.[63] The rewilding ethos emerged from collaboration between environmentalists David Foreman and Michael Soulé in the late 1980s, when they established the Wildlands Project to foster scientific and strategic support for enlarged networks of wilderness.[64] Rewilding emphasises keystone species such as apex carnivores in regulating ecosystems, and their need for extensive terrain and habitat linkages in order to thrive.[65] The Rewilding Europe Initiative, one prominent example, aims to 'restore missing species and function' to ten 100,000 ha core areas by 2020.[66] But while rewilding is commonly associated with wilderness, it can mean simply making nature relatively 'wilder', to live by its own temporalities.

Some of these interventions to support rewilding, and other forms of restoration, imply that we cannot just let nature 'run wild', at least initially. Restoration may sometimes happen through benign neglect that allows natural succession and rejuvenation,[67] as evident in the forests of the New England region of the United States that have regrown since felled

---

[62] Monbiot, *Feral. Searching for Enchantment on the Frontiers of Rewilding*.
[63] M. Bekoff, *Rewilding Our Hearts: Building Pathways of Compassion and Coexistence* (New World Library, 2014), 5.
[64] C. Sandom, et al., 'Rewilding' in D. MacDonald and K. Wills (eds), *Key Topics in Conservation Biology II* (John Wiley and Sons, 2013), 430–1.
[65] Foreman, 'The wildlands project and the rewilding of North America', 548.
[66] See E. Marris, 'Reflecting the past' (2009) 462 *Nature* 30–1; Sandom, 'Rewilding', 439.
[67] L. Navarro and H. Pereira, 'Rewilding abandoned landscapes in Europe' (2012) 15(6) *Ecosystems* 900, 904.

for agriculture in the eighteenth century.[68] But often some intervention is indispensable. As the SER explains:

> the restored ecosystem often requires continuing management to counteract the invasion of opportunist species, the impacts of various human activities, climate change, and other unforeseeable events. In this respect, a restored ecosystem is no different from an undamaged ecosystem of the same kind, and both are likely to require some level of ecosystem management.[69]

Such husbandry resonates in 'regardening' and 'conservation gardening', as advocated by restorationists working in Europe, such as Chris Smout, who sees rewilding as impractical in landscapes burdened by prolonged anthropogenic change.[70]

The methods of restoration vary depending upon the degree of degradation to overcome and the proposed future usage. When improving ecosystem services for farming (e.g. pest control and pollination), the restoration may correspondingly have more restricted ambitions. By comparison, full-blown rewilding that returns an area to a much higher level of naturalness, akin to a credible national park, can be more demanding. Its methods include increasing native vegetation and enhancing wildlife corridors, and sometimes translocation of species to an ecosystem from which they were extirpated. In the 1990s the US Fish and Wildlife Service restored wolves to Yellowstone, releasing 31 creatures captured in Canada.[71] In the following decade, the wolf population grew, with a corresponding decline in elk and an increase in vegetation benefitting from the fewer browsing herbivores.[72] The translocation of species may also assist plants and animals threatened by climate change. For globally vanished species, it may be necessary to translocate taxon substitutes – such as by substituting an Asian camel for an extinct North American equivalent. Of such efforts, the Pleistocene rewilding campaign is placing some African and Asian megafauna in wilder parts of North America and Siberia.[73] Yakutian

---

[68] A. Plaff, 'From reforestation to deforestation in New England, United States' (2000) 2 *World Forests* 67.
[69] Society of Ecological Restoration, *International Primer on Ecological Restoration*, at http://ser.org/resources/resources-detail-view/ser-international-primer-on-ecological-restoration.
[70] C. Smout, 'Regardening and the rest', in M. Hall (ed.), *Restoration and History: The Search for a Usable Environmental Past* (Routledge, 2009), 111.
[71] National Park Service, *Wolf Restoration*, at www.nps.gov.
[72] P. White and R. Garrott, 'Yellowstone's ungulates after wolves: expectations, realizations, and predictions' (2005) 125 *Biological Conservation* 141–2.
[73] D. Rubenstein, et al., 'Pleistocene park: does re-wilding North America represent sound conservation in the 21st century?' (2006) 132(2) *Biological Conservation* 23, 233.

horses, muskox, and European bison have been successfully introduced.[74] Biotechnology provides another tool. Artificial breeding methods can help 're-create' extinct species – such as the Heck cattle, which in the 1920s were bred into existence by German zoologists Lutz and Heinz Heck in an effort to breed back the extinct aurochs from modern aurochs-originated cattle. The descendants of the Heck cattle nurtured by these zoologists were later integrated into a re-wilding experiment in the Netherlands, called the Oostvaarderplassen.[75] Some contemporary researchers are seeking to bring extinct creatures back to life by recovering their degraded DNA; Professor Michael Archer of the University of New South Wales has led some of these efforts, such as to resurrect the Tasmanian thylacine.[76]

Sometimes restoration may require removal of infrastructure like dams and roads to improve wildlife habitat.[77] Worldwide, lake and river restoration is increasing, often through the decommissioning of dams. Their removal restores the natural hydrology of rivers and replenishes fish and other aquatic life. Practical difficulties to it include engineering safe dam breaches and overcoming legal and political hurdles to dismantling dams. As American lawyer Michael Blumm notes, 'some dam removal projects have proceeded relatively quickly from proposal to completion . . . other projects experience conflict, political wrangling, and serious delay'.[78] In the United States, with approximately 75,000 dams, dam removal now outpaces dam construction, with about 40 ageing impoundments dismantled annually.[79] Among examples, in 1999 the Edwards Dam was removed from the Kennebec River in Maine, after federal authorities determined that the benefits of an unobstructed river exceeded the dam's value.[80]

While restoration often connotes large-scale projects, not all large initiatives qualify as *ecological* restoration. Some grandiose interventions

---

[74] Pleistocene Park, *Pleistocene Park and the North-East Scientific Station*, at www.pleistocenepark.ru/en.

[75] J. Lormier and C. Driessen, 'Bovine biopolitics and the promise of monsters in the rewilding of heck cattle' (2013) 48(8) *Geoforum* 249, 253.

[76] H. Briggs, 'Tasmania tiger DNA "resurrected"', *BBC News* 20 May 2008, at www.bbc.com/news.

[77] M. Blumm and A. Erickson, 'Dam removal in the Pacific northwest: lessons for the nation' (2012) 42(4) *Environmental Law* 1043, 1047.

[78] Ibid, 1047.

[79] International Rivers Network, 'River revival, dam removal: the global view', 2001, at www.internationalrivers.org/resources/reviving-the-world-s-rivers-4042.

[80] J. Crane, '"Setting the river free": the removal of the Edwards dam on the Kennebec Rover' (2009) 1(2) *Water History* 131.

may simply modify a single environmental feature, such as tree cover, without consideration of the mutual influences between ecological complexity and restoration outcomes. For example, the national reforestation programme of China has over many decades planted each year millions of hectares of forests with the aim to have at least 20 per cent of the country forested.[81] The Chinese effort emphasises monoculture plantings of exotics, which yield minimal wider ecological benefits such as biodiversity improvements. Other large-scale restoration programs in China, conducted under the auspices of the Sloping Land Conversion Program and the Desertification Combating Program, which began in the early 2000s, have been more helpful in at least providing collateral benefits to reduce poverty and improve the livelihood of rural households.[82]

Recognising a need for restoration merely starts the journey, because of uncertainty or disagreement about what areas to prioritise and who should take the lead. Although few places on Earth are unscathed, some remain *relatively* intact (climate change may alter that, however). Conversely, areas drastically transformed into dense cities, intensive farms, and other uses cannot realistically recover their former naturalness (although may still benefit considerably from some repair, such as the creation of urban green spaces). The aim there is thus not to fully rewild, but at least to help people reconnect to nature and create more space for wildlife.[83] Ecological restoration seems putatively most feasible for *liminal spaces* – areas neither irreparably damaged nor so substantially intact as best left alone. A liminal space could be a fragmented landscape that retains patches of native vegetation with remnant wildlife interspersed with modest human settlement and development. Even so, not all liminal environments may warrant restoration for additional reasons, such as legal obstacles, financial costs, or cultural unacceptability. As the concluding chapter of this book addresses possible reforms, it postulates some criteria that the law should consider when encouraging restoration.

---

[81] S. Richardson, *Forests and Forestry in China: Changing Patterns of Resource Development* (Island Press, 1990).
[82] R. Yin, et al., 'China's ecological rehabilitation: the unprecedented efforts and dramatic impacts of reforestation and slope protection in western China' (2005) 7 *China Environment Series* 17.
[83] D. Brantz and S. Dümpelmann (eds), *Greening the City: Urban Landscapes in the Twentieth Century* (University of Virginia Press, 2011).

Environmental Restoration Law

International Environmental Law

A useful starting point is international standards, because they may indicate broad priorities and trends in environmental law around the globe.[84] Unfortunately, judging by their state, one might assume that Earth has suffered little damage. Restoration receives sparse attention compared to that lavished on sustainable development,[85] and the legal recognition is often limited to *environmental* restoration rather than the ecological variant.[86] Recent global initiatives, such as the inclusion of restoration in the UN Sustainable Development Goals[87] adopted in 2015 and the earlier 2011 Bonn Challenge to restore, by 2020, 150 million ha of degraded land globally,[88] and 350 million ha by 2030, may raise hopes of a new sentiment. But they are not legally binding ambitions, and without substantial funding and legal accountability such political gestures should not be assumed to reflect actual government priorities.

Many environmental treaties ignore restoration. The Convention on Long-Range Transboundary Air Pollution[89] lacks relevant provisions even though 'acid rain', a form of long-range pollution that damages trees, waterways, and buildings, can necessitate remediation. Likewise, the Convention on Environmental Impact Assessment (EIA) in a Transboundary Context,[90] which contains some progressive ideas about EIA, curiously lacks anything on cumulative assessment. This omission thus limits its scope to take

---

[84] The discussion in this section draws on B.J. Richardson, 'The emerging age of ecological restoration law' (2016) 25(3) *Review of European, Comparative and International Environmental Law* 277.

[85] J. Aronson and S. Alexander, 'Ecosystem restoration is a now a global priority: time to roll up our sleeves' (2013) 21(3) *Restoration Ecology* 293.

[86] Similarly, scholarly interest on the subject is meagre; notable exceptions are A. Akhtarkhavari, A. Cliquet, and A. Telesetsky, *Ecological Restoration in International Environmental Law* (Routledge, 2016); B. Boer, 'Global environmental restoration: the role of environmental law' (IUCN Academy of Environmental Law Annual Colloquium, University of Waikato, 24–28 June 2013); T.T. Ankersen and K.E. Regan, 'Shifting baselines and backsliding benchmarks: the need for the National Environmental Legacy Act to address the ecologies of restoration, resilience and reconciliation' in A.C. Flournoy and D.M. Driesen (eds), *Beyond Environmental Law: Policy Proposals for a Better Environmental Future* (Cambridge University Press, 2010), 53.

[87] United Nations, *Transforming our World: The 2030 Agenda for Sustainable Development*, Resolution A/RES/70/1 of 25 September 2015, goals 14 and 15.

[88] Bonn Challenge, at www.bonnchallenge.org/content/challenge.

[89] Adopted 13 November 1979, in force 16 March 1983, (1979) 18 ILM 1442.

[90] Adopted 15 February 1991, in force 10 September 1997, (1991) 30 ILM 802.

account of cumulative historic losses in its assessment of new activities. Some treaties contain provisions that may imply restoration. Nature conservation treaties with omnibus obligations for 'protecting' or 'conserving' reflect this genre.[91] Consider the Ramsar Convention on Wetlands of International Importance, which requires its parties to plan for the conservation and wise use of wetlands.[92] The terms 'conservation' and 'wise use', however, are not defined in the Convention. Also potentially relevant is that the Convention obliges parties to 'endeavor through management to increase waterfowl populations on appropriate wetlands';[93] presumably, increasing waterfowl populations may require restoration of their wetland habitat.

Of the few treaties that explicitly acknowledge restoration, we can find limitations in their goals, terminology, or tools. The Convention on the Protection and Use of Transboundary Watercourses and International Lakes obliges parties 'to ensure conservation and, where necessary, restoration of ecosystems',[94] but 'restoration' is not defined and the treaty's detailed provisions focus on controlling *future* water pollution. The Convention on the Law of the Sea, the pre-eminent treaty for the marine environment, has meagre provisions.[95] Coastal states must 'restore populations of harvested species' so that they can 'produce the maximum sustainable yield',[96] but this narrow, functional objective, couched in terms of human needs, is not equivalent to restoring a marine ecosystem. The associated 1995 UN Fish Stocks Agreement relating to the conservation and management of straddling fish stocks and highly migratory fish stocks contains similarly constricted provisions.[97]

One useful way to restore oceans is to create marine protected areas, a relatively straightforward goal in coastal waters under national jurisdiction, but tricky on the high seas, where participants require additional international cooperation. Without binding legal commitments, few will devote resources to restore marine areas beyond their jurisdiction.

---

[91] The ordinary dictionary meaning of 'conservation' is 'preservation, protection, or *restoration* of the natural environment and of wildlife', Oxford Dictionary of English, at www.oxforddictionaries.com /definition/english/conservation (my emphasis).
[92] Adopted 2 February 1972, in force 21 December 1975, (1972) 11 ILM 963, Articles 2–4.
[93] Ibid, Article 4.4.
[94] Adopted 17 March 1992, in force 6 October 1996, (1992) 31 ILM 1312, Article 2.2(d).
[95] Adopted 10 December 1982, in force 16 November 1994, (1982) 21 ILM 1261.
[96] Ibid, Articles 61 and 119.
[97] Agreement for the Implementation of the Provisions of the United Nations Convention on the Law of the Sea of 10 December 1982 relating to the Conservation and Management of Straddling Fish Stocks and Highly Migratory Fish Stocks, 4 August 1995, in force 11 December 2001, (1995) 34 ILM 1542.

The largest marine protected areas are in the Indian and Pacific Oceans around the coastal waters of some British and US overseas territories.[98] While some international biodiversity regimes, as discussed below, oblige parties to restore marine and terrestrial areas, the geographical ambit of these instruments effectively limits action to areas or actors under national jurisdiction. The growth of deep seabed mining poses further pressure on marine environments, without international obligations on its proponents to practice restoration,[99] and with only a voluntary Code for Environmental Management of Marine Mining outlining such expectations as a matter of corporate ethics.[100]

Treaties governing liability and compensation for environmental damage also matter, although these also do not amount to a framework for restoration. Marine pollution control and cleanup comes under the auspices of a number of treaties such as the International Convention on Civil Liability for Oil Pollution Damage.[101] The Antarctic treaty system contains provisions for remediation of contaminated base stations, of which several such as Australia's Casey Station have become unsightly waste dumps contaminating terrestrial soils and marine sediments. The 1991 Protocol on Environmental Protection to the Antarctic Treaty[102] requires the responsible parties to remediate waste dumps and abandoned work sites.[103] This obligation, however, does not require 'the removal of any structure or waste material in circumstances where the removal by any practical option would result in greater adverse environmental impact than leaving the structure or waste material in its existing location'.[104] This and other potential loopholes in the remediation obligations have sometimes led to complacency and lack of action.[105]

Radioactive contamination from bomb tests and leaking nuclear facilities has generated demands from victims for compensation and restoration.

---

[98] According to the Marine Conservation Institute, 'Marine protected areas', at https://marine-conservation.org/what-we-do/program-areas/mpas.

[99] C.L. VanDover, et al., 'Ecological restoration in the deep sea: desiderata' (2014) 44 *Marine Policy* 98.

[100] International Marine Minerals Society, Code for Environmental Management, 2001, revised 2011, at www.immsoc.org/IMMS_code.htm.

[101] Adopted 29 November 1969, in force 19 June 1975, (1969) 9 ILM 45.

[102] Adopted 4 October 1991, in force 14 January 1998, (1991) 30 ILM 1455, Annex III, Waste Disposal and Waste Management.

[103] I. Hodgson-Johnston, 'Antarctic rubbish tips: Australia's international obligations' (2014) 29 *Australian Environment Review* 108.

[104] Article 1(5)(b).

[105] Hodgson-Johnston, 'Antarctic rubbish tips'.

While atmospheric and underwater weapons testing ceased decades ago, the Cold War legacy of such hubris lingers in some places such as the Marshall Islands. Here the United States constructed in 1979 a massive concrete dome to store 84,000 m³ of radioactive waste from its nuclear testing programme in the 1940s and 1950s, but recently the long-term security of the dome was questioned as rising sea levels from climate change disturb the site.[106] And not all the Marshall Islands were remediated, and claims for monetary compensation continue to be heard at the Nuclear Claims Tribunal that was founded by the United States in 1988 to adjudicate grievances.[107] For other forms of radioactive contamination created wholly within the United States, such as abandoned uranium mines, communities such as the Navajo have struggled to receive redress from US authorities.[108]

International law on nuclear technology traditionally focused on safety standards and emergency preparedness. The first treaty devoted to dealing with radioactive debris specifically was the 1997 Joint Convention on the Safety of Spent Fuel Management and on the Safety of Radioactive Waste Management.[109] It applies to waste from civilian nuclear reactors and waste from military activities transferred to and managed within exclusively civilian programs. The obligations on parties include, in particular, to establish a regulatory framework to govern the safety of radioactive waste and protect people and the environment against radiological hazards. This treaty, however, does not assist the victims of bomb tests. Liability for nuclear damage is covered in several instruments: the Vienna Convention on Civil Liability for Nuclear Damage;[110] Paris Convention on Third Party Liability in the Field of Nuclear Energy;[111] and in reaction to the Chernobyl disaster, the Convention on Supplementary Compensation for Nuclear Damage.[112] These instruments suffer from a variety of limitations, including the absence of a neutral tribunal to adjudicate claims, which generally must be heard in courts where the nuclear installation is located, time limits and damage limits on liability, and a

---

[106] C. Jose, K. Wall, and J Hendrik, 'This dome in the Pacific houses tons of radioactive waste – and its leaking', *The Guardian* 3 July 2015, at www.theguardian.com.
[107] Marshall Islands Nuclear Claims Tribunal Act 1988, Public Law No. 1987-24; 1988-19.
[108] R. Tsosie, 'Indigenous peoples and the ethics of remediation: redressing the legacy of radioactive contamination for native peoples and native lands' (2015) 13(1) *Santa Clara Journal of International Law* 203.
[109] Adopted 27 September 1997, in force 18 June 2001, (1997) 36 ILM 1431.
[110] Adopted 21 May 1963, in force 12 November 1977, (1963) 2 ILM 727.
[111] Adopted 29 July 1960, in force 1 April 1968, (1960) 1041 UNTS 358.
[112] Adopted 12 September 1997, in force 15 April 2015, (1997) 36 ILM 1473.

narrow definition of damage, in addition to narrow state participation in these treaties.[113]

Among examples of international law that come closer to addressing *ecological* restoration is the Convention to Combat Desertification, which defines 'combat desertification' as including 'rehabilitation of partly degraded land' and 'reclamation of desertified land'.[114] Also relevant is that the Convention proclaims that 'rehabilitation ... of land and water' is one way to achieve its objectives.[115] These provisions appropriately target the specific environmental and economic problems that the Convention aims to address. Also notable is that the Convention on Biological Diversity obliges each party, as far as possible, to 'rehabilitate and restore degraded ecosystems and promote the recovery of threatened species'; and to 'adopt measures for the recovery and rehabilitation of threatened species and for their reintroduction into their natural habitats under appropriate conditions'.[116] The Aichi Biodiversity Targets in the Convention's strategic plan for 2010-20 include several relevant goals, including restoration of 'ecosystems that provide essential services' such as water (target 14), and to restore at least 15 per cent of degraded ecosystems with a view to improving ecosystem resilience, and combating climate change and desertification (target 15).[117] Neither the Convention nor the Aichi targets refine restoration.[118] The World Heritage Convention, of earlier vintage, also touches on restoration in its obligation on each party 'to take the appropriate legal, scientific, technical, administrative and financial measures necessary for the ... *rehabilitation*' of this heritage.[119] This reference to

---

[113] See D.E.C. Currie, 'The problems and gaps in the nuclear liability conventions and an analysis of how an actual claim would be brought under the current existing treaty regime in the event of a nuclear accident' (2008) 35(1) *Denver Journal of International law and Policy* 85.

[114] Convention to Combat Desertification in Those Countries Experiencing Serious Drought and/or Desertification, Particularly in Africa, 14 October 1994, in force 26 December 1996, (1994) 33 ILM 1328, Articles 1, and 5, 6 and 10.

[115] Ibid, Article 2.

[116] Adopted 5 June 1992, in force 29 December 1993, (1992) 31 ILM 818, Articles 8(f) and 9(c).

[117] D. Jorgensen, 'Ecological restoration in the Convention on Biological Diversity targets' (2013) 22 *Ecological Restoration* 2077.

[118] But state parties at least have recognised the need to address this lacuna: Decisions Adopted by the Conference of the Parties to the Convention on Biological Diversity at Its Eleventh Meeting, 'Ecosystem Restoration', UNEP/CBD/COP/DE/XI/16, (Hyderabad, India, 8-19 October 2012).

[119] Convention Concerning the Protection of the World Cultural and Natural Heritage, 16 November 1972, in force 17 December 1975 (1972) 11 ILM 1358, Article 5.4.

'rehabilitation' also appears in several other provisions of the Convention concerning the functions of its World Heritage Committee.[120]

Legal obligations for ecological restoration also appear in biodiversity protection directives of the EU. The definition of conservation in the 1992 Habitats Directive is to 'maintain or *restore* the natural habitats and the populations of species of wild fauna and flora at a favourable status'.[121] It also refers explicitly to restoration for the same purpose in several of its substantive obligations.[122] Also relevant are the Directive's criteria for selecting sites as special areas of conservation: one criterion is the site's 'restoration possibilities'.[123] The Habitats Directive is particularly apt for restoration given Europe's long history of environmental transformation, but yields no guidance on the historic benchmark for recovery of degraded places. The accompanying European Biodiversity Strategy sets a target that 'by 2020, ecosystems and their services are maintained and enhanced by establishing green infrastructure and *restoring at least 15 per cent of degraded ecosystems*'.[124] Concomitantly, the European Landscape Convention[125] acknowledges the importance of ecological restoration, albeit in a cursory manner.

International climate change law provides the newest arena for ecological restoration standards. The past is explicitly evoked in the Paris Agreement of 2015 with its commitment to hold the 'global average temperate... well below 2°C above pre-industrial levels and to pursuing efforts to limit the temperature increase to 1.5°C above pre-industrial levels' – although curiously the Agreement does not define the period denoted by the 'pre-industrial' baseline. But with some climate change already coming, it must be reckoned with in planning for ecological restoration. Global warming may seem an obstacle to restoration because the predicted environmental shifts may undermine any curative interventions. Restoring the habitat of endangered wildlife may be pointless if a changing climate

---

[120] Articles 22–4.
[121] Council Directive 92/43/EEC on the Conservation of Natural Habitats and of Wild Fauna and Flora, OJ L 206/7, 22 July 1992, Article 1(a) (my emphasis).
[122] Ibid, Articles 2–4.
[123] Ibid, annex III, A(c) and B(b).
[124] European Commission, *Our Life Insurance, Our Natural Capital: An EU Biodiversity Strategy to 2020*, Communication from the Commission to the European Parliament, the Council, the Economic and Social Committee and the Committee of the Regions, Com/2011/0244 Final (my emphasis).
[125] European Treaty Series No. 176, 2000, Article 1 ('Landscape planning', a term used in the Convention, is defined as 'strong forward-looking action to enhance, restore or create landscape').

alters the suitability of that habitat. The prospect of climate change may also be abused as an excuse to avoid ecological restoration. On the other hand, climate mitigation measures such as reforestation (being promoted through the Reduced Emissions from Deforestation and Degradation (REDD-plus)) may contribute to restoration.[126] Climate change must be incorporated into restoration work such as through additional buffers and safety margins to accommodate changing climatic conditions. Ecosystems are always in a state of flux: climate change accelerates that flux.

It is unnecessary to labour further on how international law deals with restoration – this discussion serves to illustrate broad patterns rather than discern all details. The key takeaway is that ecological restoration remains outside the fundamental goals of global law, a poor cousin of the philosophy of sustainability. Restoration garners acknowledgement in a piecemeal manner in some instruments, but without the necessary status as a core pillar of global governance. An international treaty dedicated specifically to ecological restoration is probably needed in order to elevate its salience. Even among 'soft law' instruments, where one commonly finds more expansive aspirations, references to ecological restoration are sparse. Both the World Charter for Nature of 1982[127] and Rio Declaration on Environment and Development of 1992[128] each contain just one relevant clause. As already noted, the UN Sustainable Development Goals of 2015 give more recognition to restoration, but without any concomitant legal changes. Overall, so far international environmental law provides limited direction or obligation on nation states to practice ecological restoration; though it does not necessarily constrain those who wish to innovate.

Domestic Law and Environmental Restoration

Laws and policies relating to environmental restoration have been around for some time. The infamous American 'Dust Bowl' of the 1930s, perhaps that country's worst environmental disaster, inspired the federal government to enact in 1935 the Soil Conservation and Domestic Allotment

---

[126] P. Kanowski, C. McDermott, and B. Cashore. 'Implementing REDD: lessons from analysis of forest governance' (2011) 14 *Environmental Science and Policy* 111.
[127] Adopted 28 October 1982, GA Res. 7, 36 UN GAOR Supp. (No. 51) at 17, UN Doc. A/51 (1982) clause 11(e) ('areas degraded by human activities shall be rehabilitated for purposes in accord with their natural potential').
[128] Adopted 14 June 1992, UN Doc. A/CONF.151/26 (vol. I), (1992) 31 ILM 874, principle 7 ('States shall cooperate in a spirit of global partnership to conserve, protect and restore the health and integrity of the Earth's ecosystem').

Act[129] and to establish the Soil Conservation Service to administer tougher soil erosion control and repair programs. Another early initiative was the US Federal Aid in Wildlife Restoration Act 1937,[130] which earmarked revenue from a new tax on firearms and ammunition for wildlife enhancement projects, although the funds flowed primarily to projects benefitting game animals prized by hunters.[131] A further precedent is Britain's National Parks and Access to the Countryside Act 1949, which empowered local authorities to acquire and restore derelict lands.[132]

In recent decades, numerous other countries have introduced relevant regulations and associated policies, including Australia, Brazil, Kenya, New Zealand, and South Africa, but most of these laws, like the early American and British initiatives, aim for *environmental* restoration rather than the ecological approach. Even where laws explicitly convey restoration goals, most commonly in nature conservation statutes, few articulate comprehensive and holistic restoration standards and duties.[133] In some nations, restoration has become a major national priority, as in Germany after the 1990 national reunification when extensive restoration programs of contaminated lands and waters in the former East Germany were initiated to address the legacies of industrial development.[134] But even here, the German approach emphasises site remediation rather than landscape restoration.

Presently, legal mandates and procedures for environmental restoration exist in seven situations, and legal recognition of the legacy of past damage provides a related eighth context. These contexts are:

1. Industry-specific regulations pertaining to the resources sector that require rehabilitation of discrete sites with discernible temporal and spatial parameters, such as a former mine or forestry coupe.[135]

---

[129] Public Law No. 74–461.
[130] 50 Stat. 917.
[131] H. Doremus, 'Restoring endangered species: the importance of being wild' (1999) 28 *Harvard Environmental Law Review* 1, 6–7.
[132] 12, 13 and 14 Geo 6, c. 97, s. 89.
[133] H. Schoukens, 'Ecological restoration as the 21st century environmental paradigm. Is EU law capable of saving our declined nature?', in J. De Bruyne, et al. (eds), *Policy within and Through Law: Proceedings of the 2014 ACCA-Conference* (Maklu, 2015), 63.
[134] P C. Wood, 'German policy response to an environmental crisis: the case of the former East Germany' in D. Soden and B.R. Steel (eds), *Handbook of Global Environmental Policy and Administration* (Marcel Dekker, 1999), 495, 501–8.
[135] G. Tordoff, A.J. Baker, and A. Willis, 'Current approaches to the revegetation and reclamation of metalliferous mine wastes' 41 *Chemosphere* (2000) 219.

2. Remediation procedures, such as obligations on owners of polluted brownfield sites, and standards for cleanup after major environmental emergencies and disasters.
3. Conservation law programs for the recovery of endangered species, in which the goal is species recovery rather than necessarily recovery of the ecosystems they inhabit.
4. Development controls that allow for biodiversity offsets or other environmental offsets that serve to restore degraded areas to compensate for losses precipitated by a new development.
5. As part of law enforcement sanctions against persons who have unlawfully damaged the environment, such as pollution of a waterway or disturbance of wildlife habitat.
6. Pursuant to civil liability suits to recover the costs of environmental damage.
7. As part of the general statutory functions of public agencies, such as under land use planning and development control legislation.
8. EIA procedures that require consideration of cumulative impacts may provide room to take account of past losses, although unlike the foregoing contexts such procedures do not necessarily require restoration.

The first listed context, which commonly involves waste removal, revegetation and measures to improve aesthetics, may be incorporated into the licence conditions of developments such as open cut mines. Examples are found in South Africa's Mineral and Petroleum Resources Development Act 2002[136] and the US Surface Mining Control and Reclamation Act 1977.[137] Forestry operations also are commonly subject to conditions for replanting, as in New Zealand's Forests Act 1949.[138] Such interventions help return land to productive use with some collateral environmental benefits, but they do not seek landscape-scale systemic improvements.

Remediation of contaminated land and water, the second context, is a significant regulatory burden in many jurisdictions because of the legacy of industrial development. The burden is commonly assigned to current landowners even if previous occupants caused the damage. England's Environment Act 1995 contains representative provisions for restoration

---

[136] Act No. 28, 2002, s. 5(c); see also the National Environmental Management Act 1998, Act No. 107, 1998, s. 24G(3).
[137] Public Law No. 95-87.
[138] Public Act 1949, No. 19, schedule 2, ss. 8 and 10 (logging of New Zealand's *indigenous* forests ceased in 2002).

of such brownfield property.[139] Kenya's Environmental Management and Co-ordination Act 1999 establishes a National Environment Restoration Fund to meet costs where perpetrators of environmental degradation cannot be identified.[140] The US 'Superfund' legislation authorises the EPA to remediate contaminated sites on private property and seek financial contribution from private owners.[141] The EU's Environmental Liability Directive of 2004 also provides for government engagement in restoration activities and cost recovery, like the Superfund scheme.[142] The goal of remediation, according to the Directive, is 'to ensure, as a minimum, that the relevant contaminants are removed, controlled, contained or diminished so that the contaminated land, taking account of its current use or approved future use . . . no longer poses any significant risk of adversely affecting human health'.[143] Apart from cleanup regulations, the common law or constitutional rights may be used to solicit court orders to oblige remediation. The Supreme Court of Argentina in *Mendoza Beatriz Silva, et al v. State of Argentina, et al.*[144] ruled that the federal government and local authorities in Buenos Aires had violated a constitutional right to a healthy environment by allowing the degradation of the Riachuelo River, and thus the authorities had an obligation to restore it.

While these interventions can be important locally, especially for reducing public health risks, they do not aim to restore the integrity, health, and function of ecosystems. The legal standards of remediation may be limited to allow intended future uses of the land, such as housing, which is very different from ecological rewilding. Imposing liability for the cost of remediation may also be frustrated when companies are bankrupt or corporate groups hide behind undercapitalised partners shouldered with responsibility for environmental compliance. Queensland's innovative Environmental Protection (Chain of Responsibility) Act 2016 (Qld) attempts to overcome these barriers by allowing environmental rehabilitation orders to be issued against 'a party' that had some relevant association with a company that was in financial distress (e.g. a parent company

---

[139] 1995, c. 25, Part 11A.
[140] 1999, c. 387, s. 25.
[141] Comprehensive Environmental Response, Compensation and Liability Act 1980, Public Law No. 96–510.
[142] Directive 2204/35/EC, of the European Parliament and of the Council of 21 April 2004 on Environmental Liability with regard to the Prevention and Remedying of Environmental Damage 2004/35/EC, 2004 OJ L 143/56, 30 April 2004.
[143] Ibid, at Annex II(2).
[144] JTS 1569, XL (9 July 2008).

or senior manager), and thereby to enable cost recovery for the cleanup. The Queensland legislation may have been influenced by allegations that mining companies were failing to provide adequate financial assurances to meet post-mine rehabilitation obligations.[145]

Recovery of endangered species is the third arena for restoration law. Capable of being undertaken *in situ* or *ex situ*, the former approach is more likely to offer broad environmental benefits such as improvements of wildlife habitat. Some species recovery programs are designed not to rebuild biodiversity for ecological benefits but to rebuild populations for harvesting, as occurs in some fisheries governance.[146] Species recovery laws typically only target part of the wider ecological niche of an endangered creature (e.g. removing a specific threatening process such as an invasive pest), and thus are usually not equivalent to full ecological restoration. The United States pioneered endangered species legislation, with the federal Endangered Species Act 1973 providing a mandate to restore wildlife populations. It directs federal agencies to further the 'conservation' of listed species, a term defined to mean more than just preventing extinction, but to take all necessary steps, including 'propagation, live trapping, and transplantation' to enable listed species to no longer require legal protection.[147] It has been a precedent for many jurisdictions. There are as yet no legal requirements in any country to restore extinct species, although some scientists experiment with resurrecting lost creatures, such as the passenger pigeon and the thylacine.[148]

The impact of endangered species laws is questionable if measured by the number of imperilled species recovering so as to be removed from statutory lists. Only 1.3 per cent of the species ever listed under the American legislation (28 out of 2105 species) have been delisted because they have recovered sufficiently, according to a 2013 report.[149] The fact that listings of endangered species have far outpaced delistings under the American legislation over the past 40 years reflects the lack of effective progress in curbing the underlying threatening process, with most species destined

---

[145] Environmental Justice Australia (EJA), *Dodgy Clean Up Costs: Six Tricks Coal Mining Companies Play* (EJA, 2016).
[146] E.g. Fisheries Management Act 1994 (NSW).
[147] Public Law No. 93–205, 16 USC s. 1532(3).
[148] M.R. O'Connor, *Resurrection Science: Conservation, De-Extinction and the Precarious Future of Wild Things* (St Martin's Press, 2015).
[149] Figures as of 2013, according to Louis Jacobson, 'Only 1 per cent of endangered species list have been taken off list, says Cynthia Lummis', *Politifact* 3 September 2013, at www.politifact.com.

to 'remain on the list forever'.[150] In some cases, the problem is the failure to list imperilled species, a lacuna that has arisen often enough with Canada's Species at Risk Act (SARA) 2002.[151] A threatened species may be overlooked despite advice from the designated scientific committee if politicians have other priorities (as they have done in Canada on at least 30 proposed listings). The polar bear, gravely at risk from climate change,[152] is listed under the Canadian legislation under the lesser category of 'special concern' (it has been listed as 'threatened' under the US legislation since 2008), thereby providing the species with the fewest available protections under the legislation. Overall, according to one evaluation of SARA in 2012, 'because of ongoing and illegal foot-dragging by the federal government, only two species listed under SARA have any more protection of their critical habitat now than they did prior to listing'.[153]

A fourth legal situation for restoration is within statutory penalties for causing environmental damage.[154] Consider Australia's Great Barrier Reef Marine Park Act 1975 (Cth), whose only mechanism for obliging restoration is in response to offences for reef damage.[155] Similarly, the Wildlife and Natural Environment (Scotland) Act 2011 authorises a restoration order against anyone who has unlawfully damaged the environment.[156] The limitation of such provisions is that they do not empower authorities to *initiate* restoration when no offence has occurred, and much damage ensues from officially authorised activities such as farms and mines. The Great Barrier Reef itself is degraded by farm runoff and has reportedly lost 50 per cent of its coral since 1985 partly due to such impacts (as well as coral bleaching from climate change), despite the reef having World Heritage status.[157]

Environmental offsets constitute the newest arena for restoration. Offsets provide environmental improvements to counterbalance the

---

[150] H. Doremus and J.E. Pagel, 'Why listing may be forever: perspectives on delisting under the U.S. Endangered Species Act' (2001) 15(5) *Conservation Biology* 1258.

[151] SC 2002, c. 29; see S. Nixon, et al., *Failure to Protect: Grading Canada's Species at Risk Laws* (Ecojustice, 2012).

[152] Two-thirds of polar bear habitat is expected to evaporate by 2050: S. Amstrup, B. Marcot, and D. Douglas, *Forecasting the Range Wide: Status of Polar Bears at Selected Times in the 21st Century* (US Department of Interior and Geological Survey, 2007), 6.

[153] S. Nixon et al., Failure to Protect, at 8.

[154] See generally M.L. Larsson (ed), *The Law of Environmental Damage: Liability and Reparation* (Martinus Nijhoff Publishers, 1999).

[155] Section 61A.

[156] 2011 asp 6.

[157] J. Eilperin, 'Great Barrier Reef has lost half its corals since 1985, new study says', *Washington Post* 1 October 2012, at www.washingtonpost.com.

residual impacts of a new activity that cannot be mitigated at its site, with the offset typically included as a condition of development approval. Environmental offsets began as informal experiments by regulators seeking creative ways to allow economic developments that otherwise would be environmentally unacceptable. They now increasingly feature in in sophisticated legislation, such as Queensland's Environmental Offsets Act 2014 (Qld), which runs to nearly 80 pages. The market for carbon offsets is also receiving legislative impetus, such as Australia's Carbon Credits (Carbon Farming Initiative) Act 2011 (Cth) which allows farmers and other land managers to earn marketable carbon credits by storing carbon or reducing greenhouse gas emissions on their property. Offsets, especially in the biodiversity context, remain controversial because of concerns of unacceptable trade-offs and difficulties in measuring equivalences in ecological values.[158] A significant temporal gap may arise between the impacting development and the offset gains, and uncertainty whether the gains, such as a replanted forest, will ever materialise. Apart from these limitations relating to the integrity of the environmental offset, as elements of markets for ecosystem services they may exclude 'goods and services that are less capable of monetization' and thus jeopardise restoration priorities.[159]

The problematic nature of offsets is illustrated by the *Briels* decision of the Court of Justice of the European Union (CJEU).[160] A Dutch authority had permitted widening of an existing motorway, which would adversely affect marshes in a nearby Natura 2000 site. The EU Habitats Directive obliges national authorities to approve projects only after a habitat assessment confirms that they will not adversely affect the integrity of the Natura 2000 sites.[161] In the *Briels* case, the Dutch authority, pursuant to a habitat assessment, allowed a habitat offset as mitigation, even though it was unclear whether the creation of new meadows would appropriately offset damage from the motorway project. The CJEU ruled against the Dutch offset plan, holding firstly that it would not provide acceptable 'mitigation' as it was aimed neither at avoiding nor reducing the adverse effects; and secondly, the proposed offset violated the precautionary principle, which underpins the habitats assessment criteria of the Habitats Directive.

---

[158] P. Gibbons and D. Lindenmayer, 'Offsets for land clearing: no net loss or the tail wagging the dog?' (2007) 8(1) *Ecological Management and Restoration* 26.
[159] Telesetsky, 'Ecoscape', 522.
[160] *Briel* v. *Minster of Infrastructur en Milieu*, Case C-521/12, 15 May 2014.
[161] Directive 92/43/EEC of 21 May 1992 on the Conservation of Natural Habitats and of Wild Fauna and Flora, OJ L 206/7, 22 July 1992, Article 6(3).

On the latter point, the CJEU noted, 'any positive effects of a future creation of a new [offset] habitat . . . are highly difficult to forecast with any degree of certainty and, in any event, will be visible only several years into the future'.[162] In effect, the *Briels* judgement suggests that restoration, in the guise of 'offsets', must be a last resort when environmental damage cannot be avoided or reduced.

The sixth legal context for environmental restoration is civil liability litigation to recover the costs of private injuries to human health or property. Since environmental regulation addresses mainly public interests, with prevention of future damage rather than reparation of past injury its priority, any individual victims may need to rely on the common law for redress. Remedies for the torts of nuisance or negligence may provide such redress, along with any legislation that allows victims to recover compensation from perpetrators. Sometimes litigation for this purpose is conducted in class action suits, often known as 'toxic tort litigation', involving hundreds or thousands of plaintiffs. The infamous 1979 'Love Canal' episode in the United States was an early example of the mounting torrent of toxic tragedies.[163] Such litigation has evolved to be used creatively to allow plaintiffs to recover in negligence or nuisance for chronic hazards, including recovery for stress and fear engendered by latent and lingering toxic exposures despite the lack of manifestation of actual damage.[164]

As a fillip for environmental restoration, civil liability litigation is quite limited. It aims to compensate victims, rather than repair damage *per se*: monetary compensation may not necessarily be spent to remediate the pollution. Second, evidential hurdles exist in meeting legal thresholds of a causative link between exposure to a hazardous substance and the resulting harm.[165] A long latency period between initial exposure and manifestation of harm in victims of toxic waste pollution is well known.[166] Latent environmental impacts are especially problematic when coupled with legislation that creates limitation periods for bringing actions, either in the form of a statute of limitations or a statute of repose. In these situations, plaintiffs with latent injuries run the risk of having their claims

---

[162] *Briel v. Minster of Infrastructur en Milieu*, para. 32.
[163] A. Levine, *Love Canal: Science, Politics and People* (Lexington Books, 1982).
[164] A.P. Rosen, 'Emotional distress damages in toxic tort litigation: the move towards foreseeability' (1992) 3 *Villanova Environmental Law Journal* 113.
[165] E. Forgotson, 'Liability for long-term latent effects of toxic agents' (1964) 50(2) *American Bar Association Journal* 142-3.
[166] J. Zinns, 'Close encounters of the toxic kind – toward an amelioration of substantive and procedural barriers for latent toxic injury plaintiffs' (1981) 54 *Temple Law Quarterly* 822.

systematically barred despite their merits; alternatively, by the time the harm materialises, the defendant may be bankrupt or otherwise judgment-proof. A statute of limitation 'restricts the amount of time in which plaintiffs may file actions in court to enforce rights after their injuries have been, or should have been, discovered' while statutes of repose 'limit the time during which a defendant may bear potential liability for injuries against plaintiffs'.[167] Statutes of repose seem to be a distinctly American phenomenon, and the number of years prescribed as the time limit varies from state to state, commonly at about one decade, while statutes of limitations run up to 6 years.[168]

Nor does a successful suit provide legal remedies to animals and plants, unless a person owns them. The question of who or what environmental law should protect was voiced by American scholar Christopher Stone in his 1972 polemic 'Should trees have standing?'.[169] He argued that only by granting legal rights to natural places could we change the culture that sees nature as an expedient resource for our use and at our disposal. A vision that evokes Stone's ideal is starting to find legal traction in some countries, such as New Zealand, where a long-running dispute between the government and Maori over management of a major waterway concluded in 2012, with the parties agreeing that the Whanganui River is a legal person with its own rights, and that two guardians, one each appointed by the local Maori tribe and government, will protect the river's interests for forever.[170] Guardianship is one means by which trees can acquire standing, and thus allow law suits to be brought on behalf of nature to recover compensation to fund its restoration.

Environmental restoration may also occur pursuant to the broad statutory functions of public agencies that manage or supervise the use of land and waters. These laws may usefully offer broad plenary powers to engage in various restorative interventions. Conversely, their often vague, aspirational tone creates room to do nothing. South Africa's lodestar National Environmental Management Act includes 'remedying' environmental damage among its

---

[167] A. Ferrer, 'Excuses, excuses: the application of statutes of repose to environmentally-related injuries' (2006) 33 *Boston College Environmental Affairs Law Review* 345, 347–8.

[168] American Council of Engineering Companies, 'Statutes of repose/statutes of limitations', at www.acec.org/advocacy/committees/pdf/statuteofreposelimitations.pdf.

[169] C.D. Stone, 'Should trees have standing? Towards legal rights for natural objects' (1972) 45 *Southern California Law Review* 450.

[170] K. Shuttleworth, 'Agreement entitles Whanganui River to legal identity', New Zealand Herald 30 August 2012, at www.nzherald.co.nz.

core principles that decision-makers must give 'consideration'.[171] The official objects of South Australia's Environmental Protection Act 1993 (SA) include that 'proper weight should be given . . . to . . . *restoration* and enhancement' and 'to ensure that all reasonable and practicable measures are taken to . . . *restore* . . . the environment'.[172] But without performance criteria or statutory definitions, we cannot readily determine whether the restoration duties receive 'proper weight' or 'consideration'. Nor does this legislation offer any specific tools for undertaking restoration. A potentially more useful law is the Environment (Wales) Act 2016, whose stated purpose is 'to promote sustainable management of natural resources',[173] and it includes a duty on public authorities to 'seek to maintain and enhance biodiversity . . . and in so doing promote the resilience of ecosystems'.[174] Commendably, the Act elaborates on the latter goal, of direct relevance to restoration, by stipulating that authorities 'must take account of' five enumerated ecological conditions including the 'adaptability of ecosystems'.[175]

New Zealand's Resource Management Act (RMA) 1991, the country's main legislation governing land use development, also has some relevant provisions. Notably, regional councils must, when preparing a land use plan, consider 'the restoration or enhancement of any natural and physical resources in a deteriorated state or the avoidance or mitigation of any such deterioration',[176] and any local planning authority may include in a resource consent 'a condition requiring . . . replanting of any tree or other vegetation or the protection, restoration, or enhancement of any natural or physical resource, be provided'.[177] But the New Zealand legislation neither defines restoration nor includes restoration among its guiding principles and objects. At least it is better than Australia's Environment Protection and Biodiversity Conservation Act 1999 (Cth), the country's premier law in its field: it lacks any explicit reference to restoration or related terms, even within its statement of objects and its definition of 'ecologically sustainable development'.[178]

---

[171] Act No. 107, 1998, s. 2(4).
[172] Section 10(1)(a)(ii) and 10(1)(b) (my emphasis). The Act contains numerous other references to 'rehabilitation'.
[173] Section 1.
[174] 2016 anaw 3, s. 6(1).
[175] Ibid, s. 6(2)(e).
[176] Public Act 1991, No. 69, s. 65(3)(f)).
[177] Ibid, s. 108(2)(c).
[178] Sections 3 and 3A. Although authorities regard the legislation as supporting restoration, since subsidiary regulations refer to restoration, such as in regard to wetlands: Environment Protection and Biodiversity Conservation Regulations 2000 (Cth), schedule 6, clauses 2.02(a), (c), (e)(iii)–(iv), (f)–(g).

The lack of statutory definition of 'restoration' in the foregoing examples brings additional confusion when legislation includes inconsistent language, including to 'remediate', 'rehabilitate', or 'repair', as occurs with the Canadian Environmental Protection Act 1999.[179] Slightly better, the Canadian Environmental Assessment Act 2012 includes 'restoration' in its definition of 'mitigation measures', but omits a separate definition of restoration itself.[180] The Environmental Trust Act 1998 (NSW), a law of the Australian state of New South Wales, creates a financial trust 'to encourage and support restoration and rehabilitation projects in both the public and private sectors',[181] but bizarrely it does not define 'restoration' or 'rehabilitation'. This undefined terminology may diminish public accountability for restoration activities as well as foster diverse and potentially counterproductive practices.

The foregoing analysis thus reveals a piecemeal approach to environmental restoration, with little evidence of its recognition as a fundamental pillar of environmental law, and a pervasive failure to define key terminology and provide implementation tools. How the legal system acknowledges past ecological losses in regulating new activities is a further metric by which we can measure the overall importance given to restoration. As noted earlier, an eighth legal context for restoration relates to environmental assessment legislation, a subject that deserves its own section as it focuses not on undertaking restoration *per se* but rather taking past losses into account when regulating future uses.

Seeing the Forest for the Trees: Environmental Assessment

Some environmental changes are immediate and obvious, such as when a new dam suddenly impounds a river. But many simmer for ages: climate modification, habitat loss and fragmentation, and pesticide accretion are examples. We might characterise the latter as 'death by a thousand cuts' or the 'tyranny of small decisions', and they are worrisome because we may not be aware of their perniciousness until too late. Adverse environmental changes from the past might not become apparent until some tipping point is breached due to an additional development pressure that alone might be viewed as innocuous. The notion of 'cumulative impacts' captures this broad context: cumulative impact is, by nature, significant over

---

[179] SC 1999, c. 33, ss 2(1), 196, 205, 234(4), 294.1
[180] SC 2012, c. 19, s. 2.
[181] Section 7(a).

either a wider time frame or a wider spatial context. We can delineate several types of cumulative effects, explains Brian Noble, a leading Canadian researcher in this field: *linear* additive effects, which are additional to each prior individual effects; *amplifying* effects, in which the incremental addition has a larger effect than the one proceeding; and *discontinuous* effects, where additional impacts do not manifest until a specific threshold is crossed.[182] One of the challenges for environmental law in acquiring better rear vision is to take into account these cumulative environmental effects and forestall them before serious or irreparable damage occurs.[183] Regulating cumulative effects is essential to avoid the twin problems of shifting baselines and the tyranny of small decisions that fuel continued environmental degradation.

Environmental impact assessment in theory meets these challenges, to enable us to see the forest for the trees. It has been a pillar of environmental law since the 1970s, when the United States pioneered the National Environmental Policy Act (NEPA) 1969: it requires federal agencies to assess the environmental effects of their proposed actions before making decisions.[184] The purpose of NEPA is not just to assess impacts and complete an Environmental Impact Study (EIS); it also aims to improve the quality of decisions, in that governing agencies will take actions that 'protect, restore, and enhance the environment'.[185] The broad range of actions NEPA covers includes permit applications, federal land management actions, and construction of public infrastructure. In theory, procedures for EIS preparation not only enable careful evaluation of the environmental and related social and economic effects of proposed actions, but also opportunities for public consultation. EIA is now practised in more than 100 countries worldwide,[186] with the particular details of EIA practices varying according to the jurisdiction and legislative context. They may also vary depending on the type of impact under evaluation. In many

---

[182] B. Noble, *Cumulative Environmental Effects and the Tyranny of Small Decisions*, Occasional Paper No. 8 (Natural Resources and Environmental Studies Institute, University of Northern British Columbia, 2010), 4.
[183] H. Spaling and B. Smit, 'Cumulative environmental change: conceptual frameworks, evaluation approaches and institutional perspectives' (1993) 17 *Environmental Management* 587.
[184] Public Law No. 91-190.
[185] A. Steinemann, 'Improving alternatives for environmental impact assessment' (2001) 21 *Environmental Impact Assessment Review* 3-4.
[186] H. Alshuwaikhat, 'Strategic environmental assessment can help solve environmental impact assessment failures in developing countries' (2005) 25 *Environmental Impact Assessment Review* 307-8.

instances, the responsible agency has significant discretion to determine the factors included in an EIA and the weight each factor will receive in the assessment and final decision.

EIA is typically regarded as an *anticipatory* environmental management tool that evaluates the environmental effects likely to arise from a project or action. Consideration of cumulative effects has tended to be rationalised to avoid further environmental losses rather than as an opportunity to cure past losses. In the Australian case of *Gray v. Minister for Planning*, Judge Nicola Pain argued that in an:

> environmental impact assessment which takes into account the principle of intergenerational equity . . ., one important consideration must be the assessment of cumulative impacts of proposed activities on the environment . . . [F]ailure to consider cumulative impact will not adequately address the environmental impact of a particular development where often no single event can be said to have such a significant impact that it will irretrievably harm a particular environment but cumulatively activities will harm the environment.[187]

The assessment of cumulative environmental effects is now a characteristic of many project-based EIA regulations around the world. It has been mandatory in Canada since 1995, for instance. The Canadian Environmental Assessment Act 2012 lists considerations during a federal EIA of a designated project, which include '(a) the environmental effects of the designated project, including . . . any cumulative environmental effects that are likely to result'.[188] The Guidelines for EIA in the Arctic prepared by the Finnish Ministry of the Environment highlight that 'in the Arctic, cumulative impacts are of special concern because of the sensitivity of the area and the long recovery times'[189] and thus 'impact assessment, particularly for assessments of cumulative impacts, may extend beyond the period of time required for the assessment of the project activities'.[190] New Zealand's RMA obliges planning authorities to assess cumulative impacts in a variety of regulatory contexts.[191] Cumulative effects must also

---

[187] *Gray v. Minister for Planning*, [2006] NSWLEC 720, para. 122
[188] SC 2012, c 19, s. 19.
[189] Finnish Ministry of the Environment, *Arctic Environmental Protection Strategy: Guidelines for Environmental Impact Assessment (EIA) in the Arctic* (1997), 9.
[190] Ibid, 21.
[191] Public Act 1991, No. 69, s. 3 of the Act defines 'effect', a pivotal term throughout the Act, to include 'any cumulative effect'. See further J. Dixon and B. Montz, 'From concept to practice: implementing cumulative. Impact assessment in New Zealand' (1995) 19(3) *Environmental Management* 445.

be considered in the United States pursuant to regulations of the Council on Environmental Quality in relation to implementation of NEPA.[192] The assessment of cumulative effects is also required by EU members pursuant to several directives, two of which deal with project-level EIA[193] and another with strategic assessment of government programs and plans.[194]

In practice, the quality of cumulative assessment can fall well short of the foregoing aspirations. With project-based EIA, the most widespread form, the potential contribution of cumulative assessment to decision-making is limited by two characteristics of the EIA process. Firstly, the assessments use truncated spatial and temporal scales, such as considering effects only in the same locality.[195] Secondly, EIA tends to measure direct, immediate impacts, rather than also synergistic interactions. Because project-based EIA focuses narrowly on the project itself, it may only successfully address simple, linear cumulative effects rather than complex interactive effects.[196]

Two contexts in which assessment of cumulative effects may do better are strategic EIA and landscape-scale planning, as both expand the assessment beyond individual projects and sites. Such methods, offering higher-tiered assessment process, should ideally occur before any project-based EIAs take place so that the latter can take into account the bigger picture. The EU's directive on strategic EIA is a well-known legal precedent, applying to a range of government plans and programmes.[197] The directive makes a strategic EIA mandatory for plans and programs in designated sectors (e.g. agriculture, energy, fisheries, transport, and waste) that set the framework for future development consent of projects listed in the separate EIA directive. The European law does not extend EIA to policies, as is possible in some countries, such as under

---

[192] Council on Environmental Quality, *Considering Cumulative Effects under the National Environmental Policy Act* (Council on Environmental Quality, Executive Office of the President, 1997).

[193] Directive 85/337/EEC on the assessment of effects of certain public and private projects on the environment, OJ L 175/40, 5 July 1985; Directive 97/11/EC amending Directive 85/337/EEC on the assessment of the effects of certain public and private projects on the environment, OJ L. 73/5, 14 March 1997.

[194] Directive 2001/42/EC of the European Parliament and of the Council of 27 June 2001 on the assessment of the effects of certain plans and programmes on the environment, OJ L 197/30, 21 July 1991.

[195] E. Joao, 'How scale affects environmental impact assessment' (2002) 22 *Environmental Impact Assessment Review* 289.

[196] Noble, *Cumulative Environmental Effects and the Tyranny of Small Decisions*.

[197] Directive 2001/42/EC of the European Parliament and of the Council of 27 June 2001 on the assessment of the effects of certain plans and programmes on the environment, OJ L 197/30, 21 July 1991.

Australia's Environment Protection and Biodiversity Conservation Act 1998 (Cth).[198] Even strategic EIA and regional planning, however, may not bring a comprehensive perspective where assessment is confined to issues within the national jurisdiction of the legislation. William Rees, the doyen of eco-footprint theory, argues that *global* constraints must also be taken into account in cumulative impact assessments.[199] Finally, it must be reiterated that EIA procedures, no matter how inclusive of different timescales, do not *per se* lead to environmental restoration; EIA aims to identify and assess the significance of impacts rather than oblige the repair of any past impacts.

Ecological Restoration Law

Legislative Frameworks

Ecological restoration is more ambitious and complex than the foregoing examples, as it aims to restore ecological structure, complexity, and integrity.[200] It also represents a radical shift beyond the 'enclave theory of conservation', in which it was once assumed that designating environmental sanctuaries and parks would suffice to meet all conservation goals while freeing the remaining, and much larger, areas for economic development.[201] Ecological restoration requires managing ecological processes across extensive land- and seascapes and taking into account numerous ecological variables, including species composition, habitat requirements, historic environmental conditions, and possible pending changes, such as global warming. Biodiversity has to be safeguarded and nurtured where it lives, which may or may not be within protected 'enclaves'. The restoration agenda has in recent years dovetailed with the 'rewilding' movement's proposals for setting aside and restoring very large areas with minimal human presence.[202]

---

[198] Section 146–54. See further S. Marsden and S. Dovers (eds), *Strategic Environmental Assessment in Australasia* (Federation Press, 2002).
[199] W. Rees, 'Cumulative environmental assessment and global change' (1995) 15(4) *Environmental Impact Assessment Review* 295.
[200] D. Hughes. 'Land conservation and restoration: moving to the landscape level' (2002–3) 21 *Vanderbilt Environmental Law Journal* 115; K. Suding, et al., 'Conservation: committing to ecological restoration' (2015) 348 *Science* 638.
[201] Sax, 'The new age of environmental restoration', 3.
[202] J.B. Mackinnon, *The Once and Future World: Nature as It Was, As It Is, As It Could Be* (Random House Canada, 2013); 'E.O. Wilson on saving half the Earth', at http://eowilson foundation.org/e-o-wilson-on-saving-half-the-earth.

Such ambition makes it difficult for ecological restoration to succeed. One obstacle is that legal boundaries, such as set by property tenure or agency jurisdiction, lead to ecologically arbitrary units for environmental management. Tenure may limit restoration to small-scale initiatives located within areas pre-defined by property law, with subsequently limited opportunities for up-scaling restoration through a landscape framework. Socially, ecological restoration is also more challenging because restoring large areas often requires the cooperation of more people – landowners, local communities, farmers, businesses, and so on. Restoration in such contexts faces obstacles if it creates too many losers or inequities. The financial cost of such restoration may also become more onerous, given the sheer size of some projects, possibly covering thousands of square kilometres. In an era where governments are in retreat due to fiscal constraints, the private sector has to shoulder more of the costs. Perhaps because of such obstacles, few examples of ecological restoration legislation exist.

Islands sometimes provide among the best opportunities for restoration because of their reasonably self-contained geography. One shining example of such restoration is Macquarie Island, a 128 km^2 subantarctic outpost controlled by the Tasmanian government. Like other subantarctic islands, Macquarie had suffered its share of feral mammals such as rats and cats, which since the mid-nineteenth century had devastated the island's vegetation and seabirds. But over several decades of intensive restoration that concluded in 2013, all the pests were eradicated by the Tasmanian Parks and Wildlife Service.[203] The efforts of the Service in restoring the World Heritage-listed island were enabled by it having legal control of the area, pursuant to Tasmania's National Parks and Reserves Management Act 2002 (Tas.) without having to contend with any other landholders or conflicting interests apart from the federal government's benign environmental oversight. Most opportunities for ecological restoration, however, lack such favourable conditions.

The United States offers the most extensive range of legislative initiatives for ecological restoration. Some projects occur under the auspices of general environmental legislation, as in places managed by the National Parks Service, while other initiatives have customised governance.[204] One example of the latter is the Collaborative Landscape Restoration Program

---

[203] J. Scott, 'Macquarie Island – exciting changes in vegetation after eradication of rabbits and rodents' (2014–15) 27 *Australian Plants* 351.

[204] Examples are discussed in W.R. Lowry, *Repairing Paradise: The Restoration of Nature in America's National Parks* (Brookings Institution Press, 2009).

(CLRP), enacted by the US Congress in 2009 under title IV of the Omnibus Public Land Management Act.[205] Its statutory objectives are to 'encourage the collaborative, science-based ecosystem restoration of priority forest landscapes' through mechanisms that encourage 'sustainability', facilitate 'the reduction of wildfire management costs', improve 'watershed health' and use 'forest restoration byproducts' to 'offset treatment costs while benefitting local rural economies and improving forest health'.[206] Administered by the federal Department of Agriculture, CLRP projects are selected by a national panel with funding of US$40 million available annually between 2010 and 2020 to meet up to half the costs of proposals that will restore at least 50,000 acres, involve collaboration with local communities and landholders, and provide local economic and social benefits, including lowering wildfire risks. The eligible lands for restoration primarily comprise national forests, but may also include lands under the jurisdiction of other federal bodies, such as the Bureau of Indian Affairs, and potentially even adjacent private lands.

Interestingly, the legislation appropriately seeks to define the environmental baseline that funded projects will seek to restore, namely:

> restoration of, the structure and composition of old growth stands according to the pre-fire suppression old growth conditions characteristic of the forest type, taking into account the contribution of the stand to landscape fire adaptation and watershed health and retaining the large trees contributing to old growth structure.[207]

Also of precedential value are the ecological outcomes prescribed by the legislation, which include to 'improve fish and wildlife habitat', 'maintain or improve water quality and watershed function', and 'prevent, remediate, or control invasions of exotic species'.[208] One example of a CFLR initiative is the Selway-Middle Fork Clearwater Project in Idaho, which covers 600,000 ha through actions that include decommissioning roads, replacing culverts to restore fish passage, reducing fuel loads in forests, and eliminating invasive plants. The project also aims to address the region's chronic unemployment by generating new opportunities, such as reusing vegetation removed by forest thinning and fuel load reduction to support local biomass energy facilities. The multi-dimensional nature of this project, including its attentiveness to social and economic context, is notable.

---

[205] Pubic Law No. 111–11; see www.fs.fed.us/restoration/CFLRP/index.shtml.
[206] Ibid, s. 4001.
[207] Ibid, s. 4003(c)(D).
[208] Ibid, s. 4003(c)(3).

A similar legal measure has been sought for the Great Lakes region.[209] The proposed Great Lakes Ecosystem Protection Act 2012, which has so far failed to secure Congressional support, would amend federal water quality legislation to include the purpose to achieve the Great Lakes Restoration Initiative Action Plan, the Great Lakes Regional Collaboration Strategy, and the Great Lakes Water Quality Agreement of 1978. This would entail adjusting the mission of the federal EPA; streamlining the funding mechanisms for restoration in the Great Lakes area; and improving accountability. The Great Lakes region, home to about 30 million people, has been severely affected by chemical pollution and the spread of invasive species. The current restoration initiatives, which target these impacts, are implemented through precarious inter-agency collaborations, goodwill, and *ad hoc* funding.

Some US eco-restoration laws have been difficult to implement. The Clean Water Act 1972 introduced an overriding obligation to 'restore and maintain the chemical, physical and biological integrity of the Nation's waters',[210] for action via a variety of means including obligations on water users to participate in compensatory mitigation for impacts to wetlands or other aquatic areas.[211] But the law stipulates that restoration should be the 'first option' because the 'likelihood of success is greater and the ... potential gains in terms of aquatic resource functions are greater, compared to enhancement and preservation'.[212] In practice, the story has unfolded differently. Administrators have focused on eliminating chemical pollutants and repairing their damage, while making only limited progress with reversing other ecological changes including dredging, levees, and invasive species.[213] The operative provisions of the Clean Water Act also have limitations, focusing on reducing water pollution and thereafter maintaining water quality 'regardless of whether the ecological integrity of the water body has actually been restored'.[214] The Clean Water Act also comes up short on qualitative standards for ecological restoration. Authorities have stipulated two metrics for restoration: 're-establishment projects' (i.e. an increase in aquatic area and in ecosystem functions) or 'rehabilitation projects' (i.e. an increase in ecosystem functions but not aquatic resource

---

[209] See Great Lakes Ecosystem Protection Act 2012, 112th Congress, 2011–13.
[210] Public Law No. 92–500, s. 101(a).
[211] Ibid, s. 404.
[212] Clean Water Act Regulations, CFR, Title 33, Ch. 2, Part 332, s. 332.3(2).
[213] R.W. Adler, 'Resilience, restoration, and sustainability: revisiting the fundamental principles of the Clean Water Act' (2010) 32 *Law and Policy* 139, 150.
[214] Ibid, 151.

area). Other than a preference for *in situ* restoration that is ecologically self-sustaining, the regulations give no further qualitative legal standards to define an appropriate ecological restoration effort.[215]

A notable state-level restoration initiative is the Everglades Forever Act 1994.[216] Administered by the Florida Department of Environmental Protection and the South Florida Water Management District, with federal support, it aims to improve Everglades water quality by reducing phosphorus levels, restoring water flows, and removing invasive plants and animals. Other goals include water resource development and supply, increased public access, and increased protection of land through conservation easements. The Comprehensive Everglades Restoration Plan – the principal policy framework – consists of over 60 civil works projects to be implemented over a 30-year period at a cost once estimated at US$7.8 billion.[217] The Everglades Forever Act has had some success, as measured by improving water quality standards (e.g. reduced farm and urban runoff) and improved storm water treatment areas,[218] but has been less successful in restoring biodiversity, such as wading bird pairs.[219] Such benefits can be compared to the huge cost of restoring the Everglades and the complex cooperation required among a number of federal and state government agencies with conflicting mandates, as well as some private sector collaboration.[220]

Dam removal has been a feature of a number of American restoration projects mandated by law. Between 2011 and 2014, the US National Park Service removed the Elwha and Glines Canyon dams located near Olympic National Park in the state of Washington in order to restore the Elwha River to its natural flow. These dams, which were built in the early twentieth century (1912 and 1927, respectively), had blocked salmon passage to vital spawning habitat and altered the river's hydromorphology significantly.[221] The process has been drawn out since 1992 when,

---

[215] Environmental Protection Agency, 'Compensatory mitigation methods', at www.epa.gov/cwa-404/compensatory-mitigation-methods.
[216] Fla. Stat. 1994, s. 373.4592.
[217] W. Perry, 'Elements of South Florida's comprehensive Everglades Restoration Plan' (2004) 13(3) *Ecotoxicology* 185.
[218] See generally T.R. Salt, S. Langton, and M. Doyle, 'The challenges of restoring the Everglades ecosystem' in M. Doyle and C. Drew (eds), *Large-Scale Ecosystem Restoration: Five Case Studies from the United States* (Island Press, 2008), 5.
[219] M.I. Cook, 'Statewide summary' (2014) 20 *South Florida Wading Bird Report* 1.
[220] M. Doyle, 'Introduction. The watershed-wide, science-based approach to ecosystem restoration' in M. Doyle and C. Drew (eds), *Large-Scale Ecosystem Restoration: Five Case Studies from the United States* (Island Press, 2008), ix, at xii.
[221] Blumm and Erickson, 'Dam removal in the Pacific northwest', 1051.

through the Elwha River Ecosystem and Fisheries Restoration Act, Congress authorised the government to purchase the Elwha and Glines Canyon dams and directed the Department of the Interior to completely restore the Elwha River ecosystem, including dealing with these dams.[222] The government's EIS released in 1995 concluded that the only way to completely restore the river system was to remove both dams. While it is still early to discern major changes in the Elwha River ecosystem, scientists predict it will take approximately 30 years before the river's normal flows and sediment loads recover.[223] The removal of these impoundments was made easier because of their age, modest power generation, and few vested interests. By contrast, a long-standing campaign to remove the 1970s-era Lake Pedder dam from Tasmania's southwest wilderness has stalled in the face of economic costs and its political salience.[224]

Recovery of depleted fisheries resources is the focus of several other American restoration laws, including the Klamath River Basin Fishery Resources Restoration Act 1876,[225] the New England Fishery Resources Restoration Act 1990,[226] and the Trinity River Basin Fish and Wildlife Restoration Act 1990.[227] These laws promote restoration for enhancing ecosystem services aligned with human interests in fish and game exploitation. The Trinity River legislation established a public fund, created a task force, and assigned responsibilities to the federal Department of Interior to restore fish and wildlife to the numbers existing before the construction of the Trinity River section of the Central Valley Project (a federal water management project in California). The New England legislation aims to restore Atlantic salmon and other fishery of selected rivers of this region. By thus prioritising the improvement of specific ecosystem services, these laws may lead to piecemeal, simplified restoration programs that do not capture the range of ecological components and relationships.

An example of aquatic restoration legislation that embraces a more holistic approach to ecological recovery is the Estuaries and Clean Waters Act 2000, providing for the restoration of estuary habitat and development of a national strategy for this purpose, along with new financing mechanisms, information sharing and research capabilities, and the establishment of

[222] Ibid, 1046.
[223] A. East, et al., 'Large-scale dam removal on the Elwha River, Washington, USA: river channel and floodplain geomorphic change' (2015) 228 *Geomorphology* 765.
[224] Richardson, 'Rewilding Tasmania's Lake Pedder'.
[225] Public Law No. 99–552.
[226] Public Law No. 101–593.
[227] Public Law No. 98–541.

an inter-agency council to coordinate action.[228] Restoration is explicitly defined in the Act as including activities that improve or create estuary habitat 'with the goal of attaining a self-sustaining system integrated into the surrounding landscape'[229] and include actions that control exotic species, reintroduce native species, and limit construction of reefs.[230] In addition to this Act, a variety of site-specific or ecosystem-specific restoration laws have been enacted by Congress, including the Lake Pontchartrain Basin Restoration Act 2000,[231] restoration of a nationally significant water body in Louisiana, and the Tijuana River Valley Estuary and Beach Sewage Cleanup Act 2000,[232] which authorises more federal investment in wastewater treatment and associated restoration measures for this river system that straddles the United States and Mexican borders.

In comparison to the American model of dedicated legislation, some jurisdictions pursue ecological restoration through general conservation statutes in which the detailed governance is fleshed out though supplementary regulations and policies. Canada's National Parks Act stipulates that 'maintenance or restoration of ecological integrity . . . shall be the first priority of the Minister' in parks management,[233] although Canadian courts have interpreted this provision less ambitiously. In one case, allowing infrastructure development in a park, Judge Gibson explained that the Act 'requires a delicate balancing of conflicting interests which include the benefit and enjoyment of those living in, and in close proximity to, Wood Buffalo National Park . . . [and] does not require that ecological integrity be the "determinative factor" '.[234] New Zealand has dealt with restoration challenges through its Conservation Act 1987,[235] administered by the Department of Conservation (DoC). The Department takes restoration very seriously and has undertaken numerous world-class pest control and habitat improvement projects to save many of New Zealand's imperilled birds and other wildlife.[236] This commitment of DoC dovetails with a wider emphasis on ecological restoration in some New Zealand

---

[228] Public Law No. 106–457.
[229] Ibid, s. 103(4)(A).
[230] Ibid, s. 103(4)(B).
[231] Public Law No. 106–457.
[232] Ibid.
[233] SC 2000, c. 32, s. 8(2).
[234] *Canadian Parks and Wilderness Society v. Canada (Minister of Canadian Heritage)*, (2002) 2 FC D-8, para. 52–3; *affirmed* (2003) 4 FC 672.
[235] Public Act 1987, No. 65, s. 2(1).
[236] D. Butler, T. Lindsay, and J. Hunt, *Paradise Saved* (Random House New Zealand, 2014).

legislation. The statutory functions of the New Zealand Game Bird Habitat Trust Board, which administers the Wildlife Act 1953, include several references to restoration.[237] The fascinating Waitakere Ranges Heritage Area Act 2008 describes the heritage features of these ranges, located near the city of Auckland, as including to 'provide opportunities for ecological restoration',[238] and the specified statutory goals include to 'restore, and enhance the area and its heritage feature', and 'restoring and enhancing degraded landscapes'.[239] One salient lesson from the New Zealand approach is the necessity of cooperation with local communities, including Maori tribes and environmental groups (e.g. Forest and Bird Protection Society), many of which have established their own eco-sanctuaries. Funding is another theme of the New Zealand experience, with the private sector increasingly called on to cover restoration costs in the face of periodic public sector budgets (DoC itself suffered severe funding cuts in 2009 and 2013, leading to the loss of about 10 per cent of its staff).[240]

Australia, with equally serious environmental restoration needs, has followed the New Zealand approach of initiating restoration projects via general rather than specific legislation. The New South Wales National Parks and Wildlife Act 1974 (NSW) specifies that the objectives of a management plan for each park include 'the *rehabilitation* of landscapes and the *reinstatement* of natural processes',[241] while the same jurisdiction's Wilderness Act 1987 (NSW) states that a designated wilderness area shall be managed 'to *restore* (if applicable) and to protect the unmodified state of the area and its plant and animal communities'.[242] But none of these terms are defined in the statutes. Occasionally natural resource management laws contain relevant provisions, such as procedures for cleanup of waterways and riparian zones and restoration of environmental flows, as provided for in Australia's Water Act 2007 (Cth) that serves mainly to manage and restore the huge Murray–Darling River Basin. The Water Act creates the Murray–Darling Basin Authority, with a mandate to develop a Basin Plan that requires the 'sustainable use of . . . water resources to protect and *restore* the ecosystems, natural habitats and species that are reliant on the Basin water resources'.[243]

---

[237] Public Act 1953, No. 31, s. 44D(b)–(c).
[238] Local Act 2008, No. 1, s. 7(2)(a)(v).
[239] Section 8(g)(ii).
[240] J. Vernon, 'DOC job cuts a threat to NZ, says Forest and Bird', Newswire.co.nz 4 April 2013.
[241] Section 72AA(1)(h) (my emphasis).
[242] Section 9(a) (my emphasis).
[243] Section 21(2)(b) (my emphasis).

Further examples could be given here, but that might create a misleading impression that many governments have embraced ecological restoration with gusto. They have not, in general, for reasons explained at the outset of this section. Three specific legal challenges (in addition to other financial, social, and scientific challenges) need attention.

First, the pervasive problem of undefined and inconsistent terminology must be overcome. The use of loose or variable language such as 'remediate', 'repair', or 'restore' can be confusing when the focus is supposedly ecological restoration rather than a less ambitious target. Confusing languages can lead to inconsistent approaches and accountability failures. Laws must enunciate clear and consistent terminology and include relevant statutory definitions so that public accountability for restoration programs is ensured. The tendency to subsume restoration within statutory definitions of 'conservation' may obscure attention to the value of restoration as a distinct practice.

Second, related to the terminology dilemma, the law must better enunciate the goals of ecological restoration and other forms of environmental improvement. Clear statutory goals help to channel efforts efficiently towards specific outcomes and provide motivations to achieve them, as well as establishing criteria for judging success. For instance, if climate change mitigation is the aim, the law can create a framework for landowners to participate in reforestation to earn marketable carbon credits, whereas if the goal is to restore landscapes for threatened species, the purpose of restoration law will be *inter alia* to revegetate landscapes, connect fragmented bush patches, and cull feral predators. Another reason to differentiate ecological restoration goals legislatively is the outcomes sought may infer different historic baselines. Reforestation to sequester greenhouse gases does not necessarily need to be done with reference to any past benchmark, whereas it is possibly crucial for a biodiversity recovery project. And just as the law should define when to undertake restoration, it may need to discourage it when it is not feasible, such as in urbanised and intensely farmed landscapes.

Third, we need better tools. The foregoing legislative survey showed that few legal instruments are used for ecological restoration. Land use planning and conservation reserve management have been the main legal contexts for articulating restoration projects. Other tools might bring more success. For instance, we need technical standards codified in legislation to ensure projects follow rigorous science, such as setting technical standards in the same manner found in pollution control regulation. Further, EIA law should be used in strategic planning to address cumulative environmental impacts. New intergovernmental forums for multi-agency and multi-stakeholder collaborations could also help given the enlarged scale of landscape restoration projects. Changes to private land tenure may also be necessary to enable restoration of ecological corridors and sites that cut across different properties. One study of wildlife corridors and habitat connectivity projects observed that 'governance and institutional arrangement for such cross-jurisdictional corridor initiatives will always be a challenge because there is such a diversity of tenures, partners and stakeholders'.[244] Overcoming the 'current inadequate regime of piecemeal restoration', explains Anastasia Telesetsky, an American law professor, requires an 'ecoscape' or place-based framework that transcends artificial politico-legal boundaries.[245] In other words, we need legal mechanisms that can integrate actors, places, and issues into comprehensive governance regimes at the landscape scale of restoration. These ideas are pursued further in the closing chapter of this book.

Ecological Restoration Beyond the State

Private Governance

Government insouciance about restoration has encouraged the private sector to get involved, especially with wildlife habitat recovery and reforestation. Many projects now occur through community groups, environmental NGOs, indigenous tribes, and other stakeholders.[246] Their formula typically includes land purchases, agreements with property owners, pest extermination, protective fencing, and vegetation replanting.[247] Some examples to follow will help us understand their aspirations and achievements. To the extent that the law informs such efforts, it is largely confined to private law techniques such as conservation covenants supplemented by public subsidies. The control, however, typically remains with the community sector to initiate and implement the projects.

Conservation covenants feature in many private restoration initiatives, as the covenant registered on the property title can help ensure indefinite

---

[244] S. Whitten, *A Compendium of Existing and Planned Australian Wildlife Corridor Projects and Initiatives, and Case Study Analysis of Operational Experience* (CSIRO, 2011), vii.
[245] Telesetsky, 'Ecoscapes', 494.
[246] See C. Fraser, *Rewilding the World: Dispatches from the Conservation Revolution* (Picador, 2009).
[247] For more examples, see Whitten, *A Compendium of Existing and Planned Australian Wildlife Corridor Projects and Initiatives*.

protection, both by obliging restoration in the first instance and by protecting its results. Conservation covenants, also sometimes known as easements, have since the 1970s become widely used in many Anglophile countries and facilitated by legislative abrogation of the unwieldy common law variety that generally restricts a covenant to negative obligations and requires the benefit of the covenant to attach to property appurtenant to the land burdened with the obligations.[248] Covenants efficiently allow additional lands to come under stricter conservation controls without the expensive financial outlays of outright property acquisition. In some jurisdictions, special legislation, such as New Zealand's Queen Elizabeth the Second National Trust Act 1977[249] and Australia's Victorian Conservation Trust Act 1972 (Vic.), create an independent body mandated to establish conservation covenants. In 2014 the UK Law Commission recommended the introduction of a special statutory scheme in England and Wales to enable the use of conservation covenants as in these jurisdictions.[250]

As a tool for restoration, covenants have strengths and limitations. Positively, landowners may feel empowered by the official legal and public recognition of their efforts to help nature, as I experienced personally when covenanting 66 acres of a Tasmanian forest that I purchased in 2015.[251] Knowing that one's efforts to care for the property will not be undone by a successor landowner provides additional motivation to invest in its conservation and restoration. The covenant, backed by legislation, is also strengthened by criminal penalties that deter third parties, such as neighbours who might allow their livestock to graze on the protected land, dump rubbish, or help themselves to some firewood.

Conversely, the limitations of a conservation covenant include that its voluntary nature means that a landowner normally cannot be obliged to enter into one. Financial incentives must therefore be provided in many instances to induce a landowner to take the initiative. Secondly, covenants tend to emphasise negative obligations, such as prohibitions on clearing vegetation or mustering stock, rather than positive duties to plant trees, restore soil, or other environmental improvements (though in principle the legislative provisions in most examples are broad enough to

---

[248] V. Adams and K. Moon, 'Security and equity of conservation covenants: contradictions of private protected area policies in Australia' (2013) 30(1) *Land Use Policy* 114.
[249] Public Act 1977, No. 102.
[250] Law Commission, *Conservation Covenants*, LAW COM No. 349 (MH Stationary Office, 2014).
[251] See www.bluemountainview.com.au.

encompass positive duties).[252] Thirdly conservation covenants may suffer from poor compliance. Any positive duties are usually couched in vague language such as to use 'best endeavours' or 'if feasible' (e.g. to eradicate weeds or feral animals),[253] and even negative obligations may be hard to supervise when government officials lack the time to monitor compliance, especially given that covenanted properties are often located in remote, rural areas. Fourthly, private landowners may lack the necessary expertise for restoration; although the terms of a covenant can provide for access to technical advice from government authorities, it may not be adequate for the same reason that monitoring the implementation of covenants can be perfunctory. A study of the New Zealand experience with covenants enacted under the Queen Elizabeth the Second National Trust Act 1977[254] found that less than half of properties were visited biannually, the Trust's own monitoring target, and there was 'no record of any cases where the QEII Trust had sought to enforce a QEII covenant'.[255]

Government financial aid provides another component of the soft governance framework to support private initiative in ecological restoration. Such aid may involve direct financial subsidies in the form of cash grants or indirect subsidies through the taxation system. Direct financial aid may be given as recurrent programme support for NGOs doing relevant environmental work or as project-based grants for specific initiatives. Attracting private donors improves when the government has already put some money on the table, as that signals both the credibility of the NGO's fundraising campaign and allows donors to be associated with potentially much larger environmental outcomes. A big driver of nature conservation funding in Australia prior to 2013 was the federal government's enrolment of private properties in the national reserve system by providing funds to induce landowners to accept a conservation covenant.[256]

Alternatively, governments can influence restoration indirectly through tax advantages. Income tax concessions benefit mostly high earners, while offering little or no incentive to the unwaged or low-income households. Restoration expenses in most jurisdictions are not tax-deductible unless

---

[252] E.g. Nature Conservation Trust Act 2001 (NSW), s. 10.
[253] E.g. Tasmanian Land Conservancy (TLC), *Nature Conservation Plan for 199 Rosedale Road, Bicheno* (TLC, June 2013), 17.
[254] Public Act 1999, No. 102.
[255] K. Ewing, 'Conservation covenants and community conservation groups: improving the protection of private land' (2008) 12 *New Zealand Journal of Environmental Law* 315, 325.
[256] Australia, Department of the Environment, 'National reserve system', at www.environment.gov.au/land/nrs/getting-involved/private-landholders.

the expenses are incurred in order to earn taxable income: this incentive effect encourages landholders to put or keep land in production rather than conserve it. Property-related taxes offer another means to incentivise environmental action in the private sector. For instance, modest tax concessions are available in Australia to support landholders who accept a conservation covenant: these comprise a federal income tax deduction equivalent to the reduced capital value of the land, state government waiver of land tax, and reduced municipal rates.[257] All these forms of tax relief have limitations. The federal tax concession requires the landholder to make an application that incurs fees including the cost of a fresh property valuation. The advantage of a land tax exemption is negated by the fact that farmers are already exempt. And municipal rates concessions are highly uneven – some local councils offer full exemptions, while many offer none or a partial rebate.

A lot more could be said about the impact of the taxation system on environmental behaviour, but that would warrant another book.[258] The fundamental impediment with the tax system is that it undervalues ecosystem services. The tax concessions reflect an outmoded mentality that assumes that nature conservation and improvement is simply about setting aside discrete pockets of land, for which altruistic landholders deserve a bit of financial recompense. This is not enough: the entire tax system needs overhaul. The current bias to fossil fuel industries that benefit from tax subsidies must be shifted towards a green tax regime in which costly environmental externalities such as greenhouse gases are punitively taxed while conservation and restoration of natural capital that generate positive externalities is rewarded through generous tax concessions and credits that benefit all, not just the high-income earners.

Such fiscal obstacles, fortunately, have not always prevented human altruism unleashing some major ecological restoration projects sustained by voluntary initiative, goodwill, and community cooperation. The following discussion highlights a few examples.

Arid Recoveries – Australia

Australia's arid 'outback' often adorns tourist brochures as a rugged, unspoilt wilderness, but the truth could not be more different. An ecological

---

[257] M. McKerchar and C. Coleman, 'The Australian income tax system: has it helped or hindered primary producers address the issues of environmental sustainability?' (2003) 6(2) *Journal of Australian Taxation* 201.

[258] See further L. Kreiser (eds), *Environmental Taxation and Green Fiscal Reform: Theory and Impact* (Edward Elgar Publishing, 2014).

tragedy, courtesy of European settlers, has unfolded in a region devastated by invasive weeds, livestock, rabbits, cats, and foxes. Medium-sized native desert fauna have suffered gravely, with many now extinct or clinging to survival elsewhere on remote offshore islands. 'Arid Recovery' is one innovative response, launched in 1997 to restore a patch of South Australian outback.[259] The 'recovery' centres on 123 km^2 of fenced reserve about 550 km north of the city of Adelaide, serving to exclude the feral pests so that reintroduced native wildlife can flourish. Part of the enclosure, one of the largest of its kind in Australia, provides a dingo pen experiment to determine whether *Canis lupus dingo* can naturally control cats and foxes. Arid Recovery also encompasses a larger 200 km^2 buffer zone where less intensive feral animal control methods apply. Several locally extinct mammals have since been successfully reintroduced to the reserve.

An additional novel feature of this project is it multi-stakeholder partnership, involving a business corporation, the South Australian government, the University of Adelaide, and several NGOs. The involvement of a business entity is unusual for voluntary ecological restoration, but was essential in this specific context because the fenced enclave sits partly on the Olympic Dam Mine Lease and adjoining pastoral properties leased by the BHP Billiton mining company. Arid Recovery's success is also due to financial assistance from the state and federal governments, the South Australian Arid Lands Natural Resource Management Board, and the Natural Heritage Trust. It functions without government regulation other than permitting the capture and relocation of endangered wildlife.

Although Arid Recovery might be dismissed as a drop in the bucket relative to the enormity of degraded lands needing restoration, it has wider positive ramifications because it generates transferable information and techniques for broad-scale landscape management of Australia's arid zone, and also because of its demonstration of how mining, pastoralism, and conservation organisations can collaborate for ecological outcomes. The Arid Recovery reserve now has five times as many small native mammals compared to neighbouring areas, and its vegetation has flourished since the rabbits were purged.[260] The critical challenge is to cost-effectively replicate the Arid Recovery model in other areas. Encouragingly, it has already inspired plans for the world's largest predator-proof enclosure at the Newhaven Wildlife Sanctuary, which when complete will provide

---

[259] The discussion of Arid Recovery draws on www.aridrecovery.org.au.
[260] B. FitzGerald, 'Olympic dam haven pays off for endangered local wildlife', *The Australian* 20 September 2014, at www.theaustralian.com.au.

a massive 65,000 ha sanctuary for endangered outback wildlife.[261] The project is led by the Australian Wildlife Conservancy, in collaboration with Aboriginal rangers from the Ngalia Warlipiri and Nyirripi peoples. In such voluntary initiatives, maintaining goodwill among stakeholders is essential. Government regulation cannot ensure it, although public seed funding, as provided in both Arid Recovery and the Newhaven sanctuary, can leverage change.

Another desert recovery in Australia is Gondwana Link, which one international expert heralds as 'one of the most concerted efforts to resurrect nature ever attempted'.[262] Gondwana Link seeks to repair a vast 1000 km strip in southwestern Australia – a region blighted by some dreadful degradation from misguided farming.[263] Parts of it still teem with biodiversity, being one of the world's 35 internationally recognised biodiversity 'hot spots' and the only one in Australia.[264] Began in 2002, the project's vision is: 'reconnected country across south-west Australia, from the Karri forests of the far [southwest] to the woodlands and mallee bordering the Nullarbor Plain, in which ecosystem function and biodiversity are restored and maintained'.[265] Gondwana Link began as an informal collaboration among environmental groups and other partners, who since 2009 have worked under the auspices of an entity called Gondwana Link Ltd. Like Arid Recovery, their project enjoys funding and technical support from a diverse cohort of private and public sponsors.

It brings properties into its plans through outright land purchase or conservation covenants, with are then subject to restoration and stewardship through conservation action plans that embrace adaptive management principles to address feral animal control, diseases, habitat fragmentation, bush fires, stock grazing, and other ecological disturbances. Land purchases typically occur where the extent of restoration is considered 'too massive to achieve through the largesse of any one landholder, or group of landholders, particularly farmers'.[266] Further, Gondwana Link cultivates with landowners a business case for restoration. It works with farmers to turn degraded soils into more viable and profitable farming opportunities

---

[261] T. Volling, '$8m plan to shut out feral cats; bid to re-create wildlife haven in Central Australia', NT News 11 December 2015, at www.ntnews.com.au.
[262] Fraser, *Rewilding the World*, 327.
[263] See www.gondwanalink.org.
[264] V. Jealous, 'Gondwana filling the gaps', *The Australian* 5 February 2011, www.theaustralian.com.au.
[265] Gondwana Link, 'Vision', at www.gondwanalink.org/aboutus/vision.aspx.
[266] Gondwana Link, 'Work we directly support', at www.gondwanalink.org.

through restoration of native vegetation. It is also supporting ecologically and economically beneficial enterprises such as growing sandalwood, a tree that produces a valuable food crop and essential oils. Planting sandalwood also aids carbon sequestration, thereby providing potential future revenue from businesses wanting to offset their carbon emissions. Another distinctive feature is the project's collaboration with Aboriginal communities and other groups beyond the standard ensemble of environmental NGOs found in many restoration initiatives. Gondwana Link negotiated a memorandum of understanding with local Aborigines to foster cooperative land management and incorporate the Noongar people's history and culture into the restoration practices. Local artists participate too; the MIX Artists have worked in local communities through workshops and exhibitions to highlight the natural wonders of areas targeted by Gondwana Link and to stir the public's environmental awareness and respect for the restoration work.

Gondwana Link is impressive for its ambition and collegiality, and although it will likely be some years before its full impact is appreciated, early signs are encouraging.[267] Fundraising for long-term strategic action remains its main challenge. A lingering question is whether and how a more comprehensive legal framework beyond conservation covenants and funding contracts with state agencies might facilitate its objectives. If Gondwana Link's activities were incorporated into local and regional land use planning systems, for instance, it might garner even greater results. More flexible legal arrangements for negotiating legal covenants and extension of legal protections to key habitat linkage areas, not just core enclaves, might also be useful, as recommended by some literature.[268]

Y2Y Conservation Initiative – North America

Even more ambitious than Gondwana Link, in terms of sheer area and jurisdictional complexity, is the project to conserve and restore a corridor of the Rocky Mountains from the United States to northern Canada. Initiated in 1997 by the non-profit Yellowstone to Yukon Conservation Initiative (Y2Y), the plan was conceived by environmental NGOs rather

---

[267] L. Morrison, 'Gondwana links to success: survey', *The Western Australian* 12 February 2014, https://au.news.yahoo.com/thewest; K. Bradby, A. Keesing, and G. Wardell-Johnson, 'Gondwana Link: connecting people, landscapes, and livelihoods across south-western Australia' (2016) 24(6) *Restoration Ecology* 827.

[268] I. Pulsford, J. Fitzsimons, and G. Wescott (eds), *Linking Australia's Landscapes: Lessons and Opportunities from Large-Scale Conservation Networks* (CSIRO Publishing, 2013).

than government agencies to improve biodiversity habitat and ecological connectivity across some 3200 km from Yellowstone National Park to the Yukon.[269] It covers terrain in two Canadian provinces (British Columbia and Alberta) and territories (Yukon and Northwest) and five US states (Idaho, Montana, Oregon, Washington, and Wyoming), and within these jurisdictions touches numerous municipal authorities and Native American communities. Road construction, forest clearance, dams, oil and gas projects, suburban sprawl, and even recreation and tourism, have spoilt much of the Rockies, especially the southern Y2Y region whose ecosystems have become highly fragmented. Among key species targeted for protection are grizzlies and wolverines, which depend on large areas of wilderness, as well as fish spawning grounds.

With over 150 participation organisations, Y2Y strategy aims to protect the Rocky Mountains habitat through collaborations with private landowners who agree to safeguard conservation values.[270] As of 2014, Y2Y has protected about 5.7 million ha of land and participated in 65 conservation and restoration projects,[271] and it claims to have directly contributed to nearly doubling by 2016 the amount of protected land in the region, to 21 per cent from 11 per cent.[272] The Y2Y is not simply about expanding public conservation areas with buffers and connectivity bridges, but also seeks restoration and reduction of development pressures. Its recent work includes decommissioning old logging roads, restoring the ecological functionality of culverts under forest roads, creating mechanisms to reduce roadkill, providing landowners with tools to coexist with predators, and eradicating invasive plants. In some cases Y2Y representatives participate in government land use planning and development decisions by making submissions to influence outcomes.[273] The Y2Y has also helped improve knowledge of the region's ecological and cultural values – an important measure to understand historic and changing environmental

---

[269] L. Wilcox and P. Aengst, 'Yellowstone to Yukon: romantic dream or realistic vision of the future?' (1999) 9(3) *Parks* 17; S.L. Levesque, 'The Yellowstone to Yukon Conservation Initiative: reconstructing boundaries, biodiversity, and beliefs' in J. Blatter and H.M. Ingram (eds), *Reflections on Water: New Approaches to Transboundary Conflicts and Cooperation* (MIT Press, 2001), 123.

[270] For more details, see Y2Y at https://y2y.net.

[271] Yellowstone to Yukon Conservation Initiative, *2014 Annual Report* (Y2Y, 2014), 5.

[272] Y2Y, 'Fact sheet: introducing Y2Y', at https://y2y.net/publications/fact-sheet.

[273] E.g. T. Foubert. 'Y2Y stands firm on minimum corridor width', *Rocky Mountain Outlook* 13 October 2016, at www.rmoutlook.com.

baselines for enabling the impact of restoration and conservation to be measured over time.[274]

Its successes are many, but Y2Y also has had its obstacles and opponents. Not all local communities and landowners have welcomed its conservation agenda, and within the Y2Y itself, which encompasses numerous partner organisations,[275] 'conflicts over goals, operations, and many other aspects of the Y2Y effort' have arisen.[276] Climate change looms as a disruptive challenge to the work of Y2Y, though its proponents believe that the continental-scale initiative will enhance the resilience of the region's ecosystems to cope with climatic shifts.[277] And despite signing memorandums of understanding with US and Canadian parks agencies, and being active in regulatory processes, Y2Y as a non-government phenomenon can only influence but not dictate environmental governance in the region.

Trees for Life – Scotland

Scotland's ancient Caledonian forest has benefited from a major ecological restoration project by Trees for Life (TfL), a local conservation charity. Initiated in 1989, TfL aspires to restore a large contiguous area of the Caledonian landscape and all its constituent biodiversity to the Scottish Highlands.[278] The region was once a vast temperate rainforest, but after centuries of plunder, by 1600 AD the forest had shrunk to about 1.5 per cent of its original extent in scattered pockets unsuitable for farming. Accompanying the deforestation much wildlife went extinct, often through hunting: the brown bear and the wild boar disappeared in the tenth and seventeenth centuries respectively, while the last wolf was shot in 1743. The introduction of sheep and a surge in red deer numbers, without predators, prevented the forests' regeneration. The remaining inaccessible remnants, many protected within the Cairngorms National Park, are populated mainly by old trees, with little regenerative capacity.

---

[274] L. Wilcox, B. Robinson, and A. Harvey, *A Sense of Place: Issue, Attitudes and Resources in the Yellowstone to Yukon Ecoregion* (Y2Y, 1998).
[275] C.C. Chester, 'Responding to the idea of transboundary conservation: an overview of public reaction to the Yellowstone to Yukon (Y2Y) Conservation Initiative' (2007) 17(1–2) *Journal of Sustainable Forestry* 103.
[276] D.J. Mattson, et al., 'Leaders' perspectives in the Yellowstone to Yukon Conservation Initiative' (2011) 44 *Policy Sciences* 103, 105.
[277] C.C. Chester, J.A. Hilty, and W.L. Francis, 'Yellowstone to Yukon, North America' in J.A. Hilty, et al. (eds), *Climate and Conservation: Landscape and Seascape Science, Planning, and Action* (Island Press, 2012), 240.
[278] See http://treesforlife.org.uk.

Some small-scale replanting began in the 1960s, but TfL recognised that: 'to restore a true forest, rather than just a few pockets of natural woodland here and there, we need a vision, and action, on a larger, more coherent and coordinated scale'.[279] Its vision is to create a contiguous stretch of forest of some 230,000 ha, and so far it has planted about 1.5 million trees. Relying on volunteers, the first stage of TfL's action plan facilitates the natural regeneration of native trees by removing deer from regenerating areas through exclusion fences. Where no existing seed source occurs, in barren areas, native trees are planted in fenced exclosures. The third strategy removes exotic trees and plants (e.g. Sitka spruce, western hemlock). Through these methods, TfL aims, in its words, to 're-establish areas, or "islands", of healthy young forest scattered throughout the barren, deforested glens. As these new trees reach seed-bearing age they will form the nuclei for expanded natural regeneration in the surrounding area'.[280] In addition to the re-vegetation, TfL collaborates with plans to reintroduce wildlife to the region, including the European beaver, which is viewed as a keystone species that improves habitat for other wildlife, such as butterflies, dragonflies, and fish, by creating dam ponds. And TfL would like to see other species re-established, including bears, wolves, and lynx.[281]

Remarkably, TfL relies entirely on persuasion and goodwill to achieve its goals with landowners on property outside of its control. In 2008 it purchased the 4,000 ha Dundreggan Estate near the famous Loch Ness where some half million new trees will restore the barren landscape and connect the property to nearby forested patches. Animal reintroductions are also planned, beginning with wild boar. TfL intends to use Dundreggan as a focus for scientific research and education programs. But most TfL work transpires on property it does not own. As of 2016, TfL had not used any legal agreements with property owners, although in the future it may need contracts to carry out initiatives funded by government environmental grants.[282] Also, the work of TfL will likely be shaped by new Scottish legislation to articulate landowners' environmental responsibilities for a region cherished as shared Scottish heritage.[283] On public lands, TfL has

---

[279] A. Watson Featherstone, 'The wild heart of the highlands' (1997) 18 ECOS 48–9.
[280] See http://treesforlife.org.uk/work/action-plan.
[281] Watson Featherstone, 'The wild heart of the highlands'.
[282] Email correspondence from Alan McDonnell, Conservation Projects Manager, Trees for Life, 4 February 2016.
[283] Land Reform (Scotland) Act 2016 asp 18.

collaborated with Forestry Commission Scotland to restore native woodlands and replace commercial exotic plantations with native species.

The success of the TfL's work so far has been attributed to its ability to marry a grand, long-term vision (over at least half a century) with shorter milestones (annually or within a decade). The inclusion of interim milestones helps to keep participants motivated, attract funding, and measure progress, while the longer, 'stretch goals' provide the bigger vision as well as a more flexible framework to respond to new information and circumstances in a changing ecological and social milieu.[284] It thus implements restoration with an adaptive governance framework.

Community Sanctuaries – New Zealand

As an increasingly environmentally committed society, it isn't surprising that New Zealand hosts numerous examples of ecological restoration initiated by government authorities and community groups that create havens for its imperilled wildlife. Shockingly, Aotearoa has already lost 42 per cent of its terrestrial birds (57 species) since human settlement 800 years ago, a particularly severe loss given that most of its avifauna is endemic. Having evolved in isolation without mammalian predators, its birds developed various levels of flightlessness, ground foraging, and nesting preferences that made them highly vulnerable to predation by human beings or their companions, such as dogs, rats, and mustelidae. According to the New Zealand Threat Classification System list, 153 species or subspecies of birds are threatened, and counting insects, plants, and other species, the national endangered total balloons to about 2800 species.[285]

While DoC spearheads many of New Zealand's restoration projects, many also rest on private, voluntary initiatives.[286] The most popular strategy is to acquire land for enclosure as a sanctuary in which exotic plants and animals are first removed through poisoning, trapping, and other methods, while fences erected around the targeted area stall any fresh intrusions. But many sanctuaries remain open and unfenced, in which the aim is not the complete removal of all vermin but to reduce them to low enough levels to enable native wildlife to survive. The strategies

---

[284] A. Manning, D. Lindenmayer, and J. Fischer, 'Stretch goals and backcasting: approaches for overcoming barriers to large-scale ecological restoration' (2006) 14(4) *Restoration Ecology* 487.

[285] New Zealand Threat Classification System, at www.doc.govt.nz/about-us/science-publications/conservation-publications/nz-threat-classification-system.

[286] The following discussion of community sanctuaries draws partially from Butler, Lindsay, and Hunt, *Paradise Saved*, 243–300.

can be expensive and rely on significant on-the-ground assistance from volunteers, often in perpetuity because of the ever-present threat of pest reinvasion. In some cases, community groups undertake restoration on DoC land, with delegated authority and technical support.

One effort is the Puketi Forest Trust, a community organisation restoring 15,000 ha of forest in northern New Zealand.[287] The Puketi Forest contains splendid stands of kauri and podocarp along with about 370 other recorded plant species. The Trust raised NZ$1 million to pay for the trapping of feral cats and mustelidae in a 5500 ha patch of forest and the eradication of rats and possums within a smaller core area. Vermin control has been credited with the revival of the forest's residual populations of long- and short-eared bats, and various birds, as well as enabling the successful reintroduction of locally extinct species including the New Zealand robin and kokako. The Trust operates a volunteer worker programme, with community helpers enlisted to check pest traps and monitor birds.

Another example, on a much smaller scale, is the Mount Tutu Eco-Sanctuary, a family-owned, eco-tourism property near the northern city of Tauranga.[288] The 6.5 ha property, with unlogged ancient rainforest, has been managed for conservation restoration since 1988 and protected under a covenant via the Queen Elizabeth the Second National Trust Act since 1993. The owners, the Short family, initiated a pest eradication programme and replanted native trees along the borders of the rainforest while removing exotic trees such as pine and poplar. Native birds also breed in the sanctuary under a government licence. Local volunteers periodically assist with the forest and bird conservation activities in the property. While the Mount Tutu Eco-Sanctuary may seem trivial given its paltry size, in combination with numerous other pockets conserved around New Zealand it contributes to the survival of its biodiversity, creating additional population reserves and adding to the gene pool, and building ecological connectivity.

Unlike the foregoing fenced sanctuaries, Friends of Flora (FoF) cares for one of the many open sanctuary projects.[289] Named after the Flora Stream catchment, the endeavour began in 2001 with the aim to restore its ecological health. The catchment is in the Kahurangi National Park, under the auspices of DoC, which allowed FoF to take the initiative in the restoration work. The FoF project concentrates on culling stoats in order to increase the number of native birds, with about 1,000 trap stations placed

---

[287] See www.puketi.org.nz.
[288] See www.mount-tutu.co.nz.
[289] See www.fof.org.nz.

in an area of 8,000 ha. Aerial baiting with 1080 poisoning, undertaken by DoC, provides another layer of pest control. Successes so far include the recovery of the rare blue duck, bell bird, and rifleman. The FoF project had also worked to translocate the great spotted kiwi, which had disappeared from the area by the 1980s. FoF is sustained by community volunteers, including scientists, and local fundraising. It offers an interesting example of public–private collaboration, and evidence of the increasing delegation of restoration roles to the community, both as a response to inadequate government funds and as a way to engage the community and build social support for environmental improvements.

Overall, at least 600 community environmental groups in New Zealand have been identified as carrying out restoration projects, many providing a significant 'citizen science' resource for ecological monitoring that enhances scientific and community environmental literacy.[290] The groups also shape environmental law, through participation in local council land use planning and development control, such as making submissions and appearing in public hearings on draft proposals in order to ensure that resource management regulation dovetails with their restoration work.[291] Some community groups have themselves been formally harnessed as agents of governance with the authority to register conservation covenants and engage with communities to bring their properties voluntarily into these regimes, as has occurred with the Banks Peninsula Conservation Trust established in 2001.[292] And some groups, such as Gecko NZ Trusts, focus on improving environmental surroundings in human communities, to build 'living neighbourhoods' that enhance both natural and social capital.[293]

Mangrove Restoration – Thailand

Sometimes known as the 'rainforests by the sea', mangroves are ecologically far-reaching. They nourish biodiversity through feeding and breeding grounds for mammals, amphibians, and birds, and provide vital spawning habitat for fish and crustaceans. Mangrove forests also physically cushion seashores from the erosive forces of storms and waves. Through their capacity to filter some pollutants, mangroves also cleanse local water

---

[290] M.A. Peters, et al., 'The current state of community-based environmental monitoring in New Zealand' (2016) 40(3) *New Zealand Journal of Ecology* 279.
[291] K. Ewing, *Ecological Restoration and the Law: A Guide for Community Conservation Groups* (University of Waikato, 2008), 43.
[292] Ibid, 62.
[293] See www.geckology.co.nz/projects.html.

quality. Not surprisingly, therefore, mangrove restoration has become a priority for environmentalists seeking to reverse the staggering losses of recent decades, estimated by the UN at 36,000 km² or 20 per cent of the world total between 1980 and 2005.[294] The primary causes include clearing for charcoal production and shrimp and other aquaculture farming. Numerous mangrove restoration projects are under way worldwide, sustained by a combination of direct replanting and restoring tidal and freshwater hydrology to enable natural succession processes to take hold.[295] Unlike the foregoing restoration examples, these projects commonly carry a strong international dimension through the guidance of global NGOs and funding from foreign governments and private foundations.

Thailand, with one of the worst records (reportedly having lost about half its mangroves since 1960), hosts several restoration projects led by international and local environmental groups. Thai mangroves are officially government tenure, but in practice often come under the auspices of coastal communities.[296] The lack of effective government oversight contributed to lawless exploitation and degradation of mangroves, but in recent decades many communities have responded with grassroots conservation and restoration. Some have also sought governance rights, such as under forestry legislation, for such activities.[297] Interestingly, it appears that community-managed mangroves in Thailand tend to achieve better environmental outcomes than in state-controlled mangroves.[298]

Increasingly, foreign environmental organisations and donors collaborate with coastal communities to support these goals. Wetlands International has worked with some since 2007 to restore mangroves in the Krabi estuary in southwest Thailand. Its approach includes fencing restored areas to prevent livestock grazing pressures and assisting local residents in finding supplementary economic activities.[299] Another internationally supported initiative in Thailand is the cluster of six projects

---

[294] UN Food and Agriculture Organization (FAO), *The World's Mangroves 1980–2005* (FAO, 2007).

[295] C. Field, 'Rehabilitation of mangrove ecosystems: an overview' (1998) 37 *Marine Pollution Bulletin* 383.

[296] C. Sudtongkong and E. Webb, 'Outcomes of state- vs. community-based mangrove management in southern Thailand' (2008) 13(2) *Ecology and Society* 27.

[297] N. Rittibhonbhun, et al., 'Community-based mangrove rehabilitation and management: a case study in Sikao district, Trang province, Southern Thailand' (1993) 14 *Regional Development Dialogue* 111.

[298] Sudtongkong and Webb, 'Outcomes of state- vs. community-based mangrove management in southern Thailand'.

[299] Wetlands International, 'Ecological mangrove restoration in Thailand', at www.wetlands.org.

undertaken by the Community-Based Ecological Mangrove Restoration consortium, which with funding from the German government and NGO donors empowers local communities to lead restoration projects.[300] The consortium emphasises training and education programs that highlight the economic advantages to local people from healthy mangrove forests. Overall, the Thai experience suggests that devolution of decision-making to local levels creates governance space for community-crafted solutions for environmental management and restoration, while international support is important for seed money and technical advice. Thailand's new Promotion of Marine and Coastal Resources Management Act 2015 may help institutionalise and strengthen the authority of coastal communities to restore and conserve mangroves.[301]

Conclusion

The foregoing showcases just a few of the many ecological restoration projects worldwide that communities and NGOs lead, sometimes with government backing. Many others, too numerous to discuss here, include: the Fouta Djallon Highlands of West Africa multinational project to restore critical watersheds for several transboundary rivers;[302] the Terai Arc Landscape programme, which involves Indian and Nepalese authorities working with local communities to restore and reconnect transborder wildlife habitat corridors, especially to protect tigers;[303] and the Algonquin to Adirondacks Collaborative, partnering Canadian and US groups to improve ecological linkages across 93,000 km^2.[304] Although community-based projects may be viewed as beyond the law, relying on goodwill and voluntary effort, they all have a governance dimension. Apart from the inherent governance in such projects that provides means for communities to collaborate and change environmental behaviour, their governance envelope includes the use of external legal tools, such as conservation covenants and contractual agreements, and regulation that disciplines the community groups themselves, such as setting lines of communication, engagement, and accountability. The entities in the foregoing examples

---

[300] See www.mangroveactionproject.org.
[301] Sections 12 and 16.
[302] J. Fischer, 'Creating common spaces: natural resource management in Fuuta Jalon, Guinea' (2000) 13(6) *Society and Natural Resources* 567.
[303] E. Wikramanayake, et al., 'The Terai Arc landscape: a tiger conservation success story in a human-dominated landscape' in R. Tilson and P. Nyhus (eds), *Tigers of the World: The Science, Politics, and Conservation of Panthera Tigris* (Elsevier/Academic Press, 2010), 161.
[304] See www.a2acollaborative.org.

often take a charitable trust or an incorporated society. Each institutional model has pros and cons, such as variable flexibility in fundraising, stakeholder relationships, and community accountability.

Fundraising itself is another common challenge, to both initiate and sustain projects over the long term. The scramble for funds is intense, and it may be hard to secure donations for projects that do not yield any commercial benefits or generate measurable outcomes for many decades. In developing countries, funding often comes from international donors. The choice of institutional structure is also relevant to funding success. Corporate sponsorship may be easier to secure for entities structured as a company, because it is a structure that these donors often already have familiarity with. Any type of dependence on external funding creates risks for the long-term financial sustainability of a restoration project. On the other hand, making restoration pay for itself is challenging because of market failures to value ecological improvements.

Thirdly, community volunteers are often the most valuable source of support for restoration. Often hundreds of volunteers work on single projects over many years, requiring coordination, recognition, and encouragement. Some volunteers are recruited for their special scientific expertise, and landowners may volunteer by making their land available for restoration projects. The voluntary nature of restoration projects, however, should not mislead us to the potentially significant opposition from landowners if they were to be expected to pay for such projects or forego development opportunities. We hear a lot about restoration projects that succeed on the efforts of volunteers, but not those that died and disappeared from view owing to apathy.

All of the foregoing considerations invite further consideration of the role of people, and specifically local communities, in ecological restoration governance. Sometimes the restoration of a community itself must also be sought, specifically including rebuilding a people's economic and cultural relations with their ancestral homelands. The following section explores this enquiry in a context relevant to many of the countries considered in this book.

Restoring Culture with Nature

Indigenous Peoples and the Environment

As some of the foregoing case studies reveal, local communities are often crucial intermediaries to restoring nature, a connection particularly strong with indigenous peoples. Indeed, ecological restoration is sometimes inseparable from restoration of people to the land, especially for those whose cultural heritage dwells in their ancestral environments.[305] Indigenous peoples remain a striking presence in many countries, including as land managers, despite the legacies of colonialism and dispossession. As Robert Nixon explains, they should be seen not as having 'some romantic, timeless, organic bond to the pulse of nature, but rather . . . acknowledge[d] that their often precarious conditions of survival depend on different combinations of temporal awareness'.[306] Environmental law is gradually respecting this indigenous temporal awareness in contexts such as management of wildlife and national parks.

According to the former UN Working Group on Indigenous Populations, they are the 'descendants of the original inhabitants of conquered territories possessing a minority culture and recognising themselves as such',[307] with some 370 million such people in the world across 90 countries today.[308] They also own or manage large areas that make them a vital collaborator in restoration: about 22 per cent of Australia is under Aboriginal control and a further 9 per cent is subject to some level of Aboriginal rights.[309] In New Zealand, Maori organisations hold 6 per cent of the country,[310] while Native Americans own about 4.5 per cent of the United States, with a particularly large share of Alaska.[311] One researcher in 1999 estimated that worldwide 'as many as three quarters of all protected areas overlap indigenous territories'.[312] Given such numbers, it is not surprisingly that SER in 1995 launched an Indigenous Peoples' Restoration Network to support

---

[305] C.A. O'Neill, 'Restoration affecting native resources: the pace of native ecological science' (2000) 42 *Arizona Law Review* 343; L. Godden and S. Cowell, 'Conservation planning and indigenous governance in Australia's Indigenous Protected Areas' (2016) 24 *Restoration Ecology* 692.
[306] Nixon, *Slow Violence and the Environmentalism of the Poor*, 61–2.
[307] UN Working Group on Indigenous Populations, *Preliminary Report on the Study of the Problem of Discrimination against Indigenous Populations*, UN Doc. E/CN4/Sub2/L 566, 1982.
[308] 'Who are indigenous peoples?' Factsheet (UN Permanent Forum on Indigenous Issues, 2015).
[309] J. Altman and F. Markham, 'Values mapping indigenous lands: an exploration of development possibilities' (Seminar, Native Title Research Unit, Australian Institute of Aboriginal and Torres Strait Islander Studies, 1 May 2013), 6.
[310] Controller and Auditor-General, *Maori Land Administration: Client Service Performance of the Maori Land Court Unit and the Maori Trustee* (Audit Office, 2004), 8.
[311] NCAI Policy Research Center, *Geographic and Demographic Profile of Indian Country* (National Congress of American Indians, 2012).
[312] M. Colchester, *Indigenous Peoples and Forests: Main Issues, Analytic Paper for the Forest Policy Implementation Review and Strategy Development* (World Bank, 1999), 12.

'eco-cultural restoration' by working closely with grassroots communities and promoting use of traditional ecological knowledge.[313]

Indigenous connections to and impacts on the natural environment have been interpreted in diverse ways, each with different ramifications for their role in restoration.[314] One longstanding ideal depicts indigenous peoples as ecological guardians, living harmoniously with their natural surroundings without the profligacy of Western culture.[315] An IUCN task force praises indigenous communities as 'the sole guardian of vast habitats critical to modern societies ... [and] their ecological knowledge is an asset of incalculable value'.[316] Several features of indigenous livelihoods might verify these claims, including spiritual veneration of the natural world, and traditional environmental knowhow honed by years of practice.[317] Indigenous groups may thus protect natural sites dedicated to ancestral spirits or deities,[318] and deploy their traditional knowledge to live sustainably within nature's limits.[319] Even more relevant to restoration, such peoples are sometimes construed as environmental architects, having co-evolved with and moulded natural systems over millennia.[320] Through fire burning, selective hunting and gathering, and other forms of husbandry, indigenous peoples have left an important legacy in many landscapes. Australia has some of the best evidence; the seasonal burnings of woodlands and scrub contributed to a mosaic of vegetation that enhanced biodiversity, and contemporary efforts to repair it sometimes involve the traditional

---

[313] See www.ser.org/iprn.
[314] For a more detailed account, from which part of this discussion draws on, see B.J. Richardson, 'The ties that bind: indigenous peoples and environmental governance' in B.J. Richardson, S. Imai, and K. McNeil (eds), *Indigenous Peoples and the Law: Comparative and Critical Perspectives* (Hart Publishing, 2009), 337.
[315] See F. Berkes, 'Traditional ecological knowledge in perspective' in J.T. Inglis (ed), *Traditional Ecological Knowledge: Concepts and Cases* (International Development Research Centre, 1993), 1.
[316] IUCN Inter-Commission Task Force on Indigenous Peoples, *Indigenous Peoples and Sustainability: Cases and Actions* (IUCN, 1997), 35.
[317] D. Posey, 'Culture and nature: the inextricable link' in UNEP *Cultural and Spiritual Values of Biodiversity* (UNEP, 2000), 1, 4; R. Johannes (ed), *Traditional Ecological Knowledge: A Collection of Essays* (IUCN, 1989).
[318] S. Bhagwat and C. Rutte, 'Sacred groves: potential for biodiversity management' (2006) 4 *Frontiers in Ecology and the Environment* 519.
[319] G.M. Morin-Labatut and S. Akhtar, 'Traditional environmental knowledge: a resource to manage and share' (1992) 4 *Development Journal of the Society for International Development* 24; E. Sherry and H. Myers, 'Traditional environmental knowledge in practice' (2002) 15(4) *Society and Natural Resources* 345.
[320] B. Orlove and S.B. Brush, 'Anthropology and the conservation of biodiversity' (1996) 25 *Annual Review of Anthropology* 329.

custodians.[321] This symbiotic relationship between some indigenous cultural practices and maintenance of biodiversity makes these communities key partners in restoration.[322]

Not all hunter–gatherer livelihoods were benign, however, given historical evidence of wildlife expirations and other legacies.[323] Tim Flannery, a scientist who studies such impacts in Oceania, describes a 'blitzkrieg extinction' following the first human settlers in New Zealand, with some nine species of moa (some much larger than ostriches) perishing within a few centuries, along with extensive deforestation.[324] The Clovis hunters of North America dispatched 35 species, including even the behemoth mammoths.[325] While such ancient evidence might seem absurdly irrelevant to debates about contemporary indigenous peoples, some research documents more recent indiscretions of hunter–gatherer lifestyles.[326] Low population densities and technological constraints might thus best explain the lighter environmental burden of *some* hunter–gatherers rather than any innate conservation ethos.[327] For ecological restoration, the foregoing claims suggest a case-by-case approach rather than making sweeping assumptions about indigenous environmental practices.

Whatever the historical evidence, some researchers emphasise that indigenous environmental livelihoods have changed irreparably.[328] The

---

[321] D. Yibarbuk, et al., 'Fire ecology and Aboriginal land management in central Arnhem Land, Northern Australia: a tradition of ecosystem management' (2001) 28 *Journal of Biogeography* 325.

[322] N. Mitchell and S. Buggey, 'Protected landscapes and cultural landscapes: taking advantage of diverse approaches' (2000) 17 *George Wright Forum* 1.

[323] L.M. Shields, 'Are conservation goals and aboriginal rights incompatible?' (2000) 10 *Journal of Environmental Law and Practice* 187; A.M. Stearman, 'Revisiting the myth of the ecologically noble savage in Amazonia: implications for indigenous land rights' (1994) 49 *Culture and Agriculture* 2.

[324] Flannery, *The Future Eaters*, 195.

[325] See G. Haynes, 'The extinction of North American mammoths and mastodons' (2002) 33 *World Archaeology* 391. However, the evidence of such impacts is disputed: D. Grayson and D. Meltzer, 'Clovis hunting and large mammal extinction: a critical review of the evidence' (2002) 16 *Journal of World Prehistory* 313.

[326] J.B.C. Jackson, et al., 'Historical overfishing and the recent collapse of coastal ecosystems' (2001) 293 *Science* 630; but see the robust counter arguments in R.E. Johannes, 'Did indigenous conservation ethics exist?' (2002) 14 *SPC Traditional Marine Resource Management and Knowledge Information Bulletin* 3.

[327] S. Krech III, *The Ecological Indian: Myth and History* (WW Norton, 2000) (discussing Native Americans).

[328] E.g. R. Meher, 'The social and ecological effects of industrialisation in a tribal region: the case of the Rourkela steel plant' (1998) 57 *American Journal of Economics and Sociology* 105; C. Ramirez, 'Ethnobotany and the loss of traditional knowledge in the 21st century' (2007) 5 *Ethnobotany Research and Applications* 245.

forsaken environmentalist view, as we might call this stance, depicts indigenous culture as influenced by urbanisation, migration, technology, markets, and so on.[329] The consequences may be environmentally pernicious; Alaskan natives have been implicated in destructive forestry practices,[330] while in the highlands of Papua New Guinea, population growth and modern hunting weapons have imperilled local wildlife.[331] But while it would be naïve to assume that indigenous cultures have remained untainted by the wider world, in addition to the direct impact of colonialism they also show resilience and adaptation.[332] Indigenous knowledge is not simply a relic of primeval hunter–gatherer societies, but continues to evolve and contribute to contemporary resource management. Aboriginal traditional fire management has been reintroduced in some Australian outback national parks to help restore biodiversity.[333] In Canada, the National Aboriginal Forestry Association has issued guidelines for involving Aboriginal peoples in forest management.[334] Likewise, some indigenous tribes in the Amazon have responded to threats such as illicit logging and over fishing to safeguard their local environments.[335] The environmental innovation thesis, as we can call this idea, presents one of the most forceful arguments for bolstering the indigenous voice in restoration work.

The suffering and human rights violations incurred by many indigenous peoples are often coupled with environmental damage.[336] Environmental justice scholars Laura Westra and Richard Howitt have focused on the conscription of indigenous territories into the market economy, such

[329] M. Colchester, *Salvaging Nature: Indigenous Peoples, Protected Areas and Biodiversity Conservation* (World Wide Fund for Nature, 1994), 26.
[330] F. Cassidy and N. Dale, *After Native Claims: The Implications of Comprehensive Claims Settlements for Natural Resources in British Columbia* (Oolichan Books, 1988), 104–7.
[331] T. Flannery, *Throwim Way Leg: Tree-Kangaroos, Possums, and Penis Gourds – On the Track of Unknown Mammals in Wildest New Guinea* (Atlantic Monthly Press, 1998)
[332] See K. Mishra (ed), *Traditional Knowledge in Contemporary Societies: Challenges and Opportunities* (Pratibha Prakashan, 2007); M. Gadgil, F. Berkes, and C. Folke, 'Indigenous knowledge for biodiversity conservation' (1993) 22 *Ambio* 151.
[333] R. Kimber, 'Black lightning: Aborigines and fire in central Australia and the western desert' (1983) 18 *Archaeology in Oceania* 38.
[334] National Aboriginal Forestry Association (NAFA), *Aboriginal Forest Land Management Guidelines: A Community Approach* (NAFA, 1995).
[335] M. Montoya and K.R. Young, 'Sustainability of natural resource use for an Amazonian indigenous group' (2013) 13 *Regional Environmental Change* 1273.
[336] E.g. D. Brook, 'Environmental genocide: Native Americans and toxic waste' (1998) 57 *American Journal of Economics and Sociology* 105; R. Niezen, 'Power and dignity: the social consequences of hydro-electric development for the James Bay Cree' (1993) 30 *Canadian Review of Sociology and Anthropology* 510.

as through dams, mines, and forestry projects that have been ruinous for both people and nature.[337] Long-range environmental impacts on remote indigenous communities have also been tracked, including toxic contamination in the Arctic food chain and adverse climatic changes.[338] Even seemingly benign policies can hurt, such as the creation of conservation parks that displace local peoples from their traditional hunting and foraging grounds.[339] These and other examples that could be given make clear that environmental restoration can be an essential prerequisite to the well-being of some indigenous peoples, and that restoration must be linked to wider initiatives to improve their legal status to reject unwanted economic development.

Legal Governance

The law has leveraged greater indigenous participation in environmental governance in recent years. While indigenous peoples have long cared for lands and waters according to their legal customs, the increasing recognition of indigenous rights by international and national legal systems has given more legal weight to indigenous involvement in environmental protection and restoration. In both international and domestic law, acknowledgment of these peoples in environmental governance has grown in line with their solidifying legal status as distinct 'peoples'.[340] The International Labour Organization's (ILO) Convention Concerning Indigenous and Tribal Peoples in Independent Countries[341] 1989 and the UN Declaration on the Rights of Indigenous Peoples[342] 2007 represent the principal global instruments in this field. The Declaration proclaims indigenous peoples' rights to own, develop, and conserve their traditional lands,[343] as well as the need for indigenous consent for any development affecting their

---

[337] R. Howitt, *Rethinking Resource Management: Justice, Sustainability and Indigenous Peoples* (Taylor and Francis, 2001); L. Westra, *Environmental Justice and the Rights of Indigenous Peoples – International and Domestic Law Perspectives* (Earthscan Publishers, 2007).

[338] D.L. Brown, 'Toxic-tainted Arctic animals passing poisons on to Inuit', *Seattle Times* 22 May 2001, at www.seattletimes.com; R. Abate and E.A.K. Warner, *Climate Change and Indigenous Peoples: The Search for Legal Remedies* (Edward Elgar Publishing, 2015).

[339] See examples detailed in World Rainforest Movement, 'Protected areas: protected against whom?' (January 2004); E. Kemf (ed), *Indigenous Peoples and Protected Areas. The Law of Mother Earth* (Earthscan, 1993).

[340] S.J. Anya, *Indigenous Peoples and International Law* (Oxford University Press, 2004).

[341] ILO Convention No. 169, 27 June 1989, in force 5 September 1991, (1989) 28 ILM 1382.

[342] UN Doc. A/61/L.67, 7 September 2007.

[343] Ibid, Article 26.

territories.[344] The ILO Convention contains similar standards, including an obligation on state parties to 'respect the special importance for the cultures and spiritual values of the peoples concerned of their relationship with the lands or territories'.[345] Also, some environmental conventions acknowledge indigenous peoples, with particular emphasis on their *traditional* practices. The Convention on Biological Diversity 1992,[346] ratified by some 190 states, obliges its parties to 'respect, preserve and maintain knowledge, innovations and practices of indigenous and local communities embodying traditional lifestyles relevant for the conservation and sustainable use of biological diversity'.[347] These and other provisions may stimulate improvements to domestic legislation for similar ends including restoration projects.

Securing land rights has been the gold standard for most indigenous communities. Particularly since the 1970s, judicial case law, special legislation, and treaties have affirmed their entitlement to their traditional territories. In the seminal 2014 decision in *Tsilhqot'in Nation* v. *British Columbia*,[348] the Supreme Court of Canada declared that the Tsilhqot'in Nation hold Aboriginal title over certain lands in British Columbia, the first declaration of its kind in Canadian judicial history. Interestingly, the Court construed Aboriginal land title as having an intergenerational environmental dimension, noting that it cannot 'be developed or misused in a way that would substantially deprive future generations of the benefit of the land'.[349] Recognition of indigenous tenures also occurs in numerous developing countries, such as Papua New Guinea and the Philippines.[350] The Philippines Indigenous Peoples' Rights Act 1997 facilitates acquisition of communal ownership of ancestral land, with some 3 million ha held by indigenous groups as of 2004 under these provisions,[351] and some of these areas are included in the government's 2011 Tree Planting Plan to restore 1.5 million ha of degraded lands. Indigenous land rights do

---

[344] Ibid, Article 30.
[345] ILO Convention No. 169, Article 13.
[346] Adopted 5 June 1992, in force 29 December 1993, (1992) 31 ILM 818.
[347] Ibid, Article 8(j).
[348] [2014] 2 SCR 257.
[349] Ibid, para. 74.
[350] R. Crocombe (ed), *Land Tenure in the Pacific* (University of the South Pacific, 1994); T. van Meijl and F. von Benda-Beckmann (eds), *Property Rights and Economic Development: Land and Natural Resources in Southeast Asia and Oceania* (Kegan Paul, 1999).
[351] Republic Act No. 8371; M. Colchester, 'Indigenous peoples and communal tenures in Asia', in UN Food and Agricultural Organization (FAO), *Land Reform, Land Settlement and Cooperatives* (FAO, 2004) 28, 38.

not always amount to exclusive ownership; instead, some hold usufruct resource rights to areas traditionally harvested, as in Scandinavia, where courts have affirmed Sámi rights to reindeer herding, game hunting, and fishing.[352]

While the foregoing advances strengthen indigenous peoples' role in environmental decisions, including restoration projects, such rights may not extend to the protection of the habitat that supports the wildlife or other resources. The Canadian case of *Mikisew Cree First Nation* recognised that an Aboriginal treaty right to trap and hunt has geographical limits, and loses its value without the preservation of the wider, enabling wildlife habitat.[353] Some US law confirms implied water protection rights for the maintenance of fishing on tribal reservations, based on the *United States v. Adair* and *Kittitas Reclamation District v. Sunnyside Valley Irrigation District* cases.[354] However, in all these cases, the traditional harvesting territory of the tribal group was near the environmental damage. For Aboriginal peoples harvesting migratory species, a much larger habitat area would need protection – such accommodation has not been judicially recognised. One solution, taken in New Zealand, is specific provisions in environmental legislation to safeguard indigenous interests. The RMA affirms as of 'national importance' the 'relationship of Māori and their culture and traditions with their ancestral lands, waters, sites,'[355] as well as the Maori stewardship principle of 'Kaitiakitanga,'[356] which government decision-makers must respect when administering the legislation.[357] The Act has led to municipal authorities routinely consulting with Maori groups when reviewing development applications.[358]

---

[352] C. Allard and S. Funderud Skogvang (eds), *Indigenous Rights in Scandinavia: Autonomous Sami Law* (Routledge, 2015), 99–102.
[353] *Mikisew Cree First Nation v. Canada (Minister of Canadian Heritage)*, [2005] SCC 69, para 47. The Mikisew's treaty right to hunt in the national park was threatened by the Crown's plans to build a road.
[354] *United States v. Adair*, 478 F Supp 336 (D Or, 1979); *United States v. Adair*, 187 F Supp 2d 1273 (D Or, 2002); *Kittitas Reclamation District v. Sunnyside Valley Irrigation District*, 763 F 2d 1032 (9th Cir. 1985).
[355] Public Act 1991, No. 69, Section 6(e).
[356] Ibid, s. 7(a).
[357] See generally P. Beverley, 'The mechanisms for the protection of Māori interests under part II of the Resource Management Act 1991' (1998) 2 *New Zealand Journal of Environmental Law* 121.
[358] Ministry for the Environment, *Case Law on Tangata Whenua Consultation* (Government of New Zealand, 1999).

Another legal trend is tribal governance that gives communities not only access to natural resources, but authority to manage them. Native American tribes have long been judicially recognised as distinct political entities retaining inherent sovereign powers to the extent not ceded to or removed by the US Congress.[359] Tribes such as the Navajo regulate timber and mineral resources on their reservations, and can control hunting and fishing. In 1984 the US EPA adopted a Federal Indian Policy to recognise tribal governments as the appropriate authority for setting environmental standards, issuing permits, and managing environmental programs within tribal reservations.[360] In Canada, a co-management model has engaged First Nations in the governance of wildlife, forests, waters, and other natural resources, especially in the Arctic and other northern regions. Canada's pioneering Comprehensive Land Claims Process (CLCP) has led to 26 major settlements (as of early 2017) since it began in 1973, with more under negotiation.[361] The CLCP agreements typically cover financial compensation, co-management of Aboriginal lands, wildlife management, and regional development.[362] Each CLCP deal creates *sui generis* institutions for environmental affairs managed jointly by indigenous and governmental representatives. Some agreements acknowledge the scope for restoration; the Nunavut Agreement 1993, one of the largest in geographical scope provides that land use plans will include measures to 'protect, and where necessary, to *restore* the environmental integrity of the Nunavut Settlement Area'.[363] The 2003 Tlicho Agreement contains numerous provisions dealing with environmental conservation, a term defined as 'maintenance of the integrity of ecosystems by measures such as the protection and *reclamation* of wildlife habitat and, where necessary, *restoration* of wildlife habitat'.[364] First Nations outside the CLCP framework may participate in the First Nations Land Management Act 1999, which allows for limited tribal control over environmental management

---

[359] Beginning with *Johnson v. McIntosh*, (1823) 21 US (8 Wheat) 543, 572–88.
[360] W. Ruckelshaus, *EPA Policy for the Administration of Environmental Programs on Indian Reservations* (American Indian Environmental Office, 1984).
[361] C. Alcantara, *Negotiating the Deal: Comprehensive Land Claims Agreements in Canada* (University of Toronto Press, 2013).
[362] Indian and Northern Affairs Canada, *Comprehensive Claims Policy and Status of Claims* (Government of Canada, 2003).
[363] Agreement between the Inuit of the Nunavut Settlement Area and Her Majesty the Queen in Right of Canada, 25 May 1993, clause 11.3.2 (my emphasis).
[364] Land Claims and Self-Government Agreement among the Tlicho and the Government of the Northwest Territories and the Government of Canada, 2003, clause 1.1.1 (my emphasis).

on Indian reservations.[365] The federal funding to support participating First Nations can extend to remediation projects.[366]

In Australia, the Aboriginal voice was traditionally limited to token advisory committees and consultation mechanisms, but in recent decades a variety of legal reforms have strengthened their participation in environmental decisions, albeit with much more needed.[367] Prior to the 1992 *Mabo* decision of the High Court,[368] recognition of Aboriginal land rights was confined to a few statutory schemes of limited ambition except for the Northern Territory's legislation.[369] The joint management of the Kakadu and Uluru national parks in the Northern Territory introduced an innovative model of collaborative governance: each provided for Aboriginal ownership and lease-back of the land to the government conservation agency, an Aboriginal majority on the board of park management, and financial payments to the traditional owners.[370] Jointly managed parks have also facilitated cross-cultural education, training, and employment for Aboriginal peoples in order to share in the economic benefits of eco-tourism.

In the wake of *Mabo* and the enabling Native Title Act 1993 (Cth), further legal changes have ensued, One is indigenous Land Use Agreements, which allow native title claimants to negotiate resource management, such as for biodiversity conservation and restoration, in places under claim.[371] One was negotiated in 2005 between the South Australian government and the Adnyamathanha people over land in the Vulkathunha-Gammon Ranges National Park, with these agreements enabling indigenous participation in various restoration activities in the park.[372] The creation of Indigenous Protected Areas is another institutional mechanism for both cultural and environmental restoration. Aboriginal-owned places that are

---

[365] SC 1999, c. 24; see T. Isaac, 'First Nations Land Management Act and third party interests' (2005) 42 *Alberta Law Review* 1047.

[366] First Nations Lands Advisory Board, *Annual Report 2003-2004* (First Nations Lands Management Resource Centre, 2004), 19.

[367] G. Nettheim, G.D. Meyers, and D. Craig, *Indigenous Peoples and Governance Structures: A Comparative Analysis of Land and Resources Management Rights* (Aboriginal Studies Press, 2002), 393.

[368] *Mabo and Others v. Queensland (No 2)*, (1992) 175 CLR 1.

[369] Aboriginal Land Rights (Northern Territory) Act 1976 (Cth).

[370] T. De Lacy and B. Lawson, 'The Uluru-Kakadu model: joint management of Aboriginal-owned national parks in Australia' in S. Stevens (ed), *Conservation through Cultural Survival: Indigenous Peoples and Protected Areas* (Island Press, 1997), 155.

[371] D. Craig, 'Native title and environmental planning; indigenous land use agreements' (2000) 17 *Environmental and Planning Law Journal* 440.

[372] As explained in Department of Environment and Heritage, *Management Plan: Vulkathunha-Gammon Ranges National Park* (Government of South Australia, 2006).

voluntarily included in such areas comprise almost 7 per cent of Australia and 40 per cent of Australia's overall area set aside for conservation.[373] Through protocols such as 'Healthy Country Planning', the Indigenous Protected Areas provide a framework to restore Aboriginal relationships to the land and harness Aboriginal knowledge and custom in culturally appropriate ways for ecological restoration and other management activities.[374] The Karajarri people of the Kimberley region are among those who use Healthy Country Planning for their country, such as a new ranger programme for removing weeds and feral animals, protecting cultural heritage, and educating about traditional ecological knowledge.[375] Healthy Country Planning builds on the earlier co-management approach to enhance indigenous-led environmental stewardship, and with Indigenous Protected Areas helps to move away from the enclave model of conservation premised on unadulterated 'wilderness'.

Indigenous places thus powerfully illustrate the intertwined and often inseparable ecological and cultural dimensions of restoration. Such places also provoke debates about what is the 'natural', baseline condition of the environment to be restored and the place of people within it. As restoration governance is often just as much about 'healing relationships',[376] it requires other ingredients beyond scientific knowhow or government direction to succeed. An 'intercultural' approach to restoration, explains Catherine O'Neill, a Seattle University academic who specialises in this subject, must accept the validity of indigenous environmental knowledge in restoration and involve such peoples as equal partners in the design and execution of such projects.[377] In some cases, these considerations may lead to bespoke strategies negotiated with individual communities and tailored to different milieux rather than reliance on any general legislative template. Australian commentators Lee Godden and Stuart Cowell conclude that 'the challenge for ecological restoration efforts is not to lock in a model that gives priority to either ecological values or static "traditional" management but rather to adopt a flexible approach that allows for "bottom up" indigenous community management'.[378]

---

[373] Cited in Godden and Cowell, 'Conservation planning and indigenous governance'.
[374] Ibid.
[375] Karajarri Traditional Lands Association, *Karajarri Healthy Country Plan 2013–2023* (Kimberley Land Council, 2014), 18.
[376] N. Tucker, 'Healing country and healing relationships' (2005) 6 *Ecological Management and Restoration* 83.
[377] O'Neill, 'Restoration affecting native resources'.
[378] Godden and Cowell, 'Conservation planning and indigenous governance'.

Reflections

The pace of ecological degradation around the world continues to exceed efforts to repair it. Global warming, species decline, and ocean acidification are among the barrage of grim news we daily encounter. According to the authoritative *Living Planet Report*, a biennial comprehensive assessment of the planet's health, by 2014 humanity's overall ecological footprint had more than doubled since 1961 – a period ironically coinciding with the advent of modern environmental law.[379] Given pervasive environmental decay over long periods, measures to conserve or sustain natural systems will not suffice to safeguard ecosystem functions, services, and habitat for biodiversity. The philosophy of sustainable development that guides much legislation has served largely as a defensive stance to prevent further degradation rather than as a fillip for improving natural capital. As such, a strategy to maintain as opposed to enhance ecosystems may often leave ecosystems and biodiversity vulnerable to further decline. Unless human numbers and consumption dramatically fall in the near future, we have no alternative but to invest in nature's restoration and enhancement.

Of further concern, while many parts of the world now host ecological restoration projects, some doubt their efficacy. The examples discussed in this chapter, such as Arid Recovery and the New Zealand community sanctuaries, showcase the better efforts. A 2012 global study of 621 wetland restoration schemes found that many did not achieve the expected results or match the character of equivalent natural systems, even after many decades.[380] A 2014 study of river restoration learned that 75 per cent had not achieved their minimum performance goals.[381] A 2009 meta-review of 240 studies of ecological recovery in aquatic and terrestrial systems, both passively and actively restored, concluded that 35 per cent had complete recovery while the remaining had either moderate to limited recovery (35 per cent) or no recovery (30 per cent).[382] But encouragingly, studies

---

[379] *Living Planet Report*, 2014 Facts, at www.footprintnetwork.org/en/index.php/gfn/page/living_planet_report_2014_facts.

[380] D. Moreno-Mateoos, et al., 'Structural and functional loss in restored wetland ecosystems' (2012) 10(1) *PLoS Biology* e1001247.

[381] M.A. Palmer, K.L. Hondula, and B.J. Koch, 'Ecological restoration of streams and rivers: shifting strategies and shifting goals' (2014) 45 *Annual Review of Ecology, Evolution, and Systematics* 247.

[382] H. P. Jones and O.J. Schmitz, 'Rapid recovery of damaged ecosystems' (2009) 4(5) *PLoS One* 4e5653.

also typically show that ecological recovery will more likely succeed when there is active restoration rather than indifference.[383]

The reasons for the success or failure of restoration projects remain under further research,[384] but the quality of governance matters.[385] That some community-initiated projects (as considered in this chapter) have flourished should not imply that the law is a bystander to their success, as some benefit from legal undergirding (e.g. statutory conservation covenants, delegated authority from government agencies, and public grants). The community projects also verify how social participation strengthens restoration, and emphasises why we should construe such involvement and local oversight as a form of governance in its own right. But they may not be replicable on a broad scale without legal interventions to overcome recalcitrant landowners or competing economic pressures.

The mixed fortunes of restoration ventures may also reflect failures to address uncertainty in the way that natural systems behave, an unrealistic belief that nature can be made a carbon copy of what it once was, and reliance on overly short timescales in which to expect results.[386] Defining 'successful recovery' in restoration ecology elicits many views, because the criteria can vary widely in goals, ambition, and rationale.[387] Contentious issues include the choice of historic baseline for restoration, the extent to which restoration should accommodate human use and disturbance, and how to value restoration-related ecosystem services in order to attract financial and political support. Environmental law shows limited cognisance of such issues, and little rear vision overall. It needs a deeper sense of nature's history, and the massive injuries inflicted on it, in order to fulfil our responsibilities to restore the planet. Environmental law also needs to articulate more explicitly the role of people as key partners in restoration projects, as against treating restoration as largely a matter of government prescription and scientific knowhow. Most examples of restoration

---

[383] J.M. ReyBenayas, et al., 'Enhancement of biodiversity and ecosystem services by ecological restoration: a meta-analysis' (2009) 325 *Science* 1121.

[384] L. Wortley, J.M. Hero, and M. Howes, 'Evaluating ecological restoration success: a review of the literature' (2013) 21 *Restoration Ecology* 537.

[385] J. Aronson, et al., 'What role should government regulation pay in ecological restoration? Ongoing debate in Sao Paulo state, Brazil' (2011) 19 *Restoration Ecology* 690; M.C. Ruiz-Jaen and T.M. Aide, 'Restoration success: how is it being measured?' (2005) 13 *Restoration Ecology* 569.

[386] R.H. Hilderbran, A.C. Watts, and A.M. Randle, 'The myths of restoration ecology' (2005) 10(1) *Ecology and Society* 19.

[387] K.N. Suding, 'Toward an era of restoration in ecology: successes, failures, and opportunities ahead' (2011) 42 *Annual Review of Ecology, Evolution and Systematics* 465, 467.

mandated by legal systems should be described as 'environmental' restoration, addressing discrete legacies such as pollution spills or abandoned mines, but not rebuilding natural and cultural systems. The pioneering initiatives in the United States and New Zealand, as considered in this chapter, herald future directions for restoration governance.

Still, success is never assured given the uncertain and dynamic behaviour of ecosystems as well as the complex social setting of restoration. Adaptive management, with continual monitoring of restoration projects and making adjustments over time to improve outcomes, will help.[388] Ecological restorations are often not one-time projects, but sometimes continual efforts, and global warming introduces a further dynamic to contend with. Nature does not stand still, and a restored nature will likewise shift in years to come. Climate change does not imply that we should shy away from ecological restoration; rather, it becomes another layer of environmental change to reckon with so that restored land and seascapes can survive additional pressures. If we can meet these challenges, some of nature's ghosts may reappear and once again enrich our surroundings.

---

[388] See C.R. Allen and A. Garmestani (eds), *Adaptive Management of Socio-Ecological Systems* (Springer, 2015).

5

Rallentare

Life in the Fast Lane

Some of Earth's remotest wild places, such as Antarctica, a Pacific atoll, or an equatorial rainforest, can evoke in visitors a timeless bliss, where time wafts away. I often feel so when I elope from my university office to cogitate at Blue Mountain View, my Tasmanian eco-sanctuary.[1] This unhurried tempo can not only inspire contemplation about nature's cycles and sequences, such as observing the seasonal changes in its flora and fauna, as I often do, it can also provoke reflection on the jarringly different social time that disciplines our daily lives. The tempo of modern life, especially for city dwellers, bears little resemblance to nature's biorhythms. While Earth can occasionally unleash a violent tempest, its temporalities usually meander much more gradually than those of human culture. The cult of speed ripples throughout our 'advanced' civilisation, from fast food to speed dating.[2] The accelerating tempo also intensifies environmental pressure as we plunder natural resources more quickly than they can regenerate, while hastiness usurps any legal controls by truncating due diligence. This chapter explores how the pace of time contributes to the widening gap between social and natural timescales, and thereby impairs environmental governance. It also celebrates how some social movements seek to slow us down, or as the Italians would say, *rallentare*, from the country that gave birth to Slow Food.

The compression of time has a technology edge, through 'time saving' innovations like the Internet and mobile phones and, earlier, wireless telegraphy.[3] We live in a digitally accelerated time in which the instant connectivity of social media constantly tempts and distracts us. The slightest

---

[1] See www.bluemountainview.com.au.
[2] For further examples, see H. Rosa and W.E. Scheuerman (eds), *High-Speed Society: Social Acceleration, Power, and Modernity* (Penn State University Press, 2008).
[3] N. Green, 'On the move: technology, mobility, and the mediation of social time and space' (2002) 18(1) *The Information Society* 281.

delays, such as a 'slow' online connection, or queuing at a bank, easily frustrate many. 'The exponential acceleration of technological change combined with instant connectivity have a direct influence on human temporal perception', explains US commentator Brian Stewart, 'resulting in either conscious or subconscious acceleration of many processes along with an expectation that events should unfold rapidly'.[4] The opportunities to constantly interact in 'real time' with individuals across the globe makes one accustomed to unprecedented temporal immediacy.[5] Technological advances in transportation, such as airline travel, have also dramatically shrunk both space and time by putting nearly every nook of the globe within a day's reach for the *hoi polloi*. Perversely, however, all this time-saving technology has not given us more 'free' time; instead, we feel perpetually rushed and short of time, turning to bookstore displays providing tips on better time management, such as enticing volumes on *Make Ahead Meals: Over 100 Easy Time-Saving Recipes*,[6] *Successful Time Management*,[7] *500 Time-Saving Hints for Every Woman*,[8] and *Time Efficiency Makeover*.[9] This ethos also inhabits the world that academics know, as the motto to 'publish or perish' squeezes out the tradition of patient research to produce one's *magnum opus*.

Broader cultural and economic changes are intertwined with this haste, as observed for over a century. In 1877, English essayist William Greg acknowledged, 'beyond doubt, the most salient characteristic of life in this latter portion of the nineteenth century is its SPEED – what we may call its hurry, the rate at which we move, the high-pressure at which we work'.[10] He was lamenting how capitalism's ascent had fostered a convergence of time keeping and industrialisation that was transforming the experience of time from the subjective realm to an invariant, commoditised value.[11] In the early twentieth century, the emergence of Taylorism and Fordism as frameworks for industrial production intensified the breakdown of time

---

[4] B.M. Stewart, 'Chronolawgy: a study of law and temporal perception' (2012) 67 *University of Miami Law Review* 303, 310.
[5] See W. Scheuerman, *Liberal Democracy and the Social Acceleration of Time* (John Hopkins University Press, 2004).
[6] M. Smith, *Make Ahead Meals: Over 100 Easy Time-Saving Recipes* (Penguin Canada, 2015).
[7] P. Forsyth, *Successful Time Management* (Kogan Page, 2003).
[8] E. Barnes, *500 Time-Saving Hints for Every Woman* (Harvest House Publishers, 2006).
[9] D.K. Breininger and D.S. Bitticks, *Time Efficiency Makeover* (Health Communications, 2005).
[10] W.R. Greg, 'Life at high pressure' (1877) 2 *Literary and Social Judgments* 262.
[11] R. Hassan, *Empires of Speed* (Brill, 2009), 55–6.

into ever-smaller units that were monetised as ways of better measuring production and worker efficiency.[12] As time became correlated more closely with the dynamic of capitalism to extract surplus value from labour, it in turn drove more investment in time-saving efficiencies to maximise productivity.

That the etymology of 'business' relates to the quality of being busy is telling, for the corporate world is the most frenetic and time-conscious milieu. Because time is money in the economic system, speed is its yardstick of efficiency. Measurements of economic 'productivity' reflect doing more in less time. As American Internet pioneer James Gleick explains, 'the modem economy lives and dies by precision in time's measurement and efficiency in its employment ... Pruning minutes and seconds and hundredths of seconds has become an obsession in all but a few segments of our society'.[13] In textile sweatshops, companies have distilled workers' time into mere fractions of a second: in Nike's factories in Central America, the assigned time frames for fabric makers on the production line are not expressed in minutes per task but in ten-thousandths of a second.[14] Not only has time being diced into ever smaller fragments to extract greater productivity, it has also become permanently 'available' to be worked. With the advances in information and communication technologies since the 1970s, notably the Internet and satellites, as well as the emergence of 24-hour global markets that never sleep, the tempo of modern life accelerates further.[15]

In aggregation, the economy-wide dimensions of this imperative crystallise in revered indicia such as GDP, economic growth, productivity, sales, and so on. Their acceleration in some emerging economies has been staggering. China's meteoric rise over the past four decades to become the world's second largest economy has come with an average growth rate of real GDP between 1978 and 2012 of 9.4 per cent.[16] When China's economic growth 'slowed' to 6.8 per cent in 2015, the international press took notice, calling it 'gloomy'[17] and 'painful'.[18] In 2016 India was hailed

---

[12] B. Dorey, *From Taylorism to Fordism: A Rational Madness* (Free Association, 1988).
[13] J. Gleick, *Faster: The Acceleration of Just About Everything* (Hachette Book Company, 2000), 11–12.
[14] Figures quoted in the film *The Corporation* (2003).
[15] Hassan, *Empires of Speed*.
[16] A. Cheremukhin, et al., *The Economy of People's Republic of China from 1953*, NBER Working Paper No. 21397 (National Bureau of Economic Research, 2015).
[17] Z. Xin, 'Top Chinese think tank warns of gloomy economic prospects for 2016', *South China Morning Post* 21 December 2015, at www.scmp.com.
[18] K. Vaswani, 'China economic growth slowest in 25 years', *BBC News* 19 January 2016, at www.bbc.com/news.

when it overtook China as the world's fastest economy, at 7.1 per cent per year.[19] The environmental connotations of such breakneck growth become clearer when its ecological footprint gets broken down into specific economic sectors. For instance, Chinese cities have become car-clogged as residents discard their bicycles; in 2009 China surpassed the United States in the highest number of new car sales,[20] and in 2015 China's private motor vehicle numbers reached 172 million, up from a mere 3.2 million in 1985.[21] China's real estate boom yields a similar picture, with massive investment in new apartment complexes, shopping malls, and other urban infrastructure over recent decades.[22] In turn, this economic juggernaut disgorges colossal ecological impacts: China is the world's largest contributor to marine plastic debris,[23] and the world's largest emitter of greenhouse gases,[24] though on a per capita basis it might seem less culpable.

Brevity and speed also infect politics. Politicians believe they need to be ever more succinct to garner our fleeting attention. Prior to television, political speeches in the United States broadcast on radio typically averaged one hour, while today they rarely last more than 20 minutes and many are just pithy 30 second advertisements.[25] A parallel trend towards succinctness and economy is the fewer days that legislatures are sitting: the Canadian House of Commons has dropped from 165 days in the 1969–73 period to 105 days per year over 2004–8.[26] A similar trend is observed in Great Britain.[27] With fewer sitting days, governments are also fast-tracking new laws by imposing time limits on parliamentary scrutiny and

---

[19] C. Riley, 'India's economic growth is still the envy of the world', *CCN Money* 31 August 2016, at http://money.cnn.com.
[20] 'China overtakes US as world's biggest car market', *The Guardian* 9 January 2010, at www.theguardian.com.
[21] T. Shaohui, 'China's car ownership reaches 172 million', *Xinhua* 25 January 2016, at http://news.xinhuanet.com/en; X. Deng, *Private Car Ownership in China: How Important Is the Effect of Income?* (Centre of Regulation and Market Analysis, University of South Australia, 2007), 1.
[22] S.X. Zhao and B. Michael, *How Big is the Chinese Real Estate Bubble and Why Hasn't It Yet Burst: A Comparative Study between China and World Major Financial Crises 1980-2014*, Working paper WP16SZ2 (Lincoln Institute of Land Policy, 2016).
[23] According to J.R. Jambeck, 'Plastic waste inputs from land into the ocean' (2015) 347, *Science* 768-9.
[24] R. Meyer, 'China, the world's biggest polluter, commits to cap-and-trade carbon emissions', *The Atlantic* 25 September 2015, at www.theatlantic.com.
[25] G. Ritzer, *The McDonaldization of Society* (SAGE, 2015), 165.
[26] C.E.S. Frank and D. Smith, 'The Canadian House of Commons under stress: reform and adaptation' in H. Bakvis and M. Jarvis (eds), *From New Public Management to New Political Governance* (McGill-Queen's University Press, 2012), 70, 85.
[27] 'Britain's idle parliament', *The Economist* 5 April 2014, at www.economist.com/news.

packing massive legislative changes into single Bills; the Canadian government's omnibus budget legislation of 2012, known simply as 'Bill C-45', contained some 450 pages that amended or repealed about 60 separate statutes (most having nothing to do with the financial budget). In April 2017 the Republican-controlled US Congress used the 'nuclear' option to force confirmation of Supreme Court nominee Neil Gorsuch in defiance of a threatened Democrat-filibuster. The shortening attention span of politics and the tempo of the electoral cycle encourages policies that yield results before the next election, which may be only 1 or 2 years away. As governments become side-tracked by expedient and short-term concerns, they are less likely to generate policies oriented to the very long term.

The accelerating pace of life, while widely felt, exerts itself unevenly across cultures. Psychologist Robert Levine has devoted his career to this subject, discerning big differences between the tempo of the United States (fast) and Brazil (slower), as well as in-country differences between rural (slow) and urban (faster).[28] Levine also finds places where people still live according to 'nature time', such as diurnal and seasonal rhythms, in contrast to the more prevalent 'event time' structured around happenings such as work and meetings. Latin American and Mediterranean countries are the most somnolent lifestyles, according to his research.[29] Important correlations with tempo found by Levine include that cities with warmer climates are slower than cooler ones, places with more dynamic economies are faster, and collectivist cultures flow more slowly than those that glorify individualism. Big cities spawn particularly fast cultures,[30] and Richard Wiseman's 'Pace of Life Project' suggests that the tempo of global metropolises has increased by 10 per cent on average in the past two decades since the early 1990s, with Singapore presently the world's most frenetic.[31]

Life in the fast lane also can have serious repercussions for ordinary people. Paradoxically, time-saving technologies have tended to hasten, not lessen, our sense of being busy and stressed.[32] As British social

---

[28] R. Levine, *A Geography of Time: The Temporal Misadventures of a Social Psychologist* (Basic Books, 1998).

[29] R. Levine and A. Norenzyan, 'The pace of life in 31 countries' (1999) 30(2) *Journal of Cross-Cultural Psychology* 178.

[30] See also I. Hoch, 'City size effects, trends and policies' (1976) 193 *Science* 856.

[31] Pace of Life Project, at www.richardwiseman.com/quirkology/pace_home.htm.

[32] Interestingly, however, technological innovation has also empowered people to investigate their past much better, thus reducing the omnipresence of the present. The Internet and new computing technologies have fuelled massive interest in family history, with public and private research portals available for amateur researchers to trace their genealogy (e.g.

commentator Claudia Hammond explains, 'the invention of the car hasn't saved us hours of travelling, instead we travel further. Social-networking sites haven't saved us time seeing people; instead we stay in touch with more people and communicate with them more often'.[33] Hackneyed phrases such as 'time deficit', 'time poverty', 'time pressure', 'time scarcity', 'time squeeze', and 'time stress' speak to this ubiquitous stress.[34] Our predecessors' dream of the future 'leisure society' has never materialised. Ironically, despite time being our most valued commodity, economists David Hamermesh and Jungmin Lee found that the richest people suffer the most from lack of time.[35] Time poverty, believe health experts, fuels many ailments, including an epidemic of binge drinking, anxiety, irritability, weight gain, insomnia, and reduced sex drive, among many others.[36] People sleep less well than they did two centuries ago.[37] Our hurried culture also increases familial strife and marital breakdowns.[38] Rushing motorists precipitate traffic accidents.[39] Social psychologist Stanley Milgram's theory of 'urban overload' holds that the rapidity of city life has lowered social civility as busy people become less respectful of strangers.[40] Similarly, time theorist Robert Levine surmises that 'people who move quickly are less likely to find time for social responsibilities particularly when those responsibilities involve strangers'.[41]

The antidote to some of these ailments and attitudes, suggest some health therapists, is to reconnect people to nature. Building on Edward

---

www.ancestry.com, www.myheritage.com, www.archives.com, and www.nationalarchives .gov.uk). Many people still long to give meaning to their lives by placing them within longer time frames. However, some postmodernist scholars such as Jean Baudrillard and Fredric Jameson evaluate the trend as an impoverished 'simulacra' of real historical experiences: F. Jameson, *Postmodernism, or, the Cultural Logic of Late Capitalism* (Duke University Press, 1991); J. Baudrillard, *Simulacra and Simulation* (University of Michigan Press, 1994).

[33] C. Hammond, *Time Warped: Unlocking the Mysteries of Time Perception* (House of Anansi Press, 2012), 280–1.

[34] Cited in A. Szollos, 'Toward a psychology of chronic time pressure' (2009) 18 *Time and Society* 332, 336.

[35] D.S. Hamermesh and J. Lee, *Stressed Out on Four Continents: Time Crunch or Yuppie Kvetch?* Working paper No. 10186 (National Bureau of Economic Research, 2003).

[36] L. Kreitzman, *24 Hour Society* (Profile Books, 1999).

[37] A.R. Ekirch, *At Day's Close: Night in Time* (WW Norton, 2006) (explaining that before the nineteenth century, people in Western society more commonly slept in two segments, as aligned with circadian rhythms).

[38] K.J. Daly, *Families and Time: Keeping Pace in a Hurried Culture* (SAGE, 1996).

[39] P.J. Tranter, 'Speed kills: the complex links between transport, lack of time and urban health' (2010) 87(2) *Journal of Urban Health* 155.

[40] S. Milgram, 'The experience of living in cities' (1970) 167 *Science* 1461.

[41] Levine, *A Geography of Time*, 202.

O. Wilson's biophilia thesis,[42] research into nature-based healthcare and education touts such benefits as better recovery times in hospitals, fewer behavioural disorders in children, and improved emotional and cognitive outlook.[43] Likewise, so-called 'eco-therapists' recommend taking regular work breaks so as to connect oneself to nature,[44] and some even choose a 'sea change' or 'tree change', leaving the bustling city and hectic workplace altogether to seek bucolic bliss. One quaint option is the 'Decelerator Helmet', a high-tech headgear designed by Lorenz Potthast to slow down the user's sense of hustle and bustle in the modern city.[45] The viewer wearing this bizarre device, shaped like an inverted ice bucket, will see a computer monitor showing the surroundings in real-time. By operating a wireless mouse, the viewer can slow down the video feed and thereby create a sensation of more leisurely surroundings.

Nature not only offers palliative care for the time stressed, but itself needs solace from our hurried culture. As we internalise the tightening discipline of time, the 'tyranny of the moment',[46] we risk losing sight of how our behaviour affects the environment, especially impacts manifesting gradually over the long term. In our daily routines, busy people can find environmental civility too inconvenient, thus buying their coffee in disposal cups, shopping with single-use plastic bags, driving rather than walking to the local corner store, and other selfish habits that cumulatively degrade the planet. In the marketplace, arguably life's most frenetic domain, many economic transactions have little time for environmental due diligence. Corporate environmental reports, though increasingly common, betray their hurried drafting by the frequent absence of detailed analysis of ecological impacts. Monitoring environmental conditions or assessing potential impacts are time-consuming commitments that most busy developers prefer to avoid. Likewise, investing in environmental improvements of long-term value may not appeal to a company that cannot gain a pay-off immediately. Consumer education about the environmental

---

[42] E.O. Wilson, *Biophilia* (Harvard University Press, 1984).
[43] L. Buzzell and C. Chalquiet (eds), *Ecotherapy: Healing with Nature in Mind* (Counterpoint, 2009).
[44] See E. Darier, 'Time to be lazy. Work, the environment and modern subjectivities' (1998) 7(2) *Time and Society* 193; M. Jalas, 'Debating the proper pace of life: sustainable consumption policy processes at national and municipal levels' (2012) 21(3) *Environmental Politics* 369.
[45] K. Buchan, 'Decelerator helmet: viewing the world in slow motion', *The Guardian* 10 July 2014, at www.theguardian.com.
[46] T. Hylland-Eriksen, *The Tyranny of the Moment: Fast and Slow Time in the Information Age* (Pluto Press, 2001).

qualities of products and services is often reduced to vacuous labels such as 'free range' or 'dolphin safe': there is no time (and perhaps no motivation) to explain the environmental context of these purchases. Environmental legislation itself faces incessant demands from business managers wanting quicker approvals, as though it is a foregone conclusion that their developments will get the go-ahead. Prestigious or politically sensitive development projects may even be shepherded through, with customised 'fast-track' legislation that offers only cursory environmental scrutiny.

The social and environmental sequelae of fast time have not gone unnoticed or unchallenged. Time-related strategies for slowing down have entered debates about sustainable living. A plethora of slow and simplicity movements are defying our culture of busyness, with names such as Slow Technology, Slow Design, Slow Cities, and Slow Travel. They offer guidance for personal lifestyle redemption as well as institutional changes to tackle systematically the sources of hurriedness and freneticism.[47] The two slow life movements of environmental significance that this chapter explores are Slow Food and Slow Money (also closely related to socially responsible investing). The former seeks more environmentally responsible farming and consumption, while the latter aims to shift financial markets towards more patient and enduring investing practices aligned with sustainable development. Before looking at the movements for slow time, this chapter probes the influence of fast time on environmental decisions. This includes the culture of fast consumption and the accelerated depletion of natural resources, such as forests. The phenomenon of 'fast track' legislation particularly illustrates the pernicious effects of accelerated governance. A pulp mill proposal in Tasmania, Australia, yields interesting insights into this phenomenon. The subsequent sections investigate Slow Food and Slow Money, and their governance, as ways to align human timescales with nature's.

Keeping Up with the Joneses

All Consuming

Nature fares badly in our throwaway, shopaholic society, in which consumption defines our economic and cultural personality.[48] Numerous products have planned, inbuilt obsolescence or become socially obsolete

---

[47] C. Honoré, *In Praise of Slowness: Challenging the Cult of Speed* (HarperOne, 2005).
[48] See generally, C. Hamilton and R. Denniss, *Affluenza: When Too Much Is Never Enough* (Allen and Unwin, 2005); K.M. Ekström and H. Brembeck, *Elusive Consumption* (Bloomsbury, 2004); B.B. Barber, *Consumed – How Markets Corrupt Children, Infantilize*

as fashion dictates that 'newer' is 'better'. This fast consumption, in which the populace is sweet-talked to shop, consume, and discard way beyond any basic needs, has soared. Household consumption expenditures worldwide grew from US$4.8 trillion in 1960 to US$24 trillion in 2005 (in 1995 dollars), an increase of 400 per cent compared to the global population increase of 124 per cent over the same period.[49] The dynamic of capitalism to stimulate ever-increasing consumption to sustain business profitability drives intense exploitation of natural resources and their return to the environment as trash. Fast consumption makes a mockery of corporate social responsibility (CSR) claims about being eco-friendly when their wares have limited life expectancy – consider plastic bottled water, for instance.[50] If businesses were genuine about sustainability, they would discourage consumption and produce durable goods that last for ages. Governments have been complicit in the religion of consumerism; during the Cold War, the West stimulated mass consumption as a way to 'prove' capitalism's economic superiority, and since the 1970s consumerism has dovetailed with neoliberal ideologies that accentuate the primacy of individual choice through the 'free' market.[51] Tellingly, shortly after 9/11 President George Bush exhorted Americans to 'go shopping' in order to show the terrorists that they would not be intimidated.

The ethos of fast consumption has older roots. In the 1920s, light bulb manufacturers such as Philips and Osram conspired to reduce the longevity of incandescent bulbs in order to boost sales volumes.[52] Although light bulbs invented in the nineteenth century could last for decades, such longevity didn't make business sense when seldom burnt-out bulbs would rarely need replacement. Thus, the manufacturers actively lowered the life span of light bulbs from about 2,500 hours to 1,000 hours. The cartel eventually broke up, but it had demonstrated how lowering product quality and durability could boost consumption and profits. Many examples of

---

Adults and Swallow Citizens Whole (WW Norton, 2007); N. Lawson, *All Consuming* (Penguin, 2009).

[49] A. Leonard, *The Story of Stuff* (Free Press, 2010), 146.
[50] P.H. Gleick, *Bottled and Sold: The Story behind Our Obsession with Bottled Water* (Island Press, 2010).
[51] M.S. Rosenberg, 'Consumer capitalism and the end of the Cold War', in M.P. Leffler and O.R. Westad (eds), *The Cambridge History of the Cold War*, Volume III (Cambridge University Press, 2010), 489.
[52] *The Light Bulb Conspiracy*, film, 2010, directed by C. Dannoritzer and S. Michelson.

intentionally defective products can still be found.[53] Apple's iPod, a portable media player introduced in 2001, had an effective lifespan of just 18 months, as that was the durability of its 'rechargeable' battery.[54] To replace it (but it wasn't easily removable) would cost US$250, or one could buy another iPod for US$400. Computer ink cartridges are another gripe; they can cost more than the printer, and some are engineered with a disabling device to stop printing before their pigment is exhausted.

While the lifespan of some products has increased owing to technological innovation or consumer pressure, companies have found another ploy to keep people shopping – by rendering products socially obsolete. Businesses can make subtle design and cosmetic adjustments to impress consumers with 'new' products marketed as necessary to stay abreast of trends. This social obsolescence is not restricted to designer sunglasses or must-have handbags; as the useful life of cars has extended, the automobile industry has also focused on reducing their fashionable life.[55] The industry embellishes its models frequently, even annually, cajoling buyers to trade up for the latest styles even though the new models usually retain similar quality.

Super-sizing everything has become another metric by which consumers can keep track of the Joneses. McMansions, SUVs, and giant plasma televisions, along with bigger servings of junk food, have become hallmarks of conspicuous consumption. Expanding portion sizes in US takeaway joints and restaurants since the 1970s has correlated with the nation's obesity crisis.[56] The 2004 *Super Size Me* documentary film tracked Morgan Spurlock's deteriorating health as he gorged only on McDonald's food for 1 month, including any super-size meals offered to him. Houses have also been getting bigger, perhaps to store all this extra stuff and their fatter residents. US houses are palatial, averaging 2,646 feet^2 (or 245 m^2) in 2013 compared to 1,660 feet^2 (154 m^2) in 1973. European houses on average seem compact: about 85 m^2 in Britain, 115 m^2 in the Netherlands, and

---

[53] See G. Slade, *Made to Break: Technology and Obsolescence in America* (Harvard University Press, 2006).

[54] H. Steuver, 'Battery and assault', *Washington Post* 20 December 2003, at www.washingtonpost.com.

[55] T. McCarthy, *Auto Mania: Cars, Consumers, and the Environment* (Yale University Press, 2007).

[56] L.R. Young and M. Nestle, 'The contribution of expanding portion sizes to the US obesity epidemic' (2002) 92(2) *American Journal of Public Health* 246.

137 m² in Denmark.[57] In recommending that the UK government legislate larger minimum house sizes, the not impartial Royal Institute of British Architects argued: 'a lack of space has been shown to impact on the basic lifestyle needs that many people take for granted, such as having enough space to store possessions or even to entertain friends'.[58] The appetite for swanky housing has also been a major driver of home renovations and soaring house prices, especially in salubrious cities such as Sydney and Vancouver.

Advertising has an insidious influence here. Television programs, now even on some supposed 'public' channels, bombard viewers with irritating commercials. Advertising can be particularly effective when consumers are not even aware of it, such as Hollywood films that include product placements or embedded marketing. Marketers increasingly rely on interactive advertising on social media such as Twitter and Facebook. Advertisers have also capitalised on popular environmental concerns through 'green' marketing that aims to induce consumers to buy more stuff on the assumption that it is safe and clean. The foregoing contributes to social alienation, generating more information but less meaning; it's an abstract world that French sociologist Jean Baudrillard called 'hyperreality', in which consumers are flooded with images that blur the line between truth and fiction.[59]

Cheap credit, and its lax regulation, has also stimulated fast consumption. When wages growth failed to keep pace with the consumption goals of the market, the financial sector stepped in to enable consumers to buy now and pay later. Home loans today are within the reach of many, sometimes even for those without a deposit. Credit cards, introduced in the 1950s, sit in most individuals' wallets: 72 per cent of adult Americans have them, as do 60 per cent from British. Loose credit policies have allowed consumer debt to soar. Australian household debt was estimated in 2015 as equivalent to 130 per cent of GDP, the then highest ratio of any country.[60] Canadians are also awash with debt: the ratio of household debt to disposable income touched a record 164.5 per cent in late 2015, amounting

---

[57] R. Roberts-Hughes, *The Case for Space: The Size of England's New Homes* (Royal Institute of British Architects, 2011), 10.
[58] Ibid, 4.
[59] Baudrillard, *Simulacra and Simulation*.
[60] M. Mulligan, 'Australian households awash with debt: Barclays', Sydney Morning Herald 16 March 2015, at www.smh.com.au.

to C$1.92 trillion.[61] At the close of 2014, Americans typically each held US$7,200 in credit card debt, an increase of US$57.1 billion over the preceding 12 months.[62] The personal debt binge has spread to many other countries, such as Thailand and South Korea.[63] Such credit may cause shoppers to succumb to their impulses, allowing them to live beyond their means (though not indefinitely).

Just as credit cards seduce shoppers to buy what they can't afford, retailers entice them with cheap prices. Buyers flock to outlet malls populated by Wal-Mart, Ikea, Home Depot, and other discounters. Ellen Ruppel Shell, in her bestseller *Cheap*, found that Chinese sweatshop-built 'bargains' such as flimsy furniture, tacky gadgets, and ill-fitting clothes pack the shelves of these shopping factories.[64] Thrift stores are brimming with even cheaper second-hand wares, often discarded by consumers to make way for their new purchases. The obsession with cheapness potentially shrinks the market for quality, well-crafted goods, thereby making them increasingly expensive. Food is also notoriously retailed as cheap and fast. As discussed later this in this chapter, fast-food chains such as McDonald's and Subway cater to consumers on the go, who can 'enjoy' meals at knockdown prices thanks to low staff wages and agricultural subsidies.[65]

This unprecedented cornucopia of material stuff doesn't make us happier or healthier. The emotional uplift of retail therapy is momentary, as we soon become habituated to the new sofa or shoes. In fact, 'oniomania', the medical term for compulsive shoppers, can wreak emotional havoc for sufferers, including depression and financial ruin. Instead, purchasing non-material 'experiences', such as enrolling in a yoga class or trying a new hobby such as gardening tends to be more fulfilling and lasting, suggest psychologists.[66] Findings from the World Values Survey, which annually polls individuals in over 65 countries on their life satisfaction, indicate that prosperity promotes happiness until about US$13,000 annual income

---

[61] Statistics Canada, 'National balance sheet and financial flow accounts, fourth quarter 2015' (Statistics Canada, 11 March 2016).
[62] 'America's skyrocketing credit card debt', *CBS News* 10 March 2015, at www.cbsnews.com/news.
[63] J. Fernquest, 'Household debt makes economy fragile', *Bangkok Post* 11 November 2015, at www.bangkokpost.com; K. Jun, 'South Koreans are on a debt binge', *Wall Street Journal* 25 February 2015, at www.wsj.com.
[64] E.R. Shell, *Cheap: The High Cost of Discount Culture* (Penguin Press, 2011).
[65] As discussed in E. Schlosser, *Fast Food Nation: The Dark-side of the American Meal* (Houghton Mifflin, 2001).
[66] J. Hamblin, 'Buy experiences, not things', *The Atlantic* 7 October 2014, at www.theatlantic.com.

per person (in 1995 dollars).[67] Beyond that, additional wealth yields only modest increments in well-being. There is a curious exception, however; spending one's wealth on others, such as for philanthropy, can make one happier than spending it on oneself.[68] Such insights have encouraged economists to devise alternative measures of economic vitality and well-being to replace GDP.[69]

All this consumption takes a heavy toll on Earth. Huge quantities of fossil fuels, minerals, water, and other resources are exploited to make and transport growing amounts of products and services. Researchers in 2009 estimated that humankind extracts and uses about 50 per cent more natural resources than 30 years earlier.[70] While resource use efficiency has improved, especially in Europe, population and economic growth have offset it. The most familiar environmental consequences of consumerism are mountains of trash. Despite public campaigns to 'reduce, reuse, and recycle', the garbage accumulates. In 2012 American households generated about 251 million tonnes of it (or 1,591 pounds per person annually) compared to 87 million tons (551 pounds per person) that was recycled or composted.[71] While recycling rates have shot up, from 6.4 per cent in 1960 to 34.5 per cent in 2012, the volume of waste in 1960 was much lower at 88 million tons, or 678 pounds per person (nearly half that of today). Europeans are less wasteful, according to Eurostat data: in 2012, 492 kg (or 1,084 pounds) of municipal waste was generated per person, and the recycled or composted share grew from 18 per cent in 1995 to 42 per cent in 2012.[72] According to the World Bank, per capita waste volumes in South Asia are the lowest anywhere (averaging 164 kg per person annually, as of 2011).[73]

---

[67] See www.worldvaluessurvey.org/index.html.

[68] E.W. Dunn, L.B. Aknin, and M.I. Norton, 'Spending money on others promotes happiness' (2008) 319(5870) *Science* 1687.

[69] Alternative measures of prosperity include the Index of Sustainable Economic Welfare, www.neweconomics.org, and the Happy Planet Index, www.happyplanetindex.org.

[70] Sustainable Europe Research Institute, Global 2000, and Friends of the Earth Europe, *Overconsumption? Our Use of the World's Natural Resources* (Sustainable Europe Research Institute, 2009), 3.

[71] US Environmental Protection Agency (EPA), *Municipal Solid Waste Generation, Recycling, and Disposal in the United States: Facts and Figures for 2012* (EPA, 2014), 1.

[72] 'In 2012, 42% of treated municipal waste was recycled or composted', Eurostat news release 25 March 2014, at http://ec.europa.eu/eurostat/web/products-press-releases.

[73] D. Hoornweg and P. Bhada-Tata, *What a Waste: A Global Review of Solid Waste Management* (World Bank, 2012), 9.

The environmental impacts of trash are troubling, including climate change, soil contamination, and marine pollution. A 2015 study attributed about 60 per cent of global greenhouse gases to household consumption.[74] Most waste ends up in smelly, rat-infested landfills. The global *Waste Atlas Report* published in 2014 identified 50 behemoth landfills that hold 200–300 times the volume of the Great Pyramid of Giza.[75] One of America's largest, the Fresh Kills landfill in New York, closed in 2001 and was reputedly the largest human-made structure in the world, bigger than China's Great Wall.[76] Decaying organic material in landfills generates methane, a potent greenhouse gas. Growing electronic waste (e-waste) in dumpsites has left a toxic time bomb, leaching lead, cadmium, mercury, and other toxic metals into the surrounding soil and groundwater. Incinerators are often no safer, belching ash and fumes. Much consumer waste finds its way to the oceans. Of 280 million tons of plastic produced in 2013, some 10–20 million tons became marine debris.[77] The ecological costs include poisoned seabirds and fish, entanglement of marine life, especially turtles, and flow-on costs to people from contaminated food.

The law is complicit in fast consumerism. It begins with the lacklustre regulation of natural resources harvesting, whether it is forestry, farming, or mining, in addition to the feeble control of fossil fuels use. Later, this chapter delves into forestry to illustrate one example. Further along the economic spectrum, consumer regulation that limits product warranties for short periods results in shoppers discarding defective products because the repair costs can be greater than buying a replacement. European Union law requires 2-year warranties on consumer goods, well below the reasonable lifespan of numerous products such as televisions and computers.[78] Some jurisdictions, such as Australia, innovatively tie warranty periods to the stipulation that goods be 'fit for purpose',[79] but retailers routinely mislead customers on their rights or make them pay for legally unnecessary

---

[74] D. Ivanova, et al., 'Environmental impact assessment of household consumption' (2016) 20(3) *Journal of Industrial Ecology* 536.
[75] D-Waste, *Waste Atlas Report: The World's 50 Biggest Dumpsites* (D-Waste, 2014), 4.
[76] Leonard, *The Story of Stuff*, xiii.
[77] United Nations Environment Programme (UNEP), *Valuing Plastics: The Business Case for Measuring, Managing and Disclosing Plastic Use in the Consumer Goods Industry* (UNEP, 2014), 7.
[78] European Directive 1999/44/EC of the European Parliament and of the Council of 25 May 1999 on certain aspects of the sale of consumer goods and associated guarantees, O.J 1999, L 171/12, 7 July 1999, Article 5(1).
[79] Competition and Consumer Act 2010 (Cth), s. 54.

extended warranties.[80] In any event, challenging a retailer or manufacturer in court is too expensive and troublesome for most shoppers. The law also contributes to fast consumption through lax product labelling standards. Advertising law targets overtly misleading or deceptive conduct, such as an agri-business advertising produce as 'organic' that in fact contains artificial chemicals.[81] However, apart from specialist regulations for discrete sectors, few jurisdictions mandate positive obligations on businesses to disclose the environmental qualities or impacts of their products and services. A business is thus often not obliged to tell prospective consumers of its carbon footprint or treatment of animals.

Solutions to these and other governance gaps will require wide-ranging responses, such as rewarding resource-efficient behaviour, more mandatory recycling, higher waste charges, longer product warranty periods, cradle-to-grave product stewardship, and improved product labelling to disclose environmental impacts. Environmentally destructive fast consumerism can also be tackled through social activism. Already, an array of grassroots movements are educating consumers and forging alternative lifestyles for those wishing to live more simply and slowly, including the tiny house movement, community farmers' markets, and various slow living networks.[82] However, the challenges to overcome go beyond the wasteful consumption of modern lifestyles, extending to some deep-seated avarice.

The Scramble for Nature's Bounty

Our all-consuming ways are older than the recent post-war affluence. Humankind has plundered nature unsustainably for ages, and some of the butchering has been sickening in its enormity and rapidity. The famed Galápagos tortoise's (*Geochelone nigra*) population plunged from about 250,000 before the seventeenth century to about 3,000 by the 1970s, a collapse mainly attributable to hungry sailors and settlers. The North American bison (*Bison bison*) once swarmed in numbers of between 30 and 60 million, but was reduced by 1890 to less than 1,000 stragglers, a slaughter that government authorities encouraged to weaken Native Americans who relied on the creatures for food and clothing. Bison numbers have

---

[80] A. Kollmorgen and J. Castle, 'Consumer law and extended warranties', *Choice* 27 November 2013, at www.choice.com.au.
[81] E.g. Competition and Consumer Law Act 2010 (Cth), s. 18.
[82] K. Humphrey, *Excess; Anti-consumerism in the West* (Polity Press, 2010).

'recovered' to about half a million today, though only 20,000 roam wild and only 8,000 have not genetically hybridised with cattle.[83]

The bloodshed is not mere history. Today, about 73 million sharks die at human hands annually, mostly for their fins.[84] In Australia, some 3-5 million kangaroos are culled yearly for commercial purposes.[85] The carnage is not limited to wildlife. Deforestation, to enable palm oil plantations, cattle grazing, and other 'productive' uses, destroys about 7.3 million ha of forest annually, about the size of Panama, according to the UN Food and Agricultural Organization (FAO).[86] More bad news awaits us. Less freshwater is predicted by 2025, with 1.8 billion people living with absolute water scarcity, due to such short-sighted practices as depleting water aquifers for irrigated farming and building sprawling cities like Phoenix in deserts.[87] What's extraordinary about much of this greed and insouciance is that it has occurred with the blessing of the law or at least the absence of any legal control. Natural resources open to all without social control have, as Garrett Hardin predicted, become susceptible to a tragedy of the commons.[88] Even scientific knowledge about nature's limits – we know much better today than our predecessors – has not been enough to deter human rapacity.

Harvesting nature's resources is not itself a problem (we would perish without them); rather, it is the *speed* with which the exploitation occurs, leaving nature gasping for survival. Time, in other words, is the crucial part of the equation. Sustainable harvesting of renewable resources depends on limiting what we take out of nature to less than it can reproduce. That harvestable surplus, whether it is water, trees, or fauna, differs spatially and temporally as environmental conditions vary.[89] Seeds planted in poor soils

---

[83] See further: C.B. Stanford, *The Last Tortoise: A Tale of Extinction in Our Lifetime* (Belknap Press, 2010); A.C. Isenberg, *The Destruction of the Bison: An Environmental History, 1750-1920* (Cambridge University Press, 2000).

[84] S.C. Clarke, et al., 'Global estimates of shark catches using trade records from commercial markets' (2006) 9(10) *Ecology Letters* 1115.

[85] Department of the Environment and Heritage, *Background Information: Commercial Kangaroo and Wallaby Harvest Quotas* (Commonwealth Government, April 2010).

[86] UN Food and Agricultural Organization (FAO), *The Global Forest Resources Assessment 2005* (FAO, 2005), Deforestation, according to the FAO, in fact removes 13 million ha per year, but because of planting and natural expansion of existing forests, the net loss is 7.3 million ha.

[87] International Fund for Agricultural Development, 'Water facts and figures', at www.ifad.org/english/water/key.htm.

[88] G. Hardin, 'Tragedy of the commons' (1968) 162 *Science* 1243.

[89] R. Hilborn, C.J. Walters, and D. Ludwig, 'Sustainable exploitation of renewable resources' (1995) 26 *Annual Review of Ecology and Systematics* 45.

with limited moisture will produce limited reproductive surplus compared to plantings in receptive terrain. Or ducks thriving in good habitat with few predators may tolerate substantial game hunting compared to a population without such favourable conditions. However, many of the major targets of harvesting, such as great whales and old-growth forest, operate on such long timescales that they can sustain only very low rates of harvesting. In essence, environmental management must adaptively aim for a sustainable yield that takes account of variable conditions and variable sensitivities depending on the resource in question, while allowing a margin of safety to take account of uncertainty.

While the concept of sustainable development has been familiar to environmental governance for about 30 years, the notion of sustainable yield has a long history in the management of fish, wildlife, and forests: since 1930 (for fisheries) and 1849 (forestry).[90] Regulations to control resource harvesting have evolved over an even longer time. Freshwater fishing has been regulated in Europe since at least the medieval period.[91] The vulnerability of marine fisheries to overexploitation became recognised more slowly because of their seeming abundance and the difficulties of regulating beyond coastal waters. Laws to protect forests in England date to about the twelfth century.[92] Similar restrictions arose in China much earlier, in the Western Zhou dynasty (1046–771 BCE).[93] Through European colonisation, environmental laws that promoted 'orderly' exploitation of forests, fisheries, minerals, and other resources spread throughout much of the world.[94]

The choice of regulation is important. Initially, simple prohibitions such as closed seasons and excluded areas were the preferred means of imposing some order. Later, the methods of harvesting became controlled, such as the size of fishing vessels or type of nets. Some spectacular collapses in 'regulated' harvests, such as Canada's east coast cod fishery in the early 1990s that left 35,000 fishers jobless, spurred adoption of other governance

---

[90] P.A. Larkin, 'An epitaph to the concept of maximum sustained yield' (1977) 106(1) *Transactions of the American Fisheries Society* 1.
[91] R. Hoffmann, *An Environmental History of Medieval Europe* (Cambridge University Press, 2014), 263–77.
[92] C.R. Young, *The Royal Forests of Medieval England* (University of Pennsylvania Press, 1979).
[93] Z. Shijun, 'Forest resources law' in Q. Tianbao (ed), *Research Handbook on Chinese Environmental Law* (Edward Elgar Publishing, 2015), 255, 260.
[94] R.H. Grove, *Green Imperialism: Tropical Island Edens and the Origins of Environmentalism, 1600–1860* (Cambridge University Press, 1995).

techniques.[95] Property rights approaches have become increasingly popular, including transferable rights to resources such as fish stock or water to aid in the development of environmental markets. The assumption is that private ownership incentivises users to manage resources wisely and efficiently. Because the collapse of some harvested resources owed partly to scientific assessment blunders, as with Canada's cod fishery, regulators have also become interested in adaptive management techniques that allow for some experimentation to find the optimal sustainable take.[96] Adaptive management confronts the limited knowledge of dynamic ecosystems and endorses the periodic recalibration of regulatory decisions to take account of new information and changing circumstances. Such flexibility, however, is anathema to the custom of environmental governance to 'front load' decision making to the initial approval phase with limited scope for revisiting initial decisions.

The core challenges for sustainable management of renewable resources are to overcome the impatient and myopic biases that exploit resources under harvest cycles insufficient to allow resources to recover and, as noted in Chapter 3, to retain enough flexibility to adjust management edicts in the light of changing circumstances, including new scientific knowledge. These challenges tend to arise because governance decisions reflect economic and political criteria that can deviate from ecological considerations, in addition to deficiencies in scientific knowledge. Forestry provides a good case study to illustrate these issues further.

Around the world, forest management has been one of the most divisive environmental issues for regulators and communities.[97] Logging has diverse impacts on water, climate, biodiversity, and many other ecological dimensions. Conversely, forestry can economically sustain 'timber towns', and thus the industry attracts political salience when jobs and livelihoods are at stake. Time infuses these tensions: the time intervals by which forests are cut influences the type and scale of ecological disturbances they experience, while such cutting cycles also affect the economic viability of logging operations. Time also informs any brokered political compromises, in which the negotiated shift to a new forestry regime or

---

[95] R.A. Myers, J.A. Hutchings, and N.J. Barrowman, 'Why do fish stocks collapse? The example of cod in Atlantic Canada' (1997) 7(1) *Ecological Applications* 1.
[96] C. Walters, *Adaptive Management and Renewable Resources* (Blackburn Press, 1986), iv.
[97] See J. Ajani, *The Forest Wars* (Melbourne University Press, 2007); N. Turvey, *Terania Creek: Rainforest Wars* (Glasshouse Books, 2006); D. Salazar and D.K. Alper (eds), *Sustaining the Forests of the Pacific Coast: Forging Truces in the War in the Woods* (UBC Press, 2000).

the cessation of logging altogether may be phased in over many years in order to ease the economic pain.

The severity of the environmental impacts of forestry depends largely on the type of forest ecosystem and the harvesting methods. Clear felling is often the most destructive: it removes all trees and other vegetation within the logged coupe, leaving a barren landscape of tree stumps and sticks. Although clear felling is often associated with emerging economies, such as Indonesia or Brazil, it also occurs in some developed nations, such as Canada.[98] The amount of clearing and its frequency affect the environmental outcomes: clear felling may involve only a small fraction of a forest (coupes) in any year, with long rotation times between repeated cuttings. However, the impact of a single logged coupe can, in aggregate with many other areas harvested over a full rotation cycle, be significant, resulting in reduced structural complexity of the ecosystem and a 'highly homogenized landscape'.[99] Such homogenisation accrues particularly in tree plantations, which are often established over 'less productive' native vegetation. Plantations typically grow a single species chosen purely for its economic benefits. Radiata pine (a native tree of North America) is one of the most common softwood plantation timbers around the world, a choice that reflects not only pine's wood quality but also its rapid growth to maturity for harvesting (about 30 years). Eucalyptus hardwoods (from Australia) are among the fastest growing hardwood trees, and may reach a harvestable size in as little as 8 years, but more commonly 30–80 years, depending on the species and its management.

Selective logging, which tends to be less injurious, removes only some trees of designated species while preserving the majority of the vegetation and thus retaining much of the original ecosystem. However, repeated selective logging can over time have cumulative effects, as the structure of the forest is altered with consequential disruption to some biota.[100] Selective logging often removes the largest and oldest trees because of their significant volume of wood, but these may be the most important for local biodiversity because of their hollows that provide nesting spaces of birds and arboreal animals.

---

[98] J. Cooperman, 'Cutting down Canada' in B. Devall (ed), *Clearcut: The Tragedy of Industrial Forestry* (Sierra Club Books, 1995), 55.

[99] D. Lindenmayer and W. Laurance, 'A history of hubris – cautionary lessons in ecologically sustainable forest management' (2012) 151 *Biological Conservation* 11, 13.

[100] See D. Lindenmayer and J.F. Franklin, *Conserving Forest Biodiversity: A Comprehensive Multiscaled Approach* (Island Press, 2002).

The forestry industry prefers short rotation cycles because of their economic benefits.[101] Frequent rotations allow more trees to be harvested over the long term, and thereby generate more woodchips and timber to sell. Another reason is the physical risk: as the stand matures, it becomes increasingly expensive to protect and insure the trees against fire, storms, and pest and pathogen infestations. Delaying the cut may also expose growers to adverse changes in wood prices. These considerations weigh most strongly on small-scale growers who lack the capacity to diversify their business but have greater need for ongoing cash flow to survive. Thus, trees are felled when the best rate of returns will occur, well before the trees' maximum average growth is reached.

Another important temporality of forestry management relates to 'shifting baselines', a concept introduced earlier in this book. Because the baseline of a forest ecosystem may shift over long periods under the influence of logging operations, contemporary forest managers may not appreciate the forest's underlying, natural condition. Managers of forests in Scandinavia that have been logged for over three centuries have failed to recognise that forests naturally had more abundant and diverse deciduous trees and wood debris.[102] The creation of new forestry regimes may thus need to take into account deep historical changes that continue to reverberate on biodiversity and other environmental values.

So far, we have only touched on the environmental impacts of forestry in general terms. A few details warrant further comment. Biodiversity tends to fare poorly, as logging endangers species with a low tolerance of habitat disturbance. Some eucalypts do not mature to form hollows that support wildlife such as possums and owls until 150 years, a time interval well in excess of industrial cutting rotations. While shifting logging operations to timber plantations is one popular solution to this conflict, plantation forestry itself carries a large environmental burden. Clearance of native forests to create plantations can lead to a biological desert; the large chemical and water inputs degrade or deplete the local environment (and such costly inputs can necessitate big public subsidies to make plantations economically viable). Logging may also engender ecological disturbances far beyond the area cut, such as making forests more fire-prone, becoming

---

[101] P. Maclaren, 'What age should you harvest?' *New Zealand Tree Grower* August 2003, at www.nzffa.org.nz/tree-grower.
[102] P. Angelstam, P. Majewski, and S. Bondrup-Neilsen, 'West–East cooperation in Europe for sustainable boreal forests' (1995) 82 *Water, Air, and Soil Pollution* 3.

vulnerable to more severe and more frequent wild fires.[103] The impact of both clear-felling and selective logging is also exacerbated far beyond the actual logging sites by the construction of logging roads, which can become pathways for spread of invasive weeds and feral animals. In the United States, the expanded edge effects in logged areas have been identified as exacerbating the spread of gypsy moths and tent caterpillars.[104] In tropical forests in developing countries, logging roads also facilitate sharp increases in wildlife poaching, farming, and human settlement.[105] The roads themselves can become killing fields for naïve animals, a problem at its worst in Tasmania, a logging hotspot dubbed the 'roadkill capital of the world'.[106]

Forestry is moreover a source of carbon emissions, which involves another interesting temporal dimension. Because young forests usually grow faster than old forests, proponents of logging old-growth strands sometimes argue that their replacement with fast-growing trees is environmentally beneficial from a climate perspective. The reasoning is that some of the carbon from old forests will be stored indefinitely in timber products such as buildings and furniture, while the carbon released into the atmosphere will soon be sequestered by the new, growing forests.[107] A public relations campaign sponsored by Forest and Wood Products Australia describes forestry as 'one of the most greenhouse-friendly sectors of the Australian economy' for these reasons.[108] But such claims, explain scientists, 'confuse rates of carbon sequestration with carbon storage'.[109] A comprehensive carbon accounting of forestry would reveal large fugitive emissions that are not captured or stored.[110] These associated carbon

---

[103] D. Lindenmayer, et al., 'Effects of logging on fire regimes in moist forests' (2009) 2 *Conservation Letters* 271.

[104] J. Roland, 'Large-scale forest fragmentation increases the duration of tent caterpillar outbreak' (1993) 93 *Oecologia* 25.

[105] W. Laurence, 'As roads spread in rainforests, the environmental toll grows' (2012) 19 January *Yale Environment 360* 1.

[106] A. Jones, 'Welcome to Tasmania, the roadkill capital of the world', ABC Radio National (Off Track) 14 December 2014, at www.abc.net.au/radionational/programs/offtrack.

[107] Y. Pan, et al., 'A large and persistent carbon sink in the world's forests' (2011) 333 *Science* 988.

[108] C. Walters, 'Sequester carbon in a piano: forestry advert hits bum note', *Sydney Morning Herald* 2 May 2009, at www.smh.com.au.

[109] Lindenmayer and Laurance, 'A history of hubris', 14.

[110] M.E. Harmon, W.K. Ferrell, and J.F. Franklin, 'Effects on carbon storage of conversion of old-growth forests to young forests' (1990) 247 *Science* 699; R.C. Dewar and M.G.R. Cannell, 'Carbon sequestration in the trees, products and soils of forest plantations: an analysis using UK examples' (1992) 11 *Tree Physiology* 49.

emissions from logging and subsequent processing operations include: accelerated decay of some of the living biomass at the logging coupe; carbon lost from soil disturbance; emissions involved in managing plantations; and further emissions from industrial processes associated with wood processing and retailing. Logging of native forests can result in long-term loss of 40–60 per cent of the carbon stored in those forests, and depending on the type of forest ecosystem, it can take over a century to recapture most of that lost carbon (e.g. at least 150 years to recapture 90 per cent of all the lost carbon in an Australian eucalyptus forest).[111]

The foregoing temporal issues are ostensibly subject to legislative controls, which can shape forestry practices through licensing conditions, management plans, and outright prohibitions. It is typically only at the operational level within site-based management plans that the quality of environmental controls can be discerned, because forestry legislation tends to set broad procedures and principles.[112] By shifting the minutiae of regulation to operational controls negotiated between industry bosses and government regulators, opportunities arise for unscrupulous behaviour known as 'regulatory capture'.[113] It results in the special commercial interests of the industry prevailing over the public interest that the regulator is meant to uphold. While new governance scholarship has highlighted how industry participation in environmental regulation can bring additional resources and expertise,[114] such cosy relationships can also be corrupting if they lead to weaker regulations or lax enforcement, as has been documented in the Australian forestry industry.[115] In Tasmania, the state government has gone so far as to actually remove the application of some key environmental legislation from the forestry sector altogether: the Forest Practices Act 1985 (Tas.) governs forestry on public and private lands, and wherever a forestry operation is approved under the Act it has the effect of normally removing the application of the state's Threatened Species Act 1995 (Tas.).

Even the most ostensibly progressive forestry laws in the world seem to come undone when translated into practice. Ontario's Crown Forest

---

[111] S. Roxburgh, et al., 'Assessing the carbon sequestration potential of managed forests: a case study from temperate Australia' (2006) 43 *Journal of Applied Ecology* 1149.
[112] See e.g. Tasmania's Forest Practices Act 1985 (Tas.).
[113] E.D. Bo. 'Regulatory capture: a review' (2006) 22(2) *Oxford Review of Economic Policy* 203.
[114] I. Ayres and J. Braithwaite, 'Tripartism: regulatory capture and empowerment' (1991) 16 *Law and Social Inquiry* 435.
[115] T. Baxter, *A Law Unto Themselves? Australian Regulation of Forestry Operations* (PhD thesis, University of Tasmania, 2015).

Sustainability Act 1994, arguably one such example, sets a sophisticated vision for the province's public forests, by directing that forests be managed 'to meet [the] social, economic and environmental needs of present and future generations'.[116] According to the Act, every forestry operation must follow a management plan; the plan must 'have regard to the plant life, animal life, water, soil, air and social and economic values, including recreational values and heritage values, of the management unit';[117] and the Minister 'shall not approve a forest management plan unless . . . satisfied that the plan provides for the sustainability of the Crown forest, having regard to the plant life, animal life, water, soil, air and social and economic values . . .'.[118] The legislation also created a Forestry Futures Trust sourced from forest industry revenues to fund ongoing management and recovery of Ontario's forests damaged by pests, fires, and other impacts, as well as to fund independent forest audits.

In practice, the implementation of the Ontario legislation has come up short. The provincial government has been criticised by its own Environmental Commissioner for having 'never undertaken a comprehensive assessment to see if the management system is working'.[119] Among the Commissioner's own findings, the forestry industry has benefited from over C$1 billion in public subsidies between 2005 and 2014 to prop it up, yet insufficient funding has been provided for environmental monitoring of forestry operations. Such monitoring is needed given assertions by others that the industrial logging in the province's southern boreal forests has put at risk some biodiversity, such as the rare woodland caribou.[120] Respected Ontario environmental lawyer Dianne Saxe (and appointed as the province's Environmental Commissioner in December 2015) is among those who have despaired at some of the so-called 'sustainable' forestry practices authorised by the legislation, such as the logging of up to 70 per cent of the Algonquin Provincial Park (yes, a supposed 'park'), including much of its old growth. A core barrier to having integrity in the system, explains Saxe, is that the 'forest management plans can be challenged if they fail to comply with the Forest Management Manual, but the Act and

---

[116] SO 1994, c. 25, s. 1.
[117] Ibid, s. 8(2)(b)).
[118] Ibid, s. 9(2).
[119] Environmental Commissioner of Ontario (ECO), *The Crown Forest Sustainability Act, 1994: 20 Years Later* (ECO, 2014), 3.
[120] See www.greenpeace.org/canada/global/canada/report/2011/06.

the Manual are more process than content'.[121] In other words, 'a plan to slash wildlife habitat and old-growth forest can be called "sustainable", and "in accordance with the Manual", regardless of its actual effect on the trees, the animals, the water, or the park'.[122]

The foregoing complaints should not imply that we need to end forestry. Rather, the timber and other resources obtained from forests must be managed more sustainably, over much longer timescales, in which environmental, economic and social values are managed coherently to achieve long-term benefits for human communities and nature itself. We need to prevent further conversion of forests into monotonous tree plantations or agriculture with the corresponding dissipation of biodiversity and ecosystem services. Furthermore, as the previous chapter emphasised, we need to invest in massive reforestation to restore degraded landscapes that currently support little biodiversity.

Compressing Time in Law

Fast-Track Law

Environmental regulation not only accelerates the depletion of natural resources, such as forests, it has itself become a victim of the cult of speed, as pressure from political and business elites intensifies to quicken licensing decisions, environmental assessments, and other procedures that may delay economic development. Their effect is to 'compress' time, enabling more to be done quicker. No doubt some environmental decisions can be frustratingly time-consuming. A US Government Accountability Office Report found that the average completion time in 2012 for an EIS under the National Environmental Policy Act was 4.6 years.[123] A major mining project in Australia typically takes 3 years to obtain all environmental approvals.[124] Approvals for mines and other large development proposals can require detailed environmental impact assessments (EIAs), consideration of applications for licences and permits, periods for public consultation and, potentially, post-approval court

---

[121] D. Saxe, 'Algonquin Park and the Crown Forest (Un)Sustainability Act', Slaw 15 April 2011, at www.slaw.ca/2011/04/15/algonquin-park-and-the-crown-forest-unsustainability-act.
[122] Ibid.
[123] US Government Accountability Office, *National Environmental Policy Act: Little Information Exists on NEPA Analyses* (GAO-14-370, 2014), 14.
[124] M. Santhebennur, 'Miners see red over double green tape', *Australian Mining* 8 July 2013, at www.miningaustralia.com.au/news/miners-see-red-over-double-green-tape.

appeals by aggrieved persons. The preparation of new environmental legislation itself can be quite time-consuming, especially if politically controversial, owing to the public consultation and cost-benefit studies needed to test the law's acceptability and utility. The seemingly long intervals associated with developing and implementing environmental law thus make it a target for frustrated corporate managers, politicians, and other stakeholders interested in accelerating development.

In response, many governments have 'streamlined' and 'harmonised' their environmental regulations to reduce perceived temporal bottlenecks.[125] Examples abound. The state of Queensland in Australia in 2012 legislated the Environmental Protection (Greentape Reduction) and Other Legislation Amendment Act (Qld) to create an integrated approval procedure for all environmentally relevant activities – one of a plethora of initiatives of the former Newman government that was deeply hostile to environmental restrictions on business.[126] The European Commission in 2013 issued guidance on plans to streamline some of its environmental regulations, especially EIA processes for energy infrastructure.[127] New Zealand's highly acclaimed Resource Management Act (RMA) 1991 has also not escaped revision, with a right-wing government elected in 2008 making this statute's reform a key priority for its 'first 100 days' in office. Landholders and resource developers had criticised the Act for imposing unreasonable costs and delays. The ensuing reforms included a fresh national approval process under the auspices of a new agency, the Environmental Protection Authority, to oversee expedited processes, including a stricter 9-month limit for issuance of consents.[128]

The compression of time in environmental decision-making is most virulent in 'fast-track' legislation. It aims to expedite approval of economic development, often projects of particular significance or controversy, in a manner that limits public scrutiny and accountability. The rushed approval process can result in developments proceeding, without robust environmental due diligence, that carry dangerous environmental risks, or impose onerous impacts on specific communities. The very use of

---

[125] E.g. Office of Best Practice Regulation, *Measuring and Reducing the Burden of Regulation* (Queensland Competition Authority, 2013), passim.

[126] I. Lowe, 'Queensland's big step back from environmental assessment', The Conversation 13 September 2012, at http://theconversation.com.

[127] European Commission, *Streamlining Environmental Assessment Procedures for Energy Infrastructure Projects of Common Interest (PCIs)* (European Commission, 24 July 2013).

[128] Resource Management (Simplifying and Streamlining) Amendment Act 2009, Public Act 2009, No. 31.

expedited approvals typically reflects a calculated decision by politicians to circumvent ordinary environmental controls out of fear that their application would block the proposal in question. The asserted justifications for fast-tracking may include the utility of a more 'sophisticated', tailored regulatory process; and the need to ensure a more 'objective' assessment of major proposals by limiting ideological-motivated challenges by parochial interest groups.

Fast-track legislation is now prevalent in many countries. Ireland's Planning and Development (Strategic Infrastructure) Act 2006 was adopted in order, claim politicians, to address perceived delays to strategic infrastructure due to the planning consent process.[129] It achieves this by establishing a new division within Ireland's planning appeal board (An Bord Pleanála) to which applications for designated strategic infrastructure developments are made directly, thereby bypassing local planning authority requirements. Important features of the accelerated consent procedure include a modest 6-week public consultation followed by an 18-week assessment period (though extendable), and mandatory consideration of the 'national interest' when assessing the project. Overall, the Irish legislation reduces the approval timelines for large projects from typically up to 40 weeks to 24 weeks.[130] England's planning legislation contains a comparable mechanism for major infrastructure projects. The Planning Act 2008 allows streamlined, quicker decisions on energy, waste, and transport developments designated as 'nationally significant infrastructure projects'.[131] The Growth and Infrastructure Act 2013 extended this fast-track approach to extractive industries such as oil and gas exploration and development, while relaxing permitted development rights (without needing additional approvals).[132]

The United States has likewise introduced measures to expedite approval of important projects. From its inception in early 2017, the Trump Administration has made fast tracking, and even complete elimination of many environmental regulations, its priority. Earlier, in 2015 the US Congress amended the National Environmental Policy Act to provide for expedited environmental review and permitting for complex transportation and other major infrastructure projects, which will be considered

---

[129] Act No. 27 of 2006.
[130] B. Slattery and N. O'Higgins, 'Speed boost for strategic infrastructure projects', 22 August 2006, at www.internationallawoffice.com/newsletters.
[131] 2008, c. 29, s. 14.
[132] 2013, c. 27, ss. 18–21.

by a new oversight entity, the Federal Permitting Improvement Steering Council, and improved coordination of such permitting with collateral state-level assessments and approvals.[133] An earlier US initiative is Executive Order 13,604 of 2012, by which federal government agencies were encouraged to prioritise and quicken approvals for specific sectors and projects.[134] Through efficiency measures, such as improved data sharing between agencies and better coordination of permitting processes, the initiative aims to 'reduce aggregate timelines for major infrastructure projects by half'.[135] This initiative of President Obama was also carefully rationalised for its potential to improve environmental and community outcomes. Some US states have enacted similar measures, such as Maryland's 'Made Easy Initiative' for development licensing[136] and North Carolina's Regulatory Reform Act 2013,[137] the latter being one of the most aggressive examples waged against so-called greentape.

Among other examples, the former Canadian government under Stephen Harper eviscerated a number of lodestar environmental statutes with the aim of curbing many restrictions on economic development.[138] The gravest blow was replacing the Canadian Environmental Assessment Act with a weaker version that expedited approval processes through truncated timelines, narrower assessment criteria, and reduced scope for public consultation. The resulting Canadian Environmental Assessment Act 2012 imposed fixed timelines of up to 24 months for major oil and gas and mining projects.[139]

Australian governments rely heavily on fast-track legislation for similar purposes. Indeed, fast-tracking has become a national priority of the Council of Australian Governments' Reform Agenda.[140] The federal government (Commonwealth) is entering into fast-track agreements with each state to transfer its powers of assessment and approval under the

---

[133] Fixing America's Surface Transportation Act 2015, Public Law No. 114–94.
[134] 'Executive Order 13604 – Improving performance of federal permitting and review of infrastructure Projects' (2012) 77 Federal Register 18887.
[135] The White House, 'Presidential memorandum – modernizing federal infrastructure review and permitting regulations, policies, and procedures' 17 May 2013, at www.whitehouse.gov/the-press-office/2013/05/17.
[136] Implemented by Governor's Executive Order 01.01.2011.12, at http://easy.maryland.gov/fasttrack.
[137] SL 2013-413, HB 74.
[138] Bill C-38, An Act to implement certain provisions of the budget tabled in Parliament on March 29, 2012 and other measures, 1st Sess, 41st Parl, 2011.
[139] SC 2012, c. 19.
[140] See further www.coag.gov.au/reform_agenda.

Environment Protection and Biodiversity Conservation Act 1999 (Cth) (EPBCA). The delegated authority to states covers many developments apart from those that affect World Heritage sites, federal marine waters, and nuclear actions. By removing the Commonwealth's role from many assessments, the 'reform' promises to facilitate assessments and enable developments to get under way more quickly.

Individual state governments in Australia are also doing their bit. The state of Victoria's Major Transport Projects Facilitation Act 2009 (Vic.) quickens decision-making in a process that concentrates authority in the Minister for Planning and the Governor-in-Council.[141] The scope for abuse of this process became evident in the public outrage over the fast-tracked East West Link highway in 2014 (but subsequently cancelled with a change of government).[142] The project was designated for the purpose of applying the assessment, approvals and delivery powers under the Act. Queensland's Economic Development Act 2012 (Qld) introduced measures to streamline the environmental assessment and approvals process for major projects, including creation of a new Minister for Economic Development to oversee the ramping up of economic development in the state. The Queensland government also convened a 'Fast Tracking Taskforce' to identify opportunities for further such initiatives, with the Taskforce issuing a 37-point action plan to reduce approval timeframes by up to 50 per cent.[143]

Many other jurisdictions have embraced the trend, including Greece (Acceleration and Transparency of Implementation of Strategic Investments or Fast Track Law),[144] South Africa (Infrastructure Development Act),[145] the state of Gujarat in India (Gujarat Infrastructure Development Act),[146] and Indonesia (One-Stop Integrated Service).[147] The apotheosis of fast tracking is the special economic zone (SEZ), a juridically bounded area designated by governments for foreign investment and export-oriented

---

[141] See further, Department of Planning and Community Development, 'Major transport projects', at www.dpcd.vic.gov.au/planning/environment-assessment/major-transport-projects.
[142] P. Newman, 'The East-West Link is dead – a victory for 21st-century thinking', The Conversation 3 December 2014, at http://theconversation.com.
[143] Minister for State Development, Infrastructure and Planning the Honourable J. Seeney, 'LNP progresses record number of major projects' (Media statement, Queensland Government, 13 November 2012).
[144] Law 3894 of 2010.
[145] Act No. 23 of 2014.
[146] Act No. 11 of 1999.
[147] 'Jokowi inaugurates BKPM one-stop integrated service', *Jakarta Post* 26 January 2015, at www.thejakartapost.com.

industrialisation, to which is conceded a more liberal regulatory milieu that commonly includes tax holidays, free trade concessions, and expedited development approvals. Numerous countries, especially in the developing world, have introduced SEZs to catalyse their economic development: since they were first established in the 1950s the number of SEZs worldwide has soared to approximately 4,300 as of 2015.[148] Given the policy emphasis on reduced regulatory oversight within SEZs, the quality of environmental regulation in the zones can be inferior except where an SEZ is established explicitly to show-case high-quality green development.[149]

Some fast-track measures are occasionally welcomed by environmentalists where they facilitate action on pressing environmental issues, such as investment in the renewable energy sector. An example is Maine's Wind Energy Act 2008,[150] which offers expedited approval of grid-scale, wind energy projects. The legislation reduces appeal rights for those objecting to approved wind power projects, which can now be located in many areas of the state previously designated as out of bounds. Adopted in the immediate aftermath of the 2008 Global Financial Crisis (GFC), the legislation was justified also for its potential to generate jobs and income in this economically depressed region. In Canada, Ontario's Green Energy Act 2009 uses similar expedited approval processes for facilitating renewable energy initiatives. More commonly, however, the law fails to respond expeditiously to environmental imperatives: governments' enthusiasm to slash greentape usually exceeds their willingness to introduce credible legal controls on climate change or other serious ecological problems. International and domestic law on climate change mitigation is deeply contentious primarily because of disagreements over the time periods within which to reduce carbon emissions, with EU members generally pushing for faster phaseouts than what other Western nations or the Global South favours. Thus, because patience *per se* is not always determinative for addressing urgent environmental problems, such as climate change, the policy goal is not just to act slower but to get the *timing* right, to act at the appropriate time for the issue at stake.

---

[148] 'Special economic zones: not so special', The Economist 4 April 2015, at www.economist.com; A.G. Schweinberger, 'Special economic zones in developing and/or transition economies: a policy proposal' (2003) 11(4) *Review of International Economics* 619.
[149] B.J. Richardson, 'Is East Asia industrializing too quickly? Environmental regulation in its special economic zones' (2005) 22 *UCLA Pacific Basin Law Journal* 150.
[150] Title 35-A, c. 34.

Debacle of a Rushed Pulp Mill

Although fast-tracking promises the benefits of quicker and more efficient decision-making, by restricting public scrutiny and environmental due diligence, the fast-track process can undermine its own *raison d'etre* by spawning costly public protests and extra-legal challenges, in addition to the costs of addressing any future environmental impacts that could have been eschewed. It is worthwhile to elaborate on these risks, with a story from Australia. It is about the ignominious approval given for a bleached kraft pulp mill proposed for northern Tasmania by the then forestry behemoth Gunns.[151] Had the project proceeded, it would have been the world's fourth largest pulp mill.

Tasmania is well known to many scholars of environmental law for its turbulent history of conflicts over use of natural resources, especially hydropower dams and industrial forestry.[152] Tasmanian politics have a dyadic quality, with the state being both a powerful incubator of progressive environmental activism (it gave birth to the world's first Green Party in March 1972) and unsavoury alliances between local political and business elites wedded to industrial-scale exploitation of the island's natural resources. Ostensibly, the state's environmental law is impressive, modelled partly on New Zealand's famed RMA.[153] Tasmania's ostensibly principled and integrated approach is anchored in the object of sustainable development common to its suite of statutes such as the Environmental Management and Pollution Control Act 1994 (Tas.) and the Land Use Planning and Approvals Act 1993 (Tas.). But the exclusion of some economic sectors, notably forestry, from many of these standard controls provides a clue to the potential for a different reality in practice.

For the Gunns pulp mill, Tasmanian law already offered a methodical process for EIA of major infrastructure projects by an independent, quasi-judicial agency called the Resource Planning and Development

---

[151] This discussion draws on: T. Baxter, '(Dis)integrated assessment: the pulping of an integrated assessment process', *Proceedings of the Conference of the Australia New Zealand Society for Ecological Economics*, Darwin, 27–30 October 2009; M. Stokes, 'Legal issues arising from the pulp mill permit issued under the Pulp Mill Assessment Act 2007 (Tasmania)' (2011) 30(2) *University of Tasmania Law Review* 75; A. Macintosh and M. Stokes, 'Tasmania and the Gunns Pulp Mill' in T. Bonyhady and A. Macintosh (eds), *Mills, Mines and Other Controversies: The Environmental Assessment of Major Projects* (Federation Press, 2010), 16; F. Gale (ed), *Pulp Friction: A Review of the Environmental Impact Assessment of Gunns Proposed Mill* (Pencil Pine Press, 2011).
[152] G. Buckman, *Tasmanian Wilderness Battles: A History* (Jacana Books, 2008).
[153] Public Act 1991, No. 69.

Commission (RPDC) constituted under the Resource Planning and Development Commission Act 1997 (Tas.). A bilateral assessment agreement between the governments of Tasmania and Australia had accredited this EIA process for the purposes of the national EPBCA. The Tasmanian government initially committed itself to assessing Gunns' proposal under this process, which itself embodies elements of the streamlined regulatory process found in fast-track legislation.[154] In November 2004, the Tasmanian government declared the Gunns project of 'State significance' under section 8(2) of the State Policies and Projects Act 1993 (Tas.), and referred it to the RPDC for assessment (and federal authorities concurred). The RPDC assessment panel eventually concluded, in March 2007, that Gunns was not compliant with important requirements of the assessment process (such as failing to provide relevant information), and it appeared unlikely that the panel would recommend approval of the pulp mill. Gunns then dissented the RPDC process, alleging lengthy 'delays' in assessing its project that it superciliously believed was entitled to be approved. In fact, Gunns itself was responsible for the delays because of its reluctance to provide information to enable a full assessment; undoubtedly, the forestry company feared that its project was doomed.

As forestry was Tasmania's perceived economic bedrock, with special political influence,[155] the government colluded with Gunns to introduce the Pulp Mill Assessment Act 2007 (Tas) (PMAA) to get the project under way. This wasn't the first time that Tasmanian politicians had tried to fast-track a pulp mill; in 1989 the Wesley Vale project was assessed through the special Northern Pulp Mill Agreement Act 1988 (Tas.), which displaced the standard controls of the then Environment Protection Act 1973 (Tas.). The Gunns pulp mill required a separate EIA and approval by the federal government, which was undertaken pursuant to the EPBCA. However, with a conservative government in power, and it being deferential to state governments on most environmental matters, the federal assessment was not particularly rigorous or comprehensive.

Because of its intrinsic flaws, the only way Tasmanian leaders and Gunns believed the project would secure approval was through special

---

[154] The RPDC assessment looks at all environmental, social, and economic impacts of a proposal. The breadth of the assessment, which displaced other state laws, saves the development proponent from making numerous applications to multiple authorities for various permits and other approvals.

[155] For analysis of the incestuous relationship between Gunns and the state government, see Q. Beresford, *The Rise and Fall of Gunns Ltd* (NewSouth Books, 2014).

legislation to insulate the pulp mill from rigorous assessment. The proposal was flawed because of the proposed technology and its wood source. Gunns had originally claimed that 'only world's best technology utilising a low impact Total Chlorine Free mill will be looked at'.[156] However, Gunns later advised that it would build an elemental chlorine-free mill, thereby allowing the use of dangerous chlorine compounds. On the wood supply, Gunns sought to deflect concerns that native forests, especially old growth ones, would be logged, by committing to a plantation-based wood supply. But the pulp mill would only have been economically viable had Gunns harvested non-plantation forests.

The Tasmanian approach to fast-tracking is particularly obnoxious given that the legislation invoked was designed solely for Gunns' pulp mill. Astonishingly, the PMAA was enacted within just 33 days of Gunns' withdrawal from the RPDC, suggesting that the government had already colluded with the company. The assessment process and accountability mechanisms provided by the PMAA were problematic. The Act provided for the Minister to appoint a consultant to assess the entire project against 'guidelines'. However, these 'guidelines' were not the RPDC's guidelines but rather the different 'Recommended Environmental Emission Limit Guidelines for any new Bleached Eucalypt Kraft Pulp Mill in Tasmania', which academic Tom Baxter (an expert on this case study) describes as 'inherently far narrower in scope, more generic than, and had been superseded by, the RPDC's later work'.[157] The PMAA also provided that if the hand-picked consultant recommended approval at the conclusion of the assessment, then the Minister was to prepare a permit for consideration and approval by the parliament. Once it had endorsed the permit, the project would be deemed as approved, notwithstanding any other Tasmanian law.

Another ignominious feature of the PMAA is its disdain of public consultation and scrutiny. The federal government's separate assessment of the pulp mill allowed for public hearings and submissions, though they were restricted to 20 days. Not only did the PMAA remove all public hearings, which the RPFC had determined as essential, but the Act precluded all appeal and review rights to any court, tribunal, or other

---

[156] Gunns Limited, 'Gunns Limited announces their plans to investigate pulp mill potential in Tasmania', news release, 2004, cited in A. Krien, *Into the Woods: The Battle for Tasmania's Forests* (Black Inc, 2012), 304.
[157] Baxter, '(Dis)Integrated assessment', 11.

entity. It is worthwhile to quote the relevant provision of the Act because of its staggering breadth:

> a person is not entitled to appeal to a body or other person, court or tribunal; or no order or review may be made under the Judicial Review Act 2000; or no declaratory judgment may be given; or no other action or proceeding may be brought — in respect of any action, decision, process, matter or thing arising out of or relating to any assessment or approval of the project under this Act.[158]

While this section aimed to stop challenges to the validity of the permit issued to Gunns, such as because of the dubious EIA process, the section has wider consequences. It would prevent any business enterprise, whether in farming, fishing, or tourism, seeking legal redress for damage to itself from the pulp mill. And similarly, no resident or landholder in the vicinity of the pulp mill could get redress for any damage.

Despite the trenchant efforts of Gunns and its political friends, the project was scuttled; the fast-track process simply inflamed rather than deterred the opposition. While the state government approved the project, the federal government only conditionally approved it, subject to Gunns meeting 48 permit conditions and completing further studies.[159] The turning point in environmentalists' campaign came when they successfully courted financial investors to boycott Gunns. With the backing of an influential local businessman, the pulp mill opponents targeted the boardrooms and shareholders of the financiers whose backing the project needed with the message that to support it would violate their professed commitment to CSR. A breakthrough occurred in May 2008 when the ANZ bank rejected the A$1.4 billion loan sought by Gunns.[160] In its *Corporate Responsibility Report*, ANZ conceded that the pulp mill had 'attracted wide-spread attention over concerns about the potential social and environmental impacts of the mill . . . and a number of shareholders and customers [had] questioned our commitment to responsible lending'.[161] As a signatory to the

---

[158] Section 11. The State Policies and Projects Act 1993 (Tas.), under which the pulp mill could have been assessed and determined, is nearly as restrictive as the PMAA in this regard (see s. 28). However, the former Act offers a more thorough and consultative assessment processes than the PMAA.

[159] J. Peacock, *Chief Scientist's Report on the Gunns Limited Pulp Mill Proposal* (Australian Government, Department of Environment and Water Resources, 2007).

[160] M. Wilkinson and B. Cubby, 'ANZ exit from pulp mill project confirmed', *The Age* 28 May 2008, 3.

[161] ANZ, at www.anz.com/aus/Corporate-Responsibility-2007/Customers/managing-social-and-environmental-risks.asp.

Equator Principles, an international voluntary code for socially responsible financing, ANZ had promised to observe high standards of environmental due diligence. Other financiers similarly shunned Gunns, and it failed to secure the necessary project loans before the company slipped into bankruptcy in 2012 in the wake of increasingly unfavourable conditions in the Australian woodchip industry.

In sum, the Tasmanian story suggests fast-track legislation leads counter-productively to slow track when it destroys public trust and inflames opposition. The actions of Gunns itself greatly aggravated the situation, especially when its management sought to silence 20 prominent opponents with a 'SLAPP' lawsuit seeking A$6.9 million in damages to its business and reputation (a lawsuit that was not successful).[162] Gunns and its allies ultimately failed to win the public debate about the merits of industrial logging and polluting the environment, and the economic rationale for a staggeringly expensive project. Fast-tracking may be beneficial when genuinely motivated by the public good rather than merely serving private interests, such as to facilitate investment in renewable energy projects and other important environmental improvements. In all cases, however, there should be checks and balances such as access to judicial review.

Environmental Emergencies

Emergencies ensuing from environmental calamities can also trigger fast decision-making because of the need for often swift and far-reaching responses by governments. Emergency powers thus provide another important case study of the acceleration of time in legal governance. Most states allow for exceptions to their standard procedures and rules during national crises. Natural disasters, economic turmoil, public health scares, civil unrest, and other emergencies can trigger suspension of normal legal arrangements in order to allow authorities to expeditiously bring the threat, disturbance or commotion under control. In recent years, some very serious environmental emergencies have erupted, such as Hurricane Katrina, the Fukushima nuclear meltdown, and the 2016 Albertan wildfires.[163] The justifications for invoking emergency powers, and the adequacy of legal constraints to their use, have been the foci of

---

[162] 'The Gunns 20 litigation', ABC Radio National (Law Report) 25 January 2005, at www.abc.net.au/radionational/programs/lawreport.

[163] D.A. Farber and J. Chen, *Disasters and the Law: Katrina and Beyond* (Aspen Publishers, 2006); R. Stone, 'Fukushima cleanup with be drawn out and costly' (2014) 331 *Science*

debates among legal scholars. In the environmental context, the preparedness and resilience of society to deal with sudden adversity is a further important governance issue.

Both domestic and international law generally make provision for emergencies, such as obliging authorities to have contingency plans, and allowing extraordinary powers to be invoked in crises. In common law jurisdictions, the Crown has prerogative powers to act in emergencies where the existence or sovereignty of the country is endangered, though such prerogative powers are usually codified in legislation such as Britain's Civil Contingencies Act[164] or New Zealand's Civil Defence Emergency Management Act.[165] Martial law is one of the oldest procedures for suspending legal privileges in the name of national security.[166] The recent 'war on terror' in the United States and its allies that has intensified since 9/11 is another way in which security threats are used to invoke sudden and sometimes indefinite restrictions to civil liberties, such as increased domestic surveillance, interrogation policies that use torture, and harsh detention.[167] In the history of the United States, such sweeping actions are not unprecedented; civil liberties have been tested many times, such as the Alien and Sedition Acts of the late eighteenth century, the internment of Japanese Americans during the Second World War, and the McCarthyism era of the Cold War. While controversial, such emergency powers are not necessarily contrary to fundamental international legal norms. For instance, the 1966 International Covenant on Civil and Political Rights allows states to derogate from its provisions in 'time of public emergency which threatens the life of the nation'.[168] Exercise of emergency powers, however, does not necessarily entail unrestrained executive action. Judicial oversight may apply, such as court's ruling on whether an emergency exists or whether the executive has acted within its exceptional powers.

Environmental and public health law itself habitually include provisions for dealing with emergencies, notably provisions directing regulators to address hazardous pollution, industrial accidents, natural disasters, or

---

1507; T.T. Ha, 'Alberta wildfire will take "weeks and weeks" to extinguish', *Globe and Mail* 6 May 2016, at www.theglobeandmail.com.

[164] 2004, c. 36.
[165] Public Act 2002, No. 33.
[166] C. Fairman, 'The law of martial rule and the national emergency' (1942) 55(8) *Harvard Law Review* 1253.
[167] R.A. Posner, *Not a Suicide Pact: The Constitution in a Time of National Emergency* (Oxford University Press, 2006).
[168] Adopted 16 December 1966, in force 23 March 1976, (1967) 6 ILM 368, Article 4.

infectious diseases. In Canada, the Environmental Emergency Regulations under the Canadian Environmental Protection Act 1999 aim to reduce the occurrence and impact of accidental releases of hazardous substances into the environment.[169] Similarly, Queensland's Chemical, Biological and Radiological Emergency Powers Amendment Act 2003 (Qld) has sweeping powers to address perceived risks to public safety. A number of international agreements include relevant provisions. The Liability Annex to the Antarctic Treaty contains obligations on its parties to undertake measures to prevent emergencies and protect the Antarctic environment.[170] The Chernobyl disaster led in 1986 to the Convention on Early Notification of a Nuclear Accident, obliging states to notify of any nuclear accident within their jurisdiction that could affect others.[171] The World Heritage Convention includes provisions for listing world heritage property 'in danger', a mechanism that triggers additional scrutiny and potential assistance to alleviate the threat.[172]

While decisive action is often needed to mitigate emergencies, such action can damage the integrity of governance systems. Not only may a national 'emergency' become an excuse for invoking sweeping and disproportionately intrusive responses, the very nature of enlightened despotism is that it may usurp judicial review, public consultation, due process, and other checks and balances of legality. As explained by Jocelyn Stacey, a leading Canadian legal scholar on this subject, 'the problem of emergencies – including the environmental emergency – is that their unforeseeable and potentially catastrophic nature necessitates unconstrained executive discretion'.[173] Much literature has debated emergency powers, focusing especially on whether and how they can be exercised within meaningful legal constraints.[174] The wellspring for

[169] SOR 2003-307.
[170] Annex VI, Liability Arising From Environmental Emergencies, Protocol on Environmental Protection to the Antarctic Treaty, 14 June 2005, (2005) 45 ILM 5; see further E. Geddis, 'Liability for environmental emergencies in Antarctica' (2006) 3 *New Zealand Yearbook of International Law* 201.
[171] Adopted 26 September 1986, in force 27 October 1986, (1986) 25 ILM 1369.
[172] Convention Concerning the Protection of the World Cultural and Natural Heritage, 16 November 1972, in force 17 December 1975, (1972) 11 ILM 1358, Article 11(4).
[173] J. Stacey, 'The environmental emergency and the legality of discretion in environmental law' (2015) 53(1) *Osgoode Hall Law Journal* 985.
[174] E.g. V. Ramraj and A.K. Thiruvengadam (eds), *Emergency Powers in Asia: Exploring the Limits of Legality* (Cambridge University Press, 2010); N.C. Lazar, *States of Emergency in Liberal Democracies* (Cambridge University Press, 2009); O. Gross and F.N. Aoláin, *Law in Times of Crisis: Emergency Powers in Theory and Practice* (Cambridge University Press,

much of this literature is the contentious writings of German jurist Carl Schmitt, who examined the Weimar and Nazi regimes. Schmitt argued that unforeseeable and severe emergencies that threaten society, which cannot be anticipated by law, require that the sovereign do whatever is necessary to overcome the crisis.[175] While many scholars dispute the assumption that emergencies will inevitably lead to unsupervised executive action that undermines the rule of law,[176] dealing with emergencies undoubtedly introduces a faster tempo into legal governance.

Many environmental problems have long been identified as having, if not emergency dimensions, at least some aspects provoking the need for more authoritarian rule. Some decades ago several commentators, such as William Ophuls and Garrett Hardin, believed that the intensification of societal conflict over diminishing natural resources could be dampened only through enlightened despotism.[177] Since then, the prospect of climate change-related disasters has added to these governance challenges.[178] While some of the scholarly concern relates to rule-of-law issues, of equal concern is the complacency and lack of preparedness in some societies to deal with impending environmental calamities. Environmentalists often use alarmist language that evokes a sense of crisis and urgency, such as the 'population bomb', 'carbon bomb', 'end of nature', and 'extinction crisis', each of which suggests a grave threat requiring immediate government intervention.[179] The notion of 'emergency' conjured up by environmentalists here is much wider than the popular understanding of an emergency as a single catastrophic event, such as an oil spill or nuclear accident. As already discussed in this book, the Anthropocene symbolises this emergency-like condition on a planetary scale for which traditional

---

2006); R.J. Daniels, P. Macklem, and K. Roach (eds), *The Security of Freedom: Essays on Canada's Anti-Terrorism Bill* (University of Toronto Press, 2001).

[175] C. Schmitt, *Political Theology: Four Chapters on the Concept of Sovereignty*, trans. by G.D. Schwab (MIT Press and University of Chicago Press, 1985; original in 1922).

[176] E.g. B. Pardy, 'The unbearable license of being the executive: a response to Stacey's permanent environmental emergency' (2016) 12(3) *Osgoode Hall Law Journal* 1029.

[177] W. Ophuls, 'Leviathan or oblivion?' in H.E. Daly (ed), *Toward a Steady-State Economy* (WH Freeman, 1973); G. Hardin, *Exploring New Ethics for Survival* (Viking Press, 1972).

[178] R. Lyster, *Climate Justice and Disaster Law* (Cambridge University Press, 2016).

[179] P. Ehrlich, *The Population Bomb* (Ballantine Books, 1968); K. Mathiesen, 'Permafrost "carbon bomb" may be more of a slow burn, say scientists', *The Guardian* 9 April 2015, at www.theguardian.com; B. McKibben, *The End of Nature* (Random House, 1989); A. Vaughan, 'Humans creating sixth great extinction of animal species, say scientists', *The Guardian* 19 June 2015, at www.theguardian.com.

emergency powers, such as those for addressing toxic spills, seem to be completely inadequate.

The complex and dynamic qualities of ecosystems and their components that make it hard to predict their response to anthropogenic influences can engender, argues Stacey, an ongoing state of emergency for environmental regulators.[180] The likelihood of extreme events such as droughts, wildfires, or storms is becoming harder to predict under global climate change, and degraded ecosystems may cross critical thresholds towards irreversible change. The spread of invasive species with their devastating and often unpredictable impacts is one example of the new generation of environmental emergencies. In Australia, climate change is allowing invaders such as cane toads, fire ants, and European wasps to flourish, each precipitating widespread ecological and economic damage.[181] There are as yet no effective ways to remove these invaders, nor full scientific understanding of their long-term effects and extent. As the precautionary principle recognises, many environmental problems suffer from some level of indeterminacy and unpredictably that make them dangerous risks not easily addressed through conventional environmental regulation based on *ex ante* standards and rules.[182]

So far, however, the principal concern is surely not the growth of unchecked environmental emergency powers but the insouciance and complacency of societies in the face of the Anthropocene. Governments' swift response to the 2008 GFC to restore market stability was starkly different to their lethargic response to climate change and biodiversity extinctions. It is the lack of action, rather than sovereign power overreaction, that should be our main concern. The problem of 'slow justice' for environmental wrongs, as examined in the next section, is one dimension of this insouciance. Thus, rather than dwell on the raging debates about how emergency powers may threaten the rule of law, the focus of this book is on how to minimise the very inception of environmental emergencies. The later sections of this chapter explore some attempts to inculcate slower lifestyles that are less likely to engender catastrophic environmental decline.

---

[180] Stacey, 'The environmental emergency and the legality of discretion in environmental law'.
[181] L.H. Ziska and J.S. Dukes (eds), *Invasive Species and Global Climate Change* (CAB International, 2014).
[182] Stacey, 'The environmental emergency and the legality of discretion in environmental law'.

Slow Justice

The speed with which the law facilitates economic development contrasts with its slowness in redressing its environmental and social fallout. Slow justice is the alter ego of fast regulation. While slowness, as discussed later in this chapter, has many virtues for environmental decision-making, it has negative connotations when it delays justice for the victims of environmental harm.

Slow justice may begin with the gradual gestation of many environmental impacts. They may manifest, in human judgement, only over many decades because it is through cumulative additions and the crossing of critical tipping points that some environmental pressures are rendered harmful. In *Slow Violence and the Environmentalism of the Poor*, Robert Nixon details how this temporal displacement falls hardest on the most economically vulnerable.[183] Unlike some natural calamities, such as Hurricane Katrina, this slow environmental violence often remains obscured because it lacks the explosive and sensational qualities that we commonly expect of a 'disaster'. The Bhopal tragedy in India and the ravaged Niger Delta, both legacies of corporate hubris, are among examples Nixon cites of this incremental and accretive environmental damage that hurts those least able to protect themselves. Other examples could be the Anishnawbe people of Canada's 'Chemical Valley' in southern Ontario,[184] or the toxic poisoning of the Inuit's Arctic homelands.[185]

The tragic consequence of slow violence is that it may not gain legal recognition. Nixon speaks of its victims embodying 'displacement without movement', suffering 'the loss of the land and resources beneath them, a loss that leaves communities stranded in a place stripped of the very characteristics that made it inhabitable'.[186] For him, the law underestimates – 'in advance and in retrospect' – the environmental and human costs of slow violence.[187] To accomplish it in advance, EIA and risk assessment procedures are available, but they may be ineffective because they are not comprehensive in assessing all risks and impacts, and they may rely on

---

[183] R. Nixon, *Slow Violence and the Environmentalism of the Poor* (Harvard University Press, 2011).
[184] L.M. Schell, et al., 'Health disparities and toxicant exposure of Akwesasne Mohawk young adults: a partnership approach to research' (2005) 113(12) *Environmental Health Perspectives* 1826.
[185] M. Cone, *Silent Snow: The Slow Poisoning of the Arctic* (Grove Press, 2005).
[186] Ibid, 19.
[187] Nixon, *Slow Violence and the Environmentalism of the Poor*, 7.

dubious cost-benefit methodologies that underweight the risks involved. To accomplish the retrospective dimension, civil liability in tort law or environmental legislation may provide compensation for victims. But the barriers are legion, including litigation costs, statutes of limitation, evidential difficulties, doctrinal complexities, and even non-retroactive liability for previously authorised activities.

Slow justice is also prolonged by under-resourced judicial systems mired in byzantine and pedantic procedures that lead to ever-lengthening caseload backlogs. India is one of the worst offenders, with some 30 million cases backlogged as of 2009, with the chief justice of its High Court warning (or joking?) that it could take 466 years to clear the inventory just in his court.[188] Brazilian courts are also swimming against the tide, with more proceedings initiated annually than are decided.[189] Clogged court lists exist in many other countries with backlogs growing faster than they can be cleared.[190] Judicial backlogs also exist in countries, such as the UK, that have ratified the Aarhus Convention on Access to Justice,[191] which commits its parties to guaranteeing citizens 'timely' access to courts in environmental matters.[192]

Some individual cases have ground their way through the courts with agonising slowness. The reasons include the predominance of scientific and other technical issues requiring special expertise in environmental cases, and the high stakes when class action litigants seek substantial compensation. Australia's most drawn-out product liability lawsuit, involving the Copper Seven IUD contraceptive, which damaged the health of 300 women, ended with an out-of-court settlement after a 14-year legal saga involving two trials.[193] Even slower, attempts to hold Union Carbide responsible for the Bhopal cleanup and provide compensation for its victims have dragged on in Indian and US courts for at least 30 years, with

---

[188] 'Indian PM plea on justice backlog', BBC News 17 August 2009, at www.bbc.com/news.
[189] L. McAllister, *Making Law Matter: Environmental Protection and Legal Institutions in Brazil* (Stanford University Press, 2008), 171.
[190] M. Dakolias, 'Court performance around the world: a comparative perspective' (2014) 2(1) *Yale Human Rights and Development Journal* 87.
[191] Convention on Access to Information, Public Participation in Decision-Making and Access to Justice in Environmental Matters, 25 June 1998, in force 30 October 2001, (1999) 38 ILM 517.
[192] Working Group on Access to Environmental Justice, *Ensuring Access to Environmental Justice in England and Wales* (WWF, May 2008), 5.
[193] L. Sales, 'Copper-7 liability case settled out of court', ABC News 30 August 2001, at www.abc.net.au.

many victims dying before they received a penny.[194] International cases can also be time-consuming despite the relatively light case load on the International Court of Justice (ICJ): the whaling case brought by Australia and New Zealand against Japan took nearly 4 years for the Hague Court to decide.[195]

The epic *Exxon Valdez* case rivals these for slow justice.[196] In 1989 the tanker, steered by a drunk captain, ran aground in Prince William Sound, Alaska, spilling nearly 11 million gallons of crude oil and creating the then largest oil spill in US waters (the 2010 *Deepwater Horizon* catastrophe disgorged about 200 million gallons). The *Exxon Valdez* spill decimated about 28,000 km^2 of ocean and 2,400 km of Alaskan coastline, degrading the habitat of numerous sea mammals, fish, and birds. A flurry of lawsuits ensued, as Native Americans, fishers, local businesses, and other victims sought recompense. The initial jury verdict and judgement in 1994 awarded US$287 million for compensatory damages and US$5 billion in punitive damages, but the latter punishment was appealed and reduced to US$2.5 billion by the Ninth Circuit Court of Appeals in 2006, and eventually slashed to US$507 million by the federal Supreme Court in 2008. Among other litigation in the case, in 1991 Exxon reached a civil settlement with the federal and Alaskan governments to pay US$900 million in payments, a US$25 million criminal fine and US$100 million in restitution. That agreement also contained a 'reopener window' to allow the governments to claim a US$100 million top-up for any unforeseen additional ecological restoration, and this provision was invoked in 2006. But Exxon legally challenged this request and eventually in late 2015 the weary governments dropped their claim.[197]

Conversely, slow justice is also associated with environmentalists' efforts to stymie unwanted projects, though ironically such tactics have sometimes spurred governments to introduce countervailing fast-track measures. The delays may ensue from environmentalists targeting politicians to postpone controversial decisions, to judicial review applications to challenge approved developments. The Keystone XL pipeline, proposed in

---

[194] See International Campaign for Justice in Bhopal: at www.bhopal.net/what-happened/contamination/court-cases-environmental-liability.
[195] *Whaling in the Antarctic (Australia v. Japan; New Zealand intervening)*, [2004] ICJ Reports 226.
[196] See J. Fisher, 'The Exxon Valdez case and regularizing punishment' (2009) 26 *Alaskan Law Review* 1.
[197] Y. Rosen, 'Exxon Valdez oil spill saga reaches anticlimactic end in federal court', Alaska Dispatch News 15 October 2015, at www.adn.com.

2008 to funnel crude oil from Alberta through Nebraska and other states to refineries on the Gulf Coast, was one of the most environmentally contentious decisions for an American President. After 6 years of review, Obama announced on 6 November 2015 that he rejected the proposal. However, shortly after his inauguration, in March 2017 President Trump reversed his predecessor's position and approved Keystone XL. Unsurprisingly, delays in issuing approvals because of environmental assessments and public consultations may give rise to a grievance by developers.[198] In Australia, environmentalists' feisty legal challenges to the proposed Adani coal mine in Queensland prompted the federal government to try amending the applicable environmental legislation, the EPBCA, to limit *locus standi* in future cases.[199] Environmentalists were directly targeted in the protracted 'McLibel case' in England. This lawsuit between McDonald's and two environmental activists spanning a decade from 1986 to 1997 resulted in neither side victorious after three court judgements.[200] While McDonald's ultimately won £40,000 compensation from the activists for publishing a partially libellous pamphlet attacking the fast food company, McDonald's attracted negative publicity from the drawn-out litigation and intense media scrutiny.

One solution to some of these problems has been boutique environmental courts and tribunals, equipped with more relevant expertise, flexible procedures, and efficient case management. The first such court was established in New South Wales, Australia in 1979: the Land and Environment Court has jurisdiction to review the merits of government decisions on planning, environmental, and related matters.[201] The Court has civil and criminal enforcement functions concerning a variety of environmental laws, and it hears appeals from local courts imposing criminal sanctions under environmental laws. It has successfully minimised delay for environmental cases, a major hindrance to the resolution

---

[198] From Canada, in *Carhoun and Sons Enterprises Ltd.* v. *Canada (Attorney General)*, (2015) BCCA 163, a commercial property developer sued the federal government for economic losses it allegedly sustained when fisheries regulators took nearly 3 years to issue a permit to fill in two ravines that are potential fish habitat. The British Columbia Court of Appeal refused a federal government motion to strike out the claim, which then proceeded to trial. More often, the delays arise from post-approval legal challenges.

[199] M. McKenna and C. Merritt, 'Activists to delay Adani's Carmichael mine until 2017', The Australian 22 August 2015, at www.theaustralian.com.au.

[200] *McDonald's Corporation* v. *Steel and Morris*, [1997] EWHC QB 366.

[201] B. Preston, 'Operating an environment court: the experience of the Land and Environment Court of New South Wales' (2008) 25 *Environmental and Planning Law Journal* 385.

of environmental disputes by courts of general jurisdiction in many nations; it has contributed substantially to jurisprudence on environmental law; and it has provided consistency in implementation of environmental law within its jurisdiction.

The administration of environmental justice, while highly important, is nonetheless in the bigger picture not the most important temporal dimension of environmental governance. More critical is the urgent need to slow the pace of economic development, particularly the resource intensive and materialistic kind, and use that additional time to foster more sensible environmental practices.

Slowness

The name of this chapter, *Rallentare*, means slowing down in Italian – an apt title that acknowledges the Italian origins of Slow Food. Numerous social movements devoted to slowness have arisen since the late twentieth century, including Slow Technology, Slow Design, Slow Cities, and Slow Travel. Some speak to personal lifestyles while others address systemic and institutional factors that are sources of hurriedness and freneticism.[202] The slow movements have flourished without any central, coordinating hub, although some specific slow campaigns utilise networks to foster collaboration. Canadian journalist Carl Honoré attempted to synthesise the philosophy of slowness in his 2004 book, *In Praise of Slowness*.[203] In advocating slowness for many fields of human endeavour, Honoré stresses that slow philosophy is not about living at a snail's pace but about acting at the correct speed, with an emphasis on quality rather than quantity. Thus, the call to act slowly must be linked to understanding *when* to act, and to get the *timing* right in environmental decisions, such as when to sustainably harvest natural resources or take action to forestall a pollution threat.

Slow movements, engrossed with time, share some affinity with the earlier 'small' movements, dealing with space and scale. Ever since Ernst Schumacher proclaimed in 1973 that 'small is beautiful',[204] which evoked Gandhian economics to challenge the belief that bigger is better, localism and small-scale have become powerful leitmotifs for many

---

[202] C. Honoré, *In Praise of Slowness: Challenging the Cult of Speed* (Vintage Canada, 2004).
[203] Ibid.
[204] E.F. Schumacher, *Small is Beautiful: Economics as if People Mattered* (Blond and Briggs, 1973).

community-based development and environmental strategies. They emphasise grassroots, community participation, and autonomy as alternatives to direction by nation-states and business corporations.[205] The asserted advantages of smallness include less bureaucracy, more democracy, and social and economic policies and practices that are community-centred. Particularly since the 1980s, development policies in many states and international organisations have ostensibly embraced this ethos and decentralised decision-making to local government and community groups.[206] Major international environmental policy statements in the 1980s and 1990s routinely called for increased community involvement in environmental decisions.[207] The Treaty of the European Union has codified this commitment in the 'subsidiarity' principle, which postulates delegating authority to the lowest level of government that is competent to manage the assigned responsibilities.[208]

Although smaller scale decision-making has benefits for tackling many environmental problems, it was the slow movements that enabled a more comprehensive perspective of such problems and other social ailments by examining them through the lens of time. Slowness has many avowed benefits. It gives more time for contemplation and reflection, which can enable more careful, effective decisions that avoid costly mistakes. Slowness facilitates environmental due diligence to prevent irreparable pollution, species extinctions, or other impacts. Because of time lags between action and effect, it can sometimes take ages to see the effect of our actions on the natural environment or whether our laws and policies achieve the outcomes sought.[209] By not rushing, we also allow more time for public consultation and the building of trust that can help ensure the legitimacy

---

[205] N.P. Spyke, 'Public participation in environmental decision-making at the new millennium: structuring new spheres of public influence' (1999) 26 *Boston College Environmental Affairs Law Review* 263, 269–70.

[206] B.J. Richardson, 'Environmental law in postcolonial societies: straddling the local-global institutional spectrum' (2000) 11(1) *Colorado Journal of International Environmental Law and Policy* 1, 45–7.

[207] See e.g. World Commission on Environment and Development, *Our Common Future* (Oxford University Press, 1987); World Conservation Union, *Caring for the Earth* (IUCN, 1990); and Convention on Access to Information, Public Participation in Decision Making and Access to Justice in Environmental Matters (Aarhus Convention), 25 June 1998, in force 30 October 2001, (1999) 38 ILM 517.

[208] Article 5(3), Consolidated versions of the Treaty on European Union and the Treaty on the Functioning of the European Union O.J. C 326, 26/10/2012, 0001-0390.

[209] Idea expressed by G. de Brouwer, 'Science in Australia's environmental policy', *Presentation to the Australian Academy of Science*, 12 June 2015.

of environmental decisions – and this also helps minimise the risk of costly disputes erupting later. The timescales over which natural resources such as forests or fish are harvested also benefit from slowness, so that renewable resources have enough time to recover. Importantly, slowness should not simply be an aspiration for how we govern our environmental behaviour; it must also infuse the very core of human economic and social affairs that fuel environmental pressures. From the financial market to the food economy, hastiness is a pervasive burden on Earth's systems.

The fast, unsustainable trajectory of modern life is not for want of scientific knowledge about many of its environmental consequences, but knowledge itself is insufficient without the time for critical reflection on its meaning and application. This includes reflection on the appropriateness of our underlying values and priorities about economic growth, materialism, and mastery of nature. Time for such reflective, meditative thought is rare in our busy lives. Writing in 1955, German philosopher Martin Heidegger lamented that modern 'man today is in flight from thinking' due to the 'forces of technology'.[210] We are dominated, he continues, by a 'calculative thinking' that 'computes ever newer, ever more promising . . . more economical possibilities', and that 'races from one prospect to the next', without stopping to collect itself'.[211] The results of this mentality are quite familiar to us: the commodification of all experiences and things and the subjugation of nature as a mere instrument of human need without intrinsic value. The use of Cost Benefit Analysis (CBA) to make environmental decisions is one of many manifestations of this mentality. Instead, Heidegger demands we commit to a meditative thinking, a thinking that is deeply contemplative of 'the meaning which reigns in everything that is'.[212] Meditative thinking is slow thinking, allowing us to extricate ourselves from the haste and business of modern life to reflect on our values, goals, and other determinants that contribute to environmental actions.

Behavioural scientists have tested the innate benefits of patient, reflective decision-making. Some have conducted experiments to identify how the habit of delaying important decisions can contribute to long-term success in life. Perhaps the most famous is the 'marshmallow test', devised in the 1960s by Stanford University psychologist Walter Mischel to assess

---

[210] M. Heidegger, 'Discourse on thinking-memorial address' (1955), trans. by J.M. Anderson and E.H. Freund, in M. Stassen (ed), *Martin Heidegger: Philosophical and Political Writings* (Continuum International Publishing, 2003), 88.
[211] Ibid, 89.
[212] Ibid.

children's temperament for patience.[213] The subjects were offered two marshmallows (or other displayed treats) if they could wait, or one now if they could not. Only 30 per cent of the children could wait the necessary 15 minutes – a lifetime to most 4-year-olds – to earn a second marshmallow. Later in their lives, Mischel checked whether the more patient children in his study had enjoyed superior academic success in high school. He found they had. The study confounded assumptions that intelligence is the best predictor of success; the marshmallow test suggests intelligence is often at the mercy of impulsivity. Numerous follow-up studies have found the test similarly valid for predicting long-term social, cognitive, and mental health outcomes.[214] More recently, Frank Partnoy's bestseller, *Wait*, verifies the benefits of delay.[215] Challenging the 'go with your gut instincts' advice of Malcolm Gladwell in *Blink*,[216] or tolerance of the three seconds in which we habitually make first impressions, explained by Les Parrot in *3 Seconds*,[217] Partnoy suggests that in many contexts delaying decisions until the last moment leads to better outcomes. The art of knowing how long one can delay before committing to a decision is pivotal to effective decisions, from a business deal to a marriage proposal.

The benefits of slowness extend to environmental governance. The very inception of modern environmental law implied the need to slow down, such as by conducting an environmental assessment of proposed developments, allowing for consultation with the affected public, and providing rights of appeal and review for aggrieved persons – procedures that slow initiation of development activities to allow for proper due diligence and securing community acceptance. But environmental law has generally not articulated an explicit ethos of slowness, and to the contrary the pressure is intensifying to accelerate decision procedures that are perceived as hindering necessary economic development.

One domain in which slowness fares well in environmental law is public inquiries. Governments establish them in order to solicit more extensive public consultation in a less adversarial forum, and additional fact finding and analysis, but also sometimes disingenuously to sideline an issue and neutralise discontent. Compared to courts, public inquiries can allow for greater in-depth research and more generous public consultation such

---

[213] W. Mischel, E. Ebbesen, and A. Zeiss, 'Cognitive and attentional mechanisms in delay of gratification' (1972) 21(2) *Journal of Personality and Social Psychology* 204.
[214] See a summary of such research in W. Mischel, et al., '"Willpower" over the life span: decomposing self-regulation' (2011) 6(2) *Social Cognitive and Affective Neuroscience* 252.
[215] F. Partnoy, *Wait: The Art and Science of Delay* (PublicAffairs, 2012).
[216] M. Gladwell, *Blink: The Power of Thinking without Thinking* (Back Bay Books, 2007).
[217] L. Parrot, *3 Seconds: The Power of Thinking Twice* (Zondervan, 2007).

as through open submissions and community hearings, thereby fostering more informed and socially acceptable decisions. Not surprisingly, public environmental inquiries can take many months or even years. The Ranger Uranium Environmental Inquiry was instituted by the Australian government in July 1975 to investigate its potential involvement in the nuclear industry, with the inquiry finishing in May 1977.[218] Australia's former Resource Assessment Commission's Forest and Timber Inquiry was longer, from late 1989 until March 1992.[219] Even longer, an inquiry into an expansion of London's Heathrow airport concluded in 1999 after nearly 4 years.[220] While some public inquiries undoubtedly have been used wastefully to deflect political controversies or to stall inevitable decisions, they can sometimes improve the quality of environmental decision-making, with outcomes that enjoy greater public legitimacy and are supported by better scientific research.[221]

Their use to deal with environmental issues took off after the pioneering Mackenzie Valley Pipeline Inquiry, also known as the 'Berger Inquiry' after its chair Justice Thomas Berger. The inquiry was commissioned by the Canadian government in 1974 to investigate the social, environmental, and economic impacts of a proposed gas pipeline that would traverse through northwest Canada. The inquiry's final report, given in June 1977 at a cost of C$5.3 million and containing some 40,000 pages in 283 volumes, recommended that no pipeline be built through the environmentally sensitive northern Yukon, while a pipeline through an alternate route in the Mackenzie Valley should be delayed for 10 years.[222] The Berger Inquiry was pioneering for its sensitive engagement with the Aboriginal people who would have been most affected by the pipeline. Berger personally travelled throughout northern Canada to preside over many of the public hearings. Unlike the formal meetings convened to hear the opinions of some 300 experts, Berger's meetings in the 35 Aboriginal communities were conducted over a lengthy period in an informal style within the communities themselves; he listened to almost 1,000 people. While few environmental inquiries conducted since then match the Berger

---

[218] Ranger Uranium Environmental Inquiry, *Fox Report: Second Report* (Australian Government Publishing Service, May 1977).

[219] Resource Assessment Commission, *Forest and Timber Inquiry Final Report* (Australian Government Publishing Service, 1992).

[220] 'Long-haul Heathrow inquiry ends', *BBC News* 17 March 1999, at www.bbc.com/news.

[221] B.J. Richardson and B. Boer, 'Contribution of public inquiries to environmental assessment' (1995) 2(2) *Australian Journal of Environmental Management* 90.

[222] Justice T. Berger, *Northern Frontier, Northern Homeland; the Report of the Mackenzie Valley Pipeline Inquiry*, Volume 1 (Minister of Supply and Services Canada, 1977).

Inquiry's patience and deliberation, elements of this approach continue in some environmental regulatory processes, such as EIAs.

With environmental law worldwide under unprecedented pressure to reduce its regulatory burden on business and landowners, there is less political appetite for such lengthy public inquiries. Instead, inculcating slowness in environmental decision-making is increasingly coming from other societal sectors. Two movements of environmental significance, Slow Food and Slow Money, that explicitly challenge fastness are worth examining in detail.

Slow Food

From the Fast to Slow Food Economy

Farmers, because they work the land, should be among the most attuned to nature's timescales. They must choose the right times to plant and harvest their crops, and they must know the life cycles of their livestock to achieve optimal management. Time is also a source of risk that they must manage carefully: for vintners, a grapevine usually takes at least 3 years to mature before it can yield viable grapes, during which time droughts, pests, diseases, or other natural disturbances might wreak havoc. However, drawn into the commercial economy rather than subsisting from their own produce, farmers face pressure to shift from nature's temporalities to a contrived temporality dictated by the market. To stay in business, farmers must maximise production, and thus tender crops and manage animals by means that get food from the paddock to the plate by the quickest and most economical route.

This imperative is epitomised by the growth of factory farming and the consolidation of smallholder farms into large agri-businesses, with about two-thirds of livestock in the world raised in factory farms.[223] In Australia, between 1971 and 2003, meat production increased by 130 per cent while the number of pig producers dropped from 40,000 to about 2,300.[224] In the United States, the average size of factory-farmed dairies reportedly grew from 1,114 head in 1997 to 1,481 in 2007, while the number of dairy farms declined by 52,000 over this period.[225] The number of pig producers declined by 70 per cent, from about 240,000 in 1992 to fewer than 70,000

---

[223] See generally UN Food and Agriculture Organization (FAO), *Livestock's Long Shadow: Environmental Issues and Options* (FAO, 2006).
[224] Productivity Commission, *Australian Pigmeat Industry*, Report No. 35 (Commonwealth of Australia, 2005), xvi.
[225] Food and Water Watch, *Factory Farm Nation* (Food and Water Watch, 2007), 4.

in 2007, while the number of farmed pigs rose from 46 million to nearly 63 million in the decade to 2007.[226] Aquaculture, such as marine shrimp farming, has also become big business, with global aquaculture production expanding by a factor of 12 between 1980 and 2010, and increasing from about 47 million tonnes in 2006 to 63 million tonnes in 2011 – with most of this surge coming from China.[227] The Global Alliance Against Industrial Aquaculture is one of several groups challenging these trends, especially in salmon and shrimp farming.[228] Even the organic foods sector – the seeming apotheosis of environmental sustainability – is increasingly engineered on an industrial scale and integrated into global supply chains that expose it to fast time pressures. Large corporate producers (e.g. Heinz) and retailers (e.g. Whole Foods) have entered the organics sector, thereby shifting many producers into big business networks.[229]

The strategies to accelerate production include new inputs to stimulate the growth of crops and livestock: genetically modified plants, pesticides and synthetic fertilisers, food and hormone growth supplements, and antibiotics. Factory-farmed chickens raised under intensive systems can reach slaughter weight at 5–7 weeks of age, whereas in the pre-industrial farming era before the 1950s, that time span was 15–30 weeks. Likewise, a couple of generations ago, beef cattle were not slaughtered until 5 years old; today, they live for about 15 months. Similar patterns occur with other intensively farmed creatures, from pigs to salmon. Crop yields have also soared through inputs such as superphosphate, artificial irrigation, and pesticides. Between 1950 and 2000, US agricultural productivity soared, the average yield of corn – the country's most important crop – rose from 39 bushels to 153 bushels per acre.[230] Genetically modified maize, such as corn with enhanced resistance to pests and herbicides, has aided such gains. Adam lambasts the genetic engineering of food staples as 'the crowning glory of a long history of time rationalization'.[231] This control of time has been achieved by disciplining 'maturing, ripening, ageing and

---

[226] Ibid, 9.
[227] UN Food and Agricultural Organization (FAO), *The State of World Fisheries and Aquaculture* (FAO, 2012), 3, 25.
[228] See http://salmonfarmingkills.com.
[229] L.F. Clark, *The Changing Politics of Organic Food in North America* (Edward Elgar Publishing, 2015).
[230] K.O. Fuglie, J.M. MacDonald, and E. Ball, *Productivity Growth in U.S. Agriculture*, Economic Brief Paper 9 (US Department of Agriculture, 2007), 1.
[231] B. Adam, 'The temporal gaze: the challenge for social theory in the context of GM food' (2000) 51(1) *British Journal of Sociology* 125, 139.

decaying; controlling the seasonality of animals and plants; [and] controlling generational sequence and reproduction'.[232]

Beyond the farm gate, centralised food-processing centres such as abattoirs are achieving unprecedented economies of scale on round-the-clock 24/7 schedules. Rapid global transport systems enable the transportation and sale of food worldwide; one can easily find New Zealand apples or lamb chops for sale in a British or Canadian supermarket at any time, although they are unlikely to be sold 'fresh', as retailers add chemicals to delay natural discolouring or keep produce in deep freezers for months. But some products, such as oysters, are picked, air-freighted, and sold fresh to consumers in distant lands within a matter of days.[233] The massive popularity of fast and takeaway food is no doubt the most overt sign of the fast food economy. Since the first junk chain opened in the United States in 1921, today over 230,000 fast-food joints service more than 50 million Americans daily.[234] Subway, the world's largest fast food franchise, had in 2016 some 44,500 restaurants in 111 countries, with some 27,000 outlets in the United States alone.[235]

The environmental impacts of these trends are shocking and well-publicised thanks to literature with titles such as the *Last Harvest*, *Empty Harvest*, and *Bitter Harvest*.[236] Most of the meat, eggs, and dairy products consumed come from factory farms in which animals endure cruel, cramped conditions that deprive them of their ability to enjoy normal behaviours. The chemical supplements fed to animals can lead to painful and debilitating conditions. Factory farms also generate mountains of waste: the hormones, drugs, and fertilisers used to expedite production seep into waterways, thereby contributing to waterborne illnesses, ecological dead zones, and other hazards. Irrigation systems are sucking water from reservoirs faster than they are replenished. Genetically engineered crops pose risks that have yet to be fully understood. Modern agriculture also degrades the soil, such as by salting, contaminating, eroding, and waterlogging. The food economy also contributes to climate change: livestock generate methane emissions, most agrichemicals are

---

[232] Ibid.
[233] 'Oysters in Tokyo', Japan Times 2014, at www.japantimes.co.jp/best-of-city-guide.
[234] For further data and trends, see Schlosser, *Fast Food Nation*.
[235] Subway, at www.subway.com.
[236] P. Raebrun, *The Last Harvest: The Genetic Gamble That Threatens to Destroy American Agriculture* (Bison Books, 1996); B. Jensen and M. Anderson, *The Empty Harvest* (Avery, 1995); A. Cooper and L. Holmes, *Bitter Harvest: A Chef's Perspective on the Hidden Dangers in the Foods We Eat and What You Can Do About It* (Routledge, 2000).

derived from oil, and food processing and transport carry large carbon footprints. Deforestation, another source of carbon emissions, is increasing in some countries as land is cleared for pasture or crops. On the retail side of the food economy, food packaging, such as styrofoam containers and plastic wrapping, pollutes the environment, taking hundreds of years to decompose safely. These environmental impacts add to the numerous social ailments of the fast food economy, including sweatshop abuses and unhealthy diets. Many of these costs of industrial agriculture have been hidden or ignored in expedient calculations of profit and productivity.

Consumer awareness of some of these impacts has fostered interest among some landholders in sustainable farming systems, whose elements commonly emphasise organic, local, and small-scale features. Permaculture and natural sequence farming are among this new wave of ecologically designed agricultural and garden systems that aim to restore degraded land and utilise natural processes holistically. While these approaches challenge industrial agriculture, the Slow Food movement more explicitly challenges its temporal dimensions. It began in Italy in 1986, when journalist Carlo Petrini became concerned about the planned opening of a McDonald's franchise in Rome's cherished Spanish Steps. In public protest against the fast food behemoth's intrusion into Italian food culture, Petrini and his followers presented bowls of home-made Italian pasta dishes in a unique form of demonstration to highlight the importance of traditional, local cuisine.[237] Subsequently, in 1989, the Slow Food Manifesto, written with co-founder Folco Portinari, was signed in Paris by representatives from 15 countries.[238] The movement, headquartered in Petrini's hometown, Bra, has blossomed into an international phenomenon with over 100,000 members in 1,300 local chapters in about 150 countries.

Slow Food primarily aims to enhance the public appreciation of locally produced foods and culinary traditions.[239] The philosophy of the movement is articulated in the term 'eco-gastronomy', denoting the pleasure of good food, the importance of protecting traditional and sustainable foods,

---

[237] A. Gallo-Brown, 'A history of slow food: the Italian-born movement gains steam' (2010) 6(10) *Tusker Geografica* at www.enewsbuilder.net/tusker.
[238] Slow Food Manifesto, at www.slowfood.com.
[239] I. Kjorstad, 'Slow food: counteracting fast food and fast living' in U. Tischner, et al. (ed), *System Innovation for Sustainability 3: Case Studies in Sustainable Consumption and Production: Food and Agriculture* (Greenleaf, 2010), 141; R. Sassatelli and F. Davolio, 'Consumption, pleasure and politics: slow food and the politico-aesthetic problematization of food' (2010) 10(2) *Journal of Consumer Culture* 202, 210.

and the interconnectedness of food, nature, and culture.[240] Conviviality, meaning the enjoyment of cooking and eating, and sharing such experiences with others, is also a pivotal sentiment of slow fooders.[241] In regard to the agriculture economy itself, the Slow Food philosophy espouses three interconnected principles: good, clean, and fair. The first principle means that food should be fresh and flavourful. The second refers to the consumption and production of food without damaging the health of the environment, animals, or people. The last emphasises reasonable food prices for both consumers and producers.[242] Slow Food is thus not just a time-related strategy for the food economy, but includes considerations of space and scale. Its emphasis on community or local food production aims to connect people more closely to where their food is sourced, and family dining is a second spatial context promoted by slow fooders as valuable for the shared enjoyment of food.

The Slow Food network has several levels. Locally, the 'convivia', or local chapters, organise conferences, cooking demonstrations, food and wine tasting sessions, and other public events. The convivia also build relationships with local producers, encourage chefs to source their foods locally, and work within schools to promote their cause. Most of the local chapters act independently, which seems to have made it difficult for Slow Food to capture the attention of politicians and influence public policy.[243] Slow Food operates increasingly at national and international levels to educate and connect producers and consumers.[244] The Slow Food Foundation for Biodiversity aims to protect food biodiversity and encourage sustainable agriculture.[245] The Foundation's largest project is the Presidia, launched in 2000, which offers local producers marketing assistance to sustain quality production of products at risk of extinction and to recover traditional processing techniques. The Foundation also convenes the Ark of Taste, which catalogues forgotten products so as to reintegrate them into food production practices in an effort to promote biodiversity and preserve unique foods.[246]

While the concept of 'time' itself is rarely explicitly conveyed in the literature or work of Slow Food, it deeply infuses the movement. The guiding

---

[240] Slow Food 'Our philosophy', at www.slowfood.com/international/2/our-philosophy.
[241] Gallo-Brown, 'A history of slow food'.
[242] Slow Food, 'Manifesto for quality', at www.slowfood.com.
[243] B. White, 'The challenges of eating slow', Wall Street Journal 2 September 2008, www.wsj.com.
[244] Slow Food Canada, 'About us' at, www.slowfood.ca/about.
[245] Slow Food Foundation for Biodiversity, at www.slowfoodfoundation.org.
[246] Slow Food 'Biodiversity', at www.slowfood.com/international/11/biodiversity?-session=query_session:42F942811b6b60FBF6jrk2CF8540.

Slow Food International Statute doesn't define 'slowness', but elaborates that the movement's agenda embraces a number of time-sensitive strategies including to 'promote a different quality of life, based upon respect for natural rhythms', to 'support animal welfare', 'safeguarding of biodiversity', and to 'fight climate change'.[247] In addition to this respect for nature's timescales, time is also pivotal to Slow Food's veneration of cultural tradition and heritage in local food cuisine and farming practices. In Europe particularly, Slow Food celebrates using local products in traditional recipes that might take more time to prepare, and taking time to enjoy eating meals with others rather than quickly consuming processed foods to satisfy hunger. In contrast, Slow Food adherents in North America tend to pay more attention to the environmental agenda, including organic production methods to protect health and biodiversity.

From the Plate to the Planet

The Slow Food manifesto promotes a gastronomic association connecting an improved culinary experience with local traditions and regional environmental health. Begun as a reaction to the intrusion of McDonald's into Rome, the movement initially promoted the classic Italian *osterie* and *trattorie* (i.e. traditional eateries). It has since reached beyond gastronomy to concern itself increasingly with environmental conservation and social justice in the agrarian context. The Slow Food Foundation for Biodiversity was established in 2003 to support and coordinate projects that protect local biodiversity, and it has emerged as a core pillar of the Slow Food mission, as reflected in the Foundation's annual 'Social Reports'.[248] The 2013 Social Report, for instance, declared that:

> The protection of biodiversity is the most important insurance policy we can take out to guarantee our future. Biodiversity is what allows plants and animals to react to unforeseen events, to adapt to a changing climate and to resist the attacks of parasites and diseases. A biologically varied system has the antibodies necessary to react to harmful organisms and to maintain its equilibrium.[249]

Although Slow Food is institutionally distinct from the organic movement, it generally supports the principles of organic food production. The latter industry has enjoyed robust growth over the past 20 years: sales of

---

[247] Slow Food International Statute, Article 3.
[248] Available at www.fondazioneslowfood.com/en/what-is-the-foundation/social-report.
[249] Slow Food Foundation for Biodiversity (SFFBD), *Social Report 2013* (SFFBD, 2014), 8.

organic produce in the United States increased from US$3.6 billion in 1997 to over US$39 billion in 2014 (and comprised four per cent of total food sales in 2014).[250] The Australian organic market grew 15 per cent annually over 2009 to 2014,[251] while the organic farmed area of New Zealand grew by 13.4 per cent annually between 2007 and 2012.[252] Likewise, the European organic food market has rapidly expanded production and consumption, with growth rates of nearly 10 per cent annually.[253] Not all of these trends are necessarily associated with Slow Food, and indeed its leaders maintain that organic agriculture on an industrial scale and integrated into global supply chains resembles monoculture cropping that is not compatible with its values.[254] In Australia, for instance, about 50 per cent of certified organic primary producers operate with large agri-businesses and 20 per cent of Australian organic produce is exported globally.[255]

Slow Food has recently begun to give more attention to animal welfare. The US chapter in 2014 launched 'Slow Meat', an initiative that does not ask consumers to be vegetarians, but calls for farms to raise their animal welfare standards. The Slow Food International policy paper on animal welfare declares that it 'does not support practices involving the close confinement of livestock, the use of genetically modified animals or their offspring, long distance transport, routine mutilations, the use of antibiotics, and slaughter without pre-stunning'.[256] Slow Food is also getting interested in seafood, and has sponsored the spinoff movement for 'Slow Fish', which emphasises sustainable harvesting of fish, supporting local, artisanal fishing practices, and remunerating workers fairly. A commitment to animal welfare is an important time-related strategy because it implies raising poultry and livestock in conditions that allow for more natural behaviours, including longer lifespans: by contrast, industrial animal production raises animals to slaughter age as quickly as possible.

Slow Food's prescriptions for systemic change are not as well articulated as its underlying values. They generally include education of producers

---

[250] Data from Organic Trade Association, 'State of the industry' (2015), at http://ota.com/sites/default/files/indexed_files/StateOfOrganicIndustry_0.pdf.
[251] Australian Organic, *Australian Organic Market Report 2014* (Australian Organic, 2015), 2.
[252] Organics Aoteoroa New Zealand (OANZ), *New Zealand Organic Market Report 2012* (OANZ, 2013), 6.
[253] MarketLine, '*Organic food in Europe*' (MarketLine, 2015).
[254] Slow Food 'FAQs', at www.slowfood.ca/about.
[255] Australian Organic, *Australian Organic Market Report 2014*.
[256] A.M. Matarrese, *Slow Food Policy Paper on Animal Welfare* (Slow Food Foundation for Biodiversity, 2013), 7.

and consumers, and improved food labelling that empowers consumers to make ethical choices. Slow Food's animal welfare policy, for instance, explains: 'education is one of Slow Food's core tools. By understanding where our food comes from, how it was produced and by whom, adults and children can learn how to combine pleasure and responsibility in their daily choices'.[257] To achieve this goal, the paper recommends improved animal welfare labelling, as 'consumers [have] the right to know where their food comes from and how it was produced'.[258] Slow Food has even launched its own 'narrative label', based on the idea that food labels should tell the story of where food comes from, as against merely providing a list of ingredients or other non-contextual information. But Slow Food has been less interested in developing its own animal welfare codes or laws and instead tends to rely on those developed by major animal welfare groups.

The social justice agenda of Slow Food is even less concretely translated into policy action. Indeed, the movement is criticised as elitist because the local, organic foods it promotes generally cost more than the mass-produced alternatives found in supermarkets.[259] In addition, Slow Food is questioned for lacking ethnic and cultural diversity among its participants.[260] Despite the movement's declared ethos of 'good, clean and fair', the 'fair' principle is often not given as much importance as the other elements.[261] Leitch suggests that the movement is overly 'concerned with the commodification of rural and proletarian nostalgia' rather than actual protection of local farm production cultures.[262] The fair trade movements, such as fair trade coffee, much more overtly and effectively champion the social justice dimension of agricultural production. The Slow Food movement is also dismissed for being unrealistic and harmful to feeding the world's poor, for which large-scale, industrial farming is touted as the best way to feed the growing global population.[263] Such criticisms however ignore the long-term social and environmental cost of 'cheap' food, in

---

[257] Ibid, 9.
[258] Ibid.
[259] Gallo-Brown, 'A history of slow food'.
[260] K. Severson, 'Slow food savors its big moment', *New York Times* 23 July 2008, at www.nytimes.com.
[261] R. Zurayk, 'Global views of local food systems' (2010) 1(1) *Journal of Agriculture, Food Systems, and Community Development* 27.
[262] A. Leitch, 'Slow food and the politics of pork fat: Italian food and European identity' (2003) 68(4) *Ethnos: Journal of Anthropology* 456.
[263] B. Walsh, 'Can slow food feed the world?', *Time Magazine* 4 September 2008, at http://content.time.com/time/magazine.

which the externalities of food production such as greenhouse gas emissions, reduced biodiversity, and contaminated soils, become a costly legacy for posterity to repair.

Governing Slow Food – Legislation

Although Slow Food itself expresses environmental governance for the agricultural sector, it operates with a legal context shaped by states. Because of its multi-faceted agenda, Slow Food governance cannot be captured discretely within a single legislative instrument. Rather, a number of regulations and public policies will shape the Slow Food economy. They include animal welfare regulations, greenbelt laws to conserve peri-urban farmlands, financial assistance to farmers, intellectual property law to protect farming knowledge and practices, and environmental food labelling. Detailed analysis of each and all of these legislative domains would require several further books, so only some brief remarks follow.

Slow Food depends on protecting the traditional knowledge and customs embodied in farming and culinary practices. Such knowledge is threatened by the profound socio-economic changes unleashed by globalisation, and may lack legal recognition or protection. Intellectual property law in Western jurisdictions emphasises individual property rights, which can be traded and serve to stimulate commercial innovation and economic growth. These systems are conceptually limited in their capacity to recognise and protect intellectual knowledge and custom that is pre-existing and held communally. Limited protection flows to traditional farmers' rights such as to the genetic resources in local seed varieties used to support subsistence agriculturalists.[264]

The global Agreement on Trade-Related Aspects of Intellectual Property Rights[265] (TRIPS) has encouraged states to develop legal frameworks that protect the intellectual property of business corporations, such as trademarks and patents that are perceived to contribute to economic innovation and growth.[266] TRIPS is silent on recognition of farmers' rights,

---

[264] C. Oguamanam, 'Intellectual property rights in plant genetic resources: farmers' rights and food security of indigenous and local communities' (2006) 11 *Drake Journal of Agricultural Law* 273; H.M. Haugen, 'The right to food, farmers' rights and intellectual property rights: can competing law be reconciled?' in N. Lambek, et al. (eds), *Rethinking Food Systems: Structural Challenges, New Strategies and the Law* (Springer, 2014), 195.

[265] Adopted 15 April 1994, in force 1 January 1995, (1994) 33 ILM 1197.

[266] S. Sell, *Private Power, Public Law: The Globalization of Intellectual Property Rights* (Cambridge University Press, 2003).

perhaps implying that such rights have lesser significance than other species of intellectual property. On other hand, TRIPS does not prohibit the protection of additional intellectual subject matter for the purpose of safeguarding local knowledge and informal innovations relating to plant genetic resources. But while states can in their own laws recognise and protect farmers' rights in their national legislation, this has not been widely done; Zambia and the Philippines are examples.[267]

The International Union for the Protection of New Varieties of Plants (UPOV) Convention, adopted in 1961, is also relevant to farmers' rights to plant varieties.[268] Article 9.1 affirms that parties to the Treaty:

> recognise the enormous contribution that the local and indigenous communities and farmers of all regions of the world, particularly those in the centres of origin and crop diversity, have made and will continue to make for the conservation and development of plant genetic resources which constitute the basis of food and agriculture production throughout the world.

Article 9.2 places the responsibility for realising farmers' rights with national governments. Each state party should, 'as appropriate' and 'subject to national legislation', 'take measures to protect and promote farmers' rights including . . . protection of traditional knowledge relevant to plant genetic resources for food and agriculture'. Further, by Article 15.1, acts that would otherwise constitute an infringement of intellectual property rights are exempted if the protected plant variety is used for private and non-commercial reasons. According to UPOV in its own explanation of this clause, the 'propagation of a variety by a farmer exclusively for the production of a food crop to be consumed entirely by that farmer and the dependents of the farmer living on that holding, may be considered to fall within the meaning of acts done privately and for non-commercial purposes'.[269] Hence this interpretation protects subsistence farming but does not permit the exchange of seed among smallholder farmers (although Article 9.3 suggests that saving, using, and exchanging seeds is lawful, subject to national laws). Curiously, a recently published FAQ on the

---

[267] Zambian Plant Breeder's Right Act, 2007, Article 8.2; Philippines, Plant Variety Protection Act 2002, Article 43.
[268] Adopted 2 December 1961, in force 10 August 1968, 815 UNTS 89 (amended extensively since).
[269] International Union for the Protection of New Varieties of Plants. Explanatory notes on exceptions to the breeder's right under the 1991 Act of the UPOV Convention, UPOV/EXN/EXC/1, 22 October 2009, at www.upov.int/edocs/expndocs/en/upov_exn_exc.pdf.

UPOV website advises that Article 15,1 does allow 'subsistence farmers to exchange this against other vital goods within the local community'.[270]

Indigenous peoples' environmental livelihoods are another context where intellectual property law is not easily adapted to indigenous knowledge.[271] The modern intellectual property law system is designed to promote innovation and the commercialisation of knowledge, whereas indigenous communities tend to be more interested in preserving the integrity of existing traditional knowledge. The legal requirements of authorship and novelty also pose difficulties where traditional knowledge has evolved gradually from generation to generation and is owned collectively. The idea of communal ownership, which is embraced by indigenous peoples and their customary laws, stands in stark contrast to the aim of copyright legislation to vest ownership of the copyright of any literary, dramatic, musical, or artistic work in an individual author.[272] Furthermore, many forms of indigenous cultural expression derive from pre-existing clan designs, oral histories, and dances that have been handed down for generations. Thus the resulting works might lack the requisite 'originality' for protection under conventional intellectual property legislation.

Currently, there are few international or national legal instruments that create specific intellectual property standards tailored to indigenous knowledge or cultural practices. The Convention on Biological Diversity requires states to conserve and protect indigenous peoples' knowledge, innovations, and practices relevant to the conservation of biological diversity.[273] The UN Declaration on the Rights of Indigenous Peoples of 2007 affirmed their right:

> to maintain, control, protect and develop their cultural heritage, traditional knowledge and traditional cultural expressions, as well as the manifestations of their sciences, technologies and cultures, including human and genetic resources, seeds, medicines, [and] knowledge of the properties of fauna and flora.[274]

At a national level, one of the most intriguing efforts to acknowledge indigenous peoples' culture and traditional knowledge is the report of

---

[270] UPOV, at www.upov.int/about/en/faq.html#Q30.
[271] F. Yamin and D. Possey, 'Indigenous peoples, biotechnology and intellectual property rights' (1997) 2 *Review of European Community and International Environmental Law* 141.
[272] E.g. Australia's Copyright Act 1968 (Cth), s. 35(2).
[273] Adopted 5 June 1992, in force 29 December 1993, (1992) 31 ILM 818, Article 8(j).
[274] UN Doc. A/61/L.67, 7 September 2007, Article 31(1).

New Zealand's Waitangi Tribunal into the Wai262 claim brought by Maori seeking recognition of their culture, identity, and knowledge relating to the natural environment. The Waitangi Tribunal's recommendations to the government included the establishment of a commission to protect Maori cultural works, new Maori advisory bodies relating to patents and environmental protection, and amendments to legislation to protect Maori environmental interests, including treasured flora and fauna.[275] The New Zealand approach seeks to circumvent the limitations of European-based intellectual property law's interpretations of knowledge, authorship, private property, and monopoly privilege by creating *sui generis* approaches that recognise the cultural patrimony of Maori in a way that leaves untouched conventional intellectual property doctrine.

Governments also influence agriculture through land use planning regulations. Legal protection of peri-urban land, such as designation of 'greenbelts' or 'greenspaces' can help farmers to produce for local consumers. Greenbelts are natural or open land surrounding urban areas, often comprising a mix of public estate and privately held land, on which development restrictions are placed.[276] Such land may be protected to support the ecological, cultural, and economic linkages across landscapes.[277] Another motivation is to curb environmentally damaging rapid urban sprawl.[278] Furthermore, greenbelts can sustain agricultural and rural landscapes by including agricultural lands within permissible activities in the protected areas. Greenbelts are thus potentially powerful tools to support Slow Food livelihoods close to major urban centres.

Greenbelt legislation dates from the first half of the twentieth century. The UK established greenbelts around London pursuant to the Green Belt (London and Home Counties) Act 1938.[279] The Town and Country Planning Act 1947 allowed local authorities around Britain to designate greenbelts in their land use plans: they now cover 13 per cent of England's

---

[275] W. Tribunal, *Ko Aotearoa Tēnei: A Report into Claims Concerning New Zealand Law and Policy Affecting Māori Culture and Identity. Te Taumata Tuatahi* (Ministry of Justice, 2011).
[276] M. Carter-Whitney and T.C. Esakin, *Ontario's Greenbelt in an International Context* (Canadian Institute for Environmental Law and Policy, 2010).
[277] F. Fung and T. Conway. 'Greenbelts as an environmental planning tool: a case study of southern Ontario, Canada' (2007) 9(2) *Journal of Environmental Policy and Planning* 101.
[278] T. Daniels and M. Lapping, 'Land preservation: an essential ingredient in smart growth' (2005) 19(3) *Journal of Planning Literature* 316.
[279] 1938, 1 and 2 Geo. 6, c. xciii.

landmass and also occupy other parts of the UK.[280] Recent legislation in other jurisdictions include Ontario's Greenbelt Act 2005, which protects about 1.8 million ha of land surrounding Toronto,[281] and it has been identified as an important mechanism to promote local farmers' markets.[282] Many American municipalities and states, perhaps surprisingly given the country's passion for urban sprawl, have adopted greenbelt legislation, including in Florida, Tennessee, and Oregon. The city of Portland, Oregon, is a national leader here and in 1979 adopted an urban growth boundary policy that has helped curbed (though not eliminate) the ravenous sprawl that afflicts many US metropolises. Portland was also reputedly the first city in the United States to adopt a local climate change policy,[283] and has encouraged commuters to ditch their cars by building bike lanes and expanding light rail lines.[284] In Brazil, the São Paulo City Green Belt Biosphere Reserve was designated in 1994 to contribute to the protection of the region's threatened Atlantic forests. The massive greenbelt, overseen by a management council with equal government and non-governmental representatives, extends through 73 municipalities including São Paulo metro and covers about 17,000 km².[285] The city of Melbourne, Australia, secured legal protection in 2003 for 12 'green wedges' surrounding the city, thereby limiting the affected 17 municipal authorities' capacity to allow for urban development in these mainly rural and natural environmental spaces.[286]

Fiscal instruments can also stimulate Slow Food. The European Union's Common Agricultural Policy (CAP) has since 1962, provided financial subsidies to farmers to support local production and rural development. The CAP has evolved beyond the original focus on stabilise farmer's incomes to serve collateral policy goals, including environmental

---

[280] 1947, 10 and 11 Geo. 6, c. 51; and see C. Miles, 'Scaremongers like Bill Bryson reinforce harmful green belt myths', *The Guardian* 26 November 2015, at www.theguardian.com.

[281] SO 2005, c. 1; Ontario Ministry of Municipal Affairs and Housing, *Greenbelt Background*, at www.mah.gov.on.ca/Page1381.aspx.

[282] D. Gurin, *Farmers' Markets: Opportunities for Preserving Greenbelt Agriculture* (Friends of the Greenbelt Foundation Occasional Paper Series, 2006).

[283] H.M. Osofsky and J.K. Levit, 'The scale of networks? Local climate change coalitions' (2008) 8 *Chicago Journal of International Law* 409, 415.

[284] City of Portland and Multnomah County, *Climate Action Plan 2009: Year One Progress Report* (City of Portland and Multnomah County, December 2010), 8.

[285] R.R. Ramos-Ribeiro, 'Green belt biosphere reserve in the Brazilian city of São Paulo' (2014) 20 *Ecological Questions* 93.

[286] Department of Infrastructure, *Melbourne 2030: Planning for Sustainable Growth* (State of Victoria, 2002), 9.

protection and animal welfare standards, and recipients of subsidies risk losing them if they fail to comply with such standards. The CAP 2014–20 includes 'green direct payments' to farmers to facilitate environmental goals, such as maintenance of permanent pasture and preservation of natural landscapes.[287] Since 2000, the CAP has been linked to the European Union's Rural Development Policy (RDP), which includes environmental improvement objectives, such as projects to improve water quality and revegetation to prevent erosion, and measures to diversify and strengthen local rural economies. The recent reforms to the CAP and the introduction of the RDP have helped mitigate some longstanding concerns from Slow Food proponents that European Union (EU) policies for the agricultural sector have spurred ecologically unsustainable industrial production methods.[288]

Animal welfare legislation is a further plank in the legal framework for Slow Food. The first modern piece of legislation relating to animal welfare was, according to Kathryn Shevelow, the 1822 Act to Prevent the Cruel and Improper Treatment of Cattle, passed by the UK Parliament.[289] In the following 200 years a plethora of animal welfare legislation has been adopted in numerous countries, which aims to protect animals from overt, deliberate harm, but it has hardly dented the rise of factory farming. The prevailing legal framework treats animals as human property, whose interests are subordinate to those of the people who exploit them. Animals' protection from institutionalised violence varies with the value people place on each species.[290] In Canadian law, for instance, cruelty to animals is a criminal offence in each province, but generally accepted farming practices are specifically exempt (thus, harm to a farm animal is not an offence so long as it is a standard operating procedure in the industry).[291] World Animal Protection rated Canada a lowly D grade in its 2014 animal protection index, which rates 50 countries on a scale of A to G on the quality of their legislative commitments to animal welfare.[292]

---

[287] European Commission, 'Overview of CAP reform 2014–2020', in *Agricultural Policy Perspectives Brief* 5 (European Commission, December 2013).
[288] A. Olmo (ed), *Towards a New Common Agricultural Policy: Slow Food Policy Paper on CAP* (Slow Food, 2011).
[289] 1822 3 Geo. IV c. 71; K. Shevelow, *For the Love of Animals: The Rise of the Animal Protection Movement* (Henry Holt, 2008).
[290] A. Linzey (ed), *The Global Guide to Animal Protection* (University of Illinois Press, 2013).
[291] E.g. British Columbia's Prevention of Cruelty to Animals Act, RSBC 1996, c. 372 ss. 23.2 and 24.02.
[292] C. Perkel, 'Canada given 'D' rating in animal protection, welfare', CTV News 30 November 2014, at www.ctvnews.ca.

The animal movement has articulated a number of alternative philosophical understandings of animals' entitlement to legal protection. Utilitarian Peter Singer, in *Animal Liberation*,[293] rejected the belief in any morally salient differences between sentient creatures – in regard to race, sex, or species – that justify differential treatment. Consequently, Singer argued that animals and human beings should be treated the same, with any differential treatment being ethically defensible only if it produces greater pleasure over pain. The animal welfare model promoted by Singer that tacitly condoned the 'humane' exploitation of animals was challenged by American legal academic Gary Francione, who argued for animal rights.[294] He insisted that animals are morally valuable in their own right and should not be exploited or treated as the property of human beings. The animal rights approach thus demands liberation of domesticated animals and allowing wildlife to live unmolested. A third philosophical shift came with Canadian academics Sue Donaldson and Will Kymlicka's book *Zoopolis*,[295] which argues that the animal rights agenda focuses on negative rights, such as the right not to suffer cruelty, without accommodating the positive obligations owed to animals because of the historical and geographical patterns of animal–human interactions which have engendered some dependency of animals on humans, such as pests, farm animals and even wild creatures that coexist with people in cities by exploiting the new habitat niches.

Food labelling to educate consumers and allow producers to emphasise the qualities of their products is another relevant policy instrument. The Slow Food Foundation for Biodiversity has developed its own narrative label that 'provides precise information on the producers, their companies, the plant varieties or animal breeds used, cultivation techniques, breeding and processing, animal welfare, and areas of origin'.[296] An example of the narrative label for an Italian dairy product includes the following details:

> The company processes the milk in Sordevolo (Piedmont, Italy) in Alto Elvo: from March to May and from October to November in the Croce farm, 700 meters above sea level; from June to September in the Muanda Alps, 1,470 meters above sea level, on the slopes of Mount Mucrone.

---

[293] P. Singer, *Animal Liberation* (HarperCollins, 1975).
[294] G. Francione, *Animals as Persons: Essays on the Abolition of Animal Exploitation* (Columbia University Press, 2008).
[295] S. Donaldson and W. Kymlicka, *Zoopolis: A Political Theory of Animal Rights* (Oxford University Press, 2011).
[296] Slow Food Foundation for Biodiversity, *Narrative Label: A Revolution in Food Communication* (Slow Food, 2014), 2.

> We raise 35 Alpine Brown cows and, during the summer, they graze on pasture of about 200 hectares (about 494 acres). For the rest of the year the animals are kept in the barn, but they have one hectare (almost 2.5 acres) of land that they can graze on and are fed with hay (70% produced on the farm). Locally bought certified GMO free grains are also integrated into their diet.[297]

A number of other food labels are emerging around the world to alert consumers to the geographical origins of certain food products. The Cojote Rojo eco-label (relating to the highlands of Michoacán, Mexico) and the Local Food Plus (a label designed to promote regional products in Canada for local consumers) are examples.[298] This bottom-up approach to food labelling through the private and community sectors is important for overcoming the limitations of government regulation. Regulation of packaged food labels covers numerous elements, including place-of-origin, nutritional qualities, safety, allergens, presence of genetically modified organisms (GMOs), and sometimes information on how the food was produced. The wealth of information can be confusing and has led to calls from consumer and public health groups for simpler label systems, such as a traffic light system. But some groups, such as the Slow Food movement, prefer more detailed labels. The EU's 2011 Regulation on Provision of Food Information to Consumers[299] has disappointed Slow Food leaders for its 'lack of more detailed information that can indicate a food's real quality'.[300]

Governing Slow Food – CSR

Without legal prescriptions for Slow Food practices – such as food labelling laws, greenbelt laws, improved animal welfare standards, and financial subsidies for small-scale farmers – the movement's reach may be constrained in a food economy increasingly under the sway of big companies and global markets geared to an accelerated tempo. Even family-managed farms are drawn into their web through trading and supply chains. While it is inconceivable that industrialised agriculture will embrace Slow Food,

---

[297] Ibid, 3.
[298] H. Friedmann and A. McNair, 'Whose rules rule? Contested projects to certify "local production for distant consumers"' (2008) 8(2–3) *Journal of Agrarian Change* 408.
[299] Regulation (EU) No. 1169/2011 of the European Parliament and of the Council of 25 October 2011 on the provision of food information to consumers, OJ L 304/18, 22 November 2011.
[300] Slow Europe, 'Labelling', at www.slowfood.com/sloweurope/en/topics/etichette.

it may be able to accommodate a niche for it without legal compulsion. CSR is the banner under which companies voluntarily make environmentally positive gestures. CSR has made inroads into many economic sectors, including motor vehicles (e.g. electric cars), textile production (reducing sweat shops), and also increasingly the food economy.[301] The latter sector includes Whole Foods (North American retailer selling organic produce, respecting animal welfare standards, and promoting sustainably harvested seafood) and Earthbound Farm (Californian organic food crop producer). Food conglomerates sometimes also cooperate with environmental groups, such as the example of the Marine Stewardship Council (MSC) (a global certification regime for sustainable ocean fisheries, co-established by Unilever) and *ad hoc* affiliations such as that between WWF and the Australian supermarket chain Coles to promote responsibly sourced seafood.

CSR initiatives ultimately depend on participating companies perceiving financial advantages for themselves, either directly through market demand (e.g. for eco-friendly food) or indirectly through reputational benefits from improved stakeholder relationships or a company's general social licence. The voluntary nature of CSR offers firms the opportunity to innovate and take the initiative, but also room for insouciance or even delinquency. The motivations and impact of corporate self-regulation have already been researched extensively,[302] which do not need to be rehearsed other than to emphasise that many CSR regimes lack independent monitoring and enforcement capacity, and omit robust performance metrics. Consequently, a business casually judged as socially responsible might mislead us. Consider British Petroleum (BP); despite sculpting a 'green' reputation – it was once listed on the Dow Jones' Sustainability Index and is a signatory to the United Nations Global Compact – BP caused the appalling *Deepwater Horizon* disaster in 2010.[303]

---

[301] The range of companies engaging with CSR can be gauged by the membership of major CSR codes, such as the UN Global Compact: www.unglobalcompact.org/what-is-gc/participants.

[302] E.g. I. Maitland, 'The limits of business self-regulation' (1995) 27(3) *California Management Review* 132; J. Moon, 'The firm as citizen? Social responsibility of business in Australia' (1995) 30(1) *Australian Journal of Political Science* 1; R. Gibson (ed), *Voluntary Initiatives: The New Politics of Corporate Greening* (Broadview Press, 1999); S. Wood, 'Voluntary environmental codes and sustainability' in B.J. Richardson and S. Wood (eds), *Environmental Law for Sustainability* (Hart Publishing, 2006), 229.

[303] J. Balmer, 'The BP *Deepwater Horizon* débâcle and corporate brand exuberance' (2010) 18 *Journal of Brand Management* 97.

While many treat CSR as purely within the realm of market pressures and stakeholder relations, its uptake and impact cannot be wholly divorced from its legal context. Apart from environmental law itself providing inducements to companies to raise their game, business law influences their environmental performance.[304] Corporate law is not prescriptive about business management including consideration of environmental or social issues. Indeed, a company's shareholders may adopt articles of association that enshrine a social mission for their firm, which would legally bind its managers and directors. Even without such a mission, company law itself does not oblige a company to be governed by any unadulterated, profit-making imperative. In Anglo-American jurisdictions generally, directors essentially owe three main duties to corporations: to act lawfully, carefully, and loyally. The latter, also known as the fiduciary duty, is owed to the company, as a distinct legal personality, rather than its shareholders. American corporate law is sometimes viewed as more congruent with the popular sentiment that the interests of a company and its shareholders coincide.[305] However, there is no legally enforceable duty to maximise profits. Moreover, US courts have long consented to corporate executives sacrificing profits for philanthropic and humanitarian purposes; as New Jersey's Supreme Court once stated, 'modern conditions require that corporations acknowledge and discharge social as well as private responsibilities as members of the community within which they operate.'[306] In recent years, Canada,[307] Britain,[308] and South Africa[309] have led the way among Anglophile jurisdictions in articulating a more socially responsible standard of corporate governance, a trend labelled 'enlightened shareholder value'.[310]

Another relevant feature of company law in many jurisdictions is the business judgement rule, which provides a defence against civil liability

---

[304] B. Sjafjell and B.J. Richardson (eds), *Company Law and Sustainability: Legal Barriers and Opportunities* (Cambridge University Press, 2015).

[305] In the widely quoted 1919 case of *Dodge v. Ford Motor Co*, the Michigan court that held that 'a business corporation is organized and carried on primarily for the profit of the stockholders': 170 NW 668 (Mich, 1919), 684.

[306] *A.P. Smith Manufacturing and Co. v. Barlow*, 98 A.2d 581, 586 (NJ 1953).

[307] E.g. *Peoples Department Stores v. Wise*, [2004] 3 SCR 461.

[308] Companies Act 2006, c. 46, s. 172.

[309] Institute of Directors Southern Africa, *King Code of Governance Principles for South Africa* (Institute of Directors Southern Africa, 2009).

[310] C. Williams and J. Conley, 'An emerging third way? The erosion of the Anglo-American shareholder value construct' (2005) 38 *Cornell International Law Journal* 493.

claims against managers and directors who make decisions in good faith and on an informed basis that they believed was in the best interests of their company.[311] The resulting judicial deference to business acumen means that courts will not readily overturn any impugned business decision unless there is persuasive evidence of bad faith or procedural lapses, for instance. Consequently, companies could lawfully take environmentally positive measures such as to be 'carbon neutral' or 'fossil fuel free' if their managers reasonably believe that such measures will benefit their company's reputation and business success. More difficult to legally defend, however, would be an environmental policy adopted for potential long-term financial advantages, but incurring short-term economic pain for the company. This temporal mismatching would require companies to undertake some research to validate the projected net gains over time.

Despite the foregoing latitudes, company law is also a potential impediment to Slow Food and other environmentally responsible actions because the discretion to act altruistically is also the discretion to act self-interestedly. Company law, in other words, is a two-edged sword. The latter driver is stronger because of the competitive pressures of the marketplace, and particularly affects public companies that raise money from shareholders and bondholders. A company constituted as a private, family-run company, is slightly more insulated from such market pressures, though it must still achieve commercially success to survive. Because the market focuses on near-term performance in how it values companies, it imposes a temporality on business to act for the near-term and act fast rather than slow. The anti-corporate rhetoric of the Slow Food movement is thus not entirely misplaced, given that company law gives space for prejudices against the environment to flourish in business decision-making.

On the other hand, it is conceivable that with fair-minded management, and a financially viable business model, a company could operate to provide sustainable agriculture in a manner sympathetic to Slow Food values. And as social investors become more numerous in the market, they may exert increasing influence on companies to raise their environmental performance. The movement for Slow Money is one expression of the social investing impetus.

---

[311] E.g. Australia's Corporations Act 2001 (Cth), s. 180(2).

Slow Money

The Roaring World of Finance

The proverbial 'time is money' is particularly apt to the financial world. Time, to most financial investors, is a scarce, valuable resource that necessitates acting quickly. News about a company's economic fortunes, such as its latest quarterly results, or updates about a nation's economic health such as the newest jobs or trade data, will spark an immediate reaction from investors: a company's share price can plunge or soar within minutes or a country's currency can gyrate wildly. Global market deregulation has helped eradicate spatial boundaries that would otherwise curb or slow some of these practices. Technology has also had a hand in reducing temporal friction and delay. Whereas in pre-industrial agrarian economies trading was often time-consuming drudgery because of the physical conveyance of goods over long distances, financial transactions can now occur instantly across the entire globe at low cost. Since the 1970s the uptake of mathematical methods in finance coupled with the rise of computerised trading have enabled time intervals to contract drastically, to the point of being infinitesimal. Continuous live trading in the global market is now possible in which any asset, including future options for commodities, has an instantaneous value.[312] The compression of time also pervades the real, productive economy. As supply chains have spread globally, corporate managers have needed to invest greater effort in temporal coordination and efficiency to remove bottlenecks.[313] The result is ever-decreasing intervals of time and space in the world of late capitalism.[314]

The cult of speed in the financial world is also tied to its short-term outlook.[315] Although investing generically aims to sacrifice use of existing wealth in order to reap greater future reward, the myopic and hasty tendencies of financial markets can direct investors otherwise. Near-term financial risks and performance count much more than long-term prospects, partly because companies report their financial performance

---

[312] S.M. Sundaresan, 'Continuous-time methods in finance: a review and assessment' (2000) 55(4) *Journal of Finance* 1569.

[313] J. Magretta, 'Fast, global and entrepreneurial: supply chain management, Hong Kong style' (1998) 76(5) *Harvard Business Review* 102.

[314] See further D. Harvey, *The Condition of Postmodernity: An Enquiry into the Origins of Culture Change* (Wiley, 1992).

[315] See generally K.J. Laverty, 'Economic "short-termism": the debate, the unresolved issues, and the implications for management practice and research' (1996) 21 *Academy Management Review* 825.

over short-term intervals against which corporate bosses' and financial managers' performances are measured. The modern stock exchange also enables instantaneous trading for investors, thus exposing listed companies to short-term performance pressures. Other sources of mischief are gaps and deficiencies in financial models about the economic value of long-term performance, and the intensely competitive organisational culture in financial and corporate management.[316] Shorter-term investments also appeal to people holding the assumption that in doing so they may avoid the pitfalls of the future's uncertainty, such as shifting consumer demand or regulatory changes. The resulting pressures may tempt corporate managers to inflate current profits at the expense of the long-term health of their business, for example by investing in assets with concealed risks and borrowing excessive debt to deceptively boost short-term profits.[317]

Over recent decades the financial world has become faster, not slower; and more myopic, not far-sighted. One powerful sign is the accelerating turnover of corporate securities. The average holding period for shares listed on the New York Stock Exchange plunged from about 7 years in the 1940s to just over 5 years in 1970 and down further to 6 months in 2009.[318] The average holding period for British corporate shares dropped from 5 years in the mid-1960s to 7.5 months in 2007.[319] Among emerging markets, such as China, similar trends are evident.[320] Concomitantly, high-speed frequency traders have emerged who use computer algorithms to trade corporate stocks and bonds in nanoseconds with minimal human intervention, with the aim of gaining minute profits on each trade that in aggregation can be substantial. Approximately 55 per cent US stocks and 40 per cent of European stocks were traded in this manner by 2015.[321] Because of their lack of transparency and potentially market destabilising effects, high-frequency trading systems have begun to attract regulators'

---

[316] L.L. Dallas, 'Short-termism, the financial crisis, and corporate governance' (2012) 37(2) *Journal of Corporation Law* 266, 267; K.A. Froot, A.F. Perold, and J.C. Stein, 'Shareholder trading practices and corporate investment horizons' (1993) 5(2) *Journal of Applied Corporate Finance* 542; CFA Centre for Financial Market Integrity and Business Roundtable Institute for Corporate Ethics, *Breaking the Short-Term Cycle* (CFA, 2006).

[317] Dallas, 'Short-termism, the financial crisis, and corporate governance', 267.

[318] H. Blodget, 'You're an investor? How quaint', *Business Insider* 8 August 2009, at www.businessinsider.com.

[319] A. Haldane, *Patience and Finance* (Oxford China Business Forum, September 2010), 6.

[320] Ibid, 17.

[321] R.S. Miller and G. Shorter, *High Frequency Trading: Overview of Recent Developments* (Congressional Research Service, 2016), 1.

scrutiny.[322] In 2013 Italy introduced a levy of 0.02 per cent on equity transactions lasting less than 0.5 seconds.[323] Another approach is that of the IEX stock exchange in the United States, which announced plans, to the annoyance of Wall Street traders, to introduce a 'speed bump' that slows trading by 350 microseconds.[324] Hastiness is also evident in fund managers' limited-time mandates, typically for 3 years, with regular performance reviews.[325] Their compensation package is tied to quarterly or other short-interval financial performance metrics relative to market index benchmarks or other asset managers in a similar field.[326] A 2004 survey by the UK's National Association of Pension Funds and the Investment Management Association found that British fund managers were normally appointed on 3-year terms (in 69 per cent of examples), while 16 per cent were given a term of less than 3 years, and none longer than 5 years.[327]

The long-term impacts of the foregoing are wide ranging. For the market as a whole, these managerial incentives are a zero-sum game; competition among fund managers to outperform one another by anticipating fluctuating market sentiments is largely at the expense of each other, without contributing collectively to the absolute performance and value of companies.[328] Studies have found that firms that reduce research and development investment and other discretionary spending in order to beat market quarterly forecasts accrue short-term gains in stock price, yet underperform over the subsequent 3 years.[329] A survey of corporate managers conducted by the *Wall Street Journal* in 1986 found that 82 per cent blamed 'the stock market's attention to quarterly earnings' for diminished long-term business investment and 'the loss of America's competitive edge'.[330]

---

[322] S. Mamudi, 'Trading on speed', Bloomberg QuickTake 8 July 2016, at www.bloomberg.com/quicktake/automated-stock-trading.
[323] M. Clinch. 'Italy launches tax on high-frequency transactions', CNBC 2 September 2013, at www.cnbc.com.
[324] N. Popper, 'IEX Group, critical of Wall St., gains approval for stock exchange', *New York Times* 17 June 2016, at www.nytimes.com.
[325] E.P. Davis and B. Steil, *Institutional Investors* (MIT Press, 2001), 136.
[326] T. Hebb, *No Small Change: Pension Funds and Corporate Engagement* (Cornell University Press, 2008), 95.
[327] National Association of Pension Funds (NAPF) and the Investment Management Association (IMA), *Short-termism Study Report* (NAPF and IMA, 2004), 3.
[328] Innovation Advisory Board, *Innovation: City Attitudes and Practices* (Department of Trade and Industry, 1990).
[329] S. Bhojraj, et al., 'Making sense of cents: an examination of firms that marginally miss or beat analyst forecasts' (2009) 64(5) *Journal of Finance* 2361.
[330] Laverty, 'Economic "short-termism": the debate, the unresolved issues, and the implications for management practice and research', 831.

A 2006 study by the CFA Centre for Financial Market Integrity and the Business Roundtable Institute for Corporate Ethics concluded, 'the obsession with short-term results by investors . . . and corporate managers collectively leads to the unintended consequences of destroying long-term value, decreasing market efficiency, reducing investment returns, and impeding efforts to strengthen corporate governance'.[331]

As money traverses global markets with dramatic speed and callous scrutiny, it carries risks of serious fallout. The GFC that erupted in 2008 demonstrated the enormous collateral damage that myopic, malfunctioning financial markets can wreak.[332] The GFC had complex underpinnings in various regulatory and market failures, but was essentially rooted in the irrational exuberance about the continuing appreciation in certain asset values that had become widely divorced from their underlying risks and limitations. Because of globally interconnected financial markets – connected through space and time – one player's financial crisis quickly led to contagious financial losses and collapses far from the initial fire. Since the GFC there have been numerous investigations and analyses, many of which point to the malevolent forces of speed and myopia in the financial economy.[333] While the GFC aftermath spawned numerous recommendations and occasional reforms, the frenetic and myopic tempo of the financial world remains largely unabated.

The natural environment may also be squandered by these dynamics.[334] The money economy has some environmentally unsustainable drivers that differ from the productive, 'real' economy. The separation of capital and control of business enterprise, the hallmark of corporate capitalism, can also separate investment decisions from environmental responsibility.[335] Global investors, who typically hold passive stakes in companies rather than exerting active ownership, can become physically remote from activities they fund that directly impact the environment, thus weakening their sense of responsibility for taking corrective action. Further, the imperative to invest and lend – capital does not appreciate while stashed under the bed – injects additional money into the market that fuels further

---

[331] CFA Centre for Financial Market Integrity, *Breaking the Short-Term Cycle*, 1.
[332] R.E. Hall, 'Why does the economy fall to pieces after a financial crisis?' (2010) 24(4) *Journal of Economic Perspectives* 3.
[333] E.g. J. Kay, *Kay Review of UK Equity Markets and Long-Term Decision-Making* (Department of Business Innovation and Skills, 2012).
[334] Sjåfjell and Richardson, *Company Law and Sustainability*.
[335] See B.J. Richardson, 'Putting ethics into environmental law: fiduciary duties for ethical investment' (2008) 46(2) *Osgoode Hall Law Journal* 243.

growth and development that not only spawns speculative asset bubbles but may carry adverse environmental consequences. Further fraying the ties between those who manage companies and contribute capital, investors (such as pension funds or insurance companies) typically own tiny fractional stakes in a multitude of companies that comprise their investment portfolio, and the ease of selling corporate securities helps diminish the perceived importance of being a member of the company.

As awareness grows of the financial sector's complicity with environmentally injurious development, within the financial realm itself a movement for socially responsible, 'slow' money, is gaining ascendancy. It has yet to fundamentally transform financial markets, but it has acquired followers and offers an alternative vision.

Socially Responsible Investing

Coinciding with the evolution of Slow Food, a movement for Slow Money emerged advocating more patient and socially responsible finance that supports social justice, community development, and sustainability. Slow Money arose in the early 1980s in France,[336] but the movement is more visibly associated with American social entrepreneur Woody Tasch, whose bestseller *Slow Money*,[337] published in 2008, called for financial support for local food enterprises and organic farms. Tasch's mantra led to creation of the non-profit Slow Money organisation to catalyse financial flows for slow farming.[338] Slow Money's principles can apply to other causes associated with the longstanding movement for socially responsible investing (SRI). Also sometimes known as 'ethical investment' and 'sustainable finance',[339] SRI purports to consider a wide variety of social and environmental dimensions of investments, loans, and other financial decisions. While SRI's agenda is diverse, many followers apparently share an aspiration for long-term, patient investing. Through this temporal orientation, social investors hope that economic decisions will reinforce sustainable development.

---

[336] A. Ashta, 'An introduction to slow money and its Gandhian roots' (2014) 20(2) *Journal of Human Values* 209–10.
[337] W. Tasch, *Slow Money: Investing as If Food, Farms and Fertility Mattered* (Chelsea Green Publishing, 2008).
[338] See https://slowmoney.org.
[339] W. Ransome and C. Sampford, *Ethics and Socially Responsible Investment: A Philosophical Approach* (Ashgate Publishing, 2011).

SRI has much older roots than Slow Money, dating from the eighteenth century, when the Quakers discouraged their devotees from having financial ties to the global slave trade.[340] During the early twentieth century, other religious groups began screening their financial portfolios to avoid alcohol, tobacco, and other 'sin stocks'.[341] In the 1970s, a global divestment campaign led by religious groups tried to unseat South Africa's apartheid regime by divesting from companies that profited from it.[342] These early forms of SRI that presented themselves as moral crusades relied mainly on negative investment screens and shareholder activism. Today, SRI spans a much larger portfolio of causes and issues, including animal welfare and sweatshops, and environmental issues such as climate change have become increasingly perhaps the primary concern for many social investors. In Western Europe and North America the SRI market has started to become mainstream.[343] Like the fair trade movement and ethical consumerism, SRI has become a means for enlightened individuals and institutions to express their values in an economic system that governments have failed to adequately regulate.

The tools of social investors include screening investments for their social and environmental characteristics and engaging with businesses, such as through shareholder activism or direct dialogue with managers, to encourage better behaviour. Both tactics may use enhanced environmental due diligence to assess the long-term risks and opportunities of investments. Another SRI strategy that addresses systemic change beyond individual companies involves the development of codes of conduct for investors.[344] Prominent examples include the Equator Principles,[345]

---

[340] Examples of the pioneering literature are A. Domini and P. Kinder, *Ethical Investing* (Addison Wesley, 1984); P. Kinder, S. Lydenberg, and A. Domini, *The Social Investment Almanac: A Comprehensive Guide to Socially Responsible Investing* (Henry Holt, 1992); R. Sparkes, *The Ethical Investor* (HarperCollins, 1995); M. Jeucken, *Sustainable Finance and Banking: The Financial Sector and the Future of the Planet* (Earthscan, 2001).

[341] J. Brill and A. Reder, *Investing from the Heart* (Crown Publishers, 1992).

[342] Ecumenical Diary, 'World Council ends relations with three banks over apartheid' (1982) 34(1) *Ecumenical Review* 82; R.K. Massie Jr., 'Corporate democracy and the legacy of divestment' (1991) 108(22) *Christian Century* 716.

[343] See evidence in European Social Investment Forum (Eurosif), *European SRI Study 2014* (Eurosif, 2015); US SIF (Forum for Sustainable and Responsible Investment), *Report on Sustainable and Responsible Investment Trends in the United States 2012* (US SIF, 2012).

[344] B.J. Richardson, 'Socially responsible investing through voluntary codes' in P.M. Dupuy and J.E. Viñuales (eds), *Harnessing Foreign Investment to Promote Environmental Protection: Incentives and Safeguards* (Cambridge University Press, 2012), 383.

[345] See www.equator-principles.com.

the UN Principles for Responsible Investment (UNPRI)[346] and the UN Environment Programme's Finance Initiative (UNEP-FI).[347] These voluntary initiatives, to which institutions may subscribe on a take-it-or-leave-it basis, furnish both principles for improved performance and procedures for more transparent and accountable financial decisions.[348] As social investors seek to exert influence, they become in effect means of market governance supplementing official regulation. Since many companies rely on bank loans or money from shareholders to grow their business, they may be vulnerable to any demands from investors to improve their environmental and social behaviour.[349] The SRI codes of conduct themselves codify new governance standards that investors and their portfolio companies should follow.

Not all SRI is so enlightened or ambitious. Some cautious social investors consider SRI as financially risky, and they may be disinclined to 'police' the market.[350] Although some mainstream capitalists have embraced SRI, they have done so for less altruistic reasons including to deflect pressure from NGOs or to stave off unwelcome regulation. These investors have also purged SRI's radical overtones and refashioned it into a pragmatic strategy for managing financial risks. This SRI 'industry' – now a more accurate expression than 'movement' – has become preoccupied with the financial returns of SRI rather than its social and environmental returns.[351] Certainly, any thought of remaking capitalism to address the fundamental drivers of unsustainability is off most social investors' agenda. Even the fossil fuels divestment movement, the most radical wing of SRI today,

---

[346] See www.unpri.org.

[347] See www.unepfi.org.

[348] K. Miles, 'Targeting financiers: can voluntary codes of conduct for the investment and financing sectors achieve environmental and sustainability objectives?' in K. Deketelaere, et al. (eds), *Critical Issues in Environmental Taxation*, Volume 5 (Oxford University Press, 2008), 947; O. Perez, 'The new universe of green finance: from self-regulation to multipolar governance' in O. Dilling, M. Herberg, and G. Winter (eds), *Responsible Business. Self-Governance and Law in Transnational Economic Transactions* (Hart Publishing, 2008), 151.

[349] P. Rivoli, 'Making a difference or making a statement? Finance research and socially responsible investment' (2003) 13(3) *Business Ethics Quarterly* 271.

[350] J.M. Leger, 'Socially responsible funds pique interest, but results often have been unimpressive', *Wall Street Journal* 18 November 1982, 33; H. Shapiro, 'Social responsibility mutual funds: down the down staircase' (1974–5) 12 *Business and Society Review* 90.

[351] Although the 'business case' has become the dominant theme of the SRI narrative only since the early 2000s, it was present as early as the mid-1980s: e.g. A.L. Domini and P.D. Kinder, 'Your money or your ethics: a choice investors no longer have to make' (1985) 17 *Environmental Action* 16.

displays some insouciance about the importance of systemic institutional and economic change to stave off environmental devastation.[352]

In very recent years the SRI movement has paid more attention to time and advocated long-term, patient investing.[353] A World Economic Forum report published in 2005 explains why:

> Responsible investment requires an orientation towards strategies that optimize long-term returns, both because this delivers better financial returns over the time profile that interests intended beneficiaries, and because over these periods social and environmental issues become more material and so can be better considered.[354]

One financial group dedicated to this task is the UK-based Marathon Club,[355] formed in 2004 by a cohort of pension funds to draft practical guidance for trustees on long-term investment management.[356] Another convert is the Long-Term Investors Club, established in 2008 by the French state-owned bank Caisse des Dépots et Consignations.[357] With membership open to an array of public and private funds, as well as financial regulators, the Club's participants agree to follow seven key investing principles that include taking greater consideration of ESG (environmental, social, and governance) issues.

Furthermore, some social investors recognise an important spatial dimension to their agenda. For large institutional investors, such as pension plans and insurance companies, the concept of the 'universal owner' explains why they should practice SRI. American academics James Hawley and Andrew Williams contend that institutional investors who invest widely across the market will benefit financially by taking into account the social and environmental externalities of their portfolios.[358] As economy-wide investors, they should 'have no interest in abetting behavior by any

---

[352] But some acknowledge these concerns; e.g. G. Dembicki, 'Fossil fuel divestment's true aim? To remake capitalism', *The Tyee* 20 February 2015, http://thetyee.ca/News/2015/02/20/Fossil-Fuel-Divestment-True-Aim.

[353] Hebb, *No Small Change*; M. Staub-Bisang, *Sustainable Investing for Institutional Investors* (John Wiley and Sons, 2012); E.M. Zarbafi, *Responsible Investment and the Claim of Corporate Change* (Gabler Verlag, 2011).

[354] World Economic Forum (WEF), *Mainstreaming Responsible Investment* (WEF and AccountAbility, 2005), 10.

[355] See www.uss.co.uk/UssInvestments/Responsibleinvestment/marathonclub.

[356] Marathon Club, 'Guidance note for long-term investing', spring 2007, at www.unpri.org/the-marathon-club.

[357] See www.ltic.org.

[358] J. Hawley and A. Williams, *The Rise of Fiduciary Capitalism: How Institutional Investors Can Make Corporate America More Democratic* (University of Pennsylvania Press, 2000).

one company that yields a short-term boost while threatening harm to the economic system as a whole'.[359] Any 'externality' of an individual company may result in a costly 'internality' for a universal investor's global portfolio. A report prepared for the UNPRI Secretariat evaluated the price of environmental damage worldwide to which the companies in a representative investment portfolio contribute, and estimated these in 2008 as US$6.6 trillion, or 11 per cent of global GDP.[360] While the theory of universal ownership thus introduces a vital spatial dimension to the practice of SRI, the theory does not explain how investors can in fact influence companies to prevent such environmental externalities.

While Slow Money shares the foregoing emphasis on long-term investing, its spatial character differs from universal investing. Rather than investing broadly across the entire economy, Slow Money targets specific agricultural, artisanal, or sustainable development projects within communities.[361] In other words, the spatial context is much narrower and more discrete, and involves a more intimate relationship between financiers and beneficiaries. Slow Money strategies include micro-finance and micro-enterprise structures, financial cooperatives, and impact investing into local businesses in rural communities. In recent years some Slow Money has begun to be scaled up because of involvement by large financial intermediaries such as pension plans and banks; their participation has the advantage of tapping into larger pools of financial capital, but may detract from the grassroots character of Slow Money.[362]

These qualities infuse the Slow Money network's manifesto.[363] The first of its six principles – 'we must bring money back down to earth' – means that we should invest money in farms and food. The second principle, which begins 'there is such a thing as money that is too fast', goes on to call for slowing down the velocity of money. The third questions the profit maximisation ethos, calling instead for maximising natural capital. The fourth principle emphasises the value of investment that directly and meaningfully links local communities with financiers. Avoiding speculative

---

[359] S. Davis, J. Lukomnik, and D. Pitt-Watson, *The New Capitalists. How Citizen Investors are Reshaping the Corporate Agenda* (Harvard Business Press, 2006), 18.

[360] Principles of Responsible Investment (PRI) Association and UNEP-FI, *Universal Ownership: Why Externalities Matter to Institutional Investors* (PRI Association and UNEP-FI, 2010), 2.

[361] See https://slowmoney.org.

[362] P. Jayashankar, A. Ashta, and M. Rasmussen, 'Slow money in an age of fiduciary capitalism' (2015) 116 *Ecological Economics* 322, 328.

[363] See www.slowmoney.org/principles.

ventures and favouring the creation of real wealth is the intention of the fifth principle. The last principle advocates giving back to local communities and the environment what people have taken from them.

Governing Slow Money

The SRI movement, along with its Slow Money niche, has blossomed over the past two decades and given hope it can catalyse environmental innovation and sustainability through the economy. As a source of corporate finance and having the opportunity to engage with companies in their capacities as lenders or shareholders, investors may influence enterprises' environmental practices.[364] The influence may even enable a development to be vetoed, as occurred with the Gunns pulp mill in Australia (considered earlier in this chapter). But like its twin, CSR, the voluntary nature of SRI gives investors scope to behave unscrupulously.[365] SRI may even foster complacency that further reform of environmental law or business law is unnecessary.[366] Thus the important question to consider is whether SRI can discipline the market or whether SRI itself should be regulated by governments to make it more effective and influential.

On several indicators SRI appears to be flourishing. As of May 2017, over 90 per cent of global project finance lenders had signed the Equator Principles, while the UNPRI boasted about 1,700 signatories managing over US$60 trillion of assets.[367] And over 31,000 individuals had signed the Slow Money Principles. Such numbers alone, of course, don't reveal how signatories actually implement these commitments. Another indicator comes from market surveys: while recent surveys in North America, Oceania, and Western Europe find the SRI sector capturing from 10 to 50 per cent of these investment markets,[368] these numbers are misleading

---

[364] J. Froud, A. Leaver, and K. Williams, 'New actors in a financialised economy and the remaking of capitalism' (2007) 12(3) *New Political Economy* 339.
[365] D. Vogel, *The Market for Virtue: The Potential and Limits of Corporate Social Responsibility* (Brookings Institution, 2005); M. Haigh, 'Camouflage pay: moral claims in financial products' (2006) 30(3) *Accounting Forum* 267.
[366] M. Haigh and J. Hazelton, 'Financial markets: a tool for social responsibility?' (2004) 52(1) *Journal of Business Ethics* 59; J. Bakan, *The Corporation: The Pathological Pursuit of Profit and Power* (Free Press, 2004); S. Beder, *Global Spin: The Corporate Assault of Environmentalism* (Green Books, 2002).
[367] Data from www.unpri.org. See also The UN Principles for Responsible Investment (PRI), *Annual Report 2016: From Awareness to Impact* (UNPRI, 2016), 8.
[368] Eurosif, *European SRI Study 2016* (Eurosif, 2016); US SIF Foundation, *2016 Report on Sustainable and Responsible Investing Trends* (US SIF Foundation 2016); Responsible

due to their overly inclusive survey criteria, such as counting an entire investment portfolio as 'socially responsible' when only one or two social criteria (e.g. to exclude tobacco stocks) apply. Further, that a financial institution has an SRI policy or signed a code does not necessarily correlate with its influence in the market in shaping the behaviour of companies. A multitude of factors may muzzle social investors' influence, including: the free-rider effect, countervailing market pressures, and imperfect information about companies' environmental performance.[369]

The pathways by which SRI might influence the market primarily comprise: (1) altering the cost of capital of targeted companies, such as by divestment, and thereby creating pressure on management to improve corporate behaviour; (2) advocating change within companies, using shareholder rights or creditor relationships (known as 'corporate engagement'); (3) introducing codes of conduct that prescribe systemic changes; and (4) hurting the social licence to operate, such as by stigmatising investors who fund fossil fuel industries.[370] These methods have generally yet to show their efficacy in the case of the fossil fuels divestment campaign, the most serious push to date to use investor leverage change in the business community.[371]

The reasons require some elaboration. Social investors' capacity to discipline recalcitrant companies by divesting is limited when more numerous, conventional investors enter the market to buy those companies' stock.[372] Furthermore, many investors avoid SRI because they doubt its business case. Although both the CSR and SRI movements emphasise the 'win–win' gains for market actors and wider society, the attractiveness of the win–win gains diminishes when the timing of the gains is misaligned:

Investment Association Australasia (RIAA), *Responsible Investment Benchmark Report 2016 Australia* (RIAA, 2016), 4 and 9.

[369] P. Dauvergne and J. Lister, *Eco-Business: A Big-Brand Takeover of Sustainability* (MIT Press, 2013); J. Confino and J. Drummond, 'Why CSR is not enough to create a sustainable world', *The Guardian* 26 April 2010, at www.theguardian.com; H. Glasbeek, 'The social responsibility movement: the latest in Maginot Lines to save capitalism' (1988) 11 *Dalhousie Law Journal* 363.

[370] B.J. Richardson, 'Are social investors influential?' (2012) 9(2) *European Company Law* 133.

[371] B.J. Richardson, 'Universities unloading on fossil fuels: the legality of divestment' (2016) 10(1) *Carbon and Climate Law Review* 62; A. Ansar, B. Caldecott, and J. Tilbury, *Stranded Assets and the Fossil Fuel Divestment Campaign: What Does Divestment Mean for the Valuation of Fossil Fuel Assets?* (Smith School of Enterprise and the Environment, University of Oxford, 2013).

[372] W. Davidson, D. Worell, and A. El-Jelly, 'Influencing managers to change unpopular corporate behavior through boycotts and divestitures' (1995) 34(2) *Business and Society* 171.

the costs of environmental improvements occur upfront while the promised benefits of superior economic returns appear less certain and long term, which will trouble business managers sensitive to near-term performance pressures. Even if social investors remain a minority in the market, Pietra Rivoli's research predicts that they may alter the cost of capital when the stock is particularly unique (i.e. has few substitutes) or trades in small, restrictive markets.[373] Such conditions do not exist for many economic sectors that have serious environmental impacts, such as the ubiquitous fossil fuels industry. Of tested empirical evidence, the South African boycott had only a modest effect on the economic performance of targeted companies,[374] and the more recent crusade against the tobacco industry has also hardly dented its fortunes.[375] The huge challenges social investors face in curbing ubiquitous fossil fuels dwarfs the foregoing discrete contexts confined to one nation or one economic sector. Banks can sometimes wield decisive influence, especially over small, private enterprises with few financing options, as well as established firms seeking big loans.[376] One example already noted in this chapter was the actions of the ANZ bank against the proposed Gunns pulp mill. Positive or 'impact investing' for specific sustainable development and community-based projects, as extolled by Slow Money, is more promising, but while it rewards leaders it leaves the laggards untouched.[377]

Corporate engagement, the now most prevalent method of SRI, has also had mixed results. The rise of large institutional investors in global financial markets over recent decades had raised hopes that the greater concentration of shareholder power would foster more concerted shareholder oversight of corporate management. The GFC dashed such hopes, with widespread evidence of a passive and insouciant investment culture

---

[373] Rivoli, 'Making a difference or making a statement? Finance research and socially responsible investment'.
[374] S. Teoh, I. Welch, and C.P. Wazzan, 'The effect of socially activist investment policies on the financial markets: evidence from the South African boycott' (1999) 72 *Journal of Business* 35; but compare to R. Kumar, W. Lamb, and R. Wokutch, 'The end of South African sanctions, institutional ownership, and the stock price of boycotted firms' (2002) 41(2) *Business and Society* 133.
[375] S. Chaudhuri, 'Soaring tobacco stocks prompt Calpers to reconsider investment strategy', *Wall Street Journal* 29 April 2016, at www.wsj.com.
[376] Jeucken, *Sustainable Finance and Banking*; P. Thompson, 'Bank lending and the environment: policies and opportunities' (1998) 16(6) *International Journal of Bank Marketing* 243.
[377] A. Bugg-Levine and J. Emerson, *Impact Investing: Transforming How We Make Money While Making a Difference* (Jossey-Bass, 2011).

contributing to the financial meltdown.[378] Institutional shareholders can lapse into being lapdogs rather than watchdogs owing to the costs involved, difficulties of coordinating action with competitors, and potential conflicts of interest.[379] Studies of SRI engagement reveal diverse findings. Research by Proffitt and Spicer,[380] and Lee and Lounsbury,[381] on the ascendance of institutional investors highlights their occasional victories as active shareholders that challenge corporate management on SRI issues. Riskmetrics and others found in 2009 that 'the institutional investor community consists of two distinct parts: a small active minority and a majority of more passive investors'.[382] Choi and Fisch observed that many pension funds maintain a low and non-confrontational profile.[383] Jurisdictional differences also occur in the extent of investor activism: it remains predominantly a North American tradition, while still uncommon in Europe and Oceania.[384] Because corporate engagement takes time and energy, such as meeting with business managers, participating in shareholder meetings, and follow-up correspondence, it usually occurs quite selectively. For instance, the Norwegian Government Pension Fund Global (NGPFG), the world's largest SRI fund, in 2012 held shares in approximately 8,300 companies yet engaged with about 100 firms annually.[385] Research by Megan Bowman on the banking industry and climate change found examples of banks engaging with clients on climate change concerns, which may be

---

[378] European Commission, *Green Paper: Corporate Governance in Financial Institutions and Remuneration Policies* (COM, 2010), 285 final, 8.

[379] J. Parkinson, *Corporate Power and Responsibility: Issues in the Theory of Company Law* (Clarendon Press, 1995), 168–9; B.S. Black, 'Shareholder activism and corporate governance in the United States' in P. Newman (ed), *The New Palgrave Dictionary of Economics and the Law* (Palgrave, 1998), 459; A. Shleifer and R.W. Vishny, 'Value maximization and the acquisition process' (1988) 2(1) *Journal of Economic Perspectives* 7.

[380] W.T. Proffitt, Jr. and A. Spicer, 'Shaping the shareholder activism agenda: institutional investors and global social issues' (2006) 4(2) *Strategic Organization* 165.

[381] P. Lee and M. Lounsbury, 'Domesticating radical rant and rage: an exploration of the consequences of environmental shareholder resolutions on corporate environmental performance' (2011) 50(1) *Business Society* 155.

[382] Riskmetrics Group, *Study on Monitoring and Enforcement Practices in Corporate Governance in the Member States* (Riskmetrics Group, 2009), 15.

[383] S. Choi and J.E. Fish, 'On beyond CalPERS: survey evidence on the developing role of public pension funds in corporate governance' (2008) 61 *Vanderbilt Law Review* 315, 329.

[384] Corporate Monitor, *Responsible Investment: A Benchmark Report on Australia and New Zealand by the Responsible Investment Association Australasia* (Corporate Monitor, 2008), 23.

[385] Interview with Ola Mestad, Chair, Council on Ethics, NGPFG, 12 October 2012.

more feasible for lenders given their often larger financial stake in a single client or project.[386]

Thirdly, the SRI sector may exert influence through its global codes of conduct, of which there are now about 15, including the popular UNPRI and the Equator Principles.[387] They promise to coordinate action among investors on common concerns, facilitate exchange of information, nurture best practices, and build a network for peer pressure to minimise unscrupulous practices. The market-wide scope of some codes is especially valuable in moving SRI beyond its traditional preoccupation with discrete issues, such as tobacco or weapons. The SRI codes span a range of methods and objectives that roughly divide into two models: normative frameworks that enunciate substantive principles and guidance on desirable performance (e.g. as in the Collevecchio Declaration on Financial Institutions);[388] and process standards, enabling the assessment, verification, and communication of performance (e.g. Equator Principles).[389] The codes' biggest impact has been to induce more disclosure of corporate social and environmental performance, such as pursuant to the Carbon Disclosure Project (a process-based mechanism).[390]

The most obvious limitation of these codes from a governance perspective is their *voluntary* character.[391] Considerable literature has scrutinised the motivations and impact of corporate self-regulation, which does not need rehearsing here.[392] One can easily sign up to most codes, as they generally lack threshold performance criteria, and while some require signatories to periodically report on their performance, such reporting commonly occurs without independent verification (except perhaps informally by NGO watchdogs) and any potential sanctions would be limited to delisting the offending signatory (which potentially could hurt its social licence). The lack of stringency thus creates opportunities for deceptive or perfunctory behaviour. The most successful codes – although the

---

[386] M. Bowman, *Banking on Climate Change: How Finance Actors and Transnational Regulatory Regimes are Responding* (Wolters Kluwer, 2015).
[387] Richardson, 'Socially responsible investing through voluntary codes'.
[388] See www.foe.org/camps/intl/declaration.html.
[389] See www.equator-principles.com/index.shtml.
[390] See www.cdp.net.
[391] See Maitland, 'The limits of business self-regulation'.
[392] E.g. Moon, 'The firm as citizen? Social responsibility of business in Australia'; Gibson, *Voluntary Initiatives*; Wood, 'Voluntary environmental codes and sustainability'; R.D. Morgenstern and W.A. Pizer (eds), *Reality Check – The Nature and Performance of Voluntary Environmental Programs in the United States, Europe and Japan* (Routledge, 2007).

empirical evidence of impact defies easy quantification – appear to possess the following attributes: they were drafted through a multi-stakeholder process; they are embedded in a wider institutional regime for ongoing dialogue, education, and monitoring; and they offer participants win–win environmental and financial gains in the near term. These forms of civic or co-regulation, as some commentators describe them, provide frameworks for business and non-profit NGOs to work collaboratively.[393] The UNEP-FI regime perhaps best exemplifies these traits, and it has garnered considerable support from many investors.[394] Research by John Conley and Cynthia Williams on the Equator Principles, which apply to project financing, suggests that they have had generally a positive influence in changing the culture of lenders and they identify the presence of NGO watchdogs as instrumental in making the Principles function well.[395]

Rather than seek influence only through the market, SRI can target regulators to improve the enforcement of existing laws and to adopt new, better laws. The legal measures currently available to stimulate SRI primarily comprise incentive and informational policy instruments that aim to nudge investors to reflect on their social and environmental impacts and to seek out win–win opportunities for themselves and society. Among examples, the UK's Charities (Protection and Social Investment) Act 2016 introduced an explicit authorisation for charities to engage in SRI,[396] and the Charity Commission, which supervises British charities, advises that they can choose investments that do not maximise financial returns if the preferred investments better advance the organisation's philanthropic goals.[397] Another example is the obligation on financial institutions to disclose their policies for SRI. Such reforms have been introduced in several EU states, as well as in Australia and New Zealand, and they target pension funds and other savings institutions.[398] Setting a precedent that

[393] D.J. Vogel, 'Private global business regulation' (2008) 11 *Annual Review of Political Science* 261; N. Gunningham, 'The new collaborative environmental governance: the localization of regulation' (2009) 36(11) *Journal of Law and Society* 145.
[394] UNEP-FI, at www.unepfi.org.
[395] J. Conley and C. Williams, 'Global banks as global sustainability regulators? The Equator Principles' (2011) 33(4) *Law and Policy* 542.
[396] Amending the Charities Act 2011, c. 25, s. 292A-C.
[397] Charity Commission (UK), 'Charities and investment matters: a guide for trustees', Guidance, 1 August 2016, 3.3, at www.gov.uk/government/publications/charities-and-investment-matters-a-guide-for-trustees-cc14/charities-and-investment-matters-a-guide-for-trustees.
[398] E.g. UK's Occupational Pension Schemes (Investment) Regulations, 2005, cl. 2(3)(b)(vi)–(3)(c); Australia's Corporations Act 2001 (Cth), s. 1013D(1)(l); France's Projet de loi sur

some others have emulated, Australian superannuation fund legislation also allows beneficiaries to choose where their contributions are invested, thereby enabling social investors to choose funds aligned with their values.[399] Another reform, adopted in Canada and the United States, requires mutual funds to disclose their shareholding proxy voting policies and voting records.[400] Its purpose is to discourage fund managers from colluding with corporate management, and to improve the quality of corporate governance through an active shareholder proxy process. In practice, the disclosures sometimes have been vague and perfunctory, without illuminating the implementation or impact of investment decisions.[401] Companies themselves incur some environmental reporting obligations in most jurisdictions, and misrepresentations by companies can trigger lawsuits by damaged investors; Volkswagen, for instance, was sued by the NGPFG for misleading investors about its fuel emissions.[402] Economic incentives for SRI have also been introduced. The leading example was the Netherlands' green investment directive,[403] which several studies credit as having greatly boosted funding for local eco-friendly projects,[404] although the scheme, introduced in 1995, was phased out by 2014. Conversely, economic incentives can discourage financing of environmentally unsound projects when financiers may be liable for pollution connected to their companies, as occurred in the United States for some time under the

---

l'épargne salariale, 7 February, 2001, No. 2001-152, Articles 21, 23; and New Zealand's KiwiSaver Act 2006, Public Act 2006, No. 40, s. 205A.

[399] Superannuation Legislation Amendment (Choice of Superannuation Funds) Act, 2005 (Cth).

[400] Securities and Exchange Commission (SEC), *Disclosure of Proxy Voting Policies and Proxy Voting Records by Registered Management Investment Companies* (SEC, 31 January 2003); Canadian Securities Administrators (CSA), *National Instrument 81-106 Investment Fund Continuous Disclosure and Companion Policy 81-106CP* (CSA, 2005).

[401] UK Sustainable Investment and Finance Association (UKSIF), *Focused on the Future: 2000–2010 Celebrating Ten Years of Responsible Investment Disclosure by UK Occupational Pension Funds* (UKSIF, 2010).

[402] 'Volkswagen to be sued by Norway fund over emissions scandal', BBC News 16 May 2016, at www.bbc.com/news.

[403] The scheme was revamped and extended in 2002 and 2005: Regeling groenprojecten buitenland, Staatscourant 1, 2 January 2002, 31; Regeling groenprojecten, Staatscourant 131, 11 July 2005, 13.

[404] Vereniging van Beleggers voor Duurzame Ontwikkeling (VBDO), *Socially Responsible Savings and Investments in the Netherlands: Developments in Volume and Growth of Socially-responsible Savings and Investments in Retail Funds* (VBDO, 2005), 11; KPMG, *Sustainable Profit. An Overview of the Environmental Benefits Generated by the Green Funds Scheme* (KPMG, 2002), 6.

Superfund legislation:[405] its drastic effects in dampening bank lending to the chemical industry contributed to modification of the scheme in 1996 to limit lenders' potential liability.[406]

Many areas of regulation of financial markets that can hinder SRI remain unreformed, and despite the GFC many states remain taciturn to take action. Of great importance, they should align fiduciary and trusts law with SRI.[407] These areas of law provide the broad legal standards governing how trustees, fund managers, and other custodians of investment assets must act on behalf of their beneficiaries. They problematically treat financial institutions such as pension funds as essentially private entities despite their social impacts. Trustees' duties to invest 'prudently' and act in beneficiaries 'best interests' are typically interpreted by courts to exclude consideration of social and environmental 'returns' unless they can offer at least comparable financial benefits.[408] Furthermore, the law does not encourage investment decisions that defer for many decades benefits to beneficiaries (such as climate-friendly investments). Fiduciary and trusts law expects fund beneficiaries to benefit in a direct, quantifiable way, rather than amorphously, for instance as members of the greater public may benefit from cleaner air or purer water.[409]

While prominent CSR critic David Vogel concludes that the 'most effective strategy for reconciling private business goals and public social purposes remains what it has always been, namely effective government regulation',[410] the choice is not simply between regulation and voluntary approaches. Collaborative or partnership forms of governance can combine state and non-state actors in advancing Slow Food and Slow Money, as well as other initiatives considered in this book, such as ecological restoration. The final chapter delves further into these and other possibilities.

---

[405] Comprehensive Environmental Response, Compensation and Liability Act, 1980, Public Law No. 96–510.

[406] M. Greenberg and D. Shaw, 'To lend or not to lend – that should not be the question: the uncertainties of lender liability under CERCLA' (1992) 41(4) *Duke Law Journal* 1211; and, on the 1996 statutory amendments, see: O. de and S. Domis, 'New law finally limits environmental liability' (1996) 161(189) *American Banker* 3.

[407] See B.J. Richardson, *Fiduciary Law and Responsible Investing: In Nature's Trust* (Routledge, 2013).

[408] B.J. Richardson, 'Fiduciary and other legal duties' in K. Baker and J.R. Nofsinger (eds), *Socially Responsible Finance and Investing* (John Wiley and Sons, 2012), 69.

[409] *Cowan v. Scargill*, (1985) 1 Ch. 270, 296.

[410] D. Vogel, 'The limits of the market for virtue', Ethical Corporation 25 August 2005, at www.ethicalcorp.com/content/limits-market-virtue.

Patience and Timing

Slow Food and Slow Money have become focal points for the growing interest in slower lifestyles. With slowness, we hope that consumption of natural resources should decline, people's health will improve, and society will become more attuned to nature's timescales. Slowness gives more time for due diligence, reflection, and learning, as well as enhancing accountability. Fastness, however, dominates human activity especially the economic variety and the law facilitates it.

This chapter's focus on slow and fast time and their environmental consequences, shares a common conceptual basis. It is patience, and its alter ego, impatience. Inter-temporal decisions to use or protect environmental resources reflect how individuals and social institutions, such as the law and markets, exemplify patience or impatience. The proverbial wisdom that 'patience is a virtue', a pronouncement of philosophers and clerics since time immemorial, speaks to the innate human quality for far-sighted behaviour, whether it be saving for a rainy day or studying for years to pursue a desired vocation. Humans are not alone in their disposition for thinking beyond the immediate – birds migrate for the winter and beavers build dams – but our decisions reflect evidence, analysis, and choices rather than genetically pre-programmed instinct. Human patience also has a biological basis, in the lateral pre-frontal cortex of the brain, an area that neurologists believe gives us our capacity for self-control and patience.[411] These qualities undoubtedly have had important implications for the development of human culture. Max Weber's celebrated work examined how the Protestant values of thrift and industriousness were conducive to the development of modern capitalism in northern Europe.[412] Today, patience informs the spread of global slow movements in which patience brings benefits not only to its practitioners but also to the natural world.

But, as with the proverbial forewarning that 'for every virtue there is a vice', so too patience has another side. Just as the pre-fontal cortex controls impatient behaviour, other neural substrates respond preferentially to immediate rewards and less so to the prospect of future benefits.[413] Indeed, impatience is, at least initially, the stronger twin in human development, as the impulsive behaviour of many toddlers and adolescents

---

[411] J.P. Mitchell, 'Medial prefrontal cortex predicts intertemporal choice' (2011) 23(4) *Journal of Cognitive Neuroscience* 857.

[412] M. Weber, *The Protestant Ethic and the Spirit of Capitalism* (Allen and Unwin, 1930).

[413] S.M. McClure, et al., 'Separate neural systems value immediate and delayed monetary rewards' (2004) 306 *Science* 503.

shows. The famous marshmallow test predicts quite well which youngsters will evolve into more patient adults. Becoming future-oriented and investing resources in activities whose benefits may not arise for some time is an acquired skill. This dyadic quality to our biological makeup fascinates researchers such as behavioural economists interested in the human tendency to discount future benefits (i.e. humans prefer a benefit that arrives sooner rather than later).[414] Inter-temporal choices frustrate individuals when the timing of costs and benefits are not aligned, especially when the costs arise before the benefits.

Impatience affects economic and environmental decision-making as much as its benign twin can. In the business world, it generates myopic and busy behaviours, as people seek instant profits. This has adverse implications for long-run investment in real wealth creation. For the environment, impatience results in long-term costs of climate change, biodiversity extinctions, and other ecological functions and services becoming undervalued and over-utilised. Legislative protection is watered down, such as by enabling important economic projects to be fast tracked for approval.

Because the interplay between our patient and impatient tendencies depends heavily on their context, cultural norms and systems such as the law can influence individuals' behavioural choices. Impatience does not have to prevail over patience, and if patience can be set in train, it should shape a cycle of self-improving behaviour in individuals and institutions. Conversely, impatience can generate its own self-reinforcing cycle once it gets going, such as when we judge corporate heads and fund managers on short-term performance metrics. Chapter 2 explored in more detail how the law can reinforce or counteract human behavioural tendencies.

Presently, impatience is the dominant sibling in our economic and environmental systems, in which we value short-term goals and quick results more highly than long-term benefits. The globalisation of economic markets, especially in the financial sector, has unshackled impatience, spurring over-trading and underinvestment. Similarly, the food economy, powered by petrochemicals and factory farms, pursues ever-faster growth, but without a serious commitment to sustaining the environment on which our food depends. The impatience of modern life fosters a discontinuous sense of time, in which awareness of the interrelationships between the past, present, and future becomes fragmented and downplayed. Time

---

[414] E.g. R.H. Thaler and H.M. Shefrin, 'An economic theory of self-control' (1981) 89(2) *Journal of Political Economy* 392.

becomes lived for the moment, with lowered recognition of how the past shapes the present or how the future emerges from the present.

Patience alone, however, is an insufficient yardstick for environmental behaviour because it does not specify *when* to act, and sometimes we must act quickly to resolve urgent problems. Patience must thus be linked to choosing the appropriate *timing*: to remove pollutants before they cross dangerous thresholds, to harvest natural resources when they can be safely renewed and to restore damaged ecologies before they are irretrievably lost. To get the timing right, humankind must be in a relationship with the natural world that respects its cues and rhythms. As a relational concept, timing is determined by the dynamic interactions within ecological systems in which each element has its own time flows. Patience will of course help to understand these temporalities, but getting the timing right requires more. When decisions must be done quickly, such as to phase out greenhouse gas emissions now, we are not aligning ourselves with a fast culture but rather putting the brakes on it in order to build a slower society for the long term.

We must modernise governance of the economy to inculcate a more patient, appropriately timed approach to investing, farming, and other environmentally relevant activities. It requires not only environmental laws that reframe the temporal horizons of the economy, but also parallel standards embedded within economic laws such as corporate legislation to ensure that business actors operate without conflicting legal expectations. Such standards could begin with a basic duty on companies, as well as their financiers, to be managed for their long-term success.[415] Ensuring implementation of the obligation would require measurable performance criteria, and a cognate duty of subject actors to report periodically on their environmental impacts and performance. Within environmental law, the doctrine of adaptive management dovetails with the slow agenda through the careful testing of management options over sufficient years in order to determine the best solution. These and other potential legal reforms for aligning humankind with the ecological timescape are explored in the final chapter.

---

[415] N. Grossman, 'Turning a short-term fling into a long-term commitment: board duties in a new era' (2010) 43 *University of Michigan Journal of Law Reform* 905.

6

Telling the Time

On Borrowed Time

How can we tell nature's time better? People once took their cues directly from nature's temporalities about where to hunt or gather, and when to migrate or settle. Their sheer survival depended on knowing its biorhythms. While some ancestors precipitated fateful ecological changes, recent generations have exponentially increased them. While we clearly cannot return to the small-band, hunter–gatherer lifestyles that characterised most of human history, neither can we continue with our profligate lifestyles that plunder the planet beyond its life-supporting capacity. With the advent of more precise ways to calculate intervals of time, such as clocks and calendars, and their conscription into disciplining social life through deadlines, schedules, and so on, time in human affairs has not only become increasingly divorced from nature but the means of intensifying its exploitation. The 'efficiency' and speed with which natural resources are looted, and the discounted value of future environmental benefits, exemplify our manipulation of time. This social time trifurcates the past, present, and future, obscuring their connections, and time itself is increasingly opaque to a society immersed in the moment. Having unleashed new temporalities of change in nature, we imperil our own well-being and that of the rest of nature. While scientific knowledge has become immensely important to tell tells nature's time quite well, such as through the work of climatologists or biologists, in the popular consciousness time is often acknowledged simply as a motivating factor – that we live on 'borrowed time' or 'time is running out' to forestall the upheavals of the Anthropocene.

The prospect of a global crisis has thus inspired some to depict our temporal proximity to catastrophe as a spur for action. Atomic scientists invented the Doomsday Clock in 1947 to signify the risk of global nuclear war, with the precariousness represented by the clock hand's nearness to midnight. During the onset of the Cold War, the clock was set at 7 minutes to disaster, and it has since oscillated closer to or away from midnight to reflect our anxiety about annihilation (as well as other global risks such as climate change, now factored into the clock). At the time of writing this part of the book, in early 2017, it is perched at just 2 and a half minutes from doomsday.[1] The fear of climate change itself has provoked further depictions of urgency, with Bill McKibben recently twittering that 'Trump is robbing us of the time we have left to fight climate change – time we will never get back'.[2] A tracking clock called the 'One Hundred Months'.[3] conveys this sense of urgency from a final countdown to irreparable tipping points of runaway global warming if we do not unload fossil fuels within the next 100 months (calculated from August 2008).[4] Research predicts that individuals will more likely take seriously a distant event when a firm deadline must be met, as it makes the event seem closer.[5] The '2 Degrees Clock' is another timekeeper of climate change, calibrated on the estimated available time to avoid crossing this critical warming threshold.[6] Among other examples, the World Population Clock raises awareness of the exponential surge in human numbers, with the demographic data showing changes from antiquity to the present.[7] The clock continually updates in real time on the Internet to show fluctuations in births and deaths. Conversely, some have devised 'species extinction clocks' to track the demise of biodiversity under the human onslaught.[8]

Instead of the hourglass of looming calamity, many environmentalists concentrate on raising awareness of the Earth's long timescales as a motivation for action. One effort is the Tutzing Time Ecology project, a German initiative in the 1990s that sought to demonstrate the relevance of time to environmental practice from the everyday to political domains. The term 'time ecology' was coined by the project's leaders, Martin Held and Karlheinz Geissler, to mean the multiple and mutual implications of ecology and time for investigation and discussion. Through conferences and public debate, the project aimed 'to explore to what extent both the control of time and the economic approach to time – the commodification

---

[1] Bulletin of the Atomic Scientists, at http://thebulletin.org/science-and-security-board.
[2] B. McKibben, 'Trump is robbing us of the time we have left to fight climate change – time we will never get back', 20 April 2017, https://twitter.com/billmckibben.
[3] See www.onehundredmonths.org.
[4] A. Simms, 'The final countdown', *The Guardian* 1 August 2008, at www.theguardian.com.
[5] C. Hammond, *Time Warped: Unlocking the Mysteries of Time Perception* (House of Anansi Press, 2012), 285.
[6] See www.countdown2degrees.com.
[7] See www.worldometers.info/world-population.
[8] E.g. http://corchard.com.au/index.php/extinction-clock.

of time and its association with money, the speeding up of processes, ... and the cultural affirmation of the non-stop principle – are implicated' in unsustainable development.[9] By fostering academic research and policy reform, the Tutzing initiative sought a more ecologically relevant tempo for modern life.[10]

Similarly, the Long Now Foundation aims to 'creatively foster long-term thinking and responsibility in the framework of the next 10,000 years'.[11] As founding member Stewart Brand writes: 'civilization is revving itself into a pathologically short attention span . . . coming from the acceleration of technology, the short-horizon perspective of market-driven economics, the next-election perspective of democracies, or the distractions of personal multi-tasking'.[12] Established in 1996, the Foundation oversees diverse projects for fostering long-term prescience and social responsibility, including a public 'salon' for participants to brainstorm ideas. One illustration of its work is the erection of a series of monumental, multi-millennial clocks designed to tick for 10,000 years and help civilisation view itself as being on a longer journey; the first such clock was chiselled into a Texan mountain. Another initiative is Long Bets, began in 2003 as a forum where bets on matters of societal or scientific importance are cast (e.g. about website usage or stock market performance). Gamblers do not retain the winnings, which become philanthropic gifts invested into a special-purpose endowment portfolio called the Farsight Fund.[13] The most explicit environmental initiative of the Foundation is 'Revive and Restore'; harnessing genomic technology, this project seeks to recreate extinct creatures, such as the passenger pigeon, the quagga, and the dodo, for return to the wild.[14]

Despite the insights of natural science in showing our embedded dependence upon the natural world, many people seem indifferent to the alarm bells of the ecological time bomb. The annual World Values Survey,[15] which provides intriguing snapshots of popular attitudes across numerous countries, shows increasingly pro-environmental values and behaviours worldwide. But the surveys also show some 'critical gaps between what

[9] B. Adam, et al., 'Time for the environment: the Tutzing time ecology project' (1997) 6 *Time Society* 73–4.
[10] Ibid, 81–2.
[11] Long Now Foundation, at http://longnow.org.
[12] Ibid.
[13] Long Bets, at http://longbets.org/about.
[14] Revive and Restore, at http://reviverestore.org.
[15] See www.worldvaluessurvey.org/indexhtml.

people say and do'.[16] It is not just that people forget distant environmental history; much of the bad news unfolds in our midst. Nearly each successive year, declare the tabloids, is the hottest on record or some other grim threshold is breached; Australia's famed Great Barrier Reef suffered unprecedented bleaching in 2016, with 22 per cent of its corals reportedly now dead; global populations of migratory shorebirds are in free fall due to habitat destruction; and millions of tonnes of plastic debris litter the oceans, among the daily barrage of news.[17] As I finish this book, the latest scientific research estimates that in merely the past two decades the world has lost 10 per cent of its wilderness,[18] and it has shed 58 per cent of its wildlife population since 1970.[19] Such staggering losses suggest that the Anthropocene heralds even greater calamity than first surmised. The ecological crisis is not just a 'management' failure, but reflects a deeper malaise in humankind's mentality. Philosopher Timothy Morton describes it as 'a crisis for our philosophical habits of thought, confronting us with a problem that seems to defy not only our control but also our understanding'.[20] Usually only those threats that demonstrably interfere with our present well-being solicit earnest attention, such as contaminated food or our neighbour's unsightly development, while only a small minority of the most ardent activists will chain themselves to a bulldozer or take other brazen actions in defence of an old-growth forest, whales, or other ecological treasures far removed from human routines.

To comprehend and lessen time-accelerating ecological damage, environmental stewards must not only think outside their local, spatial context but also put the problems they deal with in their full temporal context. Nature is about *change*, and to tell nature's time and thereby act with the appropriate *timing*, society must understand the vast timescales and fluctuating rhythms of its ecological processes especially over deep time.

---

[16] A.A. Leiserowitz, R.W. Kates, and T.M. Parris, 'Do global attitudes and surveys support sustainable development?' (2005) 47(9) *Environment* 22, 33.

[17] D. Carrington, '2015 smashes record for hottest year, final figures confirm', *The Guardian* 21 January 2016, at www.theguardian.com; A. Stewart, 'Australian migratory bird numbers in freefall due to destruction of east Asia tidal flats: report', *ABC News* 15 January 2015, at www.abc.net.au/news; C. Samoray, 'Ocean's plastics offer a floating fortress to a mess of microbes', *Science News* 9 February 2016, at www.sciencenews.org; M. Slezak, 'The Great Barrier Reef: a catastrophe laid bare', *The Guardian* 7 June 2016, at www.theguardian.com.

[18] J.E.M. Watson, et al., 'Catastrophic declines in wilderness areas undermine global environment targets' (2016) 26 *Current Biology*, at http://dx.doi.org/10.1016/j.cub.2016.08.049.

[19] R. Morelli, 'World wildlife "falls by 58% in 40 years"', *The Guardian* 27 October 2016, at www.theguardian.com.

[20] T. Morton, *Hyperobjects: Philosophy and Ecology after the End of the World* (University of Minnesota Press, 2013), abstract.

The idea of nature being changeable, and not merely static, was observed by Aristotle, whose writings discussed the concept of nature (*phusis*) extensively.[21] In his 2013 *Encyclopedia of Environmental Change*, editor John Matthews offers over 1,000 pages of entries that reveal the astonishing changeability of nature, especially when stretched over Earth's history.[22] Some 200 million years ago, at the end of the Permian, a mass extinction calamity obliterated 70 per cent of terrestrial vertebrate species and 95 per cent of marine life. Much environmental change has also ensued since *Homo sapiens* came on the scene, from the disappearance of megafauna, likely at human hands, to recent toxic pollution and massive deforestation for which we certainly are to blame. With the Anthropocene, humankind's ascendancy portends another planet-wide mass extinction. But viewing humankind as part of nature doesn't excuse trashing it if that is our evolved cultural disposition. What is natural is not necessarily ethical: we cannot derive morals from facts, or 'ought' from 'is'. Humankind has exceptional cognitive insight and moral choice, which behoves us to limit anthropogenic change to within parameters that allow other life forms and ecological systems to adapt or recover, as well as for our own long-term welfare.

A more ethical and productive relationship with the rest of the natural world necessitates moving beyond merely 'sustaining' or 'conserving' Earth; we must also *regenerate* and *promote* its vitality. The ethos of sustainable development that ostensibly dominates environmental law has been a measured mutation rather than a maelstrom of change, too often tamed into perfunctory business-as-usual to disguise an anthropocentric mission. Because life-giving Earth restricts and influences human beings in many complex ways we don't understand, society cannot ever hope to master nature. But conversely, the deep ecology ethos, to let nature be, untouched and wild, seems naïve and ignores nature's relentless flux, in which humankind participates. The conservation agenda powered the ascendancy of many environmental laws worldwide, but conservation of wild nature, if it assumes a world without people, is not enough. Similarly, the 'rewilding' agenda, to the extent that it erases human history and bifurcates nature and culture, may be naïve and inappropriate.[23] Moving beyond these ideals, environmental law must embrace restoration and

---

[21] Aristotle, *Physics, Books I-II*, trans. by W. Charlton (Clarendon Press, 1992), book 2.1, 192b, 20-3.
[22] J.A. Matthews, *Encyclopedia of Environmental Change* (SAGE, 2013).
[23] D. Jørgensen, 'Rethinking rewilding' (2015) 65 *Geoforum* 482.

adaptation, with the aim to heal losses, help nature thrive, and promote human reconciliation with it. We must abandon the creed of a pristine and static natural world to protect and sustain in favour of understanding nature's dynamism, in which we participate. Thus in addition to scientific knowledge about nature's time, our narratives and interpretations of the natural world forged from our embeddedness within it, provide direction in telling nature's time and acting accordingly.[24] It is a natural world which influences us, but upon which we also have some influence.

Embracing this priority begins with awareness of Earth's deep time. Environmental history should inform our lives as more than just a repository of 'lessons' about the past, such as mistakes that we should recall lest we repeat them. Learning from our mistakes certainly matters, but it is not enough for telling nature's time. Rather, the past should matter for understanding the changing relationship between people and their environment over time, a relationship mediated by culture, including environmental law, as well as the agency of nature itself in this history, such as climate change or species' evolution, as well as nature's forces of decay and entropy. From this vantage, environmental history can help us to interpret nature's vicissitudes, such as shifts in vegetation patterns or animal populations, as well as their responses to anthropogenic influences. Such knowledge can help us to restore degraded places, provide guidance on their former composition and condition, and offer insights into how they have responded to human activity. When restored, Earth will reacquire qualities that make sustaining it more worthwhile. Degraded, shifted baselines should not serve as the benchmark against which we measure progress towards sustainability. Just as importantly, participation in restoration will enhance society's ecological literacy, thereby enabling people to become more attuned to nature's temporal rhythms. Restoration is not always viable, for reasons of social opposition and financial cost,[25] and it can generate unease as just another form of human mastery of nature.[26] These give reasons to ensure that restoration follows well-conceived policies.

Greater respect for the past in turn prepares us for the future. In the *Gabčíkovo-Nagimaros* case, the International Court of Justice (ICJ) observed

---

[24] See F. Clingerman, et al. (eds), *Interpreting Nature: The Emerging Field of Environmental Hermeneutic* (Fordham University Press, 2015).

[25] B.J. Richardson and T. Lefroy, 'Restoration dialogues: improving the governance of ecological restoration' (2016) 24(5) *Restoration Ecology* 668; P. Woodworth, 'What price ecological restoration?' *Scientist Magazine* 1 April 2006, at www.the-scientist.com.

[26] E. Katz, 'The big lie: human restoration of nature' (1992) 12 *Research in Philosophy and Nature* 93; R. Elliot, 'Faking nature' (1982) 25 *Inquiry* 81.

that 'in the field of environmental protection, vigilance and prevention are required on account of the often irreversible character of damage to the environment and of the limitations inherent in the very mechanism of reparation of this type of damage'.[27] To understand how the climate might change or species evolve, knowing their histories can often provide the best clues to guide our own environmental behaviour. Restoration also has a future tense, because ecological improvements should last indefinitely, and healthier, restored ecosystems should cope better with impending adversity. Replanted forests that sequester carbon can help moderate global warming, as well as improve habitat for biodiversity to flourish, for instance.[28] Likewise, restored wetlands cleanse water, moderate flood events, and enhance fish and waterfowl populations. With such improvements, restoration may also help mitigate the continuing impacts of any grandfathered developments too politically difficult to close immediately. The relicensing of projects may similarly benefit from restoration as a precondition to their continuation, especially for projects with a problematic record. In other words, restoration in various guises underpins robust environmental governance for the future. It is not an alternative to sustainability, but its necessary twin.

A slower tempo must also command our attention to enable the better timing of environmental decisions, some of which will nurture long-term benefits while others will intervene relatively more quickly to forestall urgent threats. This agenda poses a multi-dimensional challenge, from financial markets to food production, necessitating a diversity of laws and social practices tailored to different settings in which hastiness has precipitated undesirable consequences. Already, movements for Slow Food and Slow Money inspire many to live less hurriedly and with a lighter footprint, although they remain far from mainstream practices. The pace of economic development and the rapidity of resource use, especially now in emerging economies, continue to overwhelm nature's capacity to renew itself. In addition to regulations and policies designed to put the brakes on hurriedness, which we'll come to later in this chapter, restoration itself can slow development while past mistakes are undone before new activities commence. Previous damage often reflects haste, such as forests logged before they fully regenerate or development fast-tracked without

---

[27] *Gabčíkovo-Nagymaros Project (Hungary/Slovakia)*, [1997] ICJ Reports 7, 78, para. 140.
[28] On the benefits of restoration, see F.A. Comin, *Ecological Restoration: A Global Challenge* (Cambridge University Press, 2010); M. Hall, *Earth Repair: A Transatlantic History of Environmental Restoration* (University of Virginia Press, 2005).

environmental due diligence. Paying off our ecological debt should precede further borrowing of ecological capital.

Restoration, *rallentare*, adaptive management, and other actions to align society with nature's timescape require governance from national legislation to international treaties, as well as collaboration with non-state mechanisms. This book has unveiled how legal acts and omissions exacerbate poor environmental behaviour. In this chapter we consider how the law can redeem itself. Proposals for serious environmental law reform range from including environmental goals in national constitutions[29] to rewriting lodestar legislation and global treaties with a new vision.[30] The depth and range of ideas debated by scholars and policy makers is too vast to canvass intelligently here, and thus the following comments focus on the broad approach and some examples especially relevant to the temporalities of environmental governance.

Changing the law does not begin with abstract, desktop designs but rather understanding the law's relationships to social practices and their own role in leveraging change. Earlier in this book, the law's potential to civilise human behaviour was probed, and many countries show evidence of change, including improved animal welfare (in some contexts), equal rights for many women, and reduced discrimination against gays. Law directs individuals to behave in ways they otherwise would not if left to their own devices. But the law, especially in the environmental field, can be parasitic to its social and economic context, and therefore constrained if it collides with deeply entrenched habits. That the evolutionary triumph of *Homo sapiens* has reached a cul-de-sac of ecological ruin should remind us that cultural advances don't inevitably have benign outcomes. Formulating social evolution as akin to evolutionary biology overlooks that natural selection is non-teleological, without any specific purpose, and social evolution cannot be assumed to have any specific good direction. With the Enlightenment, faith in humankind's moral progress grew in Western societies.[31] That ebullience was shattered by the two World Wars and the Holocaust, but then renewed with growing affluence and the spread of democratic values in the latter decades of the twentieth century. The direction and impact of cultural change, including through law,

---

[29] E.g. L. Kotze, *Global Environmental Constitutionalism in the Anthropocene* (Hart Publishing, 2016); D.R. Boyd, *The Environmental Rights Revolution: A Global Study of Constitutions, Human Rights, and the Environment* (University of British Columbia Press, 2012).

[30] E.g. R. Fowler, et al., *The Next Generation of Australia's Environmental Laws* (Australian Panel of Experts of Environmental Law, 2015),

[31] H. Spencer, *Essays: Scientific, Political, and Speculative* (Appleton, 1891), volume I.

remains fiercely debated; Steven Pinker's *The Better Angels* contends that people have become less violent,[32] while John Gray's *The Silence Animals* excoriates 'civilisation' as a vehicle for barbarism, such as ethnic cleansing.[33] Recent signs of reversal include the war on terror, corruption, millions of unwanted refugees, Donald Trump, and global environmental decline itself.

Scientific knowledge is one of our best resources for telling nature's time. Without it, humankind would be crippled in its capacity to curb climate change or to save endangered species. Of course, science is not perfect, being prone to the biases of its researchers and sometimes lacking answers to environmental problems. In such cases, the precautionary principle, a foundational principle of environmental law worldwide, recognises the need to act cautiously to avoid serious environmental damage.[34] Scientific data is also limited in its capacity to spur changes in social values and behaviour, for which practices that stimulate people's imagination and emotions are needed. Hence, other sources of knowledge, from Indigenous traditional wisdom to new social movements, must be considered to enrich our insights into nature's time. While we cannot escape how human cognition and culture mediate our knowledge of nature's timescales, the foregoing will give humankind and the planet better prospects than current practices.

Changing environmental attitudes and practices thus requires institutional reforms to engage communities as active participants, and to motivate people to behave in ways they might not if left to their own devices. Thomas Heberlein's insightful book, *Navigating Environmental Attitudes*, reprimands environmental managers who limit their stakeholder engagement to information and education, which he argues do little to improve behaviour.[35] Heberlein shows that informing people about environmental risks, such as building their homes on floodplains, rarely induces the desired results, because social attitudinal shifts take decades and attitudes 'ebb and flow in ways we cannot predict or control'.[36] Instead, Heberlein advocates 'structural fixes' that alter the structure or context of human decisions. When law reformers work with social and economic movements, the odds of success will likely similarly improve. This book has already identified some encouraging initiatives

---

[32] S. Pinker, *The Better Angels of Our Nature: Why Violence Has Declined* (Viking Books, 2011); see also M. Ridley, *The Rational Optimist: How Prosperity Evolves* (Fourth Estate, 2010).
[33] J. Gray, *The Silence of Animals: On Progress and Other Modern Myths* (Allen Lane, 2013).
[34] J. Peel, *The Precautionary Principle in Practice* (Federation Press, 2005).
[35] T. Heberlein, *Navigating Environmental Attitudes* (Oxford University Press, 2012).
[36] Ibid, 80.

by non-state actors, including restoration projects, environmental performance codes, and public education, as well as local and transnational networks of collaboration. Indigenous peoples undertaking ecological restoration, farmers growing slow food, and financiers investing slowly help people to tell nature's time. Another global phenomenon is the fossil fuels divestment movement, a diverse entourage that includes community activists, universities, and even some mainstream financiers, collaborating to shun oil and coal companies.[37] These gestures embody governance, contributing new behavioural norms and influencing social practices. But despite their recent uptake, they generally remain on the margins of social convention.

With further growth, the contribution of non-state groups will help diffuse the *diaspora* of environmental norms throughout society. Environmental law must spread beyond discrete controls to become a 'law of the environment' in which its oeuvre is inculcated into the very fabric of all economic and social life that becomes more sensitive to nature's timescape. The old belief that environmental standards work best when quarantined in separate, special regulation is untenable. Having separate silos of governance results in confusing messages, in which the market extols the virtues of individual choice and economic development while environmental legislation speaks of restraint. Under the diaspora, by contrast, private property rights would include environmental standards; likewise, business law would invoke corporate environmental responsibility as one of its fundamental precepts. But not every aspiration will be attainable, for now. Revolutionary upheaval, such as abolishing private enterprise or banning all fossil fuels overnight would have little legal or political traction. We need to move beyond business-as-usual, but also acknowledge that the urgency of action requires some pragmatism, because capitalism and state sovereignty are not going to disappear as soon as some would wish.[38]

The following pages continue this story through three types of action: listening to nature, adjudicating for nature, and living with nature. Telling nature's time begins with listening to its signals to understand ecological conditions and changes. Listening will help determine when restoration of any damage is necessary, for instance. Adjudicating for nature concerns the conflicts over environmental issues, and how nature can have a voice

---

[37] E. Howard, 'The rise and rise of the fossil fuel divestment movement', *The Guardian* 19 May 2015, at www.theguardian.com.
[38] F. Capra and U. Mattei, *The Ecology of Law: Toward a Legal System in Tune with Nature and Community* (Berrett-Koehler Publishers, 2015).

in this social wrangling. In places dominated by human activity, we must live with nature and govern to reduce future impacts and restore past ones. Listening, adjudicating, and living are the continuum upon which governance for telling nature's time must be staged.

Listening to Nature

To 'listen' means to observe, interpret and, ultimately, act accordingly. To understand nature's time obliges us to pay more attention to our natural surroundings, including their biodiversity, climate, cleanliness, and so on, as well as their changes over both long and short periods. Listening requires investment in environmental research to decipher nature's temporalities, research their history, and monitor future shifts. The knowledge gaps to address range from the big picture, such as global climatic trends, where some progress has already occurred, to the micro-level, such as local biodiversity. More knowledge will help counter the scourge of shifting baselines, enable identification of cumulative environmental decline, and inform realistic benchmarks to measure the efficacy of new environmental laws. Listening also helps design appropriate adaptation responses to environmental impacts that cannot be reversed, such as the climate change already with us.[39] The science–policy interface must improve to ensure that the acquisition of knowledge disseminates beyond academia and informs environmental standards and rules. Such dissemination includes public dialogue, because scientific knowledge is a resource for making decisions rather than the decisions themselves: research methods may be questioned or the interpretation of results disputed, in addition to societal disagreements about the ultimate significance of environmental knowledge and its implications for human behaviour. Furthermore, this greater knowledge must inform economic analyses of environmental problems and choices, so that the assessment of costs and benefits respects ecological values over long timescales.

Listening to nature will help determine when restoration is biologically feasible, a fundamental issue warranting some elaboration here. Determining feasibility hinges closely on the historic reference point for restoration, on which opinions vary widely. Tony Pitcher and Daniel Pauly identify environmental conditions before large-scale agriculture as the

---

[39] J.M. Verschuuren (ed), *Research Handbook on Climate Change Adaptation Law* (Edward Elgar Publishing, 2013).

ideal baseline,[40] while John Pinnegar and Georg Engelhard recommend an even earlier time, since subsistence and artisanal resource uses have had detrimental environmental effects.[41] Conversely, Eric Higgs contends 'there is no original condition for an ecosystem in any meaningful sense; one cannot fix a specific point in time'.[42] American science journalist Emma Marris agrees.[43] Further difficulties in choosing a baseline include accounting for the complexity of background change in ecosystems over time; understanding the actual biological composition of past ecosystems; and accommodating future changes, especially global warming.[44]

As we listen to nature it may become apparent that restoration is biologically impossible, such as when key species have perished or ecosystems irreparably altered – a phenomenon called 'hysteresis'. The 'novel ecosystems' theory advanced by Richard Hobbs and others builds on this insight, suggesting that some degraded places have irreversibly shifted to a different regime.[45] To restore them has been analogised as trying to put the toothpaste back into the tube.[46] Evidence of hysteresis abounds. Australian and Canadian coastal waters invaded by sea urchins have lost their kelp forests, leaving barren wastelands struggling to recover even after removal of the urchins.[47] In Tasmania's World Heritage-listed wilderness, devastating fires in early 2016 incinerated unique subalpine flora, including pencil pines and king billy pines, some over 1,000 years old, and ecologists predict

---

[40] T. Pitcher, 'Fisheries managed to rebuild ecosystems? Reconstructing the past to salvage the future' (2001) 11(2) *Ecological Applications* 601; D. Pauly, 'Anecdotes and the shifting baseline syndrome of fisheries' (1995) 10(10) *Cell* 430.
[41] J. Pinnegar and G. Engelhard, 'The "shifting baseline" phenomenon: a global perspective' (2008) 18(1) *Reviews in Fish Biology and Fisheries* 1.
[42] E. Higgs, *Nature by Design* (MIT Press, 2003), 38.
[43] E. Marris, *Rambunctious Garden: Saving Nature in a Post-Wild World* (Bloomsbury, 2013).
[44] R. Craig, 'Perceiving change and knowing nature: shifting baselines and nature's resiliency' in K. Hirokawa (ed), *Environmental Law and Contrasting Ideas of Nature: A Constructivist Approach* (Cambridge University Press, 2013), 1, 25; P.S. Alagona, J. Sandlos, and Y.F. Wiersma, 'Past imperfect: using historical ecology and baseline data for conservation and restoration projects in North America' (2012) 9(1) *Environmental Philosophy* 49–50.
[45] L.M. Hallett, et al., 'Towards a conceptual framework for novel ecosystems' in R.J. Hobbs, E. Higgs, and C. Hall (eds), *Novel Ecosystems: Intervening in the New Ecological World Order* (Wiley-Blackwell, 2013), 18. For a contrary view, see C. Murcia, et al., 'A critique of the "novel ecosystem" concept' (2014) 29 *Trends in Ecology and Evolution* 548.
[46] J. Mascaro, 'Origins of the novel ecosystems concept', in R.J. Hobbs, E. Higgs, and C. Hall (eds), *Novel Ecosystems: Intervening in the New Ecological Order* (Wiley-Blackwell, 2013), 45, 51.
[47] K. Filbee-Dexter and R.E. Scheibling, 'Sea urchin barrens as alternative stable states of collapsed kelp ecosystems' (2014) 495 *Marine Ecology Progress Series* 1.

they will never recover when virulent eucalypts invade the vacant niche.[48] Novel ecosystems might thus suit other types of management that focus on the functional benefits that these ecosystems yield, such as aesthetic qualities, pollination, clean water, and food production.[49] Thus, we might accept a restored wetland despite differences in its appearance, location, and biodiversity if it replicates most of the original ecological services.[50]

The foregoing debate includes humanity's place in nature, and specifically what anthropogenic environmental changes to condone or reverse. Returning Earth to an unimpaired, pre-human epoch is surely unrealistic for most of the planet. Consider New Zealand, having lost half its avifauna: one might ask, should the restoration clock be set to when Europeans colonised, in the early 1800s, or even earlier, before the first Polynesians came, around 1200 AD?[51] In fact, unless we can reverse extinction both baselines seem fanciful. In the more intensively and longer occupied regions, such as East Asia and Western Europe, these challenges seem daunting. Still, in some of the most densely parts of Europe one can find creative semi-rewilding projects, such as in the Oostvaardersplassen nature reserve in Holland. Less inhabited places are not free of challenges, as even seemingly 'wild' landscapes may have been socialised by indigenous peoples. Some 50,000 years of indigenous stewardship, particularly through fire, fundamentally altered the vegetation and biodiversity patterns of Australia.[52] Thus, a return to some historical condition (e.g. pre-human/pre-Industrial) or the rehabilitation of degraded landscapes to novel but functional ecosystems represent the furthest contrasts along a spectrum of options that policy-makers might aspire to achieve.

Looking to the future, we must also monitor climate change and its implications for restoration. Some experts believe that, because of global warming, 'it may be costly and futile to attempt to maintain a particular

[48] M. Slezak, 'Tasmanian bushfires "worst crisis in decades" for world heritage forests', *The Guardian* 22 January 2016, at www.theguardian.com.
[49] R. Costanza, et al., 'The value of the world's ecosystem services and natural capital' (1996) 387 *Nature* 253; N. Shackelford, et al., 'Primed for change: developing ecological restoration for the 21st century' (2013) 21 *Restoration Ecology* 297.
[50] C.C. Holling, F. Berkes, and C. Folke, 'Science, sustainability and resource management' in F. Berkes, C. Folke, and J. Colding (eds), *Linking Social and Ecological Systems: Management Practices and Social Mechanisms for Building Resilience* (Cambridge University Press, 1998), 342, 354.
[51] E. Pawson and T. Brooking, *Environmental Histories of New Zealand* (Oxford University Press, 2002).
[52] B. Gammage, *The Biggest Estate on Earth: How Aborigines Made Australia* (Allen and Unwin, 2011).

ecosystem configuration or species in a particular location'.[53] Many restoration ecologists acknowledge such concerns,[54] but believe that 'restoration and related land-management projects offer potential tools for mitigating some of the effects of global change on ecosystems'.[55] Replanted forests may help sequester carbon dioxide and create habitat corridors that assist species to migrate to more hospitable environments. These possibilities informed the Society for Ecological Restoration's (SER) position statement on climate change, which advocates restoration as a vital tool for adapting to and mitigating warming trends.[56] Evidence already exists of the value of passive ecological restoration in mitigating global warming; a large recent increase in the carbon sink of some boreal forests of the northern hemisphere has ensued from land use changes, particularly abandonment of agricultural land and reduced forest harvesting.[57]

We must also listen to the oceans, as marine environments are not so easily reinstated. Disturbances from climate change, such as ocean acidification and lower oxygen levels, will have severe and essentially irreparable effects on marine life.[58] Already, warming sea currents along Australia's southern coast have decimated its giant kelp forests, one of the Earth's most productive marine ecosystems.[59] Likewise, the predicted melting of polar ice sheets, along with other drivers of sea level rise such as thermal expansion of warmer oceans, could lead under current emission scenarios to a global average sea level rise by 2100 of 0.28 m and as much as 1 m (compared to the 1986–2005 baseline).[60] Even greater sea level rises loom in centuries beyond. Such changes, as well as restoring the lost ice sheets,

---

[53] A.E. Johnson, 'The key to halting climate change: admit we can't save everything', *The Guardian* 17 February 2016, at www.theguardian.com.

[54] J.A. Harris, et al., 'Ecological restoration and global climate change' (2006) 14(2) *Restoration Ecology* 170.

[55] B. Lavendel, 'Ecological restoration in the face of global climate change: obstacles and initiatives' (2004) 21(3) *Ecological Restoration* 199–200 (quoting ecologists John McCarty and Joy Zedler).

[56] Society for Ecological Restoration, 'Ecological restoration: a global strategy for mitigating climate change', Position Statement (SER, August 2007), at www.ser.org/resources/resources-detail-view/ecological-restoration-a-global-strategy-for-mitigating-climate-change.

[57] Y. Pan, et al., 'A large and persistent carbon sink in the world's forests' (2011) 333 *Science* 988.

[58] K.P. Helm, N. Bindoff, and J.A. Church, 'Observed decreases in oxygen content of the global ocean' (2011) 38 *Geophysical Research Letters* 1.

[59] T. Wernberg, et al., 'Climate-driven regime shift of a temperate marine ecosystem' (2016) 353(6295) *Science* 169.

[60] J.A. Church, et al., 'Sea level change' in *Climate Change 2013: The Physical Science Basis* (Intergovernmental Panel on Climate Change, 2013), chapter 13, 1137.

could not in any practical sense be reversed. Prevention, not restoration, should prevail here. But in the governance of fisheries, cetaceans, and other marine life, restoration can yield major benefits.

Consideration of environmental knowledge, and its translation into governance, requires public participation; the science itself cannot make the final decisions for reasons already explained. John Dryzek's notion of 'ecosystemic reflexivity' provides relevant guidance for designing institutions for these ends. Drawing upon Jurgen Habermas' communicative ethics for public deliberation,[61] Dryzek advocates institutions planned for 'listening more effectively to an active Earth system, [with the] capacity to reconsider core values such as justice in this light, and ability to seek, receive and respond to early warnings about potential ecological state shifts'.[62] An ecologically reflexive institution not only observes and monitors nature, it facilitates changes to policies and laws informed by that knowledge. Although ecological restoration is not his focus, Dryzek's prescriptions for institutional design dovetail with its requirements, such as determining the biological feasibility of interventions.

Such public participation should include citizen science projects, in which lay people partake in environmental monitoring to help researchers understand environmental baselines and changes that can then feed into management actions. Citizens' science taps into a valuable community resource while enhancing participants' ecological literacy and commitment. Monitoring wildlife populations, such as bird counts, is a popular form that helps to reveal the species composition and abundance in surveyed localities. I am personally involved in one such project: the Southeast Tasmania Pilot Program 2016, orchestrated by a consortium of local community groups and government partners, which recruits landowners in the region to establish wildlife monitoring sites on their properties. Provided with bird recorders and camera traps, and given training, landowners periodically record information about local biodiversity and habitat conditions which 'will be used to design better conservation programs and target feral animal control in the landscape'.[63] Citizen science has over the past two decades expanded into a huge variety of niches,

---

[61] J. Habermas, *The Theory of Communicative Action 1: Reason and the Rationalization of Society*, trans. by T. McCarthy (Beacon Press, 1984).
[62] J.S. Dryzek, 'Institutions for the Anthropocene: governance in a changing Earth system' (2014) *British Journal of Political Science*, 1, 17.
[63] Tasmanian Land Conservancy (TLC), *Community Wildlife Monitoring Manual: SE Tasmania Pilot Program* (TLC, 2016).

including tracking marine plastic debris,[64] bird counts,[65] butterfly counts,[66] and cetacean sightings,[67] among numerous projects. Advances in information technology, both in recording and sharing the data such as GPS and remote camera monitoring, have greatly expanded opportunities for citizen science to engage larger audiences of volunteers. Overall, citizen science is a superb participatory tool to help communities tell nature's time, working from the grassroots up, and concerns about the quality and reliability of data are outweighed by the cost-effectiveness of citizen science projects if well managed.[68]

States must also make listening to nature not merely a grassroots endeavour but a national priority. Just as the commanding heights of the economy are stewarded through the central bank, treasury, and other mechanisms of strategic oversight, so too environmental policy needs equivalent national steering. Each country should have a national environmental commission for this purpose, empowered to research and gather information about environmental conditions, including places needing restoration, according to robust metrics, in the same manner that governments track inflation, employment, and other indicia of the economy's health. This information should also factor into measures of national economic progress, notably Gross Domestic Product; thus, identified biophysical changes and their impacts, such as waste, deforestation, and carbon emissions, would enable a more holistic picture of progress towards sustainability, restoration, and other societal goals.[69] Listening to nature will also be improved through environmental reporting standards for the private sector, obliging companies and other actors to disclose periodically their environmental activities and impacts.[70] Not only can such information contribute to better monitoring of environmental law outcomes, it

---

[64] P.E. Duckett and V. Repaci, 'Marine plastic pollution: using community science to address a global problem' (2015) 66(8) *Marine and Freshwater Research* 665.

[65] J. Greenwood, 'Citizens, science and bird conservation' (2007) 148 *Journal of Ornithology* 77.

[66] E. Howard and A.K. Dais, 'Documenting the spring movements of monarch butterflies with Journey North, a citizen science program' in K.S. Oberhauser and M.J. Solensky (eds), *The Monarch Butterfly: Biology and Conservation* (Cornell University Press, 2004), 105.

[67] Wild Whales, http://wildwhales.org/sightings-network/about-wild-whales.

[68] M.M. Gardiner, et al., 'Lessons from lady beetles: accuracy of monitoring data from US and UK citizen-science programs' (2012) 10(9) *Frontiers in Ecology and the Environment* 471.

[69] W.D. Nordhaus and E.C. Kokkelenberg, *Nature's Numbers: Expanding the National Economic Accounts to Include the Environment* (National Academy Press, 1999).

[70] N. Oraee-Mirzamani and Z. Makuch, 'Corporate environmental disclosure law, fiduciary Duties and the Aarhus Convention' (2011) 20(1) *European Energy and Environmental Law Review* 18.

can inform corporate social responsibility (CSR) and socially responsible investment/investing (SRI) codes of conduct.

Concomitantly, the national environmental commission should have oversight of all governmental departments and agencies to ensure that such information informs their policies. Procedures for interagency consultations, disclosures, and deliberations should facilitate the sharing and analysis of environmental knowledge. Such horizontal linkages must be matched by vertical ones down to local government for similar ends, as adaptive governance and restoration require knowledge of local conditions. Already a few states have established integrative, oversight mechanisms: Israel and Hungary have an environmental ombudsman with 'advisory authority to review legislation and executive acts to assess their impact on future generations and to make recommendations',[71] and so too have Canada and New Zealand established environmental commissioners with similar functions.[72] Their modest success so far reflects limitations in their mandates, powers, and funding, rather than innate flaws in the model. Such linkages can help disseminate the environmental law diaspora into all spheres of the state.

Furthermore, this environmental knowledge must be codified into regulatory standards to discipline performance and improve accountability. Current restoration law lacks clear terminology and cognate standards: the legal mandates and procedures to restore ecosystems presently often omit reference to criteria of biological feasibility, with these matters typically left as discretionary judgements for governing agencies.[73] While discretion may seem desirable for its flexibility, it has drawbacks when regulators attach a low priority to environmental concerns or may act capriciously and unreasonably without accountability. The law must clarify what 'restoration' means and how it differs from the narrower approaches of remediation or reclamation; thereby, it can better ensure that on-the-ground practices occur within legally acceptable parameters.

Listening to nature will also inform managing a changing future, especially because knowledge of the natural world remains ashamedly so

---

[71] International Human Rights Clinic, *Models for Protecting the Environment for Future Generations* (Harvard Law School, 2008), 2.

[72] New Zealand Parliamentary Commissioner for the Environment, at www.pce.parliament.nz; Environmental Commissioner of Ontario, at http://eco.on.ca.

[73] Regulators often set arbitrary time periods as reference points for environmental management. The New South Wales Native Vegetation Act 2003 (NSW) bans clearing of native vegetation on private property without a permit, and 'native vegetation' is defined as that living 'before European settlement' (namely before 1788), (s. 6(2)).

incomplete. Under the rubric of 'adaptive management' and 'reflexive environmental law',[74] scholars have advocated legal regimes that respond nimbly to shifting circumstances, but challenges persist in institutionally articulating this agenda. Richard Lazarus, a US law professor, has outlined some interesting ideas for achieving such flexibility without relinquishing ever-more rigorous environmental goals. He recommends that institutions include 'recommitment strategies' that 'make it hard (but never impossible) to change the law in response to some kinds of concerns', coupled with contrasting 'precommitment strategies that deliberately make it easier to change the law in response to other longer-term concerns that are in harmony with the law's central purpose'.[75] Interested in similar institutional challenges, Sidney Shapiro and Robert Glicksman propose 'back-end' adjustments to regulation to give it greater adaptive qualities.[76] They believe that 'back-end' adjustments have advantages over the guesswork involved in rationalising new regulations at the outset or 'front-end' of decisions. Such a regulatory system, believe Shapiro and Glicksman, should enhance resilience because of its iterative, learning process. To make it work, they argue that administrative laws must be modified to include waivers, extensions, and exceptions that enable *ad hoc* changes, but subject to rigorous transparency stipulations, including tracking systems and annual public reports.

At the global level, similar institutional challenges arise for listening to nature. Already the international system has several entities that help, including global environmental monitoring and reporting mechanisms such as the IPCC (for climate change trends) and the Intergovernmental Science-Policy Platform on Biodiversity and Ecosystem Services. Also, the United Nations Environment Programme (UNEP) and the UN Food and Agricultural Organization (FAO) are major knowledge generators on some global environmental trends, including water, forests, and fisheries. Launched in 1995, UNEP's periodic Global Environmental Outlooks provide insights into global megatrends supported by open access to data, with input from experts nominated by governments and other stakeholders.[77] Multilateral development banks such as the World Bank have since the

---

[74] E.W. Orts, 'Reflexive environmental law' (1995) 89 *Northwestern University Law Review* 1227.

[75] R.J. Lazarus, 'Super wicked problems and climate change: restraining the present to liberate the future' (2009) 94 *Cornell Law Review* 1153, 1158.

[76] S.A. Shapiro and R.L. Glicksman, 'The APA and the back-end of regulation: procedures for informal adjudication' (2004) 56 *Administrative Law Review* 1159.

[77] See UNEP, 'The GEO-6 process', at http://web.unep.org/geo/assessments/geo-6-process.

1980s improved their environmental knowledge, through commissioning environmental due diligence and environmental impact assessment (EIA) for project lending decisions,[78] for example, although multilateral finance remains within a pro-market framework that encourages economic growth, free trade, and other structural forces of environmental pressure.

Some environmental treaties have established scientific advisory and fact-finding committees, whose recommendations may get actioned through periodic conferences of the state parties and the adoption of supplementary instruments such as treaty protocols. The Commission for the Conservation of Antarctic Marine Living Resources is one example; it facilitates detailed scientific research into Southern Ocean fisheries for the purposes of setting catch limits. In accordance with the Convention on the Conservation of Antarctic Marine Living Resources, the Commission's members apply an ecosystem-based and precautionary approach to inform long-term sustainability of the fishery.[79] Another approach is the 2015 Paris Agreement.[80] It includes quinquennial performance reviews that enable adjustment of the Agreement in the light of new information about global warming trends and parties' emission-reduction efforts; and concomitantly, the Paris Agreement does not allow parties to lower their nationally determined contribution in future years.[81] One potential downside to such regime flexibility is uncertainty over the rules of the game, which can undermine enduring policy-making and the desire for a predicable regulatory milieu. On the other hand, the more serious problem remains that global governance lacks mechanisms to ensure that environmental knowledge is acted on; the IPPC has warned of devastating climate change since its inception, but without commensurate progress in international law.

Adjudicating for Nature

Aligning ourselves with nature's time has social and political consequences, creating winners and losers. 'While it might be technically possible to achieve certain restoration outcomes through science and engineering',

---

[78] E.g. World Bank, *Environmental and Social Framework: Setting Environmental and Social Standards for Investment Project Lending* (World Bank, August 2016).
[79] Adopted 20 May 1980, in force 7 April 1982, (1980) 19 ILM 841.
[80] Conference of the Parties, United Nations Framework Convention on Climate Change, Adoption of the Paris Agreement, 21st sess, UN Doc. FCCC/CP/2015/L.9 (12 December 2015), Annex.
[81] For more analysis, see M. Doelle, 'The Paris Agreement: historic breakthrough or high stakes experiment?' (2016) 6(1–2) *Climate Law* 1.

explains US academic Anastasia Telesetsky, 'these results could be as easily reversed through partisan politics and self-interested governance'.[82] Statutory mandates for restoration, adaptive governance, and other agendas must thus engage with affected communities and earn their support.[83] This imperative, however, does not mean surrendering to mob rule, as different stakeholders must be heard and their participation must respect knowledge from listening to nature. The legal principle of intragenerational equity behoves decision-makers to manage the costs and benefits of their actions equitably across time. The ethos of environmental justice speaks to similar aspirations, including that decisions be reached democratically with vulnerable stakeholders protected from inequities such as not bearing the brunt of meeting new environmental restraints.[84] The legal system thus has important responsibilities to foster transparent, equitable deliberation and negotiation in environmental issues, a task I call adjudicating for nature.

Community participation and support, especially in restoration projects, matter for several reasons. Because such projects can displace people or generate burdensome costs, local opposition can easily stir. Farmers were angered by the reintroduction of wolves to some American national parks in the 1990s and the return of beavers to British waterways in the early 2000s.[85] A restoration project that hurts one community disproportionately should obviously be managed to offset or mitigate the pain, such as by financial compensation, depending on the legal rights at stake. On a global scale, these considerations play out in the longstanding conflicts between developing and developed countries, particularly over climate change mitigation and biodiversity protection, which international law has tried to reconcile through its principle of 'common but differentiated responsibility' that obliges the richer nations to provide

---

[82] Telesetsky, 'Ecoscapes', 503.
[83] D. Egan, E. Hjerpe, and J. Abrams, 'Why people matter in ecological restoration' in D. Egan, E.E. Hjerpe, and J. Abrams (eds), *Human Dimensions of Ecological Restoration: Integrating Science, Nature, and Culture* (Island Press, 2011); R.H. Horwich and J. Lyon, 'Community conservation: practitioners' answer to critics' (2007) 41 *Oryx* 376; J.E. Reyes, 'Public participation and socioecological resilience' in D. Egan, E.E. Hjerpe, and J. Abrams (eds), *Human Dimensions of Ecological Restoration: Integrating Science, Nature, and Culture* (Island Press, 2011), 79.
[84] K. Shrader-Frechette, *Environmental Justice: Creating Equality, Reclaiming Democracy* (Oxford University Press, 2002).
[85] A. Vaughan, 'Rewilding Britain: bringing wolves, bears and beavers back to the land', *The Guardian* 19 September 2014, at www.theguardian.com; J. Hamann, 'Wolves' return to Yellowstone sparks controversy', *CCN News* 12 November 1997, at http://edition.cnn.com.

financial and technical aid to Global South societies to help them contribute to shared environmental actions.[86] Global restoration initiatives, such as the 2011 Bonn Challenge to restore 350 million ha of degraded forest landscapes by 2030, depend on securing the support of developing countries, where most of this restoration will occur.[87]

Another reason is that communities provide a valuable management resource. Restoration in particular often requires many hands, with some projects mobilising grassroots assistance for years. Restoration ecologists may have the technical skills to design projects, but they do not supply the personnel for planting trees, fencing reserves, weeding, culling pests, and so on.[88] Furthermore, these are not one-off tasks: many projects require subsequent environmental monitoring and potentially further interventions. Some communities, such as indigenous peoples, may have special environmental knowledge and stewardship skills;[89] some have already played a formative role in restoration projects, such as Gondwana Link in Western Australia.[90] Adaptive management can also benefit from community participation, such as where local resource users provide knowledge of changing environmental conditions.

Furthermore, ecological restoration and many other environmental actions have cultural and emotional dimensions that make community participation essential. Restoration can improve individuals' passion for Earth, or as Harvard biologist Edward O. Wilson would say, enrich their biophilic impulse.[91] The intimate grassroots participation of communities in restoration projects, such as planting trees or tendering wildlife, can enhance their intimacy with the nonhuman world. Yet biophilia, like any affection, is unlikely to flourish if left unnurtured.[92] If people's experience

---

[86] S. Alam, et al., *International Environmental Law and the Global South* (Cambridge University Press, 2015), 217–19.

[87] See www.bonnchallenge.org.

[88] M. Lee and P. Hancock, 'Restoration and stewardship volunteerism' in D. Egan, E.E. Hjerpe, and J. Abrams (eds), *Human Dimensions of Ecological Restoration: Integrating Science, Nature, and Culture* (Island Press, 2011), 23.

[89] M.K. Anderson, *Tendering the Wild: Native American Knowledge and the Management of California's Natural Resources* (University of California Press, 2005); W. Barbour and C. Schlesinger, 'Who's the boss? Post-colonialism, ecological research and conservation management on Australian indigenous lands' (2012) 13 *Ecological Management and Restoration* 36.

[90] N. Burrows, A. Burbidge, and P. Fuller, 'Integrating indigenous knowledge of wildland fire and western technology to conserve biodiversity in an Australian desert', at www.millenniumassessment.org/en/Bridging.Proceedings.aspx.

[91] E.O. Wilson, *Biophilia* (Harvard University Press, 1984).

[92] S.K. Allison, *Ecological Restoration and Environmental Change: Renewing Damaged Ecosystems* (Routledge, 2012), 199.

of nature is limited to desolate landscapes that harbour few species – rats, pigeons, and feral cats – they will probably not appreciate biodiversity. Equally, if people's daily routines habituate them to car parks, electricity pylons, and shopping centres, they will hardly understand Earth's complexity and richness. Restored ecosystems, especially those near towns, can help reengage individuals with nature, improving their ecological literacy. One such example is 'Zealandia', a restored bird-rich sanctuary located within Wellington, the capital city of New Zealand.[93] While the 235 ha sanctuary is not a perfect re-creation of the site of 1,000 years ago, before the Maori, Zealandia evokes among its visitors a sense of awe and respect for their natural surroundings.[94] Another example is Environment Tasmania's 'Community Forest Walks' programme, creating environmentally sensitive trails to enable the public to enjoy and learn about the ecosystems that this NGO is helping to regenerate.[95] These considerations matter even more for natural places of special cultural significance to communities, such as their ancestral lands and waters. The reintroduction of western quolls to South Australia's Flinders Ranges in 2014 after over a century's absence, for instance, was attended by the local Adnyamathanha people, who regard the endangered *dasyurid* as a totem species and part of their Dreamtime.[96]

Such initiatives dovetail with 'reconciliation ecology', an idea pioneered by Michael Rosenzweig,[97] which aims to enhance biodiversity and improve ecosystem functionality in human-dominated landscapes such as cities and farms. Its methods include restoration of local wildlife habitat and innovations such as green roofs, wildlife highway crossings, and anti-collision windows to reduce bird deaths. Marine environments may also be improved, such as disposing old ships to create artificial reefs. Urban and peri-urban areas can surprisingly harbour much biodiversity, as one international study of birds in 54 cities found that they support one-fifth of the world's bird diversity, although bird density in concrete jungles is diminishing except for their highly resilient denizens, such as pigeons and starlings.[98] Reconciliation ecology also benefits people,

---

[93] Zealandia, at www.visitzealandia.com
[94] R. Kirkman, 'Transitory places' (2012) 9(1) *Environmental Philosophy* 95.
[95] M. Hawes, *Community Forest Walks Project Evaluation* (Environment Tasmania, 2016).
[96] E. Jackson, 'Endangered western quolls thriving in SA after 100 year absence', *ABC News* (The World Today) 26 September 2014, at www.abc.net.au/worldtoday.
[97] M. Rosenzweig, *Win–Win Ecology* (Oxford University Press, 2003).
[98] M.F.J. Aronson, et al., 'A global analysis of the impacts of urbanization on bird and plant diversity reveals key anthropogenic drivers' (2014) 281 *Proceedings of the Royal Society B*, doi: 10.1098/rspb.2013.3330.

including aesthetic and recreational gains though stronger personal interactions with nature. Environmental psychologists such as James Miller emphasise that 'the environment encountered during childhood becomes the baseline against which environmental degradation is measured later in life', leading to increasing isolation of people from natural systems and apathy about their condition and conservation.[99] Through reconciliation activities, the scourge of drifting baselines may diminish as people become more aware of their degraded surroundings and the opportunities to improve them. And because of the collaborative nature of reconciliation projects, via community groups and partnerships with urban planners and ecologists, they can also strengthen social capital.

We should not get carried away here in presuming that environmental stewardship is only about communities blissfully collaborating; far from it, in fact. Environmental decisions are among the most politically toxic and contentious. An old-growth forest to some evokes a priceless natural wonder, but to others it represents strands of timber of value only as newspaper or building lumber. Business and industry often reflect the latter perspective, but the allegiances can vary; local communities that economically depend on specific resources, as in timber towns, can be as staunchly myopic as the forestry companies; and conversely, some entrepreneurs genuinely embrace CSR and sustainable development for posterity. This inter-temporal tension in environmental decision-making is among the most difficult to govern. Although many profess altruistic concern for enduring ecological well-being, vested interests against conservation laws can dominate regulatory processes, an influence sometimes called 'rent seeking' or 'regulatory capture'.[100] Bureaucrats and legislators frequently succumb to it. In addition, once parliaments enact a law to solve a societal problem it can be much harder to change it, for reasons related to path dependency and the power of interest groups who come to rely on the status quo. The habit of grandfathering resource users and polluters illustrates this pattern.

Overcoming such temporal inertia begins with more transparent and inclusive decisions to reduce the influence of unscrupulous interests. The leading international standard is the Aarhus Convention on Access to Information, Public Participation in Decision-Making, and Access to

---

[99] J.R. Miller, 'Restoration, reconciliation and reconnecting with nature nearby' (2006) 127 *Biological Conservation* 356, 431.

[100] A. Krueger, 'The political economy of the rent-seeking society' (1974) 64(3) *American Economic Review* 291; E. Dal Bo, 'Regulatory capture: a review' (2006) 22(2) *Oxford Review of Economic Policy* 203.

Justice in Environmental Matters.[101] It has three pillars: the public rights to participate in executive programs, receive environmental information from governments, and challenge unlawful practices in court. The Aarhus Convention, however, does not directly apply to private entities, and thus corporations need not be governed by these accountability mechanisms unless individual states choose to act. Other international instruments share this focus on public institutions. The International Labour Organization (ILO) Convention Concerning Indigenous and Tribal Peoples in Independent Countries[102] and the UN Declaration on the Rights of Indigenous Peoples,[103] enacted in 1989 and 2007, respectively, affirm a variety of indigenous rights that signatory governments should respect, including rights to territory and natural resources, and to participate in environmental decisions. The 1994 Desertification Convention also has extensive stipulations on community involvement in programs to combat soil erosion.[104] All these elements can, if implemented by governments, advance public adjudication for nature.

Environmental law in most countries typically accommodates some public participation, from rights to make submissions in EIAs and licensing applications, to opportunities to have one's day in court.[105] Ample literature has already researched the value of democratising environmental governance, which does not need review here.[106] But one institution worth pausing to highlight is the public inquiry. When used to their full potential, inquiries can elicit lively public participation and undertake and test scientific research in the crafting of policies and laws.[107] Environmental

---

[101] Adopted 25 June 1998, in force 30 October 2001, (1999) 38 ILM 517.
[102] International Labour Organization (ILO), Convention No 169, 27 June 1989, in force 5 September 1991, (1989), 28 ILM 138.
[103] UN Doc. A/61/L.67, 7 September 2007.
[104] UN Convention to Combat Desertification in Those Countries Experiencing Serious Drought and/or Desertification, Particularly in Africa, 14 October 1995, in force 26 December 1996, (1994) 33 ILM 1328; K.W. Danish, 'International environmental law and the "bottom-up" approach: a review of the desertification convention' (1995) 3(1) *Indiana Journal of Global Legal Studies* 133.
[105] B.J. Richardson and J. Razzaque, 'Public participation in environmental decision-making' in B.J. Richardson and S. Wood (eds), *Environmental Law for Sustainability* (Hart Publishing, 2006), 165.
[106] E.g. T.C. Beierle and C. Cayford. *Democracy in Practice: Public Participation in Environmental Decisions* (Routledge, 2002); U. Etemire, *Law and Practice on Public Participation in Environmental Matters* (Routledge, 2016); F. Coenen (ed.), *Public Participation and Better Environmental Decisions* (Springer, 2008).
[107] B.J. Richardson and B.W. Boer, 'Federal public inquiries and environmental assessment' (1995) 2(2) *Australian Journal of Environmental Management* 90, 92.

inquiries have demonstrated their value in several jurisdictions. Australia's former Resource Assessment Commission (RAC) conducted several inquiries into controversies with the aim of generating new policy directions. Unlike a court's typically narrow jurisdiction over the specific issues under dispute, the Commission's remit was to investigate wide-ranging natural resources conflicts, such as in forestry and coastal management, and in the national context.[108] Canada's former National Roundtable on the Environment and the Economy performed similar functions as an independent policy advisory agency to the Canadian government. Their ability to gather and sift through diverse scientific evidence, consult with the public, and make recommendations for government action – qualities redolent of Dryzek's 'ecosystemic reflexivity' – suggest that the public inquiry should have a special place in adjudicating for nature. But that both the Australian and Canadian examples were abolished, in 1993 and 2013 respectively, demonstrates their political vulnerability when their masters no longer consider them useful. This limitation is not unique to public inquiries, as numerous institutions can similarly succumb to political machinations. An example discussed in Chapter 3 was Australia's Murray–Darling Basin Authority, whose efforts to develop an innovative plan to restore the basin's damaged ecology were undermined by myopic water users and their political envoys.

Negotiated agreements offer another fillip for participatory and patient environmental governance, quite the antithesis of fast-tracking. Negotiation beneficially allows bespoke governance where a homogeneous approach would be counterproductive. Negotiation has been the preferred method of governance for indigenous peoples in Canada, Australia, New Zealand, and many other countries for settling historic grievances and forging new partnerships for management of natural resources. The Great Bear Rainforest Agreement demonstrates this approach successfully. It was negotiated over a decade in regard to an area of coastal British Columbia, with involvement from First Nations, environmental NGOs, and industry stakeholders such as forestry companies. The Agreement, signed in 2006 and applying to 6.4 million ha, increased the conservation reserves from 9 per cent to 28 per cent of the region; defined and operationalised an ecosystem-based management framework, based on adaptive management principles for most of the remaining area; and established the

---

[108] E.g. Resource Assessment Commission, *Coastal Zone Inquiry: Final Report* (Australian Government Publishing Service, 1993); Resource Assessment Commission, *Forest and Timber Inquiry: Final Report* (Australian Government Publishing Service, 1992).

Coast Opportunity Fund for adapting the social and economic activities of First Nations communities to the management objectives.[109] The success of the Agreement is due to many factors, especially its twin-track strategy of negotiating overarching, macro-governance principles and micro-governance of operational details. The slow negotiations, over more than a decade, may seem impractical in a world addicted to fast time, but they may prove to be superior over the long term by reducing future conflict.

Another governance institution, the trust, may also alleviate the risk of unscrupulous political interference while ensuring nature's long-term stewardship beyond the limited temporal purview of existing laws for sustainability. With ancient roots in Roman, Salic, and Islamic law, the trust today enjoys extensive recognition in the Anglophile jurisdictions.[110] The trust ingeniously separates legal and beneficial ownership of the underlying assets – held by the trustees on behalf of the designated beneficiaries. Trust law also serves, in conjunction with fiduciary law, to align the behaviour of trustees with the interests of beneficiaries through the duty to act loyally.[111] The trust has evolved dramatically from its origins as a means for intergenerational transfer of familial assets – for instance, pension plans commonly use financial trusts for managing their financial portfolios. Some scholars of environmental law, notably luminaries Joseph Sax, Edith Brown Weiss, and Klaus Bosselmann, have advocated the trust for intergenerational environmental stewardship.[112] In this case, a natural asset such as a forest or river can be managed on behalf of a given community or managed for its own benefit, as occurs with philanthropic trusts established to advance an environmental mission without any designated (human) beneficiaries.

Already, some jurisdictions use trusts to manage high-value conservation lands, often in conjunction with protective covenants.[113] Trusts feature in national parks governance, as well as some community-managed

---

[109] H. Saarikoski, K. Raitio, and J. Barry, 'Understanding "successful" conflict resolution: policy regime changes and new interactive arenas in the Great Bear Rainforest' (2013) 32 *Land Use Policy* 271.

[110] A. Avini, 'The origins of the modern English trust revisited' (1996) 70 *Tulane Law Review* 1139.

[111] M. Conaglen, 'The nature and function of fiduciary loyalty' (2005) 121 *Law Quarterly Review* 452.

[112] J.L. Sax, 'The public trust doctrine in natural resource law: effective judicial intervention' (1970) 68 *Michigan Law Review* 471; E.B. Weiss, *In Fairness to Future Generations: International Law, Common Patrimony, and Intergenerational Equity* (United Nations University Press, 1989); K. Bosselmann, *Earth Governance: Trusteeship of the Global Commons* (Edward Elgar Publishing, 2015).

[113] N.A. McLaughlin, 'The role of land trusts in biodiversity conservation on private lands' (2001–2) 38 *Idaho Law Review* 453.

reserves. Some US examples include the Alabama Forever Wild Land Trust,[114] and the Maryland Environmental Trust.[115] A 2015 nationwide census found land trusts with some 207,000 active volunteers managing some 56 million acres in the United States, up from 46 million acres a decade earlier, and a tally over twice the area of national parks in the country (excluding Alaska and other non-contiguous areas).[116] Likewise, environmental trusts feature increasingly in Great Britain, with purposes that include conservation of heritage sites and landscape management. Some private trusts have international responsibilities, such as the Global Environmental Trust[117] and World Land Trust.[118]

Another modality for nature stewardship is the public trust doctrine. It represents the fiduciary mandate of the state as custodian of the nationally significant resources that it manages in perpetuity for the benefit of its citizens. As interpreted by Mary Wood, a leading American advocate of it, 'the focus of the doctrine is not on some amorphous ... conception of the "public interest", but rather on the measurable abundance of the natural assets themselves'.[119] The doctrine's paramount requirement obliges authorities to manage natural resources for public benefit rather than private advantage. Building on environmental legislation that prescribes specific standards and procedures, the public trust doctrine supplies a reservoir of responsibility that can discipline agencies wielding discretionary powers. The doctrine has been revived since the 1970s, and the constitutions of at least half a dozen US states, such as Nevada and Pennsylvania, include provisions that express government trusteeship responsibilities of key natural resources.[120] The public trust has also enjoyed considerable recognition in India's courts.[121] But the doctrine has yet to garner extensive uptake around the world, and even the US courts have restricted its application to a few natural resources.

---

[114] See www.outdooralabama.com/forever-wild-land-trust.
[115] See http://dnr.maryland.gov/met.
[116] K. Chang, *2015 National Land Trust Census Report* (Land Trust Alliance, 2016), 23.
[117] See www.globalenvironmentaltrust.org.
[118] See www.worldlandtrust.org.
[119] M.C. Wood, 'Advancing the sovereign trust of government to safeguard the environment for present and future generations (Part ii): instilling a fiduciary obligation in governance' (2009) 39(1) *Environmental Law* 91, 103.
[120] R.M. Frank, 'The public trust doctrine: assessing its recent past and charting its future' (2012) 65 *UC Davis Law Review* 665, 685. Of case law, see *Borough of Neptune City* v. *Borough of Avon-by-the-Sea*, 294 A.2d 47, 54 (NJ 1972).
[121] E.g. *M.C. Mehta* v. *Kamal Nath and Ors* (2000) INSC 334.

Its prospective orientation may also deflect trustees' attention from any past damage to the entrusted assets. The associated doctrine of waste, which obliges a trustee to prevent the decay or waste of the assets, may not adequately address this lacuna.[122] The common law duty to prevent waste evolved to limit the power of a life tenant over property, so as to protect the property's value for its successor owner, the 'remainderman'.[123] In its modern guise, especially in US law, the doctrine of waste has acquired an economic slant whereby 'waste' is sometimes conceptualised as 'inefficient' use of a natural resource – an unhelpful interpretation for ecological purposes except where restoration directly improves the economic productivity of the land (e.g. soil rehabilitation for agriculture).[124] Such doctrinal limitations, however, do not necessarily preclude trustees from practising restoration if they wish to interpret their responsibilities broadly. Indeed, restoration figures in many land trusts, such as the Columbia Land Trust in the US northwest[125] and the Banks Peninsula Conservation Trust in New Zealand.[126] But the presence of an explicit duty to restore would surely make it a priority for all rather than discretionary for some.

Another possible aspect for law reform is the trust's capacity to adapt and respond to changing circumstances. Fidelity to the original purpose of the trust might dissuade its custodians from interpreting their responsibilities in the light of evolving social and environmental circumstances. This risk is already evident in the attitudes of some pension fund trustees, who reject SRI as incompatible with their legal responsibilities.[127] A study as recently as 2009 on UK pension trustees' attitudes found that the 'interviewees indicated that climate change did not generally feature on the agenda of their trustee meetings and that they considered it to be a relatively unimportant . . . factor'.[128] Yet a growing body of legal opinion concludes that financial trustees have ample room to take into account climate change

---

[122] J.L. Sax, et al., *Legal Control of Water Resources* (Thomson-West, 2000), 460–1.
[123] *Moore and Reinhardt v. Phillips*, 627 P 2d 831 (1981) (discussing the trustee responsibilities of a life tenant).
[124] E.B. Weiss, 'The planetary trust: conservation and intergenerational equity' (1984) 11 *Ecology Law Quarterly* 495, 513.
[125] Columbia Land Trust, *Conservation and Restoration Program* (Columbia Land Trust, 2015).
[126] See www.bpct.org.nz.
[127] B.J. Richardson, *Fiduciary Law and Responsible Investing: In Nature's Trust* (Routledge, 2013), passim.
[128] J. Solomon, *Pension Fund Trustees and Climate Change* (Association of Chartered Certified Accountants, 2009), 7.

and environmental issues.[129] Trustee responsibility is an old but adaptable legal norm, being described by a British law reform inquiry as 'susceptible to flexible and expansive interpretation',[130] and interpreted by the New Zealand High Court as 'a flexible standard' that 'will change with economic conditions and in the light of contemporary thinking'.[131] Legislative direction on trustees' environmental responsibilities could assist those who fall behind new social values. An example, from the United Kingdom, is the Charities (Protection and Social Investment) Act 2016. It explicitly authorises charities to engage in SRI,[132] and the Charity Commission, which supervises UK charities, advises that they can choose investments that do not necessarily seek to maximise financial returns if the preferred investments better advance the organisation's philanthropic goals.[133]

A trust structure will more likely achieve its potential when it has clearly prioritised objectives and enjoys independence from outside interference. The difficulties of Australia's Murray–Darling Basin Authority to secure a water plan for the long-term management of the river system are rooted in its governing legislation[134] giving the Authority conflicting goals: to protect the future ecological health of the river basin while accommodating current water users. A single environmental priority would have lessened the Authority's vulnerability to external pressure to appease the water users. The Murray–Darling Basin thus presents a cautionary tale on how to manage natural resources over the long term. Insulating environmental trusts from parochial pressures may seem at odds with the earlier stated virtue of community participation in decisions. Undoubtedly a tension simmers here, but it is tolerable once we appreciate that the trust serves to protect the voice of future generations in the adjudication for nature. It is posterity's participation that needs safeguarding.

A potentially better model of trusteeship for prioritising nature (though only time will tell) is New Zealand legislation that gives some natural places legal personhood. Under the Te Urewera Act 2014, the 208,000 ha

---

[129] Freshfields Bruckhaus Deringer, *A Legal Framework for the Integration of Environmental, Social and Governance Issues into Institutional Investment* (UNEP-FI, 2005); R. Sullivan, et al., *Fiduciary Duty in the 21st Century* (UNEP-FI, 2015).
[130] Law Reform Commission (LRC), *Trust Law: General Proposals* (LRC, 2008, 12).
[131] *Re Mulligan (Deceased)*, (1998) 1 NZLR 481, 500.
[132] Charities (Protection and Social Investment) Act 2016, c. 4, s. 15(1), inserting Charities Act 2011, c 25, ss 292A–292C.
[133] Charity Commission, *Charities and Investment Matters: A Guide for Trustee* (Guidance, 1 August 2016), cl. 3.3, at www.gov.uk/government/publications/charities-and-investment-matters-a-guide-for-trustees-cc14/charities-and-investment-matters-a-guide-for-trustees.
[134] Water Act 2007 (Cth).

Te Urewera National Park was disestablished and replaced by a legal entity named Te Urewera, with the same rights as a citizen, and the park overseen by a board of trustees composed of Maori and government representatives.[135] The enabling legislation aims 'to establish and preserve in perpetuity a legal identity and protected status for Te Urewera for its intrinsic worth, its distinctive natural and cultural values, the integrity of those values, and for its national importance'.[136] The board's statutory duties include not merely the conventional ones for a conservation reserve, such as to prepare a management plan, but also novel ones including to 'promote or advocate for the interests of Te Urewera in any statutory process or at any public forum'.[137] The legislation further describes not only Te Urewera's outstanding qualities, being 'ancient and enduring, a fortress of nature, alive with history', but also its significance to the Tūhoe tribe as 'the heart of the great fish of Maui, its name being derived from Murakareke, the son of the ancestor Tūhoe' and as the tribe's 'place of origin and return, their homeland'.[138] Such language evokes the ecological timescape missing from much environmental law, especially this veneration of the past and nature's perpetual life.

Another New Zealand precedent is Te Awa Tupua, 'an indivisible and living whole comprising the Whanganui River from the mountains to the sea, incorporating its tributaries and all its physical and metaphysical elements'.[139] The Te Awa Tupua (Whanganui River Claims Settlement) Act 2017 will similarly provide joint Maori and government stewardship of the river that has its own legal identity and right to maintenance of its environmental health and well-being. The legislation also establishes a stakeholder advisory body to support the trustees. As with Te Urewera, the personification of the land and water was introduced to neutralise conflicts between Maori and the government over ownership of the environment while overlaying management with robust governance. But unlike Te Urewera, the Te Awa Tupua is by the terms of the proposed legislation open to some resource uses, such as fishing and water extraction.

These affirmations of Maori cosmology, and specifically their ancestors embedded in nature, offer a novel form of ecological guardianship.[140] Unlike the traditional conservation paradigm that protects nature *apart*

---

[135] Public Act 2014, No. 51, s. 11.
[136] Ibid, s. 4.
[137] Section 18(1)(g).
[138] Section 3(1) and (4)–(5).
[139] Te Awa Tupua (Whanganui River Claims Settlement) Act 2017, s. 12.
[140] C. Irons Magallanes, 'Nature as an ancestor: two examples of legal personality for nature in New Zealand' (2015) 22 *VertigO - la revue électronique en sciences de l'environnement*, at https://vertigo.revues.org.

from people, the New Zealand legislation recognises 'the inseparability'[141] of the people and the land or water, as places of cultural significance and economic sustenance. How these legal precedents will work in practice remains to be determined, but they show that respect for the rights of indigenous peoples, including restoration for past wrongs and protection for their future well-being, can coincide with environmental protection. These laws may help build relationships with the natural world that enable people to tell nature's time and live by its temporalities. Perhaps indicative of a trend, in March 2017 an Indian court cited the New Zealand precedent in its decision to accord the Ganges River and its main tributary, the Yamuna, the status of living, legal entities.[142] Government officials will act as legal custodians to protect the waterways from pollution and other despoliation.

Transnationally, further examples abound of adjudicating for nature. This is not the place to get into detailed analysis of international environmental law-making processes through treaties and other instruments, for which ample literature gives insights into the *relative* successes,[143] such as the Antarctic Treaty System,[144] the Montreal Protocol,[145] and MARPOL,[146] and the failures, notably the Kyoto Protocol[147] and many of the regional fisheries agreements.[148] The pitfalls of global environmental treaties have spurred the development of alternative governance that involves non-state actors. One collaborative model is the Marine Stewardship Council (MSC), an international non-profit established in 1996 to help put the global seafood market on an ecologically sustainable footing. Worldwide Fund for Nature (WWF) and Unilever founded it, thereby combining environmental credibility with business acumen. The scheme's success centres on the MSC chain of custody certification, which helps restaurants, fishmongers,

---

[141] Te Awa Tupua (Whanganui River Claims Settlement) Bill, clause 69(2).

[142] M. Safi, 'Ganges and Yamuna rivers granted same legal rights as human beings' *The Guardian* 21 March 2017, at www.theguardian.com.

[143] E.g. A. Gillespie, *The Illusion of Progress: Unsustainable Development in International Law and Policy* (Routledge, 2001); S. Barrett, *Environment and Statecraft: The Strategy of Environmental Treaty-Making* (Oxford University Press, 2006).

[144] Antarctic Treaty, 1 December 1959, in force 23 June 1961, 402 UNTS 71.

[145] Montreal Protocol on Substances that Deplete the Ozone Layer, 16 September 1987, in force 1 January 1989, (1987) 26 ILM 1550.

[146] International Convention for the Prevention of Pollution from Ships, 2 November 1973, in force 2 October 1983, (1973) 12 ILM 1319.

[147] Kyoto Protocol to the United Nations Framework Convention on Climate Change, 11 December 1997, in force 16 February 2005, (1998) 37 ILM 22.

[148] S. Cullis-Suzuki and D. Pauly, 'Failing the high seas: a global evaluation of regional fisheries management organizations' (2010) 34(5) *Marine Policy* 1036.

and other intermediaries identify seafood from wild fisheries certified by the MSC.[149] Currently 37,000 fishing sites, as well as about 3,300 businesses (as of early 2017) meet the chain of custody standard. The affiliated MSC fishery certification programme recognises sustainable fishing practices. Together, these MSC initiatives help influence seafood consumers' purchases and motivate the industry to improve its environmental practices.

The MSC standards were developed over several years through public consultation, including with scientific experts, and the standards are periodically revised to reflect lessons learned and new information including the FAO's responsible fisheries guidelines. The credibility and impact of MSC is evident in some major supermarket chains, such as Whole Foods Market (a major retailer of organics) promoting the MSC programme. While we might doubt the quality and impact of a private sector CSR initiative, given its voluntary nature, the MSC benefits from NGO oversight, through the WWF, that ensures far greater accountability than typical CSR codes and standards. Initiatives like the MSC can supplement official governance, closing loopholes in how we listen to and act on nature's timescape.

Beyond environmental policy, an innovative global regime that exemplifies democratic collaboration is the Internet's Domain Naming System. The Internet Corporation for Assigned Names and Numbers (ICANN) is a public benefit company, incorporated in California and delegated responsibility by US President Bill Clinton in 1998 to coordinate the Domain Naming System worldwide. It relies on a collegial process of governance that brings 'together the primary stakeholders such as businesses, civil society, governments, [and] research institutions . . . to cooperate and participate in the dialogue, decision making and implementation of solutions to common problems or goals'.[150] ICANN's initial agreement with the US National Telecommunications and Information Administration also included mechanisms and timelines for ongoing reviews of ICANN's performance. Its consultative process has won praise as an innovative experiment.[151] Notionally overseen by the United States (it was due to be removed in 2017, at the time of writing, but President Trump may seek to retain

---

[149] See www.msc.org. See further F. Gale and M. Haward, *Global Commodity Governance: State Responses to Sustainable Forest and Fisheries Certification* (Palgrave Macmillan, 2011).

[150] ICANN, 'Multistakeholder model', at http://icannwiki.com/index.php/Multistakeholder_Model

[151] M. Mueller, *Ruling the Root: Internet Governance and the Taming of Cyberspace* (MIT Press, 2002); J. Malcolm, *Multi-Stakeholder Governance and the Internet Governance Forum* (Terminus Press, 2008).

US oversight), ICANN is managed by its stakeholders, such as through the Generic Names Supporting Organization and various working groups and advisory committees.[152] ICANN undertakes long-term strategic management of the Internet[153] and provides a forum for multi-party dialogue in these activities initiated from the bottom up from among representatives of Internet users. In sum, ICANN demonstrates that complex global issues can be managed collegially without necessarily being beholden to big corporate or government interests.

Living with Nature

We can't rewild the entire planet; human beings will foreseeably continue to occupy most of Earth even if ecological restoration can refurbish some of its jewels to their former splendour. From farms to factories, cities to countryside, regulators must contend with numerous entrenched developments, many grandfathered. In this mosaic of often quite intense human activity, environmental governance must focus on enabling people to live with, not apart from, nature, but a nature that while no longer wilderness at least is allowed to become 'wilder' and live by its natural tempo. Just as adjudicating for nature depends on a variety of institutions, from trusts to public inquiries, so too in this domain we need customised institutions to align human behaviour with nature's temporalities. Collaboration rather than coercion will often garner the best results, so long as the incentives to cooperate outweigh the temptation not to do so.

Globally, states must overcome the sparse affirmation of ecological restoration and affiliated goals. Cheap talk, such as the Bonn Challenge of 2011 and other international declarations of intent, does not create meaningful accountability for our Earth debt. Similarly, the rhetoric of overcoming future adversity, such as climate change, has not so far resulted in credible action; the Paris Agreement seems too weak to prevent devastating global warming. Besides strengthening environmental treaties on these issues, the diaspora must extend to global economic instruments complicit in time-distorting development. Financial governance is particularly bereft of environmental standards: the General Agreement on Trade in Services, including its subsidiary Agreement on Financial

---

[152] See ICANN's organisational structure: icann.org/sites/default/files/assets/org-chart-1800x1000-04mar14-en.png.

[153] For instance, ICANN's development of the IPv6 platform allows long-term expansion of Internet domain names.

Services of 1997,[154] as well as financial governance networks such as the Bank for International Settlements and the International Organization of Securities Commissions, lack acknowledgement of the environmental impact of financial flows.[155] If political elites shy away from decisive action, the best hope for closing the lacunae in global environmental governance may rest with social movements for (for example) social investing and multi-stakeholder collaborations, such as the Forest Stewardship Council (FSC) and the United Nations Environment Programme – Finance Initiative (UNEP-FI).

The illusion of international progress puts more responsibility on states to take the initiative in their own backyards. Living with nature requires refashioning each country's principal legislation, beginning with the basic environmental goals. The core obligations of lead agencies must include restoration, alongside existing stipulations for sustainability and nature conservation. These obligations should include creating a national ecological restoration plan and subsidiary local plans to allow for management of ecological processes across broad landscapes and to prioritise efforts and allocate resources. Some jurisdictions have already progressed towards this goal. The new Environment (Wales) Act obliges public authorities to 'promote the resilience of ecosystems'[156] and prepare a list of Welsh biodiversity of 'principal importance' for which public authorities 'must take all reasonable steps to maintain and enhance'.[157] Another Welsh innovation is the Well-being of Future Generations (Wales) Act, which obliges public authorities to engage with communities and take measures that focus on long-term sustainable development.[158] Oversight of efforts to achieve these obligations rests with the Future Generations Commissioner for Wales. Legislation such as the Welsh example may, if implemented, help communities recover some past losses, as well as enhance nature's resilience to survive adversities and preserve options for posterity. Retaining for future generations the full range of options necessary for their well-being requires legislation capable of maintaining biodiversity and ecological integrity over the long term.

---

[154] Annex on Financial Services and the Understanding on Commitments in Financial Services, are part of the Final Act Embodying the Results of the Uruguay Round of Multilateral Trade Negotiations: at www.wto.org/english/docse/legale/finale.htm.
[155] See generally K. Alexander, R. Dhumale, and J. Eatwell, *Global Governance of Financial Systems* (Oxford University Press, 2006).
[156] 2016, anaw 3, s. 6(1).
[157] Subsection 7(1) and 7(3).
[158] 2015, anaw 2.

The operational fabric of regulation also needs revamping. Development proposals must pass more rigorous environmental assessments, with the EIA process encompassing *cumulative* environmental impacts while eschewing Cost-Benefit Analysis (CBA) calculations that devalue future environmental integrity. The discount rates applied in CBA should be set by an independent entity that includes representatives like the Future Generations Commissioner for Wales. By assessing proposals against incremental impacts, governance can mitigate the scourge of shifting baselines and put environmental change in its deeper historical context. Likewise, land use planning systems must be more vigilant against attritional losses, such as by curbing urban sprawl, creating impervious greenbelts, and restoring green niches around human settlements to promote reconciliation ecology. Alan Sonfist's *Time Landscape* – his restoration of an empty lot in Manhattan, as discussed in Chapter 1 – exemplifies practices that the law should promote.

Just as importantly, EIA and land use planning must become more retrospective, to evaluate whether their predictions and assumptions were correct. The habit of front-loading regulation at the initial assessment and approval stage requires rebalancing with greater post-decision oversight. Economic activities should commence conditionally, subject to relicensing processes that may foreseeably result in the suspension or modification of any authorised development. Such recalibration might ensue where an operator has not met performance expectations, the initial EIA to support its licence made wrong predictions, or new knowledge of another environmental problem justifies changing course. Regulation can to some extent anticipate these scenarios by stipulating a staged approval processes, whereby new activities are phased in to allow time for monitoring and adjustments to operations. Acceptable activities would thereby graduate to further levels of approval in a sequential licensing process. This approach should also dovetail with the ethos of adaptive governance. Where a development warrants discontinuation, the options to backtrack depend on the type of activity. Large dams may be physically incapable of modification, and certainly can't be 'relocated', while a fishing operation might be feasible if shifted to another locality. Where an activity cannot shift or change, environmental restoration that generates *net* gains could help so long as it avoids the awful pitfalls of existing offset practices. Some existing uses, of course, may even need closure, for which financial compensation may be justified.

The foregoing can promote *rallentare*. A staged licensing process with options for backtracking or modifying activities intrinsically puts the breaks on economic activity. In many cases, just repealing or modifying existing laws, such as fast-track legislation, can augment slowness. Extending the time frames for natural resources management can curb unsustainable resource harvesting. The FSC's certification process exemplifies how resource governance can be recalibrated to longer and slower timescales. The logging protocols under FSC rules mean that the trees must reach much older ages than under conventional forestry before harvesting. The logging rules for a Tasmanian farm that in 2010 became the first here to achieve FSC certification require that the trees attain 150 years,[159] an age at which the forest supports much more native biodiversity than one harvested under the 80 years rotation cycles commonly used in Tasmania.[160] Conceivably a wide variety of other legal mechanisms can nurture the slow society, including laws promoting animal welfare and strengthening urban greenbelt protection and intellectual property rights for subsistence farmers, as well as changing business law to foster long-term, patient economic activity. Humankind must live off the interest, not the principal, of nature's capital, and thereby slow its consumption greatly.

Living with nature extends to its restoration. Current laws mainly target spatially and temporally discrete contexts, such as contaminated brownfield sites. In scaling-up restoration to entire landscapes and seascapes, several governance challenges arise.[161] One is the additional coordination of numerous landholders, each with potentially conflicting goals. Secondly, because landscapes often comprise a patchwork of ecosystems of variable condition, each requires bespoke management as well as integrated approaches that link local interventions to a broader restoration plan. Restoring ecological connectivity can allow movement of wildlife and thereby adaptation to changing environments.[162] Thirdly, scaling-up means working with layers of government, as well as NGOs and local landowners, which multi-level governance theory suggests risks introducing

---

[159] F. Breen, 'A national first', *ABC News* 10 July 2010, at www.abc.net.au/news.
[160] A. Macintosh, *Chipping Away at Tasmania's Future: Alternatives to Subsidising the Forestry Industry* (Australian Institute, 2013), 40.
[161] R.J. Hobbs, et al., 'Managing the whole landscape: historical, hybrid and novel ecosystems' (2014) 12 *Frontiers in Ecology and the Environment* 557; E. Gómez-Baggethun, et al., 'Scale misfit in ecosystem service governance as a source of environmental conflict' (2013) 26 *Society and Natural Resources* 1202.
[162] B.H. McRae, et al., 'Where to restore ecological connectivity? Detecting barriers and quantifying restoration benefits' (2012) 7 *PLOS One*, at http://dx.doi.org/10.1371/journal.pone.0052604.

rival policy goals and making negotiations more complex.[163] These considerations make collaboration with private landholders essential for ecological restoration. Land is often held privately – about 40 per cent of the United States[164] and 62 per cent of Australia[165] is held so, as well as substantial tracts held unofficially by indigenous peoples and other local communities.[166] Even marine waters in the public domain can be subject to private sector interests, such as minerals exploration rights and fisheries permits. Contracts, covenants, and other types of negotiated agreements, both legally binding and voluntary, can help articulate environmental standards and responsibilities for these actors.[167] Landholders need incentives to restore and conserve their environments, and legal security for their efforts.

Conservation covenants (sometimes known as easements), as discussed in Chapter 4, can contribute to these goals. Supplementing standard environmental regulation, covenants restrict land use and oblige positive actions, and their inclusion in the property title binds both current and future landholders. Covenants have grown markedly in popularity since the 1980s. In the United States nearly 16.7 million acres in 2015 were under covenants held by state and local land trusts, up from about 6 million acres in 2005.[168] In Australia, the number of covenants grew from less than 100 in the 1970s to 7,491 in 2014.[169] Covenants registered under New Zealand's Queen Elizabeth the Second National Trust Act 1977,[170] the country's main covenanting tool, increased from about 480 in the early 1990s to 4,505 by June 2015, with the size of covenanted area correspondingly growing from about 25,000 ha to 181,346 ha.[171] Landowners' expenditures of labour and money on replanting trees, whose lifespan may easily exceed 100 years, benefit from a covenant to ensure that they last for

---

[163] G. Winter (ed), *Multilevel Governance of Global Environmental Change: Perspectives from Science, Sociology and Law* (Cambridge University Press, 2006).
[164] US Bureau of the Census, *Statistical Abstract of the United States* (11th edition, Bureau of the Census, 1991).
[165] Australian Bureau of Statistics, *Year Book Australia 2002* (Australian Government Publishing Service, 2002).
[166] Rights and Resources Initiative, *Who Owns the World's Land? A Global Baseline of Formally Recognized Indigenous and Community Land Rights* (Rights and Resources Initiative, 2015), 1.
[167] E.g. Estuary Restoration Act 2000, Public Law. 106-457, 33 USC s. 2901.
[168] Chang, *2015 National Land Trust Census Report*, 5.
[169] M.J. Hardy, et al., 'Exploring the permanence of conservation covenants' (2016) *Conservation Letters*, doi: 10.1111/conl.12243, 1, 2.
[170] Public Act 1977, No. 102.
[171] QEII National Trust, *Annual Report 2015* (Queen Elizabeth the Second National Trust, 2015), 14–15.

their natural term.[172] Further, the presence of a covenant can contribute to the ecological 'branding' of a property, certifying its credentials, as I know personally from my own Tasmanian eco-sanctuary. Existing conservation covenant legislation in many jurisdictions needs reform, however. Many examples emphasise negative obligations, such as prohibitions on clearing vegetation, mustering stock, or building infrastructure, while positive duties to revegetate, restore soil, or do other improvements are less commonly prescribed.[173] Legislation enabling covenants sometimes even omits to mention restoration.[174] But because monitoring of compliance with covenant conditions is 'a particular challenge',[175] and depends largely on landowners' goodwill, prescriptive duties are not necessarily desirable.

As a voluntary commitment, covenants may appeal only to landholders who already care about the environment, while others may need a combination of financial incentives (as considered below) and statutory obligations to act. In Queensland, Australia, a duty of environmental care on leaseholders of Crown land is included in the Land Act 1994 (Qld),[176] which was supplemented by the Delbessie Agreement (operative from 2007 to 2012) to elaborate management criteria for the 1,800 rural leases subject to the duty, such as an expectation that landowners agree to a conservation covenant as a condition of lease renewal.[177] A stewardship duty may appear a simple solution to transform property ownership, but in practice it is fraught with difficulties. Law changes in New South Wales and Queensland to restrict landholders' authority to clear native vegetation were hugely contentious and suffered reverses.[178] In lands held by indigenous peoples, equally important considerations apply, and the evolving global principle of 'free, prior, and informed consent' implies limits to regulation of land use without indigenous permission.[179] Stewardship

---

[172] B. Lindsay, 'Legal instruments in landscape conservation: the nature and role of conservation contracts and conservation covenants' (2016) 24(5) *Restoration Ecology* 698.

[173] An example of positive obligations is in Western Australia's Soil and Land Conservation Act 1945 (WA), parts IV and V.

[174] See e.g. Australian legislation: Nature Conservation Act 2002 (Tas.), ss 34–9; Nature Conservation Act 1992 (Qld) s. 51. An example of statutory recognition of restoration is the Canadian province of Nova Scotia's Conservation Easement Act, 2001 SNS c. 28, ss. 4(c) and 7(g).

[175] Hardy, et al., 'Exploring the permanence of conservation covenants', 7.

[176] Section 199.

[177] Queensland Department of Natural Resources and Water, *Delbessie Agreement (State Rural Leasehold Land Strategy)* (Department of Natural Resources and Water, 2007).

[178] E.g. Native Vegetation Act 2003 (NSW); Vegetation Management Act 1999 (Qld).

[179] C.M. Doyle, *Indigenous Peoples, Title to Territory, Rights and Resources: The Transformative Role of Free, Prior and Informed Consent* (Routledge, 2012).

duties are hard to monitor and enforce, and without baseline environmental information (i.e. from listening to nature) it might be impossible for regulators to verify any ecological changes. Negatively framed duties, such as prohibitions against land clearance, lend themselves to compliance much better than positive custodial obligations.

Encouraging positive actions for restoration and stewardship should look to social movements such as Slow Food for inspiration. Purely voluntary approaches are no doubt as highly susceptible to performance failures as top-down regulation for several reasons, including market failures to value the environment, the opportunities for free-riding, and the absence of credible sanctions, among various misgivings. Co-regulation that combines state and non-state actors can overcome the limitations of either acting alone if well designed, such as an environmental certification scheme developed collaboratively with shared compliance control. Neil Gunningham and Peter Grabosky explain that 'recruiting a range of regulatory actors to implement complementary combinations of policy instruments, tailored to specific environmental goals and circumstances, will produce more effective and efficient policy outcomes'.[180] A certification regime modelled on the MSC or FSC might attract farmers interested in gaining market advantages with consumers willing to pay a premium for products associated with animal welfare, organics, and biodiversity conservation. The involvement of government agencies, such as through accreditation of private sector certification schemes that verify best practices, can improve outcomes.[181] A certification scheme incorporating Slow Food principles and restoration of degraded areas could supplement official land use planning, and it would have even greater leverage when linked to financial benefits such as tax concessions. Certification schemes could also encourage landholders to enter into conservation covenants. This model will not be relevant to all landholders, depending on their economic and cultural objectives, On indigenous people's territories, other governance models include Canada's First Nations Land Management Act 1998 and, more ambitiously, the comprehensive land claims settlements, both of which allow for negotiated indigenous self-management.[182]

---

[180] N. Gunningham and P. Grabosky, *Smart Regulation: Designing Environmental Policy* (Clarendon Press, 1998), 15.
[181] M.A. Lawson, *Farmers, Voluntary Stewardship Programs, and Collaborative Natural Resource Governance in Rural Australia* (PhD thesis, University of New England, 2016).
[182] SC 1999, c. 24. See further C. Alcantara, *Negotiating the Deal: Comprehensive Land Claims Agreements in Canada* (University of Toronto Press, 2013).

Business law is as important as property law in aligning environmental governance with nature's timescales because it performs a similarly constitutive function for economic activity. The conventional wisdom that environmental standards should be quarantined in separate regulation, outside of business law, lacks merit. Although dedicated environmental regulation remains essential, business law should also host some environmental standards in order to minimise the tensions that entrepreneurs incur between advancing their financial success and being socially responsible. Some businesses already see win–win opportunities where improved environmental performance offers financial advantages and a better social licence.[183] Businesses may express their environmental commitments through internal management changes or external gestures, such as joining an industry CSR code.[184] The quality of the latter is questionable for reasons already canvassed in the previous chapter.[185]

It is a myth, however, to assume that corporations must, as a matter of law, chase maximum profits. In the Anglophile jurisdictions, company law does not prescribe business goals, and indeed a firm has the discretion to adopt an internal constitution that enshrines a specific mission, such as to pursue some environmental cause. This might be seen in investment corporations that sell SRI portfolios. The business judgement rule, which partially shields managers' actions from liability claims when they act informatively and in good faith, also gives companies some leeway to be socially responsible.[186] Furthermore, in a number of jurisdictions, courts and legislatures have reinterpreted the fiduciary responsibility that boards and managers owe to their company as necessitating enlightened, long-term stewardship of the business.[187]

---

[183] K. Babiakand and S. Trendafilova, 'CSR and environmental: motives and pressures to adopt green management practices' (2011) 18(1) *Corporate Social Responsibility and Environmental Management* 11.

[184] N. Gunningham, R.A. Kagan, and D. Thornton, 'Social license and environmental protection: why businesses go beyond compliance' (2004) 29(2) *Law and Social Inquiry* 307.

[185] J. Bendell, 'In whose name? The accountability of corporate social responsibility' (2005) 15(3–4) *Development in Practice* 362; D. Dunphy and S. Benn (eds), *Corporate Governance and Sustainability: Challenges for Theory and Practice* (Routledge, 2007); B. Slew, 'Style over substance: sustainability reporting falling short', *The Conversation*, 23 September 2014, at https://theconversation.com.au.

[186] L. Johnson, 'Corporate officers and the business judgment rule' (2005) 60 *Business Lawyer* 439; *Australian Securities and Investments Commission v. Rich*, (2009) 236 FLR 1.

[187] E.g. in Canada, see *Peoples Department Stores Inc. (Trustee of) v. Wise*, [2004] 3 SCR 461; and in the UK, see the Companies Act 2006, c. 46, s. 172. And further C.A. Williams and J.M. Conley, 'An emerging third way? The erosion of the Anglo-American shareholder value construct' (2005) 38 *Cornell International Law Journal* 493.

But company law's latitude to act altruistically also carries the discretion to do otherwise.[188] The latter can easily prevail because of market pressure, especially for companies wishing to sell securities to profit-hungry investors. Company law also directly undermines environmental responsibility because it encourages risk-taking. Limited corporate liability shields shareholders against losses beyond their investment in the company, a privilege removed only exceptionally.[189] Limited liability encourages business investment and spares shareholders the time-consuming burden of closely monitoring a company for fear of personal liability.[190] But it may enable its beneficiaries to evade responsibility for environmental damage and actually encourage risky behaviour. A mother company of a corporate group might create under-capitalised subsidiaries of which it is the shareholder, to which it assigns the riskier side of its business. The actions of James Hardie Industries, a former Australian asbestos manufacturer that restructured its business to reduce its liability to mesothelioma victims, illustrate the societal repercussions of limited liability.[191] Obliging companies to post bonds or have adequate liability insurance are mechanisms by which the law can mitigate but not eliminate the doctrine's effects.

The ground-breaking decisions of Norwegian courts in the Hempel case signal how a stricter approach to corporate environmental liability might foster better due diligence, especially in corporate mergers and acquisitions involving firms harbouring environmental liabilities. The Norwegian courts found that Hempel AS, a Danish parent company, was responsible for the costs of investigation and remediation of a polluted site controlled by its subsidiary.[192] Hempel AS acquired the Norwegian subsidiary after most of the pollution had occurred (mainly due to the subsidiary's predecessor many decades earlier). The rulings in the Hempel cases are more than just a conventional interpretation of the Norwegian Pollution Control Act 1981;[193] as company law scholar Beate Sjåfjell argues, they

---

[188] See K. Greenfield, *The Failure of Corporate Law: Fundamental Flaws and Progressive Possibilities* (University of Chicago Press, 2006).
[189] K. Vandekerckhove, *Piercing of the Corporate Veil* (Kluwer Law, 2008).
[190] F.H. Easterbrook and D.R. Fischel, 'Limited liability and the corporation' (1985) 52 *University of Chicago Law Review* 89.
[191] P. Prince, J. Davidson, and S. Dudley, 'In the shadow of the corporate veil: James Hardie and asbestos compensation', in *Research Note* 12 (Department of Parliamentary Services, 10 August 2004).
[192] *Hempel AS v. Norwegian Ministry of Environmental Protection*, Rt. 2010, 306; *Hempel AS v. Norwegian Ministry of Climate and the Environment*, LG-2013-210482; *Hempel AS v. Norwegian Ministry of Climate and the Environment*, HR-2015-470-U.
[193] Act of 13 March 1981 No. 6 Concerning Protection Against Pollution and Concerning Waste.

ambitiously pierce the corporate veil.[194] The risk of liability for historic pollution in such situations should motivate companies to slow down and conduct greater environmental due diligence, as well as 'stimulat[e] . . . greater environmental awareness and sense of responsibility in the business world'.[195]

In addition to corporate responsibility for ecological restoration, positive practices should be encouraged. Some institutional alternatives to the for-profit company already exist. The cooperative is one of the oldest economic organisations in the world, enabling its members to collaboratively pursue charitable and commercial goals,[196] and whose global importance for sustainability and social innovation was acknowledged when the UN declared 2012 the 'International Year of Co-operatives'. They are popular for proponents of Slow Food, including producers (agricultural co-ops) and consumers (food co-ops), and some Slow Money financiers use the cooperative structure (community credit unions). But despite their vintage, cooperatives have never been especially popular in the business community, outside of a few niche sectors. Entrepreneurs hesitate to put money into cooperatives because of their complicated decision-making processes, which give more control to the collective membership,[197] and cooperatives lack access to some sources of financial capital to enable their market growth.[198]

The corporate 'hybrid', combining commercial and community mandates, may appeal more to such entrepreneurs.[199] Introduced already in Canada, Britain, France, Italy, and the United States, the hybrid's characteristics include (with some variations across jurisdictions): a duty to promote a community benefit, in addition to conventional financial benefits for the company; an asset lock and dividend cap (which restricts withdrawal of company assets and profits and thereby protects the firm's

---

[194] B. Sjafjell, 'The courts as environmental champions: the Norwegian Hempel cases' (2016) 13(5) *European Company Law* 199, 206.
[195] Ibid.
[196] International Co-operative Alliance, 'Co-operative identity, values and principles', http://ica.coop/en, under 'What's a co-op'.
[197] P. Davis, 'The governance of co-operatives under competitive conditions: issues, processes and culture' (2001) 1(4) *Corporate Governance* 28.
[198] C. Liao, 'Limits to corporate reform and alternative legal structures' in B. Sjafjell and B.J. Richardson (eds), *Company Law and Sustainability: Legal Barriers and Opportunities* (Cambridge University Press, 2015), 274, 290–1.
[199] J. Battilana, et al., 'In search of the hybrid ideal' (2012) 10(3) *Stanford Social Innovation Review* 51; D.R. Young, E.A.M. Searing, and C.V. Brewer (eds), *The Social Enterprise Zoo* (Edward Elgar Publishing, 2016).

solvency to meet its community purpose); an annual community contribution report that documents the company's social impact; and giving shareholders the right to take enforcement action against management who fail to fulfil the community mission.[200] With shareholders, the corporate hybrid has the advantage over cooperatives (and charitable trusts) of greater access to the capital markets. Yet, unlike a conventional corporation, the hybrid model allows, and indeed normally obliges, the company to pursue community outcomes, even if they lack a business case. The asset and dividend lock feature of the Canadian and British models is particularly beneficial in counteracting expedient business practices. The hybrid legislation, however, is not particularly prescriptive about what qualifies as an acceptable community benefit. The UK legislation, to illustrate, provides that a 'company satisfies the community interest test if a reasonable person might consider that its activities are being carried on for the benefit of the community'.[201]

Hybrids are becoming popular. In the United States as of early 2017, 31 states had enacted legislation to allow for 'benefit corporations', as they are known there, and about 1,300 such corporations were operating.[202] In Britain, nearly 12,000 'community interest companies' were active as of March 2016.[203] Some undertake environmental activities: EuCAN was founded to promote community involvement in wildlife habitat management and restoration.[204] Emory Knoll Farm, incorporated in Maryland, makes green roofs using recycled materials, and contributes to local ecological restoration projects.[205] The major benefit of hybrids will likely be to reward socially responsible companies with the brand name that comes with registration as an accredited hybrid, and thereby the reform can help raise the market profile of CSR. The hybrid is not such a novel idea once we realise that social investors themselves have long measured their success in reaping profits with a social mission. Slow Money investors such as

---

[200] Companies (Audit, Investigations and Community Enterprise) Act 2004, c. 27 (UK); Business Corporations Act, 2002, SBC c. 57 (British Columbia); An Act Respecting Community Interest Companies, 2012, SNS, c. 38 (Nova Scotia); Legge, 28 dicembre 2015, n. 208 (Italy); LOI no. 2014-856 du 31 juillet 2014 relative à l'économie sociale et solidaire (France). For a US example, see Maryland Annotated Code, Corporations and Associations Article, s 6-C-01-08.
[201] Companies (Audit, Investigations and Community Enterprise) Act 2004, c. 27, s. 35(2).
[202] Data from Benefit Corporation: http://benefitcorp.net.
[203] Regulator of Community Interest Companies, *Annual Report 2015/2016* (HM Stationery Office, 2016), 18.
[204] See www.eucan.org.uk.
[205] See www.greenroofplants.com.

Iroquois Valley Farms promote smallholder agriculture and organic production while earning returns to enable the business to continue.[206]

Because the corporate hybrid currently remains a *choice* for business, it does nothing to redeem mainstream corporations law and indeed may foster a ghetto of CSR-focused firms marginalised from the majority. Some tentative steps have begun to address this anomaly. The UK's Companies Act 2006 obliges company directors to act in good faith in a way they believe 'would be most likely to promote the success of the company . . . and in doing so have regard [to] the likely consequences of any decision in the long term'.[207] This provision goes on to refer to community and environmental outcomes as further relevant considerations for directors. Yet language such as 'he considers', 'in good faith', and 'have regard' dilutes the exhortation to a discretionary consideration that may defy judicial scrutiny. More prescriptive is India's 2013 company legislation that obliges businesses with annual revenues exceeding 10 billion rupees to donate 2 per cent of their net profits to charity (eligible areas for donations include education, environment, poverty, and gender equality).[208] After the law's enactment, India's private sector charitable contributions reportedly soared from 33.67 billion rupees in 2013 to 350 billion rupees in 2016; on the other hand, anecdotal evidence suggests that companies dishing out money to charities have generally not changed their underlying business practices.[209]

To address the latter, the law should offer additional incentives to overcome the mismatch between the long-term horizons over which environmental issues become financially material and the short-term benchmarks against which investment managers and companies measure their success. A general duty on all companies to act environmentally responsibly would signal to senior managers and directors that these are important responsibilities to address as diligently as other core statutory duties, but it would be difficult to define how to discharge such a duty beyond meeting ordinary obligations under environmental legislation, as well as ensuring that the duty prevails over competing (economic) ones that corporate bosses might otherwise prioritise. Alternatively, legislators could specify procedural changes, such as a requirement on all companies to establish an appropriate environmental management system, such as one certified by

---

[206] See http://iroquoisvalleyfarms.com.
[207] 2006, c. 46, s. 172(1)(a).
[208] Companies Act 2013, No. 18, s. 135.
[209] O. Balch, 'Indian law requires companies to give 2% of profits to charity. Is it working?', *The Guardian* 5 April 2016, at www.theguardian.com.

the International Organization for Standardization, and to adopt an environmental performance plan with targets and means to achieve ongoing improvements in their business.

Other areas of business law must also be aligned with environmental goals, which can be noted only briefly here. At the level of financial investors, further law reform should modify the fiduciary and trust law duties of fund managers to oblige them to take similar steps to mitigate environmental impacts in their financial decisions, as I have argued in another book.[210] Consumer law could be revamped to include positive environmental disclosure obligations on businesses, for instance in regard to carbon emissions, resource consumption, and waste. The tax system also has significant leverage in incentivising market actors; useful reforms here of course include carbon taxes, removal of fossil fuels subsidies, and expanding property tax concessions for landowners who promote nature conservation. For instance, to curb the throwaway attitudes of consumers, Sweden's budget for 2017 cut the goods and services tax (from 25 to 12 per cent) levied on minor repairs to a wide variety of products such as bicycles, clothes, and washing machines in the hope that consumers will reuse them.[211] The extensive literature on the role of economic instruments in environmental law has much more to say about this subject.[212]

The foregoing actions will also help mobilise the economic resources to pay for environmental improvements. Ecological restoration in particular can be expensive. While nature may recover through ecological succession and evolutionary adaptations, its healing often requires human intervention, entailing substantial labour and financial capital. And because nature's scars are often an historic legacy without identifiable responsible actors, the public at large may need to bear such costs. A 2016 study of improving water quality to repair Australia's damaged Great Barrier Reef by 2025 estimated the cost at about A$8.2 billion.[213] In 2000, the US Congress approved the largest ecological restoration project in the world – the Comprehensive Everglades Restoration Plan, to cost about US$10.5 billion

---

[210] Richardson, *Fiduciary Law and Responsible Investing*.
[211] 'Can Sweden tackle the throwaway society?', *BBC News* 21 September 2016, at www.bbc.com/news.
[212] For an introduction, see United Nations Environment Programme (UNEP), *The Use of Economic Instruments in Environmental Policy: Opportunities and Challenges* (UNEP, 2004); J.E. Milne and M.S. Andersen (eds), *Handbook of Research on Environmental Taxation* (Edward Elgar Publishing, 2012).
[213] Alluvium, *Costs of Achieving the Water Quality Targets for the Great Barrier Reef* (Alluvium Consulting Australia for Department of Environment and Heritage Protection, 2016), iii.

by its completion around 2035.[214] In 2016 Nigerian authorities launched a massive cleanup of the polluted Ogoniland, impacted by decades of oil extraction, costing about US$1 billion.[215] These examples illustrate the staggering price tag of some ecological restorations.

Another expense, also often borne by governments, flows from removal of grandfathered uses. Because authorities usually find it politically unpalatable to extinguish grandfathered rights, they may decide to buy them back. When community pressure eventually persuaded the New South Wales government to terminate BHP Billiton's coal mining lease to the agriculturally valuable Liverpool Plains, it paid the company A$220 million.[216] Another example, also from Australia, is the federal government's buying out of grandfathered water right holders in the contentious Murray–Darling River Basin. It created an 'environment special account'[217] that receives funds to purchase existing water rights and thereby enable the Authority to lower salinity levels, increase water depth, and generally support the floodplains and water-dependent ecosystems. The costs of removing grandfathered industries, however, can sometimes appear to be insurmountable; no government seems willing to close down operational coal mines or oil refineries. When governments thus fail to act, non-governmental actors may exert their own pressure, as the fossil fuels divestment movement now seeks.

The costs of restoration or removal of grandfathered rights must be evaluated relative to the benefits, both long- and short-term. The enduring benefits of productive and healthy ecosystems are very difficult to calculate, but are huge. The initial benefits of restoration projects include direct economic gain from employment opportunities and value-added activities. Data on the restoration economy suggest considerable short-term benefits alone.[218] An analysis of such benefits in Oregon's restoration economy found they had 'created jobs in construction, in technical fields such as engineering and wildlife biology, and in supporting businesses such as plant nurseries, heavy equipment companies, rock and gravel

---

[214] US National Park Service, www.nps.gov/ever/learn/nature/cerp.htm. See also http://evergladesrestoration.gov.
[215] 'Nigeria launches $1 billion Ogoniland clean-up and restoration programme', *UNEP News Centre* 2 June 2016, at www.unep.org/newscentre.
[216] P. Hannam, 'Liverpool Plains: Baird government to pay BHP Billiton $220 million for licence', *Sydney Morning Herald* 11 August 2016, at www.smh.com.au.
[217] Created by the Water Amendment (Water for the Environment Special Account) Act 2012 (Cth), ss. 86AA – 86AJ.
[218] T. BenDor, et al., 'Estimating the size and impact of the ecological restoration economy' (2015) 10(6) *PLoS ONE*, at doi.org/10.1371/journal.pone.0128339.

quarries, and other local businesses'.[219] Total investments in 6,740 ecological improvement projects completed in Oregon between 2001 and 2010 were quantified as having supported nearly 6,500 jobs.[220] These projects in turn stimulated flow-on economic activity in the community, valued at US$977 million for the decade.[221] A national study of the US restoration economy published in 2015 quantified its benefits at US$9.5 billion in direct economic output annually, and a further US$15 billion indirectly.[222]

In addition to flow-on economic activity, some studies use nonmarket valuations of the economic benefits of restoration projects, such as clean drinking water, soil enrichment, and biodiversity gains. One example concerns the restoration of the Skyline Tier forest, an area of about 350 ha in northeast Tasmania; the 2016 study priced an array of economic benefits associated with aesthetic improvements, carbon sequestration, fewer weeds, and cleaner water.[223] The aesthetic benefits for local residents alone were calculated at A$650,000 while the carbon sequestration was priced at about A$1.9 million. Many other jurisdictions, such as Germany and Britain, have enjoyed economic advantages from investing in ecological restoration, according to Storm Cunningham's book devoted to the subject.[224] Whether these economic benefits exceed the opportunity costs of foregoing the potential alternate use of regenerated land, such as forestry or mining, takes us back to Chapter 3's critique of CBA.

Whatever the benefits, someone must still pay the upfront costs. Cost recovery from corporate polluters under current environmental legislation typically targets small, discrete sites, although the behemoth sum BP paid for the *Deepwater Horizon* mess helped repair (sort of) a large swathe of the Gulf of Mexico. Governments can also directly contribute through cash subsidies to environmental NGOs undertaking restoration, but the contributions mostly fall well short of many needs. The other options rely on private sector initiative, ranging from philanthropy[225] to commercial

---

[219] C. Kellon, *Oregon's Restoration Economy* (Ecotrust, 2011), 2.
[220] Ibid.
[221] Ibid.
[222] T. BenDor, et al., 'Estimating the size and impact of the ecological restoration economy'.
[223] Gillespie Economics, *Economic Benefits of Restoring Skyline Tier Scamander Plantation, Tasmania* (Gillespie Economics, 2016).
[224] S. Cunningham, *The Restoration Economy: The Greatest New Growth Frontier* (Berrett-Koehler Publishers, 2002).
[225] Australian Department of Environment and Water Resources, *Encouraging Environmental Philanthropy: Lessons from Australian Case Studies and Interviews* (Commonwealth of Australia, 2007).

approaches that pay for themselves through market demand. Available philanthropic support is also not enough, even though some NGOs such as the Nature Conservancy have amassed huge war chests (it had net assets of US$6.712 billion as of June 2015).[226] Commercial strategies may help bridge the funding gap.[227] They hinge on entrepreneurs being able to *directly* capture the economic benefits of their investments or *indirectly* capture such benefits through reputational gains that a company accrues by being perceived socially as a good corporate citizen. But pervasive market failures to reflect the economic value of environmental improvements can deter business commitments.[228] The collapse of Earth Sanctuaries, Australia's first public company dedicated to wildlife conservation and recovery, provides evidence.[229]

Some hybrid approaches that combine philanthropy and commercial contributions show promise. Established in 2015, the Murray–Darling Basin Balanced Water Fund is accumulating about A$100 million from the Nature Conservancy, private individuals, and institutional investors to buy and lease water rights while protecting wetlands.[230] Though water trading has been a feature of the basin's governance for some years, this commercial and philanthropic partnership is novel. Kilter Rural, a large Australian water fund manager, oversees the Balanced Water Fund, and it buys water when water levels are high (and needed for wetlands to thrive) and the price is low, and sells water to irrigation farmers when water levels drop but the price is high. Another innovative precedent is the Coast Opportunity Funds, established in 2007 to safeguard rainforests in British Columbia, Canada.[231] The Coast Opportunity Funds consists of the Coast Conservation Endowment Fund and the Coast Economic Development Fund, which together assist indigenous peoples to transition to environmentally sustainable development and to help implement the Great Bear

---

[226] Nature Conservancy, *Consolidated Financial Statements for the Year Ended 30 June 2015 and Report Thereon* (Nature Conservancy, 2015), 3.
[227] J. Fitzsimons and G. Wescott, 'The role and contribution of private land in Victoria to biodiversity conservation and the protected area system' (2001) 8(3) *Australian Journal of Environmental Management* 142; L. Pasquini, et al., 'The establishment of large private nature reserves by conservation NGOs: key factors for successful implementation' (2011) 45(3) *Oryx* 373.
[228] J. Scorse, *What Environmentalists Need to Know about Economics* (Palgrave-Macmillan, 2010).
[229] B. Aretino, et al., *Creating Markets for Biodiversity: A Case Study of Earth Sanctuaries Ltd* (Australian Productivity Commission, 2001).
[230] K. Rural, et al., *Information Memorandum: The Murray-Darling Basin Balanced Water Fund* (Kilter Rural, October 2015).
[231] See www.coastfunds.ca.

Rainforest Agreement. The Funds were launched with C$120 million from the Nature Conservancy and other private and public finance, and it generates further money by selling carbon credits from the rainforest.

Another success story is the Mount Misery Habitat Reserve in southern Tasmania, comprising a 700 ha network of private properties with conservation covenants and intervening public lands that protect a diversity of forest communities and wildlife. Its centrepiece is the Huon Bush Retreats, an eco-tourism venture comprising secluded eco-designed cabins nestled in the forest and educational walking trails with interpretative signage about the area's Aboriginal and natural values including the scenic Mount Misery sub-alpine ecotone.[232] Rescued from loggers in the early 2000s, the lands have since been managed sustainably for low-impact tourism and human habitation, as well as some ecological restoration including providing release grounds for rehabilitated native animal orphans. The Huon Nature Trust owns the Bush Retreats operation and some surrounding covenanted properties, and provides a mechanism to manage the financial eco-investments efficiently. The Mount Misery Habitat Reserve exemplifies how private landowners can collaborate to create an alternative to destructive forestry operations, and some of these landowners were involved in the famous 'Battle of Bakers Creek' of 2002, in which community residents successfully blockaded logging operations sought by Gunns (the company discussed in Chapter 5's case study of fast-track legislation).

Fundraising at the international level has become a familiar theme in global environmental conferences and treaty deliberations. The principle of 'common but differentiated responsibilities' has informed these negotiations, essentially aiming to get Western states to contribute more funds to enable the poorest countries to fulfil their side of the bargain, such as reducing deforestation or adapting to global warming.[233] Many eco-funds have been created, and the Global Environment Facility, established in 1991, has become the largest public funder in this domain. Some environmental treaties manage funds to assist developing countries, such as the World Heritage Fund established under the World Heritage Convention.[234]

---

[232] P. Dimmick, 'Huon Bush Retreats: ethical investment meets private conservation' (February–March 2008) *Owner Builder* 50; see further www.huonbushretreats.com.

[233] The principle is affirmed in the Rio Declaration on Environment and Development, 14 June 1992, (1992) 31 ILM 874, principle 7.

[234] Convention Concerning the Protection of the World Cultural and Natural Heritage, 16 November 1972, in force 17 December 1975, (1972) 11 ILM 1358, (1972) 11 ILM 1358.

But still, the available money has never come close to meeting needs.[235] The largest untapped avenues for fundraising are, as within countries, in the private sector either through special taxes or voluntary contributions such as the SRI sector. The Tobin tax is one option that could make a dramatic difference: in 1971 Canadian economist James Tobin proposed a novel financial tax (set at less than 0.5 per cent) on global financial flows in order to reduce currency exchange rate volatility, and his idea has since been seized by environmentalists as useful for generating revenue for new global environmental actions.[236] Another strategy, already utilised, is linking development finance to SRI criteria, as demonstrated by the practices of some sovereign wealth funds such as the Norwegian Government Pension Fund Global.

Living with nature demands wide-ranging governance reforms from many actors, and from the local to global spheres. The foregoing pages touch briefly on just some of the pathways to realign human environmental behaviour with nature's timescape. Much more could be said, but that will require another book. There is no singular solution to the contrived social time of human civilisation, but law will have to contribute. The failure to tell nature's time is rooted deeply in the cultural, economic, and institutional fabric of human society, sourced in practices and attitudes such that changes to regulations or international treaties alone will not be sufficient to overcome it. But embedding governance in the progressive forces of social change, such as movements for ethical investing, slow living, and grassroots ecological restoration, will help extend the environmental law diaspora into new spheres and leverage greater results.

Arcadia

To tell nature's time behoves us to observe, understand, and live with environmental *changes*. As Aristotle deduced, time is perceptible only in relation to noticing the 'before' and 'after' of events. Ecological changes, especially when stretched over eons, may be imperceptible or so glacial as not to be taken seriously. While scientific advances give unprecedented insight into nature's evolution, their influence on the popular consciousness and social norms has lagged. Our struggle to notice nature's time begins with social conditioning that emphasises what to watch or

---

[235] J. Vidal, 'Rich nations failing to meet climate aid pledges', *The Guardian* 21 February 2009, at www.theguardian.com.
[236] R. Falk, *(Re)imagining Humane Global Governance* (Routledge, 2013), 48.

disregard. Fortunately, not all are so blinded, and around the world scattered communities and households strive to tell nature's time.

For some individuals, nature's tempo informs their personal lifestyle. The horse-drawn eco-caravan constructed by two French travellers is one quaint example. Their story, posted on the Shelter blog, describes a caravan they fashioned from recycled materials costing €600.[237] They journeyed slowly through their home country for 9 months, and afterwards kept the caravan and a second that they built for their permanent home. Another individual who respects the ecological timescape is Australian agriculturalist Peter Andrews, whose former property Tarwyn Park was restored into a thriving farm with its biodiversity and ecological tempo rehabilitated.[238] Tarwyn Park was resurrected by following 'natural sequence' farming that works with natural systems, including the water cycle, carbon cycle, and biodiversity.

At the group level, the Global Ecovillage Network links an ensemble of independent communities to share best practices. One of its founding members is Findhorn, in northeast Scotland, whose 450 permanent residents implement many tenets of sustainable living, including eco-friendly farming, eco-designed housing, and renewable energy sourcing, and numerous international visitors swarm to Findhorn for its spiritual and environmental enlightenment.[239] It also has an entrepreneurial side, hosting businesses such as an alternative medicine centre and publishing company, and Findhorn has even issued its own local currency, the Eko. The Findhorn Foundation, a charitable trust, and the New Findhorn Association, a locally constituted body, represent the bucolic community's ethical and environmental goals. Although Findhorn might be slighted as indulgent New Age communalism, its achievements have independent affirmation. In 1998 it was awarded a UN Habitat Best Practice designation from the UN Centre for Human Habitats, and in 2005 it was measured as having the lowest ecological footprint of any community in the developed world, and half that of Britain's average.[240] Findhorn has also

---

[237] L. Lewandowski, 'A horse-drawn caravan', *The Shelter Blog* 29 May 2015, at www.theshelterblog.com/a-horse-drawn-caravan.

[238] P. Andrews, *Back from the Brink: How Australia's Landscape Can Be Saved* (ABC Books, 2008). Unfortunately, under duress the property was later sold to a mining company, but Andrews' legacy remains in the new model of eco-friendly farming that he pioneered.

[239] Findhorn Community, *The Findhorn Garden Story* (Findhorn Press, 1975, 4th edn, 2008).

[240] S. Tinsey, 'Ecological footprint of the Findhorn Foundation and community', www.ecovillagefindhorn.com/docs/FF%20Footprint.pdf&gt.

won praise for ecological restoration via its collaboration with Scotland's Trees for Life.[241]

The south Indian township of Auroville, also in the Global Ecovillage Network, is worth mentioning. Established in 1968 as a multinational community committed to social justice and ecological regeneration, Auroville's 2,500 residents now live under the Auroville Foundation Act 1988, which created a unique local government structure to allow the experiment to flourish.[242] Like Findhorn, the community finances many of its activities through local entrepreneurism, including organic agriculture. Ecological restoration is pivotal to Auroville's vision, and the community grew a substantial greenbelt through reforestation of degraded farmlands, with benefits to local biodiversity and the community itself, including building materials and as a source of natural medicinal products. The reforestation effort, involving millions of tree plantings, has spread to neighbouring regions, thereby creating ecological connectivity for wildlife to thrive.[243] Like virtually any community, Auroville has had its internal conflicts and controversies,[244] but as an intercultural township committed to sustainability it presents a model for many, as acknowledged in resolutions of support from the UNESCO General Assembly.[245]

As the future belongs to city dwellers, unlike the rural demography of human history, arcadia must also flourish in the large metropolises. They might seem an unlikely place to tell nature's time. Rapid urbanisation, especially in the Global South, intensifies environmental and social stress, including food supply, housing, infrastructure, energy, and environmental amenities. Around the world, many governments have pioneered experimental eco-cities, from China's Tianjin to Portugal's PlanIT Valley,[246] while long established cities, such as Copenhagen and Oslo, show

---

[241] Act No. 54 of 1988. See further 'Reconnecting with nature and history of co-creation', at www.findhorn.org/2014/09/reconnecting-with-nature-2/#.V4jB20sskpE

[242] See www.auroville.org. And further, E.F. Kent, *Sacred Groves and Local Gods: Religion and Environmentalism in South India* (Oxford University Press, 2013), 119–59; R. Kapoor, 'Auroville: a spiritual-social experiment in human unity and evolution' (2007) 39(5) *Futures* 632; M. Miles, *Urban Utopias* (Routledge, 2008), 189–94.

[243] See further www.green.aurovilleportal.org/agro/46-the-auroville-forest.

[244] E.g. 'Local concerns over Indian utopia', *BBC News* 24 May 2008, at www.bbc.com/news.

[245] E.g. Director-General of UNESCO, 'Thirty-fifth anniversary of the founding of Auroville', 11 April 2003, at http://portal.unesco.org/en/ev.php-URLID=11235&URLDO=DOTOPIC&URLSECTION=201.html.

[246] W. Pentland, 'The rise (and demise) of Earth's eco-cities', *Forbes* 21 January 2011, at www.forbes.com.

how conurbations can also be retrofitted for eco-living.[247] They combine principles of green building design, generous public transport networks, recycling schemes, greenbelts, and densification to curb sprawl. Some also embrace environmental restoration; Tianjin itself emerged from a desolate wasteland once blighted by chemical pollution from neighbouring factories, but cleaned up by government authorities. But Tianjin, like some of its peers, requires huge financial investments beyond the reach of most municipalities. A better role model might be Brazil's Curitiba, hailed by some as the world's greenest city,[248] graced with numerous parklands, an extensive bus network used by 80 per cent of its residents for their daily commuting, grassroots recycling schemes, and many other green attributes obtained through astute city planning and community participation rather than expensive high-tech outlays.

In the business world, the seeming antithesis of communal environmentalism, innovation flourishes in some quarters. The Tasmanian Land Conservancy is an environmental NGO that has had astonishing success since 2001 in raising funds from donors and partnering with corporate entrepreneurs to purchase high-value properties, some of which are re-sold with a conservation covenant through its revolving fund.[249] The Conservancy's fundraising also supports its engagements with other landowners to enhance their capacity to protect critical ecological values, as has occurred with my Blue Mountain View.[250] Internationally, the Coalition for Environmentally Responsible Economies (CERES) has brought investors, environmental, and social advocacy groups, and other parties together to catalyse sustainable business practices.[251] Its climate campaign has highlighted the ominous risks to shareholders from global warming (e.g. litigation, physical damage, and reputation impacts) and CERES has coordinated the filing of shareholder resolutions and engagements with institutional investors on climate change, as well as lobbying market regulators to achieve broader governance changes.[252] It has maintained a critical eye on the US Securities and Exchange Commission's implementation of the 2010 corporate climate change disclosure regulations that CERES

---

[247] A. Pantsios, 'Top to greenest cities in the world', *EcoWatch* 24 October 2014, at www.ecowatch.com.
[248] B. Barth, 'Curitiba: the greenest city on Earth', *Ecologist* 15 March 2014, at www.theecologist.org/greengreenliving.
[249] See http://tasland.org.au.
[250] See www.bluemountainview.com.au
[251] See www.ceres.org/about-us/coalition.
[252] J. Cook, 'Political action through environmental shareholder resolution filing: applicability to Canadian oil sands?' (2012) 2(1) *Journal of Sustainable Finance and Investment* 26, 35–7.

lobbied for.[253] These and other examples hopefully contain the seeds of wider, systemic change.

Of course, not everyone chooses to live like a Findhornian or fund the Tasmanian Land Conservancy, and it's how the majority behave that really challenges environmental governance. Leveraging social change requires more than legal prescriptions, and an ensemble of social and economic institutions will need to participate, along with traditional regulatory authorities, in the new governance agenda. The ensemble will also include artists. In his book *Ecology without Nature*, Timothy Morton contends that people's image of nature is the main obstacle to progressive environmental behaviour.[254] He investigates the value of art in reimagining our environmental relationships for a better future, arguing that it can help overcome the artificial bifurcation of nature and civilisation. So too, this book began with acknowledgement of the consciousness-altering power of the visual arts to articulate nature's timescape, and it is fitting to conclude with another anecdote.

British landscape photographer Jem Southam tells nature's time well. He is not a photographer in a hurry, taking his time to know his subject matter, often returning again and again to re-photograph sites months or even years later. Southam tells stories about places, whether it is a village pond or a coastal escarpment, exploring their history, continuity, change, and memory. Avoiding images of nature that are comforting and sentimental, Southam examines landscapes that might strike one as mundane or bland, but in fact deftly capture intriguing changes. His *Red River Valley* series of a dirty stream engages with one legacy of Victorian industrialisation. Southam's *Upton Pyne* series tracks the variable condition of a neglected small, village pond, which oscillates through cycles of decay and renewal that he photographed over 6 years. Alternatively, omitting humankind from nature's timescales, Southam's *Rockfalls* and *Rivermouths* series embrace the diverse passages of time etched in the landscape: from the deep geological history evident in weathered cliffs to the daily ebb and flow of an estuary's tidal waters. These and other works also reveal Southam's personal fidelity to slow time, his hundreds or thousands of hours spent perambulating through the countryside searching for the ideal vantage for his next image.

---

[253] J. Coburn and J. Cook, *Cool Response: The SEC and Corporate Climate Change Reporting* (CERES, 2014).

[254] T. Morton, *Ecology without Nature: Rethinking Environmental Aesthetics* (Harvard University Press, 2007).

Environmentalists increasingly recognise the power of the visual arts to help tell nature's time. A restoration programme in the Tasmanian Midlands to re-establish wildlife corridors solicited local artists to assist the local community see and understand the ecological changes, from the past to the future, that the project encompasses.[255] Likewise, artists helped engage the public in the US Nature Conservancy's restoration of a wetland in the Emiquon Preserve in Illinois; in this project, unusually, the public were recruited as the artists themselves, invited to draw, paint, photograph, or otherwise represent the restoration process and its results.[256] Through such actions the arts can also help culturally overcome the invisibility of cumulative environmental damage and thus build the political will to legislate change. Scientific knowledge alone will not leverage behavioural changes if unaccompanied by other social endeavours that inspire people's imagination and compassion to tell nature's time.

Humankind cannot change the nature of time, but we can alter how we perceive, value, and use it. Individual consciousness creates its own time, intertwined with the collective consciousness of time that societies create by which our lives are organised, history interpreted, and destiny contemplated. Living within nature, humankind's understanding of time must dovetail with the natural timescales and biorhythms on which all life flows so as to improve the timing of our environmental decisions. Recognising the anthropomorphic construction of time does not imprison us within the environmental destructiveness of industrial clock time, but rather yields opportunities to re-imagine time, to see nature's temporalities as heterogeneous and changing. Environmental law can help inculcate a new culture of time, one that tells nature's time better, by opening new knowledge, communication, and social practice that bring communities closer to nature's biorhythms. We must embrace both the recent and deep histories of places and the perpetual cycles of life, as well as their future potentials. An understanding of time aligned with the ecological timescape cannot dispense with clocks and calendars, but they should not fixate us. Restoring ecological damage, responding to a dynamic future, and relaxing the pace of life can help align us with Earth's complex temporalities much better than the ever-present now. Telling nature's time will enable humankind to have further time on Earth.

---

[255] Greening Australia, 'Tasmanian Midlands restoration project', at www.greeningaustralia.org.au/project/tasmanian-midlands-restoration-program.

[256] Allison, *Ecological Restoration and Environmental Change*, 188.

INDEX

A

Aarhus Convention, 98, 303, 372–73
Accountability, 7, 116, 137, 200, 206, 222, 234, 288, 347, 366, 381–82
'Acid rain', 206
Acts of god, 151–52
Adaptive governance, 14, 16, 41, 44, 245, 366, 369, 384
Adaptive management, 132, 147–48, 149–50, 151, 357, 367, 370
Advertising, 193, 274, 278
Agreements, 160, 168, 171, 235
Air pollution, 51, 206
Alabama Forever Wild Land Trust, 376
Alberta, 195, 242, 297, 305
  Forest Act, 128–29
  Wood Buffalo National Park in Alberta, 195, 232
Algonquin to Adirondacks Collaborative, 249
A Line in the Himalayas, Richard Long, 6
Amazon, 27, 46, 197, 254
Amboseli National Park, 192
Amnesia, environmental, 16, 71–77
Amplifying effects, 223
Anglophile jurisdictions, 43, 236, 328, 375, 389
Animal rights, 324–25
Antarctic treaty system, 208, 299, 380
Anthropocene, 2, 7, 36, 39, 48, 52–53, 98–99, 123, 129, 144, 180, 196, 278–87, 300–01, 351–54
Aquaculture, 248, 312
Arcadia, 399
  business world, 402–03
  ecological changes, 399–400
  Global Ecovillage Network, 400–01
  rapid urbanisation, 401–02
Arctic, 197

Argentina, 215
Arid Recovery, 238–41, 261–62
Aristotle, 22, 354, 399
Australia, 105, 111–12, 117, 124, 129, 159, 168, 177, 182, 208, 238–41, 274, 277, 284, 287, 304, 311, 317, 344–45, 386, 390, 394, 400. *See also* Queensland, New South Wales, South Australia, and Tasmania
  Environment Protection and Biodiversity Conservation Act, 134–35, 169, 221, 226, 305
  Carbon Credits (Carbon Farming Initiative) Act, 218
  Council of Australian Governments' Reform Agenda, 290
  Covenants, 386–87
  Fast-tracking, 290–91
  Government's CBA, 139
  Great Barrier Reef, 217, 353, 394
  Great Barrier Reef Marine Park Act, 217
  Indigenous peoples, 1, 18, 28, 33, 40, 58, 76, 86, 197, 251–52, 254, 259–60, 374
  Intergovernmental Agreement on the Environment, 102
  Joint management of national parks, 259
  Mabo case, 86, 259
  Murray–Darling Basin Authority (MDBA), 158, 159n182, 233, 374, 378, 395
  Native Title Act, 259
  Ranger Uranium Environmental Inquiry, 310
  Resource Assessment Commission (RAC), 102, 310, 374
  Tobacco Plain Packaging Act, 166

405

INDEX

Australia (*cont.*)
　Water Act, 159, 233
　Wildlife, 50, 74, 187, 279, 301, 353, 361–63, 397
　Yorta Yorta case, 18

B
'Back-end' adjustments, 367
Bioarchaeology, 63, 67
Biodiversity, 15, 54, 57, 73, 111, 171, 196–98, 211, 216, 218, 226, 230, 240–46, 254, 259, 281–87, 316, 325, 360–71, 383, 388, 400
Biological change, 47, 77
　to cultural change, 77–79
Blank slate, 61–62
Bolivia, 130
Brazil, 160, 213, 268, 282, 303, 323, 402
British Columbia, 13, 168, 242, 256, 397
　Great Bear Rainforest Agreement, 374, 397
British Petroleum (BP), 73, 122, 199, 327, 396
Brown Weiss, Edith, 137–38
Brundtland Commission. *See* World Commission on Environment and Development
Business. *See also* corporate governance; corporate social responsibility (CSR)
　community, 165, 177–79, 183, 340, 391
　elites, 105, 117, 124–26, 287, 293
　judgement rule, 328, 389, 394
　law, 93, 96, 106, 117, 165, 170, 173, 182, 328, 339, 346, 349, 359, 385, 389, 391–94
　time, 121–24, 179, 266, 271–72, 329, 341

C
California, 74, 231, 327, 381
California Public Employees' Retirement System, 178, 184
Canada, 96, 102, 104–05, 129, 153, 170, 280–81, 292, 302, 324, 345, 391. *See also* Alberta, British Columbia and Ontario
　Berger Inquiry, 310

Canada National Parks Act, 129, 195, 232
Canadian Environmental Assessment Act, 101–02, 224, 290
Canadian environmental law, 43, 101–02, 105, 124, 129, 170, 224, 217, 292, 299, 310, 366, 374
Canadian Environmental Protection Act, 222, 299
Comprehensive Land Claims Process (CLCP), 258–59
First Nations Land Management Act, 258–59, 388
Mikisew Cree First Nation case, 257
National Energy Board Act, 118
National Round Table on the Environment and the Economy, 101, 374
Species at Risk Act (SARA), 118, 217
Tsilhqot'in Nation v. British Columbia, 256–57
CAP. *See* European Union, Common Agricultural Policy (CAP)
Capitalism, 27, 29, 38, 122, 126, 131, 180–83, 266, 272, 330, 336, 347, 359
Carbon
　tax, 104, 124, 177, 179, 394
　trading systems, 155
Carson, Rachel, 114
CBA. *See* Cost-benefit analysis (CBA)
CERCLA. *See* United States, Comprehensive Environmental Response and Compensation Liability Act (CERCLA)
CERES. *See* Coalition for Environmentally Responsible Economies (CERES)
Certification schemes, 97, 174, 177, 327, 381, 385, 388
Change management, 146–54
　acts of god, 151–52
　adaptive management, 147–50
　modern societies, 152–53
　polycentric regulation, 148–49
　precautionary approach, 150–51
　societies, 153–54

INDEX

Chernobyl, 15, 34, 56, 199, 209, 299
China, 17, 47, 47, 104, 160, 205, 266–67, 280, 312, 331, 401
Chlorofluorocarbons, 34, 51
Choice modelling, 140–41
Chronophage, 19, 20
Citizen science projects, 247, 364–65
CJEU. *See* Court of Justice of the European Union (CJEU)
CLCP. *See* Canada, Comprehensive Land Claims Process (CLCP)
Cleavages in conceptualisations of time, 21–22
Climate change, 18, 55–56, 69, 93, 115, 177, 351, 355. *See also* Global warming
CLRP. *See* Collaborative Landscape Restoration Program (CLRP)
Club of Rome, *Limits to Growth* report, 48–49, 125
Coal mining, 129, 165, 177, 180, 305, 395
Coalition for Environmentally Responsible Economies (CERES), 402
Coast Opportunity Funds, 375, 397
Code for Environmental Management of Marine Mining, 208
Cojote Rojo eco-label, 326
Cold War, 209, 272, 298, 350
Collevecchio Declaration, 343
Common law, 15, 85, 87, 89, 92, 96, 99, 110, 219, 236, 377
Community sanctuaries, 245–47
Community-Based Ecological Mangrove Restoration consortium, 249
Company law, 93, 181, 328–29, 389–90
Conservation covenants, 236–41, 247, 362, 375, 386–88, 398
Conservation gardening, 203
Constitutional law, 86, 89, 92, 133, 138, 215
Consumerism, environmental impacts, 271–78
Contingent valuation, 140–41
Contractual agreements, 107, 146, 163, 170–71, 249, 259, 374

Convention on Biological Diversity, 148, 210, 256, 321
Convention on Civil Liability for Nuclear Damage, 209
Convention on Supplementary Compensation for Nuclear Damage, 209
Convention on the Protection and Use of Transboundary Watercourses and International Lakes, 207
Convention on Third Party Liability in the Field of Nuclear Energy, 209
Convention to Combat Desertification, 210
Corporate engagement, 179, 340–42
Corporate governance, 92, 328, 333, 345
Corporate initiative, responding to change via, 172
  business community, 178–79
  climate change, 177–78
  contribution of NGOs, 179–80
  environmental regulation, 172–73
  participation in CSR codes, 176–77
  social licence, 174–76
  World Business Council for Sustainable Development, 174
Corporate social responsibility (CSR), 126–27, 174–77, 272, 326–29, 346, 366, 381, 389, 392, 393
Corpus Clock, 19
Cost-benefit analysis (CBA), 44, 128, 139–46, 288, 303, 308, 384
  environmental regulation, 145–46
  execution, 140–41
  NSW Government, 143
  precautionary principle, 144–45
  public policy, 139–40
  subsidiary rationales, 142
Courts, 81, 84–87, 92–93, 100, 110, 112, 133, 195, 215, 218, 268, 278, 296, 303–05, 329, 373–74, 390
Critical legal studies, 11, 88
CSR. *See* Corporate social responsibility (CSR)
Cultural change, 26, 47, 59, 118
  biological to, 77–79

Cultural heritage, 189, 251, 260, 321
Cumulative effects, 222–25
Customary international law, 87, 89
Cyclical time, 29, 37

D

Dams, 166–68, 182, 188, 204, 230–31, 293, 384
Dedham Vale Morning, John Constable, 189
Deepwater Horizon, 55, 73, 114, 122, 199
Deforestation, 46, 55, 58, 142, 212, 243–44, 253, 279, 314, 354, 398
Denmark, 177
Derrida, Jacques, 20
Diaspora of environmental norms, 359
Dichlorodiphenyltrichloroethane (DDT), 114
Discontinuous effects, 223
Discounting, 69, 141–45, 348, 350, 384
Discretionary language, in law, 127, 148
Domes of Yosemite, Albert Bierstadt, 189
Doomsday Clock, 351
Dow Jones Sustainability Index, 327
Due diligence, 8, 95–96, 163, 264, 309
  environmental, 174, 270, 288, 293, 297, 307, 335, 357, 368, 391
  financial, 178
  slowness, 347
Duration of law, 85
'Dust Bowl', 212–13

E

Earth
  Earth jurisprudence, 130–31
  timescales, 2, 4–5, 7, 30–36, 39, 42
Earth Charter, 130
Easements. *See* Conservation covenants
Eco-footprint theory, 77, 79, 226
Eco-labels, 271, 278, 318–19, 325–26
Eco-therapists, 270
Ecocentric approach, 98–99, 130
Ecological integrity, 53, 98, 129, 145, 179, 195, 200, 232, 383

Ecological modernization, 122–23
Ecological restoration, 8, 15, 39, 45, 72, 130, 145, 147, 197, 210–11, 363–64, 401. *See also* Environmental restoration
  arid recoveries, 238–41
  community sanctuaries, 245–47
  ecological restoration projects worldwide, 249–50
  ecosystems change, 200–01
  ecological restoration beyond state, 235–50
  legislative frameworks, 226–35
  mangrove restoration, 247–49
  past environmental desecration, 198–99
  private governance, 235–38
  rehabilitation, 199–200
  societal commitment, 197–98, 370–72
  TfL, 243–45
  voluntary nature of restoration projects, 250
  Y2Y Conservation Initiative, 241–43
Ecological serial killer, 53
Ecological timescape, 15–16, 36–41, 44, 88, 120, 379, 400, 404
Economy-wide investors, 337–38
Ecosystem function, 229, 240, 261, 371
Ecosystemic reflexivity, 364, 374
Ecuador, 102, 104
Eden Besieged, 52
  ancient legacy, 59
  Deepwater Horizon oil spill, 55
  ecological systems, 56
  greenhouse gas emissions, 57
  grim prognosis, 53
  hypothesis of Anthropocene, 54
  vivid depictions of animals, 58
EEZ. *See* Exclusive economic zone (EEZ)
EIA. *See* Environmental impact assessment (EIA); US Energy Information Administration (EIA)
EIS. *See* Environmental Impact Study (EIS)
El Nino/LaNina Southern Oscillation (ENSO), 32

Einstein, Albert, 22–23
Electronic waste (e-waste), 277
Empire, Andy Warhol, 4
Emissions trading system (ETS), 57, 156–57
Empirical-inductive approach, 42
Enclave theory, 196, 226
   of conservation, 192–97, 260
Endangered species, 44, 49–50, 78, 100, 129, 136, 358
   recovery, 83, 214, 216
Enlightenment, 29, 61, 121, 357
ENSO. *See* El Nino/LaNina Southern Oscillation (ENSO)
Environmental *acquis*, 98
   Canada, 104–05
   global environmental rules, 107–08
   natural resources, 99–100
   'non-regression' principle, 106
   sustainable management, 102
   timeline of environmental law milestones, 103–04
   transatlantic gap, 101–02
Environmental amnesia, 16, 71–77
   Deepwater Horizon, 73
   human colonization, 74
   manifestations of group self-deception, 76–77
   shifting baseline syndrome, 72
Environmental and public health law, 298–99
Environmental assessment, 163–64, 222–26, 287, 290, 305, 384
   cumulative effects, 224–26
   EIA, 223–24
   environmental changes, 222–23
Environmental due diligence, 174, 270, 288, 293, 297, 307, 335, 357, 368, 391
Environmental emergencies, 297–301
Environmental generational amnesia, 72
Environmental impact assessment (EIA), 83, 127–28, 206, 214, 223–24, 287, 310–11, 368, 384
Environmental Impact Study (EIS), 223, 231, 287
Environmental justice, 15, 82, 131–32, 254, 306, 369

Environmental law, 3, 7, 41, 42, 46, 60, 98–108, 124–25, 147–48, 152–53, 160–61, 184, 200, 251, 355, 359, 373–74, 404. *See also* Ever-present now of environmental law; Space and time in environmental law; Time and space in environmental law
Environmental liability, 14, 84, 92, 101, 113–14, 208–09, 215, 219, 299, 303, 390–91
'Environmental leaders' programs, 170
Environmental licences, 164–65, 169, 173
Environmental protection, 122–25, 129, 141, 145–46, 172–73, 196, 255, 380
Environmental restoration, 197, 263. *See also* Ecological restoration
   domestic law and, 212–22
   ecosystems change, 200–01
   domestic law and environmental restoration, 206, 212–22
   environmental assessment, 222–26
   international environmental law, 206–12
   past environmental desecration, 198–99
   rehabilitation, 199–200
   societal commitment, 197–98, 370–72
Environmental risks, 14, 49, 55, 67–70, 76, 127, 134, 136, 199, 215, 288, 301–02, 313, 335, 358
EPA. *See* United States, Environmental Protection Agency (EPA)
EPBCA. *See* Australia, Environment Protection and Biodiversity Conservation Act (EPBCA)
Equator Principles, 297, 335, 339, 343–44
Ethical investment, 334, 399
Ethics, 9, 42, 77, 126, 138, 142, 145, 186, 202, 318, 325, 354
ETS. *See* Emissions trading system (ETS)
EU. *See* European Union (EU)
EuCAN, 392

Europe
  climate change policy and emissions, 57, 135
  ecological restoration, 202–03, 362
  environmental agreements, 170–71
  environmental law milestones, 103–04, 280
  fur trade, 75
  Landscape Convention, 211
  national parks, 194
  SRI, 335, 339, 342
European Commission, 135, 140, 157, 288
European Union (EU), 43, 100–01, 122–23, 277, 324
  Common Agricultural Policy (CAP), 323–24
  Court of Justice of the European Union (CJEU), 218–19
  EIA Directive, 225, 288
  Environmental Liability Directive, 215
  ETS, 156–57, 162
  Habitats Directive, 211, 218–19
  Subsidiarity principle, 307
  Regulation on Provision of Food Information to Consumers, 326
  Rural Development Policy (RDP), 324
Ever-present now of environmental law. *See also* Environmental law governing change
  frozen in time, 154–63
  managing change, 146–54
  relicensing and recalibrations, 163–72
  responding to change via corporate initiative, 172–80
  CBA and intergenerational trade-offs, 139–46
  prospective governance, 132–38
  sustainable development, 125–32
  pull of the future; drag of the present, 121–25
  ungrandfathering system, 180–86
Evolutionary psychology, 62–63, 66, 70
Evolutionary time lags, 59
  biological to cultural change, 77–79

environmental amnesia, 71–77
foresight, 62–71
primitive mind and modern civilization, 59–62
Exclusive economic zone (EEZ), 110, 112–13
Exxon Valdez oil tanker spill, 199, 304

F
Factory farms, 17–18, 311–13, 324, 348
FAO. *See* UN Food and Agricultural Organization (FAO)
Farsight Fund, 352
Fast-track(ing) law, 287–92, 297
Fiduciary law, 137, 328, 346, 375–76, 389, 394
Finance, roaring world of, 330–34
Financial due diligence, 178
Financial self-interest, 174, 329
Finland, 5, 104, 224
Fisheries and fishing, 3, 15, 47, 72, 101, 110, 150, 157–58, 216, 231, 280–81, 327, 364, 368, 380–81, 386
Florida, 230, 323
FoF. *See* Friends of Flora (FoF)
Fordism, 30, 265–66
Foresight, 8, 62
  evolutionary psychology, 63
  H. neanderthalensis, 64
  hazardous consequences, 71
  indirect reciprocity, 66–67
  marine plastic pollution, 68–69
  statistical probabilities, 69–70
  time perception, 65
Forest Stewardship Council (FSC), 177, 383, 385, 388
Forestry, 213–14, 248, 254, 280–81, 293–95, 385, 398
Fossil fuels divestment movement, 130, 148, 175–77, 180–81, 336, 359, 395
Foucault, Michel, 27
France, 1, 13, 58, 334, 391
Friends of Flora (FoF), 246–47
FSC. *See* Forest Stewardship Council (FSC)
'Future Orientation Index', 122

G

Gabcikovo-Nagymaros case, 87, 115, 133, 355–56
Genetically modified organisms (GMOs), 312–13, 326
GEO5. *See* Global Environmental Outlook 5 (GEO5)
Germany, 122, 170–71, 213, 249, 300, 351, 396
GFC. *See* Global Financial Crisis (GFC)
Global Ecovillage Network, 400–01
Global Environmental Outlook 5 (GEO5), 102n282
Global environmental rules, 107–08
Global Environmental Trust, 376
Global Financial Crisis (GFC), 29, 123–24, 131, 180, 292, 301, 333, 341, 346
Global restoration initiatives, 370
Global South, 102, 292, 370, 401
Global warming, 18, 52, 55, 137, 143, 150, 178–79, 183, 211, 226, 261, 351, 356, 362–63, 368, 398, 402. *See also* Climate change
Glover, John, 5
GMOs. *See* Genetically modified organisms (GMOs)
Go Fossil Free networks, 177–78
Gondwana Link, 131, 240–41, 370
Government bureaucracy, 92, 307
Grandfathering, 83, 116–17, 125, 132, 153–63. *See also* Ungrandfathering system
   Clean Air Act, 155–56
   environmental law reform, 160–61
   environmental licenses, 164–65
   ETS, 156–57, 162
   ITQs, 157–58
   Murray–Darling Basin Authority, 159
   Social licence, 176
Great Acceleration, 54
Great Lakes Water Quality Agreement, 229
Greece, 291
Greenbelts, 322–23, 326, 384–85, 401–02
Greenhouse gases, 234, 238, 277
   emissions, 2, 129, 148, 179, 180–81, 267
Green marketing, 274
Green washing, 177
Greentape, 288, 290, 292
Gross Domestic Product (GDP), 54, 266, 274, 276, 338, 365
Gunns pulp mill, 294–95

H

Harnessing genomic technology, 352
HFCs. *See* Hydrofluorocarbons (HFCs)
History, environmental, 10–13, 28, 40, 48, 50, 76, 190, 193, 198, 353–55
Hobbes, Thomas, 61, 67
Holocene, 36, 52–53
Homicide, 82
Homo neanderthalensis, 64
Homo sapiens, 1–2, 35, 40–41, 59–60, 63–65, 78, 354, 357
   evolutionary legacy, 47, 60, 119, 357
Hourglass of looming calamity, 351
Hungary, 366
Hydrofluorocarbons (HFCs), 160
Hysteresis, 361

I

IASB. *See* International Accounting Standards Board (IASB)
ICANN. *See* Internet Corporation for Assigned Names and Numbers (ICANN)
ICJ. *See* International Court of Justice (ICJ)
ILO. *See* International Labour Organization (ILO)
Impatience, 347–48
India, 86, 90, 104, 160, 160, 199, 249, 291, 302–03, 376, 380, 393, 401
   Auroville, 401
   Bhopal disaster, 15, 114, 199, 302–03
Indigenous peoples and environment, 1, 8, 18, 27, 29, 33, 44, 66, 84, 131, 188, 240–41, 250–60, 321, 362, 370, 373–74, 378–80, 387, 397

Indigenous people's land rights, 18–19, 131, 200, 256, 259
Indirect reciprocity, 66–67
Individual transferable quotas (ITQs), 157–58
Indonesia, 55, 166, 189, 282, 291
Industrial capitalism, ungrandfathering, 183–84
Industrial Revolution, 27, 38, 53, 121
Institutional investors, 337–38
Intellectual property law, 83, 319–22
Interdisciplinary approaches, 41
Intergenerational equity, 14, 49, 91, 122–23, 133–34, 138, 142, 186, 224, 375
Intergenerational trade-offs, 139–46
Intergovernmental Panel on Climate Change (IPCC), 56, 135, 367
International Accounting Standards Board (IASB), 116
International climate change law, 211–12. *See also* Paris Agreement
International Court of Justice (ICJ), 87, 112, 115, 133, 304, 355
International environmental law, 112, 148, 308. *See also* Environmental law
  corporate observance, 173
  ecological restoration, 206–11
  EIA, 206–07
  international climate change law, 211–12. *See also* Paris Agreement
  nuclear technology, 209–10
  radioactive contamination, 208–09
  restoring oceans, 207–08
International Labour Organization (ILO) Convention Concerning Indigenous and Tribal Peoples in Independent Countries, 255, 373
International Union for Conservation of Nature (IUCN), 49–50, 104, 198, 252
Internet Corporation for Assigned Names and Numbers (ICANN), 381–82
Internet's Domain Naming System, 381
Investor–state dispute settlement (ISDS), 108, 165–66
IPCC. *See* Intergovernmental Panel on Climate Change (IPCC)
Israel, 64, 366
Ireland, 289
Italy, 306, 314–16, 332, 391
ITQs. *See* Individual transferable quotas (ITQs)
IUCN. *See* International Union for Conservation of Nature (IUCN)

J

Japan, 122, 140, 171, 297, 304
Judiciary, 85–86, 89, 183. *See also* Courts
Jurisdictions, 43, 102–04, 173, 193, 208, 226, 232, 291, 298, 319, 328, 342, 374–75, 389, 391, 396

K

Kaldor, Nicholas, 139–40
Kant, Immanuel, 22
Kenya, 64, 187, 192, 196, 213, 215
Keystone XL pipeline, 108, 304–05
Kyoto Protocol, 102, 104, 136–37, 380

L

Land use planning, 96, 116, 234, 384
  authorities, 18
  grandfathering, 158
  law, 185
  regulations, 322
'Learning by doing', 156–57
Legal governance, 3, 255–60
Legal pluralism, 96, 98, 149
Legal protection of peri-urban land, 322
Legal system, 89
  cudgel against legal positivism, 88
  environmental management, 83
  fundamental legal norms, 81
  homicide, 82
  legal governance at international level, 86–87
  results of law-making, 85
  time, 80–98
Leopold, Aldo, 9, 149

Licensing, 164, 185–86. *See also* Relicensing
Life in fast lane, 264–71
Linear additive effects, 223
Linear progression of time, 29
Lingering spaces, 18–19
Listening to nature, 360
  citizen science projects, 364–65
  global warming, 362–63
  institutional challenges, 367–68
  knowledge of natural world, 366–67
  marine environments, 363–64
  national environmental commission, 365–66
  restoration, 360–62
Local Food Plus, 326
Locke, John, 61, 161
Long Now Foundation, 352

M
Maine, 292
Malaysia, 122
Mangrove restoration, 247–49
Marine plastic pollution, 68–69, 267, 365
Marine Stewardship Council (MSC), 327, 380–81, 388
MARPOL, 380
Martial law, 298
'Mastery' of time by modern society, 2, 38
MDBA. *See* Australia, Murray–Darling Basin Authority (MDBA)
Megafauna extinctions, 53, 58, 354
MEAB. *See* Millennium Ecosystem Assessment Board (MEAB)
Milankovitch cycles, 36
Millennium Ecosystem Assessment, 152
Millennium Ecosystem Assessment Board (MEAB), 105n284
Millennium Ecosystem Assessment Panel, 153–54
Minors Oposa v. Secretary of Department of Environment and Natural Resources, 91, 133–34
Modernity, 29, 121

Monbiot, George, 202
Monetary policy, 181–82
Montreal Protocol, 137, 160, 380
Mount Corcoran, Albert Bierstadt, 189
MSC. *See* Marine Stewardship Council (MSC)
Multi-scalar regulation, 148–49
Multilateral development banks, 367

N
National Aboriginal Forestry Association (NAFA), 254
National Association of Pension Funds (NAPF), 332
Natural law principles, 81
Nature
  restoring culture with, 250–60
Nature, time in, 30, 359
  adjudicating for nature, 368–82
    ecological restoration, 370–71
    environmental law, 373–74
    international standard, 372–73
    jurisdictions, 375–76
    law reform, 377–78
    Maori cosmology, 379–80
    MSC, 380–381
    negotiation, 374–75
    'reconciliation ecology', 371–72
    restoration, 368–70
    trusteeship, 378–79
  Arcadia, 399–404
  borrowed time, 359
    civilise human behavior, 357–58
    Earth's long timescales, 351–52
    environmental decisions, 356–57
    environmental law, 354–55
    environmental risks, 358–59
    Gabčikovo-Nagimaros case, 355–56
    global crisis, 350–51
    natural science, 352–53
    types of action, 359–60
  Earth's timescales, 2, 4–5, 7, 30–36, 39, 42
  listening to nature, 360–68
  living with nature, 382–99
    business law, 389
    conservation covenants, 386–87

Nature, time in (*cont.*)
    cost recovery, 396–97
    ecological restoration, 394–95
    entrepreneurs, 391–92
    environmental legislation, 393–94
    environmental standards, 382–83
    Hempel case, 390–91
    hybrids approaches, 392–93, 397–98
    negotiations, 398–99
    rallentare, 384–85
    respecting ecological timescape, 36–41
    restoration economy, 395–96
    scaling-up restoration, 385–86
    social changes, 399
    voluntary commitment, 387–88
Nature's enclaves, 192
    'enclave' view of environmental protection, 196–97
    national park, 192–94
    tourism, 194–95
    US national parks system, 195–96
Nature's ghosts, 187
    environmental history, 190–91
    environmental impacts, 191–92
    social history, 189–90
    toponyms, 187–88
Negotiated rule-making, 170–71
Negotiation, 374–75
NEPA. *See* National Environmental Policy Act (NEPA)
Netherlands, 104, 122, 170–71, 204, 218, 273, 345, 362
Neuroscience, 25
New South Wales (NSW), 50, 141, 169, 191, 194, 387, 395
    Environmental Planning and Assessment Act, 182–83
    Environmental Trust Act, 222
    Government's CBA, 141, 143
    Gray v. Minister for Planning case, 224
    Land and Environment Court, 133, 305
    Liverpool Plains, 395
    National Parks and Wildlife Act, 194, 233
    Royal National Park, 192
    Wilderness Act, 233
New Zealand, 158, 233, 245–47, 322
    Civil Defence Emergency Management Act, 298
    Climate Change Response (Moderated Emissions Trading) Amendment Act, 157–58
    Department of Conservation (DoC), 232–33
    Emissions Trading Scheme, 157
    Fisheries Amendment Act, 157–58
    Maori, 29, 193, 220, 233, 251, 257, 322, 371, 379
    Queen Elizabeth Second National Trust Act, 237
    Regulatory Impact Analysis, 139–40
    Resource Management Act (RMA), 102, 104, 128, 135, 166–67, 221–24, 288, 293
    Te Urewera Act, 378–89
    Waitakere Ranges Heritage Area Act, 233
    Waitangi Tribunal, 322
    Whanganui River, 104, 220, 379
    Wildlife Act, 233
Newhaven Wildlife Sanctuary, 239–40
Newton, Isaac, 20
New York, 4–5, 129, 277, 331
NGPFG. *See* Norwegian Government Pension Fund Global (NGPFG)
Nigeria, 395
Non-biodegradable plastics, 2, 56
'Non-regression' principle, 106
North America (Y2Y Conservation Initiative), 241–43
North American Free Trade Agreement, 108
Norway, 390–91
Norwegian Government Pension Fund Global (NGPFG), 342
'Novel ecosystems' theory, 361–62
NSW. *See* New South Wales (NSW)
Nuclear accident, 209, 297–300
Nuclear waste, 33, 51, 69, 209

INDEX

O

OANZ. *See* Organics Aotearoa New Zealand (OANZ)
'Occupy' protest movement, 131, 180–81
OECD. *See* Organisation for Economic Cooperation and Development (OECD)
Offsets, 111, 214, 217–19, 241, 369, 384
Ontario, 170, 286
   Chemical Valley, 302
   Crown Forest Sustainability Act, 285–86
   Green Energy Act, 292
   Greenbelt Act, 323
Open-ended commitments, 134
Oregon, 242, 323, 395–96
Organics Aotearoa New Zealand (OANZ), 317n252
Organisation for Economic Cooperation and Development (OECD), 127n31, 135n74
Ostrom, Elinor, 149
Outcomes-based regulation, 169, 393
Ozone layer, 51, 105, 137, 150

P

Palaeolithic, 1, 64
Paleoneurology, 63
Papua New Guinea, 254, 256
Paris Agreement, 122, 136, 148, 177, 211, 368, 382
Partially Buried Woodshed, Robert Smithson, 5
Past perspectives in environmental law
   ecological restoration law, 226–50
   environmental restoration law, 206–26
   nature's enclaves, 192–97
   nature's ghosts, 187
   environmental history, 190–91
   environmental impacts, 191–92
   social history, 189–90
   toponyms, 187–88
   reflections, 261–63
   restoring culture with nature, 250–60

   restoring environment, 197–205
Path dependency theory, 91–93, 106, 186, 372
Patience, 17, 292, 309, 347–49, 374, 385
Permian, 35, 354
Philippines, 91, 133–34, 256–57, 320
Philosophical theories of time, 21–23
Pilgrim's Way, Hamish Fulton, 6
Pond at Upton Pyne, Jem Southam, 6
Place name etymologies, 188
Planck time, 22
Planetary ecological systems, 46
Planetary orbital cycles, 36
Pleistocene, 36, 50, 203
PMAA. *See* Tasmania, Pulp Mill Assessment Act (PMAA)
Policy principles, 122, 127
Politics and time, 11, 85, 87, 117, 267–68
Polycentric governance, 149
Polycentric regulation, 148–49
Population growth, 32, 54, 123, 138, 172, 254, 276
Positive time preference, 142
Postmodernism, 11, 88, 94, 120–21
Precautionary approach, 17, 150–51, 368
Precautionary principle, 14, 17, 49, 115, 122, 127–28, 144–45, 151, 218, 301, 358
Precommitment strategies, 367
Prescriptive planning, 124, 173
Primitive mind and modern civilization, 59–62
Private governance, 97, 235–38
Project eXcellence and Leadership (Project XL), 170
Property rights, 10, 15, 18, 105, 109–10, 123, 132, 161, 281, 319, 359, 385
Prospective governance, 132–38
Prudent business planning, 165
Public environmental inquiry, 111, 310–11, 373–74, 378
Public trust doctrine, 86, 103, 138, 376
Pulp mill regulation, 293–97

Q

Quasi-contractual agreements, 170–71
Queensland, 50, 117, 128, 215–16, 288, 291, 305
  Chemical, Biological and Radiological Emergency Powers Amendment Act, 291
  Economic Development Act, 291
  Environmental Offsets Act, 218
  Land Act, 387
  mining legislation, 128–29
Quota shares, 158

R

RAC. *See* Australia, Resource Assessment Commission (RAC)
Radioactive contamination, 208–09
Rallentare, 264, 357, 384–85
  compressing time in law, 287–306
  consumerism, 271–87
  life in fast lane, 264–71
  patience and timing, 347–49
  slow food, 311–29
  slow money, 330–46
  slowness, 306–11
Ramsar Convention on Wetlands of International Importance, 207
Rapid urbanisation, 401–02
RDP. *See* European Union, Rural Development Policy (RDP)
Recalibrations of governance, 163–72
Recommitment strategies, 367
Reconciliation ecology, 371–72
Red List criteria, 49–50
Red River Valley series, Jem Southam, 403
Reduced Emissions from Deforestation and Degradation (REDD-plus), 212
Reflexive environmental law, 364, 367
Reflexive law, 97
Regulatory capture, 92, 117, 145, 183, 285, 372
Rehabilitation, 199, 201, 210
Reinventing Environmental Regulation initiative, 170
Relicensing, 125, 146, 163–69, 185, 356, 384. *See also* Licensing
  ad hoc relicensing, 167–68
  empower enterprises, 170
  Environment Agency, UK, 168
  environmental licenses, 164–65
  governance challenge with, 171–72
  ISDS, 165–166
  negotiated rule-making, 170–71
  New Zealand's RMA, 166–67
Remediation, 44, 199, 201, 208, 213–15, 366, 390
Resilience, 16, 18, 44, 132, 201, 210, 221, 243, 298, 367, 383
Restoration, 252–53, 356–57. *See also* Environmental restoration; Ecological restoration
Restoring
  culture with nature, 250–60
  ecological connectivity, 385
  degree of degradation, 203–04
  environmental and ecological restoration, 197–201
  indigenous peoples and environment, 250–55
  legal governance, 255–60
  removal of infrastructure, 204–205
  rewilding, 202–03
  SER, 201–02
Rewilding, 44, 130, 201–05, 215, 226, 354, 362, 382
Rio Declaration on Environment and Development, 133, 212
Rivers and Tides, Andy Goldsworthy, 4
RMA. *See* New Zealand, Resource Management Act (RMA)
Rockfalls and Rivermouths, Jem Southam, 403
Rousseau, Jean-Jacques, 61
Russia, 197

S

Sabi Game Reserve, 192
SARA. *See* Canada, Species at Risk Act (SARA)
Scale decision-making, 307
Science–policy interface, 360

Science, 8–9, 12, 31, 36, 41, 46, 48, 59, 67, 78, 100, 137, 147, 165, 234, 279–81, 301, 308, 350, 352, 355, 358, 360, 364, 404
Scotland, 191, 243–45
  Findorn community, 400–01
  Trees for Life (TfL), 243–45, 401
  Wildlife and Natural Environment (Scotland) Act, 217
Scramble for Nature's Bounty, 278–87
  carbon emissions, 284–85
  deforestation, 279
  forest management, 281–82
  forestry industry, 283
  forestry laws, 285–86
  implementation of Ontario legislation, 286–87
  sustainable development, 280
Scream, The, Edvard Munch, 189
Selective logging, 129, 282, 284
SER. *See* Society for Ecological Restoration (SER)
SEZ. *See* Special economic zone (SEZ)
SFFBD. *See* Slow Food Foundation for Biodiversity (SFFBD)
Shifting baseline, 72, 223, 283, 360, 384
Short time frame, 134
Singapore, 122, 268
Slow food, 311–29, 347
  animal welfare policy, 318
  biodiversity considerations, 316–19
  from fast to slow food economy, 311–16
  governing slow food–CSR, 326–29
  governing slow food–legislation, 319–26
  social movement, 98
Slow Food Foundation for Biodiversity (SFFBD), 315–16, 325
Slow justice, 302–06
Slow money, 17, 44, 271, 330–347, 356, 391–92
  governing slow money, 339–46
  roaring world of finance, 330–34
  SRI, 334–39

'Slow violence' of environmental trauma, 50–51
Slowness, 4, 302, 306–11, 347
Social capitalism, 183–84
Social investors, 335, 337. *See also* Socially responsible investment (SRI)
Social licence, 174–76, 181, 327, 340, 343, 389
Social time, 8, 26–27, 30–31, 37, 39–40, 81, 99, 350, 399
Socially responsible investment (SRI), 145, 174–77, 334–46, 377–78, 389, 399
  codes, 366
Societal collapse, 46, 71, 151–53, 190
Society for Ecological Restoration (SER), 201, 363
South Africa, 190, 192, 196, 213, 291, 328, 335, 341
  Kruger National Park, 192, 196
  Mineral and Petroleum Resources Development Act, 214
  National Environmental Management Act, 220–21
South Australia
  Environmental Protection Act, 221
  Flinders Ranges, 371
  Vulkathunha-Gammon Ranges National Park, 259
Southeast Tasmania Pilot Program, 364
South Korea, 275
Space and time in environmental law, 9–19, 108–18. *See also* Environmental law; Time and space in environmental law
  climate change and loss of biodiversity, 113
  crude metrics, 111
  economic advantages, 117
  EEZ, 110
  environmental governance, 108–09
  environmental history, 12–13
  legislative reform, 112
  pollution emissions, 116–17
  sustainable development, 118
  temporal proximity, 114
  time-extended phenomena, 115

Special economic zone (SEZ), 291–92
Species extinction clocks, 351
'Species' evolution, 3, 20, 32–35, 59, 119, 355, 357
SRI. *See* Socially responsible investment (SRI)
Stakeholders, 131, 170, 174, 176, 198, 235, 327–28, 369, 381–83
Stare decisis (precedent), 12, 81, 86–90
Statute of limitations, 82, 90, 116–17, 219–20, 303
Stern Review on the Economics of Climate Change, 143–44
Sustainability. *See* Sustainable development
Sustainable development, 3, 10, 49, 122–23, 125, 198, 228, 354, 375, 401
  business approaches, 126–27, 179, 272, 327
  ecocentric approach, 130–31
  environmental justice issues, 131–32
  in environmental law, 41, 49, 78, 97, 184
  environmental legislation, 122, 127–28, 383
  gravity of Anthropocene, 129–30
  principles of, 133–34
  natural resources management, 16, 128–29
  reports, 176–77
  sustainable development philosophy, 132–33
Sustainable finance, 334. *See* Socially responsible investment (SRI)
Sustainable management, 102, 221, 281
Sweden, 103, 394
Switzerland, 102, 122, 199
Systemic stability, 89
Systems theory, 26, 97

T

TAC. *See* Total allowable catch (TAC)
Tainter, Joseph, 152–53
Tasmania, 5, 171, 182, 187, 194, 227, 231, 236, 284, 361, 371, 385, 396, 398, 404

Blue Mountain View, 264, 402
Climate Change (State Action) Act, 136
Environmental Management and Pollution Control Act, 293
fast-tracking, 136, 285, 295
Forest Practices Act, 285
Land Use Planning and Approvals Act, 293
Pulp Mill Assessment Act (PMAA), 294–96
Resource Planning and Development Commission (RPDC), 293–94
State Policies and Projects Act, 294
Tasmanian Museum and Art Gallery, 190
Threatened Species Act, 285
Thylacine, 36, 75, 190, 204, 216
Tasmanian Land Conservancy (TLC), 136, 285, 237n253, 402–03
Taxation system, 237–38
Taylorism, 27, 30, 265–66
Technology and time, 17, 24–27, 29–30, 37–38, 59, 78, 121, 264–66, 268, 271, 306, 308, 330, 352
Temporal inertia and motion in law, 88–98, 372
  cultural change, 96
  evolutionary processes, 91
  legal governance, 95
  legal system, 89
  relationship between law reform and social change, 94
  rules-driven path dependence, 92
  Slow Food movement, 98
  stabilising legal processes, 90
  systems theory, 97
  theory of path dependence, 93
Temporal proximity, 110, 113–15, 350
Temporal personality types, 24–25
Temporalities of environmental change, 20, 47
  Eden Besieged, 52–59
  evolutionary time lags, 59–79
  time and law, 80–98
  time-lapsed environmental change, 46–52

timelines of modern environmental law, 98–120
'Tensed' time, 22–23
'Tenseless' time, 22–23
Terai Arc Landscape programme, 249
Terra nullius, 28, 197
TfL. *See* Trees for Life (TfL)
Thailand, 34, 247–49, 275
   Estuaries and Clean Waters Act, 231–32
Theory of natural selection, 35
'Tide of history', 18
Time
   archaic *Homo sapiens* burial sites, 1
   Chronophage, 19, 20
   cleavages in conceptualisations of, 21–22
   Corpus Clock, 19
   debate over 'tensed' and 'tenseless' time, 22–23
   denominations of, 20–21
   detaching time from organic cycles and sequences, 2
   direction and tempo, 28–29, 264–66
   Earth's timescales, 2, 4–5, 7, 30–36, 39, 42
   ecology, 351
   empirical-inductive approach, 42–43
   features, 26–27
   fields, 21
   frames, 136
   hermeneutical approach to nature, 9
   humankind's timescales, 6–7
   in industrial production, 30
   linear progression, 29
   in nature, 30–41
   nature's tempo, 7
   nature's time, 3
   plasticity of space, 2
   pregnancy calendar, 1
   sense of time in nature, 4
   social practice of time, 6
   social time with nature's timescape, 8
   and space in environmental law, 9–19, 108–18
   study of past societies, 27
   substantival concept of, 22
   Time Perspective Inventory, 24–25
   timescales and temporal orientations, 41
Time and law
   temporal inertia and motion in law, 88–98
   temporalities of legal system, 80–88
Time and space in environmental law, 9. *See also* Environmental law; Space and time in environmental law
   architecture of environmental law, 14–15
   ecological timescape, 8, 15–16, 36, 44, 120, 379, 400, 404
   emergence of modern environmental law, 13
   legal doctrines, 14
   multi-stranded approach to time, 18
   'pace' of time, 17
   with philosophy of sustainable development, 9–10
   scholarly discipline of environmental history, 12
   scholars of law, 11
   space in doctrinal and theoretical development, 10, 108–14
   sparse commitment to ecological restoration, 15–16
   under-appreciated temporalities of environmental law, 19
Time compression in law, 264, 287
   environmental emergencies, 297–301
   fast-track law, 287–92
   rushed pulp mill, 293–97
   slow justice, 302–06
Time Landscape, Alan Sonfist, 5, 384
Time-extended phenomena, 115
Time-lapse footage, 46–47, 109
Time-lapse sequences, 46
Time-lapsed environmental change, 46
   environmental change accelerating, 52
   nuclear waste, 51
   Red List criteria, 49–50
   temporal trajectories, 49
   time-lapse imagery, 47
   turning point, 48

Time-related strategies, 271
Time-shifted rationality, 78–79
Timelines of modern environmental law
 anthropogenic disturbances, 118–19
 evolving environmental *acquis*, 98–108
 law reform, 120
 social factors, 119–20
 space and time in environmental law, 108–18
Timing, 4, 7, 20–21, 82, 117, 292, 306, 347–49, 351, 356
TLC. *See* Tasmanian Land Conservancy (TLC)
Tobin tax, 399
Torrey Canyon oil tanker spill, 48
Tort law, 91, 99, 110, 303
Total allowable catch (TAC), 158
Toxic tort litigation, 84, 219
Tracking clock, 351
Trade-Related Aspects of Intellectual Property Rights (TRIPS), 319–20
'Tragedy of the commons', 60, 109, 113, 279
Trail Smelter case, 87, 103, 112–13
Travel cost method, 140–41
Treaty on the Non-Proliferation of Nuclear Weapons, 94
Tree Mountain–A Living Time Capsule, Agnes Denes, 5
Tree Piece, John Davis, 6
Trees for Life (TfL), 243–45, 401
'Triple bottom line' approach, 126–27
TRIPS. *See* Trade-Related Aspects of Intellectual Property Rights (TRIPS)
Trusts law, 44, 137–38, 346, 375–78
Turning point, 48, 296
Tutzing Time Ecology project, 351
'2 Degrees Clock', 351

U
Ukraine, 199. *See also* Chernobyl
UN Food and Agricultural Organization (FAO), 55n43, 248n294, 256n351, 279, 311n223, 367
UN Framework Convention on Climate Change, 136–37, 160
UN Principles for Responsible Investment (UNPRI), 174, 177, 336, 338–39, 343
UN Working Group on Indigenous Populations, 251–52
UNEP. *See* United Nations Environment Programme (UNEP)
UNEP-FI. *See* United Nations Environment Programme-Finance Initiative (UNEP-FI)
Ungrandfathering system, 180–86. *See also* Grandfathering
 environmental behaviour, 181–82
 environmental law, 184
 Environmental Planning and Assessment Act, 182–83
 greenhouse gas emissions, 180–81
 licensing process, 185–86
 'ungrandfathered', 162–63
 ungrandfathering industrial capitalism, 183–84
Union for Protection of New Varieties of Plants (UPOV), 320
United Kingdom, 75, 103, 178, 188, 236, 267, 273–74, 303, 328, 332, 337, 376–77, 391–92, 396, 400. *See also* Scotland and Wales
 Act to Prevent the Cruel and Improper Treatment of Cattle, 324
 Alkali Act, 99
 Bank of England, 183
 Cambridge Water case, 92
 Charities (Protection and Social Investment) Act, 344, 378
 Civil Contingencies Act, 298
 Climate Change Act, 136–37
 Community interest companies, 392
 Companies Act, 328, 393
 English forests, 188, 192
 Environment Act, 168, 214–15
 Green Belt (London and Home Counties) Act, 322
 Heathrow airport inquiry, 310
 National Parks and Access to the Countryside Act, 213

Planning Act, 289
Public Health Act, 99
Town and Country Planning Act, 322–23
War Damage Act, 86
United Nations Convention on the Law of the Sea, 207
United Nations Declaration on the Rights of Indigenous Peoples, 255, 321, 373
United Nations Environment Programme (UNEP), 87, 102n282, 367
United Nations Environment Programme–Finance Initiative (UNEP-FI), 336, 344, 382
United Nations Sustainable Development Goals (2015), 127, 131, 206, 212
United States, 57, 72, 76, 93, 100, 102, 112, 170, 187, 189, 202, 204, 209, 251, 267, 345, 398, 381, 386. *See also* California, Florida, Maine, New York and Oregon
  Benefit corporations, 391–92
  Clean Air Act, 100, 155–56
  Clean Water Act, 229–30
  Collaborative Landscape Restoration Program (CLRP), 227–28
  Comprehensive Everglades Restoration Plan, 230, 394
  Comprehensive Environmental Response and Compensation Liability Act (CERCLA), 135
  Council of Environmental Quality, 225
  Ecological restoration legislation, 232
  Endangered Species Act, 136, 216
  Energy Information Administration (EIA), 57n56
  Environmental Protection Agency (EPA), 100, 139, 170, 258
  Factory farms, 311–13
  Fast-track legislation, 289–90
  Federal Aid in Wildlife Restoration Act, 213
  Federal Energy Regulatory Commission (FERC), 167–68
  Florida, Everglades Forever Act, 230
  Geological Survey, 46
  Government Accountability Office, 287
  Government's CBA, 139
  Great Lakes Ecosystem Protection Act, 229
  Growth and Infrastructure Act, 289
  Kittitas Reclamation District case, 257
  Land trusts, 376, 386
  'Love Canal' disaster, 219
  Microbead-Free Waters Act, 163
  National Environmental Policy Act (NEPA), 100, 223, 225, 289–90
  National Parks Service Organic Act (1916), 195
  national parks system, 195–96, 227
  NASA, 46
  Our Children's Trust litigation, 138
  Project XL (for eXcellence and Leadership), 170
  Securities and Exchange Commission, 116, 402
  Sierra Club v. Morton, 112
  Snail Darter case, 100
  Stock exchanges, 331–32
  Superfund scheme, 215, 245, 346
  Surface Mining Control and Reclamation Act, 214
  United States v. Adair case, 257
Universities Superannuation Scheme, 178
UNPRI. *See* UN Principles for Responsible Investment (UNPRI)
UPOV. *See* Union for Protection of New Varieties of Plants (UPOV)
US Nature Conservancy, 397–98, 404

V

Victoria, 196
  Conservation Trust Act, 236
  Major Transport Projects Facilitation Act, 291
  National Parks Act, 136
Vintage differentiated regulation (VDR), 155
'Vulnerable' species, 49–50

W

Wales, 236, 383–84
　Environment (Wales) Act, 221, 383
　Well-being of Future Generations (Wales) Act, 383
Water pollution, 51, 9, 207, 229
Waterfall, Marzena Wasikowska, 4
WBCSD. *See* World Business Council for Sustainable Development (WBCSD)
WCED. *See* World Commission on Environment and Development (WCED)
WEC. *See* World Energy Council (WEC)
Wetlands, 111, 207, 229, 247–49, 261, 356, 362, 397
Weymouth Bay, John Constable, 189
Wild law, 130–31
Wilderness, 193–97, 202, 233, 238, 242, 353, 361, 382
World Bank, 276, 367
World Business Council for Sustainable Development (WBCSD), 174, 174*n*248
World Charter for Nature, 130, 212
World Commission on Environment and Development (WCED), 104, 125–26, 135*n*71
World Economic Forum, 337
World Energy Council (WEC), 135*n*75
World Heritage Convention, 194, 210, 299, 398
World Land Trust, 376
World Population Clock, 351
World Values Survey, 275, 352
Worldwide Fund for Nature (WWF), 327, 380–81

Y

Yellowstone Park, 103, 192, 203
Yellowstone to Yukon (Y2Y), 241–43

Z

'Zealandia', 371
Zoning, 110, 292